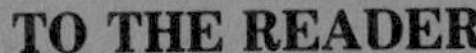

TO THE READER

§ Scientology is a religious philosophy containing spiritual counseling procedures intended to assist an individual to attain peace of mind and Spiritual Freedom. The mission of the Church of Scientology is a simple one: to help the individual attain full awareness of himself as a Spiritual Being, and of his relationship to the Supreme Being. The attainment of the benefits and goals of Scientology requires each individual's dedicated participation as only through his own efforts can he himself, as a Spiritual Being, achieve these.

§ This is part of the religious literature and works of the Founder of Scientology, L. Ron Hubbard. It is presented to the reader as part of the record of his personal research into Life, and should be construed only as a written report of such research and not as a statement of claims made by the Church or the author.

§ Scientology and its substudy, Dianetics, as practiced by the Church, address only the "Thetan" (Spirit). Although the Church, as are all churches, is free to engage in spiritual healing, it does not, as its primary goal is increased *spiritual awareness* for all. For this reason, the Church does not wish to accept individuals who desire treatment of physical or mental illness but prefers to refer these to qualified specialists of other organizations who deal in these matters.

§ The Hubbard Electrometer is a religious artifact used in the Church confessional. It in itself does nothing, and is used by Ministers only, to assist parishioners in locating areas of spiritual distress or travail.

We hope the reading of this book is only the first stage of a personal voyage of discovery into the new and vital world religion of Scientology.

This book belongs to ______________________

Date ______________________

THE BOARD OF DIRECTORS
CHURCH OF SCIENTOLOGY
OF CALIFORNIA

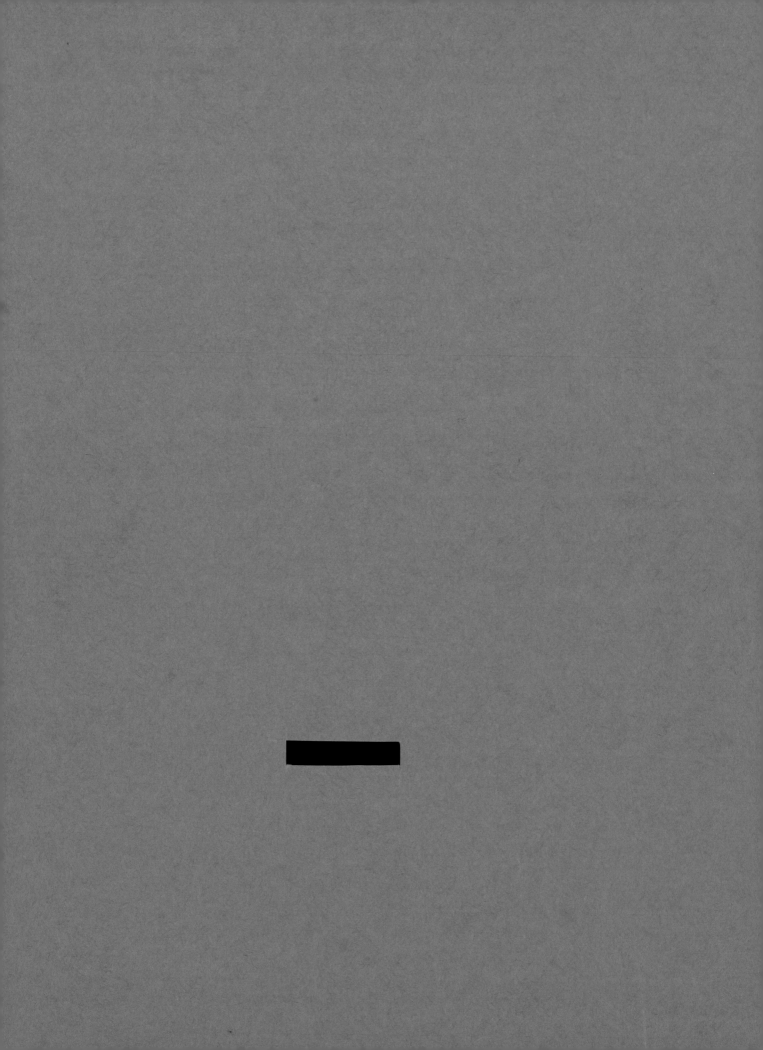

YOU CAN ALWAYS WRITE TO RON

All mail addressed to me shall be received by me.

I am always willing to help. By my own creed, a being is only as valuable as he can serve others.

Any message addressed to me and sent to the address of the nearest Scientology Church listed in the back of this book, will be forwarded to me directly.

The Volunteer Minister's Handbook

The Volunteer Minister's Handbook

by

L. Ron Hubbard

Published in
the United States of America
by
CHURCH OF SCIENTOLOGY OF CALIFORNIA
Publications Organization United States
2723 West Temple Street
Los Angeles, California 90026

and in all other countries
by
AOSH DK Publications Department A/S
Jernbanegade 6
1608 Copenhagen V
Denmark

The Church of Scientology of California is a non-profit organization.

Scientology is an Applied Religious Philosophy.
Dianetics® and Scientology® are registered names.

First Printing 1976

Compiled by the LRH Personal Compilations Bureau
Editors: Pat Brice/Alethiea C. Taylor
Design and Artwork: André Clavel
Compilations Staff:
Ernie Ryan
Maggie Sibersky
Barbara de Celle
Cliff Von Shura
Pat Broeker
Photography by L. Ron Hubbard
Contributing Photographer: Terri Armstrong
Library of Congress Catalog Card No. 76-27819
ISBN 0-88404-039-9

Printed in the United States by Kingsport Press, Inc.
Typeset by Freedmen's Organization, Los Angeles
Color Illustrations Printed by George Rice and Sons, Los Angeles

How to Use This Book

As you will see there are twenty-one different packs in the book, each covering a specific subject. Each pack has a checksheet which must be done by you as you progress through this manual.

The first pack in this book contains the basic rules and principles for successful study from Scientology study technology. You must learn these well and apply them throughout your study of the entire book.

Pack A Study, amplifies what a checksheet is and how a student does a checksheet.

In order to acquire the skills of a successful Volunteer Minister it is essential to follow and do the steps outlined in each of the checksheets.

In some instances in the packs of this handbook an asterisk (*) appears against the reference for an item in the pack. This indicates the material of that section was written by someone other than L. Ron Hubbard the Founder of Dianetics and Scientology.

A new and happy and purposeful career is before you now with the publication of this book. We wish you well.

The Editors

Contents

Preface

The Nature of Scientology

Scientology (from Latin *scio* knowing in the fullest sense of the word, and Greek *logos* to study) is a religious philosophy containing spiritual counseling procedures intended to assist an individual to become more himself and enhance his personal well-being.

Scientology encompasses a broader scope than any Eastern or Western religion ever has, but it should be realized that a great deal of what we know, with an added exactness of understanding, was already known and lost thousands of years ago. So we are not dealing with something new in Scientology.

What we are DOING with this data is new, and the technology for bringing about a new state in Man as it appears today in Scientology, is thousands of years old. When we call Scientology a religion we are calling it a religion out of a much deeper well than the last two thousand years.

The truth is that in Scientology we are studying an extension of the work of Gautama Siddhartha (Buddha), begun about 2500 years ago. He sought to end the endless cycle of birth and death and birth, and this led to an effort to show Man that he was a spirit and did not have to be a body and did not have to go on being clay.

Gautama Siddhartha found out how to move the spirit out of the body. The trouble he had with his work was how to *stably* do this or *continue* somebody in this exterior condition. He did not know how to do this.

Lamaism which began in Tibet after the time of Gautama Siddhartha, was actually developed by Gautama Siddhartha who went to Tibet and worked there to develop what is called Lamaism in an effort to produce a methodology to reach the basis of the mind and permit an individual to be spiritually free. Now that work, too, was relatively unsuccessful. We were more successful than that in Scientology. We can show an individual that he is a human spirit more easily than has been done before. And, of course, today we have been totally successful in achieving for the individual, his own awareness of his spiritual nature and abilities. Yet the work of Gautama Siddhartha, although looked upon as a failure, produced a sufficiency of wisdom on this planet to bring civilization to three-quarters of Asia.

People poured out of China for centuries over tortuous and dangerous mountains and snow-filled passes to drop down into India, just to come closer to the area where Gautama Buddha had taught that there is hope and that the endless cycle of life and death does not have to continue, that an individual can be free even from this. The ignorant deified him and made idols of him but Gautama Siddhartha never pretended to be anything but a man. And due to him a great deal of this work was handed on and an enormous amount of what we call religion in this Western Hemisphere today was given to us directly by Gautama Siddhartha.

Buddhism is the oldest and most numerous religion on this planet at this moment and predates Christianity by 500 years. Probably the shreds of Buddhism coming into the Middle East with the silk and spice merchants sparked a religious revival and a considerable amount of messianic activity in the Middle East. The spice and silk merchants of India and China now, after the contact of Alexander in about 333 BC, found out there was a Europe, followed on the trail of his retreating conquest and made a trade contact with Europe. From there on, Asia supplied Europe with spices and silks and other goods on an overland route. Along with them undoubtedly came Buddhism.

"Love thy neighbor" was one of the first lessons taught by Gautama Siddhartha and it is that lesson which we have received from the Middle East, though it is probably more popularly known as a Christian lesson.

There is even a tradition that Christ studied in India and at the age of thirty came into the West bringing wisdom and hope. This was the beginning of a further spread of religion through Christianity. The early monks of Christianity brought this religion into the greater parts of Europe. These people, then, handed on the torch of wisdom, of information, generation to generation. And right on down to this time we are indebted to them.

Scientology can demonstrate that it can attain the goals set for man by Christ, which are: wisdom, good health and immortality.

Now, regardless of any truths or prophecies or prophets or anything else that happened as an independent endeavor, all this was sparked off by Buddhism. Gautama Siddhartha Buddha predicted that in 2500 years the entire job would be finished in the West. This is stated in the Pali Canons.

Well, we finished it. Were somebody to claim that Scientology was not a religion or that religion was a disguise, this would be about the most erroneous statement he could make because it is an extension, a direct extension, of the work of Gautama Siddhartha Buddha.

Everyone, anyone, of any race, color or creed, could be a member of the Buddhist Church. It was not limited to one caste or class or race or nationality. It was the first international religious movement, but although it has carried forward until today it actually has not moved its technology one inch further than it was pushed in Tibet until the advent of Scientology.

The spirituality of man is the basis of religion and it is the one thing that all religions have in common. They have different creators, different gods, different alters of worship, but in one thing they hold a common truth and that is that man is a spiritual being. Only in Buddhism was this ever proven and it is proven now again in Scientology.

This proof and the inherent potential ability of the spirit of man you will find for yourself as you walk the well-marked road that is Scientology today.

Scientology is a religion by its basic tenets, practice, historical background and by the definition of the word "religion" itself. The following will help clarify the philosophical and practical aspects of religion.

Religious practice implies ritual, faith-in, doctrine based on a catechism and a creed.

Religious philosophy implies study of spiritual manifestations;

research on the nature of the spirit and study on the relationship of the spirit to the body; exercises devoted to the rehabilitation of abilities in a spirit.

Scientology is a religious philosophy in its highest meaning as it brings man to real knowingness of himself and truth. Our confessional relieves the being of the encumbrances which keep his awareness as a being limited to the physical aspects of life.

Scientology is also a religious practice in that the Church of Scientology conducts basic services such as sermons at church meetings, christenings, weddings and funerals.

Scientology does not conflict with other religions or religious practices as it clarifies them and brings understanding of the spiritual nature of Man.

Scientology has amongst its members people of all the major faiths, including many priests, bishops and other ordained communicants of the major faiths.

A Scientology auditor is an ordained minister in the Church of Scientology. Auditor means "one who listens." He or she is a highly trained person well versed in an understanding of the spirit. Auditing is a term used to mean the application of Scientology processes and procedures to someone by a trained auditor. Auditing is spiritual counseling.

Auditors have since the beginning of Scientology, been the only individuals on this planet, in this universe, capable of freeing Man.

At times, some forget or choose to ignore the fact that the auditor is not just another fellow or a guy who works in Scientology. An auditor is a highly trained specialist, no matter what level of training. He or she is the only one who can give man the truth that man knows.

An auditor does spiritual counseling and hears confessions in such a way as to make vital improvements in the lives of those receiving counseling. The auditor audits the spiritual beingness of the individual, increasing the individual's understanding, enabling him or her to discard aberrations and to be more effective in all aspects of life and livingness.

The Auditor is handling the reactive mind of the individual.

The reactive mind is a portion of a person's mind which works on a totally stimulus-response basis which is not under his volitional control, and which exerts force and the power of command over his awareness, purpose, thoughts, body and actions and is the single source of human aberration and psychosomatic ills.

It had managed to bury itself from view so thoroughly that ONLY inductive philosophy, travelling from effect back to cause, served to uncover it.

If you really want to know more about the reactive mind you should study *Dianetics: The Modern Science of Mental Health* thoroughly. It's enough here to say it still exists and still accounts for all one's "unaccountable" actions.

Since the perfection of the technology in Scientology to handle this reactive mind, freedom from mental torment is now a certain, attainable state and has been achieved by thousands of Scientologists.

We can demonstrate to human beings that they are spiritual beings and that is the essence of religion. Man is a spiritual being. Where he came from and how and why and where he is going, are questions developed in religion.

Auditing is directly concerned with increasing the ability of the individual to survive, with increasing his sanity or ability to reason, his physical ability, and his general enjoyment of life.

The higher a person can rise on this scale, the righter he is in terms of reason, in terms of survival, and in terms of general well-being. The higher he is, the happier. The lower he is, the sadder.

As a Volunteer Minister, you are the auditor of your community.

Happiness is important. The ability to arrange life and the environment so that living can be better enjoyed, the ability to tolerate the foibles of one's fellow humans, the ability to see the true factors in a situation and resolve problems of living with accuracy, the ability to accept and execute responsibility, these things are important. Life is not much worth living if it cannot be enjoyed. The ability to live well and fully and to enjoy that living is the gift of a Scientologist.

The auditor might liken his job to removing the rocks and shoals from the hidden depths of a turbulent river and making of it a smooth-flowing and powerful stream. The auditor is not changing the preclear by evaluation and suggestions. He is simply making it easier for the mind to do what the basic personality—the individual naturally wants the mind to do. This might be said to be the end goal of auditing.

A fact which has been forgotten in this time of war and spiritual pestilence is that there have been times in Man's history and prehistory when he *has succeeded.* It has not all been gloom and hopelessness, else we would not be here today—even as poorly as we are. Men have lived to conquer all other forms of life, from the mastodon to the microbe. Men have lived to build walls and roads and pyramids which have defied the elements for thousands of years. Men have lived to write music which has pleased the gods and lines which have made the angels sigh and the devil weep. This is a time for man to succeed again. Here is the word, the technology, the goal. The job is cut out and its name is *Survive!*

Illustrations

Throughout the ages the essence of every religion has been inseparably connected with Man's striving to rise above himself toward greater wisdom and spiritual attainments. Thus the mission of every religion has been the civilizing of brutal, unhappy and crime-ridden cultures.

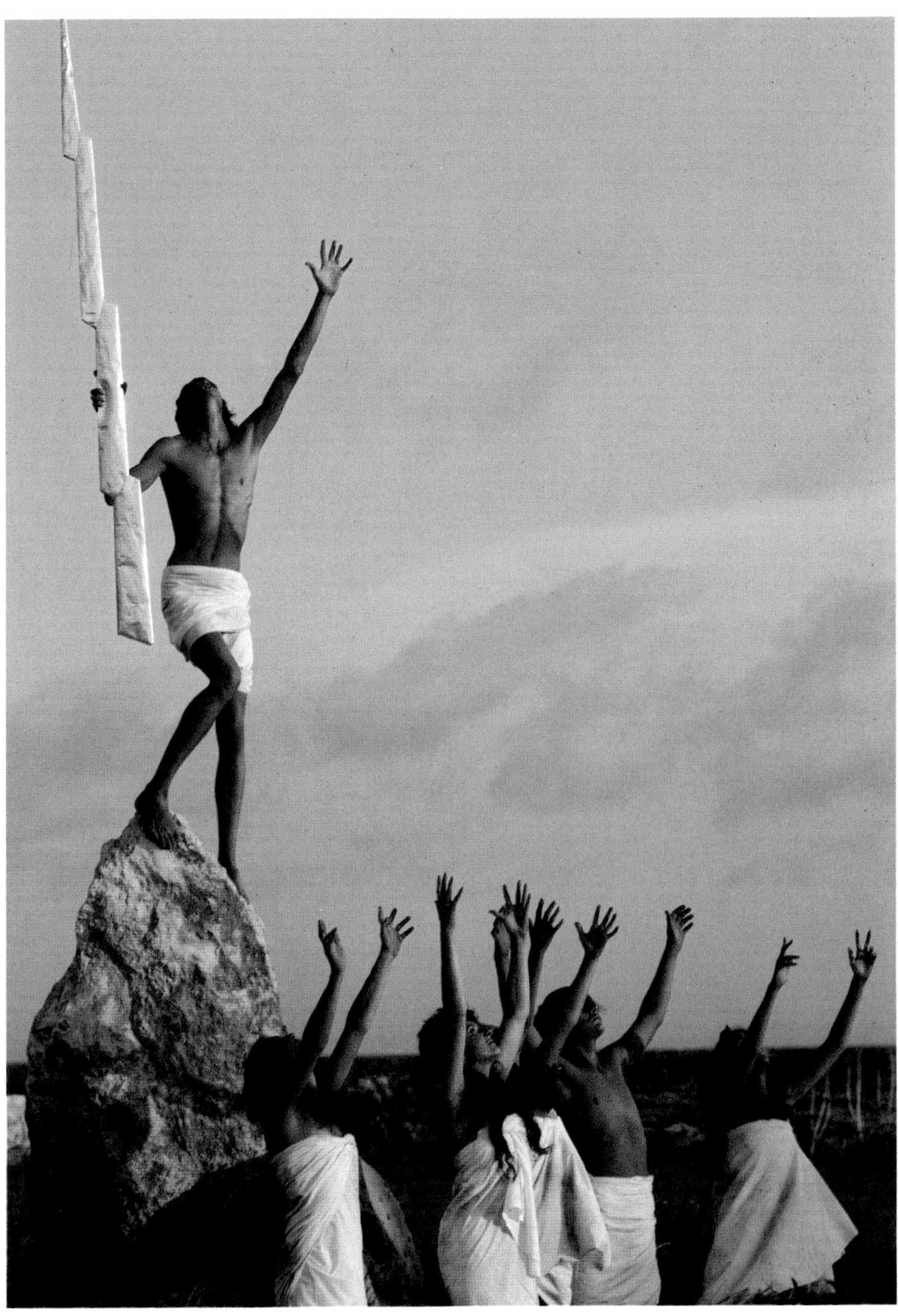

Sun worshippers sought glory in celestial bodies and the physical universe, placing devout trust in the sun as source of light and symbol of the deity.

Never far removed from Man's existence on earth has been his fight for raw survival and the effort to surmount his adversaries, both near and distant.

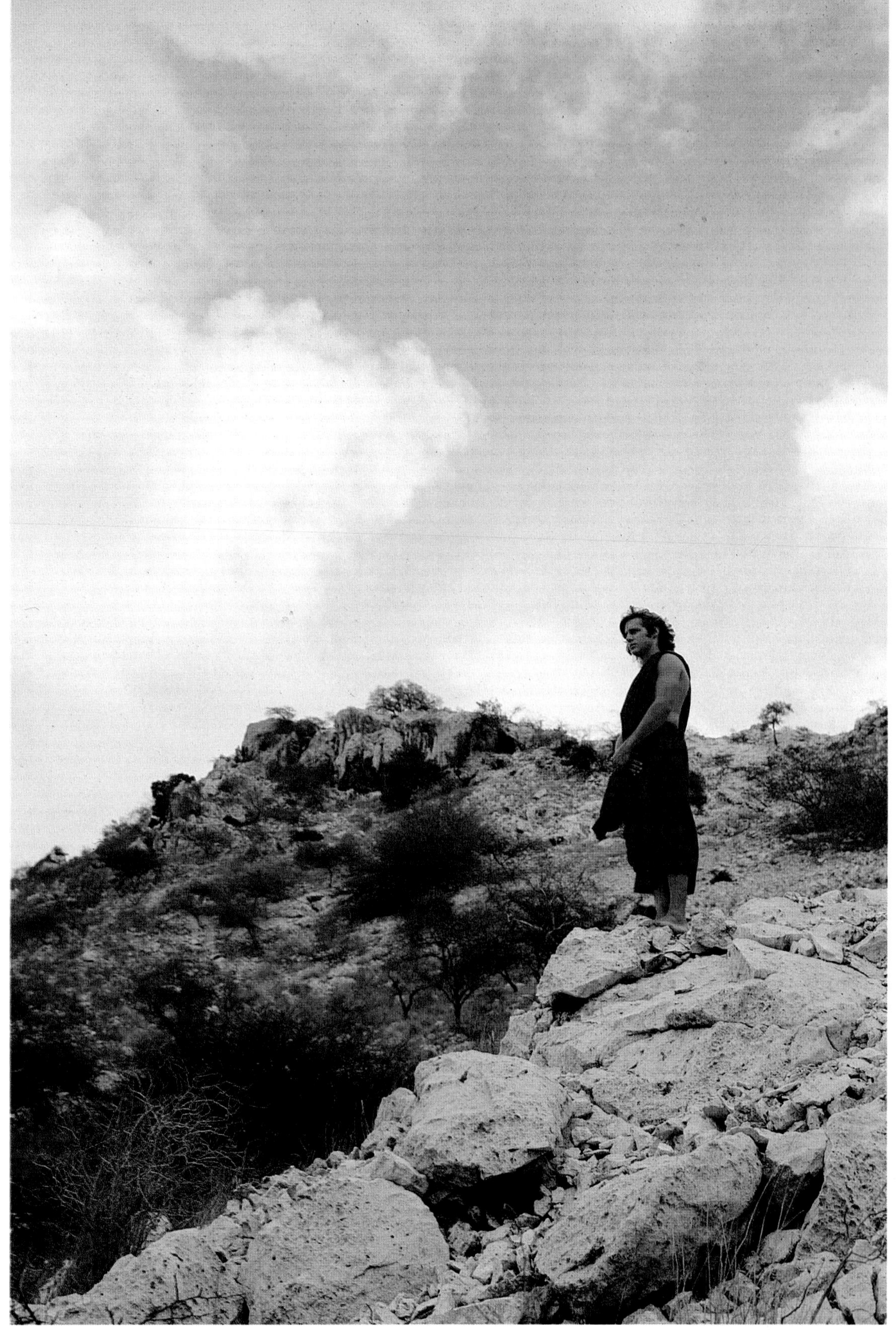

With the coming of Gautama Siddhartha and Buddhism, Asian peoples became greatly enlightened, his followers travelling and teaching throughout the villages for hundreds of years to come and bringing to the East a new civilization.

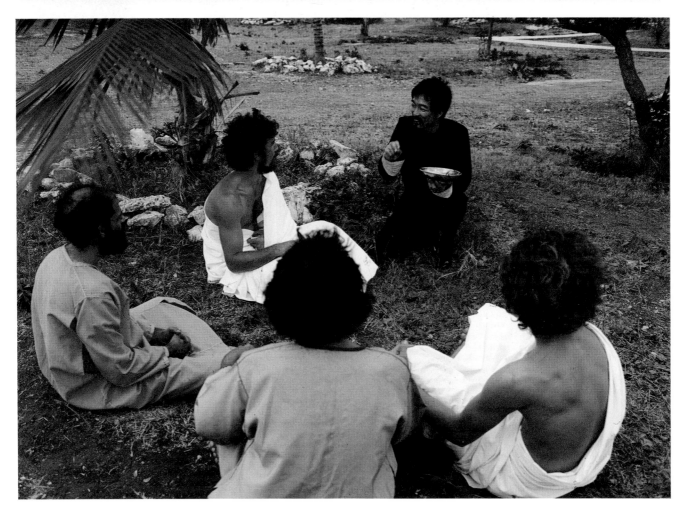

Buddhist monks discussed Man's eternal questions at length, and communicated Gautama Siddhartha's teachings of intellectual and ethical perfection by human means.

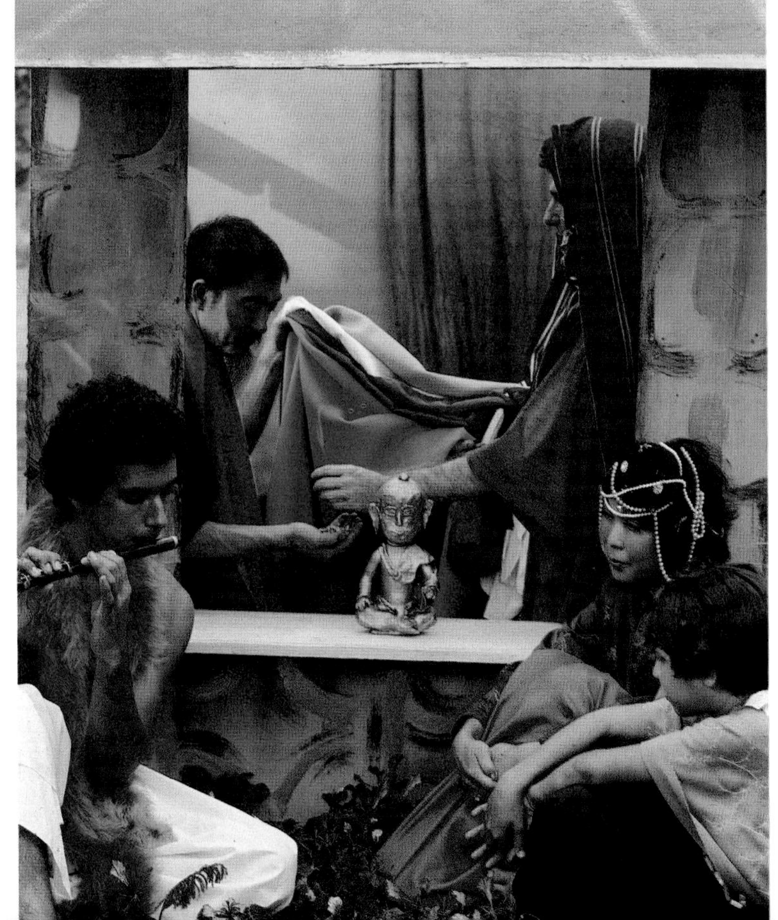

A rich and accomplished society came into being in the Buddhist world.

In time Buddhist supremacy declined and was marked by degrading influences borne within its own ranks.

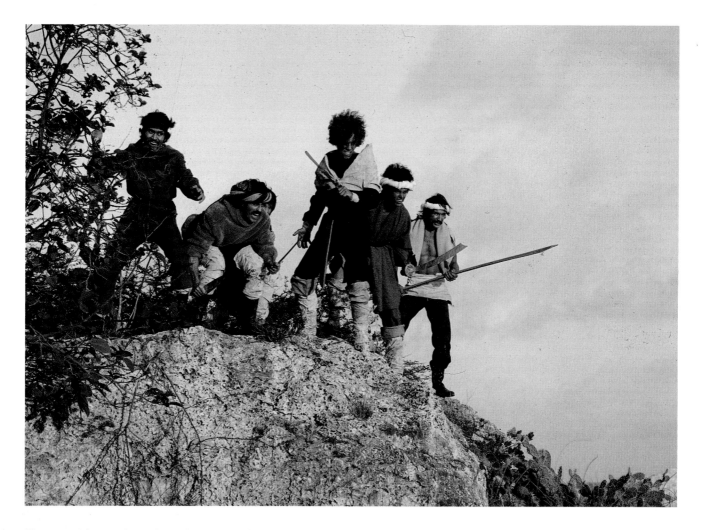

From without, invasions by Mongol hordes brought further disruption to the Buddhist culture.

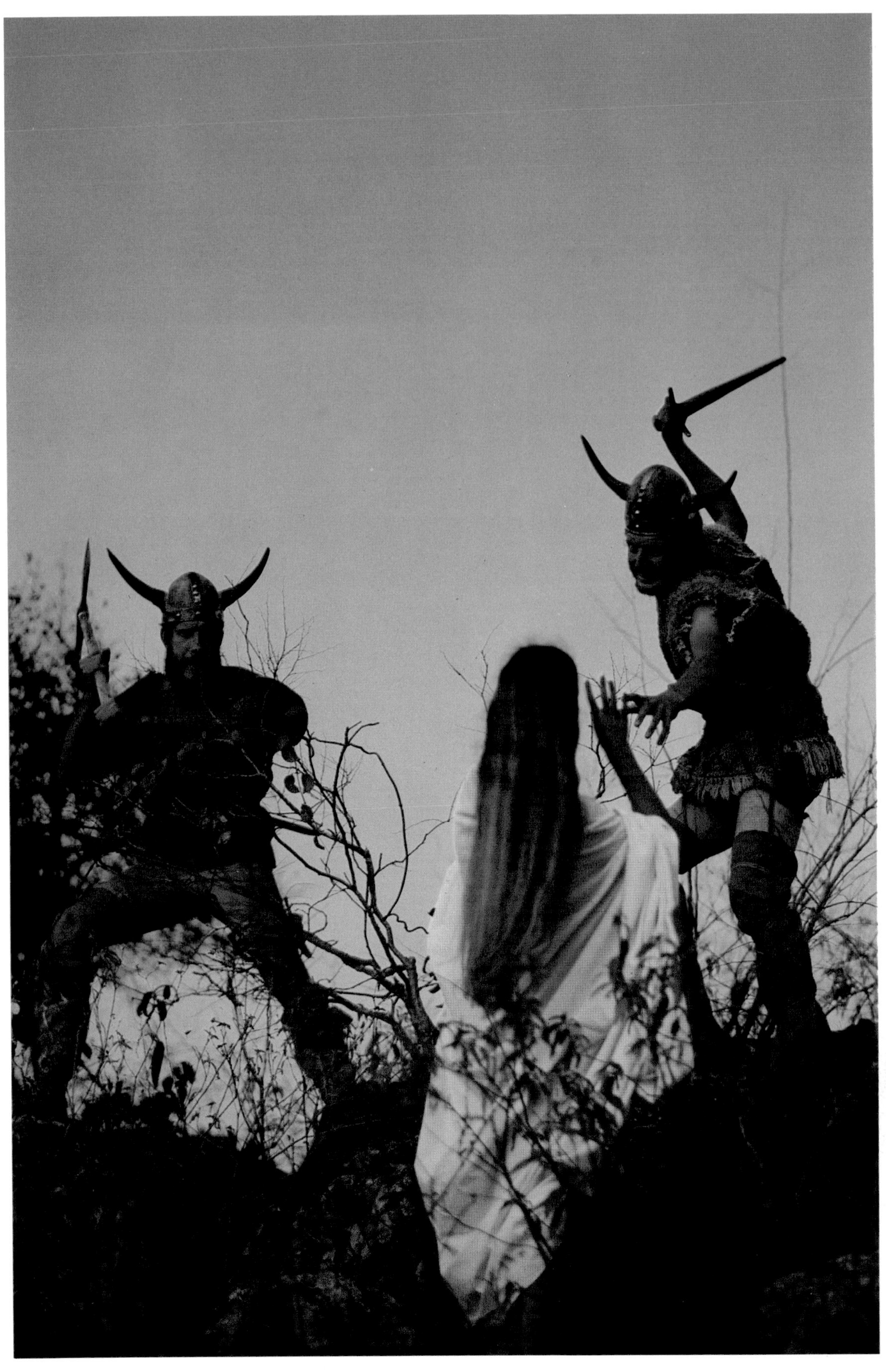

In northern and western Europe, hostile Viking bands made countless raids on established churches, lasting from the eighth through the tenth century.

Used even in many pre-Christian religions, the cross has long been a trusted religious symbol, and in the coming of Christ, the cross endured.

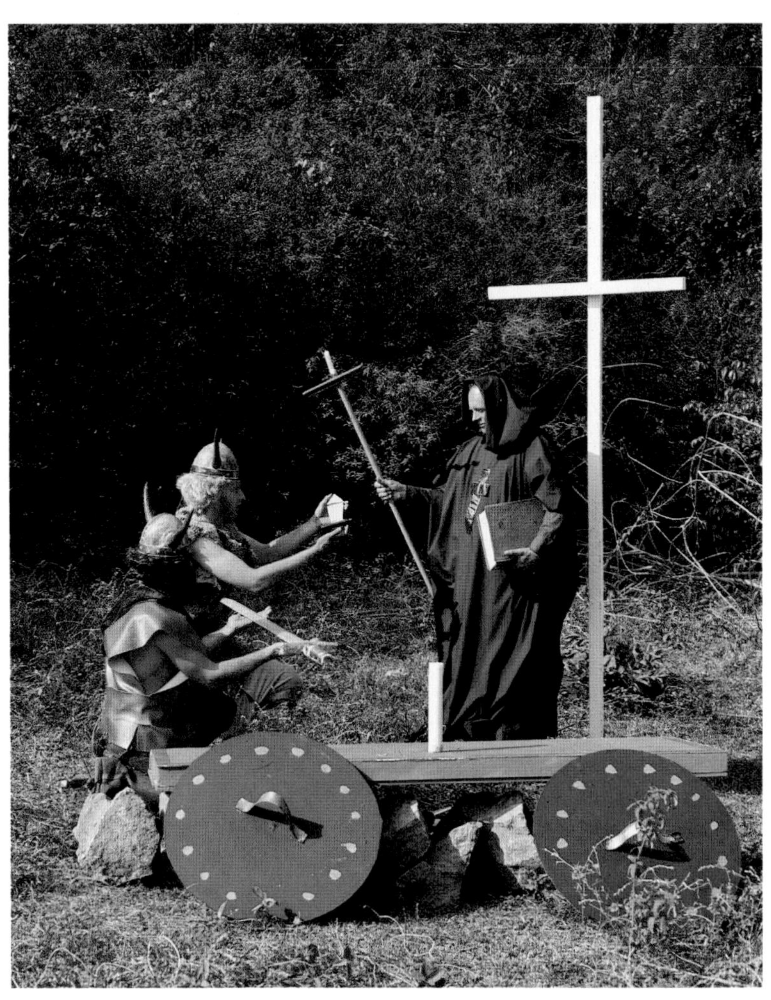

With the further emergence of Christianity and its way of understanding life, many disbelievers eventually converted to their ranks.

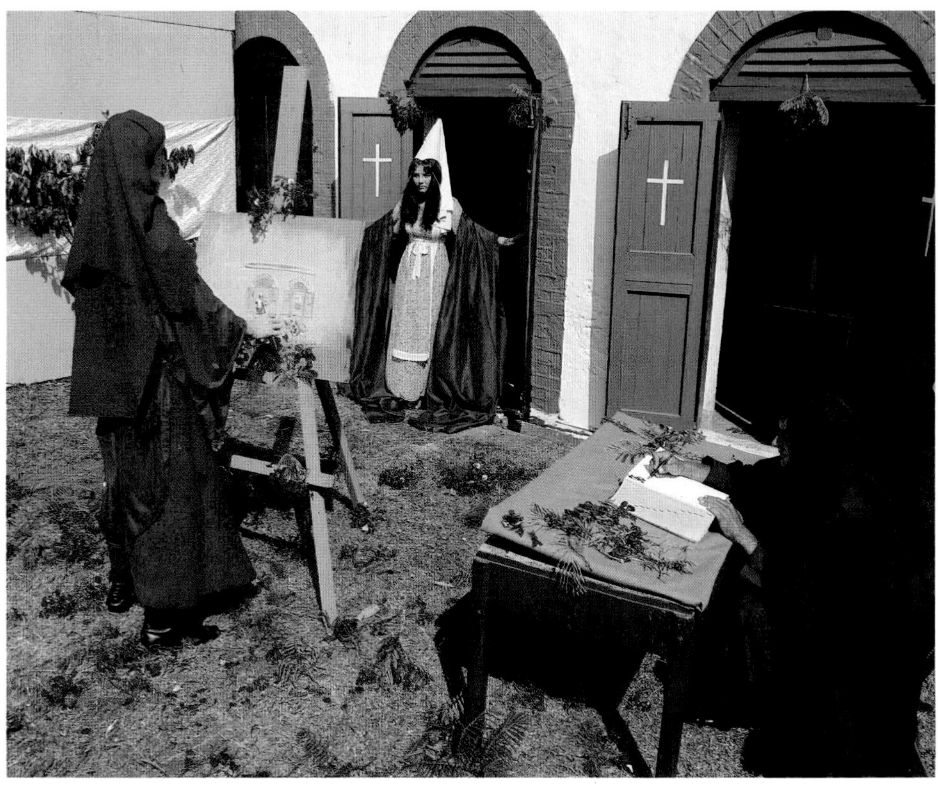

Christianity grew, its beliefs bringing help to numerous individuals and in turn, whole communities prospered and were nourished by a renaissance of learning and the arts.

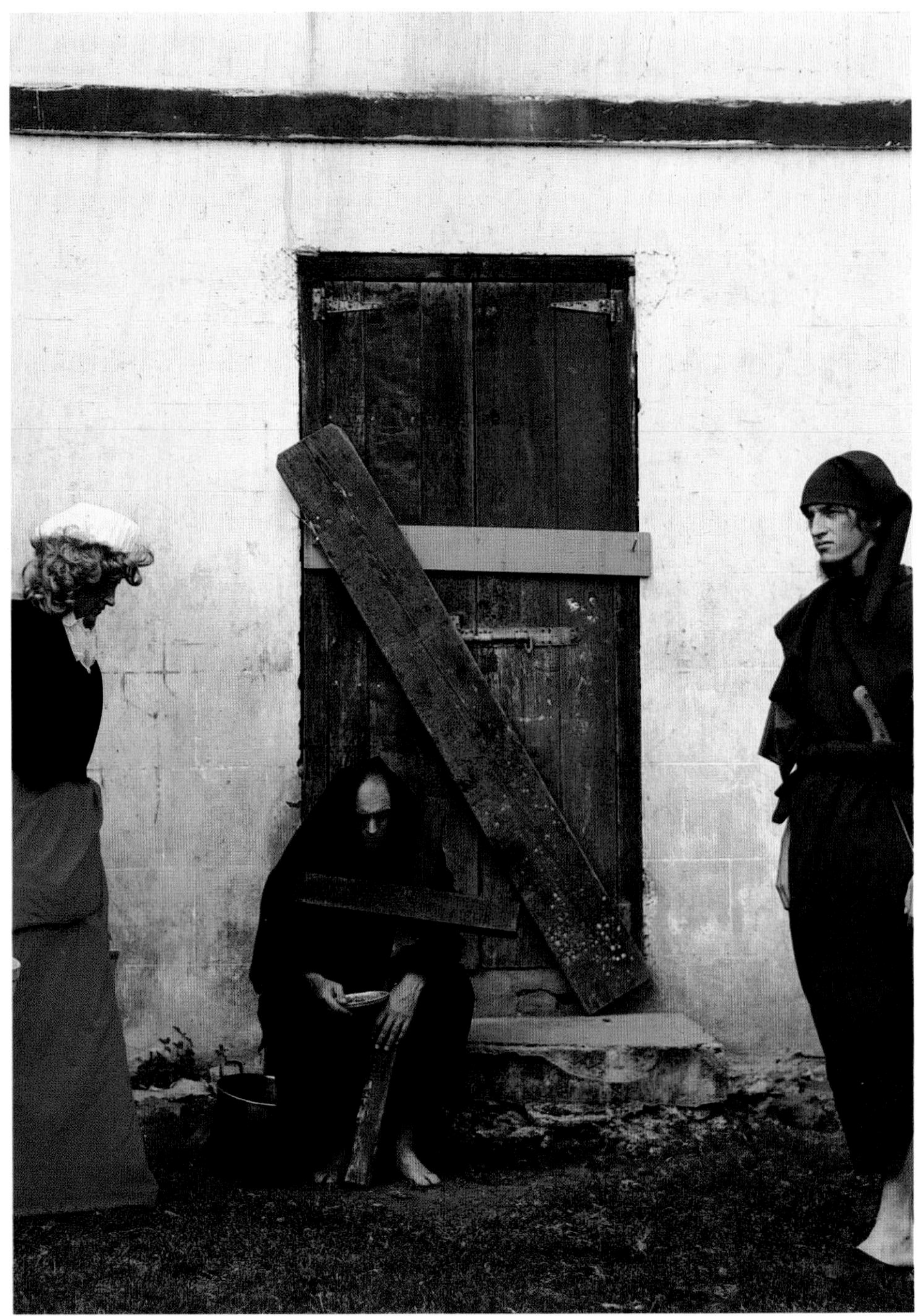

Later, even the strength of Christianity waned becoming less viable in that for some people its faith was lacking in an applied technology, meaning exact and inclusive methods of application of Christianity to livingness. Thus men came to abandon the Christian church and continued their religious searchings.

Terribly enough, with some rests the vision that we are racing toward certain oblivion and that there will be no planet earth. With many more, however, there is perpetuated Man's immortal hope for world peace. The choice is clear.

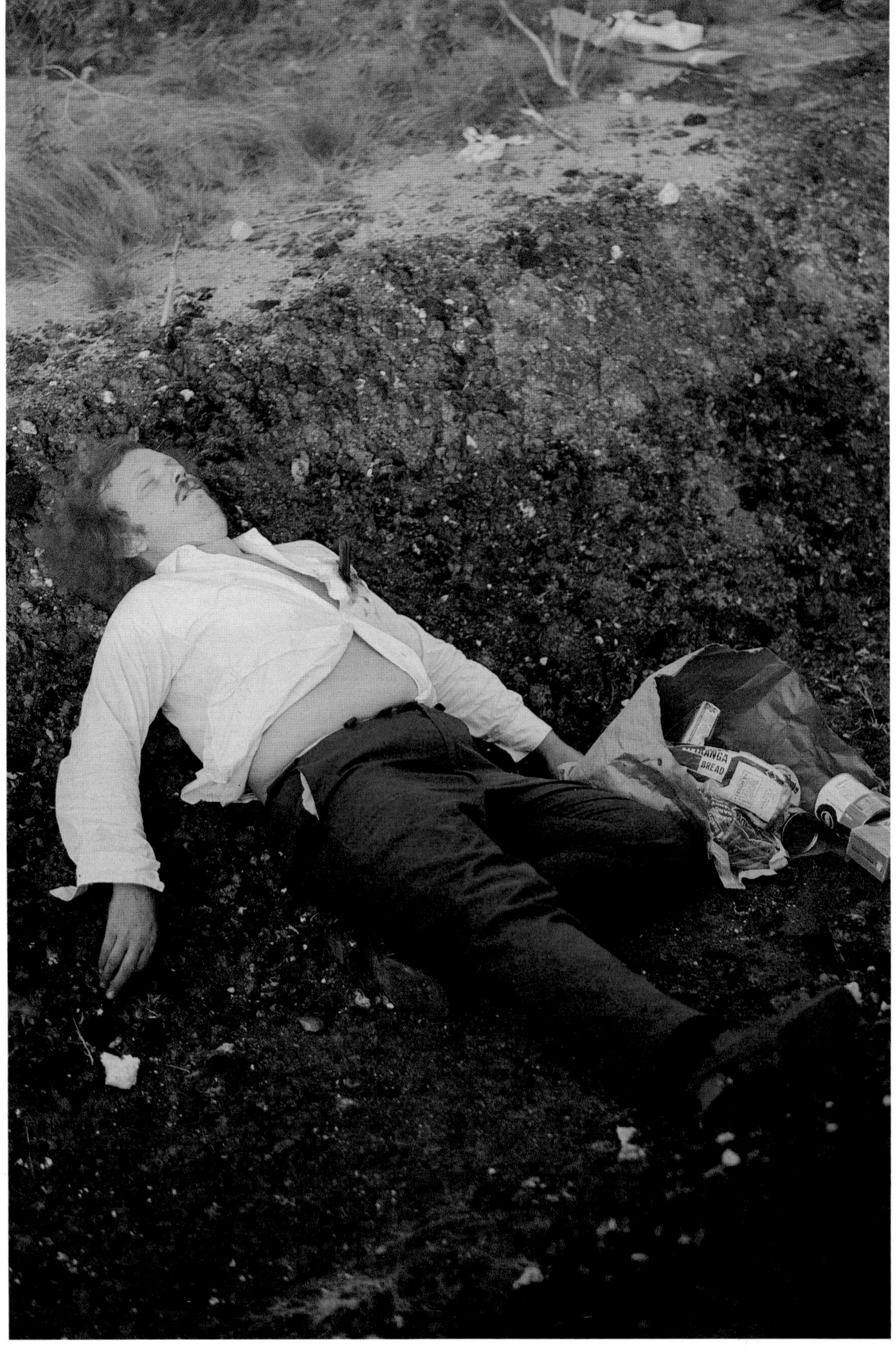

Today we are faced with a world of criminality, war, and bondage in one form or another. Do you know that among the aims of Scientology is a civilization without insanity, without criminals and without war? And that placed beneath these goals is Man's first foundation for their attainment, based on Scientology technology which is in fact a body of truths that put to practice will attain for all men these long-desired ideals.

Today's society, where there are many signs of frenzy and delirium and but bare hopes for the future, does not provide a safe, sane environment — either for adults or for children.

In a computerized society where individuality is diminished, there are those who find little or no satisfaction in strict conformity to stereotyped living and are searching for their *own* answers to life's questions and how best to live, work and find happiness.

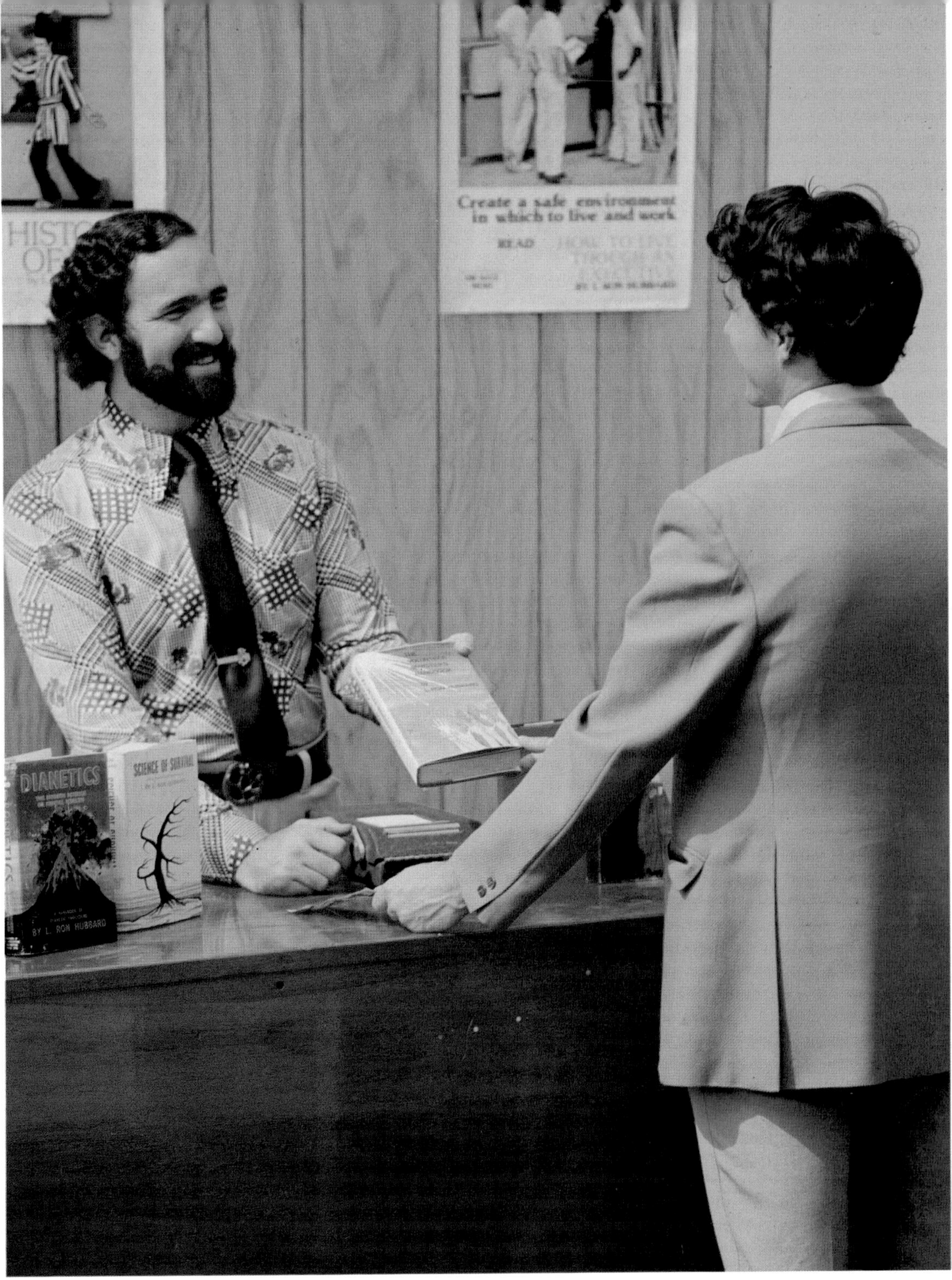

Such a person buys the *Volunteer Minister's Handbook* which in its philosophic scope and presentation of the mastery of techniques delivers to the individual a technology that he can apply to his own life and the lives of others to help his fellow man toward well-being, physically and mentally, and the rewards of personal gratification.

The *Volunteer Minister's Handbook* is particularly designed for HOME STUDY, presenting step-by-step a program based on Scientology, an applied religious philosophy, and the application of its technology. Upon completing the *Handbook's* study and drills, you will receive a Volunteer Minister's certificate issued by the Church of Scientology.

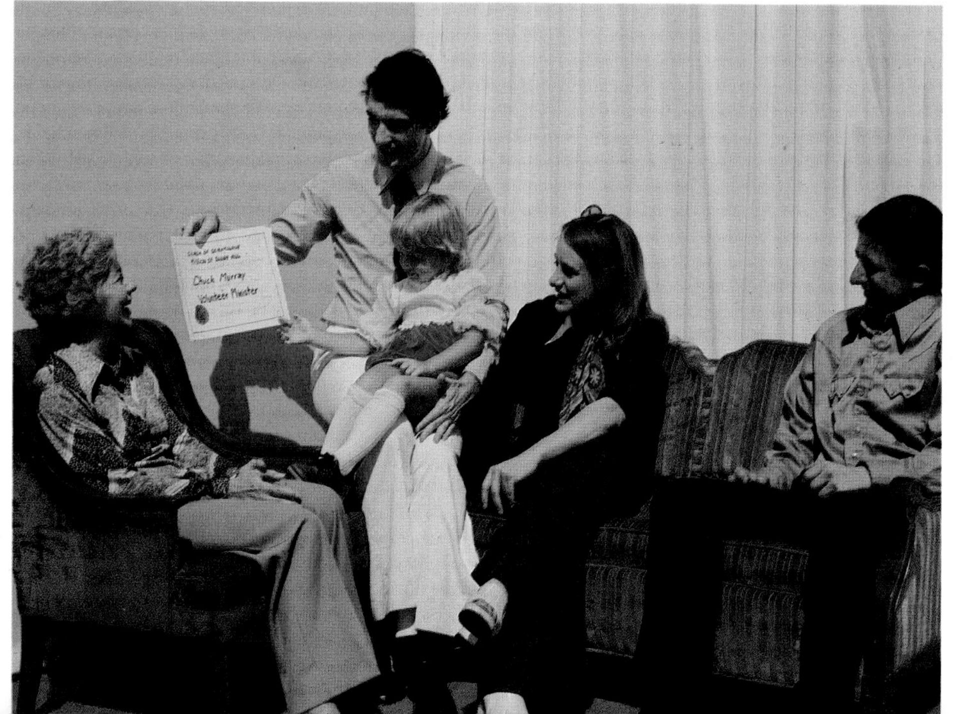

An able Volunteer Minister is easily one of the most popular persons in his community, enjoying a variety of contacts and bringing changes to many lives for the betterment of the whole of society.

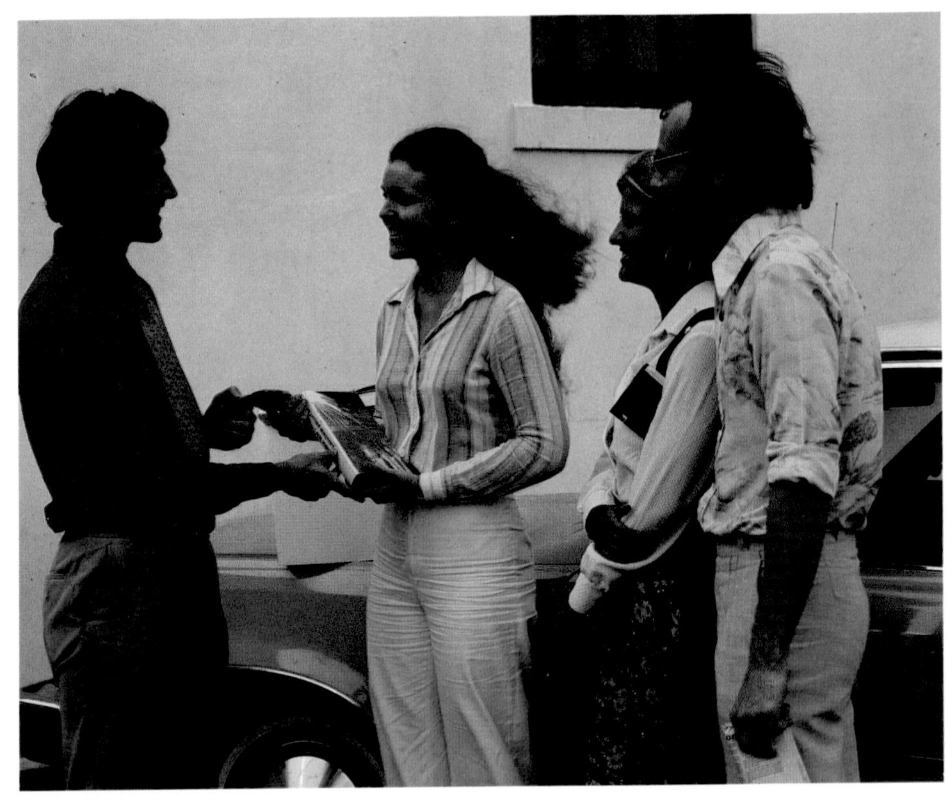

A Volunteer Minister's role includes disseminating Scientology to all those persons reaching for more knowledge. He sells them the books of Dianetics and Scientology containing all the original data and which will answer any of their questions.

In his spare moments, he continues to refer to his *Volunteer Minister's Handbook*, a compendium of specific techniques used to help others out of difficulties in life.

The art of listening is renewed in the Volunteer Minister who receives young and old into his counsel and who may, with the assurance of Scientology technology, bring to each situation the qualities of affinity, shared reality and communication. In this way a person's problems can be exactly duplicated and understood with the person himself resolving his own difficulties and achieving individual resurgence.

Falsities such as the generation gap are revealed as deceptive barriers when people are counseled by an able Volunteer Minister. Such misrepresentation is replaced with the truth evident in two people talking together sincerely without thought of age difference — only that each is aware of the other wholly as an individual — one professionally trained to be of help, and the other there to be helped.

You, as a Volunteer Minister, will take special notice of even those "usual" boyhood squabbles — for you genuinely care for others and you know how to help.

A Volunteer Minister trained in the Communication Formula steps in as a friend, has the boys go over what happened to cause a misunderstanding. Thus the boys are brought back into good communication and comradeship.

Has this happened to you — while visiting with friends a sudden unexpected quarrel breaks out between two people, such as this husband and wife? As a trained Volunteer Minister, you will understand what's happening to people in times of argument — and act effectively.

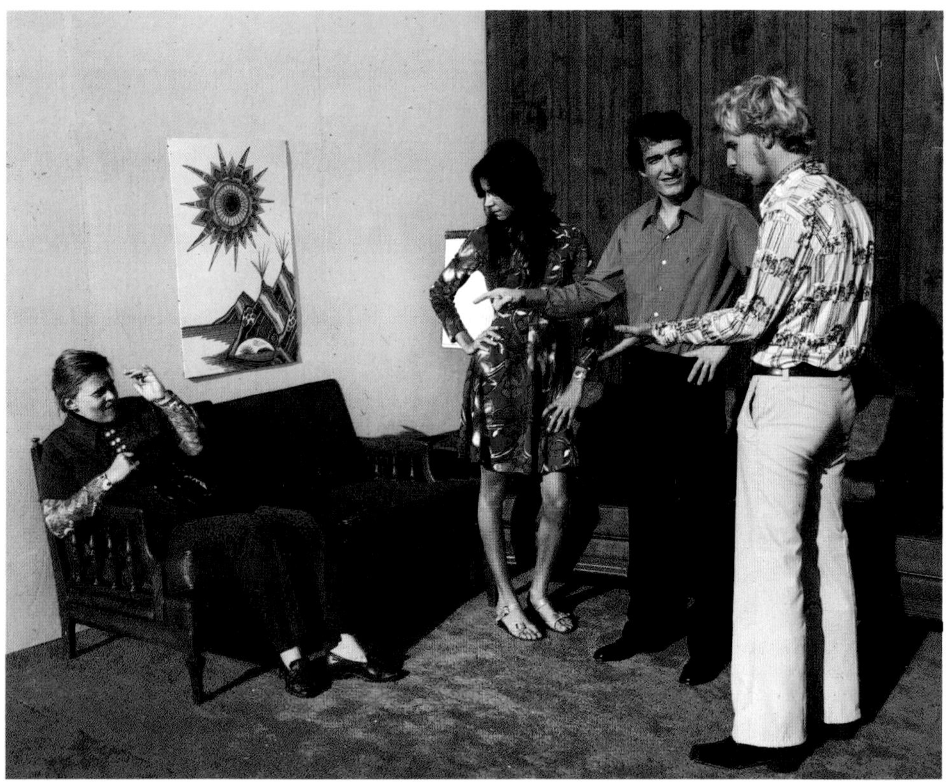

A Volunteer Minister knows the Third Party Law, carefully documented in Scientology research, that answers up to such a situation. Using this technology he is able to trace down the true instigator of this domestic conflict.

Having made a third party discovery that is affirmed by the husband and wife (until now the person was unsuspected by both combatants), the situation rights itself — and the Volunteer Minister enjoys the fruits of his training.

It is likely that you could have a similar encounter to this one — finding a young woman who has just caught and hurt her hand when slamming the door of her car.

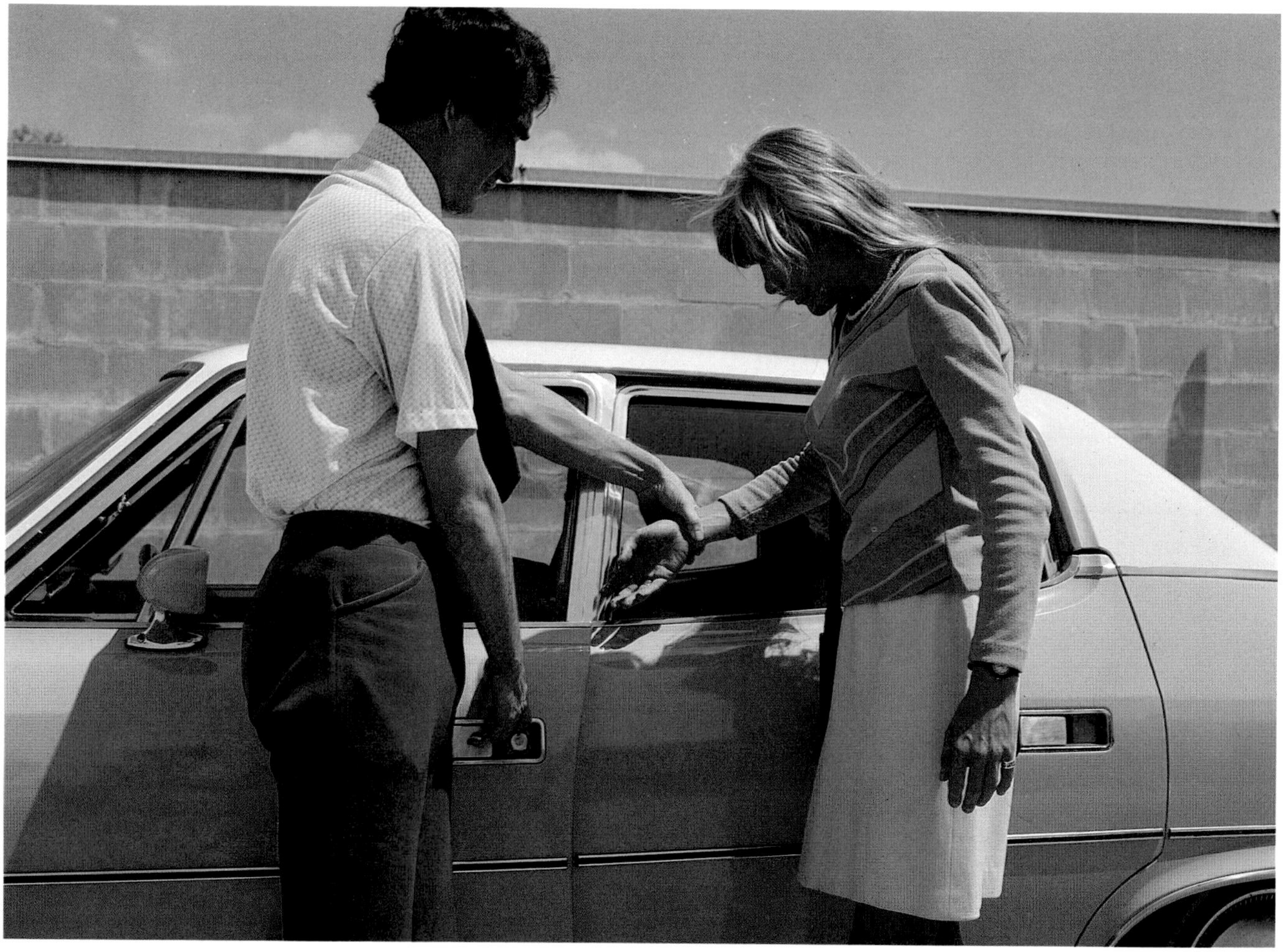

This is where you will use the precise technique of a Contact Assist. Your *Volunteer Minister's Handbook* contains numerous techniques from within the wide range of Scientology assists technology.

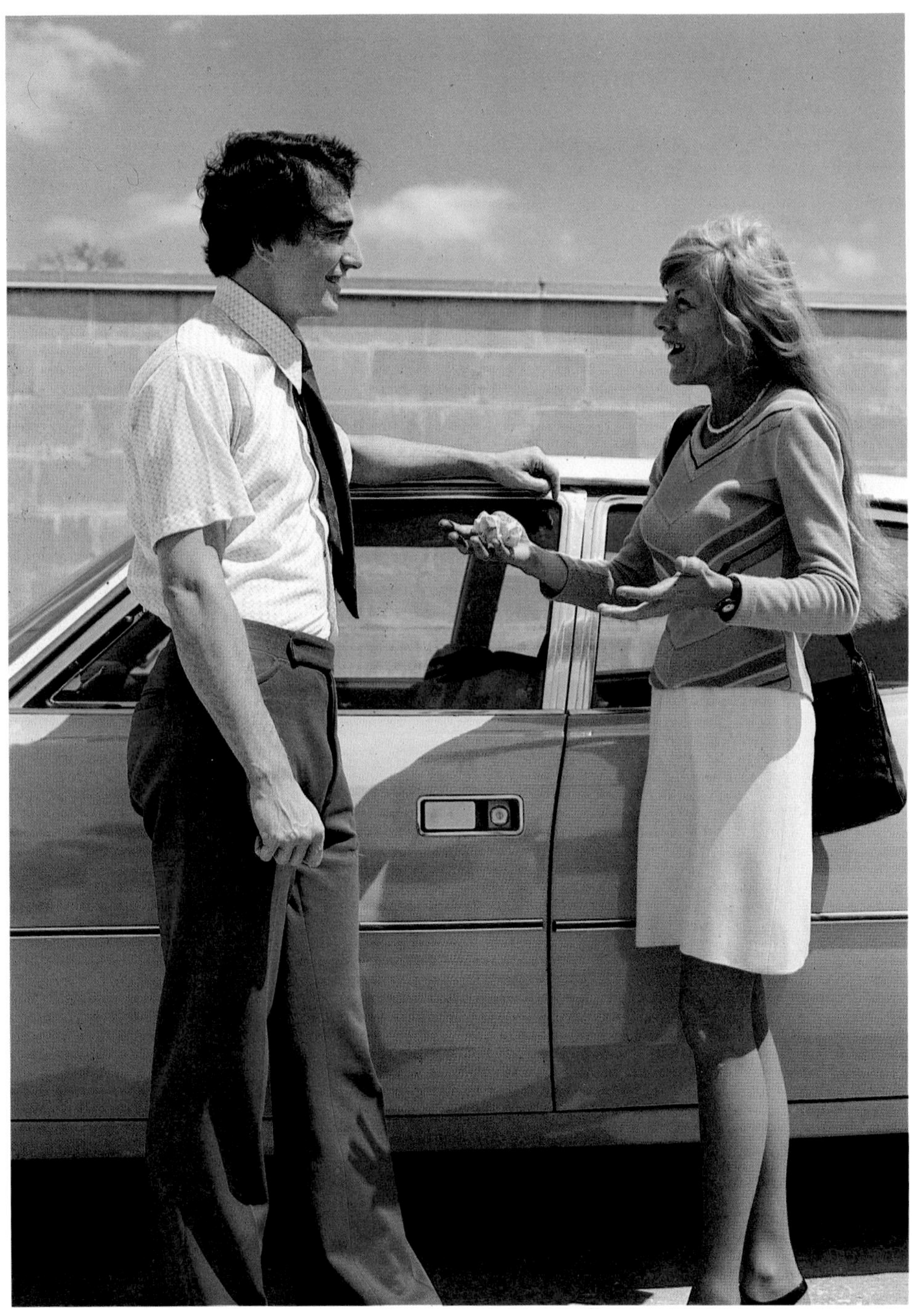

A double reward! — for you, the Volunteer Minister who have helped someone and for the young woman who has just learned of the amazing relief that is possible when you've hurt yourself.

Today heavy drinking is not uncommon at parties and often the inebriated person needs help which you, as a Volunteer Minister, are trained to also deliver.

A Locational Assist given by you orients the person again to his surroundings.

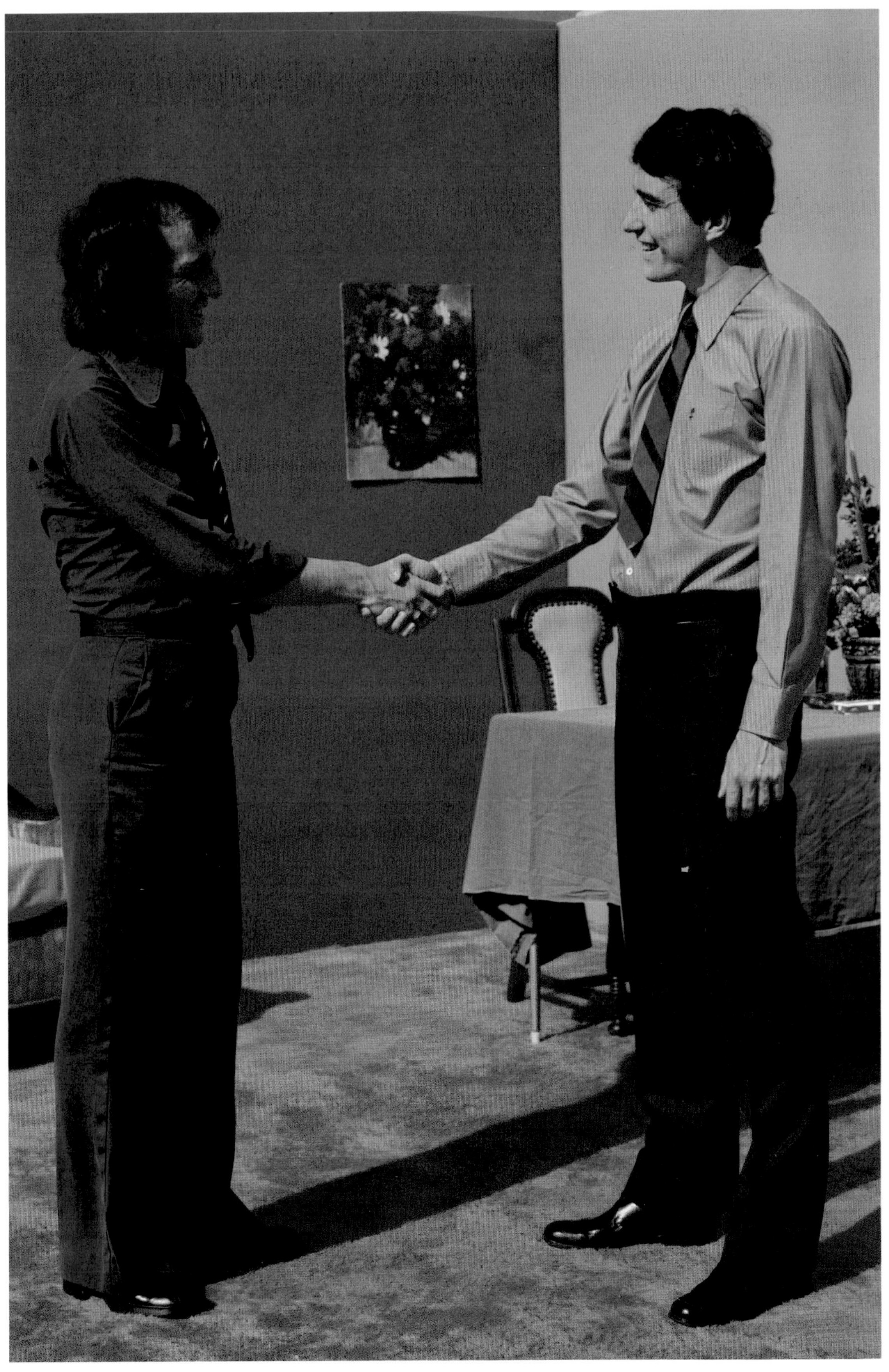

You will find that the Locational Assist and the precise way you handled it will not have in any way invalidated the person but instead will have renewed his awareness of himself as a worthwhile person and of you as a friend.

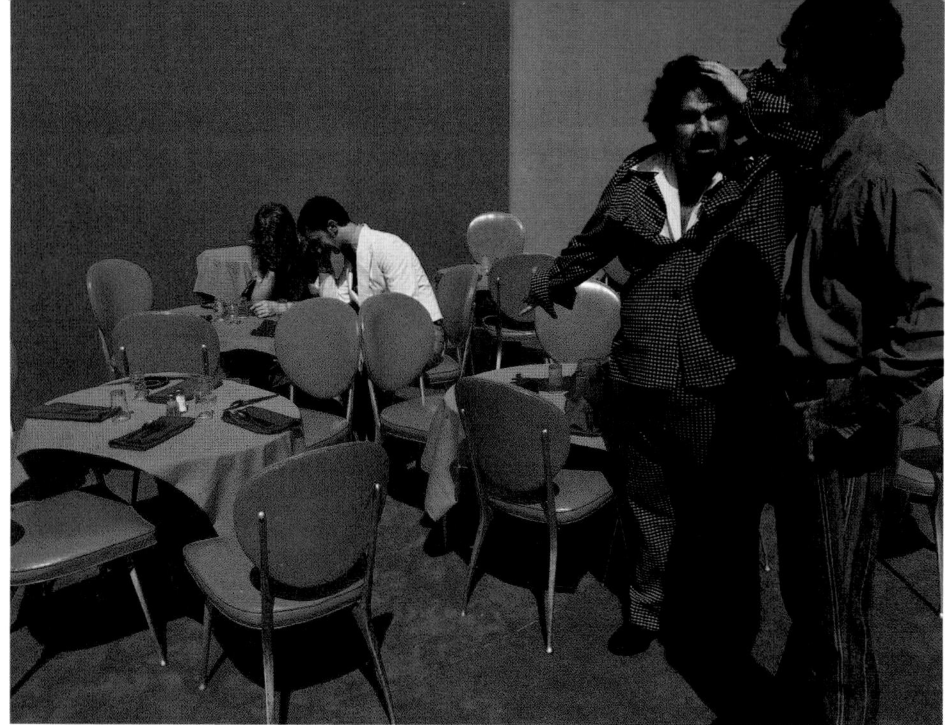

In travels about the community you will become involved with businessmen and, using investigatory technology, you will be able to direct them to solutions of their particular organizational problems. Here an owner, in danger of losing his restaurant, tells a Volunteer Minister of his impending business failure — no patrons.

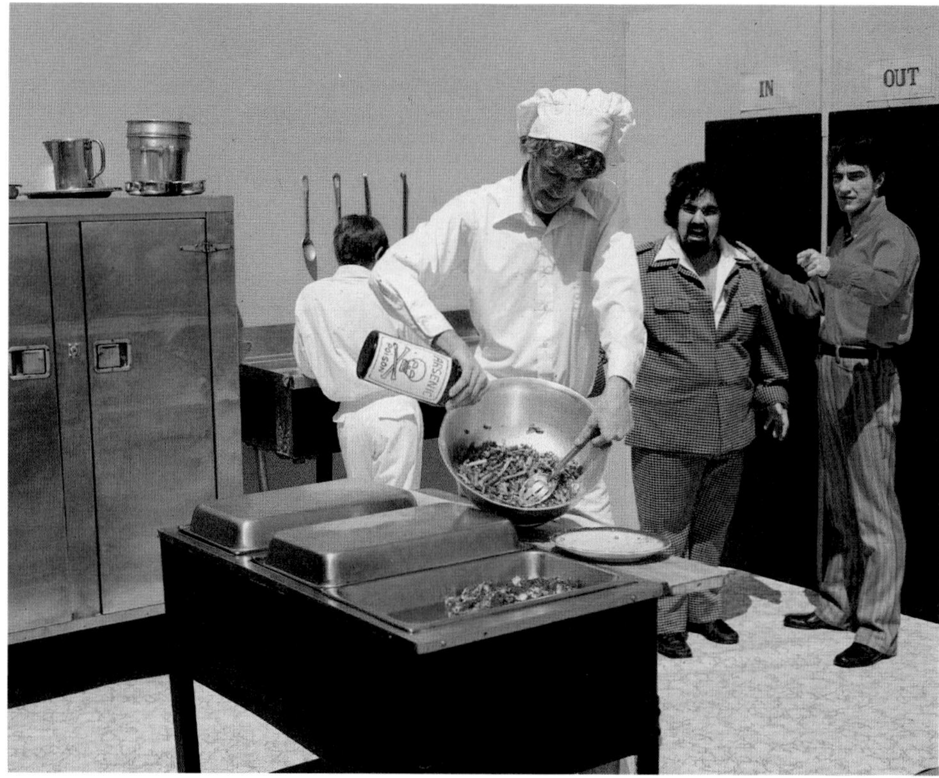

After hearing the story, the Volunteer Minister isolates the factors of the situation to find the actual source of the problem. With the precise Scientology procedure for making an investigation, he finds the right target — an employee who is actively working against the employer, and people in general, by poisoning the food.

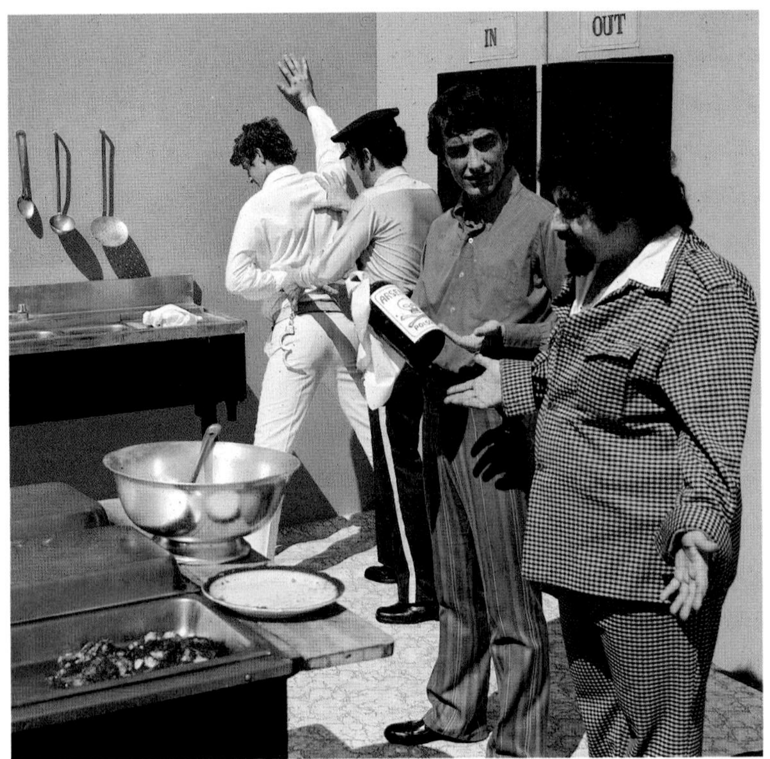

In handling to finality, the Volunteer Minister works with not only the owner and the offender but with the law enforcement people.

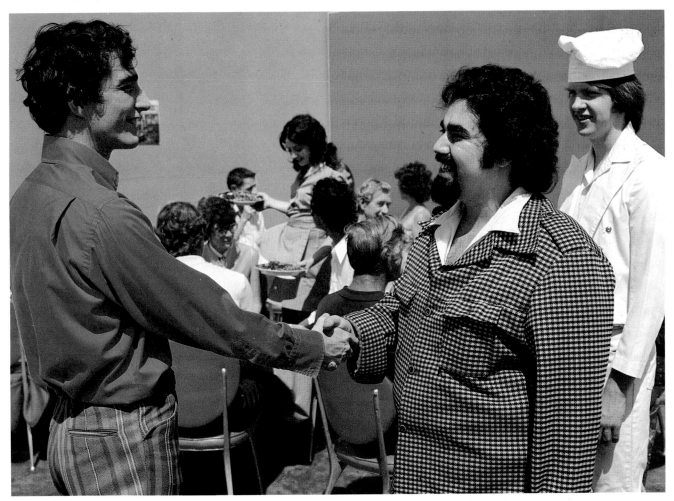

A handshake between the Volunteer Minister and the restaurant owner cements their friendship, as a new qualified cook is engaged and many patrons fill the restaurant, now restored to prosperity.

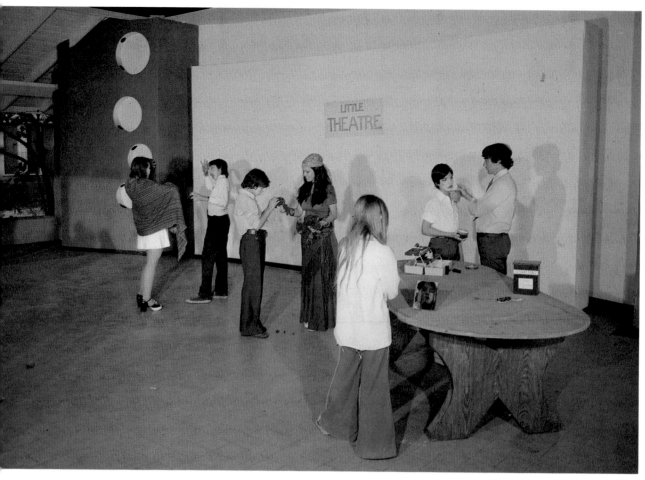

Once a Volunteer Minister, you will find yourself involved in community projects of all types, including the pastimes and endeavors of young people, who enjoy a Volunteer Minister's friendliness and participation, and who do look up to those who set an example of successful "growing up."

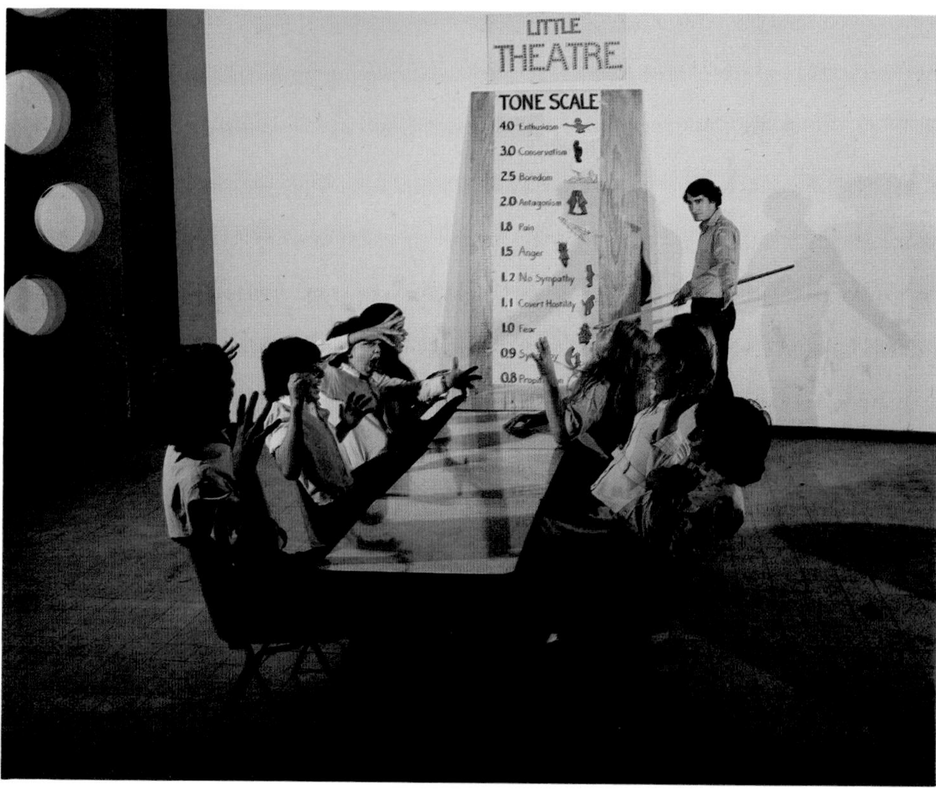

Part of the fun of contributing to the young will be in using Tone Scale technology and teaching it to them. Such training is invaluable to young thespians whose acting talents make them delight in doing the drills.

Young performers glow in these new accomplishments and bring added attention and donations to the worthwhile work that is done in Little Theatres throughout many communities.

Using his knowledge of effective public relations and targetting, the Volunteer Minister presents a police officer with a specific program to combat crime and strengthen police/community relations.

The Volunteer Minister influences the community as a whole by preparing a special campaign for his local Chamber of Commerce, an activity that he was trained to do through applying Scientology survey and targetting technology.

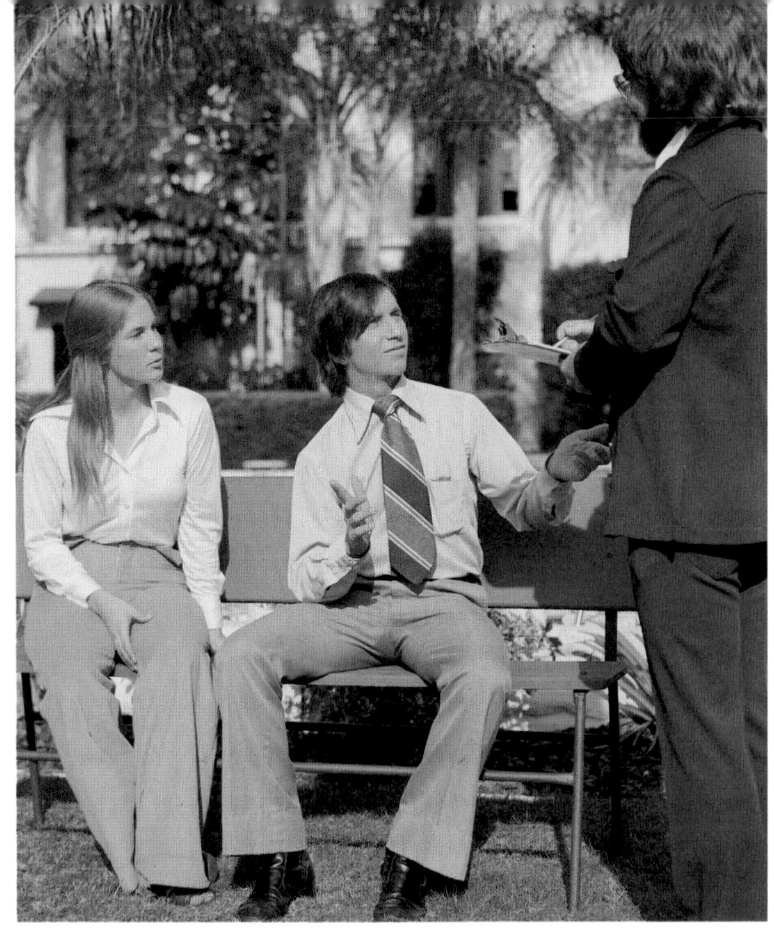

Employing survey techniques given in the *Volunteer Minister's Handbook,* he's able to create different types of survey campaigns, each directed to different publics, to find out what is needed and wanted and valuable to the community, then working out a series of targets to deliver according to survey results.

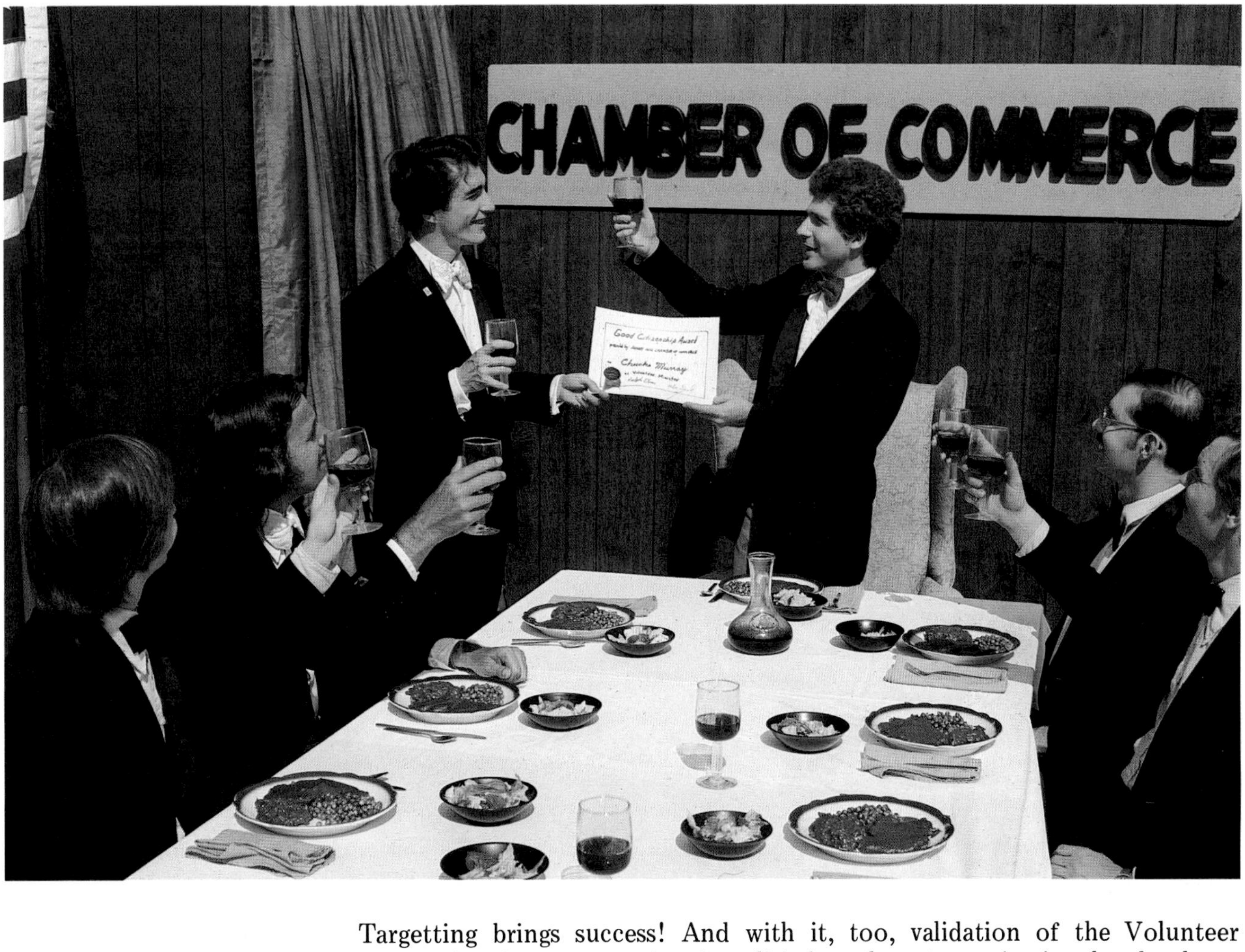

Targetting brings success! And with it, too, validation of the Volunteer Minister's role as a trusted and qualified teacher of organizational technology.

A Volunteer Minister has an understanding of other religions that enables him to work well with ministers of various other denominations for the improvement of religious interaction. He knows that Scientology is the science of human affairs which treats the livingness and beingness of Man, and demonstrates to him a pathway to greater freedom.

With his organizing abilities derived from his studies in management technology, which covers among other things the precise make and break items of any group, a Volunteer Minister is able to lead the way at ministerial conferences and be a prime contributor to harmonious actions taken within the religious community.

With his increased powers of communication, he outflows freely and exchanges ideas with other sects, and shepherds the way toward greater co-operation among all religions.

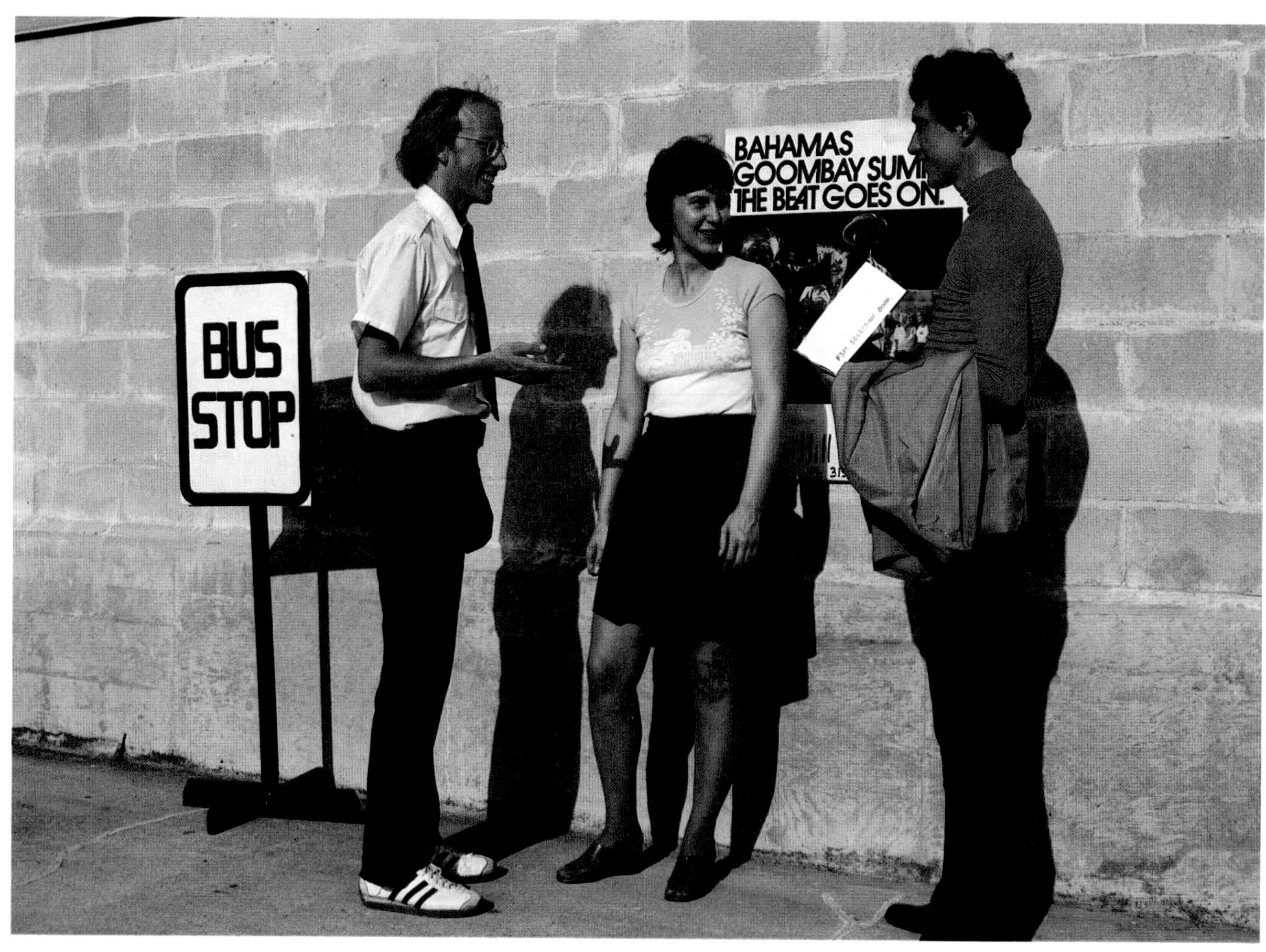

Becoming a Field Staff Member is another step taken by the Volunteer Minister. He lets friends and acquaintances know about the extensive processing and training services offered by the local Church of Scientology and selects them for their services.

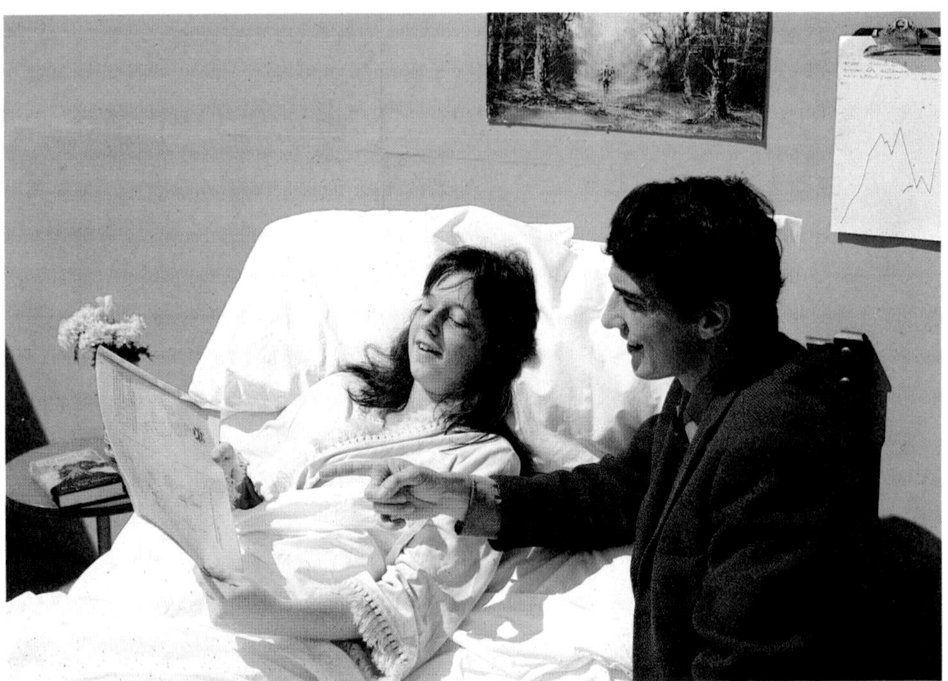

Visiting in hospitals, he brings patients' hopes up by showing them the road to full recovery through Scientology counseling and studies. The Volunteer Minister/Field Staff Member advises the person on the way that will be most helpful.

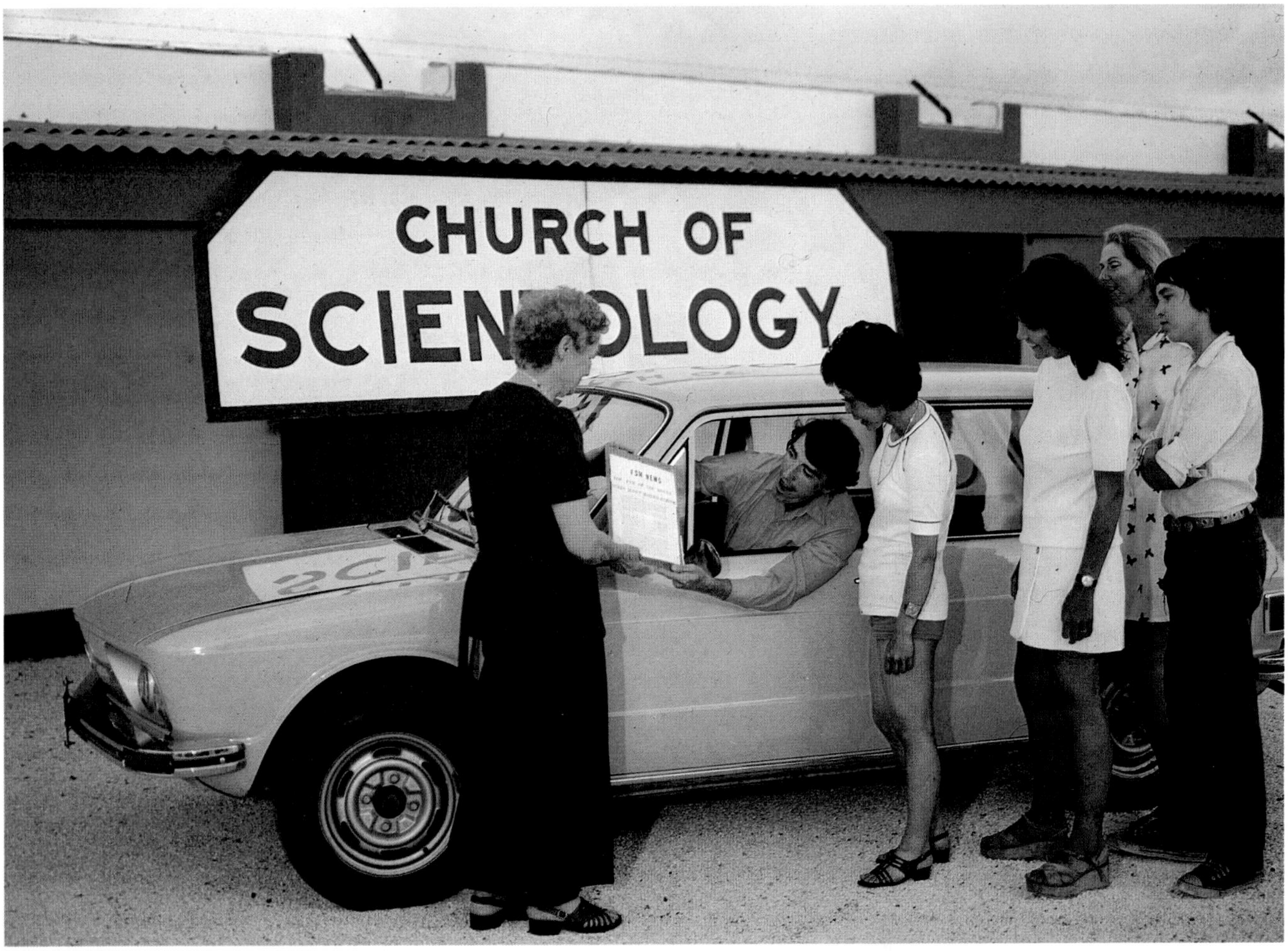

From activities in the community, the Volunteer Minister brings many more people into the Church of Scientology. In having touched so many lives for the better, he often receives special recognition for his FSM work.

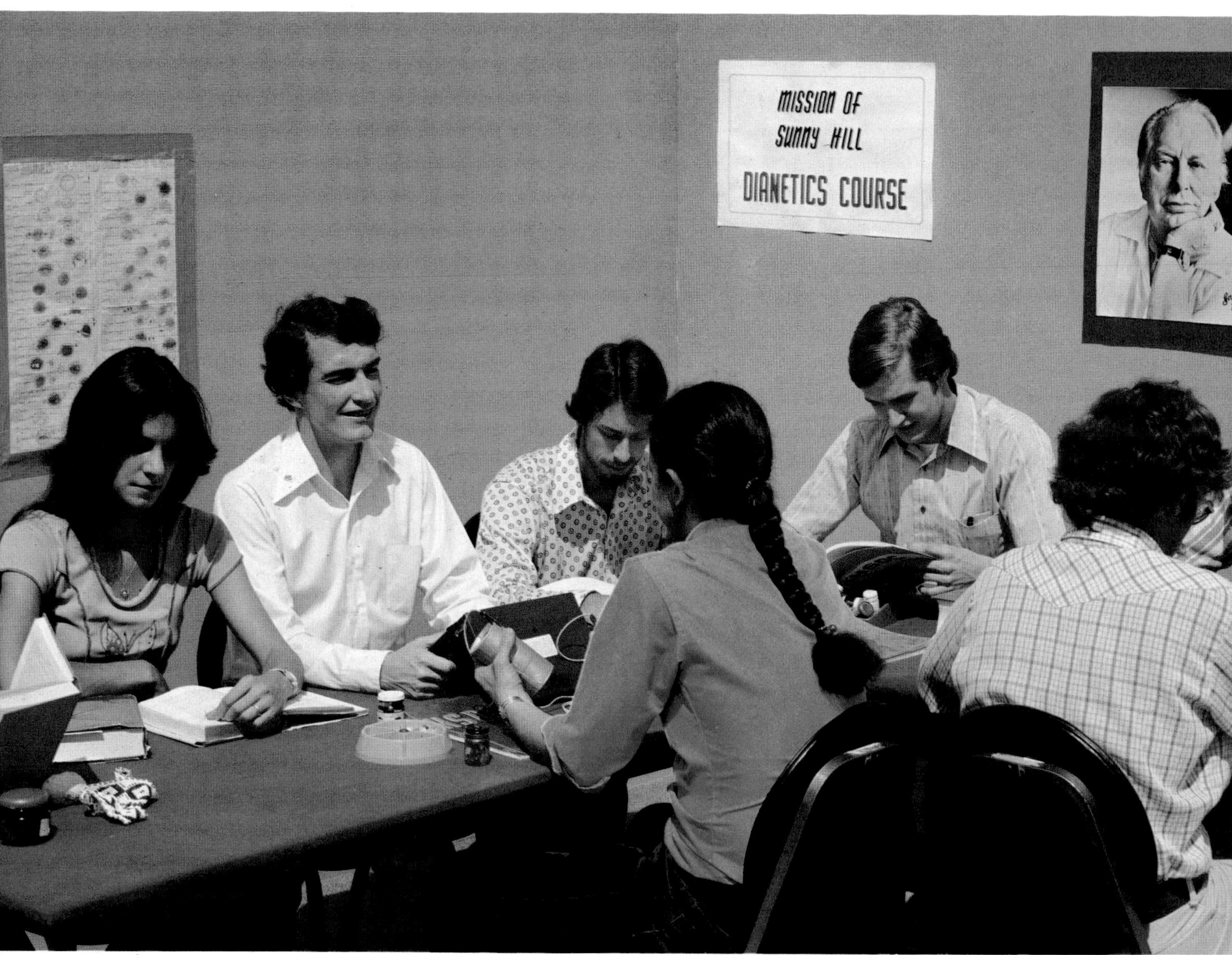

Customarily, the Volunteer Minister wants to learn further about Scientology processing in order to become a pastoral counselor, or auditor. Here he begins his training on how to use an E-Meter and the more advanced technological procedures so that he may handle an even wider range of human problems.

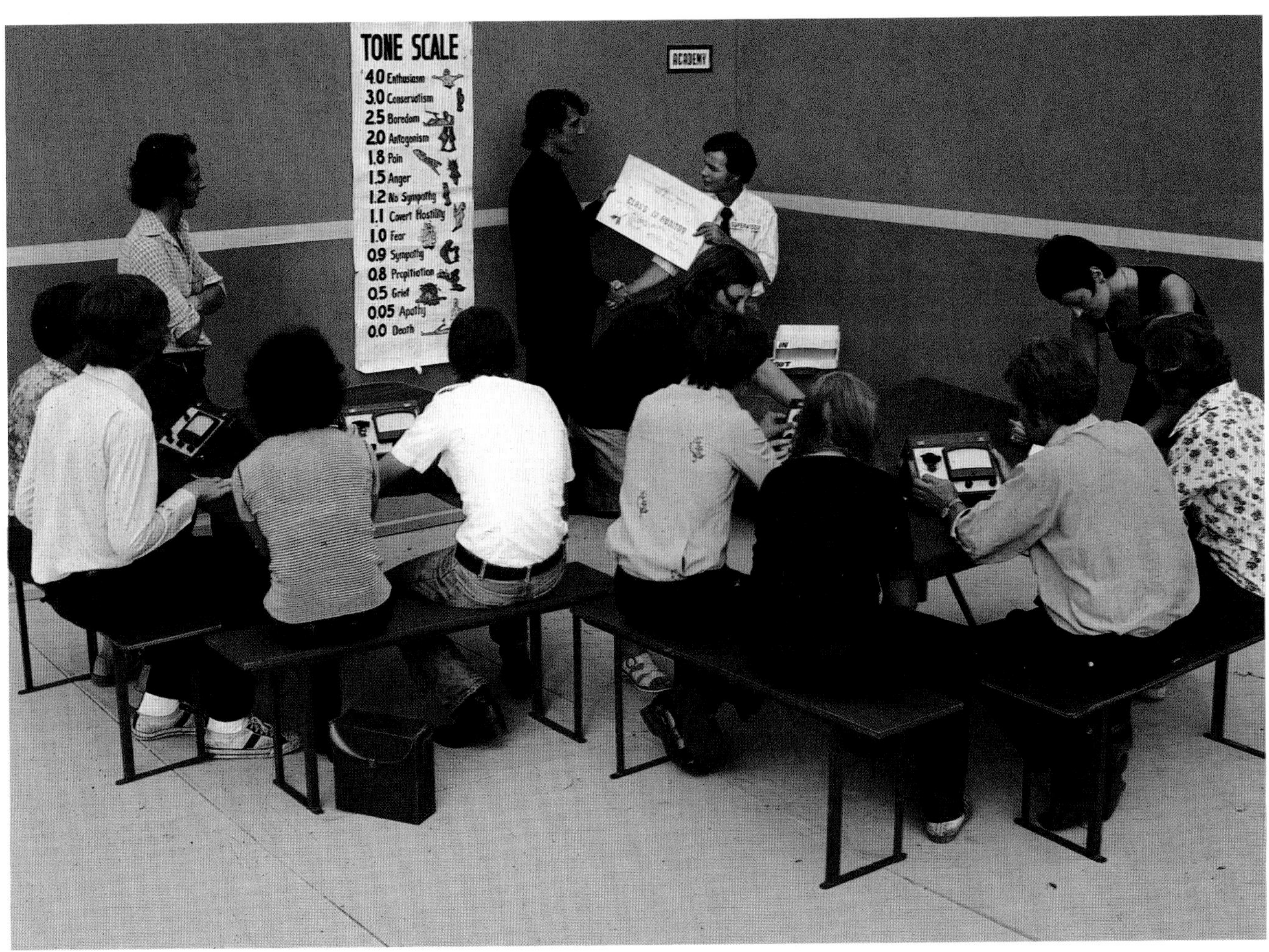

Working with others who have similar goals, the Volunteer Minister graduates as a trained auditor, competent in delivering Scientology processes to numerous people — the only effective spiritual counseling technology known to Man.

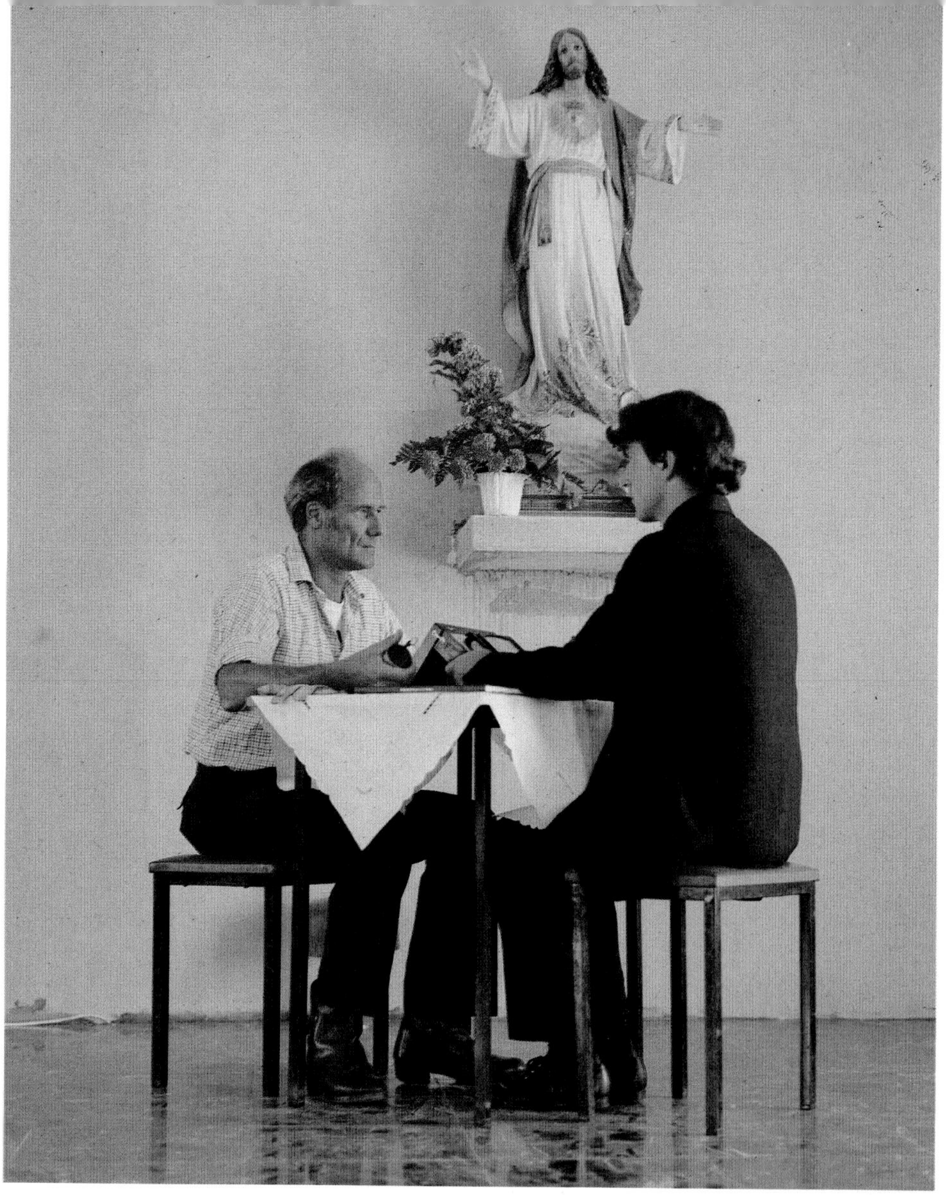

An auditor is an excellent listener, intrinsic in having mastered Scientology technology and being able to apply precisely what he has learned, and thereby truly help his preclear toward new awarenesses and viewpoints.

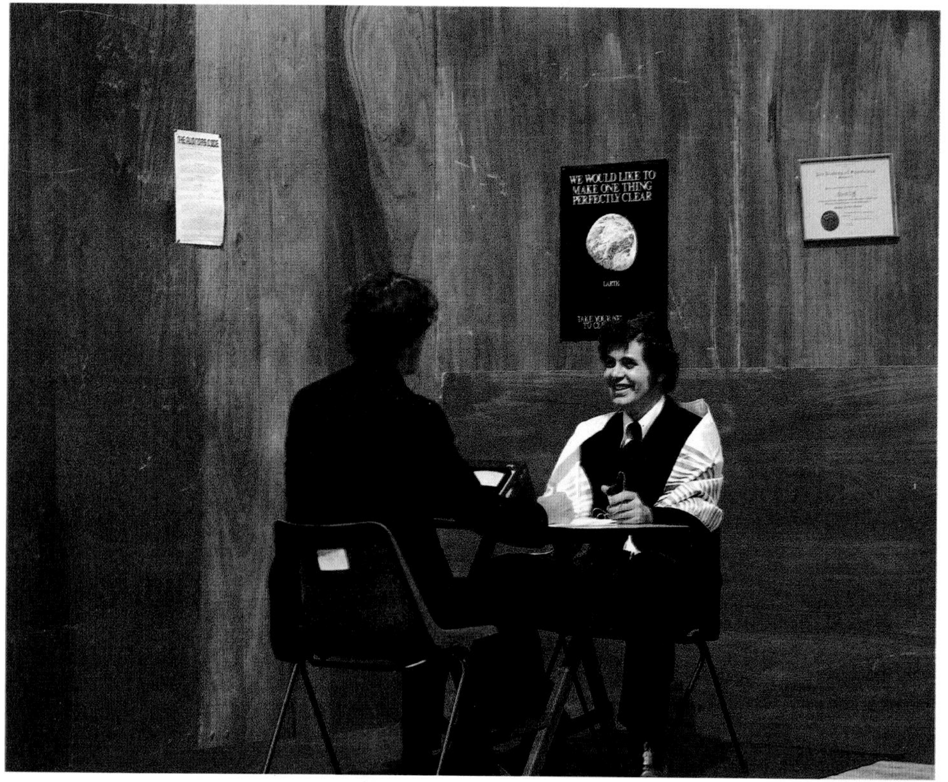

Having helped the preclear and seeing his good indicators, the Volunteer Minister/ Auditor wins too!

The Volunteer Minister/Auditor receives fair monetary exchange for his help and acquires a regular following of preclears.

Even in the case of heavy drug usage which we witness today, you as a Volunteer Minister will have special drug rehabilitation knowledge and training with which to deal with this widespread problem.

What you can tell those on drugs will interest them — that through proper vitamins and learning Scientology training drills to bring up their confront and communication level, they are able to come off drugs without having harsh withdrawal symptoms or suffering inhumane treatment.

Along with taking vitamins, they start on training drills, a gradient program of confronting each other, face to face, then handling a variety of communication cycles, so that they will gradually regain awareness of themselves as able people who can be contributing members of the society.

A cause for celebration! Two completely rehabilitated drug users and you, their Volunteer Minister.

A Volunteer Minister holds regular services in his home, talking to his congregation and teaching them more and more about themselves and life through applying Scientology, "the science of knowing how to know answers." People of all religious practices are welcome to these talks.

Among his duties, he performs marriages using the finely-worded ceremonies of the Church of Scientology.

He presides over funerals and is a wise counselor for family and friends.

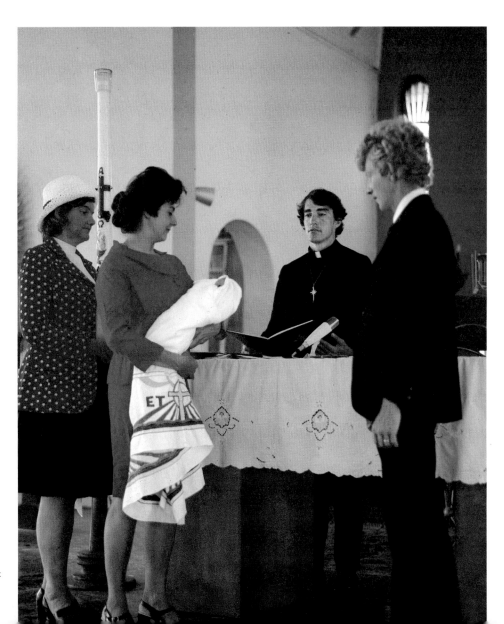

And he welcomes the newborn into the world with recognition of each baby as a loved being, as he performs the Naming Ceremony of the Church of Scientology.

Thus the Volunteer Minister, in the tradition of this new world religion, is a leader who brings greater freedom to people so that they may go out and free others, happier all in their understanding of themselves and life itself, and in the pleasure and accomplishments of living.

You, as a Volunteer Minister, are entrusted to help bring to earth this new day, through the religious philosophy and applied technology that is Scientology. Every age and religion has had its technology. The technology of today and tomorrow is Scientology.

The Volunteer Minister's Handbook

Introduction

Religious Influence in Society

An early 20th century philosopher spoke of the impending decline of the West. What he failed to predict was that the West would export its culture to the rest of the world and thus grip the entire world in its death throes.

Today we are witnessing that decline and since we are involved in it, it is of utmost importance to us. At stake are whether the ideals we cherish will survive or some new abhorrent set of values win the day.

These are not idle statements. We are today at a watershed of history and our actions today will decide whether the world goes up from here or continues to slide into some new dark age.

It is important to understand bad conditions don't just happen. The cultural decay we see around us isn't haphazard. It was caused. Unless one understands this he won't be able to defend himself or reach out into the society with effectiveness.

A society is capable of surviving for thousands of years unless it is attacked from within or without by hostile forces. Where such an attack occurs, primary targets are its religious and national gods and heroes, its potential of leadership and the self-respect and integrity of its members.

Material points of attack are finance, communications, technology and a denial of resources.

Look around today and you will find countless examples of these points. They scream at us every day from the newspapers.

Probably the most critical point of attack on a culture is its religious experience. Where one can destroy or undermine religious institutions then the entire fabric of the society can be quickly subverted or brought to ruin.

As you read on in this book you will discover why this is such an important factor and what can be done about it.

Religion is the first sense of community. Your sense of community occurs by reason of mutual experience with others. Where the religious sense of community and with it real trust and integrity can be destroyed then that society is like a sand castle unable to defend itself against the inexorable sea.

For the last hundred years or so religion has been beset with a relentless attack. You have been told it's the "opiate of the masses," that it's unscientific, that it is primitive; in short, that it is a delusion.

But beneath all these attacks on organized religion there was a more fundamental target: the spirituality of man, *your own basic spiritual nature, self-respect and peace of mind.* This black propaganda may have been so successful that maybe you no longer believe you have a spiritual nature but I assure you you do.

In fact, you don't have a soul, you *are* your own soul. In other words, you are not this book, your social security card, your body or your mind. You are you. This will become more apparent, if it isn't already clear, as you read this book.

Convince a man that he is an animal, that his own dignity and self-respect are delusions, that there is no "beyond" to aspire to, no higher potential self to achieve, and you have a slave. Let a man know he is himself, a spiritual being, that he is capable of the power of choice and has the right to aspire to greater wisdom and you have started him up a higher road.

Of course, such attacks on religion run counter to man's *traditional* aspirations to spiritual fulfillment and an ethical way of life.

For thousands of years on this planet thinking man has upheld his own spirituality and considered the ultimate wisdom to be spiritual enlightenment.

The new radical thought that man is an animal without a spiritual nature has a name: totalitarian materialism. Materialism is the doctrine that "only matter matters." The apostles of this new thought are trying to sell everybody on the idea that people really down deep are just a mass and what the person wants to do is cohese with this mass and then be protected by the mass.

This philosophical position was very handy to militaristic and totalitarian governments and their advocates of the last hundred years who wished to justify their atrocities and subjugation of populaces.

One of the tricks of the game has been to attack religion as unscientific. Yet science itself is merely a tool by which the physical universe can be better controlled. The joke is that science itself can become a religion.

Gerhard Lenski on page 331 of his *The Religious Factor, a Sociologist's Inquiry,* defines religion as "a system of beliefs about the nature of force(s), ultimately shaping man's destiny, and the practices associated therewith, shared by members of a group."

Scientific activities can be as fanatical as religious ones. Scientific groups can themselves be religious "orthodox science" monopolies. The Einsteinian concept of space and time can itself become a holy writ, just as Aristotle's writings were converted into dogmas by the orthodoxy to squash any new ideas in the Middle Ages. (Einstein himself until late in his life was looked upon as a maverick and denied admittance into learned societies.)

Science in itself can become a new faith, a brave new way of overcoming anxiety by explaining things so there is no fear of God or the hereafter.

Thus science and religion are not a dichotomy (pair of opposites). Science itself was borrowed from ancient religious studies in India and Egypt.

Religion has also been attacked as primitive. Too much study of primitive cultures may lead one to believe religion is primitive as it is so dominant in them and that "modern" cultures can dispense with it. The truth of the matter is that at no time is religion more necessary as a civilizing force than in the presence of huge forces in the hands of Man, who may have become very lacking in social abilities emphasized in religion.

The great religious civilizing forces of the past, Buddhism, Judaism, Christianity, and others, have all emphasized differentiation of good from evil and higher ethical values.

The lowering of Church attendance in the United States coincided with a rise in pornography and general immorality, and an increase in crime which then caused a rise in numbers of police without a subsequent decline in actual moral aberration.

When religion is not influential in a society or has ceased to be, the state inherits the entire burden of public morality, crime and intolerance. It then must use punishment and police. Yet this is unsuccessful as morality, integrity and self-respect not already inherent in the individual, cannot be enforced with any great success. Only by a spiritual awareness and inculcation of the spiritual value of these attributes can they come about. There must be more reason and more emotional motivation to be moral etc., than threat of human discipline.

When a culture has fallen totally away from spiritual pursuits into materialism, one must begin by demonstrating they are each a soul, not a material animal. From this realization of their own religious nature individuals can again come to an awareness of God and become more themselves.

Medicine, psychiatry and psychology "solved" the whole problem of "human nature" simply by dumping it into the classification of material nature—body, brain, force. As they politically insist on monopoly and use social and political propaganda to enforce their monopoly, they debar actual search for real answers to human nature.

Their failures are attested by lack of result in the field of human nature. They cannot change man—they can only degrade. While asserting dominance in the field of human nature they cannot demonstrate results—and nowhere do they demonstrate that lack more than in their own persons. They have the highest suicide rate and prefer the use of force on others. Under their tutelage the crime rate and antisocial forces have risen. But they are most condemned by their attacks on anyone who seeks answers and upon the civilizing influences of religion.

Of course, if one is going to find fault with something, it implies that he wishes to do something about it and would if he could. If one does not like the crime, cruelty, injustice and violence of this society, he *can* do something about it. He can become a VOLUNTEER MINISTER and help civilize it, bring it conscience and kindness and love and freedom from travail by instilling into it trust, decency, honesty and tolerance.

Briefly, a Volunteer Minister fulfills the definition of religion in this increasingly cynical and hopeless world.

Let's look again at the definition of religion.

In a few words, religion can be defined as belief in spiritual beings. More broadly, religion can be defined as a system of beliefs and practices by means of which a group of people struggles with the ultimate problems of human life. The quality of being religious implies two things: first, a belief that evil, pain, bewilderment and injustice are fundamental facts of existence; second, a set of practices and related sanctified beliefs that express a conviction that man can ultimately be saved from those facts.†

Thus, a Volunteer Minister is a person who helps his fellow man on a volunteer basis by restoring purpose, truth and spiritual values to the lives of others.

A Volunteer Minister does not shut his eyes to the pain, evil and injustice of existence. Rather, he is trained to handle these things and help others achieve relief from them and new personal strength as well.

How does a Volunteer Minister accomplish these miracles? Basically, he uses the technology of Scientology to change conditions for the better—for himself, his family, his groups, friends, associates and for mankind.

A society to survive well, needs at least as many Volunteer Ministers as it has policemen. A society gets what it concentrates upon. By concentrating on spiritual values instead of criminality a new day may yet dawn for Man.

†Reference *A Scientific Study of Religion* by J. Milton Yunger, Oberlin College.

A

Study

Study Checksheet

Purpose:

To learn the rules, concepts and demonstration of study techniques so that the student will never go past a misunderstood word nor lack the ability to apply the data he is studying.

a Study Section 1 Vital Data on Study. ________

b Drill: Write out the *rule* pertaining to the role the misunderstood word plays *invariably* in studying. ________

c Drill: Write an example of how a confused idea stems from a misunderstood word. ________

d Study Section 2 Definition of a Student. ________

e Study Section 3 The Intention of the Student. ________

f Drill: Look up the word "intention" in a good dictionary. Use it in several sentences of your own, related to the goals you have. ________

g Study Section 4 Learning Processes, Education by Evaluation of Importance. ________

h Study Section 5 Barriers to Study. ________

i Drill: If at any time as you're studying this Volunteer Minister's Handbook you find yourself (1) spinny or bored, (2) having particular difficulty in assigning and applying doingness or action to an idea in the text or (3) feeling blank, what are the three stumbling blocks you know you've encountered? (Write them down.) What remedies will you use? (Write them down.) ________

j Study Section 6 Study Phenomena. ________

k Drill: Regarding misunderstood words, draw a diagram of the second phenomena cycle. ________

l Study Section 7 Simple Words. ________

m Study Section 8 Words, Misunderstood Goofs. ________

n Drill: Without reference to Section 8 again, write down the *rule* that explains the relationship between earliest and later misunderstood words. ________

o Study Section 9 How to Use a Dictionary. ________

p Drill: Look up the words "word," "concept" and "idea" in a good dictionary. Now draw a diagram that illustrates their relationship. How does this apply to or affect your own study habits? ________

q Study Section 10 Dinky Dictionaries. ________

r Study Section 11 Demo Kits. ________

s Drill: Put together a demo kit of your own. ________

t Drill: Demonstrate what happens to a student when he goes past a misunderstood word (using pieces of your demo kit for each of these): the student, the text book, the part he's having difficulty with, the misunderstood word, the various ways the student feels. ________

u Drill: Now demonstrate in the same way, using a separate piece from your demo kit to represent each separate thing involved, what the student does to find and correct a misunderstood word. Move the pieces about to show all the actions or steps he takes. Do this until you feel good about using a demo kit. ________

v Study Section 12 What is a Checksheet. ________

Study Pack

The Organization
Executive Course
Basic Staff Volume 0
page 9

1
Vital Data on Study

One of the biggest barriers to learning a new subject is its nomenclature, meaning the set of terms used to describe the things it deals with. A subject must have accurate labels which have exact meanings before it can be understood and communicated.

If I were to describe parts of the body as "thingamabobs" and "whatsernames," we would all be in a confusion, so the accurate naming of something is a very important part of any field.

A student comes along and starts to study something and has a terrible time of it. Why? Because he or she not only has a lot of new principles and methods to learn, but a whole new language as well. Unless the student understands this, unless he or she realizes that one has to "know the words before one can sing the tune," he or she is not going to get very far in any field of study or endeavor.

Now I am going to give you an important datum:

The only reason a person gives up a study or becomes confused or unable to learn is because he or she has gone past a word that was not understood.

The confusion or inability to grasp or learn comes AFTER a word that the person did not have defined and understood.

Have you ever had the experience of coming to the end of a page and realizing you didn't know what you had read? Well, somewhere earlier on that page you went past a word that you had no definition for.

Here's an example. "It was found that when the crepuscule arrived the children were quieter and when it was not present, they were much livelier." You see what happens. You think you don't understand the whole idea, but the inability to understand came entirely from the one word you could not define, *crepuscule* which means twilight or darkness.

This datum about not going past an undefined word is the most important fact in the whole subject of study. Every subject you have taken up and abandoned had its words which you failed to get defined.

Therefore, in studying Scientology be very, very certain you never go past a word you do not fully understand. If the material becomes confusing or you can't seem to grasp it, there will be a word just earlier that you have not understood. Don't go any further, but go back to BEFORE you got into trouble, find the misunderstood word and get it defined.

That is why we have a dictionary. It will not only be the new and unusual words that you will have to look up. Some commonly used words can often be misdefined and so cause confusion. So don't depend on our dictionary alone. Use a general English language dictionary as well for any non-Scientology word you do not understand when you are reading or studying.

2

*BTB 26 October 1970
Issue II

Definition of A Student

A student is one who studies. He is an attentive and systematic observer. A student is one who reads in detail in order to learn and then apply.

As a student studies he knows that his purpose is to understand the materials he is studying by reading, observing, and demonstrating so as to apply them to a specific result.

He connects what he is studying to what he will be doing.

3
The Intention of the Student

*BTB 27 October 1970
(Extracted from Study Tapes)

The state of mind with which a student approaches study will determine the results that student gets from the study.

The student *must* determine what he is going to do with the materials he is studying. He *must* determine what he is going to do with the information he is absorbing.

If a student's intent is to study the materials so he can pass the exam he will be very incapable of doing anything with the subject once the exam is over. He might be a great theoretician, but he will not be able to use the subject.

Some students don't have any intention other than getting through the course. They are just there studying away. They balk at doing demos or looking up words for their exact meaning. Even when forced to demonstrate something they maintain the attitude that it has nothing to do with them. "It's all very interesting to read but . . . ."

Non-involvement is the primary barrier in the ability to apply the materials of a course.

There can be many reasons for study. Points, exams, status, speed, glory, whatever.

There is only one valid reason: Studying for understanding, application and practice.

4

*BTB 14 September 1969
Issue I

Learning Processes, Education by Evaluation of Importance

Education by importance is all right as long as you are in terrific ARC with your people. If you are not in terrific ARC with the people you have, you have to get them to relax about the body of data you are teaching before the importance of data shows up.

A person can be hung up on the all-importance and everythingness of a subject. He is so nervous of dire consequences that he will eventually have an accident. People are often thoroughly educated into this attitude. It is all so important it will kill him if he doesn't know. This inhibits his power of choice and ability to evaluate data. Education today is taught by consequence, not by the fact it is a sensible thing to do. In the world, importance essentially means punishment.

To teach someone a subject just have him select out the unimportances of the subject. He will start to think everything is important but coax him on with ARC and control and he will eventually come up with something unimportant, i.e., you are teaching him how to drive a tractor. He will find the coat of paint on the crank unimportant. You acknowledge and ask him to find something else unimportant. Keep at this repeating it and repeating it and eventually "all-ness" will start to disintegrate. He will select down to the most important controls of the tractor and the next thing you know he can drive a tractor! He won't have a craving-to-know anxiety and won't be nervous at all. You are teaching by de-evaluation of importance.

It is interesting that a person who never selected out the importances of Scientology or any subject, and believes every datum must be memorized, you will find, has a history of being punished within an inch of their lives. There is a direct coordination here.

Education is basically, fixing data, unfixing data, and changing existing data, either by making it more fixed or less fixed.

This technology using importances can undo to a marked extent a very thorough education in some subject and return it to the power of choice of an individual.

5 Barriers to Study

HCOB 25 June 1971
Word Clearing Series 3

There are three different sets of physiological and mental reactions that come from three different aspects of study. They are three different sets of symptoms.

(1) Education in the absence of the *mass* in which the technology will be involved is very hard on the student.

It makes him feel physiologically condensed. Actually makes him feel squashed. Makes him feel bent, sort of spinny, sort of dead, bored, exasperated.

If he is studying the doingness of something in which the mass is absent this will be the result.

Photographs help and motion pictures would do pretty good as they are a sort of promise or hope of the mass but the printed page and the spoken word are not a substitute for a tractor if he's studying about tractors.

You have to understand this data in its purity—and that is that educating a person in a mass that they don't have and which isn't available produces physiological reactions. That is what I am trying to teach you.

It's just a fact.

You're trying to teach this fellow all about tractors and you're not giving him any tractors—well, he's going to wind up with a face that feels squashed, with headaches and with his stomach feeling funny. He's going to feel dizzy from time to time and very often his eyes are going to hurt.

It's a physiological datum that has to do with processing and the field of the mind.

You could therefore expect the greatest incidence of suicide or illness in that field of education devoted to studying absent masses.

This one of studying the something without its mass ever being around produces the most distinctly recognizable reactions.

If a child felt sick in the field of study and it were traced back to this one, the positive remedy would be to supply the mass—the object or a reasonable substitute—and it would clear it up.

(2) There is another series of physiological phenomena that exist which is based on the fact of too steep a study gradient.

That's another source of physiological study reaction because of too steep a gradient.

It is a sort of a confusion or a reelingness that goes with this one.

You've hit too steep a gradient.

There was too much of a jump because he didn't understand what he was doing and he jumped to the next thing and that was too steep and he went too fast and he will *assign* all of his difficulties to this new thing.

Now differentiate here—because gradients sounds terribly like the third one of these study hang ups, definitions—but remember that they are quite distinctly different.

Gradients are more pronounced in the field of doingness but they still hang over into the field of understanding. In gradients however it is the *actions* we are interested in. We have a plotted course of forward motion of actions. We find he was terribly confused on the second action he was supposed to do. We must assume then that he never really got out of the first one.

The remedy for this one of too steep a gradient is cutting back. Find out when he was not confused on the gradient, then what new action he undertook to do. Find what action he understood well. Just before he was all confused what did he understand well—and then we find out that he didn't understand it well.

It's really at the tail end of what he understood and then he went over the gradient you see.

It is most recognizable and most applicable in the field of doingness.

That's the gradient barrier and one full set of phenomena accompanies that.

(3) There is this third one. An entirely different set of physiological reactions brought about through a bypassed definition. A bypassed definition gives one a distinctly blank feeling or a washed out feeling. A not-there feeling and a sort of an hysteria will follow in the back of that.

The manifestation of "blow" stems from this third aspect of study which is the misunderstood definition or the not comprehended definition, *the undefined word.*

That's the one that produces the blow.

The person doesn't necessarily blow on these other two—they are not pronouncedly blow phenomena. They are simply physiological phenomena.

This one of the misunderstood definition is so much more important. It's the make up of human relations, the mind and subjects. It establishes aptitude and lack of aptitude and it's what psychologists have been trying to test for years without recognizing what it was.

It's the definition of words.

The misunderstood word.

That's all it goes back to and that produces such a vast panorama of mental effects that it itself is the prime factor involved with stupidity and the prime factor involved with many other things.

If a person didn't have misunderstoods his *talent* might or might not be present but his *doingness* would be present.

We can't say that Joe would paint as *well* as Bill if both were unaberrated in the field of art, but we can say that the *inability* of Joe to paint compared with the *ability* of Joe to do the motions of painting is dependent exclusively and only upon definitions.

There is some word in the field of art that the person who is inept didn't define or understand and that is followed by an inability to act in the field of the arts.

That's very important because it tells you what happens to doingness and that the restoration of doingness depends only upon the restoration of understanding on the misunderstood word.

That is very fast processing. There is a very swift wide big result obtainable in this.

It has a technology which is a very simple technology.

It enters in at the lower levels because it has to. This doesn't mean it is unimportant; it means it has to be at the entrance gates of Scientology.

It is a sweepingly fantastic discovery in the field of education and don't neglect it.

You can trace back the subject a person is dumb in or any allied subject that got mixed up with it. The psychologist doesn't understand Scientology. He never understood a word in psychology so he doesn't understand Scientology.

Well, that opens the gate to education. Although I've given this one of the misunderstood definition last, it is the most important one.

HCO PL 24 September 1964 *Instruction & Examination: Raising the Standard of*
HCO PL 4 October 1964 *Theory Checkout Data*

6 Study Phenomena

There are two phenomena here.

First Phenomenon: When a student misses understanding a word, the section right after that word is a blank in his memory. You can always trace back to the word just before the blank, get it understood and find miraculously that the former blank area is not now blank in the bulletin. The above is pure magic.

Second Phenomenon: The second phenomenon is the overt cycle which follows a misunderstood word. When a word is not grasped, the student then goes into a non-comprehension (blankness) of things immediately after. This is followed by the student's solution for the blank condition which is to individuate from it—separate self from it. Now being something else than the blank area, the student commits overts against the more general area. These overts, of course, are followed by restraining himself from committing overts. This pulls flows toward the person and makes the person crave motivators. This is followed by various mental and physical conditions and by various complaints, fault-finding and look-what-you-did-to-me. This justifies a departure, a blow.

But the system of education, frowning on blows as it does, causes the student to really withdraw self from the study subject (whatever he was studying) and set up in its place a circuit which can receive and give back sentences and phrases.

We now have "the quick student who somehow never applies what he learns."

The specific phenomena then is that a student can study some words and give them back and yet be no participant to the action. The student gets A+ on exams but can't apply the data.

The thoroughly dull student is just stuck in the non-comprehend blankness following some misunderstood word.

The "very bright" student who yet can't use the data isn't there at all. He has long since ceased to confront the subject matter or the subject.

The cure for either of these conditions of "bright non-comprehension" or "dull" is to find the missing word.

But these conditions can be prevented by not letting the student go beyond the missed word without grasping its meaning.

The "Bright" Ones

Demonstration is the key here. The moment you ask this type of student to demonstrate a rule or theory with his hands or the paper clips on your desk this glibness will shatter.

The reason for this is that in memorizing words or ideas, the student can still hold the position that it has nothing to do with him or her. It is a total circuit action. Therefore, very glib. The moment you say *"demonstrate"* that word or idea or principle, the student *has* to have something to do with it. And shatters.

One student passed "Itsa" in theory with flying colors every time even on cross-check type questions, yet had never been known to listen. When the theory instructor said, "Demonstrate what a student would have to do to pass Itsa," the whole subject blew up. "There's too many ways to do Itsa auditing!" the student said. Yet on the bulletin it merely said "Listen." That given as a glib answer was all right. But "demonstration" brought to light that this student hadn't a clue about listening to a preclear. If *he* had to demonstrate it, the non-participation of the student in the material he was studying came to light.

Don't get the idea that demonstration is a practical section action. Practical gives the *drills.* These demonstrations in theory aren't drills.

Demonstration

Giving a bulletin or tape check by seeing if it can be quoted or paraphrased proves exactly nothing. This will not guarantee that the student knows the data or can use or apply it nor even guarantees that the student is there. Neither the "bright" student nor the "dull" student (both suffering from the same malady) will benefit from such an examination.

So examining by seeing if somebody "knows" the text and can quote or paraphrase it is completely false and *must not be done.*

Correct examination is done only by making the person being tested answer: (a) the meanings of the words (redefining the words used in his own words and demonstrating their use in his own made up sentences), and (b) demonstrating how the data is *used.*

7

HCOB 4 September 1971
Issue III, Word Clearing
Series 20

Simple Words

You might suppose at once that it is the BIG words or the technical words which are most misunderstood.

This is NOT the case.

On actual test, it was English simple words and NOT Dianetics and Scientology words which prevented understanding.

For some reason Dianetics and Scientology words are more easily grasped than simple English.

Words like "a," "the," "exist," "such" and other "everybody knows" words show up with great frequency when doing word clearing.

It takes a BIG dictionary to define these simple words fully. This is another oddity. The small dictionaries also suppose everybody knows.

It is almost incredible to see that a university graduate has gone through years and years of study of complex subjects and yet does not know what "or" or "by" or "an" means. It has to be seen to be believed. Yet when cleaned up his whole education turns from a solid mass of question marks to a clean useful view.

A test of school children in Johannesburg once showed that intelligence DECREASED with each new year of school!

The answer to the puzzle was simply that each year they added a few dozen more crushing misunderstood words onto an already confused vocabulary that no one ever got them to look up.

Stupidity *is* the effect of misunderstood words.

In those areas which give Man the most trouble you will find the most alteration of fact, the most confused and conflicting ideas and of course the greatest number of misunderstood words. Take "economics" for example.

The subject of psychology began its texts by saying they did not know what the word means. So the subject itself never arrived. Professor Wundt of Leipzig University in 1879 perverted the term. It really means just "a study (ology) of the soul (psyche)." But Wundt, working under the eye of Bismarck, the greatest of German military fascists at the height of the German war ambitions, had to deny man had a soul. So there went the whole subject! Men were thereafter animals (it is all right to kill animals) and Man had no soul, so the word psychology could no longer be defined.

THE EARLIEST MISUNDERSTOOD WORD IN A SUBJECT IS A KEY TO LATER MISUNDERSTOOD WORDS IN THAT SUBJECT.

Then come words like "a" "the" and other simple English as the next words that are often misunderstood.

In studying a foreign language it is often found that the grammar words of one's *own* language that tell about the grammar in the foreign language are basic to not being able to learn the foreign language.

That a person *says* he knows the meaning is *not* acceptable. Have him look it up no matter how simple the word is.

8

HCOB 10 March 1965
Scientology 0,
Scientology VI

Words, Misunderstood Goofs

It has come to my attention that words a student misunderstands and looks up can yet remain troublesome.

It's this way: The student runs across a word he or she doesn't understand. He or she looks it up in a dictionary, finds a substitute word and uses that.

Of course, the first word is still misunderstood and remains a bother.

Example: (Line in text) "The size was Gargantuan." Student looks up Gargantuan, finds "like Gargantua, huge." Student uses "huge" as a synonym and reads the text line "The size was 'huge'." A short while later is found still incapable of understanding the paragraph below "Gargantua" in the text. Conclusion the student makes—"Well, it doesn't work."

The principle is that one goes dull after passing over a word one does not understand and brightens up the moment he spots the word that wasn't grasped. In actual fact, the brightening up occurs whether one defines the word or not.

But to put another word in the place of the existing word is to mess it all up.

Take the above example. "Huge" is not "Gargantuan." These are synonyms. The sentence is "The size was Gargantuan." The sentence was *not,* "The size was huge." You can't really substitute one word for another and get anything but an alteration. So something remains not understood.

The *correct* procedure is to look over, get defined well and understand *the* word that was used.

In this case the word was "Gargantuan." Very well, what's that? It means "like Gargantua" according to the dictionary.

Who or *what* was Gargantua? The dictionary says it was the name of a gigantic king in a book written by the author Rabelais. Cheers, the student thinks, the sentence meant "The size was a gigantic king." Oops! That's the same goof again like "huge." But we're nearer.

So what to do? Use Gargantuan in a few sentences you make up and bingo! You suddenly understand *the* word that was used.

Now you read it right. "The size was Gargantuan." And what does that mean? It means "The size was Gargantuan." And *nothing* else.

Get it?

There's no hope for it, mate. You'll have to learn real English, not the 600 word basic English of the college kid, in which a few synonyms are substituted for all the big words.

9

*BTB 4 September 1971R
Word Clearing Series 22R

How to Use a Dictionary

You use a dictionary when word clearing. The misunderstood word is looked up in the dictionary and you learn what the word means so that you know it without again referring to the dictionary. Then the word is used in several sentences which clearly indicate that you understand it.

Words sometimes have different or more than one meaning. You have to know every different meaning so all definitions are looked up and the word is fully defined. You also must choose the definition in use in the sentence so that the materials are understood.

The Alphabet

Knowledge of the alphabet is the key to finding words quickly. The alphabet must be known cold. The person who has to figure out which letter comes first, m or n or u or v, wastes many precious minutes which can add up to many wasted hours.

Words are arranged in alphabetical order in all dictionaries. All words beginning with the letter A would be in the first section, all words beginning with the letter B in the second section, and so on. Within these sections the words themselves are arranged so that each second letter in the word is in alphabetical order. (For example, the word "fall" precedes the word "few," which precedes the word "field," etc.)

Near the top of each page, printed in bold type, are the first word and the last word on the page (in very large dictionaries it's every two columns). You can use this as a guide to quickly find the page that contains the word you are looking for.

How to Break up a Word

Many words are in a combined form and by separating the word you can look up each part in the dictionary. By doing this, the meaning of the word often becomes clearer. Take the word Theo-logy.

The first part, Theo- means God or Gods and the second part of the word, -logy means discourse or expression or the science, theory or study of. When you put the two parts together, you have the science, theory or study of God. Sometimes in combining forms of words, a letter is changed, as in the word in-dividu (e)-ate.

Look up Words in the Definition

Many times when looking up a word, you will find in its definition other words which need to be looked up in order to understand the meaning of the original word. Therefore, each word given in the definition must also be clearly defined and understood so that there are no underlying misunderstood words on the word you are looking up. Large children's dictionaries are good as the definition words are simple.

The so-called "Merriam Webster" dictionaries in the US are almost useless and give out more misunderstoods in definitions than they clarify in clearing, don't bother with them. The *World Book Dictionary* available from Field Enterprises, Merchandise Mart Plaza, Chicago, Illinois, 60654, is a huge and very good child's dictionary. In the UK the 18 Volume Oxford series are good.

Use a Big Enough Dictionary

The smaller dictionaries (paperback or junior) seldom contain complete definitions of a word. Sometimes a most vital part of a definition is omitted. This can involve running around to look for another dictionary or missing the real meaning of the word. So always use a big enough dictionary.

Get the Word Used in Sentences

The word, when cleared with the dictionary, is then used over and over in sentences until you understand it.

The dictionary usually has several examples of use. These are not enough. The person has to make up several of his own before he really knows the word.

Words of a special technology require a dictionary of it if possible.

Many students have been or are engaged in technical professions outside of Scientology such as engineering, computer programming, architecture etc., and you would need a glossary or dictionary of the terms involved in these technologies.

Foreign Words—Get a Dictionary of that Language

There are two kinds of foreign language dictionaries. One is a dictionary entirely in the foreign language. The other is the English/foreign language dictionary, in which one half of the dictionary is English words with the foreign word next to it, and the other half is the foreign word with its English counterpart next to it. You would use the all foreign dictionary only with a person who knew that language fluently.

You use a dictionary. It is always a misunderstood word, never a concept or idea.

10

HCOB 19 June 1972
Word Clearing Series 37

Dinky Dictionaries

In learning the meaning of words small dictionaries are very often a greater liability than they are a help.

The meanings they give are often circular: Like "CAT: An Animal." "ANIMAL: A Cat." They do not give enough meaning to escape the circle.

The meanings given are often inadequate to get a real concept of the word.

The words are too few and even common words are often missing.

HUGE dictionaries can also be confusing as the words they use to define are often too big or too rare and make one chase through twenty new words to get the meaning of the original.

The best dictionaries are the very large children's dictionaries like *The World Book Dictionary* (A Thorndike-Barnhart Dictionary published exclusively for Field Enterprises Educational Corporation, Merchandise Mart Plaza, Chicago, Illinois 60654 or Doubleday and Company. Thorndike-Barnhart has a whole series of dictionaries of which this is a special one. Field Enterprises has offices in Chicago, London, Rome, Sydney, Toronto. The *World Book Dictionary* is in two volumes, each 28 1/2 cm (11 1/4 inches) by 22 cm (8 5/8 inches) by 5.8 cm (2 1/4 inches), so it is no small dictionary!) (Also it defines Dianetics correctly and isn't determined on a course of propaganda to re-educate the public unlike Merriam Webster's dictionaries).

Little pocketbook dictionaries may have their uses for traveling and reading newspapers, but they *do* get people in trouble. I have seen people find a word in them and then look around in total confusion. For the dinky dictionary did not give the full meaning or the second meaning they really needed.

So the dinky dictionary may fit in your pocket but not your mind.

11 Demo Kits

|*BTB 29 October 1970R

All students are required to have their own demonstration kit.

A demo kit is a bunch of rubber bands, batteries, fuses, corks, caps, paper clips, coins or whatever will do. These are kept in a box or container (tobacco tins and dairy cartons are good).

A demo kit is to be used for all study. It is to be used frequently while coaching, doing checkouts, studying alone or listening to tapes.

A demo kit adds mass, reality and doingness to the significance.

The pieces of the kit represent the things one is demonstrating.

Thus the idea of an auditor, a pc, a meter and a procedure become real with a demo kit. They can be seen and felt.

Demo kits are for use. They will get you much better results.

12 What is a Checksheet

|*BPL 27 July 1969R

The "checksheet" is a Scientology development in the field of study.

A checksheet is a list of materials, often divided into sections, that give the theory and practical steps which, when completed, give one a study completion. The items are selected to add up to the required knowledge of the subject. They are arranged in the sequence necessary to a gradient of increasing knowledge of the subject. After each item there is a place for the initial of the student or the person checking the student out. When the checksheet is fully initialed it is complete, meaning the student may now take an exam and be granted the award for completion.

The data of the course is studied and the drills performed *in the order given* on the checksheet. The student does not "jump around" or study the material in some other order. The materials are set out in the checksheet in the best order for study by the student so that he covers all the material on a proper gradient.

Further, following the exact order of the checksheet has a disciplinary function which assists the student to study.

The student's initial beside an item is an attestation that he knows in detail AND can apply the material contained in that bulletin, policy letter or tape, or that he has done and can do that drill.

"Through a checksheet" means through the entire checksheet—theory, practical, all drills—and done in sequence.

NUMBER OF TIMES OVER THE MATERIAL EQUALS CERTAINTY AND RESULTS (a major study datum which has been proven beyond any question in Dianetics and Scientology).

This handbook is comprised of 21 packs, each devoted to a different subject, with a checksheet given at the beginning of each pack for your use.

Follow the instructions above for getting through a checksheet and check off each item on the checksheets as you progress through the packs.

Ensure you study thoroughly each section of the pack you are on and do each drill before proceeding onto the next section.

Glossary

An extensive glossary containing all the Dianetic and Scientology terms dealing specifically with the text is provided in the back of this book. It is essential to your ultimate success with this text that you do use the glossary.

Scientology words and their definitions are the gateway to a new look and understanding of life. Understanding them will help you live better, and will assist you along the road of truth that is Scientology.

B

Orientation

Orientation Checksheet

Purpose:

To delineate for the Volunteer Minister his purpose, abilities, duties and the guidelines he uses to operate in the society.

a	Study Section 1 Conditions.	______
b	Study Section 2 Volunteer Minister.	______
c	Drill: Look up the word "restoring" in your dictionary, and write out three sentences using this word.	______
d	Drill: Look up the word "spiritual" in your dictionary and write out three sentences using this word.	______
e	Drill: Look up the word "values" in your dictionary and write out three sentences using this word.	______
f	Drill: Write an essay on the benefit of "restoring spiritual values" to society.	______
g	Study Section 3 Abilities of a Volunteer Minister.	______
h	Study Section 4 Technology.	______
i	Drill: Find some examples in your own neighborhood, town, or city of actual moral and spiritual decline you have seen.	______
k	Drill: Turn to the back of this book and locate on the church and mission list, your nearest Church of Scientology or Mission of the Church.	______
l	Drill: If you were asked by a Minister of another Church how you could give a sermon in his Church without violating his Church's beliefs what would your answer be? (Write it down).	______

Orientation Pack

1 Conditions

| Ability Magazine 174

A condition is any problem or difficulty encountered in life. It can also be any state of existence under which the individual is surviving.

The conditions which one desires to change are those conditions considered by the individual to be hindering his survival. The conditions which one desires to continue are those conditions which are considered by the individual to be enhancing or increasing his survival.

It is the nonsurvival or nonoptimum conditions of life which Scientology addresses, either by assisting the individual to know more about himself and life through the study of Scientology or by assisting the individual to handle his problems and difficulties through counseling.

Any person with problems or difficulties has two solutions for these:

1. To become more aware of existence in order to handle life.
2. To become less aware of existence in order to handle life.

It is obvious that the latter solution will result in a lessened ability to function in life. A person can become less and less aware of his problems and difficulties to the point where these become so overwhelming that he is completely immersed with a lessened ability to enjoy life. A lowered awareness will result also in an inability to perceive and enjoy those things in life which the individual desires and finds pleasurable. The most unaware individual is one who can experience nothing any longer because he is dead.

Therefore, the only solution to problems or difficulties is to become more aware—more aware of yourself, others, and existence—so that you can handle problems and difficulties easily—your own and others' with confidence, and so that you and your fellow man can continue to find pleasure in hobbies, work, family, interests and life.

The way for you personally to do this is through use of Scientology technology as a Volunteer Minister.

2 Volunteer Minister

Excerpts from Briefing Tapes 7312TC10 and 7402MC19

A Volunteer Minister is a person who helps his fellow man on a volunteer basis by providing fundamental counseling which is not readily available to the public and by *restoring spiritual values.*

Continue your normal daily life, your work and use this technology to help your family, friends, relations, children, business associates, colleagues. They need advice and assistance; you can give it, you can help change conditions for the better for your fellow man.

3 Abilities of a Volunteer Minister

Excerpts from Briefing Tapes 7312TC10 and 7402MC19

As a Volunteer Minister, you will be able to:

Make people happy and gain respect for themselves.
Bring about renewed interest in life for others.
Get people off drugs without convulsions.

Help alleviate physical discomfort and assist people effectively who are injured physically and/or spiritually.

Save lives and assist injured people in an emergency.

Assist an unconscious person to regain consciousness.

Make a drunk person sober quickly but gradiently.

Help someone who is in a coma.

Better people's memories.

Make someone look and act younger.

Communicate and listen effectively to others.

Increase a person's awareness of himself and life.

Restore purposefulness in life for others.

Find the source of and handle problems in life.

Give peace of mind by bringing relief from the sufferings and hostilities of life.

Restore a person's integrity.

Arrest criminal tendencies in the community.

Help others to feel safer and more secure in their environment.

Increase the ability of the individual to survive.

Increase sanity and ability to reason.

Increase physical capability and general enjoyment.

Perform marriages, christenings, burials and other ministerial duties.

Keep families together.

Heal broken marriages.

Get delinquent children back in the fold.

Restore children's self-determinism and get them to contribute to the family unit.

Increase love in the family and make the family more secure.

Competently do investigations and help others investigate to find the actual source of difficulties within the family, groups, clubs, businesses.

Find the real reasons for any failing projects within your own neighborhood or town or city.

Make it safe for children to grow by alleviating the dangerousness of the environment.

Handle dissident elements in the community.

Discover the source of and handle suppressions.

Persuade people in the community to become more ethical and more responsible.

Locate the source of sudden departures and prevent people from making sudden departures from the family and from jobs.

Bring about friendly relations where conflicts have existed.

Give aid to hospitals as a community servant.

Organize for increased individual production.

Using exact formulas, improve the statistics and conditions of any individual's personal life and any groups, businesses or organizations.

Improve the quantity and quality of individual production on a job.

Increase morale.

Using exact organizational technology, improve any endeavor and indeed can save failing groups, businesses, organizations—commercial or otherwise.

Target and get personal programs executed to accomplish set goals for people and groups.

Increase the sanity of a group.

Administer and provide true justice.

Increase today the spiritual values of Man.

Get your ideas and actions as a Volunteer Minister easily accepted by the community.

Help others improve their image and get more acceptability for them in their community.

By using exact technology, be able to predict what the various publics of the community will find acceptable from any individual or group in the community.

Contact, handle, salvage and save from ruin, your friends and associates.

The Volunteer Minister can do these *things and more.*

4 Technology

Excerpts from Briefing Tapes 7312TC10 and 7402MC19

Never before on this planet has the minister had this much technology at his grasp to apply and use on his family, friends, relatives, community and nation. With this technology you will be able to perform daily miracles.

Anyone can be a Volunteer Minister.

In order to arrest today the moral and spiritual decline of the societies of the earth, many thousands of Volunteer Ministers are needed. Volunteer Ministers are needed to take up their duty to help their fellow man and to deliver help, spiritual guidance and truth to Man. Most of all to deliver religious technology to Man that works invariably and produces results. You are needed in this task. And you can do this by being a Volunteer Minister.

You start out as a student minister. Read and do home study of this book. Then go to your nearest Church of Scientology where you will get any assistance you need in ensuring you understand and can apply the data.

The Church will provide you with a helpful examination on the material so that you are certain; they will answer any questions you have and will issue you a student ministerial identification card.

You can advance beyond the status of "Student Minister" in the church hierarchy to Volunteer Minister, Pastor, Bishop and in fact you should. Your service and advanced expertise are also needed by humanitarian groups and other churches.

A Volunteer Minister visits these humanitarian groups and churches and as a guest speaker, can give speeches and sermons on fundamentals about life and persuades people to come to church.

The substance of a Volunteer Minister's sermons do not violate general beliefs, rather they confirm them and are in essence the fundamental truths about life and the spirit of man from the religious philosophy of Scientology.

We are not in the road of any church. Scientology is the only religion which embraces all churches and all religions. There is no other church that does that. The goal of Scientology is spiritual betterment and a world without insanity, without war or crime. We are with all other churches achieving this. So you must persuade people to go to church and get their firm agreement to go.

It is your prime concern that any persons you counsel attend the church of their choice each Sunday. You must see to it that they do. Call the minister to verify attendance of those you encourage to go to church. At the same time, you are also interested to find out *who else* of their family, friends and acquaintances need spiritual help and direction.

Persuade, do not try to overcome by enforcing will. Never engage in controversy for your power lies in the fact that you speak truth.

You will be called upon to perform marriages, christenings, burials and other ministerial duties. Training to become a fully ordained minister so you can provide these services is available from any Church of Scientology.

Any member of any church denomination, any race, any nationality, any political affiliation, can become a Scientology church member or minister, and still retain his membership in his regular church. Anyone can be a Volunteer Minister.

Persuade others to become Volunteer Ministers if they feel the same way about today's society and Man's lot.

Man not only wishes help for himself, he is basically good and wants to help his fellow man.

Sociologists have been predicting for years that when things went to pieces culturally, a new religion would pick up these pieces. That's Scientology.

A *trained* minister is someone with special knowledge in the handling of life.

The factories, the marts of trade, the homes, the neighborhoods, these are the places we want Volunteer Ministers. In that way alone, we're on the busy, still healthy communication lines of the world.

This is the way to serve. The Volunteer Minister is part of tomorrow.

Scientology is the only game on earth where everybody wins.

So let's help the world win.

C

The Eight Dynamics

The Eight Dynamics Checksheet

Purpose:

To provide real knowledge of life by understanding and observing the eight main divisions of life.

a	Study Section 1 The Dynamics.	________
b	Drill: Go spot some people's activities—like at a park or beach—and name what dynamics they are actively participating in at that time.	________
c	Drill: Talk to some people and using good communication find out which dynamics they have in and which dynamics are not in or are unattended.	________

The Eight Dynamics Pack

The Fundamentals of Thought, Chapter 4, page 36

1
The Dynamics

As one looks out across the confusion which is life or existence to most people, one can discover eight main divisions.

There could be said to be eight urges (drives, impulses) in life. These we call DYNAMICS. These are motives or motivations. We call them THE EIGHT DYNAMICS.

There is no thought or statement here that any one of these eight dynamics is more important than the others. While they are categories (divisions) of the broad game of life they are not necessarily equal to each other. It will be found amongst individuals that each person stresses one of the dynamics more than the others or may stress a combination of dynamics as more important than other combinations.

The purpose in setting forth this division is to increase an understanding of life by placing it in compartments. Having subdivided existence in this fashion, each compartment can be inspected as itself and by itself in its relationship to the other compartments of life. In working a puzzle it is necessary to first take pieces of similar color or character and place them in groups. In studying a subject it is necessary to proceed in an orderly fashion. To promote this orderliness it is necessary to assume for our purposes these eight arbitrary compartments of life.

THE FIRST DYNAMIC is the urge toward existence as one's self. Here we have individuality expressed fully. This can be called the SELF DYNAMIC.

THE SECOND DYNAMIC is the urge toward existence as a sexual or bisexual activity. This dynamic actually has two divisions. Second Dynamic (a) is the sexual act itself and Second Dynamic (b) is the family unit, including the rearing of children. This can be called the SEX DYNAMIC.

THE THIRD DYNAMIC is the urge toward existence in groups of individuals. Any group or part of an entire class could be considered to be a part of the third dynamic. The school, the society, the town, the nation are each part of the third dynamic, and each one is a third dynamic. This can be called the GROUP DYNAMIC.

THE FOURTH DYNAMIC is the urge toward existence as mankind. Whereas the white race would be considered a third dynamic, all the races would be considered the fourth dynamic. This can be called the MANKIND DYNAMIC.

THE FIFTH DYNAMIC is the urge toward existence of the animal kingdom. This includes all living things whether vegetable or animal. The fish in the sea, the beasts of the field, or of the forest, grass, trees, flowers or anything directly and intimately motivated by life. This can be called the ANIMAL DYNAMIC.

THE SIXTH DYNAMIC is the urge toward existence as the physical universe. The physical universe is composed of matter, energy, space and time. In Scientology we take the first letter of each of these words and coin a word, MEST. This can be called the UNIVERSE DYNAMIC.

THE SEVENTH DYNAMIC is the urge toward existence as or of spirits. Anything spiritual, with or without identity, would come under the heading of the seventh dynamic. This can be called the SPIRITUAL DYNAMIC.

THE EIGHTH DYNAMIC is the urge toward existence as Infinity. This is also identified as the Supreme Being. This is called the Eighth Dynamic because the symbol of infinity stood upright makes the numeral "8." This can be called the INFINITY or GOD DYNAMIC.

Scientologists usually call these by number.

A further manifestation of these dynamics is that they could best be represented as a series of concentric circles wherein the first dynamic would be the center and each new dynamic would be successively a circle outside it. The idea of space adjoining enters into these dynamics.

The basic characteristic of the individual includes his ability to so expand into the other dynamics, but when the seventh dynamic is reached in its entirety one will only then discover the true eighth dynamic.

As an example of use of these dynamics one discovers that a baby at birth is not perceptive beyond the first dynamic, but as the child grows and interests extend, he can be seen to embrace other dynamics. As a further example of use, a person who is incapable of operating on the third dynamic is incapable at once of being a part of a team and so might be said to be incapable of a social existence.

As a further comment upon the eight dynamics, no one of these dynamics from one to seven is more important than any other one of them in terms of orienting the individual.

The abilities and shortcomings of individuals can be understood by viewing their participation in the various dynamics.

D

ARC

A R C Checksheet

Purpose:

To understand the mechanics of affinity, reality and communication and be able to engage in good communication with anyone at any time.

a	Study Section 1 Understanding.	______
b	Drill: Draw a triangle and label the corners A, R, C.	______
c	Study Section 2 Affinity.	______
d	Drill: Find some examples of you feeling affinity for someone.	______
e	Drill: Find some examples of someone feeling affinity for you.	______
f	Drill: Find some examples of someone else feeling affinity for another.	______
g	Study Section 3 What is Communication?	______
h	Study Section 4 This is How to Communicate!	______
i	Drill: Demonstrate the formula of communication according to the drill given in the section.	______
j	Study Section 5 Reality.	______
k	Drill: Find some examples of you being in agreement with someone.	______
l	Drill: Find some examples of someone being in agreement with you.	______

m Drill: Find some examples of someone else being in agreement with another. ________

n Drill: Use your demo kit to show what affinity, reality and communication are and how they relate to each other. ________

o Drill: Go to a retirement home. Explain that you are a Volunteer Minister and that you would like to talk to anyone who would "just like somebody to talk to." Using ARC and the formula of communication, have a talk with the person until you have established a relationship and made a friend. Continue to maintain your relationship with the person in the future. ________

p Drill: Go to a home for juvenile delinquents or a prison and repeat drill (o) above. ________

ARC Pack

*SO WW ED 54 INT
6 October 1971
Campaign Org
Friendliness!

1 Understanding

There is a triangle of considerable importance in Scientology, and understanding of it gives a much greater understanding of life and an ability to use it.

Affinity, reality and communication (A-R-C triangle) are the three components or aspects of understanding. Affinity, reality and communication coexist in an inextricable relationship. These factors compose an ARC triangle (pronounced by saying each letter separately).

*SO WW ED 54 INT
6 October 1971
Campaign Org
Friendliness!

2 Affinity

The coexistent relationship between affinity, reality and communication is such that none can be increased without increasing the other two and none can be decreased without decreasing the other two.

Affinity is the feeling which exists between people or within a person. If affinity between two people is high we might use the word "love" as a synonym for this affinity. If the affinity is low we may use the word "hate" as a synonym for this affinity.

Affinity, as an aspect of understanding might be compared to the magnetic and gravitic forces of the physical universe. It is that which holds things together and forces them apart.

Many efforts to formulate principles of thought and life have led to the statement, in one form or another, that "love" is what makes the world go 'round. Many investigators have felt that the whole subject of thought and life can be summed up in this way and can be expressed fully in terms of "love." Such statements as "God is love," show how completely this aspect of understanding is made responsible for not only life but the entire physical universe as well.

HCOB 21 June 1971 Issue II (Extracted from HCOB 23 March 1965 Materials and Axiom 28)

3 What is Communication?

Communication is often defined as the interchange of ideas or even objects between two people.

So we need two people and an idea or something to be communicated. Now let's see what else is needed.

First of all, we have to have one person who starts the communication. We will call him the cause-point because he causes the communication to start. The other one receives the communication, so we call him receipt-point.

Now we come back to the cause-point and we know that if he is going to get his idea across he has to intend to reach the other fellow, so we put intention on his side. He also has to have some attention on the other fellow to see if he is ready to be talked to, so we also have "attention" there. Receipt-point, in order to receive the message, has to have his attention on the sender, so he has "attention" too.

There is one other factor that has to go in here for there to be a good communication. Look at this example of the message that the battle commander sent back to headquarters from the battle. This message was, "Send reinforcements. We are going to advance." But the message had to be passed by word-of-mouth from the front line and by the time it got to headquarters it said, "Send three-and-fourpence. We are going to a dance." What was the missing factor that made this an imperfect communication? *Duplication.* Each person getting the message didn't copy exactly what was said. This is where most communication breaks down. Because we didn't get the person's attention or because our own intention to get our idea across wasn't strong enough, the idea is not duplicated and is not received the way we meant it and so misunderstandings arise.

From our picture we now get the formula of communication which is: CAUSE—DISTANCE—EFFECT, with INTENTION, ATTENTION and DUPLICATION with UNDERSTANDING.

Joe is *Cause* and Bill is *Effect* and there is *Distance* between them. Joe puts his *Attention* on Bill and gets Bill's *Attention.* Joe with *Intention* gets his communication across to Bill who has the *Intention* to *Duplicate* it and does.

This is the way an idea goes across from one person to another. This is how to talk and how to listen.

HCOB 21 June 1971
Issue II (Extracted from
HCOB 23 March 1965
Level 0 Materials and
Axiom 28)

4
This is How to Communicate!

When two people are in good communication, A sends his idea across to B; B receives it, then sends his reply or answer back to A who receives it. A then does what? Mostly he does nothing. There is a missing part here that should be in a good communication. The missing thing is acknowledgment.

What is acknowledgment? It is the way you let someone know that you have his answer. It could be a nod or a smile, a "thank you" or an "okay." It simply lets the person know that you received his communication. If I ask you for the time and you reply, "It's nine o'clock," how would you know I got your reply if I don't give you some acknowledgment? You would not know if you have been heard.

Lack of acknowledgment is very frequent in society today and is the cause of a lot of communication difficulties. You will see people who do not talk at all. They have long since given up the idea that anyone has ever heard them, will listen to them, or wants to listen. Similarly the person who talks all the time is quite sure no one has heard them and is still trying to get through. If there was someone around them who could acknowledge and let them know they had been listened to, they would improve.

One also becomes very tired of doing things for someone who never acknowledges what one has done. A little acknowledgment goes a long way. It is not necessarily praise, just a sign that someone has noticed that something was done. You will see the people around you become more cheerful if you acknowledge their efforts and their communication.

"I see that you've done the lawns"; "Thank you for ironing my shirt," or to your child, "Thank you for going to bed when you were told." We are only too ready to notice a mistake or pay attention to something NOT done, or complain about a question not answered, we should be just as ready to acknowledge these things when they are done or answered.

As we have seen, the formula of communication is: Cause, Distance, Effect, with Attention, Intention and Duplication.

Let us have a look at this in more detail:

COMMUNICATION IS THE CONSIDERATION AND ACTION OF IMPELLING AN IMPULSE OR PARTICLE FROM SOURCE-POINT ACROSS A DISTANCE TO RECEIPT-POINT, WITH THE INTENTION OF BRINGING INTO BEING AT THE RECEIPT-POINT A DUPLICATION AND UNDERSTANDING OF THAT WHICH EMANATED FROM THE SOURCE-POINT.

Now demonstrate the above using bits of wood or matchboxes etc. Set up a Source-point and a Receipt-point with two of these, with some distance between them. Now take another object in your hand, and calling it the impulse or particle, push it (action of impelling) across the distance from Source-point to Receipt-point.

Now do it again including this time the *consideration* and the *intention* to bring about a *duplication* and *understanding* (at the Receipt-point) of the particle that emanated from the Source-point.

(Was it received the same as it was sent? Was it duplicated? Was it understood?)

Repeat this demonstration until you are certain you understand the formula of communication.

Communication is also within the being, of course, independent of a body. Communication includes memory, which is communication with the past—or more correctly—communication with facsimiles which, though they are independent of time, contain recordings of times which are past as far as the physical universe is concerned. The "past" is all in the "present" for a thetan. The only thing which makes a facsimile "past" is the recording of past physical universe time which it contains.

Talking is only a special division of hearing, but we have made it a very important division. So important, in fact, that a delusion has developed among men that words *are* the things they stand for, as though you could walk up to someone and say, "An iron safe is falling on you" and then see him crushed flat on the sidewalk by no visible means.

Communication in an individual has to be in a very decadent state before the idea that words are things can be entertained. Communication is in just such a state in many people.

Communication of emotion to another organism without going through the physical universe may be possible. It certainly is possible without any discernible means.

Communication of thought from one mind to another is certainly possible without dependence upon mest efforts. Thought exists without any dependence whatsoever upon the physical universe. It communicates often entirely independently of mest.

5 Reality

*SO WW ED 54 INT
6 October 1971
Campaign
Org Friendliness!

The next component of understanding is reality. Reality has been a vast and controversial subject for a long time. This writer believes that reality has been formulated better in Scientology than in any other system now known.

Reality is agreement.

Agreement with what? Agreement with anything.

Agreement is like the resonance of a sound in one of Helmholz's glass bells. An idea enters a mind, like a sound entering one of those bells, and if it finds agreement with its "wave length" it grows stronger and stronger. An idea passes near a mind, and if there is agreement in this mind for that idea, this mind begins to "resonate" to that idea.

On the negative side, agreement is the experience of not meeting resistance. When an idea is shot out into a field of thought in which there is agreement for this idea, there is nothing to stop this idea, and it will grow and grow in power and area of influence, until it produces great and magnificent efforts in the universe of mest.

If the idea meets disagreement, it grows weaker and weaker until it is heard no more.

Reality is agreement. The simple but not universally known fact which makes this so is the fact that reality, as a process, has nothing to do with the physical universe. Reality is not a function of the physical universe, it is a function of spirit. Mest does not care whether anything is "real," because mest does not think. Mest just is. It whirls around with boundless energy over limitless spaces through endless time using practically no matter at all—but it does not think. Reality is of no concern to mest.

Reality is one of the three components of understanding.

How little wonder that "philosophers" who made reality a function of matter, energy, space and time and said that thought was the only unreal thing failed to solve anything more complicated than whether to come in out of the rain.

So far as we can tell, the physical universe is real. *So far as we can tell.* But the one thing which we can KNOW is real, is the spiritual being.

The physical universe is sensed by us in a very abstract manner. We look at a great field of motion and we see, not that field, but the top of a table. This hard surface which we perceive is only an abstraction which our imperfect senses make from the detailed process which is going on at a level too minute for us to sense. The reality which we perceive is real, only because all the other people we have ever met perceive it the same way.

Naturally. They are the same kind of organism. They have developed the same physical tools for making abstractions from this process. But suppose we should encounter a different organism and try to establish the reality of this table top with this other organism. It might not work out. The other organism might say, "I see this field at which you are pointing. It is a very active field, lots of motion. Things are moving very fast." And you say to this organism, "You're crazy. There is nothing moving on that table top. It's very hot from the sun, but there is nothing moving."

You are both viewing the same phenomenon, but you perceive it as heat and he perceives it as more motion. One of you, obviously, is seeing the "reality" which the other is not—or are you?

What is the "reality" in a situation in which no two people can agree? What would be the "reality" about the color of a red dress if you were trying to establish the color to a talking dog? You would say, "See here, Fido, this dress is the same color as that apple, but it is quite different from that leaf." And the dog would say, "Yes. You are right. I do not understand this word color that you are using, but I can see clearly that the dress has the same brightness as the apple but is not so bright as the leaf." Who is seeing the "reality"—you or the dog?

The answer is that the word "reality" is misplaced. "Reality" does not and never can apply to the physical universe. It applies only to perceptions of mest by organisms. When the perceptions agree, THAT is reality. When the perceptions disagree, THAT is unreality. The mest itself stays the same, no matter how much reality or unreality is going on in the being perceiving it.

The old question, "Would the stone on the desert be a real stone if no one ever saw it?" is a silly question. We can assume that if no organism ever saw the stone, the stone would still be there. Or, we can assume that the stone would not be there. But that has nothing to do with reality. The stone cannot be either real or unreal, except as it is perceived by an organism. Reality is not a function of stones, it is a function of thought. Stones very probably exist all over the universe without ever being perceived by organisms. They are not concerned with whether they are real or not. They just go on being stones. *We* are the only ones who are concerned with whether they are real—and what we mean by that is, not "*are* they there?" but "can we *agree* about whether they are there?"

Of course, the agreement is easier if we go and look right at the stones instead of guessing about them. But the process of agreement is not different. Looking at the stones does not make them real or unreal, it only makes them easier to agree about. Two men could look at the stones, and one could say, "What pretty sponges." Poof. There goes the reality. "Well," you say, "he was just wrong."

Exactly. He was wrong—that is, one of them was. But which one?

The answer is, the "wrong" one is the one who gets the smaller number of people to agree with him when he gets home. If he cannot get anyone to agree with him, he is very likely to be locked up in an institution for living in an unreal world. But the unreality of this world consists wholly and entirely of his lack of agreement with other people.

Let us assume that there is one physical universe. Let us assume that rocks are hard and water flows and all cats are gray at night. It is easy for us to agree on this, but how can we demonstrate it in terms other than our own perceptions?

We cannot. That is the hard fact. That is the hardest fact in a universe of hard facts about matter, energy, space and time.

That is why reality is agreement.

Reality is even more important within an individual than it is between individuals. In other words, a man must agree with himself before he can agree with anyone else.

Unreality within an individual is insanity.

A man looks out the window and sees a raging, stormy sea. He turns back to his work and in a moment looks again. He sees, this time, peaceful, rolling fields, with cows grazing upon them.

This is unreality. The two sights do not agree.

The quickest way to drive someone insane is to do something to his reality, to introduce disagreements into his facsimiles. Perhaps, if our civilization were built upon affinity or communication, this might not be the quickest way. But our civilization is built solidly upon agreements about the physical universe. A man who looks at energy, space and time, and particularly matter, the way other men look at them is sane. A man who looks at them differently is nuts. People are glad to tell him so. Therefore, we can cut off communication with people and make them angry. We can reverse affinity against them and make them covert or grief-stricken. But when we produce disagreements in their facsimiles about matter, energy, space and time we drive them crazy.

"What did you do with the picture, Paula?"

"I didn't touch it."

"It was hanging right there on the wall. Now it is gone. I have asked Nancy, and she didn't touch it. I certainly didn't touch it. That leaves only you, Paula. What did you do with the picture? Where did you hide it?"

"I didn't . . . I didn't . . . I didn't . . . believe me, I didn't."

"What did you do with the picture, Paula?"

An individual who is a Clear would be annoyed by this sort of thing. An individual who was "normal" would fly into a blind, destructive rage, or plan some way to thoroughly ruin the reality of his tormentor.

An individual who was neurotic would be terrified or grief-stricken.

An individual who was psychotic would drop immediately into apathy.

An individual who invalidates the realities of others consistently is demonstrating that his own reality is very shaky.

In working with people heavily burdened with problems and

difficulties the volunteer minister will find it a great advantage to remember that affinity, reality, and communication affect each other mutually. What is good for one is good for the other two.

It is the PERSONAL TOUCH, caring for the individual, being considerate and helpful, providing a warm comforting, safe and cheerful atmosphere, being understanding, giving service with affinity, reality and communication, granting another beingness, respecting others, observing the communication cycle and agreed upon codes of conduct, accepting and granting importance to another, politeness and courtesy, really wanting that person in front of you to win and helping him to do so unselfishly and without reserve.

Tolerance and friendliness of course do not mean lack of control and effectiveness as these things are also part of the ingredients.

The SCARCE commodity in the world today is tolerance! This is one of a minister's greatest assets together with a knowledge of some fundamental truths of life as given here you as a volunteer minister can effectively aid and assist many, many people.

E

Tone Scale

Tone Scale Checksheet

Purpose:

To understand and be able to use the Tone Scale as a Volunteer Minister to improve the tone level of people.

a Study Section 1 The Tone Scale. ________

b Study Section 2 Emotional Tone Scale. ________

c Study Section 3 Tone Scale Expanded. ________

d Drill: Demonstrate the Tone Scale in full from the bottom up using your demo kit. ________

e Drill: Practice reciting the Tone Scale in full until you know where each tone is in relation to the others. ________

f Study Section 4 Obnosis and The Tone Scale. ________

g Drill: Write a short essay on how to tell the difference between social and chronic tone. ________

h Drill: Using the data in Section 4, Obnosis and The Tone Scale, go to a public park, airport, railway station or any place where people congregate. Spot the social and chronic tones of people by getting into communication with them. Do this until you are confident that you can spot anyone's social and chronic tone at will. ________

i Drill: Go to a public place and using the data in Section 1 The Tone Scale, find people to talk with and start talking to the person at the highest possible tone level, creatively and constructively, and then gradually drop the tone of one's conversation down to the point where it achieves response from the person. Once you have found a person's tone, use the Tone Scale technology to raise his tone. Do this with many people until you feel you have a full command of the Tone Scale technology. ________

Drill: Write an essay on how you as a Volunteer Minister can put the Tone Scale technology to good use in society. ________

Tone Scale Pack

The Auditor No. 60
Science of Survival
page 91

1 The Tone Scale

A person's reaction to life and the environment are represented in Scientology by the Tone Scale. This scale plots the spiral of life from half-consciousness and death up through full vitality and consciousness. The Tone Scale shows the potential of survival in terms of longevity of the organism (unless, of course, processing intervenes).

The higher the individual is on the Tone Scale, the better chance he has of obtaining the wherewithal of living, the happier he is and the healthier his body will be.

By various calculations about the energy of life, by observation and by test, this Tone Scale is able to give levels of behavior as life declines. These various levels are common to all men.

In contact with various situations and people in his environment, an individual goes up and down the scale. The accuracy of this Tone Scale you can test yourself through direct observation.

The various numbered positions are arbitrary numbers. They are a value assigned arbitrarily with no relationship to anything else except this Tone Scale. These numbers could just as well be called "a," "b," "c," "d" as positions.

In *Dianetics: The Modern Science of Mental Health* we had the Tone Scale in its embryonic form. Then in *Science of Survival,* we started moving in this line and really got behavior at its various levels.

Man is such a composite of beings that he has a few positions on the Tone Scale. We tried to explain it by harmonics and so forth; it was quite easily explained that way and, in fact, still has some truth in it. But the fact of the matter is that a man is on the Tone Scale as a social-educational unit which is part of the society—and that is his stimulus-response activity. Then, he was on the Tone Scale at an entirely different level as a thetan.

What was he as a thetan? He was conforming to or not conforming to the society to the degree that he was sane or insane as a thetan—so we have this monitoring unit and we look on the Tone Scale and we find out that we can plot the thetan on the Tone Scale independently. We find out that he is usually clear below zero.

And we can trace the social-educational strata which we can trace all the way through this way: "He went to Eton," which is merely a position on the Tone Scale.

Then we have the composite being plotted on the Tone Scale. This is the social educational environmental background modified by the thetan—the thetan's willingness to accept this or his anxiousness to reject it.

So we have the thetan on the Tone Scale and we have the body on the Tone Scale and then we have this position on the Tone Scale which was gotten because of the interaction of these two facts. So there are actually three places where a person could be on the Tone Scale.

The Tone Scale also has a chronic or an acute aspect. A person can be brought down the Tone Scale to a low level for ten minutes and then go back up or he can be brought down for ten years and not go back up. A person receives bad news and he may sink for a moment to a low tone. He falls in love for a few months and he goes way up tone. His girl leaves him and for a week he is at tone 0.5. As a person grows older his tone may drift down. As an old man, he may drift down to 0.0 and death, either slowly or swiftly.

A man who has suffered too many losses, too much pain, tends to become fixed at some lower level of the Tone Scale, and, with only slight fluctuations, stay there. Then his general and common behavior will be at that level of the Tone Scale.

A salesman, for example, may appear to be very enthusiastic with customers, but at home he is always angry. In this case, anger may well be his chronic tone level. Of course, as good news and bad, happy days and sad ones strike a person, there are momentary raises and lowerings on the Tone Scale.

The constant position on the Tone Scale is determined by three factors. The first is the accumulated entheta in the person—how much of this theta is enturbulated in engrams and analytical locks and so strikes back against him, forcing him into non-survival activities or inhibiting him in environments containing imagined dangers.

The second factor is the amount of theta the person has as life force. This would be his volume of theta. One person has more volume of theta than another and can thus stand to have more enturbulence, more engrams. One may have so little native theta that half a dozen engrams will convert it all into entheta, leaving the person insane. Another person may have so much theta that thousands of engrams still leave him with enough theta to go on living a productive life in the 2.0 plus zone.

The third factor is a ratio between the analytical mind and the reactive mind. An individual may have a reactive level of 1.0 and an analytical level of 3.5. The result is that when he is in a restimulative environment, he may be covertly hostile but in a more favorable environment, he may be analytically very productive. These two minds average out to a constant.

This Tone Scale was first tailored to apply to human behavior and, oddly enough, it has gone into parlance. Auditors know what you're talking about when you say "He's a 1.1" and "He's a 1.5" is a great picture of behavior. An auditor knows his Tone Scale well and he knows how to speak Scientology very well. "1.5?" It says to him immediately, "Holds on like mad, quite destructive yet at the same time has impulses towards helping and being upset, supposed to be doing it for everybody's good but is quite brutal about the whole thing, he probably is holding on to flocks of ridges in various patterns, if you gave him a communication line, he'd just flip it the opposite way so that it would be destructive if you let him go on at all."

At 2.0, you've got the fellow who stands in the middle of the park and lectures from a soapbox and says, "Down with the government, you've got to do something. Workers, throw off your chains . . . ." That's antagonism. They're this, they're that, they're something or other.

4.0 is enthusiasm. He's going out on the line at 4.0. He's saying "Now, what we ought to do is so and so if we get together and we do this and we do that, why we know we can do it" . . . and so on.

Let's take a look at 3.0 on the Tone Scale—conservatism. "Well, yes, Mr. Jones, if you'll come back tomorrow we'll think it over very carefully. Of course, this company has a very conservative policy and we don't want to encroach too much upon your time" . . . stop motion, stop motion, let's hold it down, let's not do anything, let's not be very advancing, let's seem calm about the whole thing because that's the nicest, stupidest trip there is in the universe. God help the young kid down in the well field if he finds out how to save the company 50% of their production costs. God help him because conservatism is a gradient scale of die. It's stop.

At .05, apathy, near death, imitates death. People with fear paralysis, catatonic psychoses, can't talk—communication is zero. If a person is almost all wrong, he approximates death. Like an opossum, he plays dead. A soldier with fear paralysis may be a catatonic. If this state becomes the permanent state of the whole being, it is close to zero—one can't communicate with him, his sense of reality is gone down to apathy, he can't feel any affinity. When you get a person in any apathy engram, you have real trouble. He says, "What's the use? All is lost."

The Tone Scale is a very clear-cut pattern and it becomes very clear-cut to us now that we can relate experience to it all the way up and down it, and so it becomes very easy to use. If you know the Tone Scale and you know the Tone Scale principles, you can do a very good job of processing. You can move someone way up the Tone Scale with Scientology.

This Tone Scale is of great use to an auditor for he can determine the position of the preclear on it and establish the reality of the preclear on it.

How do you move someone up the Tone Scale? One of the ways you move someone up is to get him to stop identifying. You get him to associate one thing with another, rather than identify with it. Then you can get him to differentiate.

Another method is simply start talking to the person at the highest possible tone level, creatively and constructively, and then gradually drop the tone of one's conversation down to the point where it achieves response from the person. An individual best responds to his own tone band; and an individual can be lifted only about half a point on the tone scale by conversation.

This then is done first by announcing something creative and constructive and seeing whether the person responds in kind, then, giving forth some casual conversation, perhaps about sports, and seeing if the person responds to that. Getting no response you then start talking antagonistically about something about which the person knows—but not, of course, about the person—to see if you achieve the response at this point. You may then give forth with a sentence or two of anger against some condition. You can indulge in a small amount of discreditable gossip, and see if there's any response to that. If this does not work, then dredge up some statements of hopelessness and misery.

Somewhere in this range the individual will agree with the type of conversation that's being offered—that is, he will respond to it in kind.

A conversation can then be carried on along this band where the individual has been discovered and from this you will rapidly gain enough information to make a good estimate of the individual's *position* on the chart.

If you wish to lift the person's tone, you should talk at about half a point above their general tone level.

The most effective means of raising an individual's tone level is, of course, Dianetics and Scientology processing and training.

Whichever way you move him up, moving him at all makes him well. Moving him up the Tone Scale restores his self-determinism.

With processing, you can address directly each of these ways and keep him coming right up on the Tone Scale. It becomes very easy to move people around on, not something which is terribly arduous. It can demonstrate to him that he *can* where he says he can't.

At the sub-zero level, he quickly rises upscale through the entire range as a thetan and generally settles at 20.0 and in command of the body and situations. The course of auditing takes the preclear quite automatically down from the false tone of the Body-Plus-Thetan Scale to the actual tone of the thetan. Then the tone of the thetan rises back up the scale level by level.

At the top of the chart, one is fully conscious of himself, his environment, other people and the universe in general. He accepts his responsibilities in it. He faces the realities of it. He deals with the problems within the limits of his education and experience.

When the individual is operating at optimum, he has almost complete freedom of activity in any situation or problem that arises. Any force directed against the activity he is pursuing, he will overcome quite easily, with a feeling of achievement and satisfaction.

The whole intent of Scientology is to raise the individual from lower to higher strata on this Tone Scale by increasing intelligence, awareness, ability and self-determinism. And it does.

2
Emotional Tone Scale

HCOB 18 September 1967

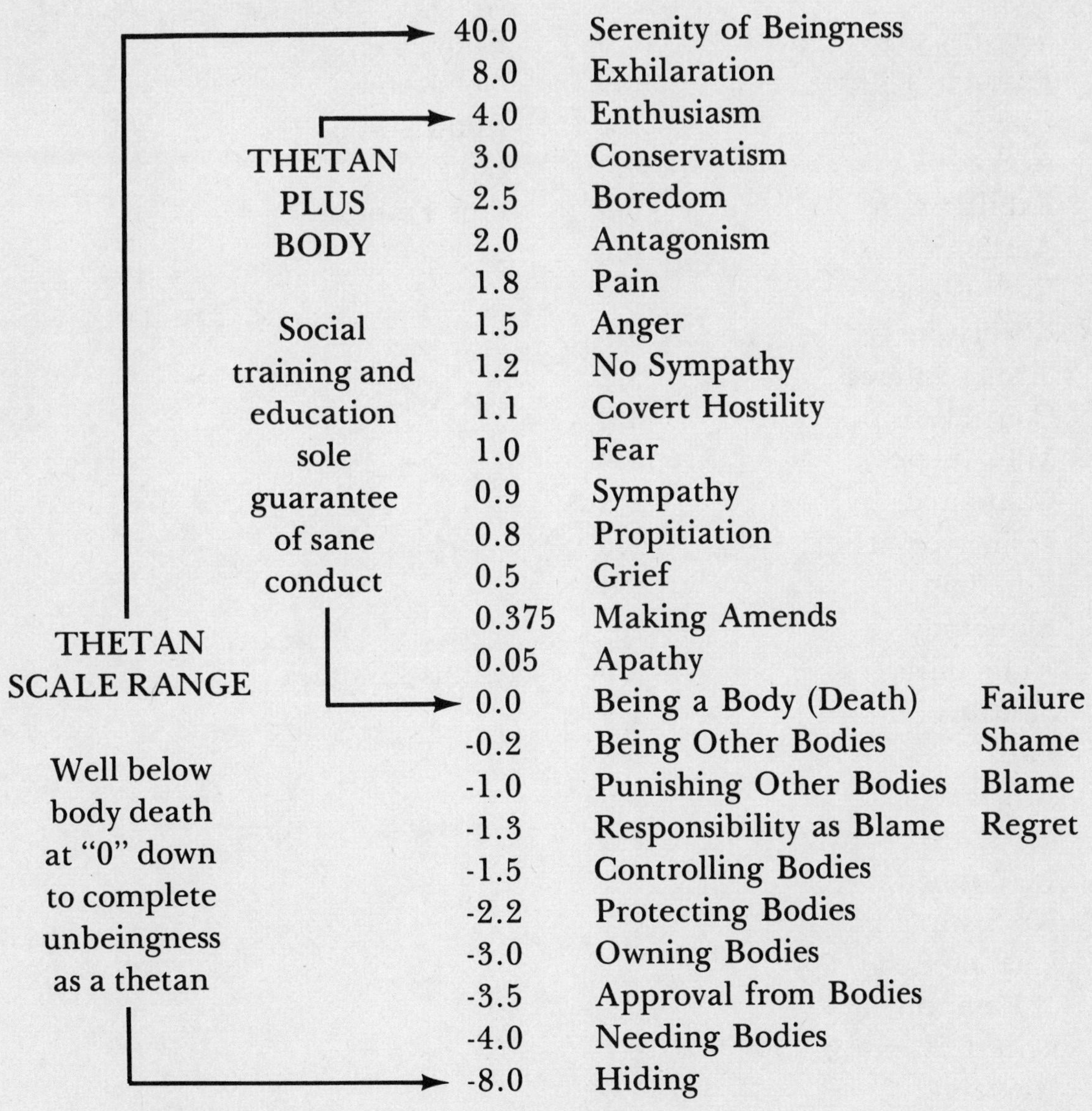

THETAN SCALE RANGE
THETAN PLUS BODY
Social training and education sole guarantee of sane conduct
Well below body death at "0" down to complete unbeingness as a thetan
40.0 Serenity of Beingness
8.0 Exhilaration
4.0 Enthusiasm
3.0 Conservatism
2.5 Boredom
2.0 Antagonism
1.8 Pain
1.5 Anger
1.2 No Sympathy
1.1 Covert Hostility
1.0 Fear
0.9 Sympathy
0.8 Propitiation
0.5 Grief
0.375 Making Amends
0.05 Apathy
0.0 Being a Body (Death) Failure
-0.2 Being Other Bodies Shame
-1.0 Punishing Other Bodies Blame
-1.3 Responsibility as Blame Regret
-1.5 Controlling Bodies
-2.2 Protecting Bodies
-3.0 Owning Bodies
-3.5 Approval from Bodies
-4.0 Needing Bodies
-8.0 Hiding

3
Tone Scale Expanded

HCOB 25 September 1971RA
Tone Scale in Full

		KNOW TO MYSTERY SCALE
Serenity of Beingness	40.0	Know
Postulates	30.0	Not Know
Games	22.0	Know About
Action	20.0	Look
Exhilaration	8.0	Plus Emotion
Aesthetic	6.0	
Enthusiasm	4.0	
Cheerfulness	3.5	
Strong Interest	3.3	
Conservatism	3.0	
Mild Interest	2.9	
Contented	2.8	
Disinterested	2.6	
Boredom	2.5	
Monotony	2.4	
Antagonism	2.0	Minus Emotion
Hostility	1.9	
Pain	1.8	
Anger	1.5	
Hate	1.4	
Resentment	1.3	
No Sympathy	1.2	
Unexpressed Resentment	1.15	
Covert Hostility	1.1	
Anxiety	1.02	
Fear	1.0	
Despair	.98	
Terror	.96	
Numb	.94	

Sympathy	.9	
Propitiation (Higher toned—selectively gives)	.8	
Grief	.5	
Making Amends (Propitiation—Can't W/H anything)	.375	
Undeserving	.3	
Self-abasement	.2	
Victim	.1	
Hopeless	.07	
Apathy	.05	
Useless	.03	
Dying	.01	
Body Death	0.0	
Failure	0.0	
Pity	- 0.1	
Shame (Being other bodies)	- 0.2	
Accountable	- 0.7	
Blame (Punishing other bodies)	- 1.0	
Regret (Responsibility as blame)	- 1.3	
Controlling Bodies	- 1.5	Effort
Protecting Bodies	- 2.2	
Owning Bodies	- 3.0	Think
Approval from Bodies	- 3.5	
Needing Bodies	- 4.0	Symbols
Worshipping Bodies	- 5.0	Eat
Sacrifice	- 6.0	Sex
Hiding	- 8.0	Mystery
Being Objects	-10.0	Wait
Being Nothing	-20.0	Unconscious
Can't Hide	-30.0	
Total Failure	-40.0	Unknowable

4 Obnosis and the Tone Scale

*BTB 26 October 1970
Issue III

The title of this section starts with an odd word: obnosis. It's been put together from the phrase: "observing the obvious." The art of observing the obvious is strenuously neglected in our society at this time. Pity! It's the only way you ever see anything; you observe the obvious. You look at the is-ness of something; at what is actually there. Fortunately for us, the ability to obnose is not in any sense "inborn" or mystical. But it is being taught that way by people outside of Scientology.

How do you teach somebody to see what is there?

Well, you put up something for him to look at, and have him tell you what he sees. That is what can be done in a class; the earlier in the course, the better. A student is asked to stand up in front of the classroom and be looked at by the rest of the students. An instructor stands by and keeps asking, "What do you see?" The first responses run about like this:

"Well, I can see he's had a lot of experience."

"Oh, can you? Can you really see his experience? What do you see there?"

"Well, I can tell from the wrinkles around his eyes and mouth that he's had lots of experience."

"All right, but what do you see?"

"Oh, I get you. I see wrinkles around his eyes and mouth."

"Good!"

The instructor accepts nothing that isn't plainly visible. A student starts to catch on and says: "Well, I can really see he's got ears."

"All right, but from where you're sitting can you see both ears right now as you're looking at him?"

"Well, no."

"Okay. What do you see?"

"I see he's got a left ear."

"Fine!"

No conjectures, no tacit assumptions will do. Nor are the students permitted to wander in the bank. For example, "He's got good posture."

"Good posture by comparison to what?"

"Well, he's standing straighter than most people I've seen."

"Are they here now?"

"Well, no, but I've got pictures of them."

"Come on. Good posture in relation to what that you can see right now."

"Well, he's standing straighter than you are. You're a little slouched."

"Right this minute?"

"Yes."

"Very good."

You see what the goal of this is? It is to get a student to the point where he can look at another person, or an object, and see exactly what is there. Not a deduction of what might be there from what he does see there. Not something the bank says ought to go in company with what is there. Just what is there, visible and plain to the eye. It's so simple, it hurts.

Along with this practice in observing the obvious about people, the students receive a lot of information about particular physical and verbal indications of tone level. Things very easy to see and hear, by looking at a person's body and listening to his words. "Thetan-watching" has no part in obnosis. Look at the terminal, the body, and listen to what's coming out of it. You don't want to get mystical about this, and start relying on "intuition." Just look at what's there.

As examples: You can get a good tip on chronic tone from what a person does with his eyes. At apathy, he will give the appearance of looking fixedly for minutes on end, at a particular object. Only thing is, he doesn't see it. He isn't aware of the object at all. If you dropped a bag over his head, the focus of his eyes would probably remain the same. Moving up to grief, the person does look "downcast." A person in chronic grief tends to focus his eyes down in the direction of the floor a good bit. In the lower ranges of grief, his attention will be fairly fixed, as in apathy. As he starts moving up into the fear band, you get the focus shifting around, but still directed downward. At fear itself, the very obvious characteristic is that the person can't look at you. Terminals are too dangerous to look at. He's supposedly talking to you, but he's looking over in left field. Then he glances at your feet briefly, then over your head (you get the impression a plane is passing over), but now he's looking back over his shoulder. Flick, flick, flick. In short, he'll look anywhere but at you.

Then, in the lower band of anger, he will look away from you deliberately. You know, he looks away from you; it's an overt communication break. A little further up the line and he'll look directly at you all right, but not very pleasantly. He wants to locate you—as a target.

Then at boredom, you get the eyes wandering around again, but not frantically as in fear. Also, he won't be avoiding looking at you. He'll include you among the things he looks at.

Equipped with data of this sort, and having gained some proficiency in looking at the is-ness of people, the students are sent out into the public to talk to strangers and to spot them on the tone scale. Usually, but only as a slight crutch in approaching people, they are given a series of questions to ask each person, and a clipboard for jotting down the answers, notes, etc.

They are public opinion poll-takers from the Church of Scientology. The real purpose of their talking to people at all is to spot them on the Tone Scale, chronic tone and social tone. They are given questions calculated to produce lags and break through social machinery, so that the chronic tone juts out. Here are some sample questions, actually used: "What's the most obvious thing about me?" "When was the last time you had your hair cut?" "Do you think people do as much work now as they did fifty years ago?"

At first, the students merely spot the tone of the person they are interviewing—and many and various adventures they have while doing this! Later, as they gain some assurance about stopping strangers and plying them with questions, these instructions are added: "Interview at least fifteen people. With the first five, match their tone, as soon as you've spotted it. The next five, you drop below their chronic tone and see what happens. For this last five, put on a higher tone than theirs."

What does a student gain from these exercises?

A willingness to communicate with anyone, for one thing. To begin with, students are highly selective about the sort of people they stop. Only old ladies. No one who looks angry. Or only people who look clean. Finally, they just stop the next person who comes along, even though he looks leprous and armed to the teeth. Confrontingness has come way up and he's just somebody else to talk to. They become willing to pin-point a person on the scale, without shilly-shallying. Then say, "He's a chronic 1.1, social tone 3.5, but real phony." That's the way it is, and they can see it. They also become quite gifted and flexible at assuming tones at will, and putting them across convincingly. Very useful in many situations, and lots of fun to do. They grow adept at punching through a communication lag in an informal situation, at sorting out apparencies from realities. The rise in certainty of communication and in ease and relaxation of manner while handling people, in the students who have been run through this mill is something which must be seen or experienced to be believed. The one most often repeated request by students is: "Can't we please have some more obnosis this week? We haven't had enough of it yet."

F

Assists

Assists Checksheet

Purpose:

To train a minister in assists technology, to enable him to perform his duty of ministering to the spiritual anguish of people, and executing his responsibility to relieve their suffering.

a	Study Section 1 Assists in Scientology.	________
b	Drill: Get some calling cards made up for yourself.	________
c	Drill: Go to a crowded area and observe any confusions. Put order into the confusion.	________
d	Study Section 2 Assist Summary.	________
e	Drill: Demonstrate why it is the minister's job to render assists and relieve anguish.	________
f	Study Section 3 Touch Assists, Correct Ones.	________
g	Drill: Find a friend who has a bruise, injury, burn or cut and give him a touch assist.	________
h	Study Section 4 Assists for Injuries.	________
i	Drill: Find a relative or friend who has recently been injured and render a contact assist at the same exact spot where the injury occurred.	________
j	Study Section 5 Unconscious Person Assist.	________
k	Drill: Go to a hospital and give an assist to an unconscious person.	________
l	Study Section 6 Sickness.	________
m	Study Section 7 Emergency Assists.	________

n	Drill: Go to a hospital on a Saturday evening and give aid in an emergency to someone in need of help.	________
o	Study Section 8 How to Make a Person Sober.	________
p	Drill: Locate a drunk person at a party or other location and make him sober.	________
q	Study Section 9 Touch Assist, An Improvement on Spinal Adjustment for Medical Doctors and Practitioners.	________
r	Drill: Locate a person with the symptoms of a slipped disc and give the assist to handle it.	________
s	Study Section 10 Exercises One, Two and Three.	________
t	Drill: Do these exercises yourself.	________
u	Drill: Find a friend and have him do these three exercises.	________

Assist Pack

1

HCOB 21 October 1971

Assists in Scientology

Definition: An Assist: An action undertaken by a minister to assist the spirit to confront physical difficulties.

An assist is not normally done in a formal session. The way the term has been used is a very simple activity to relieve an immediate troublesome difficulty.

An assist is much more specifically and definitely anything which is done to alleviate a present time discomfort.

An assist could happen almost anywhere. At the beginning of a session, no matter how formally this session is constituted, you are running an assist.

You have an auditing room. You have a preclear, and you are the auditor. You know all these things, but the preclear doesn't. Don't call it a formal session. Tell the preclear that it is an assist and that you are not intending anything very strenuous. In rendering an assist you should tell the preclear that "this is just an assist" to try and ease the pain in his hand a little, after which you are going to stop.

The handling of an assist as an auditor is different than the handling of a formal session since the factor of control is notably slackened, sometimes almost completely missing.

One of the factors in assists is that an assist has as a large part of its anatomy, "trying to help." Just remember that you are only trying to help and don't get your heart broken by the fact that the fellow's broken spine doesn't heal instantly.

Another factor is that an assist is differentiated and defined as addressing the game someone knows he is playing.

What techniques would comprise an assist? Anything that would help. And what are these? One of the easiest ones to render is locational processing. You tell the person, "Look at that chair. Look at that ceiling. Look at that floor. Look at that hand." (the auditor pointing to the objects), when he has an injured hand and the pain will diminish. This is a very easy assist.

For example, a person has a bad shoulder. You touch his hand of the same arm and say, "Close your eyes and look at my fingers." Make sure that he keeps his eyes closed. You then touch him on the elbow and say, "Look at my fingers." Do this anywhere on his body. Just touch him and say, "Look at my fingers." This is a communication process which eases his attention over from a concentration upon the injury to something else which is quite near the injury and thus doesn't result in too much of a shock. It reduces havingness but it is positive and gets positive results. It can be done by an untrained person.

You can teach this assist to anybody. You say, "If somebody has a bruise, injury, a burn, a cut, the way to handle this is to tell the person to close his eyes, and then you touch the area near and distant from the vicinity of the injured area, asking them, with their eyes closed, to look at your fingers. You contact them this way many times. They will experience sudden pains in the area, and you will discover that the 'psychic trauma' has been discharged."

You will find that most people do not have any upset about physical contact. Most people think that this is the thing to do.

Say you wanted to render an assist on somebody who had a very *indefinite difficulty.* That is the hardest one to render an assist on. The person has a pain but he cannot say where. He doesn't know what has happened to him. He just feels bad. Use *locational processing* as such.

An assist carries with it a certain responsibility. If you give an assist casually to somebody out in the public and do not shove a calling card in his pocket, you are making an error. The reason for this is that he will not know from whom and where help came. An auditor goes through life and he casts his shadow upon many people and they have really no cognizance of what has happened at all if he is rendering an assist. He says, "Do this, do that"—maybe he wins, or maybe he loses because this is the type of session least calculated to procure orderly results. But in the main these people have been helped. They don't know really by what, except some word that the auditor kept saying. They don't even know that he is an auditor. They don't know anything about it at all. Show a person where he can obtain further assistance, and by whom the assistance was given.

Be yourself. Be positive. Be professional and definite. Have a calling card and make sure the card is easily enough understood. Don't ask them for permission. Just do it. No reason to wander around and give them funny notions. If you are going to help some stranger out, help him out. Don't explain to him or any bystander, otherwise you are likely to stand there explaining, waiting for somebody's permission. Don't bother with that. You act as though you are the one in charge and you will be in charge. And this is part and parcel of the knowledge of how to do an assist. You have got to be the person in charge. This has to be so good, as far as you are concerned, that you overcome the informality of the session to a very marked degree. If you do it extremely well, the assist will amount to auditing.

Say for example, there is a big accident and a crowd of people are pressing around. The police are trying to push the people back. Well, push the people back and then push the policeman back. Say, "Officer, keep these people at a distance." Then you lean over the victim and snap him back to rights. If you are enough THERE, everybody else will realize that you are the ONE that is THERE. Therefore, such things as panic, worry, wonder, upset, looking dreamily into the far distance, wondering what is wrong or what should be done, are no part of your make-up if you are rendering an assist. Cool, calm and collected should be the keynote of your attitude. Realize that to take control of any given situation it is only necessary to be there more than anybody else. There is no necromancy (magic; conjuration of the spirits of the dead in order to predict the future) involved. Just BE there. The others aren't. And if you are there enough, then somebody else will pull himself out of it and go on living.

Understand that an auditor or minister when rendering an assist must make up with presence what he lacks in surroundings and agreements. It all comes under the heading of willingness to be there and willingness to control people.

One of the ways of convincing people of beingness and of being there is to exercise control—positive, undeniable tone 40 exercise of control. Start to control the situation with high enough ARC, enough presence and factuality—there won't be anybody present that won't step back and let you control the situation. You are entitled to it in the first place because of senior "know-how." The control of body attention or thought comprises the majority of your knowledge. The majority in Scientology simply points in this direction. The observable thing is control of attention, objects and thoughts. When you have good confidence of being able to handle these, and when you positively know how to do these, then you can make sure that everybody else knows you can do this, and you make them realize this by doing it. You have all of these things available in rendering an assist.

You might never think of a riot as being a situation which necessitated an assist, or an assist as applicable to a riot, but a riot is simply a psychosomatic momentary injury or traumatic condition on the third dynamic. Could you settle a riot? Well, if you can settle a riot, you can certainly settle one person who is in a riot. The antithesis of any pain, disturbance or tumult is order. The thing which controls tumult is order; and conversely, the thing which controls order is tumult. You need only bring order into a confused situation and bring confusion into an orderly situation to control everything in the field of motion, action and objects.

This is a fantastic simplicity and one which takes some grasping. Conceive as order, merely a fixed position, idea and attitude. A policeman knows what he is supposed to do. Maybe he will put on a tourniquet or maybe he won't. Keep the people away and stop everything is his idea of how it should be. Now you can aid or abet the order he is creating or cancel the order by creating a confusion which he cannot handle. Of the two, the first is the best in that situation. You aid and abet and cap the order he is creating. If you were to accuse him of having a confused accident scene, which is by now not at all confused, and ask him to straighten it out, you would channel his attention in the direction it is already gone, and so you control his attention.

Remember, those people are still moving a little bit; they are still breathing. There is still a tiny bit of motion going on. If you were to ask him something on the order of "can't we have it a little quieter and more orderly here?", he would at once perceive that there was far too much confusion and motion, and he would simply come under your direction because you have simply channelled his attention in the direction it was already going. Therefore, you have taken control.

If you ever want to overset a fixed order, create a confusion. If you want to overset a confusion, create a fixed order. Pick out of the scene those beings in the scene whose attention is channelled in the direction you want attention to go, and you aid and abet that attention which already exists. Or, where you have too many fixed positions and fixed ideas to overcome, you simply take those turbulent individuals in the scene who are creating the confusion against those fixed ideas and channels and you make their confusion much more confused, at the same time yourself imposing another order in another direction.

The mechanics of taking over any confused scene are simply the mechanics of trying to get a preclear to see through the morass of cross purposes, commands, ideas and environments in which he has lived. And whether that applies to the third dynamic or otherwise, the laws are still there and it tells you then that the imposition of order on a preclear comes foremost in an assist.

In an assist you always count on the fact that the thetan himself would, if he could, do the right thing. If you work on that postulate you will never be wrong. Get the idea that it is something else trying to do the wrong thing. The keynote of a thetan is order.

Where you are giving an assist to one person, you put things in the environment into an orderly state as the first step, unless you are trying to stop a pumping artery—but here you would use first aid. You should understand that first aid *always* precedes an assist. You should look the situation over from the standpoint of how much first aid is required. Maybe you will find somebody with a temperature of 106 degrees. It may very well be that he needs to lie down and be covered up, and though antibiotics are much overrated, he might be better off with a shot of one of these than with an assist at that time.

Auditing will not shut off a pumping artery, but a tourniquet will. If you are going into the zone of accidents, you are going to be in the vicinity of a great deal of destruction and chaos, and you are very foolish not to have your Red Cross First Aid Certificate. You may often have to find some method of controlling, handling and directing personnel who get in your way before you can render an assist. You might just as well realize that an assist requires that you control the entire environment and personnel associated with the assist if necessary.

An assist is auditing on several dynamics. It is therefore, much harder to do than auditing in a formal room as it requires presence. You must bring yourself to face the fact that you have to give enough presence and enough control to enough dynamics to bring the environment into a compliance with your postulate. If you postulate that somebody is going to pick up his bed and walk, then you have to be willing to move and be capable of moving around the people who are going to watch him pick up his bed and walk.

A good example of an assist would be when somebody is washing dishes in the kitchen. There is a horrendous crash and the person comes down all over the sink, hits the floor as she is going down, she grabs the butcher knife as it falls. You go in and say, "Well, let me fix that up." One of the first things you would have to do is to wind some bandage around the hand to stop the bleeding. Part of the first aid would be to pick up the dishes and put them back on the sink, sweep the pieces together into a more orderly semblance. This is the first symptom of control. She becomes introverted into the cut to the point that she wouldn't particularly notice what you were doing. But you realize the anxiety that all her blood is pouring out; your first attention to the case is attention to the environment.

Next you would make her sit down. To remove her from the scene of the accident is not as desirable as auditing her there. That is directly contrary, perhaps, to what you believe, but it is true. That is why you bring a little order into the environment. You position her and then you are ready for techniques. It is quite remarkable for you have manifested order in a much wider sphere than a cut hand in order to bring about a healing of the cut hand. If you understand that your responsibility always extends much wider than the immediate zone of commotion, you never miss. If you bring order to the wider environment you also bring it to the narrower environment. If you bring it into the narrow environment, you also bring it to the wider environment. It is a gradient scale of how much order you can bring.

In processing, you have to control or direct attention, objects, person, or thoughts of the injured person. If you are really good on the subject of assists, you will direct an additional thing: his knowingness. You can control a man's knowingness rather easily, but it is hard to see it. About the first thing that you can observe about somebody is his person. You are trying to straighten it out. Don't think even though you have this person sitting down that you have straightened it out because it is still messed up. But there is something that you can straighten out easily—and that is his attention. If you could heighten his attention and his knowingness at the same time, you would really be in wonderful circumstances. You always shift and direct his attention, hence locational processing.

Because he is injured you are not going to move his person around. You have got his attention. Don't try to shift his thoughts around at first because they are dispersed and chaotic. This leaves you his attention only.

If someone is in terrible condition and he is really writhing around, and you want to render an assist, you don't wait until he stops writhing. He is liable to stop writhing dead. What you do with him is to direct his attention. You tell him to *"shut your eyes and look at my fingers."* You press your fingers hard enough so that he can't help but put his attention on them. In this wise you can always have a successful assist because assists all come under the heading of control. The beingness of the person and his presence makes the control possible. So part of control is always presence, identity, person, the one who takes charge and has things under control. When you are able to control his attention, his body and thoughts then he will be in session and you are no longer doing an assist.

Assists dominantly require that you direct the attention of the preclear and dispose his person one way or the other and eventually take over control of his thoughts on the subject. But by the time you have all these three in line you are no longer doing an assist.

So what you really do is do an assist up to the time the person can handle the incident or pain, put him in a more favorable environment and give him auditing. So the assist is what you do on the street, and auditing is what you do in the auditing room when he comes to you after your assist has been successful.

2

HCOB 11 July 1973

Assist Summary

Injuries, operations, delivery of babies, severe illnesses and periods of intense emotional shock all deserve to be handled with thorough and complete assists.

Medical examination and diagnosis should be sought where needed and where treatment is routinely successful, medical treatment should be obtained. As an assist can at times cover up an actual injury or broken bone, no chances should be taken, especially if the condition does not easily respond. In other words where something is merely thought to be a slight sprain, to be on the safe side an X-ray should be obtained, particularly if it does not at once respond. An assist is not a substitute for medical treatment but is complementary to it. It is even doubtful if full healing can be accomplished by medical treatment alone and it is certain that an assist greatly speeds recovery. In short, one should realize that physical healing does not take into account the being and the repercussion on the spiritual beingness of the person.

Injury and illness are PREDISPOSED by the spiritual state of the person. They are PRECIPITATED by the being himself as a manifestation of his current spiritual condition. And they are PROLONGED by any failure to fully handle the spiritual factors associated with them.

The causes of PREDISPOSITION, PRECIPITATION and PROLONGATION are basically the following:

1. Postulates
2. Engrams
3. Secondaries

4. ARC Breaks with the environment, situations, others or the body part
5. Problems
6. Overt Acts
7. Withholds
8. Out of communicationness

The purely physical facts of injuries, illnesses and stresses are themselves incapacitating and do themselves often require physical analysis and treatment by a doctor or nutritionist. These could be briefly catalogued as:

A. Physical damage to structure
B. Disease of a pathological nature
C. Inadequacies of structure
D. Excessive structure
E. Nutritional errors
F. Nutritional inadequacies
G. Vitamin and bio-compound excesses
H. Vitamin and bio-compound deficiencies
I. Mineral excesses
J. Mineral deficiencies
K. Structural malfunction
L. Erroneous examination
M. Erroneous diagnosis
N. Erroneous structural treatment
O. Erroneous medication

There is another group which belongs to both the spiritual and physical divisions. These are:

i. Allergies
ii. Addictions
iii. Habits
iv. Neglect
v. Decay

Any of these things in any of the three groups can be a cause of non-optimum personal existence.

We are not discussing here the full handling of any of these groups or what optimum state can be attained or maintained. But it should be obvious that there is a level below which life is not very tolerable. How well a person can be or how efficient or how active is another subject entirely.

Certainly life is not very tolerable to a person who has been injured or ill, to a woman who has just delivered a baby, to a person who has just suffered a heavy emotional shock. And there is no reason a person should remain in such a low state, particularly for weeks, months or years when he or she could be remarkably assisted to recover in hours, days or weeks.

It is in fact a sort of practiced cruelty to insist by neglect that a person continue on in such a state when one can learn and practice and obtain relief for such a person.

We are mainly concerned with the first group, 1-8. The group is not listed in the order that it is done but in the order that it has influence upon the being.

The idea has grown that one handles injuries with touch assists only. This is true for someone who as an auditor has only a smattering of Scientology. It is true for someone in such pain or state of case (which would have to be pretty bad) that he cannot respond to actual auditing.

But a Scientologist really has no business "having only a smattering" of auditing skills that could save his or the lives of others. And the case is very rare who cannot experience proper auditing.

The actual cause of not handling such conditions is, then, to be found as iv. NEGLECT. And where there is Neglect, v. DECAY is very likely to follow.

One does not have to be a medical doctor to take someone to a medical doctor. And one does not have to be a medical doctor to observe that medical treatment may not be helping the patient. And one does not have to be a medical doctor to handle things caused spiritually by the being himself.

Just as there are two sides to healing—the spiritual and the structural or physical—there are also two states that can be spiritually attained. The first of these states might be classified as "humanly tolerable." Assists come under this heading. The second is spiritually improved. Grade auditing comes under this second heading.

Any minister (and this has been true as long as there has been a subject called religion) is bound to relieve his fellow being of anguish. There are many ways a minister can do this.

An assist is not engaging in healing. It is certainly not engaging in treatment. What it is doing is ASSISTING THE INDIVIDUAL TO HEAL HIMSELF OR BE HEALED BY ANOTHER AGENCY BY REMOVING HIS REASONS FOR PRECIPITATING, AND PROLONGING HIS CONDITION AND LESSENING HIS PREDISPOSITION TO FURTHER INJURE HIMSELF OR REMAIN IN AN INTOLERABLE CONDITION.

This is entirely outside the field of "healing" as envisioned by the medical doctor and by actual records of results is very, very far beyond the capability of psychology, psychiatry and "mental treatment" as practiced by them.

In short, the assist is strictly and entirely in the field of the spirit and is the traditional province of religion.

A minister should realize the power which lies in his hands and his potential skills when trained. He has this to give in the presence of suffering: he can make life tolerable. He can also shorten a term of recovery and may even make recovery possible when it might not be otherwise.

When a minister confronts someone who has been injured or ill, operated upon or who has suffered a grave emotional shock, he should be equipped to handle the person.

Religion exists in no small part to handle the upsets and anguish of life. These include spiritual duress by reason of physical conditions.

Ministers long before the Apostles had as a part of their duties the ministering to the spiritual anguish of their people. They have concentrated upon spiritual uplift and betterment. But where physical suffering impeded this course, they have acted. To devote themselves only to the alleviation of physical duress is of course to attest that the physical body is more important than the spiritual beingness of the person which, of course, it is not. But physical anguish can so distract a being that he deserts any aspirations of betterment and begins to seek some cessation of his suffering. The specialty of the medical doctor is the curing of physical disease or non-optimum physical conditions. In some instances he can do so. It is no invasion of his province to assist the patient to greater healing potential. And ills that are solely spiritual in nature are not medical.

The "psych-iatrist" and "psych-ologist" on the other hand took their very names from religion since "psyche" means soul. They, by actual statistics, are not as successful as priests in relieving mental anguish. But they modernly seek to do so by using drugs or hypnotism or physical means. They damage more than they help.

The minister has a responsibility to his people and those about him to relieve suffering. He has many ways to do this. He is quite successful in doing so and he does not need or use drugs or hypnotism or shock or surgery or violence. Until his people are at a level where they have no need of physical things, he has as a duty preventing their spiritual or physical decay by relieving where he can their suffering.

His primary method of doing so is the ASSIST.

As the knowledge of how to do them exists and as the skill is easily acquired, he actually has no right to neglect those for whose well-being he is responsible, as only then can he lead them to higher levels of spiritual attainment.

3

|*BTB 7 April 1972R

Touch Assists, Correct Ones

On assists when you are speaking with medicos you talk to them in terms of restoring communication in blood and nerve channels.

Normal *errors* in a touch assist are: (1) Don't go to extremities, (2) Don't equal balance to both sides, (3) Don't carry through (they go to release point only), (4) Don't repeat on following days if needed.

A guy stubs a toe, the other toe is where it is locked up.

There is a balance of the nerve energy of the body on 12 nerve channels going up and down the spine. The type of energy in the body travels at 10 feet a second.

The energy from a shock will make a standing wave in the body.

The brain is a shock cushion, that is all. It absorbs the shock from a large amount of energy. The neuron-synapse is a disconnection.

A wave one way will have a wave reacting the other way. In the sympathetic system the wave locks up on both sides of the body. So do assist thoroughly on both sides. Get both sides and unlock standing wave. The purpose of a touch assist is to unlock the standing waves that are small electronic ridges of nervous energy that is not flowing as it should.

You can unlock an impulse in the leg and it can get into spine and lock up. So this is where you get the Chiropractor fixing people. But the nerves are "telling the muscles" to hold the bone out of place.

A shock puts, via the nerves, a permanent command into a set of muscles, all different "commands" going out from the shock. The system functions through stops to try to hold that shock back. It's actually nerve to muscle to bone.

Light massage along nerve channels will get muscles unlocked to permit bone to go in place. You unlock nerve channels.

The trick is standing waves. The wave is slowed down as it goes through the body, like at each joint. There are brain cells at each joint absorbing the shock.

Inertia—when enough heavy charge goes through a nerve it stops passing the charge through and just builds it up. A touch assist will bring the flow back and the suspended pain, cold, electrical charges and muscle command will blow through.

Shock impulse goes tearing down nerve in huge volume, all accumulating nodules of standing waves all over the body, trying to stop the nerve impulse. The nerve goes into apathy with the huge volume of impulse. Like 100,000 volts of electricity over a small wire, something goes.

With auditing you are bringing back the nerve "from apathy" up through the tone scale. Like getting apathy of nerve up through the pain explosion. So the touch assist is short sessioned and always balanced.

At first you might just get an awareness of the area, then maybe after the 3rd or 4th assist (third or fourth day or many more days with one done each day) there is a large jolt that will go through.

The communication cycle is not as important in the touch assist as it is with thetan auditing. But it must be present. Here we are dealing with the body. You do give the command, get an answer from the patient and acknowledge each time.

The Assist Demo on Arthur Hubbard:

My son, Arthur had a wound on his right foot right side at ball of foot location, wound not healing quickly.

You want to get the guy where he is available. Arthur was sitting on chair with legs straight and feet on my knees, (one foot on each knee) and Arthur's hands palms down on his shins. Arthur was comfortable.

The target of all this touch assist was a pain in the wound in the side of the foot. The extremity is the top end of the big toe. Both hands and especially finger tip are also extremities. It's a sympathetic system.

On the assist you must go to corresponding extremities.

(R-factor) I'm going to touch you like this. (I touched Arthur's foot). When you feel it well tell me, okay? Okay.

"Feel my finger?"

"Yes" (Arthur).

"Good."

This was done *rapidly* alternating from one side of body to other, one command and answer and ack for each touch; assist done on each toe back and forth left to right, one for one touch on one side, touch on other side. Up foot, each toe, over to hands, left hand to right hand, one touch for one. This was done for several minutes.

I then had Arthur bend over to get to the spine. Arthur said he had some numbness in the lower spine when I asked about this area. I then did the spine touching 3 inches from spine on one side then to 3 inches on the other side alternately, up the head and around the neck and head.

I asked "How's that?"

Arthur said, "Better," gave cognition on pants being same ones he had on during accident, and I ended off.

Spine

Arthur during this assist had numbness in kidney back area. This is the midpoint between the extremities on the sympathetic system. In the future if the assist hadn't been done he might have had kidney trouble.

The impulse locks up in the spine, so you have to do the spine too to release that charge.

Extremity

The extremity is beyond the point of the body injury. Really handling the extremity furthest from the injury, the legs would strip the blocked energy out (if you get the extremity).

The way you run the touch assist is give the command then touch. Do not touch and then give the command as it's backwards. This requires a drill: "Feel my finger," Then touch a point.

Schools of Healing

The thing that's wrong with each school of healing is that it says it can do the job totally. It can't. An example of this is a Swedish masseuse saying he can cure a person. But in addition to massage, let us say, the person doesn't eat. It's not part of the cure, so doesn't cure.

The doctor's bug is diagnosis. He is even setting up a computer system in the country to figure out what is with the person. But they don't have logic or the Data Series to program from so they won't make it.

There is a big hole in Adele Davis's book on dieting. She doesn't talk enough about iodine on diets, but that is what activates thyroid which burns up the food. So her reducing diets don't always reduce.

If you block out the fields of knowledge you won't get anywhere.

To cure things a doctor should use a number of things (schools of healing) and do each one right.

Regard body with a question mark in your mind.

There is a "brain" at each joint. This is why acupuncture works. One can paralyze a whole body area with it by touching these minor "brains" with a needle. It can do other things as well if you know how.

Mesmerism

Mesmerism is no relation to hypnotism at all. Mesmerism is animal magnetism. It's a physiological rapport. Not a concentration on mental but on mental-physiological.

To have rapport with something you can *be* it.

Hypnotism is the reduction and absorption of mental power of the person. In hypnotism one takes over the person. The subject has no control.

When doing physical healing, if you stroke sympathetically (both sides) alternately inducing a rhythmic motion which is monotonous, you can mesmerize a person.

In mesmerism there is an imposition on feeling. If you mesmerize a person and pinch your back, he will get red in the same place and feel the pain of the pinch. This is physiological rapport. No words are said during mesmerism.

In assists you *don't* want rapport; *avoid* a rhythm; on stroking in massages keep person talking; keep him saying "Yes" and you acknowledging in an assist. Keep him in communication with you. That is why you use the communication cycle, or else all feeling can go out of the body. The communication cycle *prevents* a mesmeric trance occurring that would leave the patient in rapport.

Rapport is mutual feelingness.

In an assist (1) keep talking (2) break rhythms (3) end off. This is important.

Mesmerism is the transfer of the feeling and fault of operator to patient. A woman doing massages quietly and rhythmically could be giving her patient her disjointed hip. A doctor with bad eyesight can make his patients worse or vice versa possibly; if he had good eyesight, patient could get good eyesight.

4

|*BTB 9 October 1967R

Assists for Injuries

In a CONTACT ASSIST you take the person to the exact spot where the accident occurred. Then have him duplicate exactly what happened at the time of the incident.

For instance, if he hit his head on a pipe, have him go through the action of putting his head against the exact spot on the pipe, having the pipe also touch the exact spot on his head. He should be duplicating the whole thing. That is, the rest of his body should be in the position it was at the time of the accident. If the object is hot, you let it cool first, if current was on you turn it off before doing the assist.

If he had a tool in his hand, or was using one, he should be going through the same motions with it.

Have the person repeat this several times, until the somatic occurs again. It will occur and blow off when he exactly duplicates it.

Ask him how it's going; has the somatic occurred. End when you get these phenomena of it turning on and blowing off.

If the spot is not available, you do a TOUCH ASSIST.

It is run around the injury and especially below the injury, i.e., further from the head than the injury.

It is a good idea to have the person shut his eyes during a touch assist so that he is definitely looking "through" the area of the injury in order to tell that you are touching him.

Just use a simple command like "Feel my finger. Thank you."

5

HCOB 5 July 1971R
CS Series 49R
Assists

Unconscious Person Assist

An unconscious person can be assisted by taking his hand and having him touch nearby things like pillow, floor etc., or body without hurting an injured part.

A person in a coma for months can be brought around by doing this daily.

One tells them a hand signal like "Press my hand twice for 'Yes,' once for 'No' " and can get through to them asking questions and getting "Yes" and "No" hand responses. They usually respond with this, if faintly, even while unconscious.

When one has the person conscious again one can do the assists.

FIRST AID RULES APPLY TO INJURED PERSONS.

IN MAKING THEM TOUCH SOMETHING THAT *WAS* MOVING, STOP IT FIRST.

IN MAKING THEM TOUCH THINGS THAT WERE HOT, COOL THEM FIRST.

WHEN POSSIBLE MAKE THEM HOLD THE THINGS THEY WERE HOLDING, IF ANY, WHILE DOING A *CONTACT ASSIST*.

This is important technology. It saves pain and lives. Know it and use it.

6

HCOB 14 May 1969

Sickness

It will sometimes happen that a pc has a session and then three or four days later becomes physically ill.

The auditor may feel that auditing did it. It didn't. The auditing given would have to be non-standard for this to happen, but the auditing is not to blame.

According to my friend Dr. Stanley Lief, over a century ago, Hahnemann developed a healing technology known as homeopathy which administered minute doses of medicine. The original theory seems to have been that the disease or illness was still in the body and would be released. The person would be wildly ill again and then permanently recover. This is probably a poor statement of the whole subject of homeopathy and its basic techniques may have worked well but have been lost.

In any event, the phenomenon has application here.

We would say that the mental image picture of the incident was stopped at a "stuck point" and that it would "run out" of itself if it were unstabilized.

A touch assist can do this. The person may become wildly ill after one and then recover.

What apparently happens is that the chain of incidents becomes unsettled and the same incident on the chain in which the person has been stuck for a long while runs out physically. It completes itself which is to say, it finishes its cycle of action.

At a hospital where I studied, this was part of the things I observed.

Medicine sometimes will not work on a patient. It works on others but not on a particular one.

If that particular one is given mental attention even as mild as an assist, it will be found that medicine will now work on the person.

This formed one of the first application discoveries I made. From it I inferred that function monitors structure and proceeded to investigate mental actions and reactions in the field of illness. From this came Dianetics some years later.

Mental therapy prior to 1945 was so ineffective, consisting only of 19th Century psychoanalysis and Russian and East European psychiatry, that no one else seems to have observed, then or now, that "mental blocks" are able to obstruct medical treatment of a real physical nature.

The proof is that when one even reduces the mental block slightly, medicine such as antibiotics or hormones will now be effective when they were previously ineffective on some patients.

It is this factor which gives purely medical treatment a somewhat random appearance. The patient is "stuck" at some point in time. Even inadequate handling of him mentally "unsticks" the person from the frozen or fixed "stuck" point.

One of three things can now happen:

1. The person can be treated medically for his illness with greater effect.
2. The person in two or three days gets apparently sick or sicker but eventually recovers and is not subject to that exact sickness again (it "ran out").
3. No further result is noted.

If Standard Dianetics is used WITH NO DEPARTURE from its technology and procedure the phenomenon will not occur and no pcs experience a physical aftermath.

7 Emergency Assists

Tape Lecture 5406C17
6ACC 50
Assists

What do we mean by an emergency? It is something which rises up and presents such a thorough problem right now that counseling cannot proceed unless the problem is resolved, like a broken leg. The answer to that problem is an emergency assist. How do you do an emergency assist? There are a dozen ways that I can think of offhand, all of them extremely effective.

Let's say that you were a public school playground supervisor and a child falls down and wrenches his ankle. You get to the child; you want a minimum of talk in the vicinity always. You just ask the child, "Put your attention on my hand," and you put your hand below that ankle; (in other words, on his heel, his shoe, his toes and so forth), "Thank you."

"Put your attention on my hand." (Move your hand, before giving the command). "Thank you."

"Put your attention on my hand." (Move your hand). "Good."

"Put your attention on my hand. Okay. Now just give me a signal every time you've done this." And you acknowledge him always after he has signaled.

Maybe the child is writhing around in pain but he will at least try to do it. You will feel the limb tremble, you will feel the tremor abate, you will feel it cut-in again and then get quiet and for several placements no particular result. And then, you will feel the tremble and you will feel it abate except the tremble each time will be less. The person will actually feel the impact over again that caused the injury. The child will (if you do this well for about ten, fifteen minutes) quite ordinarily simply get up and walk away without a limp and no difficulty.

Now you can take, for example, somebody in a hospital. A woman lying in a hospital bed had delivered a child some fifteen days before, and she was still in the hospital bed. Nobody would let her go home because she was too weak, she couldn't stand. Obviously to a

Scientologist this woman was still stuck in the delivery; she was still hemorrhaging a little bit. In other words, she was actively, physically dramatizing (to repeat in action what has happened to one in experience; it is a replay out of its time period now of something that happened then) this delivery. He asked this woman, "Spot some spots where you're not delivering a child." That's all.

"You're sure of that one. All right. Let's get some more spots. Some more. Some more."

"All right. Now give me some places where your condition doesn't exist," just for variation.

"Some more places, some more places, some more places, and more places where you're not delivering a child and where your condition doesn't exist."

This remedied the woman in six minutes. And she got up that afternoon and went home. Everybody thought she'd taken a wonderful turn for the better and the iron shots had finally taken hold.

When you get a much more overt attitude toward life, even more overt than you have now, you can do such things as walking into a hospital during visiting hours. As you just walk through the hospital you will see some people who are in bad shape here and there in the rooms. You could stop and do assists on every one of them for a few minutes. They may want to know why you're communicating to them. You should present your nondenominational ministerial card.

One time I went down to the receiving entrance of a large general hospital in X city. I stayed there for a couple of hours at that time. I think I saved at least one life. It was just a perfectly random time. There was one individual there who although he was under tourniquet was still bleeding like mad, and what was remedied on that person was very, very simple. I simply asked this fellow to "Locate the present time environment," and to "Locate the present time environment." He finally, with good certainty, located the side of the stretcher. People can lie in emergency bays sometimes for several minutes before they take them up to the operating room or tell them where they're going to go. That's time enough for you to give him aid.

You can just stand in an emergency room of the ambulance receiving entrance of a large hospital, and speak to the people as they come in and just ask each of them to feel the floor beneath his feet. Just ask him several times, "Feel the chair, Good. Put your hand on the chair. All right, now feel that. Good. What is that? It's a chair. Okay, let's feel the floor beneath your feet. Okay, how far away is the ceiling? All right, how far away is that wall from in front of you? Okay, let's feel this chair again." You probably in a very short course of time would have saved several lives.

The real busy time for a large hospital is Saturday night from about eleven to one. There is more traffic than you could possibly take care of in quite a while usually in a large city. Automobile accidents, bar fights, all kinds of things go walking in. Of course, almost any really wide-awake period of the day discovers some traffic into the receiving ward. You have to have a fairly big hospital to get a consistent flow of traffic. You can schedule yourself to be there an hour a day for a week, and identify yourself to hospital authorities because you're a minister. This is a duty which you have called upon yourself to perform and they will think this is very nice of you because they know very well that people are often brought in already dead or dying and waiting for a priest or minister.

Then just look like you belong there and you belong there; they know they don't. You know where you are. There is a difference between you knowing where you are and them not knowing where they are. So you stay there. This also depends upon your own ability to locate yourself.

8

|*BTB 7 June 1969

How to Make a Person Sober

This assist is not used to cure a person of alcoholism. The use of locational havingness will make a drunk person sober in a very few minutes and the cause of his need for alcohol can be audited out later. As society currently has no technology for handling the drunk who is an embarrassment to the police, his family, and often to himself, this process has social value and may serve as a line of cooperation and assistance to the police.

The locational havingness process is simply the command "Look at that ________ (room object)." Use very good TR 0. A drunk is usually considered somewhat unconfrontable and he himself certainly cannot confront. One thing he cannot confront is an empty glass. He always refills it if it is empty.

Repeat the command, each time pointing out a room object, as often as required to bring the person to sobriety. Do not Q & A with the frequent comment "What object!" Just get the command carried out, acknowledge, and give the next command.

DO NOT EVER GET ANGRY WITH OR STRIKE A DRUNK WHATEVER THE PROVOCATION.

We are not particularly in the business of handling the drunk. But we are in the field of helping our fellow man. In a society where the only alternative is a night in the clink and a fine, which is not desired by either the police or the intoxicated person, we can assist both and handle the situation in a matter of minutes. The case can be fully handled later by Dianetic auditing with excellent lasting results if the person wishes it on his own determinism.

9

|*BTB 22 July 1970

Touch Assist—An Improvement on Spinal Adjustment for Medical Doctors and Practitioners

Spinal adjustments can be painful if done when the injured person is out of communication with the afflicted area. Snapping or popping a disk into place—if it is out of place—*is* the correct action, but can in some cases result in additional shock and a strained or pulled muscle.

The following method has been found to work successfully with no uncomfortable after-effects.

Intervertebral Disk

Between each two bones of the spinal column there is a soft cushion called the intervertebral disk. It serves as a ball bearing and shock absorber.

Situation

Sudden shock such as a fall, a jerk of the body or the lifting of a heavy object with the strain on the back may cause the intervertebral disk to be pinched or pushed out of place.

Symptoms of this may be pain, dull or sharp, directly on the spinal column or along any of the connecting muscles of the back. A numbness or "buzzing" sensation may be experienced on the backside below the small of the back.

The slipped or pinched disk may not always be detected by running the fingers along the spinal column, but CAN be detected by lightly running the hand or fingers along either side of the spinal column. The reason for this is that the disk itself is very small and may not be felt, but the muscles and ligaments connected to the spine will have strain on them and may be cramped or knotted. This is the reason there may be pain along these muscles and not directly on the spinal column. This can be easily felt with the lightest of touches along either side of the spine.

Method to Handle

Have the injured person recline on a flat surface.

Give him a standard touch assist, with his agreement.

Afterwards, also with his agreement, check to see if there is a pinched or slipped disk. It will more than likely be detected by the presence of a "swollen" muscle or knot on either side of a particular section of the spinal column.

Relax the muscle.

Use a light, circular motion alternated with a sliding motion towards the spinal column. This is the most important action. It is the muscle that is physically holding the disk out of place.

It is usually during the action of relaxing the muscle that the disk slides back into place. As the muscle loosens up, you will be able to feel the disk which is out of place. If it has not slipped into place with the above action, you may GENTLY slide it sideways into place. It will go easily, without a "snap," and the person will feel instant relief.

NOTE: WHEN THERE IS NO IMPROVEMENT BY GENTLE TREATMENT PROPERLY DONE AS ABOVE, HAVE THE SPINE X-RAYED AS IT MAY BE FRACTURED AND IN NEED OF MEDICAL SETTING.

10

Ability Magazine 114A, 1963

Exercises One, Two and Three

Exercise One

Look and Act Younger: Sitting somewhere near the center of a room, close your eyes and "contact" the two upper corners of the room behind you. Then, holding those corners, sit still and don't think. Remain interested only in those two corners.

You can do this for two minutes (minimum) or two hours, always with benefit. No matter *what* happens, simply hold the corners and *don't think.*

You can do this daily. It will make you look and act younger.

Exercise Two

Feel Freer: Pick out two similar objects. Then find as many differences between them as possible.

Now pick out two objects and see where they are in relation to each other and your body.

Use these two steps over and over. You will feel freer and see better.

Exercise Three

Better your memory: Go over this list many times, each time answering its questions.

"Recall a time which really seems real to you."

"Recall a time when you were in good communication with someone."

"Recall a time when you agreed to something."

"Recall a time when somebody disagreed with you."

"Recall a time when you liked somebody."

"Recall a time when someone agreed with you."

"Recall a time when someone was communicating easily to you."

"Recall a time when somebody liked you."

Use this list many times. If "holding corners" (Exercise One) disturbed you, use this list. If you are tired or confused, use it.

This exercise can be done for hours.

G

Training Routines

Training Routines Checksheet

Purpose:

To teach the Volunteer Minister the effective use of TRs to assist him in confronting, making others confront life and problems, and in handling druggies.

a	Study Section 1 Confronting.	________
b	Drill: Write an essay on what confront has to do with (1) the Volunteer Ministers (2) Problems and (3) Society.	________
c	Study Section 2 Training Drills Modernized.	________
d	Study Section 3 Coaching.	________
e	Drill: Demonstrate with your demo kit the role of the coach.	________
f	Re-study OT TR 0.	________
g	Drill: Select a friend or relative to do this drill with, and do OT TR 0.	________
h	Re-study TR0.	________
i	Drill: Select a friend or relative to do this drill with, and do TR 0.	________
j	Re-study TR 1.	________
k	Drill: Select a friend or relative to do this drill with, and do TR 1.	________
l	Re-study TR 2.	________

m Drill: Select a friend or relative to do this drill with, and do TR 2. ________

n Study Section 4 Premature Acknowledgments. ________

o Drill: In a conversation, give premature acknowledgments and observe what happens. ________

p Drill: Now give correct acknowledgments and observe what happens. ________

q Study Section 5 Tone of Voice—Acknowledgment. ________

r Re-study TR 3. ________

s Drill: Select a friend or relative to do this drill with, and do TR 3. ________

t Re-study TR 4. ________

u Drill: Select a friend or relative to do this drill with, and do TR 4. ________

v Study Section 6 Upper Indoc TRs. ________

w Re-study TR 6. ________

x Drill: Select a friend or relative to do this drill with, and do TR 6. ________

y Re-study TR 7. ________

z Drill: Select a friend or relative to do this drill with, and do TR 7. ________

aa Re-study TR 8. ________

bb Drill: Select a friend or relative to do this drill with, and do TR 8. ________

cc Re-study TR 9. ________

dd Drill: Select a friend or relative to do this drill with, and do TR 9. ________

Training Routines Pack

1 Confronting

Ability Magazine Issue 54
More Confronting

That which a person can confront, he can handle.

The first step of handling anything is gaining an ability to face it.

It could be said that war continues as a threat to man because man cannot confront war. The idea of making war so terrible that no one will be able to fight it is the exact reverse of fact—if one wishes to end war. The invention of the long bow, gun powder, heavy naval cannon, machine guns, liquid fire and the hydrogen bomb add only more and more certainty that war *will* continue. As each new element which man cannot confront is added to elements he has not been able to confront so far, man engages himself upon a decreasing ability to handle war.

We are looking here at the basic anatomy of all problems. Problems start with an inability to confront anything. Whether we apply this to domestic quarrels or to insects, to garbage dumps or Picasso one can always trace the beginning of any existing problem to an unwillingness to confront.

Let us take a domestic scene. The husband or the wife cannot confront the other, cannot confront the second dynamic consequences, cannot confront the economic burdens, and so we have domestic strife. The less any of these actually are confronted the more problem they will become.

It is a truism that one never solves anything by running away from it. Of course, one might also say that one never solves cannon balls by bearing his breast to them. But I assure you that if nobody cared whether cannon balls were fired or not, control of people by threat of cannon balls would cease.

Down on Skid Row where flotsam and jetsam exist to keep the police busy, we could not find one man whose basic difficulties, whose downfall could not be traced at once to an inability to confront. A criminal once came to me whose entire right side was paralyzed. Yet, this man made his living by walking up to people in alleys, striking them and robbing them. Why he struck people he could not connect with his paralyzed side and arm. From his infancy he had been educated not to confront men. The nearest he could come to confronting men was to strike them, and so his criminal career.

The more the horribleness of crime is deified by television and public press the less the society will be able to handle crime. The more formidable is made the juvenile delinquent, the less the society will be able to handle the juvenile delinquent.

In education, the more esoteric and difficult a subject is made, the less the student will be able to handle the subject. When a subject is made too formidable by an instructor, the more the student retreats from it. There were, for instance, some early European mental studies which were so complicated and so incomprehensible and which were sewn with such lack of understanding of man that no student could possibly confront them. In Scientology, when we have a student who has been educated basically in the idea that the mind is so formidable and so complicated that none could confront it, or perhaps so beastial and degraded that no one would want to, we have a student who cannot learn Scientology. He has confused Scientology with his earlier training and his difficulty is that he cannot be made to confront the subject of the mind.

Man at large today is in this state with regard to the human spirit. For centuries man was educated to believe in demons, ghouls, and things that went boomp in the night. There was an organization in Southern Europe which capitalized upon this terror and made demons and devils so formidable that at length man could not even face the fact that any of his fellows had souls. And thus we entered an entirely materialistic age. With the background teaching that no one can confront the "invisible," vengeful religions sought to move foreward into a foremost place of control. Naturally, it failed to achieve its goal and irreligion became the order of the day, thus opening the door for suppressive ideologies. Although it might seem true that one cannot confront the invisible, who said that a spirit was *always* invisible? Rather let's say that it is impossible for man or anything else to confront the non-existent and thus when non-existent gods are invented and are given more roles in the society we discover man becomes so degraded that he cannot even confront the spirit in his fellows, much less become moral.

Confronting as a subject in itself is intensely interesting. Indeed, there is some evidence that mental image pictures occur only when the individual is unable to confront the circumstances of the picture. When this compounds and man is unable to confront anything anywhere, he might be considered to have pictures of everything everywhere.

Man's difficulties are a compound of his cowardices. To have difficulties in life, all it is necessary to do is to start running away from the business of livingness. After that, problems of unsolvable magnitude are assured. When individuals are restrained from confronting life they accrue a vast ability to have difficulties with it.

The drill, TR 0, done for a great many hours, will be found intensely efficacious in the handling of life. A wife and a husband whose way has not been too smooth would find it extremely interesting in terms of resolution of domestic difficulties to do this training drill. Each one running it upon the other for at least 25 hours. This would have to be done, of course, on a turn-about basis of not more than two hours on one and then a switch from "coach" to "student."

To run confronting in this fashion and with considerable gain, it would be necessary to have some understanding of what a "coach" is and, in one of these training teams, what a "student" is. This is explained for you later.

It should be understood that *drill sessions* are *not* auditing sessions.

In a drill session the entire session is in the hands of the "coach." In an auditing session the entire session is in the hands of the auditor, who is the "student" in a drill session.

There is a basic rule here. Anything which the "auditor" or "student," as he is called in the drills, is holding tense, is the thing *with* which he is confronting. If the student's eyes begin to smart, he is confronting with them. If his stomach begins to protrude and becomes tense he is confronting with his stomach. If his shoulders or even the back of his head becomes tense, then he is confronting with the shoulders or the back of his head. A coach who becomes very expert in this can spot these things at once and would in this case give a "That's it," straighten the student out on it and would then start the session anew.

It is interesting that the drill does not consist of confronting *with* something. The drill consists only of confronting; therefore, confronting *with* is a "flunk."

Various nervous traits can be traced at once by *trying to* confront with something which insists on running away. A nervous hand, for instance, would be a hand with which the individual is trying to confront something. The forward motion of the nervousness would be the effort to make it confront, the backward motion of it would be its refusal to confront. Of course, the basic error is confronting *with* the hand.

The world is never bright to those who cannot confront it. Everything is a dull gray to a defeated army. The whole trick of somebody telling you "it's all bad over there" is contained in the fact that he is trying to keep you from confronting something and thus make you retreat from life. Eyeglasses, nervous twitches, tensions, all of these things stem from an unwillingness to confront. When that willingness is repaired these disabilities tend to disappear.

Of course, tumultuously married couples may encounter some knock-down and drag-out moments in doing this confronting drill. However, it should be kept in mind that it is the coach in these training drills who is bound by the rules above and that the only harm that can result would come about if the student were permitted to blow (leave) the session without the coach, even with manhandling, getting the student back into the drill. It will be found that these blows occur most frequently when the person being coached, in other words the student is being given too few wins and is being discouraged by the coach. Of course, things he does wrong should be flunked, but it will be found that the way is paved to success with wins; therefore, when he does it well for a period of time, the student should be told so. Go into this drill expecting explosions and upsets and simply refuse to give up if they occur and you will have it whipped in short order. Go into it expecting that all will be "sweetness and light" and everyone should be a little gentleman and a little lady, and disaster will loom.

2

HCOB 16 August 1971
Issue II

Training Drills Modernized

Due to the following factors, I have modernized TRs 0 to 4:

1. The auditing skill of any student remains only as good as he can do his TRs.

2. Flubs in TRs are the basis of all confusion in subsequent efforts to audit.

3. If the TRs are not well learned early in Scientology training courses, THE BALANCE OF THE COURSE WILL FAIL AND SUPERVISORS AT UPPER LEVELS WILL BE TEACHING NOT THEIR SUBJECTS BUT TRs.

4. A student who has not mastered his TRs will not master anything further.

THIS SECTION MEANS WHAT IT SAYS. IT DOES NOT MEAN SOMETHING ELSE. IT DOES NOT IMPLY ANOTHER

MEANING. IT IS NOT OPEN TO INTERPRETATION FROM ANOTHER SOURCE.

THESE TRs ARE DONE EXACTLY PER THIS SECTION WITHOUT ADDED ACTIONS OR CHANGE.

NUMBER: OT TR 0

NAME: Operating Thetan Confronting

COMMANDS: None

POSITION: Student and coach sit facing each other with eyes closed, a comfortable distance apart—about three feet.

PURPOSE: To train student to be there comfortably and confront another person. The idea is to get the student able to BE there comfortably in a position three feet in front of another person, to BE there and not do anything else but BE there.

TRAINING STRESS: Student and coach sit facing each other with eyes closed. There is no conversation. This is a silent drill. There is *NO* twitching, moving, confronting with a body part, "system" or vias used to confront or anything else added to BE there. One will usually see blackness or an area of the room when one's eyes are closed. BE THERE, COMFORTABLY AND CONFRONT.

When a student can BE there, comfortably and confront and has reached a *major stable win,* the drill is passed.

HISTORY: Developed by L. Ron Hubbard in June '71 to give an additional gradient to confronting and eliminate students confronting with their eyes, blinking, etc.

NUMBER: TR 0 CONFRONTING

NAME: Confronting Preclear

COMMANDS: None

POSITION: Student and coach sit facing each other a comfortable distance apart—about three feet.

PURPOSE: To train student to confront a preclear with auditing only or with nothing. The whole idea is to get the student able to be there comfortably in a position three feet in front of a preclear, to BE there and not do anything else but BE there.

TRAINING STRESS: Have the student and coach sit facing each other, neither making any conversation or effort to be interesting. Have them sit and look at each other and say and do nothing for some hours. Student must not speak, blink, fidget, giggle or be embarrassed or anaten. It will be found the student tends to confront WITH a body part, rather than just confront, or to use a system of confronting rather than just BE there. The drill is mis-named if confronting means to DO something to the pc. The whole action is to accustom an auditor to BEING THERE three feet in front of a preclear without apologizing or moving or being startled or embarrassed or defending self. Confronting with a body part can cause somatics in that body part being used to confront. The solution is just to confront and BE there. Student passes when he can just BE there and confront and he has reached *a major stable win.*

HISTORY: Developed by L. Ron Hubbard in Washington in March 1957 to train students to confront preclears in the absence of social tricks or conversation and to overcome obsessive compulsions to be "interesting."

NUMBER: TR 0 BULLBAIT

NAME: Confronting Bullbaited

COMMANDS: Coach: "Start" "That's it" "Flunk"

POSITION: Student and coach sit facing each other a comfortable distance apart—about three feet.

PURPOSE: To train student to confront a preclear with auditing or with nothing. The whole idea is to get the student able to BE there comfortably in a position three feet in front of the preclear without being thrown off, distracted or reacting in any way to what the preclear says or does.

TRAINING STRESS: After the student has passed TR 0 and he can just BE there comfortably, "bull baiting" can begin. Anything added to BEING THERE is sharply flunked by the coach. Twitches, blinks, sighs, fidgets, anything except just being there is promptly flunked, with the reason why.

PATTER: Student coughs. Coach: "Flunk! You coughed. Start." This is the whole of the coach's patter as a coach.

PATTER AS A CONFRONTED SUBJECT: The coach may say anything or do anything except leave the chair. The student's "buttons" can be found and tromped on hard. Any words not coaching words may receive *no* response from the student. If the student responds, the coach is instantly a coach (see patter above). Student passes when he can BE there comfortably without being thrown off or distracted or react in any way to anything the coach says or does and has reached a *major stable win.*

HISTORY: Developed by L. Ron Hubbard in Washington in March 1957 to train students to confront preclears in the absence of social tricks or conversation and to overcome obsessive compulsions to be "interesting."

NUMBER: TR 1

NAME: Dear Alice

PURPOSE: To train the student to deliver a command newly and in a new unit of time to a preclear without flinching or trying to overwhelm or using a via.

COMMANDS: A phrase (with the "he said's" omitted) is picked out of the book "Alice in Wonderland" and read to the coach. It is repeated until the coach is satisfied it arrived where he is.

POSITION: Student and coach are seated facing each other a comfortable distance apart.

TRAINING STRESS: The command goes from the book to the student and, as his own, to the coach. It must not go from book to coach. It must sound natural, not artificial. Diction and elocution have no part in it. Loudness may have.

The coach must have received the command (or question) clearly and have understood it before he says "Good."

PATTER: The coach says "Start," says "Good" without a new start if the command is received or says "Flunk" if the command is not received. "Start" is not used again. "That's it" is used to terminate for a discussion or to end the activity. If session is terminated for a discussion, coach must say "Start" again before it resumes.

This drill is passed only when the student can put across a command naturally, without strain or artificiality or elocutionary bobs and gestures, and when the student can do it easily and relaxedly.

HISTORY: Developed by L. Ron Hubbard in London, April 1956, to teach the communication formula to new students.

NUMBER: TR 2

NAME: Acknowledgements

PURPOSE: To teach student that an acknowledgement is a method of controlling preclear communication and that an acknowledgement is a full stop.

COMMANDS: The coach reads lines from "Alice in Wonderland" omitting "he said's" and the student thoroughly acknowledges them. The coach repeats any line he feels was not truly acknowledged.

POSITION: Student and coach are seated facing each other at a comfortable distance apart.

TRAINING STRESS: Teach student to acknowledge exactly what was said so preclear knows it was heard. Ask student from time to time what *was* said. Curb over and under acknowledgement. Let student do anything at first to get acknowledgement across, then even him out. Teach him that an acknowledgement is a stop, not beginning of a new cycle of communication or an encouragement to the preclear to go on.

To teach further that one can fail to get an acknowledgement across or can fail to stop a pc with an acknowledgement or can take a pc's head off with an acknowledgement.

PATTER: The coach says "Start," reads a line and says "Flunk" every time the coach feels there has been an improper acknowledgement. The coach repeats the same line each time the coach says "Flunk." "That's it" may be used to terminate for discussion or terminate the session. "Start" must be used to begin a new coaching after a "That's it."

HISTORY: Developed by L. Ron Hubbard in London in April 1956 to teach new students that an acknowledgement ends a communication cycle and a period of time, that a new command begins a new period of time.

NUMBER: TR 3

NAME: Duplicative Question

PURPOSE: To teach a student to duplicate without variation an auditing question, each time newly, in its own unit of time, not as a blur with other questions, and to acknowledge it. To teach that one never asks a second question until he has received an answer to the one asked.

COMMANDS: "Do fish swim?" or "Do birds fly?"

POSITION: Student and coach seated a comfortable distance apart.

TRAINING STRESS: One question and student acknowledgement of its answer in one unit of time which is then finished. To keep student from straying into variations of command. Even though the same question is asked, it is asked as though it had never occurred to anyone before.

The student must learn to give a command and receive an answer and to acknowledge it in one unit of time.

The student is flunked if he or she fails to get an answer to the question asked, if he or she fails to repeat the exact questions, if he or she Q and As with excursions taken by the coach.

PATTER: The coach uses "Start" and "That's it," as in earlier TRs. The coach is not bound after starting to answer the student's question but may comm lag or give a commenting type answer to throw the student off. Often the coach should answer. Somewhat less often the coach attempts to pull the student into a Q and A or upset the student. Example:

Student: "Do fish swim?"
Coach: "Yes"
Student: "Good"

Student: "Do fish swim?"
Coach: "Aren't you hungry?"
Student: "Yes"
Coach: "Flunk"

When the question is not answered, the student must say, gently, "I'll repeat the auditing question," and do so until he gets an answer. Anything except commands, acknowledgement and as needed, the repeat statement is flunked. Unnecessary use of the repeat statement is flunked. A poor command is flunked. A poor acknowledgement is flunked. A Q and A is flunked (as in example). Student misemotion or confusion is flunked. Student failure to utter the next command without a long comm lag is flunked. A choppy or premature acknowledgement is flunked. Lack of an acknowledgement (or with a distinct comm lag) is flunked. Any words from the coach except an answer to the question, "Start" "Flunk" "Good" or "That's it" should have no influence on the student except to get him to give a repeat statement and the command again. By repeat statement is meant, "I'll repeat the auditing command."

"Start," "Flunk," "Good" and "That's it" may not be used to fluster or trap the student. Any other statement under the sun may be. The coach may try to leave his chair in this TR. If he succeeds it is a flunk. The coach should not use introverted statements such as "I just had a cognition." "Coach divertive" statements should all concern the student, and should be designed to throw the student off and cause the student to lose session control or track of what the student is doing. The student's job is to keep a session going in spite of anything, using only command, the repeat statement or the acknowledgement. The student may use his or her hands to prevent a blow (leaving) of the coach. If the student does anything else than the above, it is a flunk and the coach must say so.

HISTORY: Developed by L. Ron Hubbard in London in April 1956, to overcome variations and sudden changes in sessions.

NUMBER: TR 4

NAME: Preclear Originations

PURPOSE: To teach the student not to be tongue-tied or startled or thrown off session by originations of preclear and to maintain ARC with preclear throughout an origination.

COMMANDS: The student runs "Do fish swim?" or "Do birds fly?" on coach. Coach answers but now and then makes startling comments from a prepared list (list available from your nearest Church of Scientology). Student must handle originations to satisfaction of coach.

POSITION: Student and coach sit facing each other at a comfortable distance apart.

TRAINING STRESS: The student is taught to hear origination and do three things: (1) Understand it (2) acknowledge it and (3) return preclear to session. If the coach feels abruptness or too much time consumed or lack of comprehension, he corrects the student into better handling.

PATTER: All originations concern the coach, his ideas, reactions or difficulties, none concern the auditor. Otherwise the patter is the same as in earlier TRs. The student's patter is governed by (1) clarifying and understanding the origin (2) acknowledging the origin (3) giving the repeat statement "I'll repeat the auditing command," and then giving it. Anything else is a flunk.

The auditor must be taught to prevent ARC breaks and differentiate between a vital problem that concerns the pc and a mere effort to blow session (TR 3). Flunks are given if the student does more than (1) understand; (2) acknowledge; (3) return pc to session.

Coach may throw in remarks personal to student as on TR 3. Student's failure to differentiate between these (by trying to handle them) and coach's remarks about self as "pc" is a flunk.

Student's failure to persist is always a flunk in any TR but here more so. Coach should not always read from list to originate, and not always look at student when about to comment. By originate is meant a statement or remark referring to the state of the coach or fancied case. By comment is meant a statement or remark aimed only at a student or room. Originations are handled, comments are disregarded by the student.

HISTORY: Developed by L. Ron Hubbard in London in April 1956, to teach auditors to stay in session when preclear dives out.

Training Note

It is better to go through these TRs several times getting tougher each time than to hang on one TR forever or to be so tough at start student goes onto a decline.

3 Coaching

HCOB 24 May 1968

In order to help you to do the best you possibly can as far as being a coach is concerned, below you will find a few data that will assist you:

(1) *Coach with a purpose.*

Have for your goal when you are coaching that the student is going to get the training drill correct; be purposeful in working toward obtaining this goal. Whenever you correct the student as a coach just don't do it with no reason, with no purpose. Have the purpose in mind for the student to get a better understanding of the training drill and to do it to the best of his ability.

(2) *Coach with reality.*

Be realistic in your coaching. When you give an origination to a student really make it an origination, so that it is as if the student was having to handle it exactly as you say under real conditions and circumstances. This does not mean, however, that you really feel the things that you are giving the coach, such as saying to him "my leg hurts." This does not mean that your leg should hurt, but you should say it in such a manner as to convey to the student that your leg hurts. Another thing about this is do not use any experiences from your past to coach with. Be inventive in present time.

(3) *Coach with an intention.*

Behind all your coaching should be your intention that by the end of the session your student will be aware that he is doing better at the end of it than he did at the beginning. The student must have a feeling that he has accomplished something in the training step, no matter how small it is. It is your intention and always should be while coaching that the student you are coaching be a more able person and have a greater understanding of that on which he is being coached.

(4) *In coaching, take up only one thing at a time.*

For example, using TR 4, if the student arrives at the goal set up for TR 4 then check over, one at a time, the earlier TRs. Is he confronting you? Does he originate the question to you each time as his own and did he really intend for you to receive it? Are his acknowledgements ending the cycles of communication, etc.? But only coach these things one at a time, never two or more at a time. Make sure that the student does each thing you coach him on correctly before going on to the next training step. The better a student gets at a particular drill or a particular part of a drill you should demand, as a coach, a higher standard of ability. This does not mean that you should be "never satisfied." It does mean that a person can always get better and once you have reached a certain plateau of ability then work toward a new plateau.

As a coach you should always work in the direction of better and more precise coaching. Never allow yourself to do a sloppy job of coaching because you would be doing your student a disservice and we doubt that you would like the same disservice. If you are ever in doubt about the correctness of what he is doing or of what you are doing, then the best thing is to ask the supervisor at your local church or mission. He will be very glad to assist you by referring you to the correct materials.

In coaching never give an opinion, as such, but always give your directions as a direct statement, rather than saying "I think" or "Well, maybe it might be this way," etc.

As a coach you are primarily responsible for the session and the results that are obtained on the student. This does not mean, of course, that you are totally responsible but that you do have a responsibility toward the student and the session. Make sure you always run good control on the student and give him good directions.

Once in a while the student will start to rationalize and justify what he is doing if he is doing something wrong. He will give you reasons why and becauses. Talking about such things at great length does not accomplish very much. The only thing that does accomplish the goals of the TR and resolves any differences is doing the training drill. You will get further by doing it than by talking about it.

In the training drills the coach should coach with the material given under "training stress" and "purpose" in each part of section 2 "Training Drills Modernized" and section 6 "Upper Indoc TRs."

These training drills occasionally have a tendency to upset the student. There is a possibility that during a drill the student may become angry or extremely upset or experience some misemotion. Should this occur the coach must not "back off." He should continue the training drill until he can do it without stress or duress and he feels "good about it." So, don't "back off" but push the student through whatever difficulty he may be having.

There is a small thing that most people forget to do and that is telling the student when he has gotten the drill right or he has done a good job on a particular step. Besides correcting wrongnesses there is also complimenting rightness.

You very definitely "flunk" the student for anything that amounts to "self-coaching." The reason for this is that the student will tend to introvert and will look too much at how he is doing and what he is doing rather than just doing it.

As a coach keep your attention on the student and how he is doing and don't become so interested in what you yourself are doing that you neglect the student and are unaware of his ability or inability to do the drill correctly. It is easy to become "interesting" to a student; to make him laugh and act up a bit. But your main job as a coach is to see how good he can get in each training drill and that is what you should have your attention on; that, and how well he is doing.

To a large degree the progress of the student is determined by the standard of coaching. Being a good coach produces auditors who will in turn produce good results on their preclears. Good results produce better people.

4

HCOB 7 April 1965

Premature Acknowledgements

Do people ever explain to you long after you have understood?

Do people get cross with you when they are trying to tell you something?

If so, you are suffering from premature acknowledgement.

Like body odor and bad breath, it is not conducive to social happiness. But you don't use Lifebuoy soap or Listerine to cure it, you use a proper comm formula.

When you "coax" a person to talk after he has begun with a nod or a low "yes" you acknowledge, make him forget, then make him believe you haven't got it and then make him tell you at GREAT length. He feels bad and doesn't cognite and may ARC break.

Try it out. Have somebody tell you about something and then encourage before he has completely told you all.

THAT'S why pcs itsa on and on and on and on with no gain. The auditor prematurely acknowledged. THAT'S why pcs get cross "for no reason." The auditor has prematurely and unwittingly acknowledged. THAT'S why one feels dull when talking to certain people. They prematurely acknowledged. That's why one thinks another is stupid— that person prematurely acknowledges.

The quickest way to become a social pariah (dog) is to prematurely acknowledge. One can do it in *many* ways.

The quickest way to start the longest conversation is to prematurely acknowledge for the person believes he has not been understood and so begins to explain at greater and greater length.

So this was the hidden ARC break maker, the cognition wrecker, the stupidifier, the itsa prolonger in sessions.

And why some people believe others are stupid or don't understand.

Any habit of agreeable noises and nods can be mistaken for acknowledgement, ends cycle on the speaker, causes him to forget, feel dull, believe the listener is stupid, get cross, get exhausted explaining and ARC break. The missed withhold is inadvertent. One didn't get a chance to say what one was going to say because one was stopped by premature acknowledgement. Result, missed withhold in the speaker, with all its consequence.

This can be counted on to make you feel frightened of being "agreeable with noises or gestures" for a bit and then you'll get it straight.

5

HCOB 12 January 1959

Tone of Voice—Acknowledgement

Mood can be expressed by an acknowledgement. Evaluation can also be accomplished by acknowledgement, depending on the tone of voice with which it is uttered.

There is nothing bad about expressing mood by acknowledgement, except when the acknowledgement expresses criticalness, ridicule or humor.

HCOB 7 May 68
*BTB 22 May 1971R
TR-8 Clarification
HCOB 16 November 1965
Issue II
Commands for Upper Indoctrination TR 6, TR 7, TR 9

6
Upper Indoc TRs

Following are the upper indoc TRs 6 to 9 inclusive:

NUMBER: TR 6

NAME: 8-C (Body control)

COMMANDS: Non-verbal for first half of training session. First half of coaching session, the student silently steers the coach's body around the room, not touching the walls, quietly starting, changing and stopping the coach's body. When the student has fully mastered non-verbal 8-C, the student may commence verbal 8-C.

The commands to be used for 8-C are:
"Look at that wall." "Thank you."
"Walk over to that wall." "Thank you."
"Touch that wall." "Thank you."
"Turn around." "Thank you."

POSITION: Student and coach walking side by side; student always on coach's right, except when turning.

PURPOSE: First part: To accustom student to moving another body than his own without verbal communication. Second part: To accustom student to moving another body, by and while giving commands, only, and to accustom student to proper commands of 8-C.

TRAINING STRESS: Complete, crisp precision of movement and commands. Student, as in any other TR, is flunked for current and preceding TRs. Thus, in this case, the coach flunks the student for every hesitation or nervousness in moving body, for every flub of command, for poor confronting, for bad communication of command, for poor acknowledgement, for poor repetition of command, and for failing to handle origination by coach. Stress that student learns to lead slightly in all the motions of walking around the room or across the room. This will be found to have a great deal to do with confronting. In the first part of the session student is not allowed to walk coach into walls, as walls then become automatic stops and the student is then not stopping the coach's body but allowing the wall to do it for him. The auditor points to show which wall each time.

HISTORY: Developed by L. Ron Hubbard in Camden, New Jersey in October 1953.

NUMBER: TR 7

NAME: High School Indoc

COMMANDS: Same as 8-C (control) but with student in physical contact with coach. Student enforcing commands by manual guiding. Coach has only three statements to which student must listen: "Start" to begin coaching session, "Flunk" to call attention to student error, and "That's it" to end the coaching session. No other remarks by coach are valid on student. Coach tries in all possible ways, verbal, covert and physical, to stop student from running control on him. If the student falters, comm lags, fumbles a command or fails to get execution on part of coach, coach says "Flunk" and they start at the beginning of the command cycle in which the error occurred. Coach falldown is not allowed.

POSITION: Student and coach ambulant. Student handling coach physically.

PURPOSE: To train student never to be stopped by a person when he gives a command. To train him to run fine control in any circumstances. To teach him to handle rebellious people. To bring about his willingness to handle other people.

TRAINING STRESS: Stress is on accuracy of student performance and persistence by student. Start gradually to toughen up resistance of student on a gradient. Don't kill him off all at once.

HISTORY: Developed by L. Ron Hubbard in London, England, in 1956.

NUMBER: TR 8

NAME: Tone 40 on an Object

COMMANDS: "Stand up." "Thank you." "Sit down on that chair." "Thank you." These are the only commands used.

POSITION: Student sitting in chair facing chair which has on it an ashtray. Coach sitting in chair facing chair occupied by student and chair occupied by ashtray.

PURPOSE: To make student clearly achieve Tone 40 commands. To clarify intentions as different from words. To start student on road to handling objects and people with postulates. To obtain obedience not wholly based on spoken commands.

TRAINING STRESS: TR 8 is begun with student holding the ash tray which he manually makes execute the commands he gives. Under the heading of training stress is included the various ways and means of getting the student to achieve the goals of this training step. During the early part of this drill, say in the first coaching session, the student should be coached in the basic parts of the drill, one at a time. First, locate the space which includes himself and the ashtray but not much more than that. Second, have him locate the object in that space. Third, have him command the object in the loudest possible voice he can muster. This is called shouting. The coach's patter would run something like this. "Locate the space." "Locate the object in that space." "Command it as loudly as you can." "Acknowledge it as loudly as you can." "Command it as loudly as you can." "Acknowledge it as loudly as you can." That would complete two cycles of action. When shouting is completed, then have student use a normal tone of voice with a lot of coach attention on the student getting the intention into the object. Next, have the student do the drill while using the wrong commands, i.e., saying "Thank you" while placing in the object the intention to stand up, etc. Next, have the student do the drill silently, putting the intention in the object without even thinking the words of the command or the acknowledgement. The final step in this would be for the coach to say "Start" then anything else he said would not be valid on student with the exception of "Flunk" and "That's it." Here, the coach would attempt to distract the student, using any verbal means he could to knock the student off Tone 40. Physical heckling would not be greater than tapping the student on the knee or shoulder to get his attention. When the student can maintain Tone 40 and get a clean intention on the object for each command and for each acknowledgement, the drill is flat. There are other ways to help the student along. The coach occasionally asks "Are you willing to be in that ashtray?" When the student has answered, then "Are you willing for a thought to be there instead of you?" Then continue the drill. The answers are not so important on these two questions as is the fact that the idea is brought to the student's attention. Another question the coach asks the student is, "Did you really expect that ashtray to comply with that command?" There is a drill which will greatly increase the student's reality on what an intention is. The coach can use this drill three or four times during the training on Tone 40 on an object. As follows: "Think the thought—I am a wild flower." "Good." "Think the thought that you are sitting in a chair." "Good." "Imagine that thought being in that ashtray." "Good." "Imagine that ashtray containing that thought in its substance." "Good." "Now get the ashtray thinking that it is an ashtray." "Good." "Get the ashtray intending to go on being an ashtray." "Good." "Get the ashtray intending to remain where it is." "Good." "Have the ashtray end that cycle." "Good." "Put in the ashtray the intention to remain where it is." "Good." This also helps the student get a reality on placing an intention in something apart from himself. Stress that an intention has nothing to do with words and has nothing to do with the voice, nor is it dependent upon thinking certain words. An intention must be clear and have no counter-intention in it. This training drill, Tone 40 on an Object, usually takes the most time of any drill in Upper Indoc, and time on it is well spent. Objects to be used are ashtrays, preferably heavy, colored glass ashtrays.

HISTORY: Developed by L. Ron Hubbard in Washington, D.C., in 1957 to train students to use intention when auditing.

NUMBER: TR 9

NAME: Tone 40 on a Person

COMMANDS: Same as 8-C (Control). Student runs fine, clear-cut intention and verbal orders on coach. Coach tries to break down Tone 40 of student. Coach commands that are valid are: "Start" to begin. "Flunk" to call attention to student error and that they must return to beginning of cycle, and "That's it" to take a break or to end the training session. No other statement by coach is valid on student and is only an effort to make student come off Tone 40 or in general be stopped.

POSITION: Student and coach ambulant. Student in manual contact with coach as needed.

PURPOSE: To make student able to maintain Tone 40 under any stress or duress.

TRAINING STRESS: The exact amount of physical effort must be used by student plus a compelling, unspoken intention. No jerky struggles are allowed, since each jerk is a stop. Student must learn to smoothly increase effort quickly to amount needed, to make coach execute. Stress is on *exact* intention, exact strength needed, exact force necessary, exact Tone 40. Even a slight smile by student can be a flunk. Too much force can be a flunk. Too little force definitely is a flunk.

Anything not Tone 40 is a flunk. Here the coach should check very carefully on student's ability to place an intention in the coach. This can be checked by the coach since the coach will find himself doing the command almost whether or not he wants to if the student is really getting the intention across. After the coach is satisfied with the student's ability to get the intention across, the coach should then do all he can to break the student off Tone 40, mainly on the basis of surprise and change of pace. Thus the student will be brought to have a greater tolerance of surprise and a quick recovery from surprise.

HISTORY: Developed in Washington, D.C. in 1957 by L. Ron Hubbard.

Purpose of these four training drills, TR 6, 7, 8, and 9, is to bring about in the student the willingness and ability to handle and control other people's bodies, and to cheerfully confront another person while giving that person commands. Also, to maintain a high level of control in any circumstances.

H

Drug Rehabilitation

Drug Rehabilitation Checksheet

Purpose:

To give the Volunteer Minister a knowledge of the exact effects of drugs and how to apply the only successful methods of getting someone off them.

a	Study Section 1 Pain Association.	________
b	Study Section 2 Drug Data.	________
c	Drill: Go out to a novelty shop or record store and spot some psychedelic posters and lights.	________
d	Drill: Turn on the radio to a rock station and spot some psychedelic electronic music.	________
e	Study Section 3 TRs and Drugs.	________
f	Drill: With your demo kit, demo out why a druggie would have to do TRs as his first step.	________
g	Study Section 4 Drugs.	________
h	Drill: Go to a school campus and find some people who have the characteristics of being a drug user.	________
i	Drill: Demonstrate (using your demo kit) how vitamin B1 can help a person come off drugs, without adverse reactions.	________
j	Study Section 5 Withdrawal Symptoms.	________
k	Drill: Demo out the symptoms of withdrawal actions and how to handle them.	________

l	Drill: Find a friend with muscular spasms or nervousness and make him some Cal-Mag so he relaxes.	________
m	Study Section 6 Drugs, Aspirin and Tranquilizers.	________
n	Drill: Demonstrate why a person must come off aspirins and tranquilizers.	________
o	Drill: Go out and successfully get a druggie to stop using drugs, handling any adverse withdrawal symptoms.	________
p	Study Section 7 Antibiotics.	________
q	Drill: Select a relative, friend or neighbor and using what you know about vitamins, give aid to someone who has just had an operation, dental work or delivered a baby.	________

Drug Rehabilitation Pack

1 Pain Association

HCOB 16 July 1970
The Psychiatrist at Work

As a technical action, it is of interest to any auditor to know that pain and ideas is a basic "therapy" used down the years by psychiatrists and such lot.

The practice is very general and very old.

The person is made to associate his "wrong ideas" with pain so that he "will not have these ideas," or will be "prevented from doing those things."

A crude current example is to electric shock a person every time he smokes a cigarette. After several "treatments" he is supposed to associate the pain with the idea and so "give up smoking."

Homosexual tendencies are also so "treated."

In earlier times alcoholism was "cured" by putting poison in drinks so drinking would make the person violently ill so he would "stop it."

The mechanism is "If you get this idea you will feel this pain" ZAP!

Basically this is the action of an implanter.

Current use of it will be encountered where psychiatry has been busy implanting.

This is a pinnacle, an all, of psychiatric "treatment."

Another version of it is drugs. Make the person too torpid (sluggish) to have *any* ideas. The motto of this is "too dead to act." Institutions are emptied by hooking psychotics and "community psychiatry" exists "to make them take their pills," in short to keep them hooked. This started the current drug craze that spread into "illegal" drugs.

Obsession

Most "got to's" or obsessions come from Pain Association or drug association.

People in pain or drugged can become obsessed with *doing* the idea.

What the psychiatrist does not care to publicize is that his "cures" are implantings with compulsive ideas.

The smoker so treated now MUST smoke but CAN'T smoke. These two things are opposed. That is known as frustration—a form of insanity.

Must reach can't reach, must withdraw can't withdraw, is total basic insanity.

Thus psychiatry is *making* insane people.

This is why the insanity statistic is soaring and why the crime statistic is on a wild climb.

The psychiatrist if he handled his field well and did really effective work would have a *declining* insanity and crime statistic.

That the psychiatrist and his "technology" has been in charge during the whole period of these alarming statistics is ignored by governments.

The psychiatrist argues that he needs more money and more practitioners. But he gets money by the billion. The state has to totally support them because the public will have nothing to do with them.

Psychiatry is collecting more than $44,107,306,153 a year for ruining hundreds of thousands of people.

Psychiatric treatment runs five times the total cost of every course, grade and action available in Scientology churches and missions.

Skill Level

Any HAS knows more and can do more about the mind than any psychiatrist.

There is no real level of comparison since psychiatry as used is a destructive technology.

Under a "drug treatment" engram you often find savage electric shocks of execution strength buried.

It is doubtful if one could watch an electric shock "treatment" without vomiting.

In "neurosurgery" the ice pick is used to rip and tear up peoples' brains.

Holes are drilled in skulls and the brain is sliced up.

No evidence exists that this ever helped anyone but it makes incurable invalids.

Illegal seizure of anyone and his torture is legal in most "civilized countries."

Masters

The psychiatrist has masters. His principle organization, World Federation of Mental Health, and its members, the National Association of Mental Health, the "American" Psychiatric Association and the "American" Psychological Association are directly connected to Russia.

Even the British Broadcasting Company has stated that psychiatry and the KGB (Russian Secret Police) operate in direct collusion.

A member of the WFMH sits on every major "Advisory Council" of the US government, to name one government.

Ministers of Health or Health Authorities are members of the National Association or the WFMH.

The psychiatrist has masters.

Documentation

All these statements are the subject of total documentation in the hands of Scientology.

The auditor in auditing uncovers considerable data in former psychiatric cases.

Further an auditor can put to rights a case so abused unless a fatal injury has been done.

As psychiatry circulates rumors about auditors and attempts to discourage the use of Dianetics and Scientology it is only fair for the auditor to know exactly the status of psychiatry and psychology as used today.

It goes without saying that the savagery and fraud of psychiatry must cease and that auditors must encourage in state and public and through all his connections displacing psychiatric abuses with sane auditing.

2 Drug Data

| HCOB 29 August 1968

LSD-25 is a colorless, odorless, tasteless and virtually undetectable derivative of a rye mold called ergot. The use of sugar cubes as a medium was discontinued several years ago. Dosage is fantastically small, 50 to 1000 *micro* grams per dose, so capsules and tablets are used to reduce evaporation. Price varies from 3 to 7 dollars and it is only sold on the black market. Prior to 1964 the drug was administered by psychologists and psychiatrists. However, it is now illegal for them to do so. Despite its illegal status, LSD is very popular among teenagers and college students. An entire sub-culture of psychedelic (mind-manifesting) posters, light shows and electronic music has emerged on the West Coast. Most of the pop music has hidden drug references. A recent survey indicated that over 50% of the students graduating from the Los Angeles City School System had tried either LSD or Marijuana.

Marijuana is the most popular of the psychedelic drugs. One ounce may be readily purchased for $10 and will furnish 30-50 cigarettes or "joints." A smoker quickly progresses from the one ounce "lids" to purchasing a "brick" or "kilo." This is a kilogram (2.2 lbs) and sells for $75 to $150. Marijuana may be easily identified. It has a strong characteristic odor which is similar to fresh hay or wet, freshly cut grass. Smoking some tea leaves, rolled up into a cigarette will give you a good stable datum for identifying marijuana odor. Marijuana may be physically identified as a green or greenish brown tobacco with varying amounts of brown stems and small round seeds.

Hashish, like marijuana, comes from the female hemp plant, cannabis savitus. When matured, the plant is hung upside down and resins collect which are dried into hashish. One gram of hashish sells for $10 and will supply 10 to 30 "hits" or periods of being "high." Hashish is brown, tan or black and is usually kept in tin foil. Users of both hashish and marijuana will have blood shot eyes while under the influence. Someone under LSD may be identified by very dilated pupils.

Peyote "buttons" are several inches in diameter and come from the peyote cactus of SW America. The pure form of the drug is a synthetic (white) or natural (brown) powder called mescaline. A beefed-up version of this drug was recently made available but was, as of June 1968, unnamed.

Another new drug is STP. This drug is much more powerful than even LSD. As of June 1968, STP was waning in use as people found its results too unpredictable.

One other drug worth mentioning is DMT. This drug is smoked or injected and has immediate effects which end in about an hour. It may be identified by an odor similar to moth balls and is either a white powder or soaked into a medium such as pot or tobacco.

Marijuana is basically a very mild drug which creates euphoria. Also it has the unpleasant consequence of distorting the senses of the user to the point that people on "trips" have been known to open the door of a car going 80 mph and step out "since they could walk faster."

The remaining psychedelic drugs are much more powerful and will strongly influence a person.

The "trips" that a drug user goes on tend to produce stuck points on the track with much fixation of attention on that area. Bad "trips" tend to act like Super Engrams collapsing the track at that point.

*BTB 25 October 1971R
Issue II
The Special Drug Rundown

3 TRs and Drugs

A special drug rundown (using Dianetic processes) exists to handle persons CURRENTLY ON DRUGS. Such persons have to be weaned off drugs in order to be audited. This is done by having the person do TRs further assisted by vitamins.

Those with heavy drug histories or recently or currently on drugs do not usually run well on engrams until objective processes have been run. Thus a person *currently* on drugs would require a full TR course as the first step and then objective processing. Therefore, on such a person, you can have them do TRs as their first step toward full recovery.

4 Drugs

HCOB 28 August 1968
Issue II

It is possible to come off drugs without convulsions.

Drugs essentially are poisons. The degree they are taken determines the effect. A small amount gives a stimulant. A greater amount acts as a sedative. A larger amount acts as a poison and can kill one dead.

This is true of any drug. Each has a different amount. Caffeine is a drug. So coffee is an example. 100 cups of coffee would probably kill a person. 10 cups would probably put him to sleep. 2 or 3 cups stimulate. This is a very common drug. It is not very harmful as it takes so much of it to have an effect so it is known as a stimulant.

Arsenic is known as a poison. Yet a tiny amount of arsenic is a stimulant, a good sized dose puts one to sleep and a few grains kills one dead.

But there are some drugs which have another factor. They directly affect the reactive bank. Marijuana (pot), peyote, morphine, heroin, etc., turn on the pictures one is stuck in. And they turn them on too hard to audit out.

LSD-25 is a psychiatric drug designed to make schizophrenics out of normal people. It is evidently widely distributed by psychiatrists. It looks like cube sugar and is easily made.

Drugs are considered valuable by addicts to the degree that they produce some "desirable effect."

But they are dangerous to those around because a person on drugs (a) has blank periods (b) has unrealities and delusions that remove him from present time (c) is *very* hard to audit.

Thus a drug taker can be holding a boat alongside, go into one of his blanks, think he is on Venus and let go.

A drug taker left on watch may go blank and miss a menacing situation and not handle it because he is "somewhere else."

Giving an order to a drug taker can be grim as he may simply stand and stare at one. He ARC breaks anyone with it.

It takes about six weeks apparently for LSD to wear off. After that a person can be audited. But it ruins his case to a marked degree as it builds up ridges which don't as-is well.

A drug or alcohol *burns up* the Vitamin B1 in the system rapidly. This increased speed of burning up B1 adds to his "happy state." But now his system is out of B1 so he goes depressed.

To avoid convulsions take lots of B1 daily when coming off drugs.

And wait for six weeks before one is audited.

And then lay off. It's a pretty poor trick on those who are dependent on one and get let down.

5

HCOB 5 November 1974
Drugs, More about

Withdrawal Symptoms

The most wretched part of coming off hard drugs is the reaction called "withdrawal symptoms." People go into convulsions.

These are so severe that the addict becomes very afraid of them and so remains on drugs. The reaction can also produce death.

Earlier, B1 is mentioned as a means of easing convulsions.

There is another supplementary way of handling withdrawal symptoms. This does not replace already proven Dianetic and

Scientology techniques developed to handle these symptoms and drug addiction, and at this writing is theoretical, being in a research phase. But so terrible can be withdrawal symptoms and so lacking in success has the medical and psychiatric field been, that the data should be released.

Muscular spasms are caused by lack of calcium.

Nervous reactions are diminished by magnesium.

Calcium does not go into solution in the body and is not utilized unless it is in an acid.

Magnesium is alkaline.

Working on this in 1973, for other uses than drug reactions, I found the means of getting calcium into solution in the body, along with magnesium so that the results of both could be achieved.

This was the "Cal-Mag Formula."

Cal-Mag Formula

1. Put one level tablespoon of calcium gluconate in a normal sized glass.

2. Add 1/2 level teaspoon of magnesium carbonate.

3. Add 1 tablespoon of cider vinegar (at least 5% acidity).

4. Stir it well.

5. Add 1/2 glass of boiling water and stir until all the powder is dissolved and the liquid is clear. (If this doesn't occur it could be from poor grade or old magnesium carbonate.)

6. Fill the remainder of glass with lukewarm or cold water and cover.

They will stay good for 2 days.

It can be made wrongly so that it does not dissolve. Variations from the above produce an unsuccessful mix that can taste pretty horrible.

Anything from 1 to 3 glasses of this a day with or after meals REPLACES ANY TRANQUILIZER. It does not produce the drugged effects of tranquilizers (which are quite deadly).

The application to handle muscular spasms and tics is now quite well established.

Using this to combat withdrawal symptoms is experimental.

The theory is that withdrawal symptoms are muscular spasms.

The matter should be given tests where persons suffering from withdrawal symptoms are available.

This does not supplant Dianetic and Scientology processes. These work.

But it may be that "Cal-Mag" would assist those suffering where no competent auditing is available.

As calcium and magnesium are minerals, not drugs, they form no barrier to auditing.

6

HCOB 17 October 1969

Drugs, Aspirins and Tranquilizers

Some years ago I made a real breakthrough on the action of pain killers (known as aspirin, tranquilizers, hypnotics, soporifics).

It had never been known in chemistry or medicine exactly how or why these things worked. Such compositions are derived by accidental discoveries that "such and so depresses pain."

The effects of existing compounds are not uniform in result and often have very bad side effects.

As the *reason* they worked was unknown very little advance has been made in bio-chemistry. If the reason they worked were known and accepted possibly chemists could develop some actual ones which had minimal side effects.

We will leave the fact that this could be the medical bio-chemical discovery of the century and let the Nobel prizes continue to go to the inventors of nose-drops and new ways to kill and simply ourselves use it. Bio-chemical technology is not up to the point at this time that it can utilize it.

Pain or discomfort of a psychosomatic nature comes from mental image pictures. These are created by the thetan or living beings and impinge or press against the body.

By actual clinical test, the actions of aspirin and other pain depressants are to (a) inhibit the ability of the thetan to create mental image pictures and also (b) to impede the electrical conductivity of nerve channels.

Both of these facts have a vital effect on processing.

If you process someone who has lately been on drugs, including aspirin, you will not be able to run out the Dianetic engram chains properly because they are not being fully created.

If you process someone immediately after taking aspirin for instance, you probably will not be able to find or assess the somatics that need to be run out to handle the condition. For the next day after taking the aspirin or drug the mental image pictures may not be fully available.

In the case of chronic drug taking the drugs must be wholly worn off and out of the system and the engrams of drug taking must be run out in their entirety. If this is not done, auditing will be trying to handle chains that aren't being fully created by the thetan.

In the case of auditing someone who has taken drugs—aspirin, etc.—within the last few hours or two or three days the chains of engrams definitely will be found not fully created and therefore not available.

This would all be fine except for three things:

1. Auditing under these conditions is very difficult. Auditing errors become easy to make. The bank (chains) is jammed.

2. The thetan is rendered STUPID, blank, forgetful, delusive, irresponsible. A thetan gets into a "wooden" sort of state, unfeeling, insensitive, unable and definitely not trustworthy, a menace to his fellows actually.

3. When the drugs wear off or start to wear off the ability to create starts to return and TURNS ON SOMATICS MUCH HARDER. One of the answers a person has for this is MORE drugs. To say nothing of heroin, there are, you know, aspirin addicts. The compulsion stems

from a desire to get rid of the somatics and unwanted sensations again. There is also something of a dramatization of the engrams already gotten from earlier drug taking. The being gets more and more wooden, requiring more and more quantity and more frequent use.

Sexually it is common for someone on drugs to be very stimulated at first. This is the "procreate before death" impulse as drugs are a poison. But after the original sexual "kicks" the stimulation of sexual sensation becomes harder and harder to achieve. The effort to achieve it becomes obsessive while it itself is less and less satisfying.

The cycle of drug restimulation of pictures (or creation in general) can be at first to increase creation and then eventually to inhibit it totally.

If one were working on this bio-chemically the least harmful pain depressant would be one that inhibited the creation of mental image pictures with minimal resulting "woodenness" or stupidity and which was body soluble so that it passed rapidly out of the nerves and system. There are no such bio-chemical preparations at this time.

These tests and experiments tend to prove that the majority of pain and discomfort does come from mental image pictures and that these are immediately created.

Erasure of a mental image picture by standard Dianetic processing removes the compulsion to create it.

Drugs chemically inhibit the creation but inhibit as well the erasure. When the drug has worn off the picture audited while it was in force can return.

Any habitual drug taker, applying for auditing while still on drugs should be given a six weeks "drying out" period off drugs this whole time and then the drug taking (by somatic or sensation of drugs or prior somatics or sensations to drugs—preferably both) must be run out as an early auditing action.

A person who has taken aspirin or other drugs within the past 24 hours or the past week should be given a week to "dry out" before auditing of any kind is given.

It is not fatal to audit over drugs. It is just difficult, the results may not be lasting and need to be verified afterwards.

Chronic drug takers who have not had drugs specifically handled may go back to drugs after auditing as they were too drugged during auditing to get rid of what was bothering them and which drove them to drugs.

With the enemies of various countries using widespread drug addiction as a defeatist mechanism, with pain killers so easily available and so ineffective, drugs is a serious auditing problem.

It can be handled. But when aspirin, that innocent seeming pain killer, can produce havoc in auditing if not detected, the subject needs care and knowledge.

The above data will keep the auditor clear of the pitfalls of this hazard.

To paraphrase an old quote we used to have iron men and wooden ships. We now have a drug society and wooden citizens.

Drug companies would be advised to do better research.

And auditors and ministers are advised to ask any pcs, "Have you been taking any drugs or aspirin?"

The medical aspect is an understandable wish to handle pain. Doctors should press for better drugs to do this that do not have such lamentable side effects. The formula of least harmfulness is above.

7 Antibiotics

HCOB 27 July 1969

Very often antibiotics do not function unless the illness or injury is also audited.

The basic failure of antibiotics apparently stem from a traumatic condition which prevents the medical treatment from functioning.

When a person is medically treated for an illness, it is best to back up the action with auditing.

Sometimes the patient is too ill to be fully audited. It is difficult to audit someone who is running a temperature. In such a case, let the antibiotics bring the temperature down before auditing. But if the temperature does not come down, in the interest of the patient's recovery, auditing should be done.

It is usually too late when the patient is in a coma. But one can still reach a patient who is unconscious by touching the patient's hand to parts of the bed with "Feel that (object)."

A patient will sometimes respond to commands even when "unconscious" if you tell them to squeeze your hand to acknowledge they have done the command.

Years ago the auditing of unconscious persons was worked out and successfully done.

Needless to say, auditing any sick person requires the most exact, careful auditing, strictly by the Auditor's Code.

Postoperative Auditing

A person who has been operated on or medically or dentally treated or a mother who has just delivered a child should have the engram audited out *as soon as possible* by Dianetics.

The after-effects of anaesthetics or the presence of drugs or antibiotics is to be neglected.

The usual action is to (1) get them medical treatment (2) audit them as soon as possible on the illness or injury (3) audit them again when they are well.

HEAVY DOSES OF VITAMIN B1, B COMPLEX and C should accompany all such auditing actions.

Saving Lives

All this comes under the heading of saving lives.

At the very least it saves slow recovery and bad after-effects and resultant psychosomatic illnesses.

Dianetics is the first development since the days of Rome that changes and improves the RATE OF HEALING.

Dianetics is also the first development that removes traumatic barriers from the path of healing.

Medicines and endocrine compounds quite often are effective in the presence of Dianetic auditing which were once inexplicably ineffective in many cases. The barrier to healing was the engram. With that removed, healing can occur.

Objections To Use

Any barriers or objections to using Dianetics to assist the effectiveness of medicine or to increase the rate of or even secure effective recovery place the patient at risk as certainly as failing to use antiseptics.

Such objections can be dismissed as stemming from barbaric or superstitious mentalities or from motives too base to be decent.

It would not be possible to count the number of lives Dianetics saved in the 26 years since the publication of *Dianetics: The Modern Science of Mental Health.*

Few human betterment activities have been so widely successful and so uniformly helpful as Dianetics.

I

Handling The Dangerous Environment

Handling the Dangerous Environment Checksheet

Purpose:

To assist the Volunteer Minister to help people better confront their environment.

a	Study Section 1 The Dangerous Environment.	________
b	Drill: Demonstrate with your demo kit, show how someone could create a dangerous environment.	________
c	Drill: Locate a chaos merchant in your environment.	________
d	Drill: Demonstrate with your demo kit how an SP worries about imaginary threats.	________
e	Drill: Demonstrate with your demo kit how to handle a present time problem.	________
f	Drill: Demonstrate with your demo kit how the question "What part of the environment isn't threatening?" would handle a person whose environment is hostile to him.	________
g	Drill: With your demo kit, show how using Scientology Zero can handle the person at his reality.	________
h	Drill: Find a person with a problem. Bring his confront of the problem up.	________
i	Drill: Find someone in your environment who is overwhelmed by his problems and help him by applying Scientology Zero.	________

Handling the Dangerous Environment Pack

Tape Lecture 6309C25
SH Spec 310, *Summary II, Scientology Zero*

Tape Lecture 6312C10
SH Spec 328
Scientology Zero

1
The Dangerous Environment

If you tried to tell someone today exactly what was wrong with him in specific and complex terms, he would look at you blankly. He's worried only about the fact that the stock exchange trembled and Tel & Tel rose while gold shares sank and this has implications concerning racialism in Lower Slobovia. He knows that's what's really wrong with him: it's the fact that he *might* go broke if he didn't go broke.

Here's a person facing a boa constrictor that's about to constrict. If you tried to talk to that person about his childhood, you wouldn't get much attention from him. He sits there looking fixedly at the snake. He knows what's wrong with him: he's about to be constricted.

Some religious activities have had simple solutions to this. All you do is say, "There is no substance to reality." You look at the boa constrictor and think good thoughts and say, "There ain't no boa constrictor." If you think these thoughts strongly enough while you're being constricted, you won't mind it. They've had methods of coping with this in the past, so we're not completely original.

Scientology Zero covers descriptions of the environment and what is wrong with it. It is concerned with zones of chaos, the dangerous environment and handling threats to the individual from it. This takes care of the world in which the person lives.

The whole subject of Scientology Zero is instantly summatable in the phrase "the dangerous environment." That fits into the frame of mind of the individual who is listening to you. You have immediate agreement that the environment is dangerous.

A great many people are professional dangerous environment makers, or "Chaos Merchants" (SPs). These include the politician, the policeman, the newspaperman and the undertaker. These people feel that if they didn't sell a dangerous environment they would promptly go broke. The environment is dangerous enough, but it is to their interest to make it far more dangerous than it is.

According to the Toynbee school of thought, born in an ivory tower, the reason certain peoples aren't making it in places like Africa or South America is that there is insufficient challenge in their environment.

Out in the Philippines, a brassy energetic white man says to the Igorots, "Just cut a pathway from the village to the river and take a bullock cart down to the river and fill up a water tank and bring it up here then your women will not have to walk to the river. You should engage in this public works project at once."

He is then absolutely outraged because these people do not engage in it at once. He says, "Aha. Those people have insufficient challenge in their environment. Nothing for them to measure up to. No ambition. Not like us in the West. We've got challenge in our environment."

How much challenge has this westerner had in his environment? Mama opened his mouth and spooned the cereal into it. Papa wrote all the checks as he went through college. The way was paved in all directions with machinery and vehicles and the environment had been licked. So of course he can stand up there and be brassy.

What is the real environment of the Igorot listening to this fellow tell him how he has to cut a path to the river? The Igorot has a small son, but he knows his little boy hasn't got a chance in Hades of living until he's seven because of disease, bad food, and so forth. He knows that when the rains come, they'll flood every seed out of the ground and pound the fields to pieces, and if he can salvage anything out of that he might live a few more months. He knows that all he's got to do is walk under the wrong tree and get hit by a snake and that'll be that. In other words, he already knows he can't live, so why try? The challenge of the environment is absolutely overwhelming to this man. I've studied 21 primitive races—including the white race—and the threat of the environment of such peoples is staggering. There is too much challenge and too much danger in their environments.

Then there is the young man out in Indiana who becomes a painter. But nobody in his town is buying any paintings. Nobody believes in what he's doing. He has no future in any line that he can do. His only alternative is to work in the feed store with the neighborhood bully, who has been beating him up regularly since kindergarten. He faces continual starvation and social ostracism. He's unable to communicate or contribute to his community. That's a very hostile environment, so he goes to a friendlier one: Greenwich Village. He would rather starve to death quietly down in Greenwich Village than be threatened to death in his own hometown.

We come to the conclusion that the individual, whether he be white, black, red or yellow, if he is a man and if he is on this planet, and if he has not been able to achieve his own destiny, he is in an environment that he finds overwhelming. His methods of taking care of that environment are inadequate to his survival. His existence is as apathetic or as unhappy as his environment seems to him to be overwhelming. These are the principles of Scientology Zero.

The chaos merchant wants an environment to look very disturbing. It isn't just the politician, the soldier, the militarist, the fellow making the big rockets and the newspaper reporters who are making the environment threatening. There are many who spend their whole lives as professional chaos merchants simply by worrying everybody around them to death. The percentage is probably one out of five. They spread confusion and upset. "If I can just keep Henry worried enough, he does whatever I tell him." Along with that goes, "I wonder why Henry doesn't get ahead." Because she's making Henry sick!

The chaos merchant has lots of troops in people with vested interests. A blackmailer tries to extort money by telling someone that he can make the environment far more dangerous: "I can tell people that you and Mamie Glutz were seen in the tourist cabin, but a few quick dollars will keep this environment a little less dangerous, because I won't tell."

The medico doesn't get paid by the number of people he makes well but by the number who are sick. The more sickness there is, the more doctors there are. Don't think it's any accident that the cops will take a dangerous criminal, throw him into prison, make him more antisocial and more dangerous, then release him upon the society. Don't think this prison system in use is an accident. It's a marvelous method of getting police appropriations. If there weren't that much crime, police salaries and equipment couldn't be extorted out of anyone. Without crime, there are fewer policemen; if there's lots of crime in the society, naturally there are more policemen.

Newspaper reporters operate on this basis: "If I could just run into a big story. Supposing that school across the street should catch on fire just as the children all go inside. What a story! And me right here with my cameramen. I'd become famous overnight!" That's an exaggerated case, but it is found in the society to a marked degree.

There are other individuals than the reporter or the politician who engage in this sort of thing. So the environment is not *ever* as dangerous as it is made to appear.

Anything moving forward that tends to pacify or bring peace and a calmed environment is met by and makes a ridge with the back flow of vested interest in making a disturbed environment. If Scientology moved on forward the environment would become calmer, not less adventurous, but calmer and peaceful. In other words, its potential hostile, unreachable, untouchable threat would reduce. That's for certain because when somebody who knows a few more things about life, about himself, and about others gets a grip on the situation, he has less trouble in his environment.

Even a person who has heard very little of Scientology has less turmoil in his environment. That is a movement in the right direction and would bring about the individual resurgence. Less threatened just from a standpoint of the environment, an individual tends to resurge. He gets less apathetic. He thinks he can maybe do more about life. He can reach a little further; therefore he can exert a calming influence upon his immediate environment.

As that progressed forward, there would be more and more individuals who could bring more and more calm to the environment or handle things better and better. (It's only the things which aren't handled that are chaotic.) The threat of the environment would die out. The overwhelming, overpowering environment would become tamer. People would get less afraid. There would be more and more opportunity to handle the actual problems that exist instead of people dreaming up problems in order to make a couple of quick bucks. It would be a different picture.

The chaos merchant tends to fight calming influences. A wife has been scaring her husband to death for a long time. She scares him at the breakfast table and at dinner. If nothing else works, she brings in the pile of bills after supper. She keeps putting stress on him and yet somehow consoles him about it all. She's got him completely under her thumb. Then he learns about communication in Scientology and just as an experiment he starts talking to his wife. He looks a little calmer. This is not to be borne! At that time you can expect a considerable explosion. She's a chaos merchant. The husband is less disturbed and so obviously is then less under control and can be extorted from less. That takes the food off the plate of the chaos merchant.

All disturbance and chaos folds up in the teeth of truth. For example, the Duke of Alba is dashing about losing battles left and right and talking about how horrible the enemy is. His troops and his government are getting very upset, and his king is getting more and more discouraged. Then one day the fatal shaft of truth cuts through this whole chaos: the Duke has been in the enemy's pay all the time. Immediately everything sets back to rights. The troop morale returns and they defeat the enemy.

That's a rather dramatic instance, but all truth, whether dramatic or simple, has the same effect. Don't ever try to stop truth. It's the only thing that can go through 16-inch armor plate.

To a fellow who is raving around, cutting you up one side and down the other, you say, "The reason you're mad at me is because you have a withhold (an undisclosed, harmful, contrasurvival act) from me concerning my paycheck two months ago." Watch him fold up if that is the truth. The clean blade of truth cannot be stopped.

In a universe which is kept going and continuously made disturbed by lies, all the basic and fundamental facts had been completely covered up, particularly those related to life and death. These things were completely masked. Nothing but disturbance and chaos and suppression had been dug up around them for so long that that data was gone. So many contrary data existed, it was very difficult to sift them out. What is the truth about Man? What kind of being is he? What's he here for? What am I here for? What am I trying to do? How long will I live? What will happen to me when I die? What kind of a being am I? These are the basic and fundamental questions.

Those questions and the answers thereto belonged, on a time-honored basis, in the realm of philosophy. In the West, philosophy had come to such a decadence that it was mainly somebody sitting around a cracker barrel uttering witticisms. The last time anybody really came up with a civilized philosophy he was given a nice slug of hemlock. Philosophy has been a very unpopular subject insofar as it has disturbed the merchants of chaos in society.

Philosophers who had trouble with this were luckless only to the degree that they didn't reach the truth. The road to truth is something that you must follow all the way down. There is not such a thing as a limited truth. You've got to go all the way when you start talking about the truth of life; you mustn't hold up and not find out what it is.

Philosophy is very dangerous stuff to a fellow who is supporting himself by lies. It's dangerous only to people who are dangerous to others.

The goals and targets of philosophy are inevitable. By the mere fact of peoples looking at these truths, finding they are true, applying them and achieving a higher state of existence, there would inevitably appear a calmer life, a calmer environment, a calmer civilization. There would be less disturbance, and less pay for disturbance to be built out of that civilization. Therefore the first target, when introducing Scientology to anyone, would be that person's own environment. Scientology Zero is a whole philosophy on the subject of environment, under the heading of Dangerous Environment.

An individual believes that the environment is more dangerous than it is. He certainly believes that the environment is too dangerous for him. There are zones and areas in that environment which he believes are completely overwhelming and that he will not be able personally to cope with. This we can say with absolute certainty, whether we're talking to Joe, Bill or Pete, or even a politician or a newspaper reporter or a cop. Any relatively sane person will agree that certain spheres of the environment are a bit too much for him.

The merchant of chaos is completely crazy in that he thinks the environment has to be made chaotic. He thinks the environment is too much for him and he certainly knows he's making the environment too much for others. There are real areas of danger in the environment, but also there are areas of that environment being made more dangerous than they are. Therefore, the individual could be brought in some way to inspect his environment and perceive that it was being made more dangerous than it was. And that is one of the key points of Scientology Zero.

Another operating principle of Scientology Zero is that the individual's health level, sanity level, activity level and ambition level are monitored by *his* concept of the dangerousness of the environment. He's actually not operating to the challenge of the environment; he is withdrawing from the threat of the environment.

And knowing that, we could therefore improve these things in an individual by explaining to him about his environment. We will get a minor but demonstrable amount of resurgence and betterment in the areas of his health, his physical and mental alertness, his ambition, and his amount of activity by working with Scientology Zero. But we must talk within the real reality of the individual we're talking to. What is *his* expectancy at this level? It may be this low: that he just won't be so frightened when the doorbell rings. That's a tiny improvement, but nevertheless this improvement would be quite real to him.

This is an area of high level workability. All a person has to do is study his environment a little bit, so that when he wakes up in the morning he doesn't have an agonizing feeling that something horrible is going to happen if he gets up. This may not disappear, but it will diminish. He will be a little more active in life. You can settle for those gains, but the gains will in most cases greatly exceed your expectations and his.

How would we use these various principles? The threat he is worried about is probably imaginary and not really anything to be worried about. This is the simple therapy of Scientology Zero: *"Don't read the newspapers for two weeks and see if you don't feel better."* After he does this, you say, "Now read the newspaper for a week, and at the end of that week you'll find you feel worse. And after that time make up your mind whether or not you ought to pay any attention to the newspapers." This is a simple and inexpensive experiment.

Or you could just tell him to *"look around the environment and find something that isn't a threat to him."* If he ever gets too upset or confused, have him look around and find something that isn't being a threat to him.

Another simple process is *"take a walk." "If you feel bad, go take a walk and look at things as you walk."* This is a forward progress into the environment. That works because the person finds out that the environment is not threatening. This is a whole positive education on the negative threat. He looks around to see if something is doing this to him and he finds out it's a negative threat. "Take a walk and look at things" is the mildest advice you could possibly give anybody that is almost certain to produce a result if the person will do it.

Your effort at Scientology Zero is to get the individual to inspect the environment and find out that there is some slight greater security in it. That's all.

Out of these principles, you have to work with each individual separately because he's got a different environment than any other individual. But your single approach is, *"Look, don't worry. Look and find out if the environment is as threatening as it appears to be."*

If an individual sitting at his desk is very worried, papers are piling up, and he feels completely overwhelmed, he himself ought to be able to look at the papers on his desk and find something about them that isn't a threat. The threat of course will balance out in the discovery.

To a person who feels that everybody in the environment is hostile to him, just say, *"Find something people say or do around here that isn't hostile to you."* This is done on a gradient: *"Is there one person in the organization (or office or home) who isn't actively hostile to you?" "Was there anything said today that wasn't directly and immediately hostile to you?"*

A fellow who has a present time problem (technically, a special problem that exists in the physical universe now, on which the individual has his attention fixed) usually can't get his mind disentangled from it very far. *"Is there anything around that isn't pushing this present time problem at you?"* is a good question. It sometimes takes him a few minutes to answer it. A fellow who has just lost his girl feels that the horrible sadness and loss imparts to everything. Everything in the environment talks to him about this girl. You possibly have had a similar experience. When one's concentration has been very, very heavily on one individual it is sometimes almost heroically difficult not to associate everything with that person. The trick is to find something that isn't reminding you of that person, though you might have to search a long way. This is how to recover from a love affair.

But the situation is simple. The individual has identified everything in the environment with his unrest. Everything in the environment has become identified with the threatening things in the environment, and the individual can't pull his attention off of these things. But by quite simply directing his attention to things which are not so connected by making the individual find things which are not actively reminding him, a differentiation appears where an identification existed. And where a differentiation exists, intelligence and judgment can return. Intelligence and judgment cannot exist in the face of an identification but can exist where there is differentiation.

An individual, oddly enough, usually finds data that he can work on others more workable than data which is being worked on him, unless he also has the opportunity to work it upon others. This is an interesting commentary on the actual character of Man: Man is basically good. If you can give him things which will help him help others, he'll be far more interested than if you're simply giving him things which help him.

Therefore your supplementary advice should always go on the basis of: who are you trying to help? Who are you trying to help find out that his environment is not as dangerous as he thinks it is? So Scientology Zero has to be pretty well understood by you, in order to pass it along to Joe so he can help Pete. He will actually go help Pete with it, find out that it works to some degree, and use it to help himself.

The master question of Scientology Zero is, *"What part of the environment isn't threatening?"* You're basing this on the individual's identification of everything. It's a negative question because he has everything identified with that part of the environment which *is* threatening. You get him to differentiate, find out there are some parts of the environment that aren't threatening, and he'll make considerable forward progress.

Then the individual can also arrange his life somewhat. If you make someone plan a life by which he could live calmly and unthreatened, the life he is living becomes less threatening. This even applies to the poor fellow who's on a complete treadmill: his job doesn't pay much, but he's got to stay there with no chance of his getting away. He finds that environment very hostile. He's in a sort of trap, all of his own making. If you get him to plan, no matter how wildly or how dreamily, a life which would not be so threatening, he will continue working at his present job much more happily and calmly.

People are looking for a less threatening environment or, thinking they can't escape to that, looking for a way to better endure the environment they are in. It's a two-way look. They'd love to be able to get out of it or to master it, but they don't think they can. These are basic goals and targets which are completely general to every individual there is.

And of course being basically good, any person has actually been looking for something with which he could help other people be less intimidated or less fixed so that they could escape, endure or dominate their environment. He's also been looking for something to help his friends. He never really completely forgets his friends. Even the drunk on skid row or the bum in jail never forgets that.

What you need is a level of help which requires practically no education. The discussion of a situation is all that's required. There is no special skill needed, and yet there's a potential betterment. This becomes real to the individual no matter how crudely it is put to him. That he considers the environment dangerous and overwhelming and he doesn't quite know where the danger and overwhelm are coming from—that concept alone is an enormous piece of wisdom. It's never occurred to him before, although he has felt it and has been it all the time. That concept defines for him what he was. This is his is-ness quailing back from a threatening environment that may overwhelm him at any moment, unable to progress forward into greater endurance or power that can handle that threatening environment. This is the story of his life in just those few words.

You take it from there and actually provide a therapy. This is good solid advice:

"Knock off some of the things in your life that make you upset."

"Who upsets you? Well, don't talk to him for a while."

"What activities leave you feeling worse? Don't do them for a while."

"What things in the environment aren't really a threat to you? All right, associate with those. Pay more attention to them."

You're liable to shoot that person's IQ up and snap him around with no more wisdom than this little package contained in Scientology Zero for the Volunteer Minister.

Scientology Zero concerns the identification of the zones of chaos of existence: problems, confusions and wrongnesses.

An ordinary person tends to think that the fields of medicine, mental healing, and religion are all wrapped up. However, if he lifts the cover off any one of these areas, confusions and falsities fly up like a swarm of bumblebees and hit him in the face. You want to have him lift the cover on a gradient.

For instance, if you were to mention the state of "Clear" or any other subject a person is not ready to accept, you would be opening up Scientology Zero too fast. It's just a case of degree of what you reveal or point out. That's the level of observation.

"Everything is all bad! It's all terrible, everything is going to pieces. There isn't anybody good anyplace, and there are nothing but false situations." This might make sense, it might even be factual, but the person saying it would be considered nuts. That's too much Scientology Zero—something like emptying the cough medicine down somebody's throat. And it's the wrong presentation. It's too exaggerated, insufficiently definitive, obviously opinionated, unclear, unconvincing.

Let's take a typically British approach to the situation: "Government might not be the perfect answer." That might be too small a dose.

At Scientology Zero, you merely want the people to become aware of what the problem is. But you shouldn't infer that there are no solutions and only problems.

People don't try to resolve anything or do anything if they think it's all wrapped up. You will find out that the complacency of the world is one of the basic things which keep it gorgeously aberrated. "The government's got it all wrapped up." The fact that a bureau has said something like that immediately decrees there must have been some sense to it. This is the terrific reasonability factor that drives us around the bend. And if they want 95 percent of your pay in taxes, well, there must be some good reason for it.

You might say that the last stable datum (a datum not necessarily factual which an individual uses to align a confusion) that anybody can get in, is a toleration of a terrible condition. He says it is reasonable, or there must be a reason for it, so therefore in some fashion it is all right. That keeps it off his back as a problem.

But you, being a more adventurous character, are always lifting the lids off of things. You say, "Well, maybe that isn't quite all right." You look inside this thing and not only find that it is not all right, but you also find out that there's some awful swindle connected with it.

Scientology Zero concerns simply the level of existing chaos. Here are some typical questions:

"Is your family hard to live with?"

"Do you find your home noisy?"

"Are you worried about your job?"

"Is there any part of life about which you have anxiety?"

These questions awaken a person to the possibility that his life might be better, that the condition can be improved. And that is its sole and total therapeutic action: Hope.

The lowest level of spiritual counselling is giving somebody some hope. To summate this level, "There is a problem" is its strongest statement. And the strongest process that is applied to it is, "Maybe something can be done about it."

A view of Scientology Zero is simply the world as it exists. If we had no level of Scientology that paid any attention whatsoever to the is-ness of existence—that is, the conditions and problems of the society—we would have no area to study society just as itself, and we would keep on simply trying to resolve society without ever looking at it. So this is the level of inspection.

Now if you say, "Everything is bad all over; in fact there's no place anybody can find where anything is good," you immediately go wrong with your Scientology Zero because you are omitting the process. The process is simply:

"Well, maybe it will turn out all right," or

"Maybe if everybody got busy they could do something about it," or

"Maybe if we studied this thing enough and learned something about it it wouldn't have to be that way."

That's the least statement you could make.

You'll find this very acceptable on a public level, if you don't overwhelm them and if you apply just a small amount of hope and don't get too enthusiastic about it. Don't promise them the moon with a fence around it because that isn't necessary and it's not acceptable within their reality.

A person with a pretzel for a spinal cord comes in. You say to him, "Your trouble is possibly that you're disturbed about something." You let *him* put in some Scientology Zero on it.

He says, "You're damn right I'm disturbed about something. My spine. I'm in agony all the time."

Don't sell him up too high on this because you give him too high a hill to climb on his reality. Listen to him further as he tells you all his problems. Then pick out one of the minor things that he has given you because he won't believe you on any of the strong ones. He says he can't sleep at night, for instance.

You say, "Well, maybe we can fix you up so you'll sleep better at night."

That becomes very acceptable. Now he's got a goal. He doesn't expect you to unpretzelize his spine. But he'll move ahead on this, as you have by-passed the hidden standard, a problem a person thinks must be resolved before spiritual counselling can be seen to have worked, by giving him a new little standard. He starts winning and he sleeps a bit better at night.

Wrong approach: "We'll have you walking six-foot-six and looking sixteen years of age and all the girls whistling at you as you go down the street."

That's not acceptable. It's too much. He has already learned to live with his handicap; it already has some method of making people wrong. If you try to take it away from him directly or say you are going to, he isn't going to release it; all he's going to do is make you wrong.

So all you have to do is pick out the tiniest little problem he mentions and put some hope in on it. You're working with a gradient of confront. This person could perhaps face giving up enough of his efforts at making others wrong to sleep a little better at night. After all, he didn't intend to have his rest disturbed too. He just wants to get even with people in the daytime.

On a larger scale, someone asks, "What are we going to do about the government?"

You say, "Perhaps we could get the politicians to talk less on TV."

With this gradient approach, you could probably organize quite an association, with people busy writing letters and visiting their government representative, having a marvelous time. All they want to do is limit the amount of time a politician can talk on the air.

In deciding what's confrontable, an adjudication of how much is too little and how much is too much has got to be made. In Scientology Zero, that's the judgment that you must go on: What is acceptable and confrontable by the person?

This would be a perfect formula for a Volunteer Minister. You visit Mrs. O'Leary in a tenement where everybody is crying and screaming, there are three fights going on on two landings, and the babies are falling downstairs. Mrs. O'Leary has an awful lot of problems which she fires off at you. Her husband gets drunk all the time, the furniture gets broken, things get stolen, the rent is behind.

The Volunteer Minister always has to ask himself: "What am I trying to do?" If he's trying to make somebody happier in his environment or trying to get some action, he adjudicates his actions by these formulas. He gets something done that can be confronted by the person he is trying to get to do it. Although this sounds very simple, it has fantastic workability.

Among her problems, Mrs. O'Leary says, "I just can't keep the place clean at all."

The Volunteer Minister looks around to see what she could do. You notice that she has emptied an ashtray for his cigarette while they were standing there talking. She might be able to keep the ashtrays emptied.

You say, "I would start on this a little bit at a time and get the place cleaned up. Why don't you keep the ashtrays emptied?"

She might be very critical of you but when you leave, she'll go around and empty the ashtrays. All of a sudden a fantastic resurgence of hope may occur in that woman. The first thing you know, she's liable to be getting the idea she can do something about stopping her husband from drinking, as she has gotten the idea that something could be done.

The first level of hope is *there is something to be done about it.* The second level is *that you can do.*

To show you how missing this technology is, *that* isn't the experience of the average "Social Worker." People "trained in social work" complain that they can't get anybody to do anything about anything. For lack of this piece of information, a society falls into total socialism and total indigence, and that's how big the datum is that sits at the bottom of it. Social workers don't give anybody anything they can do. They never adjudicate the problems involved in the situation and then provide a confrontable solution to those problems that the person can do something about.

Occasionally there is a social worker who has stumbled onto this data and utilizes it, but such a person is rare. Social workers at large are terribly unsuccessful.

The average social worker says, "What you want to do, Mrs. O'Leary, is clean this whole place up from top to bottom—after all, we've given you soap. And get your children cleaned up and put in those nice new pinafores we've had sent down to you. Now I'll have a talk with your husband concerning his drinking."

At that last point Mrs. O'Leary and the social worker part company violently. Even if Mrs. O'Leary would have scrubbed her whole place, even if she would have put the children in clean clothes, the social worker has then told her something she knows by experience cannot be done: Nobody can talk to her husband about his drinking. The social worker has crashed head on into Mrs. O'Leary's stable datum.

A person says to you, "I have an awful lot of trouble with my business. My secretary is always drunk and the workers won't work. The police are always walking through the place in muddy boots." You're just listening to some kind of a circuit, so you can tell him what the problem is. It doesn't matter whether you get the problem from him or you put in the problem.

Very often, by the way, somebody's liable to get mad at you. He won't be mad at anybody else in the whole world, but he'll be mad at you. As the volunteer minister, you're his best friend. He can confront getting mad at you. He would be in a screaming rage at the rest of the world if he could confront it, but he can't so he gets mad at you. It's safe, especially if you're bound by an ethical code: you can't get mad back.

A little mousy character who never so much as whispers on the streets gets into a group meeting, realizes she's amongst friends, and dares to get mad at them. I'd find something else she could get mad at.

Here's your Scientology Zero aspect of existence: You don't tell people about problems that are completely unreal to them and that they know they can't do anything about and expect them to be in a wild enthusiasm to get going in any direction at all. You could have the police shooting down rioters with machine guns right outside the door, or rioters burning down government buildings, and in the midst of all this mess a large portion of the population would be sitting calmly, knowing that everybody had it under control who was supposed to have it under control. The visual evidence means nothing to them. That explodes a favorite stable datum: "that if somebody could see it with his own eyes he would believe it."

This is customary. You can think of many instances where a person sees things with his own eyes and doesn't believe them. In fact, they're probably more numerous than the reverse, so you never count on that as a stable datum. There isn't even any sense in being terribly good just to prove to people that you are good because if they are saying you are bad, they are incapable of the power of observation to determine when you're good. Parents are notorious in this particular line.

Sometimes a son gets to be forty years old and his father still has never gotten acquainted with him. He has a theoretical symbol someplace that he calls his son. Sons behave in a certain way; therefore, his son behaves in that way. The father will even invent a whole false past and a series of false adventures to account for this image that he has. A child often becomes very confused on such unreality.

Many a child is continually challenged for things he hasn't done. He gets into a confused state of mind because he is doing things that he should be challenged for, yet nobody ever sees these. It doesn't match his reality.

When this kind of thing occurs, the power of observation is out. The easiest thing to relay in this particular line is an idea. But the idea must not violate the confrontability or the confront potential of the individual it's being brought to. Therefore, neither the problem nor the solution in Scientology Zero must exceed the reality of the person to whom it is being pointed out.

The colonel in the army wonders how the other fellows can be so involved in their company streets and their barracks, operating in their tiny little spheres. You yourself have probably wondered occasionally how somebody could work at one bench in a shop all day long, never moving out of that zone or area. That person's confront potential on problems is on problems of the zone of that little work bench. And his ability to confront solutions applies to solutions in that zone. Therefore, we say he's an effective person on the job.

When his ability to confront problems gets up to the full zone and area of the entire camp, and he really is confronting the problems of the camp (not problems he dreams up), and he can confront solutions which are actual and real solutions to these problems, then you no longer have somebody who is working at a workbench, you have a colonel.

A private with a good confront potential will have quite a coterie when he's indicating to the troops around him the things that are wrong and pointing out the solutions. What's interesting is that these are usually more real than the command decisions.

If you started filtering around through the lower levels of rank and picking up the grapevine on the problems of the camp and solutions to them, you'd generally find out that those are the real answers. But according to the staff command level, "It's very involved for an uninformed observer to realize the tremendous difficulties of coping with this situation. General Smith, here, is having a very hard time trying to keep his number in the proper rank up at the Pentagon. And that is really the basic difficulty of this camp because we've got to make a better show."

Up to that point, you thought the problem was one of morale and drains. Now you find out that they're very complicated. And if you listen to that kind of approach for a little while you get absolutely overwhelmed.

If you sat around the press office in the national administrative centers today and listened to what the problems of the world "really" were, your eyes would probably start an inch out of your skull. Their Scientology Zero is wildly out based on an inability to observe. Sometimes these inabilities to observe are quite real; in other words, one can't go there and look. But that doesn't mean he can't get the area trustworthily looked at.

For instance, all too often a person is accused of doing a bad job and it's said he should be fired. Some kind of command decision needs to be made by an executive of a higher level. As long as everybody's fate depends on this particular level of action and that person in command is not observing what really happened, there is no justice or personal security possible. If you're going to have any justice at all, you've got to have the situation observed as intelligently and unbiasedly as it can be.

You hear people say he did a bad job. Other people say no. You eventually follow this down and learn that the customer had a hangover that morning or some other factor entered in that quite often nobody suspected. A person at command level has neither the time nor the position to observe in order to settle it, so he'd better settle it with people who can observe the situation, and then abide by what they have observed. That's a solution to his predicament.

If a group is going to operate in any optimum fashion, from it you must remove nonobservation and the substitution of a generality for judgment. But you cannot totally remove those on an absolute from all situations everywhere because the very fact of removing them would become so complicated that you would now have new complications to observe. However, you can go a long way toward the ideal.

What is the situation? What part of the situation is potentially confrontable? And what part of *that* situation will somebody do something about? Then you've got the whole formula worked out to get observation and action accomplished in this universe.

For an individual, we ask: out of the total sum of the person's problems and difficulties, which one is potentially confrontable by him? Then, what could he do about that one problem or difficulty?

You've got an estimate of what the person considers his problems and difficulties. Out of these you've got the one he would find confrontable. And once you've found out what he could face doing about that problem, then get him to do it. *Become terribly militant on the subject of getting that point done.* You'll find every time that you've got agreement with a capital A, agreement with a capital Affinity. Why? Because you haven't told him anything that he thinks is false. He knows you speak true because when you're advising him on that, he has an estimate of the situation. And you have, of course, smoked it right out into the clear. He will do something about it; he will, to that degree, win.

He will then be able to see more of his problems and difficulties and to confront more, and the cycle can be repeated. A new review of the general situation shows that he has an improved idea of what's potentially confrontable amongst his problems. You can now find out what he would be comfortable doing about this new problem. He would do that, and that would give him another win.

The only difficulty is that he very often comes up tone with too great a confidence. Like a baby who has just learned to walk, he tears across the room at a high run and falls on his face about the third step. He can get much too ambitious, so as a Counselor you have to take this into consideration and say, "Don't do any more than that at this particular time."

That's giving advice; that's social counseling.

People don't know what the world is all about. They don't know how to get any further along, they know they can't make any improvement, they know it's impossible to be any better. But you could actually prove to a whole group that it is possible to get better.

Make them each write on a sheet of paper a short list of problems he thinks is wrong with his life.

Have him then write down which is the easiest for him to confront.

Then have him write down what he knows for sure he could do about that last one he's written.

Then you say, "Now see what you've written down at the bottom of the page? DO IT!"

They'll do it, and they'll win. Thus, you could increase your agreement enormously with the people you deal with in social counseling and in other ways.

If you follow the rules I've given you, you'll be a very successful minister. You'll actually be in total control of the situation before you know it because all the advice you give will be followed. And what stops people advising? The advice they give is never followed. But your advice in this wise would always be followed.

There are two actions always involved in Scientology Zero and all of its problems: your viewpoint and the other fellow's viewpoint. They always lead to two different views of the same situation. If you can get the other fellow to estimate the situation, you seldom have to which is the laziest way to look at it. Of the two, it is slightly more important for the person involved to estimate his own problems and difficulties. But you shouldn't lose your gift in this particular wise because life is successfully lived with Scientology Zero well in. And it's unsuccessfully lived with it out.

J

Investigations

Investigations Checksheet

Purpose:

To educate the Volunteer Minister in the knowledge of how to logically investigate, and therefore be able to find the real WHY for non-optimum situations in life, businesses and organizations and handle them.

a	Study Section 1 Logic.	________
b	Study Section 2 Investigatory Procedure.	________
c	Study Section 3 Narrowing the Target.	________
d	Drill: Find an area of upset, disorder or downstats and narrow the target so as to put in order.	________
e	Study Section 4 Summary of Out-points.	________
f	Study Section 5 More Out-points.	________
g	Study Section 6 Out-points, More.	________
h	Drill: Make up at least three examples of your own for each of the types of out-points.	________
i	Study Section 7 The Real Why.	________
j	Study Section 8 The Why is God.	________
k	Drill: Demonstrate the difference between an explanation and a right why.	________
l	Drill: Isolate a situation (such as the instance in the photo sequence of the empty restaurant) and find the right why that leads to a recovery of statistics.	________

m Study Section 9 The Product as an Overt Act. ________

n Drill: Visit a store and find an overt product from an assembly line of items, like cards, clothes, tools, etc. ________

o Study Section 10 Organization Misunderstoods. ________

p Drill: Look up each of the basic organizational terms listed in the glossary at the back of this book or in your regular English dictionary. Use them in sentences until you are certain you understand them. ________

q Drill: Using your demo kit, demonstrate how organizational misunderstood words can cause management and production failures. ________

r Drill: Find an associate who is not doing well at his job, find out what word connected to his job he doesn't fully understand, and get it cleaned up with a good dictionary. ________

s Study Section 11 Third Dynamic De-aberration. ________

t Drill: Make up an admin scale for your own first dynamic. ________

u Drill: Make up an admin scale for a friend or relative's second dynamic. ________

v Drill: Make up an admin scale for a friend or relative's third dynamic. ________

w Drill: Debug points on the above drills as needed. ________

x Study Section 12 Group Sanity. ________

y Drill: For each of the 11 points of success and failure, demonstrate what a group would be like when these points are out and then go in. ________

z Study Section 13 Organization & Morale. ________

aa Drill: Find a person with low morale and raise his morale. ________

Investigations Pack

1 Logic

HCO PL 11 May 1970
Data Series 2

The subject of logic has been under discussion for at least three thousand years without any clean breakthrough of real use to those who work with data.

LOGIC means the subject of reasoning. Some in ages past have sought to label it a science. But that can be discarded as pretense and pompousness.

If there were such a "science" men would be able to think. And they can't.

The term itself is utterly forbidding. If you were to read a text on logic you would go quite mad trying to figure it out, much less learn how to think.

Yet logic or the ability to reason is vital to an organizer or administrator. If he cannot think clearly he will not be able to reach the conclusions vital to make correct decisions.

Many agencies, societies, groups capitalize upon this lack of logic and have for a very long time. For the bulk of the last 2,000 years the main western educator—the Church—worked on the theory that Man should be kept ignorant. A population that is unable to think or reason can be manipulated easily by falsehoods and wretched causes.

Thus logic has not been a supported subject, rather the opposite.

The administrator, the manager, the artisan and the clerk each have a considerable use for logic. If they cannot reason they make costly and time consuming errors and can send the entire organization into chaos and oblivion.

Their stock in trade are data and situations. Unless they can observe and think their way through, they can reach wrong conclusions and take incorrect actions.

Modern man thinks mathematics can serve him for logic and most of his situations go utterly adrift because of this touching and misplaced confidence. The complexity of human problems and the vast number of factors involved make mathematics utterly inadequate.

Computers are at best only servo-mechanisms (crutches) to the mind. Yet the chromium plated civilization today has a childish faith in them. It depends on who asks the questions and who reads the computer's answers whether they are of any use or not. And even then their answers are often madhouse silly.

Computers can't *think* because the rules of live logic aren't fully known to Man and computer builders. One false datum fed into a computer gives one a completely wrong answer.

If people on management and work lines do not know logic the organization can go adrift and require a fabulous amount of genius to hold it together and keep it running.

Whole civilizations vanish because of lack of logic in its rulers, leaders and people.

So this is a very important subject.

Unlocking Logic

I have found a way now to unlock this subject. This is a breakthrough which is no small win. If by it a formidable and almost impossible subject can be reduced to simplicity then correct answers to situations can be far more frequent and an organization or a civilization far more effective.

The breakthrough is a simple one.

BY ESTABLISHING THE WAYS IN WHICH THINGS BECOME ILLOGICAL ONE CAN THEN ESTABLISH WHAT IS LOGIC.

In other words, if one has a grasp of what makes things illogical or irrational (or crazy, if you please) it is then possible to conceive of what makes things logical.

Illogic

There are five primary ways for a relay of information or a situation to become illogical.

1. Omit a fact.
2. Change sequence of events.
3. Drop out time.
4. Add a falsehood.
5. Alter importance.

These are the basic things which cause one to have an incorrect idea of a situation.

Example: "He went to see a Communist and left at 3:00 A.M." The omitted facts are that he went with 30 other people and that it was a party. By omitting the fact one alters the importance. This omission makes it look like "he" is closely connected to Communism! When he isn't.

Example: "The ship left the dock and was loaded." Plainly made crazy by altering sequence of events.

Example: "The whole country is torn by riots" which would discourage visiting it in 1976 if one didn't know the report date of 1919.

Example: "He kept skunks for pets" which as an added falsehood makes a man look odd if not crazy.

Example: "It was an order" when in fact it was only a suggestion, which of course shifts the importance.

There are hundreds of ways these five mishandlings of data can then give one a completely false picture.

When basing actions or orders on data which contains one of the above, one then makes a mistake.

REASON DEPENDS ON DATA.

WHEN DATA IS FAULTY (as above) THE ANSWER WILL BE WRONG AND LOOKED UPON AS UNREASONABLE.

There are a vast number of combinations of these five data. More than one (or all five) may be present in the same report.

Observation and its communication may contain one of these five.

If so, then any effort to handle the situation will be ineffective in correcting or handling it.

Use

If any body of data is given the above five tests, it is often exposed as an invitation to acting illogically.

To achieve a logical answer one must have logical data.

Any body of data which contains one or more of the above faults can lead one into illogical conclusions.

The basis of an unreasonable or unworkable order is a conclusion which is made illogical by possessing one or more of the above faults.

Logic

Therefore logic must have several conditions:

1. All relevant facts must be known.
2. Events must be in actual sequence.
3. Time must be properly noted.
4. The data must be factual, which is to say true or valid.
5. Relative importances amongst the data must be recognized by comparing the facts with what one is seeking to accomplish or solve.

Not Know

One can always know something about anything.

It is a wise man who, confronted with conflicting data, realizes that he knows at least one thing—that he doesn't know.

Grasping that he can then take action to find out.

If he evaluates the data he does find out against the five things above, he can clarify the situation. Then he can reach a logical conclusion.

Drills

It is necessary to work out your own examples of the five violations of logic.

By doing so you will have gained skill in sorting out the data of a situation.

When you can sort out data and become skilled in it, you will become very difficult to fool and you will have taken the first vital step in grasping a correct estimate of any situation.

Definitions

Situation: The broad general scene on which a body of current data exists.

Data: Facts, graphs, statements, decisions, actions, descriptions which are supposedly true.

Out-Point: Any one datum that is offered as true that is in fact found to be illogical when compared to the five primary points of illogic.

Plus-Point: A datum of truth when found to be true compared to the five points.

2 Investigatory Procedure

HCO PL 19 September 1970 Issue I Data Series 16

Correction of things which are not wrong and neglecting things which are not right puts the tombstone on any organization or civilization.

In auditing when one reviews or "corrects" a case that is running well, one has trouble. It is *made* trouble.

Similarly, on the third dynamic, correcting situations which do not exist and neglecting situations which *do* exist can destroy a group.

All this boils down to CORRECT INVESTIGATION. It is not a slight skill. It is THE basic skill behind any intelligent action.

Suppressive Justice

When justice goes astray (as it usually does) the things that have occurred are

1. Use of justice for some other purpose than public safety (such as maintaining a privileged group or indulging a fixed idea) or

2. Investigatory procedure.

All suppressive use of the forces of justice can be traced back to one or the other of these.

Aberrations and hate very often find outlet by calling them "justice" or "law and order." This is why it can be said that man cannot be trusted with justice.

This *or* just plain stupidity bring about a neglect of intelligent investigatory procedures. Yet all third dynamic sanity depends upon correct and unaberrated investigatory procedures. Only in that way can one establish causes of things. And only by establishing causes can one cease to be the effect of unwanted situations.

It is one thing to be able to observe. It is quite another to utilize observations so that one can get to the basis of things.

Sequences

Investigations become necessary in the face of out-points or plus-points.

Investigations can occur out of idle curiosity or particular interest. They can also occur to locate the cause of plus-points.

Whatever the motive for investigation, the action itself is conducted by sequences.

If one is incapable mentally of tracing a series of events or actions, one cannot investigate.

Altered sequence is a primary block to investigation.

At first glance, omitted data would seem to be the block. On the contrary, it is the end product of an investigation and is what pulls an investigation along—one is looking for omitted data.

An altered sequence of actions defeats any investigation. Examples: We will hang him and then conduct a trial. We will assume who did it and then find evidence to prove it. A crime should be provoked to find who commits them.

Any time an investigation gets back to front, it will not succeed.

Thus if an investigator himself has any trouble with seeing or visualizing sequences of actions he will inevitably come up with the wrong answer.

Reversely, when one sees that someone has come up with a wrong or incomplete answer one can assume that the investigator has trouble with sequences of events or, of course, did not really investigate.

One can't really credit that Sherlock Holmes would say "I have here the fingerprint of Mr. Murgatoyd on the murder weapon. Have the police arrest him. Now, Watson, hand me a magnifying glass and ask Sergeant Doherty to let us look over his fingerprint files."

If one cannot visualize a series of actions, like a ball bouncing down a flight of stairs or if one cannot relate in proper order several different actions with one object into a proper sequence, he will not be able to investigate.

If one can, that's fine.

But any drilling with attention shifting drills will improve one's ability to visualize sequences. Why? Stuck attention or attention that cannot confront alike will have trouble in visualizing sequences.

Investigations

All betterment of life depends on finding out plus-points and why and re-enforcing them, locating out-points, and why and eradicating them.

This is the successful survival pattern of living. A primitive who is going to survive does just that and a scientist who is worth anything does just that.

The fisherman sees seagulls clustering over a point on the sea. That's the beginning of a short sequence, point No. 1. He predicts a school of fish, point No. 2. He sails over as sequence point No. 3. He looks down as sequence point No. 4. He sees fish as point No. 5. He gets out a net as point No. 6. He circles the school with the net, No. 7. He draws in the net, No. 8. He brings the fish on board, No. 9. He goes to port, No. 10. He sells the fish, No. 11. That's following a plus-point—cluster of seagulls.

A sequence from an out-point might be: Housewife serves dinner. Nobody eats the cake, No. 1. She tastes it, No. 2. She recognizes soap in it, No. 3. She goes to kitchen, No. 4. She looks into cupboard, No. 5. She finds the soap box upset, No. 6. She sees the flour below it, No. 7. She sees cookie jar empty, No. 8. She grabs young son, No. 9. She shows him the set-up, No. 10. She gets a confession, No. 11. And No. 12 is too painful to describe.

Unsuccessful investigators think good fish catches are sent by God and that when cake tastes like soap it is fate. They live in unsuccessful worlds of deep mystery.

They also hang the wrong people.

Discovery

All discoveries are the end product of a sequence of investigatory actions that begin with either a plus-point or an out-point.

Thus all knowledge proceeds from plus-points or out-points observed.

And all knowledge depends on an ability to investigate.

And all investigation is done in correct sequence.

And all successes depend upon the ability to do these things.

HCO PL 19 September 1970 Issue II
Data Series 17

3 Narrowing the Target

When you look at a broad field or area it is quite overwhelming to have to find a small sector that might be out.

The lazy and popular way is to generalize "They're all confused." "The organization is rickety." "They're doing great."

That's all very well but it doesn't get you much of anywhere.

The way to observe so as to find out what to observe is by discarding areas.

This in fact was the system I used to make the discoveries which became Dianetics and Scientology.

It was obvious to me that it would take a few million years to examine all of life to find out what made it what it was.

The first step was the tough one. I looked for a common denominator that was true for all life forms. I found they were attempting to survive.

With this datum I outlined all areas of wisdom or knowledge and discarded those which had not much assisted Man to survive.

This threw away all but scientific methodology, so I used that for investigatory procedure.

Then, working with that found mental image pictures. And working with them found the human spirit as different from them.

By following up the workable, one arrived at the processing actions which, if applied, work, resulting in the increase of ability and freedom.

By following up the causes of destruction one arrived at the points which had to be eradicated.

This is of course short-handing the whole cycle enormously. But that is the general outline.

Survival has been isolated as a common denominator to successful actions and succumb has been found as the common denominator of unsuccessful actions. So one does not have to re-establish these.

From there on, to discover anything bad or good, all one has to do is discard sterile areas to get a target necessary for investigation.

One looks broadly at the whole scene. Then discards sections of it that would seem unrewarding. He will then find himself left with the area that contains the key to it.

This is almost easier done than described.

Example: One has the statistics of a nine department organization. Eight are normal. One isn't. So he investigates the area of that one. In investigating the one he discards all normal bits. He is left with the abnormal one that is the key.

This is true of something bad or something good.

A wise boy who wanted to get on in life would discard all the men who weren't getting on and study the one who was. He would come up with something he could use as a key.

A farmer who wanted to handle a crop menace would disregard all the plants doing all right and study the one that wasn't. Then, looking carefully he would disregard all the should be's in that plant and wind up with the shouldn't be. He'd have the key.

Sometimes in the final look one finds the key not right there but way over somewhere else.

The boy, studying the successful man, finds he owed his success to having worked in a certain bank seven states away from there.

The farmer may well find his hired man let the pigs out into the crop.

But both got the reason why by the same process of discarding wider zones.

Plus-points or out-points alike take one along a sequence of discoveries.

Once in a purple moon they mix or cross.

Example: Gross income is up. One discards all normal statistics. Aside from gross income being up only one other statistic is down—new customers. Investigation shows that the advertising executives were off post all week on a tour and *that* was what raked in the money. Conclusion—send out tours as well as man the advertising department.

Example: Upset is coming from the camp kitchen. Obvious out-points. Investigation discloses a 15-year-old cook holding the job solo for 39 field hands! Boy, is he a plus-point. Get him some help!

Drawn Attention

Having attention dragged into an area is about the way most people "investigate." This puts them at effect throughout.

When a man is not predicting he is often subjected to out-points that leap up at him. Conversely when out-points leap up at one unexpectedly he knows he better do more than gape at them. He is already behindhand in investigating. Other signs earlier existed which were disregarded.

Errors

The usual error in viewing situations is not to view them widely enough to begin with.

One gets a despatch which says files don't exist.

By now keeping one's attention narrowly on that one can miss the whole scene.

To just order files put back in may fail miserably. One has been given a single observation. It is merely an out-point: files omitted.

There is no WHY.

You follow up "no files" and you may find the file clerk is in another part of the organization and never goes near the files, and the category of everyone in the files is just "bad credit ratings." You really investigate and you find there's no Credit Manager and there hasn't been one for a year.

The cycle of "out-point, correct, out-point, correct, out-point, correct" will drown one rapidly and improve nothing! But it sure makes a lot of useless work and worry.

Wisdom

Wisdom is not a fixed idea.

It is knowing how to use your wits.

HCO PL 19 September
1970 Issue III
Data Series 18
Summary of Outpoints
Omitted Data

4
Summary of Out-Points

Omitted Data

An omitted anything is an out-point.

This can be an omitted person, terminal, object, energy, space, time, form, sequence, or even an omitted scene. Anything that *can* be omitted that *should* be there is an out-point.

This is easily the most overlooked out-point as it isn't there to directly attract attention.

On several occasions I have found situation analyses done which arrived at no WHY that would have made handling possible but which gave a false why that would have upset things if used. In each case the out-point that held the real clue was this one of an omitted something.

In a dozen cases it was omitted personnel each time. One area to which orders were being issued had no one in it at all. Others were undermanned, meaning people were missing. In yet another case there were no study materials at all. In two other cases the whole of a subject was missing in the area. Yet no one in any of these cases had spotted the fact that it was an omitted something that had caused a whole activity to decay. People were working frantically to remedy the general situation. None of them noticed the omissions that were the true cause of the decay.

In crime it is as bad to *omit* as it is to commit. Yet no one seems to notice the omissions as actual crimes.

Man, trained up in the last century to be a stimulus-response animal, responds to the therenesses and doesn't respond as uniformly to not-therenesses.

This opens the door to a habit of deletion or shortening which can become quite compulsive.

In any analysis which fails to discover a WHY one can safely conclude the why is an omission and look for things that *should* be there and aren't.

Altered Sequence

Any things, events, objects, sizes, in a wrong sequence is an out-point.

The number series 3, 7, 1, 2, 4, 6, 5 is an altered sequence or an incorrect sequence.

Doing step two of a sequence of actions before doing step one can be counted on to tangle any sequence of actions.

The basic outness is no sequence at all. This leads into FIXED IDEAS. It also shows up in what is called disassociation, an insanity. Things connected to or similar to each other are not seen as consecutive. Such people also jump about subject-wise without relation to an obvious sequence. Disassociation is the extreme case where things that are related are not seen to be and things that have no relation are conceived to have.

Sequence means linear, (in a line) travel either through space or time or both.

A sequence that should be one and isn't is an out-point.

A "sequence" that isn't but is thought to be one is an out-point.

A cart-before-the-horse out of sequence is an out-point.

One's hardest task sometimes is indicating an inevitable sequence into the future that is invisible to another. This is a consequence. "If you saw off the limb you are sitting on you will of course fall." Police try to bring this home often to people who have no concept of sequence; so the threat of punishment works well on well-behaved citizens and not at all on criminals since they often are criminals because they can't think in sequence—they are simply fixated. "If you kill a man you will be hanged," is an indicated sequence. A murderer fixated on revenge cannot think in sequence. One has to think in sequences to have correct sequences.

Therefore it is far more common than one would at first imagine to see altered sequences since persons who do not think in sequence do not see altered sequences in their own actions or areas.

Visualizing sequences and drills in shifting attention can clean this up and restore it as a faculty.

Motion pictures and TV were spotted by a recent writer as fixating attention and not permitting it to travel. Where one had TV raised children, it would follow, one possibly would have people with a tendency to altered sequences or no sequences at all.

Dropped Time

Time that should be noted and isn't would be an out-point of "dropped time."

It is a special case of an omitted datum.

Dropped time has a peculiarly ferocious effect that adds up to utter lunacy.

A news bulletin from 1814 and one from 1922 read consecutively without time assigned produces otherwise undetectable madness.

A summary report of a situation containing events strung over half a year without saying so can provoke a reaction not in keeping with the current scene.

In madmen the present is the dropped time, leaving them in the haunted past. Just telling a group of madmen to "come up to present time" will produce a few miraculous "cures." And getting the date of an ache or pain will often cause it to vanish.

Time aberrations are so strong that dropped time well qualifies as an out-point.

Falsehood

When you hear two facts that are contrary, one is a falsehood or both are.

Propaganda and other activities specialize in falsehoods and provoke great disturbance.

Willful or unintentional, a falsehood is an out-point. It may be a mistake or a calculated or defensive falsehood and it is still an out-point.

A false anything qualifies for this out-point. A false being, terminal, act, intention, anything that seeks to be what it isn't is a falsehood and an out-point.

Fiction that does not pretend to be anything else is of course not a falsehood.

So the falsehood means "other than it appears" or "other than represented."

One does not have to concern oneself to define philosophic truth or reality to see that something stated or modeled to be one thing is in actual fact something else and therefore an out-point.

Altered Importance

An importance shifted from its actual relative importance, up or down, is an out-point.

Something can be assigned an importance greater than it has.

Something can be assigned an importance less than it has.

A number of things of different importances can be assigned a monotone of importance.

These are all out-points, three versions of the same thing.

All importances are relative to their actuality.

Wrong Target

Mistaken objective wherein one believes he is or should be reaching toward A and finds he is or should be reaching toward B is an out-point.

This is commonly mistaken identity. It is also mistaken purposes or goals.

"If we tear down X, we will be okay" often results in disclosure that it should have been Y.

"Removing the slums" to make way for modern shops kills the tourist industry. Killing the king to be free from taxation leaves the tax collector alive for the next regime.

Injustice is usually a wrong target out-point.

Arrest the drug consumer, award the drug company would be an example.

Military tactics and strategy are almost always an effort to coax the selection of a wrong target by the enemy.

And most dislikes and spontaneous hates in human relations are based on mistaken associations of Bill for Pete.

A large sum of aberration is based on wrong targets, wrong sources, wrong causes.

Incorrectly tell a patient he has ulcers when he hasn't and he's hung with an out-point which impedes recovery.

The industry spent on wrong objectives would light the world for a millennium.

Summary

These are the fundamental out-points required in data analysis and situation analysis.

They have one infinity of variation. They should be very well known to anyone seeking third dynamic sanity.

They are the basic illogics.

HCO PL
26 November 1970
Data Series 20

5
More Outpoints

While there could be many many oddities classifiable as out-points, those selected and named as such are major in importance whereas others are minor.

Wrong Source

Wrong source is the other side of the coin of wrong target.

Information taken from wrong source, orders taken from the wrong source, gifts or materiel taken from wrong source all add up to eventual confusion and possible trouble.

Unwittingly receiving from a wrong source can be very embarrassing or confusing, so much so that it is a favorite intelligence trick. Intelligence agencies have very intricate methods of planting false information and disguising its source.

Technology can come from wrong source. For instance Leipzig University's school of psychology and psychiatry opened the door to death camps in Hitler's Germany. Using drugs these men apparently gave Hitler to the world as their puppet. They tortured, maimed and slaughtered over 12,000,000 Germans in death camps. At the end of World War II these extremists formed the "World Federation of Mental Health," which enlisted the American Psychiatric Association and the American Medical Association and established "National Associations for Mental Health" over the world, cowed news media, smashed any new technology and became the sole advisors to the US government on "mental health, education and welfare" and the appointers of all Health Ministers through the civilized world and through their graduate, Pavlov, dominated Russian Communist "mental health." This source is so wrong that it is destroying Man, having already destroyed scores of millions. (All statements given here are documented).

Not only taking data from wrong source but officialdom from it can therefore be sufficiently aberrated as to result in planetary insanity.

In a lesser level, taking a report from a known bad hat and acting upon it is the *usual* reason for errors made in management.

Contrary Facts

When two statements are made on one subject which are contrary to each other, we have contrary facts.

Previously we classified this illogic as a falsehood, since one of them must be false.

But in doing data analysis one cannot offhand distinguish which is the false fact. Thus it becomes a special out-point.

"They made a high of $12,000 that week" and "They couldn't pay staff" occurring in the same time period gives us one or both as false. We may not know which is true but we do know they are contrary and can so label it.

In interrogation this point is so important that anyone giving two contrary facts becomes a prime suspect for further investigation. "I am a Swiss citizen" as a statement from someone who has had a German passport found in his baggage would be an example.

When two"facts" are contrary or contradictory we may not know which is true but we do know they can't both be true.

Issued by the same organization, even from two different people in that organization, two contradictory "facts" qualifies as an outpoint.

These two outpoints will be found useful in analysis.

6
Outpoints, More

HCO PL 30 September 1973, Issue I
Data Series 29

I recently investigated a number of possible new out-points. Almost all of them were simply the basic outpoints in a different guise and needed no special category.

However, two new outpoints did emerge that are in addition to the basic number.

The new out-points are:

ADDED TIME. In this out-point we have the reverse of dropped time. In added time we have, as the most common example, something taking longer than it possibly could. To this degree it is a version of conflicting data = something takes three weeks to do but it is reported as taking six months. But added time must be called to attention as an out-point in its own right for there is a tendency to be reasonable about it and not see that it IS an out-point in itself.

In its most severe sense, added time becomes a very serious out-point when, for example, two or more events occur at the same moment involving, let us say, the same person who could not have experienced both. Time had to be ADDED to the physical universe for the data to be true. Like this: "I left for Saigon at midnight on April 21st 1962 by ship from San Francisco." "I took over my duties at San Francisco on April 30th 1962." Here we have to add time to the physical universe for both events to occur as a ship would take two or three weeks to get from San Francisco to "Saigon."

Another instance, a true occurrence and better example of added time, happened when I once sent a checklist of actions it would take a month to complete to a junior executive and received compliance in full in the next return mail. The checklist was in her hands only one day! She would have had to add 29 days to the physical universe for the compliance report to be true. This is also dropped time on her part.

ADDED IN-APPLICABLE DATA. Just plain added data does not necessarily constitute an out-point. It may be someone being thorough. But when the data is in no way applicable to the scene or situation and is added it is a definite out-point.

Example: Long, long reams of data on an analysis write-up, none of which is giving any clue to the out-points on the scene. By actual investigation it was found that the person doing it did not know any why (not having used out-points to find it) and was just stalling.

Often added data is put there to cover up neglect of duty or mask a real situation. It certainly means the person is obscuring something.

Usually added data also contains other types of out-points like wrong target or added time.

In using this out-point be very sure you also understand the word *in-applicable* and see that it is only an out-point if the data itself does not apply to the subject at hand.

There is more about another already named out-point:

WRONG SOURCE. This is the opposite direction from *wrong target.*

An example would be a president of a company using the opinions and congratulations of a rival company to make his point with his company's stockholders.

A more common version of this, not unknown in intelligence report grading for probability, would be a farmer in Iowa reporting a Mexican battleship on Mud Creek. The farmer would be a wrong source for accurate naval reports.

A private taking an order from a sergeant that countermands an order he had from a lieutenant would be an example of wrong source.

What is sometimes called a "Hey You organization" is one that takes orders from anyone = a repeating out-point of wrong source.

There are many examples of this out-point. It must be included as a very important out-point on its own. It produces a chaos of illogical ideas and actions when present.

Plus Points

CORRECT TIME or the expected time period is a plus-point.

ADEQUATE DATA is a plus-point.

APPLICABLE DATA is a plus-point.

CORRECT SOURCE is a plus-point.

7

HCO PL 13 October 1970
Issue II, Data Series 19

The Real Why

"WHY" as used in logic is subject to non-comprehension.

WHY = that basic outness found which will lead to a recovery of statistics.

WRONG WHY = the incorrectly identified outness which when applied does not lead to recovery.

A MERE EXPLANATION = a *"why"* given as THE why that does not open the door to any recovery.

Example: A mere explanation, "The stats went down because of rainy weather that week." So? So do we now turn off rain? Another mere explanation, "The staff became overwhelmed that week." An order saying, "Don't overwhelm staff" would be the possible "solution" of some manager. BUT THE STATS WOULDN'T RECOVER.

The *real* WHY when found and corrected leads straight back to improved statistics.

A wrong why, corrected, will further depress statistics.

A mere explanation does nothing at all and decay continues.

Here is a situation as it is followed up:

The statistics of an area were down. Investigation disclosed there had been sickness two weeks before. The report came in, "The statistics were down because people were sick." This was a mere explanation. Very reasonable. But it solved nothing. What do we do now? Maybe we accept this as the correct why. And give an order, "All people in the area must get a medical exam and unhealthy workers will not be accepted and unhealthy ones will be fired." As it's a correction to a wrong why, the statistics *really* crash. So that's not it. Looking further we find the real WHY. In the area there is no trained-in organization chart and a boss there gives orders to the wrong people which, when executed, then hurt their individual stats. We organize the place and groove-in the boss and we get a stat recovery and even an improvement.

The correct WHY led to a stat recovery.

Here is another one: Stats are down in a school. An investigation comes up with a mere explanation: "The students were all busy with sports." So management says, "No sports!" Stats go down again. A new investigation comes up with a wrong why: "The students are being taught wrongly." Management sacks the dean. Stats really crash now. A further more competent investigation occurs. It turns out that there were 140 students and only the dean and one instructor! And the dean had other duties! We put the dean back on post and hire two more instructors making three. Stats soar. Because we got the right why.

Management and organizational catastrophes and successes are ALL explained by these three types of why. An arbitrary is probably just a wrong why held in by law. And if so held in, it will crash the place.

One really has to understand logic to get to the correct WHY and must really be on his toes not to use and correct a wrong WHY.

In world banking, where inflation occurs, finance regulations or laws are probably just one long parade of wrong whys. The value of the money and its usefulness to the citizen deteriorate to such an extent that a whole ideology can be built up (as in Sparta by Lycurgus who invented iron money nobody could lift in order to rid Sparta of money evils) that knocks money out entirely and puts nothing but nonsense in its place.

Organizational troubles are greatly worsened by using mere explanations (which lead to no remedies) or wrong whys (which further depress stats). Organizational recoveries come from finding the real WHY and correcting it.

The test of the real WHY is "when it is corrected, do stats recover?" If they do that was it. And any other remedial order given but based on a wrong why would have to be cancelled quickly.

8 The Why is God

HCO PL 31 January 1972
Data Series 22

When beings operate mainly on illogics, they are unable to conceive of valid reasons for things or to see that effects are directly caused by things they themselves can control.

The inability to observe and find an actual usable WHY *is* the downfall of beings and activities. This is factually the WHY of people not finding WHYs and using them.

The prevalence of historical Man's use of "fate," "kismet (fatalism)," superstition, fortune telling, astrology and mysticism confirms this.

Having forgotten to keep seed grain for the spring, the farmer starves the following year and when asked WHY he is starving says it is the gods, that he has sinned or that he failed to make sacrifice. In short, unable to think, he says "The Why is God."

This condition does not just affect primitives or backward people.

All through the most modern organizations you can find "The WHY is God" in other forms.

By believing that it is the fault of other divisions or departments, a staff member does not look into his *own* scene. "The reason I cannot load the lumber is because the Personnel Section will not find and hire people." It does not seem to occur to this fellow that he is using a WHY which he can't control so it is *not* a WHY for his area. It does not move the existing to the ideal scene. Thus it is not a WHY for him. Yet he will use it and go on nattering about it. And the lumber never gets loaded. The real WHY for him more likely would be, "I have no right to hire day laborers. I must obtain this right before my area breaks down totally," or "My department posts are too specialized. I need to operate on all-hands actions on peak loads."

But this does not just apply on small activities. It applies to whole nations. "The reason we Germans cannot advance is because England is against us." This wrong WHY has killed many tens of millions in two world wars.

Intelligence organizations are often almost dedicated to "the why is over there." It seldom is.

Thus survival is very closely tied to logic. If one finds he is sinking into apathy over his inability to get his job done, it is *certain* that he is operating on self-conceived wrong WHYs in areas that he cannot ever hope to control.

And in living any life, most major points of decline can be traced to the person's operating on whys that do not allow him to improve his own scene.

The Greek cut open the guts of birds to find the WHY. He called this "divination" or "augury." Don't look now, but that civilization has long been dead!

Just as anyone will be whose illogic leads him to over-thereness to find his whys.

Strength and power in the individual consists of being logical enough to find WHYS *he* can use to advance his existing scene toward the ideal scene.

The Why is NOT God. It lies with YOU and your ability to be logical.

God helps those who help themselves.

9

HCO PL 14 November 1970, Org Series 14

The Product as an Overt Act

When a product is non-existent or bad it can be classified as an overt act against both the organization and any customer.

You can estimate what the existing scene of a post really is by looking at its product.

When a flubby product is observed, you can at once approximate the existing scene.

The time it takes to achieve the product is also an estimation. A long time to achieve a small flubby product gives one a good idea of the existing scene.

This also estimates the amount of "noise" in an area.

Example: Post X is supposed to sort ruddy rods. There are no sorted ruddy rods ready. That's an omitted action. The post has to be ordered to sort ruddy rods. That's ordering someone to wear his hat which is altered sequence as he should have been wearing it already. The post must be a false terminal as it isn't wearing its hat. The product so far is no sorted ruddy rods. You order them sorted. You get bent, tangled ruddy rods furnished after a long time period filled with dev-t. Estimate of existing scene—psychotic and an awful long way from any ideal scene. Actual quality of product—an overt act.

When several staff members are furnishing a poor individual product, the organization becomes difficult to handle as the person in charge is operating as correction not as establishment and organizational product.

Wherever an organization's product is low in quantity and quality one must recognize that it contains several members who unconsciously furnish overt acts in the guise of post products and begin to straighten things out accordingly.

The road to sanity for such a person or organization is a good grasp of organizing and products, making known the technology needed to produce a product, getting it properly done so that the person can then wear his hat.

If this still doesn't occur, personal processing is necessary as the personnel may well be dramatizing overt acts (harmful acts) by turning out a bad product.

The final product of an organization is the combined products of all the members of that organization directed to accomplish the final products of that organization.

Stupidity, lack of a worked out organization chart, lack of recognition of what the final organization products should be, lack of training, lack of hats can produce poor final products. In an activity not doing well the poor final product or its lack of any product is the compound errors in sub-products. An organization where the product is pretty bad or non-existent contains many elements—posts—in it which have as *their* individual "post products" not products at all but overt (harmful) acts.

Pride of workmanship is pride in one's own product.

Every post has some product. If the products of all posts in an activity are good and the product sequence is good then the final products of the organization will be good.

10 Organization Misunderstoods

HCO PL 20 November 1970, Personnel Series 12 Org Series 15

By Scientology study technology, understanding ceases on going past a misunderstood word or concept.

If a person reading a text comes to the word *Felix domesticus* and doesn't know it simply means HOUSE CAT, the words which appear thereafter may become meaningless, "uninteresting," and he may even become slightly unconscious, his awareness shutting down.

Example: "Wind the clock and put out the *Felix domesticus* and then call Algernon and tell him to wake you at 10:00 a.m.," read as an order by a person who didn't bother to find out that *Felix domesticus* means "house cat" or "the variety of cat which has been domesticated" will not register that he is supposed to call Algernon, will feel dopey or annoyed and probably won't remember he's supposed to wake up at 10:00 a.m.

In other words, when the person hit a misunderstood word, he ceased to understand and did not fully grasp or become aware of what followed after.

All this applies to a sentence, a book, a post or a whole organization.

Along the time track a crashing misunderstood will block off further ability to study or apply data. It will also block further understanding of an organization, its organizing board an individual post or duties and such misunderstoods can effectively prevent knowledge of or action on a post.

ALL THIS IS THE MOST COMMON CAUSE OF AN UNACCEPTABLE POST PRODUCT OR NO PRODUCT AT ALL.

The difficulties of an organization in functioning or producing stem from this fact.

Personal aberration is the cause of products that are in fact overt acts.

Scientology technology today easily handles the personal aberration part of the problem, IF IT IS USED AND PROPERLY APPLIED.

Employing persons of the Leipzig, Germany death camp school (psychologists, psychiatrists) to handle personal aberration is like throwing ink in water to clean it up. One does have to *handle* personal aberration in an organization and these schools were too vicious and incompetent to do so.

Those who are personally very aberrated are not about to produce anything but an overt act. They are difficult to detect as they are being careful not to be detected. Things "just sort of go wrong" around them, resulting in a product that is in fact an overt act. But these constitute only about 10 or 20 percent of the population.

The remaining 80 percent or 90 percent where they are nonfunctional or bungling are so because they do not understand what it's all about. They have in effect gone on by a misunderstood such as what the organization is supposed to do or the administrative technology they use on their posts or where they are or what their product is.

Earth organizations like governments or big monopolies get a very bad repute because of these factors:

1. Personal aberration of a few undetected and unhandled.

2. Inadequate or unreal basic education technology and facilities.

3. Inadequate or unknown organizational technology.

4. Noncomprehension of the individual regarding the activities of which he is a part.

5. Noncomprehension of the basic words with which he is working.

6. Purposes of the post uncleared.

7. Admin of the post not known or comprehended.
8. Technology in use not fully understood.
9. A lack of comprehension of products.

Out of these nine things one gets organizational troubles and the belief that it takes a genius to run one successfully. Yet all the genius in the world will fail eventually if the above nine things are not handled to some degree.

The common methods currently in use on the planet to handle these things are very crude and time-consuming as the items themselves are either dimly comprehended or not known at all.

1A. Personal aberration is met by torture, drugs or death when it is detected. Yet, only the very serious cases who are obviously screaming, muttering or unconscious are singled out, whereas the dangerous ones are neither detected nor handled at all and become with ease generals or presidents or dictators, to say nothing of lesser fry. 10 to 20 percent of any organization is stark staring mad, doing the place in so adroitly that only their actual product betrays them.

2A. Basic education as well as higher general education has become a mass-produced area crawling with bad texts and noncomprehension and used mainly by hostile elements to overturn the state or pervert the race and its ideals.

3A. Organizational technology is so primitive as to change national maps and leading companies many times a century, an extremely unstable scene for a planet.

4A. Very few individuals on the planet have any concept of the structure entities such as their country or state or company. Persons surveying the public in the U.S., pretending to advise acceptance of "new measures" already in the Constitution, were threatened for being revolutionaries. Hardly anyone knew the basic document of the nation's organization much less its rambling structure.

5A. The basic words of organization are glibly used but not generally comprehended, words like "company," "management," "policy." Vocabularies have to be increased before comprehension and communication occur and misunderstoods drop out.

6A. Post purposes are often glibly agreed with while something entirely different is done.

7A. Administrative actions involving posts are often only dimly comprehended and seldom well-followed but in this matter of communication, dispatches, etc., the planet is not as deficient as in others except that these functions, being somewhat known can become an end-all — tons of dispatches, no actual product. In some areas it is an obsession, an endless paper chain, that is looked on as a legitimate product even when it leads to no production.

8A. The planet's technology is on the surface very complex and sophisticated but is so bad in actual fact that experts do not give the planet and its populations 30 years before the smoke and fumes will have eaten up the air cover and left an oxygenless world. (The converters like trees and grass which change carbon dioxide to oxygen are inadequate to replace the oxygen and are additionally being killed by air impurities coming out of factories and cities.) If the technology destroys the base where it is done — in this case the planet — it is not adequate and may even be destructive technology.

9A. The whole idea of "product" is not in use except in commercial industry where one has to have a car that sells or a washing machine that actually washes.

It is against this primitive background that one is trying to run an organization.

If it were not for improvements made on each one of these points the task could be hopeless.

I have gone to some length to outline the lacks in order to show the points where one must concentrate in (a) putting an organization together and (b) keeping it viable.

Enthusiasm is a vital ingredient. It soon goes dull when insufficient attention is paid to resolving and getting in these nine points.

Bluntly, if they are not gotten in and handled, the task of living and running a post or an organization will become so confused that little or no production will occur and disasters will be frequent.

The, by no means complete, list of words that have to be fully cleared and understood just to talk about organization as a subject, and to intelligently and happily work in an organization EVEN AS ITS LOWEST EMPLOYEE are:

A company
A board of directors
Top management
Policy
Management
Programs
Targets
Orders
Technology
Know-how
Organizing board
Post
Hat
Cope
Purposes
Organize
Duties
A checklist
A communication channel
A command channel
A relay point
A stable terminal
Double-hatted
A product
Aberration
VIABILITY

This is key vocabulary. One could draw up a whole dictionary for these things and no one studying it would be any wiser since it would become salted with other words of far less importance.

The way to do this list is sweat it out with a dictionary until one knows each can't mean anything else than what it does mean.

Out of a full understanding of what is implied by each, a brilliantly clean view is attained of the whole subject of organization, not as a fumble but as a crisp usable activity.

Unless one at least knows these words completely so that they can be used and applied they will not buffer off confusions that enter into the activity.

Glibness won't do. For behind these words is the full structure of an activity that will survive and when the words aren't understood the rest can become foggy.

We *do* know all these needful things. We must communicate them and use them successfully.

11

HCO PL 6 December 1970
Personnel Series 13
Org Series 18

Third Dynamic Deaberration

The exact mechanism of third dynamic (group or organization) aberration is the conflict of COUNTER POLICY.

Illegal policy set at unauthorized levels jam the actions of a group and ARE responsible for the inactivity, nonproduction or lack of team spirit.

Counter-policy independently set jams the group together but inhibits its operation.

Out-reality on organizing boards, etc., is to a large degree caused by disagreements and conflicts which are caused by illegal policy.

If we had a game going in which each player set his own rules, there would be no game. There would only be argument and conflict.

At the start it must be assumed or effected that there is someone or somebody to set authorized policy for the group. Absence of this function is an invitation to random policy and group conflict and disintegration. If such a person or body exists, new proposed policy must be referred to this person or body and issued, not set randomly at lower levels or by unauthorized persons.

Policies so set by the policy authority must be informed enough and wise enough to forward the group purpose and to obtain agreement. Ignorant or bad policy even when authorized tends to persuade group members to set their own random policy.

When no policy at all exists random policy occurs.

When policy exists but is not made known, random policy setting will occur.

Ignorance of policy, the need or function of it, can cause random policies.

Hidden not stated random policies can conflict.

Correct policy can be relayed on a cutative basis—a few words left off or a qualifying sentence dropped which makes policy incorrect or null. "Children may not go out" can be made out of "Children may not go out after midnight."

Altered policy can be limitless in error.

Attributing a self-set policy to the authorized source can disgrace all policy as well as pervert the leadership purpose.

Policy can be excluded from a zone of a group that should be governed by it. "Pipe making policy does not apply to the *small* pipe shop."

Such masses of unnecessary policy can be issued that it cannot be assimilated.

Policy can exist in large amounts but not be subdivided into relevant subjects.

Disgrace of policy can occur in a subsequent catastrophe and render any policy disgraceful, encouraging self-set policy by each group member.

All authorized policy must be set or made available in master books and adequate complete policy files. This makes it possible to compile training hats and issue them.

Group surveys of "What policy are you operating on?" can reveal random policy.

All bugged (halted) projects can be surveyed for illegal policy and cleaned up and gotten going again.

Other actions can be taken all of which add up to:

1. Get existing policy used.

2. Get areas without policy crisply given policy from the authorized source.

3. Debug all past projects of false policy.

4. De-aberrate group members as per the "Organization Misunderstoods" materials.

5. Educate the group members concerning policy technology.

6. Set up systems that detect, isolate and report out-policy and get it corrected and properly set, issued and known.

7. Monitor any new policy against statistics and include policy outnesses as part of all statistical evaluations.

Admin Scale

I have developed a scale for use which gives a sequence (and relative seniority) of subjects relating to organization.

GOALS
PURPOSES
POLICY
PLANS
PROGRAMS
PROJECTS
ORDERS
IDEAL SCENES
STATISTICS
VALUABLE FINAL PRODUCTS

This scale is worked up and worked down UNTIL IT IS (EACH ITEM) IN FULL AGREEMENT WITH THE REMAINING ITEMS.

In short, for success all these items in the scale must agree with all other items in the scale on the same subject.

Let us take "golf balls" as a subject for the scale. Then all these scale items must be in agreement with one another on the subject of golf balls. It is an interesting exercise.

The scale also applies in a destructive subject. Like "cockroaches."

When an item in the scale is *not* aligned with the other items, the project will be hindered if not fail.

The skill with which all these items in any activity are aligned and gotten into action is called MANAGEMENT.

Group members only become upset when one or more of these points are not aligned to the rest and at least some group agreement.

Groups appear slow, inefficient, unhappy, inactive or quarrelsome only when these items are not aligned, made known and coordinated.

Any activity can be improved by debugging or aligning this scale in relation to the group activity.

As out-reality breeds out-communication, and out-affinity, it follows that unreal items on the scale (not aligned) produce upsets and disaffection.

It then follows that when these scale items are well-aligned with each other and the group there will be high reality, high communication and high affinity in the group.

Group mores aligned so and followed by the group gives one an ethical group and also establishes what will then be considered as overts and withholds in the group by group members.

This scale and its parts and ability to line them up are one of the most valuable tools of organization.

Debug

When orders are not complied with and projects do not come off, one should DETECT, ISOLATE and REPORT and handle or see that it is handled, any of the scale items found random or counter.

If any item below POLICY is in trouble, not moving, one can move upwards correcting these points, but certainly concentrating on a discovery of illegal or counter policy. Rarely it occurs some old but legal policy needs to be adjusted. Far more commonly policy is being set by someone verbally or in despatches, or hidden, that is bugging any item or items below the level of policy.

So the rule is that when things get messed up, jammed up, slowed or inactive or downright destructive (including a product as an overt act) one sniffs about for random or counter policy illegally being set in one's own area or "out there."

Thus in the face of any outness one DETECTS, ISOLATES, REPORTS and handles or gets handled the out-policy.

The *detection* is easy. Things aren't moving or going right.

The isolation is of course a WHAT POLICY that must be found and WHO set it.

Reporting it would mean to the executive responsible for maintaining the application of legal policies within the organization.

This administrative technology gives us our first third dynamic de-aberrater that works easily and fast.

Why?

Well, look at the Admin Scale. *Policy* is just below *purpose.*

Purpose is senior to policy.

The person who is setting random or counter illegal policy is off group purpose. He is other-purposed to greater or lesser degree.

From 1960 to 1962 I developed a vast lot of technology about goals and purposes. If we define a goal as a long long-term matter and a purpose as the lesser goal applying to specific activities or subjects we see clearly that if we clean up a person's purposes relating to the various activities in which he is involved and on the eight dynamics we will handle the obsession to set random or counter-policies!

As the universe is full of beings and one lives with them whether he likes it or not, it would be to anyone's interest to be able to have functioning groups.

The only way a group jams up and (a) becomes difficult to live in and (b) impossible to fully separate from is by random and counter-purposes.

If one thinks he can go off and be alone anywhere in this universe he is dreaming.

The first impulse of a hostile being is "to leave" a decent group. What a weird one.

The only reason he gets in jams is his inability to tolerate or handle others.

There's no road out for such a being except through.

Thus all we can do to survive even on the first dynamic is to know how to handle and be part of the third or fourth dynamic and clean it up.

Probably the reason this universe itself is considered by some as a trap is because their admin scale is out.

And the only reason this universe is sometimes a trial is because no one published its admin scale in the first place.

12

HCO PL 14 December 1970, Personnel Series 14 Org Series 19

Group Sanity

The points of success and failure, the make and break items of a group are

1. HIRING
2. TRAINING
3. APPRENTICESHIPS
4. UTILIZATION
5. PRODUCTION
6. PROMOTION
7. SALES
8. DELIVERY
9. FINANCE
10. JUSTICE
11. MORALE

These eleven items MUST AGREE WITH AND BE IN LINE WITH THE ADMIN SCALE.

Where these subjects are not well-handled and where one or more of these are very out of line, the group will suffer a third dynamic aberration.

This then is a SANITY SCALE for the third dynamic of a group.

The group will exhibit aberrated symptoms where one or more of these points are out.

The group will be sane to the degree that these points are in.

Internal stresses of magnitude begin to affect every member of the group in greater or lesser degree when one or more of these items are neglected or badly handled.

The society at large currently has the majority of these points out.

These elements become aberrated in the following ways:

1. *HIRING*

The society is running a massive can't have (denial of something to someone else) on the subject of people. Automation and employment penalties demonstrate an effort to block out letting people in and giving them jobs. Confirming this is growing unemployment and fantastic sums for welfare, meaning relief. Fifty percent of America within the decade will be jobless due to the population explosion without a commensurate expansion in production. Yet production by U.S. presidential decree is being cut back. War, birth control are two of the many methods used to reduce population. THIS THIRD DYNAMIC PSYCHOSIS IS A *REFUSAL TO EMPLOY PEOPLE.* EXCLUSION OF OTHERS IS THE BASIC CAUSE OF WAR AND INSANITY.

2. *TRAINING*

Education has fallen under the control of one-worlders, is less and less real. Data taught is being taught less well. Less data is being taught. School and college unrest reflect this. Confirmation is the deteriorated basic education found in teenagers such as writing. Older technologies are being lost in modern rewrites. THIS THIRD DYNAMIC PSYCHOSIS IS A *COVERT REFUSAL TO TRAIN.*

3. *APPRENTICESHIPS*

The most successful industries, activities and professions of earlier centuries were attained by training the person as an apprentice, permitting him to understudy the exact job he would hold for a long period before taking the post. Some European schools are seeking to revive this but on a general basis, not as an apprentice system. A THIRD DYNAMIC PSYCHOSIS IS A *DENIAL OF ADEQUATE EXPERIENCE TO SUCCEED.*

4. *UTILIZATION*

In industries, governments and armed services as well as life itself, personnel are not utilized. A man trained for one thing is required to do something else. Or his training is not used. Or he is not used at all. A THIRD DYNAMIC PSYCHOSIS IS *FAILURE TO UTILIZE PEOPLE.*

5. *PRODUCTION*

Modern think is to reward downstats. A person is paid for not working. Governments who produce nothing employ the most people. Income tax and other current practices penalize production. Countries which produce little are given huge handouts. War which destroys attains the largest appropriations. A THIRD DYNAMIC PSYCHOSIS IS *TO PREVENT PRODUCTION.*

6. *PROMOTION*

Promotion activities are subverted to unworthy activities. True value is seldom promoted. What one is actually achieving gets small mention while other things are heavily promoted. Reality and public relations (PR) are strangers. A THIRD DYNAMIC PSYCHOSIS IS *UNREAL OR NONFACTUAL PROMOTION.*

7. *SALES*

Sales actions are unreal or out of balance. Clumsy or nonfunctioning sales activities penalize producers and consumers. In areas of high demand sales actions are negligible even when heavy advertising exists. This is proven by the inability to sell what is produced even in large countries so that production cutbacks are continual threats to economies and workers. A population goes half fed in times of surplus goods. With curtailed car factories a nation drives old cars. With a cutback construction industry people live in bad houses. Sales taxes are almost universal. A THIRD DYNAMIC PSYCHOSIS IS *THE IMPEDING OF PRODUCT DISTRIBUTION TO POTENTIAL CONSUMERS.*

8. *DELIVERY*

Failure to deliver what is offered is standard procedure for groups in the humanities. Commercially it is well in hand.

9. *FINANCE*

One's own experience in finance is adequate to demonstrate the difficulties made with money. A THIRD DYNAMIC PSYCHOSIS IS *THE PERVERSION OF FINANCE.*

10. *JUSTICE*

Under the name of justice, aberrated man accomplishes fantastic injustices. The upstat is hit, the downstat let go. Rumors are accepted as evidence. Police forces and power are used to ENFORCE the injustices contained in 1 to 9 above. Suppressive justice is used as an ineffectual but savage means of meeting situations actually caused by the earlier listed psychoses. When abuses on 1 to 9 make things go wrong, the social aberration then introduces suppressive injustices as an effort to cure. Revolt and war are magnified versions of injustices. Excess people—kill them off in a war. A THIRD DYNAMIC PSYCHOSIS IS *THE SUBSTITUTE OF VIOLENCE FOR REASON.*

11. *MORALE*

A continuous assault on public morale occurs in the press and other media. Happiness or any satisfaction with life is under continuous attack. Beliefs, idealism, purpose, dreams are assaulted. INSANITY IS A REFUSAL TO ALLOW OTHERS TO BE, DO OR HAVE.

Any action which would lead to a higher morale has to be defended against the insane few. A THIRD DYNAMIC PSYCHOSIS IS *A DETESTATION OF HIGH MORALE.*

The COMMON DENOMINATOR of all these insanities is the desire to SUCCUMB.

Insanities have as their end product self- or group destruction.

These eleven types of aberration gone mad are the main points through which any group SUCCUMBS.

THEREFORE, these eleven points kept sane guarantee a group's SURVIVAL.

Seeing all this in one example permits one to see that these third dynamic insanities combine to destroy.

A. Believing it impossible to obtain money or make it, a firm cannot hire enough people to produce. So has little to sell, which is badly promoted and is not sold so it has no money to hire people.

B. Needing people for another job the firm robs them from a plant which then collapses and fails to make money so no new people can be hired. This reduces production so people have to be dismissed as they can't be paid.

C. Persons are in the firm but are kept doing the wrong things so there is little production and no promotion or sales so there is no money to pay them so they are dismissed.

D. A new product is put in. People to make it are taken from the area already making a valuable product which then collapses that area and there is not enough money to promote and selling fails so people are dismissed.

The examples are many. There are these same eleven group insanities in play upon a group, a firm, a society.

If this is a description of group aberration, then it gives the keys to sanity in a group.

1. HIRING

Letting people INTO the group at large is the key to every great movement and bettered culture on this planet. This was the new idea that made Buddhism the strongest civilizing influence the world has seen in terms of numbers and terrain. They did not exclude. Race, color, creed were not made bars to membership in this great movement.

Politically the strongest country in the world was the United States, and it was weakened only by its efforts to exclude certain races or make them second-class citizens. Its greatest internal war (1862-65) was fought to settle this point, and the weakness was not resolved even then.

The Catholic Church only began to fail when it began to exclude.

This *inclusion* is a major point in all great organizations.

The things which set a group or organization on a course of exclusion are (a) the destructive impulses of about 10 or 15 percent of the society (lunacy) and (b) opposition by interests which consider themselves threatened by the group or organization's potential resulting in infiltration (c) efforts to mimic the group's technology destructively and set up rival groups.

All these three things build up barriers that a group might thoughtlessly buy and act to remedy with no long-range plans to handle.

These stresses make a group edgy and combative. The organization then seeks to solve these three points by exclusion, whereas its growth depends wholly upon *in*clusion.

No one has ever solved these points successfully in the past because of lack of technology to solve them.

It all hinges on three points: (1) the sanity of the individual; (2) the worthwhileness of the group in terms of general area, planetary or universal survival; and (3) the superiority of the group's organization technology and its use.

At this writing, the first point is solved conclusively in Scientology. Even hostile and destructive personalities wandering into the group can be solved and, due to the basic nature of Man, made better for the benefit of themselves and others.

The worthwhileness of the group is determined by the assistance given to general survival by the group's products and the actual factual delivery of those valid products.

The superiority of a group's administrative technology and its application is at this current writing well-covered in current developments.

Thus *in*clusion is almost fully attainable. The only ridges that build up are the short-term defense actions.

For instance, Scientology currently must fight back at the death camp organizations of psychiatry whose solution is a dead world, as proven by their actions in Germany before and during World War II. But we *must* keep in mind that we fully intend to reform and salvage even these opponents. We are seeking to *in*clude them in the general survival by forcing them to cease their nonsurvival practices and overcome their gruesome group past.

There are two major stages then of *in*cluding people: one is as paid organization personnel and one as unpaid personnel. BOTH are in essence being "hired." The pay differs. The wider majority receive the pay of personal peace and effectivenss and a better world.

The contributions to the Church of Scientology of money or the money payment to the staff member is an internal economy. Pay, the real pay, is a better personal survival and a world that can live.

Plans of INclusion are successful. They sometimes contain defense until we *can* include.

Even resistance to the church can be interpreted as a future inclusion by the church. Resistance or opposition is a common way point in the cycle of inclusion. In an organization where everyone wins eventually anyway, the senselessness of resistance becomes apparent even to the most obtuse. Only those who oppose their own survival resist a survival-producing organization.

Even in commercial companies the best organization with the best product usually finds competitors merging with it.

2. TRAINING

Basic training, hats, checksheets and texts MUST exist for every member of a group.

Criminal or antisocial conduct occurs where there is no hat.

Any type of membership or role or post in the whole organization or its field requires individual and team training. Only where you have a group member who will not or cannot bring himself to have and wear a hat will you have any trouble.

Ask yourself, "Who isn't trained on his post and hatted?" and you can answer "Who is causing the trouble?"

Basic training, slight or great, is vital for *every* member of a group, paid or unpaid.

This handbook is the Volunteer Minister's hat.

This requires training.

Training begins in childhood. Often it has to be re-oriented.

Training as a group member must be done.

Training in exact technology or in the precise technology of administration is not the first stage of training. Basic training of group members, no matter how slight, must exist and be done.

Otherwise group members lack the basic points of agreement which make up the whole broad organization and its publics.

Training must be on real materials and must be rapid. The technology of how to train is expressed in speed of training.

The idea that it takes 12 years to make a mud pie maker is false. TIME in training does not determine quality of training. Amount of data learned that can be applied and skills successfully drilled determine training.

That the society currently stresses *time* is an aberrated factor.

The ability to learn and apply the data is the end product of training. Not old age.

The rate of training establishes to a marked degree the expansion factor of a group and influences the smoothness of the group during expansion.

3. APPRENTICESHIP

Training on post is a second stage of any training action.

This is essentially a familiarization action.

To have a person leave a post and another take it over with no "apprenticeship" or genning in can be quite fatal.

The deputy system is easily the best system. Every post is deputized for a greater or lesser period before the post is turned over and the appointment is made. When the deputy is totally familiar he becomes the person on the post.

Rapid expansion and economy on personnel tend to injure this step. Lack of it can be *very* destructive.

Optimumly there should be one or two deputies for every key post at all times. This is a continual apprenticeship system.

Economically it has limitations. One has to weigh the *losses* in not doing it against the cost in doing it. It will be found that the losses are *far* greater than the cost, even though it increases personnel by at least a third for a given organization.

When an organization has neglected it as a system (and has turned over too many posts without deputy or apprenticeship action) its economics may decay to where it can never be done. This is almost a death rattle for an organization.

In a two-century old highly successful industry, *only* the apprentice system was and is used (Oporto wine industry). The quality of the product is all that keeps the product going on the world market. If the quality decayed the industry would collapse. Apprenticeship as a total system maintains it.

Certainly every executive in an organization and every technical expert should have a deputy in training. Only then could quality of organization be maintained and quality of product guaranteed.

The total working organization should be on this system actually. And whenever a person is moved up off a post, the deputy taking over, a new deputy should be appointed. The last step (appointment of a new deputy) is the one that gets forgotten.

Failure to recruit new people over a period will very surely find the whole organization declining soon solely because there is no apprentice system of deputies. The organization expands, singles up the posts, promotes some unapprenticed people and begins to lose its economic advantage. Low pay ensues, people blow off, and then no one can be hired. It's a silly cycle, really, as it is prevented easily enough by hiring enough soon enough when the organization is still doing well.

The rule is DEPUTY EVERY POST AND NEWLY DEPUTY THEM WHEN PROMOTIONS OCCUR.

The most covert way to get around this is just to call each person's junior a deputy even though he has other duties. This makes it all look good on an organizing board. "Do you have each post deputied?" "Oh yes!" But the deputies are just juniors with posts of their own.

A deputy is *used* to run the same post as it is deputied for. This means a double posting pure and only.

You'd be amazed at how much production an executive post can achieve when it is also deputied and when the principal holder of the post will use the deputy and gen him in, not get him to cover an empty lower post.

4. UTILIZATION

People must be utilized.

Equipment must be utilized.

Space must be utilized.

Learning to USE is a very hard lesson for some. Untrained people, bad organization, poor machinery, inadequate space all tend to send one off utilization.

The rule is, if you've got it use it; if you can't use it get rid of it.

This most specifically applies to people. If you've got a man, use him; if you can't use him get him over to someone who can use him. If he isn't useful, handle and train.

Anyone who can't figure out how to use people, equipment and spaces to obtain valuable final products is not worthy of the name of executive.

Reversely we get what an executive or foreman is: an executive or foreman is one who can obtain, train and use people, equipment and spaces to economically achieve valuable final products.

Some are very skilled in preparing people, systems, equipment, property and spaces to be used. But if these then go to someone who does not USE them you get a bad breakdown.

The welfare state and its inflation is a sad commentary on "executive ability."

An executive whose people are idle and whose materiel is decaying is a traitor to his people and the organization, just that, for he will destroy them all.

UTILIZATION requires a knowledge of what the valuable final products are and how to make them.

Action which doesn't result in a final product that adds up to valuable final products is destructive, no matter how innocent it seems.

Man has a planet as a valuable final product. Improper *use* of the countries and seas, air and masses which compose it will wind up with the destruction of Man, all life on it and the usefulness of the planet. So *proper* utilization of anything is a very real factor.

The 19th century industrialist like the mad kings who built great structures *used up* men; they didn't properly use men.

And not using them at all, the current fad, is the most deadly of all.

UTILIZATION is a big subject. It applies to resources, capabilities and many other factors.

The question being asked in all cases is "How can we USE this to economically obtain a valuable final product?"

Failing to answer that question gives one the "mysteries of life."

5. PRODUCTION

One may be prone to believe there is no sense in any production at all. Such a one would also be likely to say, "There is no sense at all." Or, "If they keep on producing it will become impossible to destroy it all."

Production of some final valuable product is the chain of all production sequences.

Even the artist is producing a *reaction.* The reaction's service in a wider sphere to enforce it is what gives art its sense. A feeling of well-being or grandeur or light-heartedness are legitimate valuable final products, for instance.

The production areas and activities of an org that produce the valuable final products are the most important areas and activities of the org.

6. PROMOTION

The acceptance of valuable final products and of their value depends in a large degree upon (a) a real value and (b) a desire for them.

Promotion creates desire for the valuable final product.

The old saw that the man who builds a better mousetrap will have the whole world coming to his door is a total falsity.

Unless the value is made known, and the desire created, the mousetraps are going to go unsold.

Promotion is so important that it can stand alone. It can have limited success even when there is no product! But in that case it will be of short duration.

Promotion must contain reality and the final product must exist and be deliverable and delivered for promotion to be fully successful.

Public relations and advertising and all their skills cover this area of promotion.

7. SALES

It is hard to sell what isn't promoted and can't be delivered.

Economics greatly affect selling.

Anything must be sold for a price comparable to its value in the eyes of the purchaser.

COSTING is a precise art by which the total expenses of the organization administration and production must be adequately covered in the PRICING allowing for all losses and errors in delivery and adequate to produce a reserve.

PRICING (the amount being asked) cannot be done without some idea of the total cost of the final valuable product.

The sale price of one final valuable product may have to cover the cost of producing other products which are delivered without price.

PRICING however does not necessarily limit itself to only covering immediate cost of a product. A painting with a dollar's worth of paint and canvas may have a price of half a million dollars.

Also a painting used in promotion may cost two hundred dollars and be displayed at no cost at all to the beholder.

These relative factors also include the SKILL of the salesman himself and there is much technology involved in the act of selling something to someone and the world abounds in books on the subject.

Therefore, sales (once promotion is done) are bound up really in COSTING, PRICING and SELLING.

The value in the eye of the purchaser is monitored by the desire created in him for it. If this is also a real value and if delivery can occur then SELLING is made very easy—but it is still a skilled action.

The production of a valuable final product is often totally determined by whether or not it can be sold. And if it can be sold at a price greater than the cost of delivering it.

That it *gets* sold depends on the salesman.

The skill of the salesman is devoted to enhancing the desire and value in the eyes of the buyer and obtaining adequate payment.

8. DELIVERY

The subject and action of DELIVERY is the most susceptible to breakdown in any organization. Any flaw on the sequence of actions resulting in a valuable final product may deteriorate it or bar off final delivery.

There are many preparatory or hidden-from-public-view steps on a production line. When any of these break down, delivery is imperiled.

Given the raw materials and wherewithal to make some valuable final product, the valuable final product should occur.

WHEN A VALUABLE FINAL PRODUCT DOES NOT GET PRODUCED AND CANNOT BE DELIVERED REPAIR THE EARLIER STEPS OF ITS PRODUCTION

THE LAW OF THE IRREDUCIBLE MINIMUM occurs in all delivery problems. Someone is trying to produce only the visible end product of a post or production line and neglects the earlier contributory actions and products as these are not plainly visible.

When an organization or its posts operate only on an irreducible minimum, production goes bad and DELIVERY crashes.

Take a cook who has his post at an irreducible minimum. Food is appearing on the table. If he reduced one bit more the food would no longer be edible at all. He neglects purchasing, menus and preparation. That these occur is invisible to the diners. That food appears on the table is visible to the diners. If the cook operates at any less level than he is, no edible food would be visible—hence, irreducible minimum. The food served will be bad. But it will be visible. Invisible-to-the diners actions aren't being done.

To improve the food, get the less visible actions *done.* Get the sequence of actions all done. The result will be improved food.

Take training. The final valuable product is a trained mechanic. The instructor who runs his post on an irreducible minimum is simply there, appearing to instruct.

His final product may be horribly unskilled. The teaching may take "forever."

To improve this one goes earlier on the assembly line: materials, texts, lectures, student technical services, scheduling—dozens of actions including getting the instructor trained.

The visibility is still an instructor and students being taught. But with the *whole* earlier line in the final valuable product is excellent!

A being hopes lazily for instantaneous production. It doesn't happen this way in the physical universe. Things are produced in a sequence of sub-products which result in a final valuable product. Hope all you want to. When you omit the sub-products you get no valuable final product.

When the people in an organization do not know the valuable final products of the org and when a person on a post does not know the final products of his post, a condition arises where no org DELIVERY will occur, or if it does occur it will be poor or costly. It is vital that a person knows what his post final products are and what his unit, section, department and division sub-products are and how his own and each of these contribute to the valuable final products of the organization for actual delivery to occur.

Delivering other than valuable final products or useless final products or final products that need constant correction also add up to nondelivery.

A whole civilization can break down around the point of DELIVERY. So can an organization.

Since money can be looked upon as too valuable a final product it can actually prevent DELIVERY.

Failure to deliver is the one point beings do not forgive. The whole cycle hangs upon DELIVERY.

DELIVER WHAT IS PROMISED when it is expected, in sufficient volume and adequate quality is the first maxim even of a group in politics or the humanities.

9. FINANCE

Finance too often disregards the other factors in this scale or the other factors in this scale too often disregard finance for organizations to long remain viable.

Financing must be in agreement with all the other factors of this scale and all the other factors must be in agreement with finance for viability to occur.

Because money is interchangeable for commodities then people can confuse it with too many things.

If you regard money like so many beans, as a commodity in itself, you open the door to understanding it.

Money is so many beans in to get so many beans out.

When you can master this you can handle FINANCE.

The FINANCE persons of an organization, a civilization, a planet should put so many beans in and expect more beans out than they put in. This is quite correct as a viewpoint for finance.

The difference of beans in and beans out for a planet is made up by adding beans enough to those already in existence to cover new commodities.

When finance people fail to do this beans cease to be in pace with production and inflation and deflation occur.

In an organization or any of its parts, industriousness of the staff makes the difference between the beans in and beans out.

An organization has to have income greater than outgo. That is the first rule of finance. Violating it brings bankruptcy.

Now if the FINANCE people of an organization apply the same rule remorselessly to all *its* transactions (financial planning) with each person and part of an organization, finance becomes real and manageable.

So many beans in to support the first department means so many beans out of the organization back to finance because of the cooperative work of the first department.

A hectic effort to work only with production products will wind finance up in a knot.

One has to estimate (COST) the contribution of each part of an organization to the valuable final product to know what to allow what part of an organization.

Finance has to have a full reality on the valuable final products and the sub-products and post products of the whole organization to intelligently allocate funds.

This person, that department, each contribute some part of the action that results in the money received for the valuable final products.

So finance can extend so much money for each and expect that and an additional amount back. If this occurs, so will expansion.

Finance comes unstuck when it fails to "COST" an organization and fails to support valuable final product production.

Finance must not only practice "income greater than outgo" for the organization, it must practice it for each part of the organization as well.

Then solvency becomes real.

The greatest aberration of finance is that it seeks to *save* things into solvency. The real losses in an organization are the sums *never made.* These are the most important losses for finance to concentrate upon.

A business or activity that makes $500 a week that should make $5,000 a week in potential is losing the finance people $4,500 a week!

Finance can force production along certain lines by putting in funds and getting more back.

Finance becomes too easily the management of an organization but it only does that when it ceases to deal in its own commodity: money.

An organization which has executives unfamiliar with finance will fall at once into the control of the finance people in the organization. And these finance people, if they don't really know money, will fall at once under the control of outside finance people.

One has to know finance in any organization anywhere, even in a socialism. Sooner or later the books get balanced in any society.

10. JUSTICE

Without justice there can be no real organization.

Even a government owes its people an operating climate in which human transactions and business can occur.

Where insane and criminal individuals operate unchecked in the community justice is uncertain and harsh.

The society in which the insane rise to positions of power becomes a nightmare.

Justice is a difficult subject. Man handles it badly.

Justice cannot occur until insanity can be detected and cured.

The whole task of justice is to defend the honest man. Therefore the target of justice is the establishment of a sane society.

The inability to detect or cure the insane destroys civilizations.

Justice is an effort to bring equity and peace. When one cannot detect and cure insanity then sooner or later justice actions will become unjust and be used by the insane.

To us, justice is the action necessary to restrain the insane until they are cured. After that it would be only an action of seeing fair play is done.

11. MORALE

When all factors balance up in an activity and give the group a common direction and mutual viability, morale can be expected to be good.

When the Admin Scale and the ten elements described are out of balance (without proper importance given to each) and when one or many of these (Admin Scale and the Sanity Scale) are not in agreement one with another, then morale will be poor.

Morale is not made of comfort and sloth. It is made of common purpose and obstacles overcome by the group.

When the Admin Scale and these elements are not held together by similar aims, then morale has to be held up artificially.

The most ghastly morale I have ever seen was amongst "the idle rich."

And the highest morale I've ever seen was amongst a furiously dedicated common-purposed group working under fantastic stresses with very little against almost hopeless odds.

I used to observe that morale in a combat unit would never materialize before they had been through hell together.

All drama aside, morale is made up of high purpose and mutual confidence. This comes from the Admin Scale items and these elements of organization being well-aligned, one with the next, and honest, sane endeavor to achieve a final goal for all.

All this is very fundamental first and third dynamic technology.

It is the first true group technology that can fully deaberrate and smooth out and free within the group every group member and the group itself.

Thus, combined with auditing technology, for the first time we can rely wholly on technology to improve and handle group members and the group itself toward desirable and achievable accomplishment with happiness and high morale.

Like any skill or technology it has to be known and done and continued in use to be effective.

The discovery, development and practical use of this data made me very, very cheerful and confident and did the same thing on the test group.

I hope it does the same for you.

13

HCO PL 1 November 1970
Org Series 11

Organization and Morale

Morale is a large factor in organizing.

An executive is utterly dependent upon the willingness of those who work for him.

Willingness, while it is also a factor in morale is also a manifestation of morale.

Morale, the tone of the group, is the target of "do-gooders," the "one-worlders," the labor agitator, the Commie agent and a general mixed company of often well-meaning but nevertheless deadly people.

"You poor fellow. They treat you so badly . . . we will take up this great injustice . . . workers should have everything free . . . Communist imperialist aggressors against poor working people . . . You poor fellow; God will make you welcome in his Heaven from this earthly toil . . . Kill the managers . . . Down with law and order. . . ."

Well, it all winds up in revolution eventually and mounds of dead workers and a few dead managers.

So let's look this over.

If you can do something about an ill situation you do. If you can be effective you can at least make the situation easier. If you can't do that you can sympathize.

Sympathy with the abused apparently not only does no good but winds up in revolt!

How?

You have this young girl, she is wearing last year's dress. No new clothes.

So you say, "You poor thing, wearing last year's dress." Up to now she wasn't worried about it.

Now she says, "I wish I had some new clothes."

And you say, "You poor thing. Doesn't your mother ever buy you new clothes?"

"No."

"The beast!"

She goes home and revolts.

Get it?

Someone says, "Every woiker, he got to have job, house, lotsa dough."

Worker says, "Who? Me?"

"Yes, you, poor downtrodden sod."

And then someone says, "You rich. You pay!"

The one-world do-gooders say, "You pay poor fired woikers!"

Sixty-three billion dollars is paid out. You can't walk down a street. Riot and insurrection.

Why?

Sympathy. But not one brain cell worth of organization.

People want to be part of things, part of life.

If the clod-heads that pass for leaders had the ability to organize and handle an economy (in big countries or small) people could easily be part of things and build the place up. It is in fact a highly skilled activity. And currently quite beyond the heads of nations. Or they wouldn't have unemployment, riots, inflation and future death.

Let's be practical. Who is going to build this house for the poor worker? Who is going to pay the billions except the worker?

And if, as we so glaringly see, the end product of all this "poor worker" is riot and civil commotion, insurrection and piles of dead workers then mightn't there be something a bit awry with its morale value?

Sympathy is a morale depressant. And knowingly or not, a morale destroyer. If the person who sympathized was good enough to do something about it he would.

There's nothing at all wrong with righting evil conditions. Far from it. But if you want to better things KNOW HOW TO ORGANIZE. Don't just stir up a revolt that will get workers machine-gunned.

If the chronic moaner knew how to throw together an organizing board and groove in the lines, as part of the state or the opposition he could certainly change things for the better.

Organizing is the know-how of changing things.

Good morale is the product of good organization!

If you organize something well and efficiently you will have good morale. You will also have improved conditions.

Wherever morale is bad, organize!

A very careful survey of people shows that their basic protests are against lack of organization. "It doesn't run right!" is the reason they protest things.

Inequalities of workload, rewards unearned, no ownership, these are some of the things that are snarled about.

They are cured by organizing things.

Russia Siberia'ed or shot all her managers, thinking managers and capitalists were the same thing. Then she couldn't feed her people.

And you can't even discuss morale as a subject when a country has to be held together with barbed wire frontiers to hold in its own secret-policed people!

The physical universe is no rose bed. But it can be confronted and can be lived in by a group. Whenever you see bad morale, behind it you will see chaotic disorganization.

A nation or an organization follow the same laws.

Disorganization from any cause deprives people of wanted beingness, doingness and havingness.

When you deprive people of those things you're going to have pretty awful morale.

And only organization and very good organization will bring about beingness, doingness and havingness.

All three factors must be served. And purpose and reason must exist.

A bum with a handout sandwich is a bum with a handout

sandwich. You can't change anyone upward with sympathy. It is a witch's weapon, a devil's curse. But you *can* change someone upward with organization.

Bad organization equals bad morale.

Good organization equals good morale.

And good organization is something worked on by a group, not ordered under pain of death.

The only tops that get blown when effective organization starts going in are those who don't want others to have things and take delight in suppression—in other words, good organization is only opposed by those who have reason to fear others. For in organization lies the secret of a group's strength. A small group thoroughly organized can conquer the disorganized billions. And have excellent morale while they're doing it!

The handling of group morale is done in the area of accomplishing objectives along the agreed-upon group purpose line and in the sphere of group social relations.

If any organization has a chaplain with a full grasp of the subject of morale, its definitions and technology and if he works factually and successfully, group catastrophes would be averted.

Lack of this function can be very destructive to a group. Successful accomplishment of it can be the source of group success.

Skill in Scientology technology, group organizational functions and public relations are the requisites of a good minister.

K

PTS/SP

PTS/SP Checksheet

Purpose:

To train the Volunteer Minister how to recognize and handle different types of beings in society at large.

a	Study Section 1 Psychosis.	________
b	Drill: Use your demo kit to demonstrate the definition of psychosis.	________
c	Study Section 2 The Anti-social Personality, the Anti-Scientologist.	________
d	Drill: Demonstrate the traits of the social and anti-social personalities.	________
e	Study Section 3 Handling the Suppressive Person, the Basis of Insanity.	________
f	Study Section 4 Suppressed Pcs and PTS Technology.	________
g	Study Section 5 Search and Discovery.	________
h	Drill: Demonstrate the difference and relationship between a suppressive person and a potential trouble source.	________
i	Drill: Demonstrate the difference between a Type One, Type Two and Type Three PTS.	________
j	Study Section 6 Suppressives and Hidden Standards.	________
k	Study Section 7 Mistakes, Anatomy of.	________

l Study Section 8 PTS Handling. ________

m Drill: Practice doing a PTS Handling using the method in Section 8. ________

n Study Section 9 PTS Type A Handling. ________

o Drill: Practice doing a PTS Type A handling using the method in Section 9. ________

p Study Section 10 Policies on "Sources of Trouble." ________

q Drill: Demonstrate how the PTS types A-J would be sources of trouble to you as a Volunteer Minister. ________

r Drill: Find and successfully handle two PTS persons using the methods in Sections 8 and 9. ________

s Study Section 11 Robotism. ________

t Drill: Demonstrate what robotism is. ________

u Study Section 12 Alter-is and Degraded Beings. ________

v Drill: Find two examples of a degraded being in your city, town, etc. ________

PTS & SP Pack

1 Psychosis

HCOB 28 November 1970
CS Series 22

Through a slight change of procedure on certain preclears I have been able to view the underlying motives and mechanisms of psychosis.

This is the first time the mechanisms which bring about insanity have been fully viewed. I must say that it requires a bit of confronting.

The alleviation of the condition of insanity has also been accomplished now and the footnote in *"Dianetics: The Modern Science of Mental Health"* concerning future research into this field can be considered fulfilled.

Higher Per Cent

About 15% to 20% of the human race apparently is insane or certainly a much higher per cent than was estimated.

The truly insane do not necessarily act insane visibly. They are not the psychiatric obvious cases who go rigid for years or scream for days. This is observed only in the last stages or during temporary stress.

Under apparent social behavior the continual crimes knowingly committed by the insane are much more vicious than ever has been catalogued in psychiatric texts.

The actions of the insane are not "unconscious." They are completely aware of what they are doing.

All insane actions are entirely justified and seem wholly rational to them. As they have no reality on the harmful and irrational nature of their conduct it does not often register on an E-Meter.

The product of their post duties is destructive but is excused as ignorance or errors.

As cases in normal processing they roller coaster continually.

They nearly always have a fixed emotional tone. It does not vary in nearly all insane people. In a very few it is cyclic, high then low.

All characteristics classified as those of the "suppressive person" are in fact those of an insane person.

The easiest ways to detect the insane are:

1. Pretending to do a post or duties, the real consistent result is destructive to the group in terms of breakage, lost items, injured business etc.

2. The case is no case gain or roller coaster and is covered under "PTS symptoms."

3. They are usually chronically physically ill.

4. They have a deep but carefully masked hatred of anyone who seeks to help them.

5. The result of their "help" is actually injurious.

6. They often seek transfers or wish to leave.

7. They are involved in warfare with conflicts around them which are invisible to others. One wonders how they can be so involved or get so involved in so much hostility.

Types

The German psychiatric 1500 or so "different types of insanity" are just different symptoms of the same cause. There is only one insanity and from it spring different manifestations. Psychiatry erred in calling these different types and trying to invent different treatments.

Definition

Insanity can now be precisely defined.

The definition is:

INSANITY IS THE OVERT OR COVERT BUT ALWAYS COMPLEX AND CONTINUOUS DETERMINATION TO HARM OR DESTROY.

Possibly the only frightening thing about it is the cleverness with which it can be hidden.

Whereas a sane person can become angry or upset and a bit destructive for short periods, he or she recovers. The insane mask it, are misemotional continuously and do not recover. (Except by modern processing.)

The Nature of Man

Man is basically good. This is obvious. For when he begins to do evil he seeks to destroy his memory in order to change and seeks to destroy his body. He seeks to check his evil impulses by inhibiting his own skill and strength.

He can act in a very evil fashion but his basic nature then makes it mandatory that he lessens himself in many ways.

The towering "strength" of a madman is a rarity and is compensated by efforts at self-destruction.

Man's mortality, his "one life" fixation, all stem from his efforts to check himself, obliterate his memory in a fruitless effort to change his conduct and his self-destructive habits and impulses and losses of skills and abilities.

As this rationale proves out completely in processing and fits all cases observed, we have for the first time proof of his actual nature.

As only around 20% are insane, and as those who previously worked in the mental field were themselves mainly insane, Man as a whole has been assigned an evil repute. Governments, where such personalities exist, listen to the opinion of the insane and apply the characteristic of 20% to the entire hundred per cent.

This gives an 80% wrong diagnosis. Which is why mental science itself was destructive when used by states.

The only technique available at this writing which will benefit the insane is contained in the technology of Dianetics and Scientology.

Pattern of Behavior

The apparent pattern of insane behavior is to come in (ask for processing, go on staff etc.) with the advertised intention of being helped or helping, then mess up either as a pc or on post, then state how bad it all is and leave. It looks obvious enough. He came, found it bad, left.

That is only the apparent behavior. Apparent reasons.

Based on numerous cases, this is the real cycle. Hearing of something good that might help these hateful, awful, rotten, nasty people, the psycho comes in, wrecks this, upsets that, caves in this one, chops up that one and when somebody says "No!" the psychotic either:

(a) Caves himself in physically or

(b) Runs away.

The psychotic is motivated by intent to harm.

If he realizes he is harming things he shouldn't, he caves himself in. If he is afraid he will be found out, he runs.

In the psychotic the impulse is quite conscious.

Conclusion

None of this is very nice. It is hard to confront. Even I find it so.

Freud thought all men had a hidden monster in them for he dealt mainly with the psychotic and their behavior was what he saw.

All men are not like this. The percentage that are is greater than I supposed but is a long way from all men.

Sometimes one only becomes aware of these when things are getting worked on and improved. They stay on as long as it can be made bad or there is hope it can be destroyed. Then when attention is given to improvement they blow.

Artists, writers often have these types hanging around them as there is someone or something there to be destroyed. When success or failure to destroy or possible detection appears on the scene they blow, often as destructively as possible.

Scientology churches are subjected to a lot of this. A psychotic sometimes succeeds in blowing off good staff. And then sooner or later realizes how evil he is acting and sickens or leaves.

The society is not geared to any of this at all. The insane walk around wrecking the place and decent people think it's "human nature" or "inevitable" or a "bad childhood."

As of this writing the insane can be handled. The proof of any pudding is the processing. And this is successful.

For a long while I've realized that we would have to be able to handle insane people as the psychiatrist is fading. I have had opportunity to work on the problem. And have it handled.

The insane can be helped. They are not hopeless.

I trust this data will be of use.

2

HCOB 27 September 1966

The Anti-Social Personality The Anti-Scientologist

There are certain characteristics and mental attitudes which cause about 20% of a race to oppose violently any betterment activity or group.

Such people are known to have antisocial tendencies.

When the legal or political structure of a country becomes such as to favor such personalities in positions of trust, then all the civilizing organizations of the country become suppressed and a barbarism of criminality and economic duress ensues.

Crime and criminal acts are perpetuated by antisocial personalities. Inmates of institutions commonly trace their state back to contact with such personalities.

Thus, in the fields of government, police activities and mental health, to name a few, we see that it is important to be able to detect and isolate this personality type so as to protect society and individuals from the destructive consequences attendant upon letting such have free rein to injure others.

As they only comprise 20% of the population and as only 2 1/2% of this 20% are truly dangerous, we see that with a very small amount of effort we could considerably better the state of society.

Well known, even stellar examples of such a personality are, of course, Napoleon and Hitler. Dillinger, Pretty Boy Floyd, Christie and other famous criminals were well known examples of the antisocial personality. But with such a cast of characters in history we neglect the less stellar examples and do not perceive that such personalities exist in current life, very common, often undetected.

When we trace the cause of a failing business, we will inevitably discover somewhere in its ranks the anti social personality hard at work.

In families which are breaking up we commonly find one or the other of the persons involved to have such a personality.

Where life has become rough and is failing, a careful review of the area by a trained observer will detect one or more such personalities at work.

As there are 80% of us trying to get along and only 20% trying to prevent us, our lives would be much easier to live were we well informed as to the exact manifestations of such a personality. Thus we could detect it and save ourselves much failure and heartbreak.

It is important then to examine and list the attributes of the antisocial personality. Influencing as it does the daily lives of so many, it well behooves decent people to become better informed on this subject.

Attributes

The antisocial personality has the following attributes:

1. He or she speaks only in very broad generalities. "They say . . ." "Everybody thinks . . ." "Everyone knows . . ." and such expressions are in continual use, particularly when imparting rumor. When asked, "Who is everybody . . ." it normally turns out to be one source and from this source the antisocial person has manufactured what he or she pretends is the whole opinion of the whole society.

This is natural to them since to them all society is a large hostile generality, against the antisocial in particular.

2. Such a person deals mainly in bad news, critical or hostile remarks, invalidation and general suppression.

"Gossip" or "harbinger of evil tidings" or "rumormonger" once described such persons.

It is notable that there is no good news or complimentary remark passed on by such a person.

3. The antisocial personality alters, to worsen, communication when he or she relays a message or news. Good news is stopped and only bad news, often embellished, is passed along.

Such a person also pretends to pass on "bad news" which is in actual fact invented.

4. A characteristic, and one of the sad things about an antisocial personality, is that it does not respond to treatment or reform or psychotherapy.

5. Surrounding such a personality we find cowed or ill associates or friends who, when not driven actually insane, are yet behaving in a crippled manner in life, failing, not succeeding.

Such people make trouble for others.

When treated or educated, the near associate of the antisocial personality has no stability of gain but promptly relapses or loses his advantages of knowledge, being under the suppressive influence of the other.

Physically treated, such associates commonly do not recover in the expected time but worsen and have poor convalescences.

It is quite useless to treat or help or train such persons so long as they remain under the influence of the antisocial connection.

The largest number of insane are insane because of such antisocial connections and do not recover easily for the same reason.

Unjustly we seldom see the antisocial personality actually in an institution. Only his "friends" and family are there.

6. The antisocial personality habitually selects the wrong target.

If a tire is flat from driving over nails, he or she curses a companion or a non-causative source of the trouble. If the radio next door is too loud, he or she kicks the cat.

If A is the obvious cause, the antisocial personality inevitably blames B, or C or D.

7. The antisocial cannot finish a cycle of action.

Such become surrounded with incomplete projects.

8. Many antisocial persons will freely confess to the most alarming crimes when forced to do so, but will have no faintest sense of responsibility for them.

Their actions have little or nothing to do with their own volition. Things "just happened."

They have no sense of correct causation and particularly cannot feel any sense of remorse or shame therefore.

9. The antisocial personality supports only destructive groups and rages against and attacks any constructive or betterment group.

10. This type of personality approves only of destructive actions and fights against constructive or helpful actions or activities.

The artist in particular is often found as a magnet for persons with antisocial personalities who see in his art something which must be destroyed and covertly, "as a friend," proceed to try.

11. Helping others is an activity which drives the antisocial personality nearly berserk. Activities, however, which destroy in the name of help are closely supported.

12. The antisocial personality has a bad sense of property and conceives that the idea that anyone owns anything is a pretense made up to fool people. Nothing is ever really owned.

The Basic Reason

The basic reason the antisocial personality behaves as he or she does lies in a hidden terror of others.

To such a person every other being is an enemy, an enemy to be covertly or overtly destroyed.

The fixation is that survival itself depends on "keeping others down" or "keeping people ignorant."

If anyone were to promise to make others stronger or brighter, the antisocial personality suffers the utmost agony of personal danger.

They reason that if they are in this much trouble with people around them weak or stupid, they would perish should anyone become strong or bright.

Such a person has no trust to a point of terror. This is usually masked and unrevealed.

When such a personality goes insane the world is full of Martians or the FBI and each person met is really a Martian or FBI agent.

But the bulk of such people exhibit no outward signs of insanity. They appear quite rational. They can be very convincing.

However, the list given above consists of things which such a personality cannot detect in himself or herself. This is so true that if you thought you found yourself in one of the above, you most certainly are not antisocial. Self-criticism is a luxury the antisocial cannot afford. They must be right because they are in continual danger in their own estimation. If you proved one wrong, you might even send him or her into a severe illness.

Only the sane, well-balanced person tries to correct his conduct.

Relief

If you were to weed out of your past by proper interview or processing if necessary those antisocial persons you have known and if you then handle, you might experience great relief.

Similarly, if society were to recognize this personality type as a sick being as they now isolate people with smallpox, both social and economic recoveries could occur.

Things are not likely to get much better so long as 20% of the population is permitted to dominate and injure the lives and enterprise of the remaining 80%.

As majority rule is the political manner of the day, so should majority sanity express itself in our daily lives without the interference and destruction of the socially unwell.

The pity of it is, they will not permit themselves to be helped and would not respond to treatment if help were attempted.

An understanding and ability to recognize such personalities could bring a major change in society and our lives.

The Social Personality

Man in his anxieties is prone to witch hunts.

All one has to do is designate "people wearing black caps" as the villains and one can start a slaughter of people in black caps.

This characteristic makes it very easy for the antisocial personality to bring about a chaotic or dangerous environment.

Man is not naturally brave or calm in his human state. And he is not necessarily villianous.

Even the antisocial personality, in his warped way, is quite certain that he is acting for the best and commonly sees himself as the only good person around, doing all for the good of everyone, the only flaw in his reasoning being that if one kills everyone else, none are left to be protected from the imagined evils. His conduct in his environment and toward his fellows is the only method of detecting either the antisocial or the social personalities. Their motives for self are similar—self preservation and survival. They simply go about achieving these in different ways.

Thus, as Man is naturally neither calm nor brave, anyone to some degree tends to be alert to dangerous persons and hence, witch hunts can begin.

It is therefore even more important to identify the social personality than the antisocial personality. One then avoids shooting the innocent out of mere prejudice or dislike or because of some momentary misconduct.

The social personality can be defined most easily by comparison with his opposite, the antisocial personality.

This differentiation is easily done and no test should ever be constructed which isolates only the antisocial. On the same test must appear the upper as well as lower ranges of Man's actions.

A test that declares only antisocial personalities without also being able to identify the social personality would be itself a suppressive test. It would be like answering "Yes" or "No" to the question "Do you still beat your wife?" Anyone who took it could be found guilty. While this mechanism might have suited the times of the Inquisition, it would not suit modern needs.

As the society runs, prospers and lives solely through the efforts of social personalities, one must know them as *they,* not the antisocial, are the worthwhile people. These are the people who must have rights and freedom. Attention is given to the antisocial solely to protect and assist the social personalities in the society.

All majority rules, civilizing intentions and even the human race will fail unless one can identify and thwart the antisocial personalities and help and forward the social personalities in the society. For the very word "society" implies social conduct and without it there is no society at all only a barbarism with all men, good or bad, at risk.

The frailty of showing how the harmful people can be known is that these then apply the characteristics to decent people to get them hunted down and eradicated.

The swan song of every great civilization is the tune played by arrows, axes or bullets used by the antisocial to slay the last decent men.

Government is only dangerous when it can be employed by and for antisocial personalities. The end result is the eradication of all social personalities and the resultant collapse of Egypt, Babylon, Rome, Russia or the West.

You will note in the characteristics of the antisocial personality that *intelligence* is not a clue to the antisocial. They are bright or stupid or average. Thus those who are extremely intelligent can rise to considerable, even head-of-state heights.

Importance and ability or wish to rise above others are likewise not indexes to the antisocial. When they do become important or rise they are, however, rather visible by the broad consequences of their acts. But they are as likely to be unimportant people or hold very lowly stations and wish for nothing better.

Thus it is the twelve given characteristics alone which identify the antisocial personality. And these same twelve reversed are the sole criteria of the social personality if one wishes to be truthful about them.

The identification or labeling of an antisocial personality cannot be done honestly and accurately unless one *also,* in the same examination of the person, reviews the positive side of his life.

All persons under stress can react with momentary flashes of antisocial conduct. This does not make them antisocial personalities.

The true antisocial person has a majority of antisocial characteristics.

The social personality has a majority of social characteristics.

Thus one must examine the good with the bad before one can truly label the antisocial or the social.

In reviewing such matters, very broad testimony and evidence are best. One or two isolated instances determine nothing. One should search all twelve social and all twelve antisocial characteristics and decide on the basis of actual evidence, not opinion.

The twelve primary characteristics of the social personality are as follows:

1. The social personality is specific in relating circumstances. "Joe

Jones said . . ." "The Star Newspaper reported . . ." and gives sources of data where important or possible.

He may use the generality of "they" or "people" but seldom in connection with attributing statements or opinions of an alarming nature.

2. The social personality is eager to relay good news and reluctant to relay bad. He may not even bother to pass along criticism when it doesn't matter.

He is more interested in making another feel liked or wanted than disliked by others and tends to err toward reassurance rather than toward criticism.

3. A social personality passes communication without much alteration and if deleting anything tends to delete injurious matters.

He does not like to hurt people's feelings. He sometimes errs in holding back bad news or orders which seem critical or harsh.

4. Treatment, reform and psychotherapy particularly of a mild nature work very well on the social personality.

Whereas antisocial people sometimes promise to reform they do not: Only the social personality can change or improve easily.

It is often enough to point out unwanted conduct to a social personality to completely alter it for the better.

Criminal codes and violent punishment are not needed to regulate social personalities.

5. The friends and associates of a social personality tend to be well, happy and of good morale.

A truly social personality quite often produces betterment in health or fortune by his mere presence on the scene.

At the very least he does not reduce the existing levels of health or morale in his associates.

When ill, the social personality heals or recovers in an expected manner, and is found open to successful treatment.

6. The social personality tends to select correct targets for correction. He fixes the tire that is flat rather than attack the windscreen. In the mechanical arts he can therefore repair things and make them work.

7. Cycles of action begun are ordinarily completed by the social personality, if possible.

8. The social personality is ashamed of his misdeeds and reluctant to confess them. He takes responsibility for his errors.

9. The social personality supports constructive groups and tends to protest or resist destructive groups.

10. Destructive actions are protested by the social personality. He assists constructive or helpful actions.

11. The social personality helps others and actively resists acts which harm others.

12. Property is property of someone to the social personality and its theft or misuse is prevented or frowned upon.

The Basic Motivation

The social personality naturally operates on the basis of the greatest good.

He is not haunted by imagined enemies but he does recognize real enemies when they exist.

The social personality wants to survive and wants others to survive, whereas the antisocial personality really and covertly wants others to succumb.

Basically the social personality wants others to be happy and do well, whereas the antisocial personality is very clever in making others do very badly indeed.

A basic clue to the social personality is not really his successes but his motivations. The social personality when successful is often a target for the antisocial and by this reason he may fail. But his intentions included others in his success, whereas the antisocial only appreciate the doom of others.

Unless we can detect the social personality and hold him safe from undue restraint and detect also the antisocial and restrain him, our society will go on suffering from insanity, criminality and war, and Man and civilization will not endure.

Of all our technical skills, such differentiation ranks the highest since, failing, no other skill can continue, as the base on which it operates—civilization—will not be here to continue it.

Do not smash the social personality—and do not fail to render powerless the antisocial in their efforts to harm the rest of us.

Just because a man rises above his fellows or takes an important part does not make him an antisocial personality. Just because a man can control or dominate others does not make him an antisocial personality.

It is his motives in doing so and the consequences of his acts which distinguish the antisocial from the social.

Unless we realize and apply the true characteristics of the two types of personality, we will continue to live in a quandary of who our enemies are and, in doing so, victimize our friends.

All men have committed acts of violence or omission for which they could be censured. In all Mankind there is not one single, perfect human being.

But there are those who try to do right and those who specialize in wrong and upon these facts and characteristics you can know them.

HCO PL 5 April 1965
HCO Justice Data Re: Academy and Hubbard Guidance Center

3
Handling the Suppressive Person The Basis of Insanity

The suppressive person (whom we've called a Merchant of Fear or Chaos Merchant and which we can now technically call the *suppressive person*) can't stand the idea of Scientology. If people became better, the suppressive person would have lost. The suppressive person answers this by attacking covertly or overtly Scientology. This thing is, he thinks, his mortal enemy since it undoes his (or her) "good work" in putting people down where they should be.

There are three "operations" such a case seeks to engage upon regarding Scientology: (a) to disperse it, (b) to try to crush it and (c) to pretend it didn't exist.

Dispersal would consist of several things such as attributing its source to others and altering its processes or structure.

If you feel a bit dispersed reading this, then realize it is about a being whose whole "protective coloration" is to disperse others and so remain invisible. Such people generalize all entheta and create ARC Breaks madly.

The second, (b), is done by covert or overt means. Covertly a suppressive person leaves the organization door unlocked, loses the E-Meters, runs up fantastic bills, and energetically and unseen seeks to pull out the plug and get Scientology poured down the drain. We, poor fools, consider all this just "human error" or "stupidity." We rarely realize that such actions, far from being accidents, are carefully thought out. The proof that this is so is simple. If we run down the source of these errors we wind up with only one or two people in the whole group. Now isn't it odd that the *majority* of errors that kept the group enturbulated were attributable to a *minority* of persons present? Even a very "reasonable" person could not make anything else out of that except that it was very odd and indicated that the *minority* mentioned were interested in smashing the group and that the behavior was not common to the whole group—meaning it isn't "normal" behavior.

The suppressive person is hard to spot because of the dispersal factor mentioned above. One looks at them and has his attention dispersed by their "everybody is bad."

The suppressive person who is *visibly* seeking to knock out people or Scientology is easy to see. He or she is making such a fuss about it. The attacks are quite vicious and full of lies. But even here when the suppressive person exists on the "other side" of a potential trouble source, visibility is not good. One sees a case going *up* and *down*. On the other side of that case, out of the auditor's view, is the suppressive person.

The whole trick they use is to generalize entheta. "Everybody is bad." "The Russians are all bad." "Everybody hates you." "The People versus John Doe" on warrants. "The masses." "The Secret Police will get you."

Suppressive groups use the ARC break mechanisms of generalizing entheta so it seems "everywhere."

The suppressive person is a specialist in making others ARC break with generalized entheta that is mostly lies.

He or she is also a no-gain-case.

So avid are such for the smashing of others by covert or overt means that their case is bogged *and won't move under routine* processing.

The technical fact is that they have a huge problem, long gone and no longer known even to themselves which they use hidden or forthright vicious acts continually to "handle." They do *not* act to solve the environment they are in. They are solving one environment, yesterday's, in which they are stuck.

The only reason the insane were hard to understand is that they are handling situations which no longer exist. The situation probably existed at one time. They think they have to hold their own, with overts against a non-existent enemy to solve a non-existent problem.

Because their overts are continuous they have withholds.

Since such a person has withholds, he or she can't communicate freely to as-is the block on the track that keeps them in some yesterday. Hence, a "no-case-gain."

That alone is the way to locate a suppressive person. By viewing the case. Never judge such a person by their conduct. That is too difficult. Judge by no-case-*gains.* Don't even use tests.

One asks these questions:

1. Will the person permit auditing at all? or
2. Does their history of routine auditing reveal any gains?

If (1) is present one is safe to treat the person as suppressive. It is not always correct but it is always safe. Some errors will be made but it is better to make them than to take a chance on it. When people refuse auditing they are (a) a potential trouble source (connected to a suppressive person) (b) a person with a big discreditable withhold (c) a suppressive person or (d) have had the bad luck to be "audited" too often by a suppressive person or (e) have been audited by an untrained auditor or one "trained" by a suppressive person.

The last category (e)—untrained auditor—is rather slight but (d)—audited by a suppressive person—can have been pretty serious, resulting in continual ARC breaks during which auditing was pressed on without regard to the ARC break.

Thus there are several possibilities where somebody refuses auditing. One has to sort them out in an HGC (Hubbard Guidance

Center) and handle the right one. But the Church of Scientology, by policy, simply treats the person with the same admin policy procedure as that used on a suppressive person and lets HGC sort it out. Get that difference, it's "with the same admin policy procedure as" not "the same as."

For treating a person "the same as" a suppressive person when he or she is not only adds to the confusion. One treats a real suppressive person pretty rough. One has to handle the bank.

As to (2) here is the real test and the only valid test: Does their history of routine auditing reveal any gains?

If the answer is no then *there* is your suppressive person, loud and very unclear!

That is the test.

There are several ways of detecting. When fair auditors or good ones have had to vary routine procedure or do unusual things on this case in an effort to make it gain, when there are lots of notes from Ds of P in the folder saying do this, do that, you know that this case was *trouble.*

This means it was one of three things: 1. a potential trouble source 2. a person with a big withhold 3. a suppressive person.

If despite all that trouble and care, the case did not gain or if the case simply didn't gain despite auditing no matter how many years or intensives, then you've caught your suppressive person.

That's the boy. Or the girl.

This case performs continued calculating covert hostile acts damaging to others. This case puts the enturbulence and upset into the environment, breaks the chairs, messes up the rugs and spoils the traffic flow with "goofs" done intentionally.

One should lock criminals out of the environment if one wants security. But one first has to locate the criminal. Don't lock everybody out because you can't find the criminal.

The cyclic case (gains and collapses routinely) is connected to a suppressive person. We have policy on that.

The case that continually pleads "hold my hand I am so ARC broken" is just somebody with a big *withhold,* not an ARC break.

The suppressive person just gets no-case-gain on routine student auditing.

This person is actively suppressing Scientology. If such will sit still and pretend to be audited the suppression is by hidden hostile acts which includes:

1. Chopping up auditors;
2. Pretending withholds which are actually criticisms;
3. Giving out "data" about their past lives that really holds such subjects up to scorn and makes people who *do* remember wince;
4. Chopping up Scientology churches;
5. Alter-ising technology to mess it up;
6. Spreading rumors about prominent persons in Scientology;
7. Attributing Scientology to other sources;
8. Criticizing auditors as a group;
9. Giving fragmentary or generalized reports about entheta that cave people in and isn't actual;
10. Refusing to repair ARC breaks;
11. Engaging in discreditable sexual acts (also true of potential trouble sources);
12. Reporting a session good when the pc went bad;
13. Reporting a session bad when the pc went up in tone;
14. Failing to relay communication or report;
15. Making a church go to pieces (note one uses "making" not "letting");
16. Committing small criminal acts around the church;
17. Making "mistakes" which get their seniors in trouble;
18. Refusing to abide by policy;
19. Non-compliance with instructions;
20. Alter-is of instructions or orders so that the program fouls up;
21. Hiding data that is vital to prevent upsets;
22. Altering orders to make a senior look bad;
23. Organizing revolts or mass protest meetings;
24. Snarling about justice.

And so on. One does not use the catalogue, however, one only uses this *one* fact: *no case gain by routine auditing over a longish period.*

This is the fellow that makes life miserable for the rest of us. This is the one who overworks executives. This is the auditor killer. This is the course enturbulator or pc killer.

There's the cancer. Burn it out.

In short, you begin to see that it's this one who is the only one who makes harsh discipline seem necessary. The rest of the staff suffers when one or two of these is present.

One hears a whine about "process didn't work" or sees an alter-is of technology. Go look. You'll find it now and then leads to a suppressive person inside or outside the church.

Now that one knows who it is, one can handle it.

But more than that, I can now crack this case!

The technology is useful in all cases, of course. But only this cracks the "no-gain-case."

The person is in a mad, howling situation of some yesteryear and is "handling it" by committing overt acts today. I say condition of yesteryear but the case thinks it's *today*.

Yes, you're right. They are nuts. The spin bins are full of either them or their victims. There's no other real psycho in a spin bin!

What? That means we've cracked insanity itself? That's right. And it's given us the key to the suppressive person and his or her effect on the environment. *This* is the multitude of "types" of insanity of the 19th century psychiatrist. All in one. Schizophrenia, paranoia, fancy names galore. Only one other type exists—the person the suppressive person got "at." This is the "manic-depressive," a type who is up one day and down the next. This is the potential trouble source gone mad. But these are in a minority in the spin bin, usually put there by suppressive persons and not crazy at all! The real mad ones are the suppressive persons. They are the *only* psychos.

Over simplification? No indeed. I can prove it! We could empty the spin bins now. If we want to. But we have better uses for technology than saving a lot of suppressive persons who themselves act only to scuttle the rest of us.

You see, when they get down to no-case-gain where a routine process won't bite, they can no longer as-is their daily life so it all starts to stack up into a horror. They "solve" this horror by continuous covert acts against their surroundings and associates. After a while the covert ones don't seem to hold off the fancied "horror" and they commit some senseless violence in broad daylight or collapse—and so they can get identified as insane and are lugged off to the spin bin.

Anybody can "get mad" and bust a few chairs when a suppressive person goes too far. But there's traceable sense to it. Getting mad doesn't make a madman. It's damaging actions that have no sensible detectable reasons that's the trail of madness. Any thetan can get angry. Only a madman damages without reason.

All actions have their lower scale discreditable mockery. The difference is, does one get over his anger? The no-case-gain of course can't. He or she stays misemotional and adds each new burst to the fire. It never gets less. It grows. And a long way from all suppressive persons are violent. They are more likely to look resentful.

A suppressive person can get to one solid *dispassionate* state of damaging things. Here is the accident prone, the home wrecker, the group wrecker.

Now here one must realize something. The suppressive person finds outlet for his or her unexpressed rage by carefully needling those they are connected with into howling anger.

You see the people around them get dragged into this long gone incident by mistaken identity. And it is a maddening situation to be continually mis-identified, accused, worked on, double crossed. For one is *not* the being the suppressive person supposes. The suppressive person's world is pretty hard to live around. And even ordinarily cheerful people often blow up under the strain.

So be careful who you call the suppressive person. The person connected with a suppressive person *is liable to be only visible rage in sight!*

You have some experience of this: the mousey little woman who rarely changes expression and is so righteous connected to somebody who now and then goes into a frenzy.

How to tell them apart? Easy! Just ask this question:-

Which gets a case gain easily?

You see people *around* a suppressive person Q and A and disperse. They seek to "get even" with the suppressive person and often exhibit the same symptoms *temporarily.*

Sometimes *two* suppressive persons are found together. So one can't always say which is the suppressive person in a pair. The usual combination is the suppressive person and the potential trouble source.

However you don't need to guess about it or observe their conduct.

For this poor soul can no longer as-is easily. Too many overts. Too many withholds. Stuck in an incident that they call "present time." Handling a problem that does not exist. Supposing those around are the personnel in their own delirium.

They look all right. They sound reasonable. They are often clever. But they are solid poison. They can't as-is anything. Day by day their pile grows. Day by day their new overts and withholds pin them down tighter. They aren't here. But they sure can wreck the place.

There is the *true* psycho.

And he or she is dying before your very eyes. Kind of horrible.

The resolution of the case is a clever application of problems processes, never overts and withholds. What *was* the condition? How did you handle it is the key type of process.

I don't know what the percentage of these are in a society. I know only that they made up about 10% of any group so far observed. The data is obscured by the fact that they ARC break others and make them misemotional—thus one of them seems to be, by contagion, half a dozen such.

Therefore simple inspection of conduct does not reveal the suppressive person. Only a case folder puts the seal on it. No-case-gain by routine processes.

However this test too may soon become untrustworthy for now we can crack them by a special approach. However we will also generally use the same approach on routine cases as it makes cases go upward fast and we may catch the suppressive person accidentally and cure him or her before we are aware of it.

And that would be wonderful.

But still we'll have such on our lines in justice matters from now on. So it's good to know all about them, how they are identified, how to handle.

The Church must handle such cases as per the justice codes on suppressive acts when they blow Scientology or seek to suppress Scientologists or Churches. One should study up on these.

If you've wondered if you are a suppressive person while reading this—you aren't! A suppressive person never does wonder, not for a moment! THEY KNOW THEY'RE SANE!

4

HCOB 20 April 1972
Expanded Dianetics
Series 4

Suppressed Pcs and PTS Technology

(PTS means Potential Trouble Sources which itself means a person connected to a suppressive person).

All sick persons are PTS.

All pcs who rollercoaster (regularly lose gains) are PTS.

Suppressive persons are themselves PTS to themselves.

If a Volunteer Minister does not know this, have reality upon it and use it, he will have losses on people he need not have.

There is considerable *administrative* technology connected with this subject of PTS and there is a special auditing rundown which handles PTS people.

They get handled *if* the minister knows his PTS tech, if he audits well and if he uses both the auditing and administrative technology to handle.

The administrative tech requires an interview, usually by HCO and the person is required to handle the PTS situation itself *before* being audited.

5

HCOB 24 November 1965
Level IV

Search and Discovery

The process called Search and Discovery requires as well a good knowledge of ethics.

One must know what a suppressive person is, what a potential trouble source is and the mechanism of how and why a case roller coasters and what that is. Ethics is not merely a legal action—it handles the whole phenomena of case worsening (roller coaster) after processing and without this technology an auditor easily becomes baffled and tends to plunge and squirrel. The *only* reason a case roller coasters after good standard auditing is the PTS phenomena and a suppressive is present.

Three Types

There are three types of PTS.

Type One is the easy one. The SP on the case is right in present time, actively suppressing the person.

Type Two is harder for the *apparent* suppressive person in present time is only a restimulator for the actual suppressive.

Type Three is beyond the facilities of churches not equipped with hospitals as these are entirely psychotic.

Handling Type One PTS

The type one is normally handled by an ethics officer in the course of an interview.

The person is asked if anyone is invalidating him or his gains or Scientology and if the pc answers with a name and is then told to handle that person the *good indicators* come in promptly and the person is *quite* satisfied.

If however there is no success in finding the SP on the case or if the person starts naming church personnel or other unlikely persons as SP, the ethics officer must realize that he is handling a *type two* PTS and, because the auditing will consume time, sends the person to the HGC for a search and discovery.

It is easy to tell a type one PTS from a type two. The type one brightens up at once and ceases to roller coaster the moment the present time SP is spotted. The person ceases to roller coaster, he does not go back on it and begin to beg off, he does not begin to worry about the consequences of handling. If the person does any of these things, then he/she is a *type two*.

It can be seen that ethics handles the majority of PTSes in a fast manner. There is no trouble about it. All goes smoothly.

It can also be seen that the Volunteer Minister cannot afford the time to handle a type two PTS and there is no reason the type two should not pay well for the auditing.

Therefore, when you find the type one approach does not work quickly, you must send the person to the Church of Scientology for search and discovery.

Type Two

The pc who isn't sure, won't handle, or still roller coasters, or who doesn't brighten up, can't name any SP at all is a type two.

Only search and discovery will help.

Handling Type Three

The type three PTS is mostly in institutions or would be.

In this case the type two's *apparent* SP is spread all over the world and is often more than all the people there are—for the person sometimes has ghosts about him or demons and they are just more apparent SPs but imaginary as beings as well.

All institutional cases are PTSes. The whole of insanity is wrapped up in this one fact.

The insane is not just a bad off being, the insane is a being who has been overwhelmed by an actual SP until too many persons are apparent SPs. This makes the person roller coaster continually in life. The roller coaster is even cyclic (repetitive as a cycle).

Putting the person in a current institution puts him in a bedlam. And when also "treated" it may finish him. For he will roller coaster from any treatment given until made into a type two and given a search and discovery.

The task with a type three is *not* treatment as such. It is to provide a relatively *safe environment* and quiet and rest and no treatment of a mental nature at all. Giving him a quiet court with a motionless object in it might do the trick if he is permitted to sit there unmolested. Medical care of a very unbrutal nature is necessary as intravenous feeding and soporifics (sleeping and quietening drugs) may be necessary, such persons are sometimes also physically ill from an illness with a known medical cure.

Treatment with drugs, shock, operation is just more suppression. The person will not really get well, will relapse etc.

Standard auditing on such a person is subject to the roller coaster phenomena. They get worse after getting better. "Successes" are sporadic, enough to lead one on, and usually worsen again since these people are PTS.

But removed from apparent SPs, kept in a quiet surrounding, not pestered or threatened or put in fear, the person comes up to type two and a search and discovery should end the matter. But there will always be some failures as the insane sometimes withdraw into rigid unawareness as a final defense, sometimes can't be kept alive and sometimes are too hectic and distraught to ever become quiet. The extremes of too quiet and never quiet have a number of psychiatric names such as "catatonia" (withdrawn totally) and "manic" (too hectic).

Classification is interesting but non-productive since they are all PTS, all will roller coaster and none can be trained or processed with any idea of lasting result no matter the temporary miracle.

Remove a type three PTS from the environment, give him or her rest and quiet, get a search and discovery done when rest and quiet have made the person type two.

The modern mental hospital with its brutality and suppressive treatments is not the way to give a psychotic quiet and rest. Before anything effective can be done in this field a proper institution would have to be provided, offering only rest, quiet and medical assistance for intravenous feedings and sleeping draughts where necessary but not as "treatment" and where *no* treatment is attempted until the person looks recovered and only then a search and discovery as above under type two.

6

HCOB 8 November 1965

Suppressives and Hidden Standards

If you find a suppressive on a case you will also find a chronic problem.

A problem is postulate-counter-postulate.

When a person is faced with suppression he is facing a counter-postulate.

A hidden standard is a problem a person thinks must be resolved before auditing can be seen to have worked. It's a standard by which to judge Scientology or auditing or the auditor.

This hidden standard is always an old problem of long duration. It is a postulate-counter-postulate situation—the source of the counter-postuate was suppressive to the person.

Therefore you can always find a suppressive by finding a pc's hidden standard and following it back to when it began. You will find there a suppressive to the person.

Similarly if you trace back the persons and groups who have been suppressive of the individual, you will find a hidden standard popping into view.

The datum is a case that betters then worsens (a "roller coaster case" or a "roller coaster") is always connected to a suppressive person.

The roller coaster is *caused* by the hidden standard going into action. "My eyesight didn't get better." Locate a present time suppressive on the case and trace that suppressive back to others earlier and you suddenly see the pc brighten up and (apparently for no reason) state his eyesight suddenly improved.

A case that betters and worsens (a roller coaster) is *always* connected to a suppressive person and will not get steady gain until the suppressive is found on the case or the *basic* suppressive person earlier.

Because the case doesn't get well he or she is a potential trouble source. To us, to others, to himself. You can't successfully audit that pc because there is a *hidden standard*. It makes the pc think he is no better. Suppressives also suppress the pc just like that so long as a hidden standard is present.

7

|HCOB 12 March 1968

Mistakes, Anatomy Of

In the presence of suppression, one makes mistakes.

People making mistakes or doing stupid things is evidence that an SP exists in that vicinity.

8

|HCOB 10 August 1973

PTS Handling

There are two stable data which anyone has to have, understand and know are true in order to obtain results in handling the person connected to suppressives.

These data are:

1. That all illness in greater or lesser degree and all foul ups stem directly and only from a PTS condition.
2. That getting rid of the condition requires two basic actions: A. Discover B. Handle.

Persons called upon to handle PTS people can do so very easily, far more easily than they believe. Their basic stumbling block is thinking that there are exceptions or that there is other technology or that the two above data have modifiers or are not sweeping. The moment a person who is trying to handle PTSes gets persuaded there are other conditions or reasons or tech, he is at once lost and will lose the game and not obtain results. And this is very too bad because it is not difficult and the results are there to be obtained.

To turn someone who may be PTS over to an auditor just to have him mechanically audited may not be enough. In the first place this person may not have a clue what is meant by PTS and may be missing all manner of technical data on life and may be so overwhelmed by a suppressive person or group that he is quite incoherent. Thus just mechanically doing a process may miss the whole show as it misses the person's understanding of why it is being done.

A PTS person is rarely psychotic. But all psychotics are PTS if only to themselves. A PTS person may be in a state of deficiency or pathology which prevents a ready recovery, but at the same time he will not fully recover unless the PTS condition is also handled. For he became prone to deficiency or pathological illness because he was PTS. And unless the condition is relieved, no matter what medication or nutrition he may be given, he might not recover and certainly will not recover permanently. This seems to indicate that there are "other illnesses or reasons for illness besides being PTS." To be sure there are deficiencies and illnesses just as there are accidents and injuries. But strangely enough the person himself precipitates them because being PTS predisposes him to them. In a more garbled way, the medicos and nutritionists are always talking about "stress" causing illness. Lacking full technology they yet have an inkling that this is so because they see it is somehow true. They cannot handle it. Yet they recognize it, and they state that it is a senior situation to various illnesses and accidents. Well, we have the technology of this in more ways than one.

What is this thing called "stress?" It is more than the medico defines it—he usually says it comes from operational or physical shock and in this he has too limited a view.

A person under stress is actually under a suppression on one or more dynamics.

If that suppression is located and the person handles, the condition diminishes. If he also has all the engrams and ARC breaks, problems, overts and withholds audited out and if all such areas of suppression are thus handled, the person would recover from anything caused by "stress."

Usually the person has insufficient understanding of life or any dynamic to grasp his own situation. He is confused. He believes all his illnesses are true because they occur in such heavy books!

At some time he was predisposed to illness or accidents. When a serious suppression then occurred he suffered a precipitation or occurrence of the accident or illness, and then with repeated similar suppressions on the same chain, the illness or tendency to accidents became prolonged or chronic.

To say then that a person is PTS to his current environment would be very limited as a diagnosis. If he continues to do or be something to which the suppressive person or group objected he may become or continue to be ill or have accidents.

Actually the problem of PTS is not very complicated. Once you have grasped the two data first given, the rest of it becomes simply an analysis of how they apply to this particular person.

A PTS person can be markedly helped in three ways:

(a) gaining an understanding of the technology of the condition;

(b) discovering to what or to whom he is PTS;

(c) handling.

Someone with the wish or duty to find and handle PTSes has an additional prior step: He must know how to recognize a PTS and how to handle them when recognized. Thus it is rather a waste of time to engage in this hunt unless one has studied the material on suppressives and PTSes and grasps it without misunderstoods. In other words the first step of the person is to get a grasp of the subject and its technology. This is not difficult to do if you study well and understand what I have written here.

With this step done, a person has no real trouble recognizing PTS people and can have success in handling them which is very gratifying and rewarding.

Let us consider the easiest level of approach:

i) Show the person sections 1, 2, 3 and 9 of this pack and let him study them so that he knows the elements like "PTS" and "suppressive." He may just cognite right there and be much better. It has happened.

ii) Have him discuss the illness or accident or condition, without much prodding or probing, that he thinks now may be the result of suppression. He will usually tell you it is right here and now or was a short time ago and will be all set to explain it (without any relief) as stemming from his current environment or a recent one. If you let it go at that he would simply be a bit unhappy and not get well as he is discussing usually a late lock that has a lot of earlier incidents below it.

iii) Ask when he recalls first having that illness or having such accidents. He will at once begin to roll this back and realize that it has happened before. You don't have to be auditing him as he is all too willing to talk about this in a most informal manner. He will get back to some early this-lifetime point usually.

iv) Now ask him *who* it was. He will usually tell you promptly. And, as you are not really auditing him and he isn't going into past lives and you are not trying to do more than key him out, you don't probe any further.

v) You will usually find that he has named a person to whom he is still connected! So you ask him whether he wants to handle. If he can't see how he can, you persuade him to begin to handle on a gradient scale. This may consist of imposing some slight discipline on him such as requiring him to actually answer his mail or write the person a pleasant good roads good weather note or to realistically look at how he estranged them. In short what is required in the handling is a low gradient. All you are trying to do is move the PTS person from effect over to slight gentle cause.

vi) Check with the person again, if he is handling, and coach him along, always at a gentle good roads and good weather level and no H E and R (Human Emotion and Reaction) if you please.

That is a simple handling. You can get complexities such as a person being PTS to an unknown person in his immediate vicinity that he may have to find before he can handle. You can find people who can't remember more than a few years back. You can find anything you can find in a case. But simple handling ends when it looks pretty complex. And that's when you call in the auditor.

But this simple handling will get you quite a few stars in your crown. You will be amazed to find that while some of them don't instantly recover, medication, vitamins, minerals, will now work when before they wouldn't. You may also get some instant recoveries but realize that if they don't you have not failed.

A being is rather complex. He may have a lot of sources of suppression. And it may take a lot of very light auditing to get him up to where he can do work on suppressives since these were, after all, the source of his overwhelm. And what he did to them might be more important than what they did to him but unless you unburden him he may not get around to realizing that.

But you have made an entrance and you have stirred things up and gotten him more aware and just that way you will find he is more at cause.

His illness or proneness to accidents may not be slight. You may succeed only to the point where he now has a chance, by nutrition, vitamins, minerals, medication, treatment, and above all—auditing, of getting well. Unless you jogged this condition, he had no chance at all—for becoming PTS is the first thing that happened to him on the subject of illness or accidents.

So do not underestimate what you as a Volunteer Minister and an auditor can do for a PTS. And don't sell PTS technology short or neglect it. And don't continue to push off or even worse, tolerate PTS conditions in people.

You can do something about it.

And so can they.

9

HCO PL 5 April 1972
Issue I

PTS Type A Handling

The PTS type "A" is a person "intimately connected with persons (such as marital or familial ties) of known antagonism to mental or spiritual treatment or Scientology. In practice PTS persons, even when they approach Scientology in a friendly fashion, have such pressure continually brought to bear upon them by persons with undue influence over them that they make very poor gains in processing and their interest is solely devoted to proving the antagonistic element wrong."

A Source of Trouble

Such persons with antagonistic family members are a source of trouble to Scientology because their family members are not inactive.

In fact from direct experience it has been found that those who have created troubling conditions for Scientology have been the wives, husbands, mothers, fathers, brothers, sisters, or grandparents of some Scientologist. Their complaints have been full of such statements as, "My son completely changed after he went into Scientology—he no longer was respectful to me." "My daughter gave up a wonderful career as a hairdresser to go into Scientology." "My sister got these funny staring eyes the way all Scientologists have."

Their complaints were illogical and their descriptions of what occurred were untrue, but the point of the matter is that such persons did cause Scientology Churches and fellow Scientologists a great deal of trouble and difficulty.

Don't Create Antagonism

Many Scientologists in their misunderstanding and misapplication of Scientology create the conditions that bring about the antagonism in the first place. A few illustrations of how this is done are as follows:

Scientologist to mother: "I now know where you are on the tone scale—1.1 Boy are you sneaky!" (Evaluation and invalidation.)

Father to Scientologist: "Now I don't want you to borrow the car again without my permission. I have told you time and time----" Scientologist to father: "OKAY! FINE! OKAY! GOOD! THANK YOU! I GOT THAT!" (Not an acknowledgment, but an effort to shut up the father.)

Scientologist to older brother: "You murdered me in a past life, you dirty dog!" (Evaluation and invalidation.)

Mother to Scientologist: "Whatever are you doing?" Scientologist to mother: "I'm trying to confront your dreadful bank." (Invalidation.)

There are so many ways to misuse tech and to invalidate and evaluate for others in a destructive fashion to bring about ARC breaks and upset that they can not all possibly be listed. The idea is NOT to do so. Why create trouble for yourself and for your fellow Scientologists as nothing will have been gained but ill-will?

The Why

It is a violation of the policies of the Church of Scientology for a Scientologist to be or become a PTS without reporting it or taking action, or to receive processing while PTS, also a PTS may not be trained.

This means that a person who is PTS may not receive processing or training while PTS and it also means that they had better do something to handle their condition.

Each PTS individual should report to the Ethics Department of their Scientology Church and with the assistance of ethics find a WHY as to their familial antagonism and then set about actually handling the situation. The WHY could be that his parents wanted him to be a lawyer and so blame Scientology that he is not one, rather than the fact that he flunked out of law school and couldn't stand the thought of being a lawyer!

In any case the WHY should be found and the PTS individual should then do whatever is necessary to handle.

Handling

The person who is PTS should be declared as such by ethics and should not receive Scientology training or processing until the situation has been handled.

The handling could be as simple as writing to one's father and saying, "I do not complain that you are a janitor, please do not complain that I am a Scientologist. The important thing is that I am you son and that I love and respect you. I know you love me, but please learn to respect me as an adult individual who knows what he wants in life."

Again there are as many ways of handling as there are why's found. Each case is individual. Remember, too, there is always the possibility of a "no situation." And if the person thinks he's PTS and isn't he can get sick. Or if he insists he isn't and is, he can also get upset. So find if there IS a situation first.

It is the purpose of ethics to ensure that the situation is handled.

10

HCO PL 7 May 1969

Policies on "Sources of Trouble"

Policies similar to those regarding physical illness and insanity exist for types of persons who have caused us considerable trouble.

These persons can be grouped under "sources of trouble." They include:

(a) Persons intimately connected with persons (such as marital or familial ties) of known antagonism to mental or spiritual treatment or Scientology. In practice such persons, even when they approach Scientology in a friendly fashion, have such pressure continually brought to bear upon them by persons with undue influence over them that they make very poor gains in processing and their interest is solely devoted to proving the antagonistic element wrong.

They, by experience, produce a great deal of trouble in the long run as their own condition does not improve adequately under such stresses to effectively combat the antagonism. Their present time problem cannot be reached as it is continuous, and so long as it remains so, they should not be accepted for auditing by any church or auditor.

(b) Criminals with proven criminal records often continue to commit so many undetected harmful acts between sessions that they do not make adequate case gains and therefore should not be accepted for processing by churches or auditors.

(c) Persons who have ever threatened to sue or embarrass or attack or who have publicly attacked Scientology or been a party to an attack and all their immediate families should never be accepted for processing by a Church of Scientology or auditor. They have a history of only serving other ends than case gain and commonly again turn on the church or auditor. They have already barred themselves out by their own overts against Scientology and are thereafter too difficult to help, since they cannot openly accept help from those they have tried to injure.

(d) Responsible-for-condition cases have been traced back to other causes for their condition too often to be acceptable. By responsible-for-condition cases is meant the person who insists a book or some auditor is "wholly responsible for the terrible condition I am in." Such cases demand unusual favors, free auditing, tremendous effort on the part of auditors. Review of these cases show that they were in the same or worse condition long before auditing, that they are using a planned campaign to obtain auditing for nothing, that they are not as bad off as they claim, and that their antagonism extends to anyone who seeks to help them, even their own families. Establish the rights of the matter and decide accordingly.

(e) Persons who are not being audited on their own determinism are a liability as they are forced into being processed by some other person and have no personal desire to become better. Quite on the contrary they usually want only to prove the person who wants them audited wrong, and so do not get better. Until a personally determined goal to be processed occurs, the person will not benefit.

(f) Persons who "want to be processed to see if Scientology works" as their only reason for being audited have never been known to make gains as they do not participate. News reporters fall into this category. They should not be audited.

(g) Persons who claim that "if you help such and such a case" (at great and *your* expense) because somebody is rich and influential or the neighbors would be electrified, should be ignored. Processing is designed for bettering individuals, not progressing by stunts or giving cases undue importance. Process only at convenience and usual arrangements. Make no extraordinary effort at the expense of other persons who do want processing for normal reasons. Not one of these arrangements has ever come off successfully as it has the unworthy goal of notoriety, not betterment.

(h) Persons who "have an open mind" but no personal hopes or desires for auditing or knowingness should be ignored, as they really don't have an open mind at all, but a lack of ability to decide about things and are seldom found to be very responsible and waste anyone's efforts "to convince them."

(i) Persons who do not believe anything or anyone can get better. They have a purpose for being audited entirely contrary to the auditor's and so in this conflict, do not benefit. When such persons are trained they use their training to degrade others. Thus they should not be accepted for training or auditing.

(j) Persons attempting to sit in judgment on Scientology in hearings or attempting to investigate Scientology should be given no undue importance. One should not seek to instruct or assist them in any way. This includes judges, boards, newspaper reporters, magazine writers, etc. All efforts to be helpful or instructive have done nothing beneficial as their first idea is a firm "I don't know" and this usually ends with an equally firm "I don't know." If a person can't see for himself or judge from the obvious, then he does not have sufficient powers of observation even to sort out actual evidence. In legal matters, only take the obvious effective steps, carry on no crusades in court. In the matter of reporters, etc., it is not worthwhile to give them any time contrary to popular belief. They are given their story before they leave their editorial rooms and you only strengthen what they have to say by saying anything. They are no public communication line that sways much. Policy is very definite. Ignore.

To summarize troublesome persons, the policy in general is to cut communication as the longer it is extended the more trouble they are to us. I know of no case where the types of persons listed above were handled by auditing or instruction. I know of many cases where they were handled by firm legal stands, by ignoring them until they change their minds, or just turning one's back.

In applying a policy of cut-communication one must also use judgment as there are exceptions in all things and to fail to handle a person's momentary upset in life or with us can be quite fatal. So these policies refer to non-Scientology persons in the main or persons who appear on the outer fringes and push toward us. When such a person bears any of the above designations we and the many are better off to ignore them.

Scientology works. You don't have to prove it to everyone. People don't deserve to have Scientology as a divine right, you know. They have to earn it. This has been true in every philosophy that sought to better man.

All the above sources of trouble are also forbidden training and when a person being trained or audited is detected to belong under the above headings (a) to (j) he or she should be advised to terminate and accept refund which must be paid at once and the full explanation should be given them at that time. Thus the few may not, in their own turmoil, impede service to and the advance of the many. And the less enturbulence you put on your lines, the better, and the more people you will eventually help.

11 Robotism

HCO PL 10 May 1972

A technical advance has been made in relation to the inactivity, slowness or incompetence of human beings.

This discovery proceeds from a two and a half year intense study of aberration as it affects the ability to function as a group member.

The ideal group member is capable of working causatively in full cooperation with his fellows in the achievement of group goals and the realization of his own happiness.

The *primary* human failing is an inability to function as himself or contribute to group achievements.

Wars, political upsets, organizational duress, growing crime rates, increasingly heavy "justice," growing demands for excessive welfare, economic failure and other age long and repeating conditions find a common denominator in the inability of human beings to coordinate.

The current answer in vogue, in this century and growing is totalitarianism where the state orders the whole life of the individual. The production figures of such states are very low and their crimes against the individual are numerous.

A discovery therefore of what this factor is that makes the humanoid the victim of oppression would be a valuable one.

The opening lines of *Dianetics: The Modern Science of Mental Health,* comment on Man's lack of an answer for himself.

The group needs such an answer in order to survive and for its individual members to be happy.

Scale

	Pan-determined
	Self-determined
Robot	Other-determined
Band	Oblivious
	Insane

Needing Orders

The individual with an evil purpose has to withhold himself because he may do destructive things.

When he fails to withhold himself he commits overt acts on his fellows or other dynamics and occasionally loses control and does so.

This, of course, makes him quite inactive.

To overcome this he refuses any responsibility for his own actions.

Any motion he makes must be on the responsibility of others.

He operates then only when given orders.

Thus he *must* have orders to operate.

Therefore one could term such a person a *robot.* And the malady could be called *robotism.*

Perception

Studies of perception undertaken reveal that sight, hearing and other channels of awareness *decrease* in proportion to the number of overt acts—and therefore withholds—which the person has committed on the whole track.

By relieving these, sight has been remarkably brightened.

Therefore a person who is withholding himself from committing overt acts because of his own undesired purposes has very poor perception.

He does not *see* the environment around him.

Thus, combined with his unwillingness to act on his own initiative, there is a blindness to the environment.

Overt Products

Since he does not act upon orders he is taking responsibility for, he executes orders without fully understanding them.

Further he executes them in an environment he does not see.

Thus when forced to produce he will produce overt products. These are called so because they are not in actual fact useful products but something no one wants and are overt acts in themselves—such as inedible biscuits or a "repair" that is just further breakage.

Slowness

The person is slow because he is moving on other determinism, is carefully withholding himself and cannot see anyway.

Thus he feels lost, confused or unsafe and cannot move positively.

Because he produces overt products he gets slapped around or goes unthanked and so begins a decline.

He cannot move swiftly and if he does has accidents. So he teaches himself to be careful and cautious.

Justice

Group justice is of some use but all it really does is make the person withhold himself even harder and while a necessary restraint, nevertheless does not itself bring a lasting improvement.

Threats and "heads on a pike" (meaning examples of discipline) do however jar the person into giving his attention and channeling his actions into a more desirable path from the group viewpoint.

Justice is necessary in a society of such people but it is not a remedy for improvement.

Malice

Despite the viciousness of the truly insane, there is little or no real malice in the robot.

The truly insane cannot control or withhold their evil purposes and dramatize them at least covertly.

The insane are not always visible. But they are visible enough. And they *are* malicious.

The robot on the other hand does control his evil impulses to a great extent.

He is not malicious.

His danger mainly stems from the incompetent things he does, the time of others he consumes, the waste of time and material and the brakes he puts on the general group endeavor.

He does not do all these things intentionally. He does not really know he is doing them.

He looks in wounded surprise at the wrath he generates when he breaks things, wrecks programs and gets in the way. He does not know he is doing these things. For he cannot see that he is. He may go along for some time doing (slowly wasteful) well and then carelessly smashes the exact thing that wrecks the whole activity.

People suppose he cunningly intended to do so. He seldom does.

He winds up even more convinced he can't be trusted and that he should withhold harder!

False Reports

The robot gives many false reports. Unable to *see,* how can he know what is true?

He seeks to fend off wrath and attract good will by "PR" (public relations boasts) without realizing he is giving false reports.

Morale

The robot goes into morale declines easily. Since production is the basis of morale, and since he does not really produce much, left to his own devices, his morale sags heavily.

Physical Inertia

The body is a physical object. It is not the being himself.

As a body has mass it tends to remain motionless unless moved and tends to keep going in a certain direction unless steered.

As he is not really running his body, the robot has to be moved when not moving or diverted if moving on a wrong course.

Thus anyone with one or more of such beings around him tends to get exhausted with shoving them into motion or halting them when they go wrong.

Exhaustion only occurs when one does not understand the robot.

It is the exasperation that exhausts one.

With understanding, one is not exasperated because he *can* handle the situation. But only if he knows what it is.

PTS

Potential trouble sources are not necessarily robots.

A PTS person generally is withholding himself from a suppressive person or group or thing.

Toward that SP person or group or thing he is a robot! He takes orders from them if only in opposites.

His overts on the SP person make him blind and nonself-determined.

Basic Why

The basic reason behind persons who cannot function, are slow or inactive or incompetent and who do not produce is:

WITHHOLDING SELF FROM DOING DESTRUCTIVE THINGS, AND THUS UNWILLING TO TAKE RESPONSIBILITY AND THEREFORE NEEDING ORDERS.

The exact wording of this WHY must be done by the individual himself after examining and grasping this principle.

If one writes this principle down on the top of a sheet and then asks the person to word it exactly as it applies to himself, one will attain the individual why for inaction and incompetence.

Processing

Physical work in the physical universe, general confronting, reach and withdraw, locational processing and objective processes go far in remedying this condition.

Touch assists regularly and correctly given to proper end phenomena will handle illnesses of such persons.

Word clearing is vital tech to open the person's comm lines, wipe out earlier misunderstoods and increase his understanding.

PTS tech will handle the person's robotism toward SP individuals, groups or things.

End Product

The end product when one has fully handled robotism is not a person who cannot follow orders or who operates solely on his own.

Totalitarian states fear any relief of the condition as they foolishly actively promote and hope for such beings. But this is only a deficiency in their own causes and their lack of experience with fully self-determined beings. Yet some education, advertising and amusements have been designed only for robots. Even religions existed to suppress "Man's evil nature."

Lacking any examples or understanding, many have feared to free the robot to his own control and think even with horror on it.

But you see, beings are not basically robots. They are miserable when they are.

Basically they prosper only when they are self-determined and can be pan-determined to help in the prosperity of all.

HCOB 22 March 1967
Important: Admin-Know-How, Alter-Is and Degraded Beings

12
Alter-is and Degraded Beings

Alteration of orders and technology is worse than non-compliance.

Alter-is is a covert avoidance of an order. Although it is apparently often brought about by non-comprehension, the non-comprehension itself and failure to mention it, is an avoidance of orders.

Very degraded beings alter-is. Degraded ones refuse to comply without mentioning it. Beings in fair condition try to comply but remark their troubles to get help when needed. Competent higher-toned beings understand orders and comply if possible but mainly do their jobs without needing lots of special orders.

Degraded beings find *any* instruction painful as they have been painfully indoctrinated with violent measures in the past. They therefore alter-is any order or don't comply.

Thus in counseling or in organizations where you find alter-is (covert non-compliance) and non-compliance, given sensible and correct technology or instructions, you are dealing with a degraded low level being and should act accordingly.

One uses very simple low level processes on a degraded being, gently.

In administration and organizations where a staff member alter-ises or fails to comply you are also dealing with a degraded being. He cannot be at cause and staff members *must* be at cause. So he or she should not be on staff.

This is a primary senior datum regulating all handling of preclears and staff members.

A degraded being is not a suppressive as he can have case gain. But he is so PTS that he works for suppressives only. He is sort of a super-continual PTS beyond the reach really of a simple S & D and handled only by advanced Scientology techniques.

Degraded beings, taking a cue from SP associates, instinctively resent, hate and seek to obstruct any person in charge of anything or any Big Being.

Anyone issuing *sensible* orders is the first one resented by a degraded being.

A degraded being lies to his seniors, avoids orders covertly by alter-is, fails to comply, supplies only complex ideas that can't ever work (obstructive) and is a general area of enturbulence, often mild-seeming or even "cooperative" often even flattering, sometimes merely dull but consistently alter-ising or non-complying.

This datum appeared during higher level research and is highly revelatory of earlier unexplained phenomena—the preclear who changes commands or doesn't do them, the worker who can't get it straight and who is always on a tea break.

In an area where suppression has been very heavy for long periods people become degraded beings. However, they must have been so before already due to whole track incidents.

Some thetans are bigger than others. None are truly equal. But the degraded being is not necessarily a natively bad thetan. He is simply so PTS and has been for so long that it requires our highest level technology to finally undo it *after* he has scaled up all our grades.

Degraded beings are about 18 to 1 over big beings in the human race (minimum ratio). So those who keep things going are few. And those who will make it without the steam of the few in our churches behind them are zero. At the same time, we can't have a world full of them and still make it. So we have no choice.

And we can handle them even when they cannot serve at higher levels.

L

Ethics and Justice

Ethics and Justice Checksheet

Purpose:

To train the Volunteer Minister how to recognize and handle dissident elements in the community.

a	Study Section 1 Ethics.	______
b	Study Section 2 Ethics, the Design of.	______
c	Drill: Write an essay on why the Volunteer Minister is making the environment safe.	______
d	Study Section 3 Administering Justice.	______
e	Drill: Demonstrate why it's an overt not to work for the greatest good of the greatest number.	______
f	Study Section 4 Exchange.	______
g	Drill: Walk downtown and spot some people who have out exchange.	______
h	Drill: Walk downtown and notice what businesses are creating a demand.	______
i	Drill: Demonstrate why a criminal has out exchange.	______
j	Study Section 5 Rewards and Penalties.	______
k	Drill: Go walk downtown and spot some evidence of a welfare state rewarding downstats.	______
l	Drill: Select a person you know with upstats and do something to help him further.	______
m	Study Section 6 Criminality.	______

n Drill: Write an essay on how honesty is the road to sanity. ________

o Drill: Select a friend and do exchange by dynamics on him. ________

p Study Section 7 The Volunteer Minister, His Character. ________

q Drill: Demonstrate what indicators the Volunteer Minister has for locating dissident elements. ________

r Drill: Demonstrate the correct sequence when one has to choose between safeguarding the group or rehabilitating the individual. ________

s Drill: Make a list of some of the rules of conduct of the Volunteer Minister when handling ethics matters. ________

t Study Section 8 Conditions. ________

u Drill: Select a friend and do conditions by dynamics on him. ________

v Drill: Have that person improve at least two dynamics by using conditions formulas. ________

w Study Section 9 Non-Existence Formula Expanded. ________

x Drill: Start applying your own Expanded Non-existence Formula. ________

Ethics and Justice Pack

1

HCO PL 18 June 1968

Ethics

The purpose of ethics is:

TO REMOVE COUNTER-INTENTIONS FROM THE ENVIRONMENT. And having accomplished that, the purpose becomes TO REMOVE OTHER INTENTIONNESS FROM THE ENVIRONMENT. Thus progress can be made by all.

Many mechanisms can exist to mask a counter-intention.

One has an intention to expand an organization. An "expert" says it is difficult as "The building society . . . ." The impulse is to then handle the problem presented by the "expert," whereas the correct ETHICS action is to remove his counter-intentionedness or other intentionedness. If he were an EXPERT he would simply say "OK. I'll handle my end of the expansion."

There are many ways to handle counter and other intentionedness.

There is a fine line between ethics and technology.

The point where a thetan goes mad is very exact. It is the point where he begins to obsessively stop something. From this the effort becomes generalized and he begins to stop lots of other things. When this includes anyone who or anything that would help him as well as those people and things that help, the being is *suppressive.* His intentions counter any other intention, particularly good intentions.

Other intentionedness comes from unawareness or dispersal. By removing things, which disperses others. Offering bottled medicine to cure "the blues" is a direct distraction. It is the purveyor of the distraction who is the target.

The person who enters on Scientology groups to then sell other-answer is of course an enemy.

However we go about accomplishing the above is the *action* of ethics. The above is the purpose.

2

HCO PL 7 December 1969

Ethics, the Design of

It is very easy for a staff member and even a Volunteer Minister to completely misunderstand ethics and its functions. In a society run by SPs and controlled by incompetent police, the citizen almost engramically identifies any justice action or symbol with oppression.

Yet in the absence of true ethics no one can live with others and statistics go down inevitably. So a just function must exist to protect producers and decent people.

To give you an example, when a little boy this life, the neighborhood a block around and the road from home to school were unusable. A bully about five years older than I named Leon Brown exerted a very bad influence over other children. With extortion by violence and blackmail and with corruption he made the area very dangerous. The road to school was blocked by the five O'Connell kids, ranging from 7 to 15 who stopped and beat up any smaller child. One couldn't go to school safely and was hounded by the Truant Officer, a hulking brute complete with star, if one *didn't* go to school.

When I was about six I got very tired of a bloody nose and spankings because my clothes were torn and avidly learned "lumberjack fighting," a crude form of judo from my grandfather.

With this "superior tech" under my belt I searched out and found alone the youngest O'Connell kid, a year older than I, and pulverized him. Then I found alone and took on the next in size and pulverized *him.* After that the O'Connell kids, all five, fled each time I showed up and the road to school was open and I convoyed other little kids so it was safe.

Then one day I got up on a 9-foot high board fence and waited until the 12 year old bully passed by and leaped off on him boots and all and after the dust settled that neighborhood was safe for every kid in it.

So I learned about justice. Kids would come from blocks away to get help in *their* neighborhood. Finally for a mile around it was a safe environment for kids.

From this I learned two lessons:

1. Strength is nothing without skill and tech, and reversely, without skill and tech the strength of brutes is a matter of contempt.

2. Strength has two sides, one for good and one for evil. It is the intention that makes the difference.

On further living I found that only those who sought only peace were ever butchered. The thousands of years of Jewish passivity earned for them nothing but slaughter.

So things do not run right because one is holy or good. Things run right because one makes them run right.

Justice is a necessary action to any successful society. Without it the brute attacks the weak, the decent and the productive.

There are people who suppress. They are few. They often rise up to being in charge and then all things decay. They are essentially psychopathic personalities. Such want position in order to kill. Such as Ghenghis Khan, Hitler, psychiatrists, psychopathic criminals, want power only to destroy. Covertly or overtly they pay only with death. They arrived where they arrived, in charge of things, because nobody when they were on their way up said "No." They are monuments to the cowards, the "reasonable" people who didn't put period to them while they were still only small bullies and still vulnerable.

Ethics has to get there before technology can occur. So when it doesn't exist or goes out then technology doesn't occur and suppression sets in and death follows.

So if someone doesn't hold the line, all become victims of oppression.

The Volunteer Minister is making the environment safe so that production can occur and service can be given. He is making it unsafe for those who by neglect or continual errors or suppression push statistics down and get good staff members to leave.

If none of this is well understood and yet someone is making it impossible to work, find a 9-foot high board fence . . . .

The Volunteer Minister must know his ethics technology. He must understand why he is there.

And the rest of the people in the community should understand it too.

3 Administering Justice

HCO PL 17 March 1965
Issue III, HCO (Division I)
Justice Hat

There are some things to firmly keep in mind when you have to use Justice function:

(1) Only the criminally inclined desire a society in which the criminal is free to do as he pleases.

(2) Only the criminally inclined are frightened enough of justice to protest and complain that it exists.

(3) Without order nothing can grow or expand.

(4) Justice is one of the guards that keeps the channel of progress a channel and not a stopped flow.

(5) All reactive minds can exert pain and discomfort on a being. They demand the suppression of the good and the production of the bad. Therefore, in administering justice, restrain just a trifle more than a bank can compel a bad action. The external threat need be just enough to make the internal pressure to do wrong the lesser of two discomforts. Judgment lies in how much external restraint to apply.

(6) Decent people are in favor of justice. Don't confuse the opinion of the majority who wish it with the snarls of the few who fear it.

(7) A person who is dramatizing his criminal intent can become very angry if he is not prevented from hurting others.

(8) A thetan is good. He invented a bank to keep others good. That mechanism went wrong. And that's why we're here.

(9) In a session you would keep a burglar from bursting in the room and disturbing the preclear. In Scientology you keep offenders out so we can get on with our session with society.

(10) Look up the person who rails against justice most and you will have the one you have been looking for.

(11) The only overt in handling justice is not to work for the greatest good of the greatest number.

4 Exchange

HCO PL 3 December 1971
Executive Series 4

So many tricks have been entered into economics systems, and so many political fixations exist that a manager is often very hard pressed trying to bring about solvency for his activity.

Money can be manipulated in a thousand different ways.

There are "speculators" who seek to buy something (like land) cheaply and sell it dear. Or sell it dear, depress the market and buy it back cheaply. In either case they make a profit.

It is less well-understood that "speculators" also operate on the subject of money itself. By manipulating the value of one currency against another they seek to obtain a profit. This is the "international banker" at his daily work. He buys a hundred billion French francs for X dollars. Then he causes a panic about dollars. The franc gets very valuable. He sells his hundred billion French francs for 2X dollars. Then he says dollars are great. He has "made" a huge new lot of dollars for himself.

Or he finds a crummy politician like Hitler, builds him a war machine, gets paid back out of the plunder of Europe before Hitler collapses.

The banker loans George Manager $100,000 to modernize his plant. George wanted $200,000. But he takes the $100,000. The banker holds the whole plant as security. George doesn't make it as it really took $200,000 to do it. He goes broke. The banker grabs the $5,000,000 plant. This includes the $100,000 now spent on new machines. The banker sells it to a pal for $2,500,000 and makes that sum on his "loan."

The shareholders of Bide-a-Wee Biscuit are told Bide-a-Wee is busted. The stock falls. A group buys the stock up for peanuts, emerges as the owners of Bide-a-Wee which turns out not to be busted.

All these and a thousand thousand other systems for making money, indulged in too often, spoil CONFIDENCE and destroy money.

Eventually a whole ideology like communism will grow up dedicated only to the destruction of capitalism.

What has been dropped out is the idea of EXCHANGE.

Money has to *represent* something. It can represent gold or beans or hours of work or most anything as long as the thing it represents is real.

Whatever it represents, the item must be exchangeable. If money represents gold, then gold must be exchangeable. To prove this, the moment gold couldn't be individually owned, the dollar, based on it, became much less valuable.

There has to be enough of the thing that money represents. By making the thing scarce money can be manipulated and prices sent soaring.

Economics by reason of various manipulations can be made into the most effective trap of the modern slave master.

Periodically through history, not just in current times, monied classes or those believed to control money have been torn to bits, shot, stoned, burned and smashed. The ancient pharaohs of Egypt periodically lost their country through tax abuses.

Money, in short, is a passionate subject.

Modernly, the lid is coming off the economic pot which is at a high boil.

Too many speculators, too many dishonest men generating too much hate, too many tax abuses, too many propagandists shouting down money, too many fools, all add up to an explosive economic atmosphere.

A group has to be very clever to survive such a period. Their economic arrangements and policies must be fantastically wise, well-established and followed.

As it exists at this writing, the only real crime in the West is for a group to be without money. That finishes it. But with enough money it can defend itself and expand.

Yet if you borrow money you become the property of bankers. If you make money you become the target of tax collectors.

But if you don't have it, the group dies under the hammer of bankruptcy and worse.

So we always make it the first condition of a group to make its own way and be prosperous on its own efforts.

The key to such prosperity is *exchange.*

One exchanges something valuable for something valuable.

Processing and training are valuable. Done well, they are priceless.

In many ways an exchange can occur. Currently it is done with money.

In our case processing and training are the substances we exchange for the materials of survival.

To *exchange* something one must find or create a *demand.*

He must then supply the demand in EXCHANGE for the things the group needs.

If that is understood, then at once it is seen that (a) a group can't just process or train its own members and (b) a group cannot give its services away for nothing and (c) the services must be valuable to those receiving them; (d) that the demand must be established by surveys and created on the basis of what is found, and (e) that continual public contact must be maintained.

Thus by bringing the problems of viability down to the rock-bottom basics of *exchange* one can cut through all the fog about economics and money and be practical and effective.

If one is living in a money economy, then bills are solved by having far more than "enough money" and not spending it foolishly. One gets far more than "enough money" by understanding the principles of EXCHANGE and applying them.

In another type of economy such as a socialist state, the principles still work.

The principles of exchange work continuously. It does not go high and collapse as in speculation or demanding money but failing to deliver. Or delivering and not demanding money.

We see around us examples that seem to violate these principles. But they are nervous and temporary.

What people or governments regard as a valuable service is sometimes incredible and what they will overlook as valuable is also incredible. This is why one has to use surveys—to find out what people want that you can deliver. Unless this is established then you find yourself in an exchange blockage. You can guess but until you actually find out, you can do very little about it.

Once you discover what people want that you *can* deliver you can go about increasing the demand or widening it or making it more valuable, using standard public relations, advertising and merchandising techniques.

The fundamental is to realize that EXCHANGE is the basic problem.

Then and only then can one go about solving it.

HCO PL 6 March 1966
Rewards and Penalties
How to Handle Personnel and Ethics Matters

5
Rewards and Penalties

WHEN YOU REWARD DOWN STATISTICS AND PENALIZE UP STATISTICS YOU GET DOWN STATISTICS.

If you reward non-production you get non-production.

When you penalize production you get non-production.

The Welfare State can be defined as that state which rewards non-production at the expense of production. Let us not then be surprised that we all turn up at last slaves in a starved society.

Russia cannot even feed herself but depends on conquest to eke out an existence—and don't think they don't strip the conquered! They have to.

Oddly enough one of the best ways to detect a suppressive person is that he or she stamps on up statistics and condones or rewards down statistics. It makes an SP very happy for everyone to starve to death, for the good worker to be shattered and the bad worker patted on the back.

Draw your own conclusions as to whether or not Western governments (or Welfare States) became at last suppressives. For they used the law used by suppressives: If you reward non-production you get non-production.

Although all this is very obvious to us, it seems to have been unknown, overlooked or ignored by 20th Century governments.

In the conduct of our own affairs in all matters of rewards and penalties we pay sharp heed to the basic laws as above and use this policy:

We award production and up statistics and penalize non-production and down statistics. Always.

Also we do it *all* by statistics—not rumor or personality or who knows who. And we make sure every one has a statistic of some sort. We promote by statistic only. We penalize down statistics only.

We must learn and profit from what they did wrong. And what they mainly did wrong was reward the down statistic and penalize the up statistic.

The hard worker-earner was heavily taxed and the money was used to support the indigent. This was *not* humanitarian. It was only given "humanitarian" reasons.

The robbed person was investigated exclusively, rarely the robber.

The head of government who got into the most debt became a hero.

War rulers were deified and peacetime rulers forgotten no matter how many wars they prevented.

Thus went Ancient Greece, Rome, France, the British Empire and the U.S. *This* was the decline and fall of every great civilization on this planet: they eventually rewarded the down statistic and penalized the up statistic. That's *all* that caused their decline. They came at last into the hands of suppressives and had *no* technology to detect them or escape their inevitable disasters.

Never promote a down statistic or demote an up statistic.

But someone with a steadily down statistic, investigate. Accept and convert any Ethics chit to a hearing. Look for an early replacement.

Gruesomely, in my experience, I have only seldom raised a chronically down statistic with orders or persuasion or new plans. I have only raised them with changes of personnel.

So don't even consider someone with a steadily down statistic as part of the team. Investigate, yes. Try, yes. But if it stays down, don't fool about. The person is drawing pay and position and privilege for not doing his job and that's too much reward even there.

Don't get reasonable about down statistics. They are down because they are down. If someone was on the post they would be up. And act on that basis.

Any duress levelled should be reserved for down statistics.

The Volunteer Minister also investigates social areas of down statistics. Psychiatry's cures are zero. The negative statistic of more insane is all that is "up." So investigate and hang.

If we reverse the conduct of declining businesses we will of course grow. And that makes for coffee and cakes, promotion, higher pay, better working quarters and tools for all those who earned them. And who else should have them?

If you do it any other way, everyone starves. We are peculiar in believing there is a virtue in prosperity.

You cannot give more to the indigent than the society produces. When the society, by penalizing production, at last produces very little and yet has to feed very many, revolutions, confusion, political unrest and Dark Ages ensue.

In a very prosperous society where production is amply rewarded, there is always more left over than is needed. I well recall in prosperous farm communities that charity was ample and people didn't die in the ditch. That only happens where production is already low and commodity or commerce already scarce (scarcity of *commercial* means of distribution is also a factor in depressions).

If you reward non-production you get it.

It is *not* humanitarian to let a *whole* population go to pieces just because a few refuse to work. And some people just won't. And when work no longer has reward none will.

It is far more humane to have enough so everyone can eat.

So specialize in production and everybody wins. Reward it.

There is nothing really wrong with socialism helping the needy. Sometimes it is vital. But the reasons for that are more or less over. It is a temporary solution, easily overdone and like Communism, is simply old-fashioned today. If carried to extremes like drinking coffee or absinthe or even eating it becomes quite uncomfortable and oppressive. And today Socialism and Communism have been carried far too far and now only oppress up statistics and reward down ones.

By the way, the natural law in this section is the reason Scientology goes poorly when credit is extended by churches and when auditors won't charge properly. With credit and no charge we are rewarding down statistics with attention and betterment as much as we reward up statistics in the society. A preclear who can work and produces as a member of society deserves of course priority. He naturally is the one who can pay. When we give the one who can't pay just as much attention we are rewarding a down social statistic with Scientology and of course we don't expand because we don't expand the ability of the able. In proof, the most expensive thing you can do is process the insane and these have the lowest statistic in the society.

The more you help those in the society with low statistics the more tangled affairs will get. The churches require fantastic attention to keep them there at all when we reward low society statistics with training and processing. The worker pays his way. He has a high statistic. So give him the best in training and processing—not competition with people who don't work and don't have any money.

Always give the best service to the person in society who does his job. By not extending credit you tend to guarantee the best service to those with the best statistics and so everybody wins again. None is *owed* processing or training. We are not an earth-wide amends project.

No good worker *owes* his work. That's slavery.

We don't *owe* because we do *better*. One would owe only if one did worse.

If an average man adds up what he pays the government he will find *his* visits to medicos are *very* expensive. The one who benefits is only the chronically ill, whose way is paid by the healthy. So the chronically ill (down statistic) are rewarded with care paid for by penalties on the healthy (up statistic).

In income tax, the more a worker makes the more hours of his work week are taxed away from him. Eventually he is no longer working for his reward. He is working for no pay. If he got up to $500 a week the proportion of his pay (penalty) might go as high as half. Therefore people tend to refuse higher pay (up statistics) as it has a penalty that is too great. On the other hand a totally indigent non-working person is paid well just to loaf. The up statistic person cannot hire any small services to help his own prosperity as he is already paying it *via* the government to somebody who doesn't work.

Socialisms pay people *not* to grow crops no matter how many are starving. Get it?

So the law holds.

Charity is charity. It benefits the donor, giving him a sense of superiority and status. It is a liability to the receiver but he accepts it as he must and vows (if he has any pride) to cease being poor and get to work.

Charity cannot be enforced by law and arrest for then it is extortion and not charity.

Parasitism is parasitism. Whether high or low it is unlovely.

All these "isms" are almost equally nutty and their inheritors, if not their originators, were all of a stamp—suppressive.

All I beat the drum for is that the working worker deserves a break and the working manager deserves his pay and the successful company deserves the fruits of its success.

Only when success is bought by enslavement or rewards are given to bums or thieves will you find me objecting.

This is a new look. It is an honest look.

Reward the up statistic and condemn the down and we'll all make out.

HCO PL 4 April 1972
Establishment Officer
Series 14, *Ethics*

6 Criminality

Unless we want to go on living in a far nowhere, some of the facts of scenes have to be confronted.

An inability to confront evil leads people into disregarding it or discounting it or not seeing it at all.

Reversely, there can be a type of person who, like an old time preacher, sees nothing but evil in everything and, possibly looking into his own heart for a model, believes all men are evil.

Man, however, is basically good. When going upon some evil course he attempts to restrain himself and caves himself in.

The Chart of Human Evaluation in *Science of Survival* was right enough. And such people also can be found by the Oxford Capacity Analysis where the graph is low.

This sort of thing can be handled of course by auditing but the Volunteer Minister does not always depend on that alone to handle community problems.

Criminal actions proceed from such people *unless checked* by more duress from without not to do an evil act than they themselves have pressure from within to do it.

Criminality is in most instances restrained by just such an imbalance of pressures.

If you have no ethics presence, then criminality shows its head.

Such people lie rather than be made to confront. They false report—they even use "PR" which means Public Relations to cover up—and in our slang talk "PR" means putting up a lot of false reports to serve as a smoke screen for idleness or bad actions.

Unless you get ethics in, you will never get technology in. If you can't get technology in you won't get administration in.

So the lack of ethics permits the criminal impulse to go unchecked.

Yes, it could be handled with technology. But to get money you have to have administration in.

Unless there is ethics and ways to get it in, no matter how distasteful it may seem, you will never get technology and administration in.

Of course there is always the element of possible injustice. But this is provided against.

When ethics is being applied by criminal hands, it can get pretty grim.

But even then, ethics serves as a restraint to just outright slaughter.

Omitting to handle criminality can make one as guilty of the resulting crimes as if one committed them!

So criminality as a factor has to be handled.

Exchange

The unhatted, unproducing person, who is not really a criminal or psychotic can be made to go criminal.

This joins him to the criminal ranks.

The ethics system also applies to him.

However there is something a Volunteer Minister can do about it.

This lies in the field of EXCHANGE.

Exchange is something for something.

Criminal exchange is nothing from the criminal for something from another.

Whether theft or threat or fraud is used, the criminal think is to get something without putting out anything. That is obvious.

A person can be coaxed into this kind of thinking by PERMITTING HIM TO RECEIVE WITHOUT HIS CONTRIBUTING.

This unlocks, by the way, an age-old riddle of the philosophers as to "what is right or wrong."

HONESTY is the road to SANITY. You can prove that and do prove it every time you make somebody well by "pulling his withholds." The insane are just one seething mass of overt acts and withholds. And they are very physically sick people.

When you let somebody be dishonest you are setting him up to become physically ill and unhappy.

When you let a person give nothing for something you are factually encouraging crime.

Don't be surprised that welfare districts are full of robbery and murder. People there give nothing for something.

When *exchange* is out, the whole social balance goes out.

Every full scholarship ever given by a church wound up in a messy scene.

When you hire a professional preclear who just sits around making do-less motions while people audit him and contribute to him, DO NOT BE SURPRISED IF HE GETS SICKER AND SICKER.

He is contributing nothing in return and winds up in overwhelm!

Similarly if you actively prevented someone from contributing in return you could also make him ARC broken and sick.

It is EXCHANGE which maintains the inflow and outflow that gives a person space around him and keeps the bank off him.

There are numbers of ways these flows of exchange can be unbalanced.

It does not go same out as comes in. Equal amounts are no factor. Who can measure good will or friendship? Who can actually calculate the value of saving a being from death in each life time? Who can measure the reward of pride in doing a job well or praise?

For all these things are of different values to different people.

In the material world the person whose exchange factor is out, may think he "makes money." Only a government or a counterfeiter "makes money." One has to produce something to *exchange* for money.

Right there the exchange factor is out.

If he gives nothing in return for what he gets, the money does not belong to him.

It is interesting that when a person becomes productive his morale improves.

Reversely it should be rather plain to you that a person who doesn't produce becomes mentally or physically ill. For his *exchange* factor is out.

So when you reward a downstat you not only deprive upstats, you also cave the downstat in!

I don't think welfare states have anything else in mind!

The riots of the ancient city of Rome were caused by these factors. There they gave away corn and games to a populace that eventually became so savage it could only enjoy torture and gruesome death in the arena!

A lot of this exchange imbalance comes from child psychology where the child is not contributing anything and is not permitted to contribute.

It is this which first overwhelms him with feelings of obligation to his parents and then bursts out as total revolt in his teens.

Children who are permitted to contribute (not as a cute thing to do but actually) make noncontributing children of the same age look like raving maniacs! It is the cruel sadism of modern times to destroy the next generation this way. Don't think it isn't intended. I have examined the OCAs of parents who do it!

So if a person is brought up this life with the exchange all awry, the parents and the Volunteer Minister have their hands full sometimes!

He is dealing with trained-in criminality!

What You Can Do

The remedy is rather simple.

First one has to know all about EXCHANGE as covered in Section 4.

Then you have to specially clear this up with people who do not produce.

You should get them to work on it as it relates to ALL THEIR DYNAMICS IN RELATIONSHIP TO EVERY OTHER DYNAMIC.

That means you have to clear up the definitions of dynamics with *care* and then have the person draw a big chart (of his own) and say what he gives the first dynamic and what it gives him. Then what he gives the second dynamic and what it gives him. And so on up the dynamics.

Now, have him consider "his own second dynamic." What does his second dynamic give his first dynamic? What does his second dynamic give the second dynamic and what does it give him?

And so on until you have a network of these exchange arrows, each both ways.

Somewhere along the way, if your TRs are good and you have his attention and he is willing to talk to you he will have quite a cognition!

That, if it's a big one is the end phenomena of it.

And don't be surprised if you see a person now and then change his physical face shape!

Conditions by Dynamics

An ethics type "action" can be done by giving the person the conditions formulas.

Pick up any misunderstoods in the table of conditions (in Section 8).

Have the person study the *formula* of each of these conditions in the table so that he knows what they are and what the formulas are.

When he has all this now with no misunderstood words you must clear up the words related to his dynamics 1 to 8 and what they are.

Now you're ready for the billion dollar question.

Ask him what is his condition on the first dynamic. Have him study the formulas. Don't buy any glib PR.

Don't evaluate or invalidate. When he's completely sure of what his condition really is on the first dynamic he will cognite.

Now take up the second dynamic by its parts—sex, family, children. Get a condition for each.

Similarly go on up each one of the dynamics until you have a condition for each one.

Now begin with the first dynamic again.

Continue to work this way.

You will be amazed to find he will come out of false high down to low and back up again *on each dynamic*.

Somewhere along the line he will start to change markedly.

When you have a person in continual heavy ethics or who is out-ethics (ethics bait, we say) and who is floundering around, you can do an S & D on him and quite often save his future for him.

When you have such a person you do this one first before you do the Exchange by Dynamics.

In other words, you use this on "ethics bait" and then when he's come out of such, you do Exchange by Dynamics on him.

Summary

When all looks black, and you are getting false reports, and the things said done were not done and what was really being done were overt products and despite all your work, the stats just *won't* go up, you still have three answers:

(1) GET IN ETHICS.

(2) GET EXCHANGE DONE ON INDIVIDUALS.

(3) GET IN CONDITIONS BY DYNAMICS ON THE ETHICS BAIT.

You'll be amazed!

7 The Volunteer Minister, His Character

HCO PL 7 December 1969, Issue II, The Ethics Officer His Character

If a person has no confidence in his Volunteer Minister, his morale is difficult to sustain.

A safe environment is a productive environment. An unsafe environment is an empty hall.

Ethics Functions

The TECHNICAL fact is the data we have about SUPPRESSIVES. There are very few of these in proportion to decent people. That one fact is something this society's police don't know. According to extant social technology ALL people are basically bad and are only made "good" through punishment. So everyone everywhere has to be threatened. That's extant technology. It doesn't work. The crime rate soars so obviously the know-how isn't to be found out "there." People are all animals, "they" say and must be herded. Well that's the "modern social scientist's" nutty idea. Society does not know that all they'd have to do is round up their few SPs and they'd have no crime. Instead whenever they arrest criminals they prove to these that society is brutal and crime justified and just let them loose again. They don't straighten SPs up because the "social scientist," the psychologist and psychiatrist are at this writing at least mainly SPs themselves and haven't any technology but the club.

So the Volunteer Minister must understand at once that he is dealing with a new, highly precise technology. It is the technology of ethics. A meter and a knowledge of the technology on SPs and case types and PTS phenomena and you can identify an SP promptly. He makes things go wrong, hurts people, oppresses. Around him all the right actions vanish and the wrong actions appear.

Now because he or she can make others go PTS, then THEY make mistakes.

So you get a whole group making things go wrong.

The Volunteer Minister, knowing his ethics technology, can sort out the group, find the real SP, remove him or depower him and zingo the group will rebound and do great.

Careful investigation by the Volunteer Minister (and he has very exact procedures) discloses the source or sources of the trouble. He verifies all against the person's statistics.

If he is right, the scene straightens right out. If the Volunteer Minister is wrong in his investigation and action, things will get worse, i.e., statistics will go down. So he can do it all over again, exhume the body he incorrectly shot, apologize and now find the real SP!

So ethics has its own technology, very superior technology indeed.

Ethics could clean up a whole nation and make it boom, using its technology correctly.

As ethics is a powerful technology, an uninformed Volunteer Minister who thinks he is a sort of KGB—local cop—FBI—Scotland Yard sure has missed the point. They are (or are at this writing) total failures as witness the condemnation of crime statistics in their areas. They are simply oppressive terror symbols. They take psychiatric advice and get psychiatric results. The end product is mutiny and revolution by the population.

When you threaten the whole population you get riot and civil commotion. When you have riot and civil commotion the police are threatening (because of lack of ethics technology) the whole population whereas less than 10%, even as little as 1% are bad hats.

Suppressive Reasonableness

The greatest enemy of the Volunteer Minister is the reasonable person. There are no good reasons for any outnesses except:

(a) Natural catastrophes (such as earthquakes, lightning, etc.);

(b) Suppressive persons;

(c) Persons who are PTS to suppressive persons.

When a person starts to explain the "reasons" for low statistics instead of working to get high statistics he is being reasonable.

When Joe Blow has just smashed his fifth typewriter and the executive starts to explain how he's just a good boy gone a bit ARC breaky, she is being "reasonable." He's either an SP or he's PTS to someone.

The explanation is the answer to the Volunteer Minister's WHO, not the executive's WHY.

Reasonableness is suppressive since it lets oppression continue without action being taken.

Suppressive reasonableness is a common trait. It comes from THE INABILITY TO CONFRONT EVIL.

Evil takes a bit of confronting.

People who want desperately to "have no trouble" often won't confront and handle trouble.

Murder is murder. It occurs. A murder is not a frightened wish it had not occurred. It occurred. Somebody did it. There's the body.

Psychiatrists, for instance, have two major types in their ranks, both psychopathic. One is a theetie weetie who thinks all criminals are poor abused things and the other is himself a criminal psychopath who turns criminals loose on the society just to get even with people for his own fancied wrongs. Tracing several major crimes it can be found that the violent criminal was in the hands of a psychiatrist earlier and told him his intentions yet was let loose on society.

Such a criminal—a rapist, a murderer—can't be helped by psychiatry. But that isn't the point. Decent people died and some died horribly. That doesn't make a very safe environment, does it?

It is true that we could straighten this criminal out if we could keep him out of circulation for awhile. It is true the criminal is in trouble, BUT IT IS ALSO TRUE THAT HE COMMITS CRIMES.

So a Volunteer Minister doesn't want somebody in circulation in a group or a society who commits crimes.

The job of the Volunteer Minister is to disconnect and de-power the criminal and so protect the group.

The criminal, the SP (same thing) is TRYING TO GET EVEN WITH PEOPLE. That's his common denominator. He does it by covert omissions or overt violence. It all amounts to the same thing.

The Volunteer Minister works for from 90% to 99% of the group, not for the 1%.

When the Volunteer Minister has done his duty to the group he can then take up the individual. I always handle things in that order:

1. Safeguard the group.
2. Rehabilitate the individual.

You will have a mess if you only do one or the other or try to rehabilitate the individual criminal without safeguarding the group.

In actual practice you safeguard the group by removing or isolating the individual. Then you see what can be done for the individual to rehabilitate him *without* endangering the group in any way.

A Volunteer Minister can be used by an SP (with false reports or stupid orders) to needle and hurt a group. The duty of the Volunteer Minister is plain. Follow your technology.

A Volunteer Minister can be paralyzed when persons will not let him do his job either because they don't understand it or because they are suppressive. The statistics tell which one.

Volunteer Minister Conduct

A Volunteer Minister should never discuss people who are merely under investigation or act in a way to third party people. (See glossary for "third party.") A Volunteer Minister gets the *facts* and then acts.

A Volunteer Minister should himself have very high ethical standards.

A Volunteer Minister should act like a shepherd not a wolf. When the facts are in plain view he or she should act like a panther with one straight pounce.

A Volunteer Minister who is an efficient Volunteer Minister is *very* popular with the community. If he or she knows his business and carries it out effectively, the Volunteer Minister easily becomes a local hero.

A Volunteer Minister shouldn't permit a person to be nagged, threatened or given floods of ethics conditions. When he sees these things occurring he knows it's time to investigate for WHO has got people PTS and handle without other orders.

When a Volunteer Minister sees big efforts being spent on trying to get ex-wolves back into the fold he investigates for the source of the effort and having found it finds out WHO and WHY.

A Volunteer Minister trying to handle a long history of down statistics and trouble should look first only at those who have been in the area throughout the trouble period. One or more will be SP or PTS but good.

A Volunteer Minister who has had an area all calm but suddenly sees it roughed up should look only at those who came into it since it went bad.

A Volunteer Minister is only trying to make a safe environment in which people can work happily and good service is being given to the public.

A Volunteer Minister in the final analysis is answerable to me that all is well and secure with his area.

HCO PL 14 March 1968
Corrected Table of Conditions
HCO PL 9 February 1974
Ethics Condition Below Treason
HCO PL 16 October 1968
Formula for the Condition of Treason
HCO PL 23 October 1967
Enemy Formula
HCO PL 6 October 1967
Condition of Liability
HCO PL 9 April 1972
Ethics Correct Danger Condition Handling
Tape Lecture 6505C25
SH SPEC 62
The Five Conditions
*BPL 27 April 1974
Power Formulas, First and Third Dynamics

8 Conditions

A condition is an operating state, and oddly enough in the physical universe there are several formulas connected with these operating states. There are apparently certain formulas which have to be followed in this universe or you go appetite over tin cup.

It will be seen that an individual, organization or any group in any one of these *lower* conditions have counter-intentions or other-intentions. The assignment of one of these conditions to an individual or activity and the insistence upon application of these formulas is a basic tool of anyone administering justice.

The following is the complete table of conditions:

Power
Power change
Affluence
Normal operation
Emergency

Danger
Nonexistence
Liability
Doubt
Enemy
Treason
Confusion

Power is the top of the table. An individual or group in any of the lower states can move up the table with correct application of the formulas to handle these conditions. Completion of the formula for a condition moves one up to the next condition and then that formula must also be applied.

In Scientology churches, these conditions are assigned and the formulas are written up with a separate request for upgrade to the next condition.

The Volunteer Minister, in his duty of counseling, may counsel the individual or activity gradiently through the formulas by giving them one step at a time to do until the entire formula is completed or he may give the formula to the person and guide him through to upgrade to a high condition. It is up to the Volunteer Minister to determine which gradient to use.

Confusion

The lowest of these conditions is *confusion*. The formula of the condition is: FIND OUT WHERE *YOU* ARE.

The additional formula for the condition of confusion is:

1. Locational assist on the area in which one is. (To be done by the volunteer minister.)

2. Comparing where one is to other areas where one was.

3. Repeat step 1.

Lack of this condition sometimes brings about an assignment of *Treason* in which the person cannot actually apply the formula and so occasionally does not make it on up the conditions.

Many more persons are in the condition of *confusion* than is generally realized.

Treason

Treason is defined as betrayal after trust. The formula for the condition of *treason* is: FIND OUT THAT YOU ARE.

Enemy

When a person is an avowed and knowing enemy of an individual, a group, project or organization, a condition of *enemy* exists. The formula for the condition of *enemy* is just one step: FIND OUT WHO YOU REALLY ARE.

Doubt

When one cannot make up one's mind as to an individual, a group, organization or project a condition of *doubt* exists.

The formula is:

1. Inform oneself honestly of the actual intentions and activities of that individual, group, project or organization brushing aside all bias and rumor.
2. Examine the statistics of the individual, group, project or organization.
3. Decide on the basis of "the greatest good for the greatest number of dynamics" whether or not it should be attacked, harmed or suppressed or helped.
4. Evaluate oneself or one's own group, project or organization as to intentions and objectives.
5. Evaluate one's own or one's group, project or organization's statistics.
6. Join or remain in or befriend the one which progresses toward the greatest good for the greatest number of dynamics and announce the fact publicly to both sides.
7. Do everything possible to improve the actions and statistics of the person, group, project or organization one has remained in or joined.
8. Suffer on up through the conditions in the new group if one has changed sides, or the conditions of the group one has remained in if wavering from it has lowered one's status.

Liability

When the being has ceased to be simply nonexistent as a team member and has taken on the color of an enemy, a condition of *liability* exists.

Liability is assigned where careless or malicious and knowing damage is caused to projects, organizations or activities. It is adjudicated that it is malicious and knowing because orders have been published against it or because it is contrary to the intentions and actions of the remainder of the team or the purpose of the project or organization.

It is a *liability* to have such a person unwatched as the person may do or continue to do things to stop or impede the forward progress of the project or organization and such a person cannot be trusted. No discipline or the assignment of conditions above it has been of any avail. The person has just kept on messing it up.

The condition is usually assigned when several *danger* conditions and *nonexistence* conditions have been assigned or when a long unchanged pattern of conduct has been detected.

When all others are looking for the reason mail is getting lost, such a being would keep on losing the mail covertly.

The condition is assigned for the benefit of others so they won't get tripped up trusting the person in any way.

The formula of *Liability* is:

1. Decide who are one's friends.
2. Deliver an effective blow to the enemies of the group one has been pretending to be part of despite personal danger.
3. Make up the damage one has done by personal contribution far beyond the ordinary demands of a group member.
4. Apply for re-entry to the group by asking the permission of each member of it to rejoin and rejoining only by majority permission, and if refused, repeating (2) and (3) and (4) until one is allowed to be a group member again.

Non-Existence

Every new appointee to a post begins in a condition of *non-existence.* Whether obtained by new appointment, promotion or demotion.

He is normally under the delusion that now he is "THE__________ (new title)." He tries to start off in a power condition as he is usually very aware of his new status or even a former status. But in actual fact *he* is the only one aware of it. All others except perhaps the personnel officer are utterly unaware of him as having his new status.

Therefore he begins in a state of non-existence. And if he does not begin with the non-existence formula as his guide he will be using the wrong condition and will have all kinds of trouble:

The non-existence formula is:

1. Find a comm line
2. Make yourself known
3. Discover what is needed or wanted.
4. Do, produce and/or present it.

A new appointee taking over a going concern often thinks he had better make himself known by changing everything whereas he (a) is not well enough known to do so and, (b) hasn't any idea of what is needed or wanted yet. And so he makes havoc.

Sometimes he assumes he knows what is needed or wanted when it is only a fixed idea with him and is only his idea and not true at all and so he fails at his job.

Sometimes he doesn't bother to find out what is really needed or wanted and simply assumes it or thinks he knows when he doesn't. He soon becomes "unsuccessful."

Now and then a new appointee is so "status happy" or so insecure or so shy that even when his boss or his staff come to him and tell him what is needed or wanted he can't or doesn't even acknowledge and really does go into non-existence for keeps.

Sometimes he finds that what he is *told* is needed or wanted needs reappraisal or further investigation. So it is always safest for him to make his own survey of it and operate on it when he gets his own firm reality on what is needed or wanted.

If the formula is applied intelligently the person can expect to get into a zone of by-pass where people are still doing his job to fill the hole his predecessor may have left. This is a danger condition—but it is the next one higher than non-existence on the scale.

If he *defends his job* and *does his job* and then applies the first dynamic danger formula he will come through it.

He can then expect to find himself in emergency condition. In this he must follow the emergency formula and he will come through *it.*

He can now expect to be in normal operation and if he follows the formula of that, he will come to affluence, and if he follows *that* formula he will arrive at power. And if he applies the power formula he will stay there.

Danger

There are two formulas for the *danger* condition. One is for the senior terminal or the volunteer minister. The second formula is for first dynamic handling (by the individual).

When the correct formula for handling a *danger* condition is not done, an organization or activity or person cannot easily get above that condition thereafter.

A prolonged state of emergency or threats to viability or survival or a prolonged single-handing will not improve unless the actual *danger* formula is applied.

A *danger* condition is normally assigned when:

1. An emergency condition has continued too long.

2. A statistic plunges downward very steeply.

3. A senior executive suddenly finds himself or herself doing the duties of the activity because it is in trouble.

Most failures on post are occasioned by failures to follow the conditions and reorganize them and apply the formula of the condition one is in when one is in it and cease to apply it when one is out of it and in another.

The senior terminal present acts and acts according to the formula below.

1. By-pass (ignore the junior or juniors normally in charge of the activity and handle it personally).

2. Handle the situation and any danger in it.

3. Assign the area where it had to be handled a *danger* condition.

4. Handle the personnel by ethics investigation.

5. Reorganize the activity so that the situation does not repeat.

6. Recommend any firm policy that will hereafter detect and/or prevent the condition from recurring.

Ethics is a personal thing in relation to a group. Unethical people are those who do not have ethics in on themselves personally.

Dishonesty, false reports, an out-ethics personal life should be looked for and by persuasion should be corrected.

When an executive or the volunteer minister sees such things he or she must do all he can to get the person to get his own ethics in.

When an area is downstat the executive must at once suspect an out-ethics scene with one or more of the personnel and must investigate and persuade the person to be more honest and ethical and correct the out-ethics condition found.

IT IS VITAL TO ANY ORGANIZATION, TO BE STRONG AND EFFECTIVE, TO BE ETHICAL.

THE MOST IMPORTANT ZONE OF ETHICAL CONDUCT IN AN ORGANIZATION IS AT OR NEAR THE TOP.

Ethical failure at the top or just below it can destroy an organization and make it downstat.

Historical examples are many.

Out-ethics offenses are composed of

1. DISHONESTY

2. Use of false statements to cover up a situation.

3. Representing a scene to be different than it actually is to cover up crimes and escape discipline.

4. Irregular second dynamic connections and practices.

5. Drug or alcoholic addiction.

6. Encouraging out-ethics.

7. Condoning or failing to effectively handle an out-ethics situation in self or others as an in-charge, officer, manager or executive.

People with out-ethics withholds cannot see. This is proven by the brilliant return of perception of the environment in people audited effectively and at length on such processes.

Such people also seek to place a false environment there and actually see a false environment.

People whose ethics are low will enturbulate and upset a group as they are seeking to justify their harmful acts against the group. And this leads to more harmful acts.

Out-ethics people go rapidly into Treason against the group.

Happiness is only attained by those who are HONEST with themselves and others.

A group prospers only when each member in it has his own personal ethics in.

Even in a PTS (potential trouble source) person there must have been out-ethics conduct toward the suppressive personality he or she is connected with for the person to have become PTS in the first place.

People who are physically ill are PTS *and are out-ethics* toward the person or thing they are PTS to!

Thus a group to be happy and well, and for the group to prosper and endure, its individual members must have their own ethics in.

It is up to the executive or officer to see that this is the case and to DO the actions necessary to make it come about and the group an ethical group.

This is the First Dynamic Danger Formula to be used on the out-ethics person.

Step one: Inform the person personally he is in Danger condition by reason of acts or omissions, downstats, false reports or absence or Second Dynamic or whatever the circumstances are.

He is in fact IN danger because somebody is going to act sooner or later to penalize him.

He may be involved already in some other assignment of condition.

But this is between you and him.

HE IS IN DANGER BECAUSE YOU ARE HAVING TO BY-PASS HIM TO GET HIS ETHICS IN, A THING HE SHOULD DO HIMSELF.

If he cooperates and completes this formula and it comes out all right you will help him.

If he doesn't cooperate you will have to use group justice procedures.

This is his chance to get ethics in on himself with your help before he really crashes.

When he accepts this fact, step 1 is done. Go to step 2.

Step 2.

Ethics is gotten in by definition on the person.

GET IN THE DEFINITIONS FULLY UNDERSTOOD.

The following words must be thoroughly understood. Use a dictionary for any words in the definitions not understood.

"ETHICS: The study of the general nature of morals (morals (plural) (noun): *The principles of right and wrong conduct*) *and the specific moral choices to be made by the individual in his relationship with others.*

"The rules or standards governing the conduct of the members of a profession."

"JUSTICE: 1. Moral rightness; equity. 2. Honor, fairness. 3. Good reason. 4. Fair handling: due reward or treatment. 5. *The administration and procedure of the law.*"

"FALSE: Contrary to fact or truth; without grounds; incorrect. Without meaning or sincerity; deceiving. Not keeping faith. Treacherous. Resembling and being identified as a similar or related entity."

"DISHONEST: Disposed to lie, cheat, defraud or deceive."

"PRETENSE: A false reason or excuse. A mere show without reality."

"BETRAY: To be disloyal or faithless to."

"OUT-ETHICS: An action or situation in which an individual is involved contrary to the ideals and best interests of his group. An act or situation or relationship contrary to the ethics standards, codes or ideals of the group or other members of the group. An act of omission or commission by an individual that could or has reduced the general effectiveness of a group or its other members. An individual act of omission or commission which impedes the general well-being of a group or impedes it in achieving its goals."

Do not go on until all the above words are well understood without any question or confusion.

The person is now ready to apply the FIRST DYNAMIC DANGER FORMULA to himself.

Give him this formula and explain it to him.

First Dynamic Formula: The formula is converted for the first dynamic to:

1st 1. By-pass habits or normal routines.

1st 2. Handle the situation and any danger in it.

1st 3. Assign self a danger condition.

1st 4. Get in your own *personal ethics* by finding what you are doing that is out-ethics and use self-discipline to correct it and get honest and straight.

1st 5. Reorganize your life so that the dangerous situation is not continually happening to you.

1st 6. Formulate and adopt firm policy that will hereafter detect and prevent the same situation from continuing to occur.

Now usually the person is already involved in another *group* situation of downstats or overt products or bad appearance or low conditions for something.

It does not matter what other condition he was in. From you he is in *Danger.*

So 1st 1. and 1st 2. above apply to the *group* situation he finds himself in.

He has to assign *himself* a Danger condition as he recognizes now he has been in Danger from himself.

1st 4. has been begun by this formula.

It is up to him or her to finish off 1st 4. by applying the material in steps 2 and 3. He or she has to use self-discipline to correct his own out-ethics scene and get it honest and straight, with himself and his group.

1st 5. is obvious. If he doesn't, he will just crash again.

1st 6. In formulating and adopting firm policy he must be sure it aligns with the group endeavor.

When he has worked all this out AND DEMONSTRATED IT IN LIFE, he has completed the personal Danger Formula.

He can then assign himself Emergency and follow the Emergency formula.

Then review the person and his stats and appearance and personal life.

Satisfy yourself that the steps above and the out-ethics found were all of it. That no wrong out-ethics situation has been found, that the person is not PTS. Handle what you find.

If the person made it and didn't fall on his head and is moving on up now AS SHOWN BY HONEST STATISTICS AND CONDITION

OF HIS JOB AND LIFE, you have had a nice win and things will go much, much better.

And that's a win for everybody.

Emergency

Emergency is the next condition up from *danger*. There is a certain way that you handle an emergency. An *emergency* status is declared simply and only by a down statistic; that is to say, the statistics went down. It doesn't matter what statistics, if they were supposed to go up and they went down, that's an emergency.

The reverse can take place. Suppose the number of students on a course keeps going up and up and it doesn't go down. Then obviously the students aren't being graduated from the course at the same rate they're being put into the course so there must be a slowdown on that course of some kind or another. That will create a state of emergency too. So the *desirable statistic* has not been attained. The statistic which should go down goes up, or the statistic which should go up goes down.

The formula for the condition of *emergency* is:

1. Promote, that applies to an organization. To an individual you had better say produce. That's the first action regardless of any other action. That is the first thing you have to put their attention on. The first broad big action which you take is promote. Exactly what is promotion? It is making things known, it is getting things out, it is getting one's self known, getting one's products out.

2. Change your operating basis. If for instance you went into a condition of emergency and then you didn't make any changes in your operation, well you just head for another condition of emergency.

So that has to be part of it. You had better do something to change the operating basis because that operating basis led you into an emergency.

3. Economize.

4. Then prepare to deliver.

5. Part of the condition of emergency contains this little line—you have got to stiffen discipline or ethics because life itself is going to discipline the individual.

So the rule of the game is that if a state of emergency is ignored and the steps are not taken successfully then you get an announcement after a while that the condition has been continued and if the condition is continued beyond a specified time, why that's it.

Normal

The state of *normal* operation is the next condition and is supposed to be just "normal operation." You could call it a condition of stability and it probably should be called a condition of stability except for this one little factor. This universe does not admit of a *static* state, it won't admit a *no-increase, no-decrease.* You cannot have a condition in this universe where there is no increase and no decrease. That's a totally stable condition; there is no such thing in this universe from one end of it to the other. There isn't anything that always remains the same.

Take some of the hardest substances there are like plutonium and some other such elements; those things diminish or explode. Look at the lead on some churches sometime and you'll find that it's diminishing. As hardy as this element is supposed to be it still diminishes.

The condition of normal operation, then, is *not* one of stability and therefore I've not called it stability because it can't be. Normal operation must be a *routine or gradual increase.* If there is no gradual increase there will not be a condition of stability. You cannot have a total, even state of existence which does not eventually fall on its head. The second you get this *even* state in this universe it starts to deteriorate. So a state of stability would eventually deteriorate. To prevent a deterioration you must have an increase. That increase doesn't have to be spectacular but it has to be something.

The formula for a normal condition is as follows:

1. The way you maintain an increase is when you are in a state of normal operation you don't change anything.

2. Ethics are very mild, the justice factor is quite mild, there are no savage actions taken particularly.

3. A statistic betters then look it over carefully and find out what bettered it and then do that without abandoning what you were doing before.

4. Every time a statistic worsens slightly, quickly find out why and remedy it.

And you just jockey those two factors, the statistic bettering, the statistic worsening; repair the statistic worsening, and you will find out inevitably some change has been made in that area where a statistic worsens. Some change has been made, you had better get that change off the lines in a hurry.

Affluence

There is the next condition known as *affluence.* This is one of the most dangerous conditions and nobody recognizes it as such. Take some fellow out of the south side of the northeast side of lower Chicago. He had always gone along with twenty-five cents in his pocket. That is about the most money he ever had in his pocket. All of a sudden he gets in a crap game and he wins $10,000. The first impulse somebody gets when they get that much money is to get very rich indeed. So what does this fellow in south Chicago's lower north side do? He buys himself a house, the future payments of which are going to be $175 a month. He buys himself a car, the future payments of which are going to be several hundred dollars a month. He's got all the down payments for these things. He buys himself a watch and a bunch of clothes that he doesn't need. He neglects to pay off anybody that he owes, then his $10,000 is gone. He now owes another $20,000 and he hasn't got a prayer of paying that off. He has violated the condition of *affluence.*

The formula is:

1. Economize. Now the first thing you must do in affluence is economize and then make very, very sure that you don't buy anything that has any future commitment to it, don't buy with any future commitments—nothing. That is all part of that economy, clamp it down.

2. Pay every bill. Get every bill that you can possibly scrape up from any place, every penny you owe anywhere under the sun, moon and stars and pay them.

3. Invest the remainder in service facilities, make it more possible to deliver.

4. Discover what caused the condition of affluence and strengthen it.

In affluence, you must have been doing something awfully right to get in that much money. You have to discover what it is. That's the search that you go into at its proper numbered slot. Search and overhaul anything you have been doing and review it all for what caused this.

Power Change

Above affluence there is the state of *power change.*

Mr. Sykes has been promoted to the main central bank and he has left the branch bank where he was very successful. His job is taken over by Bill Smithers. Bill Smithers moves into the little local branch position and "the new broom sweeps clean." He violates the formula almost always. It just seems to be sewn into his makeup. He makes changes! The little bank must have been doing all right if its boss was able to take off and become a manager of a bigger bank. If the little bank was doing all right and if it was in a state of normal operation which it normally would have been in for anybody to have been promoted out of it, life is a beautiful song for Bill Smithers if he follows the right condition formula and that's perfectly easy. You just *don't change anything.* In *power change,* don't change anything.

It applies to the individual on the basis that the new manager of this little district bank, Bill Smithers, had been previously the chief cashier, and he has had a power change. He has gone from chief cashier to manager of the little local bank. What do people normally do when they run into this situation? The wife has to have a bigger house and they have to have a better car, that's obvious. He's got to be the part. He has to have better clothes to live up to this. He has to have a better front, and they have to have more social affairs and make more social contacts. He runs up a nice bill of expenses on entertainment. But if it were only that, it would simply be the *individual* violating it. But he goes ahead and violates the formula for the bank also.

It has always irritated him, the fact that he has had to say "Good morning, sir" when the former manager came in. So when he comes in he doesn't let his new chief cashier say, "Good morning, sir." He decides that he had better be met in the office with most of the papers of the day. The chief cashier has to be in the office with the papers. The manager never gets a chance then even to hang up his hat. He's hit with all the papers, and he gets all the chit-chat of the bank before he can even breathe.

This makes him a little bit sore and he gets mean to people in his immediate vicinity and spoils the morale. People make a few more mistakes than they ordinarily would have made in adding up the figures. He also decides he had better change the tea break time. This is a big change and there's another change, and there's another change; the new broom is busy sweeping a bank clean of being any bank.

What a song it is to inherit a pair of successful boots. There is nothing to it. Just step in the boots and don't bother to walk. But this is somehow or another considered by people reprehensible. You're supposed to strike out on your own, you're supposed to put your own personality on, etc. etc. *Put on the boots but don't walk, man.*

After you have been around for a while, immediately all of the pressure points in the organization are going to come to you at once. The fellow who had it before had all these pressure points too, but he must have resisted them successfully because they still exist. So if anybody wants anything signed that your predecessor didn't sign, don't sign it. That's an easy rule to follow. This absolutely is the laziest position that anybody ever occupied and that's the only way it can be occupied—with total laziness. Don't do anything.

Keep your eyes open, learn the ropes and depending on how big the organization is, after a certain time, see how it's running and run it as normal operating condition if it's not in anything but a normal operating condition.

Besides the little routine that's done, snoop around and find out what made it a little bit better that week, and reinforce that. Find out what worsened it a little and take that out. By that time you're so well acquainted with the operation, you now know everybody by his first and last names. You know where all the papers are and you know the favorite dodges. The operation will just keep on moving on up. It would move ahead very successfully.

Quite normally there are only two kinds of replacements, only two circumstances, not conditions which require replacement: *the very successful one* or *the very unsuccessful one.*

Now Mr. Sykes in operating the bank had operated under normal operating conditions, coped with all of its emergencies, didn't go blooey in all the affluences and he finally had assumed a position of *power* in the eyes of his own superiors. The operation was running so well, he'd actually found himself in a position of power and the reason he got promoted was of course he'd outgrown the zone that power matched, so they moved him up to a higher power position. Quite elementary in its actual look. He'd inevitably move up to a higher power position anyway; when he does so he would leave of course an operation which was in a position of power. Quite normally when the fellow was promoted creditably then the organization he left behind must have been in a condition of power.

The fellow who walks into the boots of somebody who has left it in disgrace is in an entirely different position. Very often there are two or three replacements before they finally stabilize it because every one of these guys will use a wrong formula. Maybe in the last job they had they inherited a condition of normal operation, and they found out they didn't have to do anything and it all came off all right. So the next one they inherit is in a condition of emergency—its statistics have gone down badly causing the boss to be fired. So they decided not to do anything! When he inherits one in emergency he's got to do nothing extraordinary, he just applies the state of emergency formula to it, which is immediately promote! The statistic is down.

Power

The condition above power change is of course the condition of *power.* The first step of the power formula is *don't disconnect.* You'll find out that people complain about this.

George has been a local boy in some town and all of a sudden he becomes a big boy. He's highly powerful on Wall Street. Then he never again speaks to any of his friends in the old hometown. Those people resent that. That is so much the matter of the thing that I can tell you personally that it's almost impossible to speak to them. If you've been in an area where you've been very well known and you suddenly become a celebrity or something like that, these people won't believe that you want to talk to them. They're so used to having the formula violated.

You'll find out there are certain people around who are now absolutely sure that you don't any longer want to talk to them. In other words, beings in the universe fully expect that you're going to violate the first position of the power condition. They think you're going to disconnect. In a position of power, *don't disconnect.* Even though you're promoted to general from colonel of the regiment, don't be such a fool as to think that you can totally disconnect from that regiment. Because the only way you *can't disconnect* from the regiment is to disconnect from it. You can't just deny your connections. What you've got to do is take *ownership* and *responsibility* for your *connections.*

Now the condition of power is the guy or the organization *going into* a condition of power. The condition of power change is that state of someone actually *assuming* a condition which has been held from power. There is a difference. You're replacing Bill who was in a condition of power. Now when he moves off, disconnects, then the *power change* is "*Who took over?*"

The assumption of this state of power is governed by its own formula. The second thing you have to do is make a record of all of the lines of the post and that's the only way you will ever be able to disconnect.

For instance, if you were a very successful receptionist in an organization and you were so successful that you were made the manager's secretary, the person who takes over the receptionist post won't be able to operate it in a condition of power change unless you make a total record of the post. So in a condition of power, you have to *write up your whole post.* You'll find out if you don't write up your whole post you're going to be stuck with a piece of that post till time immemorial. A year or so later somebody will still be coming to you asking you about that post you occupied because you didn't write it up. So you make it possible for the next person in to occupy the post. Whether he does it or not is beside the point, but you made it possible for the next guy in to assume that state of power change, of changing nothing because you've shown him what was there so that he knows now what not to change.

If you don't write it up then he could change it and you will be pulled back to that post continuously and that's the surest way in the world to be snapped in against some old post that you have held and that's how never to get away from the post. Just don't write up the post of receptionist, go ahead and take the post of secretary and don't be very surprised, however, if you spend fifty percent of your time answering the telephone while being a secretary.

The responsibility is write everything up and get it into the hands of the person who is going to take care of it. Now if that person doesn't take care of it, that's his track, that's not yours. Do all you can to make the post occupiable. Sooner or later somebody's going to come along and occupy the post properly.

Third Dynamic Power Formula

1. Life is lived by lots of people. And if you lead you must either let them get on with it or lead them on with it actively.

2. When the game or the show is over, there must be a new game or a new show. And if there isn't somebody else is jolly well going to start one and if you won't let *anyone* do it the game will become "getting you."

3. If you have power use it or delegate it or you sure won't have it long.

4. When you have people use them or they will soon become most unhappy and you won't have them any more.

5. When you move off a point of power, pay all your obligations on the nail, empower all your friends completely and move off with your pockets full of artillery, potential blackmail on every erstwhile rival, unlimited funds in your private account and go live in Bulgravia. And even then you may not live long if you have retained one scrap of domination in any camp you do not now control or if you even say, "I favor politician Jiggs." Abandoning power *utterly* is dangerous indeed.

6. When you're close to power get some delegated to you, enough to do your job and protect yourself and your interests, for you can be shot fellow, shot, as the position near power is delicious but dangerous, dangerous always, open to the taunts of any enemy of the power who dare not really boot the power but can boot you. So to live at all in the shadow or employ of a power you must yourself gather and USE enough power to hold your own—without just nattering to the power to "kill

Pete," in straightforward or more suppressive veiled ways to him as these wreck the power that supports yours. He doesn't have to know all the bad news and if he's a power really he won't ask.

7. And lastly and most important, for we all aren't on the stage with our names in lights, always push power in the direction of anyone on whose power you depend. It may be more money for the power, or more ease, or a snarling defense of the power to a critic.

If you work like that and the power you are near or depend upon is a power that has at least some inkling about how to be one, and if you make others work like that, then the power-factor expands and expands and expands and you too acquire a sphere of power bigger than you would have if you worked alone. Real powers are developed by tight conspiracies of this kind pushing someone up in whose leadership they have faith. And if they are right and also manage their man and keep him from collapsing through overwork, bad temper or bad data, a kind of Juggernaut builds up. Don't ever feel weaker because you work for somebody stronger. The only failure lies in taxing or pulling down the strength on which you depend. All failures to remain a power's power are failures to contribute to the strength and longevity of the work, health and power of that power. Devotion requires active contribution outwards from the power as well as in.

Summary

So one in his own personal life and in the operation of a post or state of an organization, the state of a family, the state of a civilization, or state of a planet or a sector, all come under the heading of the states of condition. If they're in one state of condition and operate into another they for sure will fail.

Contained in these is why empires become smaller. Every time they go into a state of emergency or a state of affluence, they assume the wrong formula. The second that they assume the wrong formula of course they would emerge at the other end of this situation smaller. That's always the case.

If you want to become smaller just always apply the wrong condition. Apply the wrong formula and you will shrink every time. You could probably set yourself up as a business advisory bureau and actually bring out of the woods any failing business in the world. You could set yourself up as an advisor just using these states and doing nothing but urge that they be taken.

Everything has to be *staticizable,* that is to say, you've got to be able to get a statistic on anything anywhere in an operation. If you can't, it's all on rumor. Maybe your own life is only in trouble because you don't staticize it. Very seldom does a clerk for instance ever look at his pay as a statistic. If some fellow for instance has been getting nothing but the same paycheck for the past two or three years that's a state of emergency. Although the statistic hasn't dwindled, that's the other way you can get into a state of emergency, because sooner or later it is going to dwindle. This happens to be in the woof and warp of the universe itself.

You have things like inflation where things become less valuable. So if you had the same income it won't buy as much. And actually that is a declining statistic. Although it looked level it was really declining. The civilization around it was growing so it didn't have the relative importance of the civilization around it that it should have had.

All of a sudden the clerk is in emergency and can't pay the rent. He has been receiving X number of dollars per week over the past three years and has had no raise of any kind whatsoever, no prospects of a raise or anything like that. He does not realize that he is looking at catastrophe. He thinks he's looking at security. But for sure if he has had no change of any kind in pay status for that period of time he's looking at a personal emergency, if only because inflation itself will catch up with him. His 25-cent pieces now don't buy as many cigarettes as they used to so it's actually a declining statistic. In the expansion of the world around him and the crowd that he is moving with, their statistics are changing and his isn't.

There's more recreation available to be purchased by his fellow man but he isn't now getting more money with which to purchase the recreation. These little tiny factors will enter into his life and although he hasn't watched it at all he sees this level statistic and doesn't realize he's in a state of emergency.

If you start applying one of these conditions formulas to the wrong condition you will get into the consequences of the one you are not applying. The one you *are* in is being neglected. So that if you want to *really* go into an emergency, be in an emergency and apply an affluence formula. Boy, you're in emergency! It will crash you.

Matter follows these formulas, other things follow these formulas. Of course they become a little more flexible when you apply them to life and there's a little more life can do about it. It just doesn't lie there like a rock and simply erode, see. Life has more volition and so can apply the condition very definitely.

This doesn't just apply to big organizations and big civilizations, it applies to the individual. You go into one of these conditions and you're in it without knowing. You have to be in one or another of these conditions. There aren't any other conditions, there isn't a "no-condition." And you *are* in one or another of these. The state of emergency not recovered from with no emergency formula ended is *worse.* Then that condition is continued and it's worse! There is no condition of emergency over because everything is dead. That's one of the horrible things to look at in this universe. Nothing ends. The total persistence of the universe is one of the most amazing features of it. It will persist. Survival of anything and everything is the god and watchword by which it functions.

9

HCOPL 8 November 1975

Non-Existence Formula Expanded

Many people misapply the new post non-existence formula or the non-existence formula by stats and then wonder why they seem to continue in trouble.

The answer is a misapplication of and not really doing the non-existence formula.

Experience has shown that even experienced Scientologists, executives and staff members have not in fact ever come out of non-existence. And where the area runs at all, it is carried on the back of one or two key people.

The phrase "find a communication line" is shortened down by too many (on staff) to locating somebody's in-basket and dropping a "needed and wanted" request in it. This is not really finding a communication line.

To handle ANY area you have to have INFORMATION and furnish INFORMATION. Where this is not done, the person finds himself doing projects that get rejected, projects that have to be redone, restraints put on his actions and finds himself sinking down the conditions. He gets in bad with his seniors BECAUSE HE DOESN'T ACQUIRE AND DOESN'T FURNISH the vital information of WHAT IS GOING ON.

It is the duty of the Volunteer Minister, new on post or not, TO ROUND UP THE COMMUNICATION LINES THAT RELATE TO HIS POST, FIND OUT WHO NEEDS VITAL INFORMATION FROM HIM and GET THOSE LINES IN, IN, IN as a continuing action.

When a person fails to do just that, he never comes out of non-existence. He isn't even up to danger because nobody knows they are even by-passing him. In other words, when a staff member does not do that, in the eyes of the organization or the community, he is simply a ZERO.

Orders being issued by him usually wind up CANCELLED because they are not real. Joe was already handling it. Bill's schedule was thrown out by it. Treasury yells, "How come this expensive Dev-T!"

Pretty soon, when someone hears it's so-and-so's order they just ignore it.

But what really happened?

He never applied the non-existence formula for real and so he stayed in non-existence. His actions do not coordinate because he does NOT HAVE THE LINES TO GIVE OR RECEIVE INFORMATION.

It is really and factually not up to anyone else to round up his lines for him any more than it is up to others to do his breathing for him. The inhale and exhale of an area is the take and give of VITAL INFORMATION AND PARTICLES.

Any Volunteer Minister who finds himself in apparent non-existence, liability or worse should rush around and find the comm lines that apply to his activity and post and insist that he be put on those lines.

The Volunteer Minister has to write down what information he has to have to handle his post and what information others have to have from him to do their jobs and activities.

And then arrange comm lines so that he is an information addressee from communicators on those lines.

Therefore the expanded non-existence formula is:

1. Find and get yourself on every comm line you will need in order to give and obtain information relating to your duties and materiel.
2. Make yourself known, along with your post title and duties, to every terminal you will need for the obtaining of information and the giving of data.
3. Discover from your friends and fellow community leaders and any public your duties may require you to contact, what is needed and wanted from each.
4. Do, produce and present what each needs and wants that is in conformation with policy.
5. Maintain your comm lines that you have and expand them to obtain other information you now find you need on a routine basis.
6. Maintain your origination lines to inform others what you are doing exactly, but only those who actually need the information.
7. Streamline what you are doing, producing and presenting so that it is more closely what is really needed and wanted.
8. With full information being given and received concerning your products, do, produce and present a greatly improved product routinely on your post.

I can guarantee that if you do this—and write your information concisely so it is quick to grasp and get your data in a form that doesn't jam your own lines, you will start on up the conditions for actual and in due course arrive in Power.

M

Integrity

Integrity Checksheet

Purpose:

To be able to recognize an individual in the social environment who has overts and withholds against another person or area and be able to restore that individual's integrity toward that particular person or area by getting off his overts and withholds.

a	Study Section 1 Integrity.	________
b	Drill: Demonstrate with your demo kit the definitions of Integrity, Overt, Withhold and Missed Withhold.	________
c	Drill: Write down two examples you have seen in life of an overt, a withhold and a missed withhold.	________
d	Study Section 2 Fundamentals.	________
e	Study Section 3 Overt-Motivator Definitions.	________
f	Drill: Demonstrate the relationship between overts and motivators.	________
g	Study Section 4 The Continuing Overt Act.	________
h	Study Section 5 Effectiveness of Overts in Processing.	________
i	Drill: Demonstrate how to recognize and handle when you are cleaning a clean.	________
j	Drill: Demonstrate what procedure you would use to prevent leaving an overt undisclosed.	________
k	Drill: Write a short essay on why punishment creates criminality.	________

l Drill: Demonstrate how to recognize and handle the person who "seeks the explanation of what I did that made it all happen to me." ________

m Study Section 6 Irresponsibility. ________

n Drill: Demonstrate several ways you would recognize when a person was giving generalities instead of a specific overt or withhold. ________

o Drill: Demonstrate when and how you would use the 'don't know' version of a question on a person. ________

p Drill: Demonstrate how you would handle getting off an individual's overts on a particular person or area. ________

q Study Section 7 Justification. ________

r Study Section 8 Some famous justifications. ________

s Drill: Attend the proceedings of a civil or criminal court and observe the social mechanism of justification. ________

t Drill: Write a short essay on the relationship between criticism and overts. ________

u Study Section 9 What is a Missed Withhold? ________

v Study Section 10 ARC Breaks—Missed Withholds. ________

w Study Section 11 Withholds, Missed and Partial. ________

x Study Section 12 Withholds, Other People's. ________

y Study Section 13 Blow-Offs. ________

z Drill: Demonstrate what a missed withhold is and how to recognize when a person has one. ________

aa Drill: Demonstrate how you would handle a missed withhold on a person using the sample questions previously stated in Sections 9 to 12. ________

bb Drill: Demonstrate how to handle the person who "gets off" other people's withholds. ________

cc Drill: Write a short essay on why blow-offs occur. ________

dd Drill: Find an individual who is displaying the manifestations of overts or withholds against a particular person or area. Introduce yourself as a Volunteer Minister and offer to help the individual handle that area. Ensure that the individual is willing to be helped and that you are both in a safe environment. Don't try to handle this with all his friends looking on or where interruptions will occur for example. Go over the definitions of Integrity, Overt, Withhold and Missed Withhold and ensure he understands the purpose of the action. Finally, get off any overts or withholds the individual has against the particular person or area being handled, until his integrity with that person or area is restored. ________

Integrity Pack

*BTB 4 December 1972
Integrity Processing
Series 1
Historical

1
Integrity

INTEGRITY is defined as:

1. The condition of having no part or element taken away or wanting; undivided or unbroken state; wholeness.
2. The condition of not being marred or violated; unimpaired or uncorrupted condition; soundness.
3. Soundness or moral principle; the character of uncorrupted virtue, especially in relation to truth and fair dealing; uprightness, honesty, sincerity.

This relates to ETHICS which is defined as "the principles of right and wrong conduct and the specific moral choices to be made by the individual in his relationship with others."

Thus we see that a person who acts against his own moral codes and the mores of the group violates his integrity.

Such acts are called overts. A person having committed an overt and then withholding the fact of that overt, and withholding himself from committing further overts, will individuate from the group. The group itself will then lose integrity as it becomes divided and lacks wholeness.

Integrity Processing is therefore that processing which enables a person, within the reality of his own moral codes and those of the group, to reveal his overts so he no longer requires to withhold and so enhances his own integrity and that of the group.

Historical Precedence
Religious Confession

The need for a person to be able to morally cleanse himself by confession of sins has long been recognized in religion.

The Buddhist monk 2,500 years ago was permitted to confess and seek expiation for "acts of censure." The penalty for failure to confess was loss of the rights and privileges of a monk. This was enforcement of the natural law that he who commits actions against the codes or mores of the group separates himself from that group.

The Bible, in the Books of James and John, calls for the confession of sins.

Early Christian handling of confession was largely concerned with disciplinary aspects. The sinner had to wear sackcloth, make his bed in ashes, and fast. This went on for a time proportionate to the gravity of the offense, sometimes for years.

Certain sins were previously considered too serious for forgiveness and therefore not open to confession, but a gradual leniency developed as in the case of Calixtus, Bishop of Rome 219-223, who decided to admit adulterers to exomologesis (Greek for public confession).

In the 4th century at Rome and Constantinople we hear of "penitentiaries"—priests appointed to act for the Bishop in hearing the confession of sins and deciding whether public discipline was necessary.

Due to some misuse of public confession, individual private confession became more prominent in the 5th Century.

In 1215 the Council of the Lateran ruled that everyone must make confession at least once a year before his parish priest.

In confession as now administered in Christian churches the disciplinary penance is often little more than nominal, stress being laid rather on the fullness of the confession.

Thus for at least 2500 years confession has played an important role in religious practice.

Throughout the centuries two points of question have arisen which led to some unpopularity of confession. One was the possible misuse of information disclosed in *public* confession, hence the development of private confession before an authorized person whose code of conduct prevented misuse. The other was the infliction of disciplinary action as atonement for the sins confessed. But the latter goes beyond the realm of personal morals and ethics into justice. Confession itself, and the need for some form of confession has not been in question.

With Integrity Processing Scientology follows in the tradition of religion. This processing enables the individual to confess to overts without duress. It is done with a qualified auditor bound by the Auditor's Code. Disciplinary action forms no part of the processing.

The technology by which Scientology confessionals and Integrity Processing is delivered is new. It is not the same as any earlier technology either in Scientology or other religion. It does however follow in the longstanding tradition of religion in providing a means for the individual to admit to and take responsibility for transgression against the mores of the group and so regain a spiritual and moral integrity.

*BTB 10 December 1972
Integrity Processing
Series 7

2 Fundamentals

First of all, what is a withhold? A withhold is a no action after the fact of action in which the individual has done or been an accessory to doing something which is a transgression against some moral code consisting of agreements to which the individual has subscribed in order to guarantee, with others, the survival of a group with which he is co-acting or has co-acted toward survival.

Because a withhold is a no action or a no motion after doingness, it naturally hangs up in time and floats in time due to the actions or the overts which preceded the no action or no motion of the withhold. The reactive mind is, therefore, the combined withholds stocked up which the individual has against groups from which he feels that he is individuated from but from which he has not separated due to the fact that he has these withholds in his bank and also all the combined agreements toward survival of all these groups, from which he is not separate, and which he uses reactively to solve problems now without inspection.

Example: The individual belonged at some time to the Holy Fighters. One of the mores of this group was that all should be destroyed who do not accept the Word. The Holy Fighters went out on a punitive expedition against a neighboring tribe who would not accept the Word, but accepted some other belief. There was a great battle with much killing, however, during the battle, the individual took pity upon a helpless child and did not kill him, but took the child off the field of battle, gave him food and drink, and left him, returning, himself, to the battle.

After the battle was successfully won, the Holy Fighters had their usual service during which all spoke of how they had killed all non-believers. Our individual withheld from the group that he had not only failed to kill, but had saved the life of a non-believer. Thus we have the no action of the withhold after the overt or action of saving the child, all of which added up to a transgression against the mores of the Holy Fighters.

Because of such similar transgressions, the individual finally individuated from the group of Holy Fighters and became a member of the Board of Directors of the Society for Kindness to Humans, which itself has its own agreements to survival and with which the individual agreed; however, when difficulties or problems arose, the individual instead of treating all with kindness tended to covertly try to destroy all who would not accept the tenents of kindness. So he reactively was solving the problems of the Society of Kindness with a survival more of the Holy Fighters. Due to all his transgressions and withholds of his destructive impulses while a member of the Society for Kindness, he finally individuated from this group also.

Now he is a member of Anti-emotions, Incorporated, but he finds that he can't rule out all his emotions, but tends to be destructive and kind at the same time. So he is still solving problems not only with the mores of the Holy Fighters, but with those of the Society for Kindness to Humans. And so it goes.

Processing this individual we will find that he has all these withholds of overts against the Holy Fighters, the Society for Kindness to Humans, and Anti-emotions, Incorporated. After we have pulled all these overts, he will truly be separate from these groups and no longer reactively use their survival mechanisms as solutions to problems.

Further the action of withholding is one point where the preclear does what the reactive mind does. He withholds his own overts of transgressions against the moral code of a group in order to avoid punishment, thusly enhance his own survival, and he withholds himself from the group finally in an effort to avoid committing further overts. So just as the reactive mind contains all past survival agreements which are used to solve problems threatening the survival of the individual, so does the individual decide to withhold transgressions, in order to survive himself, and withholds himself from groups to avoid committing overts.

Withholding and surviving occur at the same time. So the communication bridge between the preclear and the reactive mind is the withhold.

The pulling of overts which have been withheld then is the first step towards getting the preclear to take control of the reactive mind. The more withholds he gives up, the more the old survival mechanisms of the reactive mind are destroyed.

Further as a withhold of an overt creates a further overt act of not-know on the group with which one is co-acting with toward survival along an agreed upon moral code, so we are running off all the ignorance created for others by an individual which results in ignorance to himself. In this fashion, we are processing the individual up toward Native State or Knowingness.

Therefore, in handling overts and withholds on an individual you are really attacking the whole basis of the reactive mind. It is an activity which the auditor and minister should earnestly and effectively engage upon. In doing this you always assume that the preclear can remember his overts and can overwhelm the reactive mind. Any objections raised by the preclear as regards Integrity Processing are only a confusion being thrown up by the reactive mind, but the individual is really trying to look for what is there despite the reactive mind's doing this. This is why any failure to pull an overt is considered a crime against the preclear. In failing to pull an overt the reactive mind is given a win and the preclear a failure, and has further given the preclear another overt against the group he is now associated with, namely, that of Scientology, because he has succeeded in withholding from it.

So in Integrity Processing the auditor must get the preclear to answer the question.

In pulling overts, be careful that you do not allow the preclear to give you his justifications for having committed it. In allowing him to give you motivators or "reasons why" you are allowing him to lessen the overt.

You are only interested in what the preclear has done, not what he has heard that others have done. So never allow a preclear to get off withholds to you about others, except in the case where he has been an accessory to a criminal act.

"Other people's overts" are handled by asking the preclear, "Have you ever done anything like that yourself?"

Remember that your duty as an auditor and minister is to simply employ your skill to obtain a greater decency, ability and integrity on the part of others. You do this by performing well your function of clearing the meter and getting off all overts and withholds. An auditor is not an enforcer of public morals. If an auditor tries to make a preclear guilty, he is violating Clause 15 of the Auditor's Code, which says: "Never mix the processes of Scientology with those of various other practices." Punishment is an old practice which is not part of our activities in Scientology. Audit against the reality of the preclear and his moral code and do not try to make him guilty. The value of any withhold is only the value the preclear puts on it.

The number of withholds a preclear has available at any given time depends upon those that are available at that given time. To clarify this point, assume that all preclears have the same set number of withholds. Well, the number available within the realm of the preclear's present state of reality and responsibility will naturally vary. Preclears with a high reality and responsibility level will have more withholds available for pulling than preclears with a low reality and responsibility level. A preclear's reality and responsibility level will increase throughout processing bringing to light many new overts. If these are not pulled, the preclear will be forced into unintentionally withholding them and his case will bog down and not progress.

3

HCOB 1 November 1968
Issue II

Overt-Motivator Definitions

These are problems in FLOWS. (An impulse or direction of energy particles or thought or masses between terminals.)

They exist with or without intention.

One can add "intentional" or "unintentional" to the definitions.

An OVERT—An act by the person or individual leading to the injury, reduction or degradation of another, others or their beingness, persons, possessions, associations or dynamics.

A MOTIVATOR is an act received by the person or individual causing injury, reduction or degradation of his beingness, person, associations or dynamics.

An overt of omission—a failure to act resulting in the injury, reduction or degradation of another or others or their beingness, persons, possessions or dynamics.

A motivator is called a "motivator" because it tends to prompt an overt. It gives a person a motive or reason or justification for an overt.

When a person commits an overt or overt of omission with no motivator he tends to believe or pretends that he has received a motivator which does not in fact exist. This is a FALSE MOTIVATOR.

Beings suffering from this are said to have "motivator hunger" and are often aggrieved over nothing.

Cases which "cave in hard" suffer from false motivators and resolve on being asked for overts done for no reason.

Cases which do not resolve on actual motivators have overts that have to be handled.

There is also the case with FALSE OVERTS. The person has been hit hard for no reason. So they dream up reasons they were hit.

Cases that go into imaginary cause (imagining they do or cause things bad or good) are suffering from false overts. They resolve on "When were you hit (punished, hurt, etc.) for no reason?" using two-way communication.

HCOB 29 September 1965
Issue II
All Levels

4 The Continuing Overt Act

Pity the poor fellow who commits daily harmful acts.

He'll never make it.

A criminal pilfering the cash box once a week has himself stopped cold as far as case gains are concerned.

In 1954 I counted some noses. I checked up on 21 cases who had never had any gains since 1950. Seventeen turned out to be criminals! The other four were beyond the reach of investigation.

That gave me my first clue.

For some years, then, I watched for no-gain cases and carefully followed up those that I could. They had major or minor criminal backgrounds.

The person who is not getting case gains is committing continuing overts.

The case who continually commits overts before, during and after processing, won't make it!

One thing helps this, however.

By putting a bit of control in the Scientology environment we have enough threat to restrain dramatization.

The phenomena is this: The reactive bank can exert stress on the preclear if it is not obeyed. Discipline must exert just a shade more stress *against* dramatization than the bank does. This checks the performance of the continual overt long enough to let processing bite.

Not everyone is a continuous overt committer by about a thousand to one. But this phenomenon is not confined to the no-gain case.

The *slow* gain case is also committing overts the auditor doesn't see.

Therefore a little discipline in the environment speeds the *slow* gain case, the one we're more interested in.

The no-gain case, frankly, is one I am not panting to solve. If a fellow wants to sell his next hundred trillion for the sake of the broken toy he stole, I'm afraid I can't be bothered.

It is enough for me to know:

(1) Where bottom is, and

(2) How to help speed slow gain cases.

Bottom is the chap who eats your lunch apple and says the children did it. Bottom is the fellow who sows the environment with secret suppressive acts and vicious generalities.

The slow gain case responds to a bit of "keep your nose clean, please, while I apply the thetan-booster."

The fast gain case does his job and doesn't give a hoot about threatened discipline if it's fair. And the fast gain case helps out and the fast gain case can be helped by a more orderly environment. The good worker works more happily when bad workers see the pitfalls and desist from distracting him.

So we all win.

The no-gain case? Well, he sure doesn't deserve any gain. One pc in a thousand. And he yaps and groans and says "Prove it works" and blames us and raises hell. He makes us think we fail.

There are actually thousands upon thousands of Scientologists who each one comment on how wonderful it is and how good they feel. There are a few dozen or so who howl they haven't been helped! What a ratio! Yet I believe some on staff think we have a *lot* of dissatisfied people. These no-gain characters strew so much entheta around that we think we fail. Thousands of reports continue to pour in from around the world with hurrah! Only the few dozen groan.

But long ago I closed my book on the no-gain case. Each of those few dozen no-gains tell frightening lies to little children, pour ink on shoes, say how abused they are while tearing the guts out of those unlucky enough to be around them. They are suppressive persons, every one. I know. I've seen them all the way down to the little clinker they call their soul. And I don't like what I saw.

The people who come to you with wild discreditable rumors, who seek to tear people's attention off Scientology, who chew up organizations, are suppressive persons.

Well, give them a good rock and let them suppress it!

For had they had their way we would have lost our chance. It's too near to think about.

After all, we have to earn our freedom. I don't care much for those who didn't help.

The rest of us had to sweat a lot harder than was necessary to make it come true.

HCOB 9 December 1974
Integrity Processing
Series 6R
Effectiveness of Overts in Processing—ARC Breaks

5
Effectiveness of Overts in Processing

The commonest cause of failure in running overt acts is "cleaning cleans" whether or not one is using a meter. The pc who really has more to tell doesn't ARC break when the auditor continues to ask for one but may snarl and eventually give it up.

On the other hand leaving an overt touched on the case and calling it clean will cause a future ARC break with the auditor.

"Have you told all?" prevents cleaning a clean. On the unmetered pc one can see the pc brighten up. On the meter you get a nice fall if it's true that all is told.

"Have I not found out about something?" prevents leaving an overt undisclosed. On the unmetered pc the reaction is a sly flinch. On a metered pc it gives a read.

A pc's protest against a question will also be visible in an unmetered pc in a reeling sort of exasperation which eventually becomes a howl of pure bafflement at why the auditor won't accept the answer that that's all. On a meter protest of a question falls on being asked for: "Is this question being protested?"

There is no real excuse for ARC breaking a pc by:

1. Demanding more than is there or
2. Leaving an overt undisclosed that will later make the pc upset with the auditor.

Why Overts Work

Overts give the highest gain in raising cause level because they are the biggest reason why a person restrains himself and withholds self from action.

Man is basically good. But the reactive mind tends to force him into evil actions. These evil actions are instinctively regretted and the individual tries to refrain from doing anything at all. The "best" remedy the individual thinks is to withhold. "If I commit evil actions, then my best guarantee for not committing is to do nothing whatever." Thus we have the "lazy," inactive person.

Others who try to make an individual guilty for committing evil actions only increase this tendency to laziness.

Punishment is supposed to bring about inaction. And it does. In some unexpected ways.

However, there is also an inversion (a turn about) where the individual sinks below recognition of any action. The individual in such a state cannot conceive of any action and therefore cannot withhold action. And thus we have the criminal who can't act really but can only re-act and is without any self-direction. This is why punishment does not cure criminality but in actual fact creates it; the individual is driven below withholding or any recognition of any action. A thief's hands stole the jewel, the thief was merely an innocent spectator to the action of his own hands. Criminals are very sick people physically.

So there is a level below withholding that an auditor should be alert to in some pcs, for these "have no withholds" and "have done nothing." All of which, seen through their eyes is true. They are merely saying "I cannot restrain myself" and "I have not willed myself to do what I have done."

The road out for such a case is the same as that for any other case. It is just longer. The processes for levels above hold also for such cases. But don't be anxious to see a sudden return of responsibility, for the first owned "done" that this person knows he or she has done may be "ate breakfast."

There is another type of case in all this, just one more to end the list. This is the case who never runs O/W but "seeks the explanation of what I did that made it all happen to me."

This person easily goes into past lives for answers. Their reaction to a question about what they've done is to try to find out what they did that earned all those motivators. That of course, isn't running the process and the auditor should be alert for it and stop it when it happens.

This type of case goes into its extreme on guilt. It dreams up overts to explain why. After most big murders the police routinely have a dozen or two people come around and confess. You see, if they had done the murder, this would explain why they feel guilty. As a terror stomach is pretty grim to live with, one is apt to seek any explanation for it if it will only explain it.

On such cases the same approach as given works, but one should be very careful not to let the pc get off overts the pc didn't commit.

Such a pc (recognizable by the ease they dive into the extreme past) when being audited off a meter gets more and more frantic and wilder and wilder in overts reported. They should get calmer under processing of course, but the false overts make them frantic and hectic in a session. On a meter one simply checks for "Have you told me anything beyond what really has occurred?" Or "Have you told me any untruths?"

The observation and meter guides given in this section are used during a session when they apply but not systematically such as after every pc answer. These observations and E-meter guides are used always at the end of every session on the pcs to whom they apply.

HCOB 14 December 1972R
Integrity Processing Series 11R
Generalities Won't Do
HCOB 10 July 1964
Overts—Order of Effectiveness in Processing

6 Irresponsibility

If you want to get withholds off an "irresponsible person" you sometimes can't ask what he *did* or *withheld* and get an answer.

This problem has bugged us for sometime, I finally got very bright and realized that no matter whether the person thought it was an overt or not, he or she *will* answer up on "don't know" versions as follows:

Situation: "What have you done to your husband?" Answer, "Nothing bad." Now we know this girl, through our noticing she is critical of her husband, has overts on him. But she can take no responsibility for her own acts.

But she *can* take responsibility for his *not knowing*. She is making certain of that.

So we ask: "What have you done that your husband doesn't know about?"

And it takes an hour for her to spill it all, the quantity is so great. For the question releases the floodgates.

And with these withholds off, her responsibility comes up and she *can* take responsibility on the items.

This applies to any zone or area or terminal of a confessional.

Situation: We are getting a lot of "I thought," "I heard," "They said," "They did" in answer to a question. We take the terminal or terminals involved and put them in this blank.

"What have you done that ________ (doesn't) (don't) know about?"

And we can get the major overts that lay under the blanket of "how bad everyone is but me."

There is no reason to expect any great responsibility for his or her own overts early on. Seeking to make the person feel or take responsibility for overts is just pushing him or her down. The individual will resent being made to feel guilty. Indeed the minister may only achieve that, not case gain. And the person will ARC break.

The realization that one has *really* done something *is* a return of responsibility and this gain is best obtained only by indirect approach as in the above confessional technique.

7 Justification

HCOB 21 January 1960

When a person has committed an overt act and then withholds it, he or she usually employs the social mechanism of justification.

We have all heard people attempt to justify their actions and all of us have known instinctively that justification was tantamount to a confession of guilt. But not until now have we understood the exact mechanism behind justification.

Short of Scientology auditing there was no means by which a person could relieve himself of consciousness of having done an overt act except to try to *lessen the overt.*

Some churches used a mechanism of confession. This was a limited effort to relieve a person of the pressure of his overt acts. Later the mechanism of confession was employed as a kind of blackmail by which increased contribution could be obtained from the person confessing. Factually this is a limited mechanism to such an extent that it can be extremely dangerous. Religious confession does not carry with it any real stress of responsibility for the individual but on the contrary seeks to lay responsibility at the door of the divinity—a sort of blasphemy in itself. Confession to be non-dangerous and effective must be accompanied by a full acceptance of responsibility. All overt acts are the product of irresponsibility on one or more of the dynamics.

Withholds are a sort of overt act in themselves but have a different source. We have proven conclusively that man is basically good—a fact which flies in the teeth of old religious beliefs that man is basically evil. Man is good to such an extent that when he realizes he is being very dangerous and in error he seeks to minimize his power and if that doesn't work and he still finds himself committing overt acts he then seeks to dispose of himself either by leaving or by getting caught and executed. Without this computation police would be powerless to detect crime—the criminal always assists himself to be caught. Why police punish the caught criminal is a mystery. The caught criminal wants to be rendered less harmful to the society and wants rehabilitation. Well, if this is true then why does he not unburden himself? The fact is this: unburdening is considered by him to be an overt act. People withhold overt acts because they conceive that telling them would be another overt act. It is as though thetans are trying to absorb and hold out of sight all the evil of the world. This is wrong-headed; by withholding overt acts these are kept afloat in the universe and are themselves as withholds entirely the cause of continued evil. Man is basically good but he could not attain expression of this until now. Nobody but the individual could die for his own sins—to arrange things otherwise was to keep man in chains.

In view of these mechanisms, when the burden became too great man was driven to another mechanism—the effort to lessen the size and pressure of the overt. He or she could only do this by attempting to reduce the size and repute of the terminal. Hence, not-isness. Hence when a man or a woman has done an overt act there usually follows an effort to reduce the goodness or importance of the target of the overt. Hence the husband who betrays his wife must then state that the wife was no good in some way. Thus the wife who betrayed her husband had to reduce the husband to reduce the overt. This works on all dynamics. In this light most criticism is justification of having done an overt.

This does not say that all things are right and that no criticism anywhere is ever merited. Man is not happy. He is faced with total destruction unless we toughen up our postulates. And the overt act mechanism is simply a sordid condition man has slipped into without knowing where he was going. So there are rightnesses and wrongnesses in conduct and society and life at large, but random, carping, covert criticism when not borne out in fact is only an effort to reduce the size of the target of the overt so that one can live (he hopes) with the overt. Of course to criticize unjustly and lower repute is itself an overt act and so this mechanism is not in fact workable.

Here we have the source of the dwindling spiral. One commits overt acts unwittingly. He seeks to justify them by finding fault or displacing blame. This leads him into further overts against the same terminals which leads to a degradation of himself and sometimes those terminals.

Scientologists have been completely right in objecting to the idea of punishment. Punishment is just another worsening of the overt sequence and degrades the punisher. But people who are guilty of overts demand punishment. They use it to help restrain themselves from (they hope) further violation of the dynamics. It is the victim who demands punishment and it is a wrong-headed society that awards it. People get right down and beg to be executed. And when you don't oblige, the woman scorned is sweet tempered by comparison. I ought to know—I have more people try to elect me an executioner than you would care to imagine. And many a preclear who sits down in your pc chair for a session is there just to be executed and when you insist on making such a pc better, why you've had it, for they start on this desire for execution as a new overt chain and seek to justify it by telling people how bad the auditor was.

When you hear scathing and brutal criticism of some one which sounds just a bit strained, know that you have your eye on overts against that criticized person and next chance you get, get the person's overts off and remove just that much evil from the world.

And remember, by and by, that if you make the person write these overts and withholds down and sign them and then give them to you, he'll be less reluctant to hold on to the shreds of them—it makes for a further blow of overts and less blow of pc. And always run responsibility on a pc when he unloads a lot of overts or just one.

HCOB 8 July 1964
Scientology III & IV
More Justification

8
Some Famous Justifications

It wasn't really an overt because . . .

It wasn't me it was just my bank.

You can't hurt a thetan.

He was asking for a motivator.

He's got overts on me.

His overts are bigger than mine.

My intentions were good.

He's a victim anyway.

I was just being self-determined.

It's better than suppressing.

I've come up to being covert.

He must have done something to deserve it.

He was dragging it in.

I was in an ARC break.

He needed a lesson.

It's not against *my* moral code.

It's about time I was overt.

They weren't willing to experience it.

I don't see why I have to be the only one to take responsibility.

They are so way out they wouldn't realize it.

He's such a victim already, one more motivator won't make any difference.

I can't help it if he reacts.

He's too critical.

I'm above moral codes.

Why should I limit my causativeness.

Just because others can't take it.

It was my duty to tell the truth.

You wouldn't want me to withhold.

These show how one can get around getting off an overt and staying *sick* from it.

We have our hands here on the mechanism that makes this a crazy universe so let's go for broke on it and play it all the way out.

9

HCOB 8 February 1962
Urgent Missed Withholds

What is a Missed Withhold?

A missed withhold is not just a withhold. Please burn that into the stone walls. A missed withhold is a withhold that existed, *could have been picked up* and was MISSED.

The person with complaints has MISSED WITHHOLDS. The person with entheta has MISSED WITHHOLDS. You don't need policies and diplomacy to handle these people. Policy and diplomacy will fail. You need that person's MISSED WITHHOLDS.

Every ARC breaky preclear is ARC breaky because of a missed withhold. Every dissatisfied preclear is dissatisfied because of MISSED WITHHOLDS.

A MISSED WITHHOLD is a withhold that existed, was tapped and was not pulled. Hell hath no screams like a withhold scorned.

The withhold need not have been asked for. It merely need have been available. And if it was not pulled, thereafter you have a nattery, combative, ARC breaky person.

How to Audit It

In picking up *missed withholds* you don't ask for withholds, you ask for missed withholds.

Sample question: "What withhold was missed on you?"

The auditor then proceeds to find out what it was and who missed it.

And if the preclear considers it no overt, and can't conceive of overts, you will have "didn't know." Example: "What didn't an auditor know in an auditing session?"

Summary

If you clean up withholds that have been missed on any preclear or person, you will have any case flying.

This is vital technology that can do wonders for cases.

Any person who is giving any trouble should be gotten hold of and checked for missed withholds.

Just try it out the next time a preclear gets upset and you'll see that I speak the usual sooth.

10

HCOB 3 May 1962

ARC Breaks—Missed Withholds

After some months of careful observation and tests, I can state conclusively that:

ALL ARC BREAKS STEM FROM MISSED WITHHOLDS.

This is vital technology, vital to the auditor and to anyone who wants to live.

Conversely:

THERE ARE NO ARC BREAKS WHEN MISSED WITHHOLDS HAVE BEEN CLEANED UP.

By WITHHOLD is meant AN UNDISCLOSED CONTRA-SURVIVAL ACT.

BY MISSED WITHHOLD is meant AN UNDISCLOSED CONTRA-SURVIVAL ACT WHICH HAS BEEN RESTIMULATED BY ANOTHER BUT NOT DISCLOSED.

This is FAR more important in an auditing session than most auditors have yet realized. Even when some auditors are told about this and shown it they still seem to miss its importance and fail to use it. Instead they continue to use strange methods of controlling the pc and odd ball processes on ARC breaks.

Allergy to picking up missed withholds can be so great than an auditor has been known to fail utterly rather than do so. Only constant hammering can drive this point home. When it is driven home, only then can auditing begin to happen across the world; the datum is that important.

An auditing session is 50% technology and 50% application. I am responsible for the technology. The auditor is wholly responsible for the application. Only when an auditor realizes this, can he or she begin to obtain uniformly marvellous results everywhere.

No auditor now needs "something else," some odd mechanism to keep pcs in session.

PICKING UP MISSED WITHHOLDS KEEPS PCS IN SESSION.

There is *no* need for a rough, angry ARC breaky session. If there is one it is *not* the fault of the pc. It is the fault of the auditor. The auditor has failed to pick up missed withholds.

As of now it is not the pc that sets the tone of the session. It is the auditor. And the auditor who has a difficult session (providing he or she has used standard technology, and can run an E-Meter), has one only because he or she failed to ask for missed withholds.

Technology today is so powerful that it must be flawlessly applied. One has his TRs and E-Meter operation completely perfect. And one follows exact technology. And one keeps the missed withholds picked up.

There is an exact and precise auditor action and response for every auditing situation, and for every case. We are not today beset by variable approaches. The less variable the auditor's actions and responses, the greater gain in the pc. It is terribly precise. There is no room for flubs.

Further, every pc action has an exact auditor response. And each of these has its own drill by which it can be learned.

Auditing today is not an art, either in technology or procedure. It is an exact science. This removes Scientology from every one of the past practices of the mind.

Medicine advanced only to the degree that its responses by the practitioner were standardized and the practitioner has a professional attitude toward the public.

Scientology is far ahead of that today.

What a joy it is to a preclear to receive a completely standard session. To receive a text book session. And what gains the pc makes! And how easy it is on the auditor!

It isn't how interesting or clever the auditor is that makes the session. It's how standard the auditor is. Therein lies pc confidence.

Part of that standard technology is asking for missed withholds *any* time the pc starts to give any trouble. This is, to a pc, a totally acceptable control factor. And it totally smooths the session.

Here are some of the manifestations cured by asking for missed withholds.

(1) Pc failing to make progress.
(2) Pc critical of or angry at auditor.
(3) Pc refusing to talk to auditor.
(4) Pc attempting to leave session.
(5) Pc not desirous of being audited (or anybody not desirous of being audited).
(6) Pc boiling off.
(7) Pc exhausted.
(8) Pc feeling foggy at session end.
(9) Dropped havingness.
(10) Pc telling others the auditor is no good.
(11) Pc demanding redress of wrongs.
(12) Pc critical of organizations or people of Scientology.
(13) People critical of Scientology.
(14) Lack of auditing results.
(15) Dissemination failures.

Now I think you will agree that in the above list we have every ill we suffer from in the activities of auditing.

Now PLEASE believe me when I tell you there is ONE CURE for the lot and ONLY that one. There are no other cures.

The cure is contained in the simple question or its variations *"Have I missed a withhold on you?"*

The commonest variations: "Have I failed to find out something?" "Is there something I don't know about you?"

Don't be so confounded *reasonable* about the pc's complaints. Sure, they may all be true, BUT he's complaining only because *withholds* have been *missed.* Only then does the pc complain bitterly.

Whatever else you learn, learn and understand this please. Your future hangs on it. The fate of Scientology hangs on it. Get the missed withholds when life goes wrong. Only then can we win and grow.

If pcs, organizations, churches and even Scientology vanish from Man's view it will be because you did not learn and use these things.

11

HCOB 22 February 1962

Withholds, Missed and Partial

I don't know exactly how to get this across to you except to ask you to be brave, squint up your eyes and plunge.

I don't appeal to reason. Only to faith at the moment. When you have a reality on this, nothing will shake it and you'll no longer fail cases or fail in life. But, at the moment, it may not seem reasonable. So just try it, do it well and day will dawn at last.

What are these nattering, upsets, ARC breaks, critical tirades, ineffective motions? *They are restimulated but missed or partially missed withholds.* If I could just teach you that and get you to get a good reality on that in your own auditing, your activities would become smooth beyond belief.

It is true that ARC breaks, present time problems and withholds all keep a session from occurring. And we must watch them and clear them.

But behind all these is another button, applicable to each, which resolves each one. And that button is the restimulated but missed or partially missed withhold.

Life itself has imposed this button on us. It did not come into being with security checking.

If you know about people or are supposed to know about people, *then* these people expect, unreasonably, that you know *them* through and through.

Real knowledge to the average person is only this: a knowledge of his or her withholds! That, horribly enough, is the high tide of knowledge for the man in the street. *If* you know his withholds, if you know his crimes and acts, then you are *smart.* If you know his future you are moderately wise. And so we are persuaded toward mind reading and fortune telling.

All wisdom has this trap for those who would be wise.

Egocentric man believes all wisdom is wound up in knowing his misdemeanors.

IF any wise man represents himself as wise and fails to discover what a person has done, that person goes into an antagonism or other misemotion toward the wise man. So they hang those who restimulate and yet who do not find out about their withholds.

This is an incredible piece of craziness. But it is observably true.

This is the WILD ANIMAL REACTION that makes Man a cousin to the beasts.

Use this as a stable datum: If the person is upset, somebody failed to find out what that person was sure they would find out.

A missed withhold is a should have known.

The only reason anyone has ever left Scientology is because people failed to find out about them.

This is valuable data. Get a reality on it.

12 Withholds, Other People's

HCOB 31 January 1970

Now and then, quite rarely, you find an auditor who in being audited "gets off" other people's withholds.

Example: "Yes, I have a withhold from you. Charley said you were insane."

Example: "Yes, I have a withhold. Mary Agnes has been in prison."

One also finds public pcs trying to do this occasionally.

The facts of the case are that it doesn't do anybody any good casewise to "get off" other people's withholds.

Essentially, a withhold by definition is something the *pc* did that was an overt act, which the pc is withholding and thus keeping secret.

Thus, getting off things that somebody else did is not helpful to a case as such things aren't aberrative to the pc.

But now let's look at this more closely.

If a pc is "getting off" other people's withholds HE HIMSELF MUST HAVE A CHAIN OF SIMILAR OVERTS AND WITHHOLDS *that are his own.*

Getting off other people's withholds is then seen as a symptom of the pc withholding similar actions of his own.

Let us then complete the two examples above.

Auditor: "Do you have a withhold?"

Pc: "Charley said you were insane."

Auditor, correctly: "Do you have a similar withhold of your own?"

Pc: "Er—uh—well actually I told the class you were crazy last month."

Auditor: "Do you have a withhold?"

Pc: "Mary Agnes has been in prison."

Auditor: "Ok. Do you have a similar withhold of your own?"

Pc: "Er—uh—well—I spent two years in a reform school and I've never told anybody."

You can assume that any pc who is trying to get off withholds someone else had is a sort of out-of-valence effort to avoid giving his own withholds.

This applies, of course, to all overts as well. Somebody giving other people's overts (which aren't aberrative to him) is actually failing to give overts of his own which are aberrative to him.

This is the mechanism behind the fact that if a pc is nattering about somebody the pc has overts on that somebody. The natter is "other people's overts." Getting these off do not help the pc. Getting the pc's off does.

Never be misled by a nattering pc. Never be hooked into letting him get off other people's overts and withholds.

13 Blow-offs

HCOB 31 December 1959

Scientology technology has been extended to include the factual explanation of departures, sudden and relatively unexplained from sessions, posts, jobs, locations and areas.

This is one of the things man thought he knew all about and therefore never bothered to investigate, yet, this amongst all other things gave him the most trouble. Man had it all explained to his own satisfaction and yet his explanation did not cut down the amount of trouble which came from the feeling of "having to leave."

For instance man has been frantic about the high divorce rate, about the high job turn-over in plants, about labor unrest and many other items all stemming from the same source—sudden departures or gradual departures.

We have the view of a person who has a good job, who probably won't get a better one, suddenly deciding to leave and going. We have the view of a wife with a perfectly good husband and family up and leaving it all. We see a husband with a pretty and attractive wife breaking up the affinity and departing.

In Scientology we have the phenomenon of preclears in session or students on courses deciding to leave and never coming back. And that gives us more trouble than most other things all combined.

Man explained this to himself by saying that things were done to him which he would not tolerate and therefore he had to leave. But if this were the explanation all man would have to do would be to make working conditions, marital relationships, jobs, courses and sessions all very excellent and the problem would be solved. But on the contrary, a close examination of working conditions and marital relationships demonstrates that improvement of conditions often worsens the amount of blow-off, as one could call this phenomenon. Probably the finest working conditions in the world were achieved by Mr. Hershey of Chocolate Bar fame for his plant workers. Yet they revolted and even shot at him. This in its turn led to an industrial philosophy that the worse workers were treated the more willing they were to stay which in itself is as untrue as the better they are treated the faster they blow-off.

One can treat people so well that they grow ashamed of themselves, knowing they don't deserve it, that a blow-off is precipitated, and certainly one can treat people so badly that they have no choice but to leave, but these are extreme conditions and in between these we have the majority of departures; the auditor is doing his best for the preclear and yet the preclear gets meaner and meaner and blows the session. The wife is doing her best to make a marriage and the husband wanders off on the trail of a tart. The manager is trying to keep things going and the worker leaves. These, the unexplained, disrupt organizations and lives and it's time we understood them.

People leave because of their own overts and withholds. That is the factual fact and the hard-bound rule. A man with a clean heart can't be hurt. The man or woman who must, must, must become a victim and depart is departing because of his or her own overts and withholds. It doesn't matter whether the person is departing from a town or a job or a session. The cause is the same.

Almost anyone, no matter his position, can remedy a situation no matter what's wrong if he or she really wants to. When the person no longer wants to remedy it his own overt acts and withholds against the others involved in the situation have lowered his ability to be responsible for it. Therefore he or she does not remedy the situation. Departure is the only answer. To justify the departure the person blowing-off dreams up things done to him, in an effort to minimize the overt by degrading those it was done to. The mechanics involved are quite simple.

It is amazing what trivial overts will cause a person to blow. I caught a staff member one time just before he blew and traced down the original act against the church to his failure to defend the church when a criminal was speaking viciously about it. This failure to defend accumulated to itself more and more overts and withholds such as failing to relay messages, failure to complete an assignment until it finally utterly degraded the person into stealing something of no value. This theft caused the person to believe he had better leave.

It is a rather noble commentary on man that *when a person finds himself,* as he believes, *incapable of restraining himself from injuring a benefactor he will defend the benefactor by leaving.* This is the real source of the blow-off. If we were to better a person's working conditions in this light we would see that we have simply magnified his overt acts and made it a certain fact that he would leave. If we punish we can bring the value of the benefactor down a bit and thus lessen the value of the overt. But improvement and punishment are neither one answers. The answer lies in Scientology and processing the person up to a high enough responsibility to take a job or a position and carry it out without all this weird hokus-pokus of "I've got to say you are doing things to me so I can leave and protect you from all the bad things I am doing to you." That's the way it is and it doesn't make sense not to do something about it now that we know.

To do less than this is cruelty itself. The person is blowing himself off with his own overts and withholds. If these are not removed then anything the organization or its people does to him goes in like a javelin and leaves him with a dark area in his life and a rotten taste in his mouth. Further he goes around spouting lies about the organization and its related personnel and every lie he utters makes him just that much sicker. By permitting a blow-off without clearing it we are degrading people, for I assure you, and with some sorrow, people have not often recovered from overts against Scientology, its churches and related persons. They don't recover because they know in their hearts even while they lie that they are wronging people who have done and are doing enormous amounts of good in the world and who definitely do not deserve libel and slander.

This campaign is aimed straightly at cases and getting people cleared. It is aimed at preserving staffs and the lives of persons who believe they have failed us.

Uneasy lies the head that has a bad conscience. Clean it up and run responsibility on it and you have another better person. We'll save a lot of people that way.

And on our parts we'll go along being as good a manager, as good a church and as good a field as we can be and we'll get rid of all our overts and withholds too.

Think it will make an interesting new view?

Well, Scientology specializes in those.

N

Marriage and Children

Marriage and Children Checksheet

Purpose:

To enable the Volunteer Minister to counsel and salvage marriages and to handle children as individuals or in groups with precise technology.

a	Study Section 1 Pregnancy and Auditing.	______
b	Study Section 2 Healthy Babies.	______
c	Drill: Go out and purchase the ingredients needed for the baby formula and get it used, either by yourself or by relatives or friends who have babies.	______
d	Study Section 3 Marriage.	______
e	Drill: Demonstrate with your demo kit how childhood illness occurs.	______
f	Drill: List 10 overts which can be committed in a marriage by a husband and 10 by a wife.	______
g	Drill: Using your demo kit, demonstrate how you can tell which partner has the most overts.	______
h	Drill: Write out the steps you would take to salvage a marriage.	______
i	Study Section 4 Be-Do-Have.	______
j	Drill: With your demo kit show how to handle a child who wants to know what to do.	______
k	Study Section 5 Child Scientology.	______
l	Drill: Write out what you would do to handle a child who "boils off" while in session.	______

m Drill: Write an essay on what happens when a child's imagination is inhibited. ________

n Drill: Find a child and run him/her on *Self Analysis.* Process to a win. ________

o Drill: Observe parents handling their children. Note parents' attitudes. ________

p Drill: Arrange to run the *Self Analysis* processes on a group of children and do it according to the instructions in the "Child Scientology" section. ________

Marriage and Children Pack

1

Pregnancy and Auditing

|*BTB 24 July 1973

The proper auditing on pregnant women consists of Dianetics and preparatory auditing for delivery.

A pregnant woman should be set up for a very easy delivery.

The delivery should be silent.

When delivery occurs the engram is run out within 24 hours of the actual delivery REGARDLESS OF ANY DRUGS USED.

Nutrition

Proper nutrition including a reduction in fattening foods is vital. Vitamin D, calcium and magnesium must be given throughout term of pregnancy.

The absence of these, the woman seeking to abort the child, accidents, and improper medications are the causes of miscarriages. Today's dietary problems and the primitive state of medical practice contribute to such difficulties as are encountered during term and delivery.

Preparatory auditing makes delivery very easy and an erasure of the incident of the delivery wipes out consequences; but only providing the nutritional and vitamin-mineral deficiencies are not present and that the woman has not been physically or medicinally mishandled.

Auditing is for use. One of its important but too frequently neglected uses is in the preparatory auditing of pregnant women and post delivery auditing immediately after birth. The woman may be audited in her local area on such auditing.

Auditing saves lives. There are no instances of auditing having been responsible for a miscarriage. There are only instances where the technology was not used to prepare a woman in term and repair the effects of delivery, and instances where accidents, bad medical handling, vitamin-mineral deficiencies or dietary carelessness existed or where the woman attempted to abort herself.

There are also instances of the correct auditing having been used in conjunction with proper nutrition and care resulting in easy delivery and miraculously fast recovery of both mother and child. May there be many more.

2 Healthy Babies

The Auditor No. 6

Although the modern emphasis on trade for its own sake may have its points, there is a limit to which it should be pushed. And wrecking a baby's health, and worrying its mother to an early grave just to collect fees should be frowned upon. (Irony)

The prepared food used today is guaranteed to upset a baby. It is a powdered mess one is supposed to dissolve in water and feed to the baby.

If you ever tasted it, you would agree with the baby. It's terrible.

More than that, it is total carbohydrate and does not contain the protein necessary to make tissue and bone. It only makes fat. When you see one of these bloated, white, modern babies, know that it is being fed exactly on the doctor's orders: a diet of mixed milk powder, glucose and water, total carbohydrate.

Breast feeding babies may have a nostalgic background, particularly to a Freudian oriented medico, but real breast milk again is usually a poor ration. Modern mothers smoke and sometimes drink. Smoking makes the milk very musty. Anyway, a nervous modern mother just can't deliver the right ration. Maybe it's the pace of the times or the breed, but there are few modern Guernsey-type mothers. So even without drinking or smoking, one should forget breast feeding.

The largest cause of upset in a baby's early life is just rations. As an old hand at this, I have straightened out more babies who were cross, not sleeping, getting sick and all, than it was easy to keep a record of. These babies were all, just plain hungry. Fed, yeah. But with what? Terrible tasting, high carbohydrate powdered milk solutions, or skim breast milk from an overworked mother. And the little things were ready to toss in their chips. Some had gone into a stupor and just didn't care anymore. Some were trying to quit entirely. And they all recovered and got alert and healthy when they were given a proper ration.

A ration *must* contain a heavy percentage of *protein.* Protein is the building block for nerves and bones. A soldier, wounded, will not heal without heavy protein intake. Ulcers will not get well without a heavy protein diet being given.

To make brain, bone and tissue, the baby *must* be given protein. And from 2 days old to at least 3 years. That makes strong, pretty, alert babies that sleep well and do well.

When I first tackled this problem, it was a personal matter. I write from the viewpoint of a father, of course, a profession in which I have had experience. I had a little boy who was not going to live and I had to act fast (1) to get him *out* of the hospital and (2) to discover his trouble and (3) to remedy it. The total time available was less than 24 hours. He was dying.

So (1) I got him out of the hospital, helped by a hot temper and a trifle of promised mayhem. And (2) I found he wouldn't or couldn't eat. And (3) I recalled all my dietary and endocrine studies that I studied in those places the reporters have now agreed I never attended.

Actually I recalled further than that. Roman troops marched on barley. Barley is the highest protein content cereal. And from a deep past I called up a formula.

This formula is the nearest approach to human milk that can be assembled easily. It is an old Roman formula, no less, from maybe 2,200 years ago.

It's a bit of trouble, of course. You have to sacrifice a pot or a small kettle to cook the barley in (it really wrecks a pot, so you just have a barley pot and use only it). And you have to cook barley for a long time to get barley water, and you may forget and it burns. But even so, it's worth it in terms of a calmer house and a healthy baby.

You mix up a full 24 hour batch of this barley recipe every day, bottle it in sterilized bottles and put it where it will remain cold. And you heat a bottle up to 98.6 F or thereabouts (test it by squirting some on the back of the hand to see if it's too warm or too cool) before you give it to the baby.

And, although you *try* to keep the baby on a schedule, you are foolish not to feed him or her when the baby is hungry.

A baby, having eaten a full ration, usually sleeps for hours anyway. If they don't, there is always a reason such as a pin or a piece of coal in the bed, wet nappies, something. When a baby who shouldn't be crying, does, I always hunt and hunt until I find out why. I don't follow the schools of (1) the baby is just willful or (2) it's a serious illness that requires an immediate operation. Somewhere between we find the real reason.

But the foremost reason a baby doesn't do well is poor rations. And to remedy that, here is the formula.

Baby Food Recipe

10 ounces barley water
15 ounces pasteurized milk
2 1/2 ounces white syrup

The syrup should be varied—depending on the baby—some like it weak—some take it stronger.

On boiling the barley water, put about half a cup of *pearl barley* in a piece of muslin, tie loosely to allow for expansion, and boil *slowly* in about 4 pints of water. Barley water will turn pink. This gives about the right consistency of barley water for making formula, as above.

You don't feed the baby the actual barley, only the water mixed as above. If you don't know what to do with the barley, eat it yourself.

With sugar and cream, it's pretty good.

3 Marriage

Tape Lecture 6001C02
SMC5

Let's take a look at marriage.

You can salvage more marriages per square house than ever before. There have been a lot of marriages that have stayed together through thick and thin and people are to be congratulated on it.

My wife, Mary Sue, and I have been married now for twenty-four years. But if you look over that and a few other little things you see that I am not the philosopher in the ivory tower talking about something I know not what of. In earlier generations it seems the requisite for all philosophers and advisers was to have no experience of any kind whatsoever in any subject about which they were advising.

You can advise people about things you don't know anything about. That's perfectly easy to do. In fact, it's one of the easiest things to do Man does.

For instance, all of the confession stories written in America are written by unmarried ladies who have reached forty or fifty. Now there's nothing wrong with being an unmarried lady reaching forty or fifty, but how come all these confession stories?

As a young writer I was sitting around with a bunch of these ladies one day and I said to them, "You get pretty high rates in the confession story racket. I ought to write some of those."

They all said, "Ha, ha, ha!"

I sat down and wrote a confession story and got a thousand dollars for it. "Yes, I remember, I was just a young maid, trusting and inexperienced, and he was a handsome devil . . ." It was easy. I saw then that you could do things you didn't know anything about. They weren't necessarily good, but you could do something about them.

One of the most adventurous of these things is getting married because *when you're getting married you're doing something you don't know anything about.* And when you try it a couple of times, usually you know less about it the second time than you did the first time.

Marriage is an interesting boat to steer. It's not a third dynamic activity; and yet it is, kind of. It generally ceases to be a second dynamic activity but has to remain so. In this society and time, a family is the closest knit self-perpetuating, self-protecting unit and is necessary economically and otherwise to the society the way it's rigged at the present time. And who destroys marriage destroys the civilization, that's fairly sure. That's why the Communists try so hard.

A culture will go by the boards if its basic building block, the family, is removed as a valid building block. But this is no reason why we should get silly about what the relationship is. The familial relationship basically is a postulated relationship. When people stop postulating it, it ceases to exist, and that's what happens to most marriages. People stop creating the family unit, and the moment they stop creating it isn't. It's not that all men are evil so therefore contracts such as marriage dissolve usually in infidelity. The reverse is true: that when you have a purely postulated relationship which has no real existence in fact, you have to continue to create it. And a family which doesn't continue to create itself as a family will cease to exist as a family. And that's about all you need to know about it.

All over the world people are having lots of trouble with family because they're running on an automaticity (Scientology term for something one is doing but is unaware of, or only partially aware he is doing). They think it will hang together through no effort of their own, but it won't.

Familially there are unhappy experiences. Father takes his role very seriously: he is the arbiter of the destiny of it all. He must be totally contributed to. Actually the Greek and Roman family had the power of life and death vested in the role of father. He could order executed any family member. They must have had a lot of trouble, mustn't they have? (If you wonder how much trouble any society had, look at what laws they had to pass. The vigor of the law is directly proportional to the amount of trouble they were having. You think the Puritans were pure? Read their list of laws!)

If your own mother and father weren't making too good a go of marriage, you might say, "Now look at that. This institution, inherent in nature and unchangeable, doesn't perpetuate itself and is not much good because look, it isn't hanging together."

So you had a failure when you were a little kid. You probably tried to postulate the family into a unit. You were working at it. You were trying to get a "papa loves mama" thing going one way or the other and to show them that they had something to live for. As a matter of fact, one of the reasons you would get hurt was to make papa and mama realize they had responsibilities for the family.

Childhood illness and injury come directly after familial upsets. Just trace it down. Maybe you had some failures because it's pretty hard when you don't have very much body to make an effect on very big bodies. Or so you had it figured. Actually, you were probably something to reckon with.

But whether or not you had a good example has nothing to do with whether or not you yourself can make a marriage. The example you were looking at existed without benefit of any knowledge of how men and women worked and what they were all about. And existing without that information, how could they do anything but run along and get flat tires every quarter of a mile?

A marriage is something you have to postulate into existence and keep created, and when you stop working at it it will cease. When everything else is rigged to perpetuate it while you're not trying to keep it going, it will be a destruction. If you realize that, and if you know the technology I've given you on overts and withholds you can make any marriage stick or you can recover any facet of any marriage or plaster one back together again anyway you want to. It takes a little doing and it takes a little guts, and that's an understatement if I ever made one.

Some years ago Mary Sue and I worked at this. We decided we would take this new technology (as it was then in the early 1960s), apply it as prescribed, and straighten out all the overts and withholds. But we didn't do it because our marriage was on the rocks; compared to most, our marriage has been pretty smooth. Nevertheless, even though we had no real trouble and no overts or withholds to amount to anything, we nearly chopped each other's heads off doing this. We had withholds like the value of Christmas presents, and critical thoughts like, "He cares more about the preclear than he does about me because he's been auditing all night." We thought we were fond of each other, but after we got all this stuff cleaned up, wow!

So with an even greater magnitude of overts and withholds, patching up the marriage is going to take great fortitude indeed.

A marriage which has broken down into a super-separateness of overts and withholds is almost impossible to put back in the run again simply by postulating it into existence. After people have separated themselves out from each other, they have to unseparate themselves again.

One June day this handsome brute or not so handsome and this beautiful girl or not so beautiful come together and say, "We will . . . til death do us part" and they think they've made a marriage. Why, they haven't started yet. Now they have to find out how they look before breakfast. You think this thing has a lot to do with the second dynamic? It has mostly to do with cosmetics and razor blades. But they've got to learn to live with each other if they can.

By the act of getting married, they have to some degree wiped out, by more or less tacit consent, what they were doing before that. And they start from there. What happens from there on out is what counts. But sometimes things they have done before that that they are violently withholding from each other don't even let the marriage get started. Forty-eight hours later they're on the rocks. Why? Well, there is just too much overt and withhold before they even knew each other. Even that marriage can be salvaged.

But how about one that has ground on for years and years with the overts and withholds mounting up until the marriage has fallen apart? It's traditional at the end of three years husbands and wives don't get any kick out of each other. It's in the textbook—all the psychologists know that. But if at the end of three years this is the case, how about at the end of ten? They've learned to endure. They're both in propitiation, they're getting along somehow, and they would rather have it that way than some other way. They'd rather be married than not. They think they're making it okay, and they don't think too much anymore about the guy or the girl that they should have married instead.

Into such relationships we can introduce one of the most startling pieces of bombardism you ever heard of. *We can clear up the marriage so it really goes.*

All a divorce or an inclination or a withdrawal is, is simply too many overts and withholds against the marital partner. "I ought to go," "I ought to do something else," "We ought to split it up," and "I'd be much better off if we hadn't" are rationales by one partner that indicate his overts and withholds against the other partner. He or she is trying to protect the other partner from his own viciousness by leaving; that's the basic reason.

Usually the gradient scale of a marriage breakup is "cool it off." And that cool-off usually occurs. But we can uncool it off. Sit down across from the partner who advocates the split and say, "All right now, George (or Agnes), come clean." Get the overts and withholds off.

This process is not particularly advised, but it's terribly workable: "*What have you done? What have you withheld?* What have you done? What have you withheld?" That cleans the overts and withholds on all dynamics.

But if you're just cleaning up a marriage, it's (1) "*What have you done to . . . ?*" (2) "*What have you withheld from . . . ?*" Every time you find a big one, check for responsibility on it: "*What part of that incident could you be responsible for?*"

They will spend days not talking to each other. But the only time they really start to claw each other up doing something like this is when you as the counselor goof. So long as you are effective and winning, you're all right. But if you get detoured and talked out of handling what you should have handled, you find yourself handling some other incident that has nothing to do with the marriage, and you're in trouble.

Three or four times probably while you're trying to clean up the marriage they will undoubtedly decide that it's all over and there's no reason to go on with it because they couldn't possibly. The thing that saves the day each time is to get whichever one feels they can't go on to just remember what he or she did rather than what's been done *to* him or her.

Start clearing up a marriage by establishing two-way communication between the marital partners and you've got it made. The right way to counsel a marriage would be with the marital partners both present, otherwise a phenomenon of transference or super-sympathy or something can set in, and it just shouldn't be there. So if a person has trouble with his marriage, the best thing to do is to ask, "Are you both willing to settle up this marriage before we go any further?"

"Settle up the marriage, yes, but my wife won't have anything to do with marriage counseling."

"Is that so? Well, better bring her over."

Set them both down in the session and let them go at it back and forth. Ask them the questions I have just given you for cleaning up a marriage. First on one until he or she has very good indicators then on the other, always maintaining the communication cycle, allowing no interruptions to the communication cycle by one or the other.

You should not take one marital partner and counsel him separately and secretly. You get them both by the scruff of the neck and set them down across from each other. You sit there and ask the questions of them. Remember, they both must be present. Don't do it in absentia if you really want to keep the marriage together. They'll probably go home and beat each other's head off, but that's better than leaving each other. Almost anybody who's been deserted will tell you that.

A marriage should be cleaned up by a professional auditor but don't flinch at trying to do it using what you have learned about overts and withholds and the technique I've given you on marriage counseling. Go ahead and take a rap at it. There are enough Scientologists around now to pick you up and put you back together again. You have no real training, you're reading this book and you're determined that you're somehow going to straighten this out with Grace and Edgar.

Undoubtedly the most workable thing of all would be for the husband and wife to save up a little bit to go to a Scientology church and get trained, both of them keeping their noses clean and knowing what they were doing. When they're all finished with their training, they have at it. That requires a lot of self-restraint but that would be the most perfect fix-up.

But to take anybody who knows nothing about Scientology and have them do this alone is not such a good idea. They'd just kill each other off. In the first place, only one person would be doing it; the other would give no cooperation. It would probably be totally covert. He'd have the total idea it was what the other person had done that had wrecked the marriage. All these misconceptions would stack together to a total bust.

Maritally, the soundest plan would actually be for both of them to go through a Scientology communication course at a Church or local Mission, get the discipline from that; then get the overts and withholds off on the marriage, and get responsibility checked on each and every part of them. The marriage would go back together again, but not without a few flying frying pans. You're a perfectionist if you believe you can put it all together again in one night because the number of overts and withholds usually takes a little longer to detail.

A sound marriage, then, consists of putting together a thetan association without overts and withholds, created into existence, continued for the mutual perpetuation and protection of the members of the family. This is a very simple arrangement, and a highly satisfactory arrangement if it continues to be simple.

When it gets complex, it's not so satisfactory. For instance, when a marriage occurs in China it really doesn't occur because the oldest man of the husband's family is still the head of the family and the wife still serves the husband's mother. They are surrounded by bunches of rules.

Actually it is not important what rules they're surrounded by as long as there is free communication amongst the members of that family or group. And if there is free communication amongst the members of that group, their affinity is sufficiently high to take the shocks and hammers and pounds of life. If the individuals connected with a family are not self-supportive then the shocks can be rough indeed. But on a self-supportive, mutually co-supportive basis, people have a better chance of making it than alone. And that is one of the basic philosophies on which marriage is based. Without such a family, a little kid wouldn't make it at all.

When the state comes along and tries to supplant the family with barracks, watch out. Somebody has Man down to a criminal level.

But a marriage can exist; a marriage, no matter how strained, can be put back together. A family or group can exist, but not without two-way communication. A group cannot exist unless it continues to be created into existence by the members of the group. And when large numbers of the group are engaged in unpostulating it, or in postulating it out of existence—as revolutionary parties and that sort of thing are concerned—then of course the rest of the group has to work much harder to keep the group together. Eventually they get tired of keeping the group together and it falls apart.

But if a family or other group is to exist, it has to work at it. The group has to be clean as far as its members are concerned. There has to be free communication. There must be a continued wish to continue to postulate the group into existence. If those factors are present, then the group can survive, whether it be a family, a company, a government, or something even larger.

That's how you make a group.

HCO PL 13 November 1970
Org Series 13
Planning by Product

4
Be-Do-Have

One of the cycles or correct sequence of action in this universe is Be-Do-Have.

This sequence is often altered in individuals. Be is first in the physical universe, Do is second, Have is third.

By getting it out of sequence a considerable confusion can be generated.

A lot of riddles of human behavior can be solved by realizing this goes out of sequence or gets omissions.

The Spanish peasant and the Spanish officials go to war at the drop of a straw. Their history is jammed with revolts. The peasant knows that if he is a peasant (be) and does his work (do) he should have.

The Spanish official is stuck in BE. He *has* so he can *be and* he doesn't have to do anything. Also a degree or title in Spain is a BE and there is no *do*. So there is no have unless it comes from the peasant. The two altered cycles collide.

Juvenile delinquency and shattered lives in the West stem directly from corruptions of this cycle.

Children in the West are commonly asked "What are you going to BE when you grow up?" It is a silly question and can drive any child up the wall. Because it's the wrong question—hits the wrong end of the cycle.

He is also asked "What are you going to DO in life?" That's just as bad.It is quite difficult to answer.

If we asked children, "What do you want to PRODUCE in life?" we could probably get a workable answer. From *that* he could figure out what he'd have to do to produce that and from that he could know what he had to BE. Then, with a little cooperation he would be able to lead a happy and valuable life.

Concentrating on BE? one finds him ready to BE allright but then he stands around the next 50 years waiting for his havingness to fall out of the sky or slide to him via a welfare state.

Therefore one must ask what has to be *done* to produce that? And there may be a lot of dones figured out and put in sequence.

Now one can work on BE.

Here is a common altered cycle:

Mr. A has a Truck—HAVE. He tries to figure out what to do with it. He works it around to try to make money. He would usually go broke. As he supposes he already has a product—a truck, and he needs a product—"money," he rarely backs it up to a BE.

Some people's "think" gets all involved in altered sequences or omissions of the BE-DO-HAVE cycle.

An activity has several final products. All of them must be worked out and considered. Then one can work out the sequence of DOs (each with a product) in order to accomplish the final products. Only then can one work out a BE.

By omission or fixations on one of these points a person or an organization can fail or perhaps never even get started.

Fixation on DO without any product in view leads to bored wandering through life.

Mothers even know this one. "Mama, what shall I do?" is a long drawn refrain. Smart Mamas often say "make a cake" or "make mud pies" or "make a house." Dumb ones say "go and play and stop bothering me!"

Armies, with guard or death "products," get obsessed with DO to a point where officers and non-comms will state "get those men busy!" No product. Meaningless, often frantic, and useless do.

The above data, missing in society, contributes to juvenile delinquency, crime, the welfare state and a dying civilization.

5 Child Scientology

Scientology Journal
Issue 14G

Save the child and you save the nation.

If, in the course of the next 15 years, Scientologists were to specialize in the group processing of children, it might well follow that all of the goals of Scientology would thereby be realized. Thus, by processing children between the ages of six and ten, we would achieve in 15 years a sanity and alertness never before obtained in that portion of the populace between the ages of 21 and 26, the age bracket which contains the energy and influence most strikingly felt by civilization.

Child Scientology could very well be, in terms of practice, the most important single field of endeavor in the religion. So used, without other addresses or assistances, Scientology might well bring about the condition of world peace—even if only by eradicating, through the restoration of sanity, the enthusiasm of youth for the sham glory of war. Therefore, we address here a subject which is broader than "what will I do to cure Johnnie's sneezes." Whether or not we are interested in those sneezes, whether or not we have tolerance or intolerance for children, whether or not we care to give time to the problem of child adjustment and sanity, each of us who has a vested interest in the continuation of Earth and of Man should be willing to invest some of his industry in the investigation and application of the group processing of children.

Hence, this is written, not to those who are interested in children, not to those who have family problems, not even to those whose duty it is to instruct children, but to anyone interested in the goals of Scientology.

In order to utilize Scientology in the attainment of the goal of a sane stratum of the populace, do you need special training? No, not beyond the contents of this section and a knowledge of the book, *Self Analysis,* a simple text and *Child Dianetics* which contains Dianetic processing for children.

What passport do you need to help children? None.

What recommendations, papers, figures, historical documents, statistics, and other buffoonery do you need to assist children? None.

Is there any lack of groups of children? No. Where are groups of children to be found? In schools, in hospitals, in orphan asylums, in children's societies, in boy and girl organizations such as the Boy Scouts in the YMCA's, in Sunday schools, and anywhere that interested people forward the battle to prepare the child of today to become the sane adult of tomorrow. Theirs has been a gallant struggle in the face of almost insuperable odds. It is time these people had some help.

Historically, child therapy has been as difficult as it is now simple.

Let us be very blunt—we are not interested in the problems of the child's mind. In Scientology, we are no longer concerned with the inopportune and conceited short-circuit between epistemology and the human brain which has resulted in the "science" of psychotherapy.

The Scientologist practicing with groups of children should disabuse anyone in authority of any lingering thought that the Scientologist might be using psychotherapy. The concern of psychotherapy is with the thinking processes of the human brain. The concern of the Scientologist is purely with the beingness of the child, which is to say his spirit, his potentialities, and his happiness. A Scientologist working with children, who permits himself to be led into arguments concerning psychotherapy is permitting to exist and be part of the argument, the erroneous concept that gains in learning and behavior are attainable through a rearrangement, by direct address, of the physical habits or fears of the child.

It is possible to reform a child's attitude toward existence by working with his mind. The best results in the field of psychotherapy were obtained by Dianetics, but even prior to Dianetics, many child psychotherapists had obtained considerably improved attitudes and behavior on the part of children by directly addressing the individual child and forming with the child a personal friendship which opened the child's interest sufficiently to permit an awareness of the existing conditions of present time. This was possible because the child's awareness of present time could be suppressed by incidents, which, having force and stress contained in them, sought to represent in themselves that they were present time. But this does not say that the optimum results are obtainable by this process of addressing the past in order to heal the present. Psychotherapy could be said to be a series of processes by which the past is addressed to remedy the present or by which a physical matter, such as the human brain, is rearranged (as in a pre-frontal lobotomy) in order to inhibit odious conduct in present time. The 500 or 600 percent gains obtainable by the application of Child Scientology to groups of children are not obtainable by addressing the past to remedy the present.

Scientology increases the beingness and potentialities of beingness of the child in present time in order to secure the capabilities of the child in the future. It does this by exercising the capabilities of beingness of the child, and is about as closely related to psychotherapy as penmanship might be or, for that matter, any other subject in the school curriculum. Thus, no one can reasonably object, on the grounds that psychotherapy is being practiced, to the education of the child in present time so as to fit him for his future.

It will be very difficult for the Volunteer Minister to keep himself from being led into this snare, because tests in "child psychology" on those in his group will indicate that their reading ages leap under this process, that children who have never been able to master even rudimentary subjects begin to learn, and that behavior which, in the past, has been highly lacking in good order and discipline turns markedly for the better. These and many other advantages to be gained in the application of Child Scientology to groups of children cannot be classified as psychotherapy simply because they attain the goals of psychotherapy. Because a thing obtains the goals another thing hoped to obtain is no reason to assume that the two are identical. This obtaining of goals was never accomplished in terms of groups by psychotherapy, and, indeed, psychotherapy never obtained these goals—even on individual children. But that person who immediately proclaims that we now have child psychotherapy simply because we have Child Scientology is making an extremely bad error in thinking and in semantics.

Significantly, camping out, hiking, hobbies, and excellent and personable group leaders have obtained results similar to these, down through the ages. But one does not classify these as psychotherapy. What we have done in Scientology is render available to those in authority over groups of children the means of procuring results of magnitude in the absence of highly personable instructors, camping out, hobbies, individual attention to the child, perfect home life, and other intensely desirable but very scarce commodities. Any expert in the field of child study can inform you that it is possible to take any child and, by giving him enough time, improve him. Parents can tell you this. Anyone, in short, could have gotten results from a child by sufficiently devoting himself to the child's interests. When one realizes that this might consume dozens or thousands of hours per child, one sees immediately that without the fundamentals of Scientology the mass resolution of the problems of children is impossible. The question has been, "How do we do it without devoting this special time to each and every child, since it is not possible to devote that time?" The answer, of course, lies in the fact that a group of 30 or 500 children simultaneously can be given Child Scientology by one untrained person, and that these children will accrue the various gains to be realized in the past only by individual address and interest.

What is the process given to groups of children?

Taking a copy of *Self Analysis* the Volunteer Minister, the

Scientologist, the scout leader or other person, delivers to the assembled group imaginary scenes to envision. The children envision these scenes, one after another.

The imaginary scenes are taken from the lists found in *Self Analysis.* They are selected and reformed from these lists in accordance with the ability of the children to understand them.

This process is continued for about 20 minutes per day. It may be continued for as short a time as three weeks for any group of children with excellent results but more optimumly may be incorporated permanently into their routine activities.

The Scientologist will discover in his first session that the children in the group divide roughly into three classes: (1) Those who cannot get any mock-ups at all, (2) those who get them too fast or too slow, and (3) those who get them well. He divides his group into three sections. He gives processing—as described above—to each of the sections, processing those who cannot get mock-ups the most, and processing those who are too fast or too slow slightly more than the third group, which is given the continued routine processing. Ordinarily, it will be found that the three groups will assume a parity in a short time, and so can be continued as one group.

The person delivering the lists must know that he should not give special attention to individuals in the group simply because these individuals are having trouble, for this would mean to each child in the group that he or she would have to have trouble so as to get individual attention.

The Volunteer Minister must also know that the children often become quite active, dramatic, and emotional when they do this process, for they find it a great deal of sport and in the case of a school, he should be prepared to have complaints from adjoining rooms, should he be so unwise as not to arrange for a suitable period of the day for processing.

The Volunteer Minister or Scientologist should know that a child will occasionally "boil off." This, as a manifestation of unconsciousness, is very mild, and simply means that some period of the child's life wherein he was unconscious has been slightly restimulated. He should know that all he has to do to arouse the child from this state is to have him *"remember something that is real to him," "a time when he was in good communication with somebody,"* and *"a time when he felt that somebody loved him."*

The person applying the lists should also know that he should not rebuke, criticize, evaluate or tease the children because of their mock-ups or their troubles with them. He should also know that he must not evaluate these mock-ups or try to interpret them as dreams, since whatever relationship they may have to dreams and regardless of how fascinating they may be, their interpretation will reduce the effectiveness and ability of the child. In fact, their evaluation for the child is actually destructive to his pride and beingness, and such interpretation not only has no part in his processing but is expressly forbidden as being intensely harmful.

What else can be expected immediately?

A small percentage of the children will not respond at all. A small percentage will become worried because of the activities and noise of the other children. A small percentage will be unchanged, though responsive. The remaining 75 or 85 percent will advance variously in their intelligence quotients, their behaviors, and their personal abilities (in particular, their ability to learn).

By experience, no disabilities will occur because of this process, excepting those which are occasioned by sudden upsets in home life or by reason of teasing or evaluation on the part of the person applying the list.

By all standard tests of learning ability, reading skill, differentiation and so forth, it will be discovered that the group as a group has progressed very far beyond what anyone has ever had the right to expect from the application of any form of child improvement. This should not be labelled a wild claim; it is rather a sober fact which is based upon very wide, careful testing and observation under many differing conditions, under many types of instructors, and under many groups of children.

Quite incidentally, and certainly of no great interest except that it makes good telling, psychosomatic difficulties, perception inhibitions (such as stuttering) and various other disabilities, the correction of which is classified entirely in the field of psychotherapy, have a tendency to de-intensify or disappear in the child who is part of a group undergoing this processing. Such improvements—no matter how dramatic they may be—are not the reason why this processing is given to the group, but instead are simply an added bonus and entirely a by-product. Indeed, it is a rather grim joke that Scientology so employed and without direction toward the release of such ills, does rather routinely what medicine has been unable to do. It is of no great concern to the Scientologist that this happens. Certainly, he does not want to prevent it from happening but he must not lose sight of the fact that he is not processing a group to make it happen. He will be given his greatest thanks as a result of such cases and his benefits will be measured by them, but this should not turn his head from the main goal of the process, which is to make a group of able children far more able. Parents, for instance, who have spent thousands of dollars on little Johnny's asthma, discover one day, after he has been a part of such a group for some time that he is no longer troubled with asthma. Further, it is doubtful if he will ever be troubled with asthma again. Parents presented with such evidence have a tendency either to become angry or to be grateful, depending upon their level of sanity.

The group auditor (or the Volunteer Minister) is not there to cure, heal, repair, patch up, treat, advise, council, or otherwise to mend children. By definition, the group auditor is one who works to create a new state of beingness in a group of people by the administration of lists prepared by myself. It should be clearly understood that we are attempting something which has never happened before. We are achieving a state in people which has not previously existed. We are taking another step forward with Man. We are not trying to bring children back to normal, nor are we trying to remedy existing conditions. We are factually striking out to attain a level of culture and civilization higher than those attained before, in which we include any period of any nation anywhere. The Volunteer Minister has about as much relationship to psychotherapy as a stone mason at work on a new city has to the proprietor of a junkyard. The Volunteer Minister is not working to return children to normal. They have never been other than they are, and in the absence of what we know now, never could have been what we hope them to be. People who try to classify the group auditor as one who is making children normal by treating them are actually insulting the group auditor. In the absence of Scientology or whatever it would have been called had it been discovered in the past or future, such repair work was the best that could be done. The attainment of gains by the eradication of something, differs considerably from the attainment of gains by the creation of something. All processing in Scientology today is positive gain processing and is in fact, creative; the work of the auditor is creative whether he is working on an individual or a group.

The special problems of individual children which confront the Volunteer Minister should be referred by him to a professional auditor, or handled by himself as a professional auditor providing he is trained in that capacity. Therefore, parents or interested persons desiring special consideration for individual problems should be directed elsewhere to his local church or mission. The Volunteer Minister's interest is in terms of mass production. He is creating with his work a new state of beingness, a new type of childhood. This is a state that is desirable not simply because it contrasts with former states, but desirable because it means a better civilization or perhaps one might say, a civilization.

What theory underlies this?

The Volunteer Minister needs no more theory than that contained in this section and in *Self Analysis* to succeed in his work. Indeed, he need not even have a solid grip on that much theory for the process to work for him. However, in the absence of background data, many things may strike him as strange or unexplained and lacking the data, he may believe himself to be dealing with an imprecise thing and so wander off course. Thus, the best Volunteer Minister would be the one who is best founded in theory and who is a professional auditor as well. The next best Volunteer Minister would be one who has studied this section and *Self Analysis*.

Although this is apparently very simple—that we just get a child to imagine something and the child is then better—and although people will occasionally try to tell the Volunteer Minister that it has been long known that creative imagination plays a considerable role in the life of the child, yet mock-up processing from prepared lists is based upon fundamental precisions which are quite invariable.

With much too much simplicity, it can be stated that here the imagination is being utilized in such a way as to bring it under the control, direction, and self-discipline of the child. The knowledge that we are not actually dealing with imagination as it has been classified in the past, and that in reality we are dealing with quite another function: namely, clarification of the role of imagination, at least makes one feel himself conversant with what is happening.

In mathematics, even in that pallid thing called arithmetic, it is necessary to observe and realize the existence of a problem and the factors of the problem, and to combine these to predict an answer. In the entire field of life, it is imagination which delivers answers. If one cannot imagine he cannot predict. The factors of life are more complex than the factors of arithmetic, but they do not differ so far as mental functioning is concerned. There are simply many more of them. One can teach a child by rote that two plus two equals four, but many an instructor and many a parent with the fondest hopes for the future of a child have, after the child's education was complete, discovered that the child either cannot or will not utilize the data to resolve problems in his own existence. In such a child, the ability to imagine the answer by recombining existing factors has not been developed nor disciplined. Many an engineering school has been embarrassed by turning forth honor graduates who yet failed dismally in the reduction of rudimentary practical problems to workable solutions. Even a thing as apparently precise as mathematics yet requires, in the good mathematician, an enormous amount of imagination. In general, symbols and figures, statistics and data, serve only to assist the functioning of the mind in a solution of problems. These are at best crutches to be utilized by an active intelligence. The mind is always the servo-mechanism of mathematics, a thing which even the better mathematicians are apt to overlook. Thus, when we are trying to teach a child, whether to be proficient in geometry or in handling his body, we must teach him as well to predict a future state of beingness; if he cannot predict a future state of beingness, he cannot resolve problems. As a statement, the phrase, "prediction of a future state of beingness," almost encompasses the function of the human mind. Prediction of beingness is somewhat different from simple prediction. It is not necessary to have pictures to tell one what is going to happen, but it is necessary to have the potentiality of imagining what is going to happen to accurately assess a situation.

Thus, it may be seen that the inhibition of the imagination of a child directly results in the inhibition of the child's ability to resolve problems relating to his own environment and his own life. This nullification of imagination should not exist; however, the individual should be able to utilize this imagination, and the imagination should be under the discipline of the individual. A good instructor realizes that it is the discipline of the student's mind by the student himself which accrues to the student the benefits of education.

The discipline of the imagination is essential in any learning process. The infant and the child are peculiarly prone to utilize their imaginations in such a way as to make their imaginations utilize them. Their imaginations are not wild; they are simply not founded upon fact and are not correlated with the existing state of affairs. At night, the child is hounded by nightmares and delusions; by day his imagination conjures up for him images based upon factual and unimportant data of his environment which frighten and inhibit him. He is given to believe, then, that there is some hidden thing in his vicinity which is inhibitive to his further survival. Delusion is imagination out of control. The control and discipline of imagination and it's employment for the artistic and practical gains of the individual would be the highest goal of a training process. There have been great instructors in the past, great teachers who could lead their students forward by their own personal magnetism. Their effort was centered upon giving the student into his own hands and this was accomplished by causing the student to desire to discipline his own beingness. However, the discipline of beingness is not necessarily the limitation of beingness. It is better to be able to decide and control a few things to be, than to be under the whip of an imagination which drives one to be a great many things, none of which are under one's control. These processes then aim directly towards disciplining the imagination and bringing it under the control of the individual child.

Throughout the day and every day of his life, the child is told that things do not belong to him. If he is given a pair of shoes, he is informed that they are not his shoes by the first command from the parent that he polish them. In the case of nearly all children, even though they seem to have possessions, they themselves do not believe themselves to own anything. Their bodies, their minds, their toys, their clothes, their habits, their mannerisms, and their likes and dislikes are all under the continuous impact of the MEST universe and other intelligences. There is something, however, which a child can own—an image which he creates himself. In fact, he will only attain to those images which he does create for himself, because in his opinion any attempt to reach images created for him by others (particularly by duress) is antipathetic to his survival. At every hand he is driven from possession and driven from beingness, for the child can possess only those things which he feels free to be.

The creation and control of mental images performs another function in that it utilizes and disciplines energy. In creating mental images which he then controls, the child discovers first that he can own something, next that he can control something, next that here is something he is free to be, and next that he has control over mental functions. Dignity and purpose are native to the child; badness and uncontrol are not. Thus, by envisioning images the child comes into possession of his own beingness and is convinced that he is free to be something. The change which comes with this realization is not an ultimate or absolute thing, for there is a gradient scale of beingness and there are always new heights above any last plateau reached. This is a gradual and continuous process, this creation of beingnesses (or symbologically, mock-ups), and the process continues in any phase of life so long as the person has life in him. The direct attack on his problem by the use of mock-up processing results as one would expect; it brings the child under his own discipline and makes him capable of being what he wants to be, not what he is forced to be. At the same time, it renders him less reactive toward disciplinary actions undertaken for his own good and toward educational measures which are provided for his future security. Acceptance will be found to replace resentment of education.

The goal of an instructor is to instruct. There is an old story about the Rough Riders, a regiment in the Spanish-American War. Their most famous exploit was the taking of San Juan Hill, yet there is an incident in this which is worthy of our notice. The orders of the day were posted and stated explicitly that they were to "jump off" from El Canay at five o'clock the following morning and were to take San Juan Hill. The Rough Riders awoke at 4:30 a.m. to discover that one small thing had been omitted from their plans: they had, as yet, to take El Canay. Thus, before they could execute their orders they had to assault and take another objective, which they did take with severe losses, and from which they finally carried out the main assault, many hours overdue, again with enormous casualties. Thus it is that a military organization can suffer frightfully from trying to fight one battle when another has to be fought first. The Volunteer Minister is supposed to educate children, the camp leader is supposed to entertain them, and the hospital nurse is supposed to make them well. Yet, standing as an obstacle before each one of these and any other individuals attempting to handle children, is, in actuality, the lack of a child. Bluntly the child is not there. He is sitting in the classroom but his mind is elsewhere. He is in the hospital as a body, but is maundering about the scene of the accident which sent him there. He is supposed to be having a good time in camp, yet he is actually at home playing with his dog. Any attempt to work with a child is an attempt to contact and get into communication with the child. Unless one can get into communication with the child he cannot perform his duties as pertain to that child.

The task of communicating with a child does not begin with talking to the child. It begins with finding a child to talk to. There are many tricks which lead a child's interest sufficiently into present time to allow one to communicate with him. Anyone dealing with children knows that this is the primary problem in that task. But it is a very terrible strain trying to maintain the child's attention in present time while one communicates with the child. If one had a process which made it possible for the child to be in present time and to get him there easily, that process would, of course, be very welcome to the child. The group processing of children, or the use of the same process on an individual child, is a workable answer to this problem.

[illegible]here is no reason to go back into the past after the child (as in [illegible] therapy) if one has a modus operandi to bring the child into the [illegible]t. You certainly would not actively go after things which easily [illegible]o you. Application of these lists in this fashion to groups of child[illegible]rings them into present time and thus to their instructor or leader. Consequently, once he has used it, an instructor finds this processing as necessary a part of classroom activity as ringing the school bell. It is one thing to get the body into class, it is another thing to get the mind into class. The instructor is being paid to instruct, but before he can instruct there must be somebody there to be instructed. This is terribly elementary, but it is a problem which has been overlooked and it is a problem which, in many cases, has made education an arduous process. Children in present time are very easy to look after, very easy to instruct, and very easy to live with. Children out of present time, bent on revenge, and fresh from a quarrelsome breakfast table in an antipathetic home, form a noisy and rebellious group. The behavior of a child out of present time is not easily predicted, and this unpredictability is a considerable strain to the child's leader. A child out of present time walks off the curb into heavy traffic, falls down fire escapes, gets hit with gymnasium equipment, hurts himself in games and causes those multitudes of upsets which make the life of a child shepherd an onerous one, at times.

The problem of the parent in the home is no different from the problems of the instructor. The continual nag-nag-nag necessary with children is occasioned solely by two things: one is that the child has no real understanding of his role (for it has never been explained to him) and so has no beingness in the house as part of the family, part of an economic unit or part of a work team; and the other is that the child is not there. The more one corrects and punishes the child, the less the child is there, since, in essence, correction is "go back into the past and pick up punishment data to remind you that the future is going to be unpleasant."

The process of mocking up is peculiarly suited to children for in the main they possess brilliant ability. An adult preclear is filled with envy at the ability of a child to obtain mock-ups and control them. The time to salvage a human being and get him out of the past into the present time is when that human being is a child, for he thus benefits most from his environment and all his education within it. Out of present time, the data and experience are going nobody knows where.

All the theory one needs to know in order to apply Child Scientology to groups is contained here. There is a great deal to know in addition to this (almost all of it is as simple) and it should all be known before much individual work is done on a particular child. This, however, will suffice for groups.

What is a mock-up?

A mock-up is not a mental image but an additional beingness. One is afraid and troubled by those things which he cannot be but must fight. One's effort is mainly expended in fighting shadows in the belief that these shadows are things which one must not be or cannot be. The limitation, rather than the increase, of beingness is the common course of existence. One finds out "by experience" (most of it incorrect) that he cannot be a great many things. His ability to be is also his ability to communicate, for the things which he is are those things which demark the amount of space he can occupy.

A mock-up, then, is more than a mental picture; it is a self-created object which exists as itself or symbolizes some object in the MEST universe. It is a thing which one can be. One can be it because one can see it. Those things which one cannot see, he cannot see because he cannot be them. In terms of human experience, beingness is space. Space is a viewpoint of dimension. The points which mark an area of space are called anchor points and these, with the viewpoint, alone are responsible for space. The creation of anchor points, then, is the creation of space, which is in itself the creation of beingness. The essential in any object is the space which it occupies. Thus, the ability to be an object first depends upon the ability to be the space which it occupies.

When one puts out pictures which he himself creates, he at once demarks space and occupies, with his own creation, an area of space. Thus, he knows it is safe to occupy this space. Thus, he knows that he can be that space. Thus, he can be that object. It does not follow that he is that object simply because he creates that object, but he has assumed by its creation that there is a new thing which he can be and a new space which he can occupy.

A mock-up then is a picture, preferably in full color, with three dimensions and in motion. There is, however, an astonishing variety of disabilities connected with mock-ups. The mock-ups of one individual are flat, those of another have no color, and yet another gets them only on the far side of a black curtain. Some mock-ups have no motion in them and some have too much. The term "mock-up" embraces all these conditions.

"Mock-up" is derived from the World War II phrase which indicated a symbolized weapon or area of attack. Here, it means, in essence, "something which a person makes up himself."

The mock-up actually contains energy and mass. It occupies space. It should be under the control of the individual.

A mock-up differs from a delusion in that in order for a thing to be a mock-up, it must answer three conditions: (1) it must be created by an individual, (2) he must know that it is his, and (3) he must get it under control so that it does not do things unless he commands it.

A mock-up can be of anything and it can be located in any direction or at any distance from the individual creating it.

The ability of an individual to get a mock-up is an index of the individual's distance from present time. That person who gets very clear, brilliant mock-ups which are definitely under his control and which do not perform erratically without his consent, is in present time. This graduates on down to an inability to get mock-ups of any kind, which means one is very far from present time.

One can generally establish the quality and character of a person's mock-ups and, consequently, the distance of that person from present time.

How will other factors in the child's environment affect this process?

The child who is a member of a group can be expected to have many factors in his environment which are antipathetic to his best survival. Such things as quarrelsome homes, lack of parents, and physical disability, all occasion problems for the group member which are beyond the scope of the group auditor's application of these processes. Children who have special problems need special processing. This does not mean, however, that these special problems would not be alleviated in greater or lesser degree by the child's being a member of a group which is being given Scientology. Many remarkable gradual or sudden recoveries from disabilities, as well as adjustments to antipathetic surroundings, have been noted and logged when these techniques were in their experimental stages, but such recoveries or adjustments should not be expected of the process.

A child who receives Scientology as part of the group can be expected to cope better with those problems which are assailing him than he could in the absence of Scientology; just as a child who is poorly fed at home can be expected to do better if he receives a hot meal in the middle of the day at school.

Invalidation of the benefit he might get from group processing might be given the child by a neurotic parent. One case has been noted where the child returned to the group after a short absence and was unable to get any mock-ups of any kind whatsoever. It was discovered, however, that as the work progressed without any further special attention than noting the child was suffering from a sudden disability, the ability returned. The parental admonition, in other words, had no lasting effect upon the child. It might be a matter for caution on the part of the group auditor not to discuss the process with the parents, although this would be rather an extreme measure, taken to prevent such invalidations and resultant temporary inabilities, in a small number of cases.

One group auditor who consistently did not give end-of-session processing after having given ten minutes of mock-ups to his group, found that one child was badly out of present time as a result of the process. The error in this case was the omission of end-of-session processing as contained in the back of *Self Analysis*; the total damage involved was the momentary inability of the child to demonstrate an arithmetic problem. The child was only a little way out of present time. He had become so entranced with his mock-up that he was still with it.

Children occasionally experience sharp pains while doing mock-ups, and in such instances, they're letting go of old incidents and punishments. The end-of-session lists take care of any such occurrence.

It is noteworthy that a group undergoing this processing during an epidemic of measles had a lower loss-of-attendance rate than the other classes in the same school which were not undergoing processing.

Here's how it is done.

The Volunteer Minister opens his copy of *Self Analysis,* goes to the beginning of the list, looks for a mock-up (the first one in that list that he can use for delivery to children), and says "All right. Now let's see if we can get a picture of you enjoying something." He pauses, and as soon as it is apparent to him that the majority of the class have such a picture, he gives the next process.

After a short period of this, he asks for a show of hands to find out how many have been getting mock-ups easily. He then selects this group out of the group, and then asks for a show of hands as to how many got no mock-ups at all and selects this group out. He then has three groups. He can, himself, render processing to each of these groups separately; or he can delegate the processing of the no-mock-up group to a student of that group, and the processing of the too-fast-too-slow group to another student, retaining for himself the easy group. It is desirable that he retain the processing of the easy group for himself, because this group will be the largest group and out of it will come the very best results. He should always remember that he is trying to make the able more able, and he should repress in himself any instinctive closure with the most nearly disabled.

The two groups which are not as able as the easy group are processed exactly as the main group is processed; the reason for their separation is that the less able hold back the able, and the ability of the able rouses the envy of those who are poor at the game and tends to press them into apathy about it.

The Volunteer Minister gives approximately 15 minutes of Scientology out of the lists to his group and then gives the group the end-of-session list from the book *Self Analysis.* This consists of: (1) rapidly sketching over the session, (2) sketching over what has been going on again, with particular attention to how each member has been sitting, (3) going over the session again with regard only to present time surroundings, (4) fixing each individual's attention upon a pleasant object near to him now. This is repeated until the group is refreshed, and requires only five or ten minutes. The total period of application of the entire process is about 20 minutes, and should be done at least once a day for a period of three weeks to get a very marked change in a group. When achieved, however, such a change is then noted to be considerable. Children who have never been able to study before, or who have been very poor at their lessons will be found to be interested in and good at them.

There's a special case of the child whose school work is of a low quality, yet who has a very high I.Q. This child is found to be unable to mock-up anything he hasn't actually seen. He would be able to mock-up his instructor and he would be able to mock-up a glass of soda water, but he would not be able to mock-up his instructor drinking a glass of soda water since he has not actually seen this. This child should be watched for; it will be discovered that the mock-ups he gets are not really his. This is remedied by simply changing them until he knows they are his. He is actually a no-mock-up case although he can get pictures; a picture is not a mock-up, a mock-up belongs to the preclear. If a child cannot mock-up creatively, his work will bear no relationship to his I.Q. If a child has a high I.Q. but no creative mock-ups, then his work will be poor.

This is all the background one needs to apply Scientology to groups of children or groups of adults. Groups of adults are handled in exactly the same way, and they respond as well as but with not quite the same lucidity, as children. On this basis, an individual can build with his own experience. Such experience is essential to a deep insight into what is happening, for nothing written here beyond the basic data can supplant the actual experience of taking a group and bearing with it for several weeks and then seeing what has happened to it and in it. This, in itself, is sufficient recompense for the trouble taken.

It is expressly recommended that the Volunteer Minister take up the processing of groups of children by going to local schools and institutions and getting the consent of those in charge to conduct this game. He need have no qualms about what might happen, for, as tests have proven the institution and even the highest authority in relation to that institution will not be anything but pleased with what occurs (unless, of course, some intensely personal factor enters).

A Volunteer Minister would do well to acquire the six-hour taped lecture course on group processing which supplements the above data, and give it free-of-charge to school teachers and others in his area. First and foremost, it will accomplish the goals of Scientology and second, but sometimes important to an auditor or minister, here is opened the most certain source of preclears known, for parents who are aware of the benefits being achieved with the child are prone to see that the child gets even further benefit in the form of professional processing.

This particular highway of approach to the problems of the world has been found workable. It is extremely easy to introduce these processes into a school and to incline instructors into their use. It is easy to put these processes to work in nursing homes, in veterans' establishments, and in many other places. The amount of help an individual can deliver per capita with these processes easily is greater than with any other single method now in existence; for he is giving men back to themselves, and there is no greater gift at his command.

0

Third Party

Third Party Checksheet

Purpose:

To thoroughly understand third party technology and be able to successfully apply it as a Volunteer Minister to handle quarrels.

a	Study Section 1 The Third Party Law.	________
b	Drill: Write down several examples of conflicts you have seen between two people.	________
c	Drill: Go to a playground and observe a quarrel between two people.	________
d	Study Section 2 Justice.	________
e	Drill: Find two different examples with a friend or associate of times when a verbal or written false report by another caused him some trouble.	________
f	Study Section 3 Third Party Investigation Procedure.	________
g	Study Section 4 Third Party How to Find one.	________
h	Study Section 5 Third Party Investigations.	________
i	Drill: Find a real example of two people, marital partners or family members or friends quarrelling. Introduce yourself as a Volunteer Minister and get their agreement to let you help them clear up their disagreement. Once they agree, have them both read Section 1 entitled The Third Party Law. Ensure they both understand it. Do a third party interview and	

find the third party, making sure that both people have good indicators and are now happy that the real third party has been found. Check back several days later to see how the two people are doing. ________

Third Party Pack

1

|HCOB 26 December 1968

The Third Party Law

I have for a very long time studied the causes of violence and conflict amongst individuals and nations.

If Chaldea could vanish, if Babylon turn to dust, if Egypt could become a badlands, if Sicily could have 160 prosperous cities and be a looted ruin before the year zero and a near desert ever since—and all this in SPITE of all the work and wisdom and good wishes and intent of human beings, then it must follow as the dark follows sunset that something must be unknown to Man concerning all his works and ways. And that this something must be so deadly and so pervasive as to destroy all his ambitions and his chances long before their time.

Such a thing would have to be some natural law unguessed at by himself.

And there *is* such a law, apparently, that answers these conditions of being deadly, unknown and embracing all activities.

The law would seem to be:

A THIRD PARTY MUST BE PRESENT AND UNKNOWN IN EVERY QUARREL FOR A CONFLICT TO EXIST.

or

FOR A QUARREL TO OCCUR, AN UNKNOWN THIRD PARTY MUST BE ACTIVE IN PRODUCING IT BETWEEN TWO POTENTIAL OPPONENTS.

or

WHILE IT IS COMMONLY BELIEVED TO TAKE TWO TO MAKE A FIGHT, A THIRD PARTY MUST EXIST AND MUST DEVELOP IT FOR ACTUAL CONFLICT TO OCCUR.

It is very easy to see that two in conflict are fighting. They are very visible. What is harder to see or suspect is that a third party existed and actively promoted the quarrel.

The usually unsuspected and "reasonable" third party, the bystander who denies any part of it *is* the one that brought the conflict into existence in the first place.

The hidden third party, seeming at times to be a supporter of only one side, is to be found as the instigator.

This is a useful law on many dynamics.

It *is* the cause of war.

One sees two fellows shouting bad names at each other, sees them come to blows. No one else is around. So *they,* of course, "caused the fight." But there *was* a third party.

Tracing these down, one comes upon incredible data. That is the trouble. The incredible is too easily rejected. One way to hide things is to make them incredible.

Clerk A and Messenger B have been arguing. They blaze into direct conflict. Each blames the other. NEITHER ONE IS CORRECT AND SO THE QUARREL DOES NOT RESOLVE SINCE ITS TRUE CAUSE IS NOT ESTABLISHED.

One looks into such a case THOROUGHLY. He finds the incredible. The wife of Clerk A has been sleeping with Messenger B and complaining alike to both about the other.

Farmer J and Rancher K have been tearing each other to pieces for years in continual conflict. There are obvious, logical reasons for the fight. Yet it continues and does not resolve. A close search finds Banker L who, due to their losses in the fighting, is able to loan each side money, while keeping the quarrel going, and who will get their lands completely if both lose.

It goes larger. The revolutionary forces and the Russian government were in conflict in 1917. The reasons are so many the attention easily sticks on them. But only when Germany's official state papers were captured in World War II was it revealed that Germany had promoted the revolt and financed Lenin to spark it off, even sending him into Russia in a blacked out train!

One looks over "personal" quarrels, group conflicts, national battles and one finds, if he searches, the third party, unsuspected by both combatants or if suspected at all, brushed off as "fantastic." Yet careful documentation finally affirms it.

This datum is fabulously useful.

In marital quarrels the *correct* approach of anyone counseling is to get both parties to carefully search out the *third* party. They may come to many *reasons* at first. These *reasons* are not beings. One is looking for a third *party,* an actual being. When both find the third party and establish proof, that will be the end of the quarrel.

Sometimes two parties, quarreling, suddenly decide to elect a being to blame. This stops the quarrel. Sometimes it is not the right being and more quarrels thereafter occur.

Two nations at each others throats should each seek conference with the other to sift out and locate the actual third party. They will always find one if they look, and they *can* find the right one. As it will be found to exist in fact.

There are probably many technical approaches one could develop and outline in this matter.

There are many odd phenomena connected with it. An accurately spotted third party is usually not fought at all by either party but only shunned.

Marital conflicts are common. Marriages can be saved by both parties really sorting out *who* caused the conflicts. There may have been, in the whole history of the marriage several, but only one at a time.

Quarrels between an individual and an organization are nearly always caused by an individual third party or a third group. The organization and the individual should get together and isolate the third party by displaying to each other all the data they each have been fed.

Rioters and governments alike could be brought back to agreement could one get representatives of both to give each other what they have been told by *whom.*

SUCH CONFERENCES HAVE TENDED TO DEAL ONLY IN RECRIMINATIONS OR CONDITIONS OR ABUSES. THEY MUST DEAL IN BEINGS ONLY IN ORDER TO SUCCEED.

This theory might be thought to assert also that there are no bad conditions that cause conflict. There are. But these are usually REMEDIAL BY CONFERENCE UNLESS A THIRD PARTY IS PROMOTING CONFLICT.

In history we have a very foul opinion of the past because it is related by recriminations of two opponents and has not spotted the third party.

"Underlying causes" of war should read "hidden promoters."

There are no conflicts which cannot be resolved unless the true promoters of them remain hidden.

This is the natural law the ancients and moderns alike did not know.

And not knowing it, being led off into "reasons" whole civilizations have died.

It is worth knowing.

It is worth working with in any situation where one is trying to bring peace.

2 Justice

HCO PL 24 February 1969
An Ethics Policy Letter—
Justice

In an extension of third party technology I have found that false reports and suppression are very important.

We know that a third party is necessary to any quarrel. Basically it is a three terminal universe.

In reviewing several organizational upsets I have found that the third party can go completely overlooked even in intensive investigation.

A third party adds up to suppression by giving false reports on others.

In several cases an organization has lost several guiltless staff members. They were dismissed or disciplined in an effort to solve enturbulation. Yet the turbulence continued and the area became even more upset by reason of the dismissals.

Running this back further one finds that the real third party, eventually unearthed got people shot by FALSE REPORTS.

One source of this is as follows:

Staff member X goofs. He is very furious and defensive at being accused. He blames his goof on somebody else. That somebody else gets disciplined. Staff member X diverts attention from himself by various means including falsely accusing others.

This is a third party action which results in a lot of people being blamed and disciplined. And the real third party remaining undetected.

The missing point of justice here is that the disciplined persons *were not faced with their accusers* and were not given the real accusation and so could not confront it.

Another case would be a third party simply spreading tales and making accusations out of malice or some even more vicious motive. This would be a usual third party action. It is ordinarily based on false reports.

Another situation comes about when an executive who can't get an area straight starts to investigate, gets a third party false report about it, disciplines people accordingly and totally misses the real third party. This enturbulates the area even more.

The basis of all really troublesome third party activities is then FALSE REPORTS.

There can also be FALSE PERCEPTION. One sees things that don't exist and reports them as "fact."

Therefore we see that we can readily run back an investigation by following a chain of false reports.

In at least one case the third party (discovered only after it was very plain that only he could have wrecked two divisions, one after the other) also had these characteristics:

1. Goofed in his own actions
2. Furiously contested any reports filed on him
3. Obsessively changed everything when taking over an area;
4. Falsely reported actions, accusing others
5. Had a high casualty rate of staff in his division or area.

These are not necessarily common to all third parties but give you an idea of what can go on.

After a lot of experience with ethics and justice I would say that the real source of upset in an area would be FALSE REPORTS accepted and acted upon without confronting the accused with all charges and his or her accusers.

An executive should not accept any accusation and act upon it. To do so undermines the security of one and all.

What an executive should do, on being presented with an accusation or downstats or "evidence" is conduct an investigation of false reports and false perceptions.

An area is downstat because of one or more of the following:

1. No personnel
2. Personnel not trained
3. Cross orders (senior orders unattended because of different junior order)
4. Area doing something else than what it is supposed to do
5. An adjacent area dumping its functions
6. False perception leading to false statistics
7. False reports by rumor or misunderstanding
8. False reports from a single rare instance becoming accepted as the condition of the whole
9. False reports on others defensively intended
10. False reports on others maliciously intended (real third party)
11. Injustices cumulative and unremedied
12. Actions taken on others without investigation and without confronting them with their accusers or the data.

This is a list of probable causes for an upset or downstat area.

Security

The personal security of the staff member is so valuable to him apparently that when it is undermined (by false accusations or injustice) he becomes less willing and less efficient and is the real reason for a PTS condition.

The only thing which can actually remedy a general insecure feeling is a renewed faith in justice.

Justice would consist of a refusal to accept any report not substantiated by actual, independent data, seeing that all such reports are investigated and that all investigations include confronting the accused with the accusation and where feasible the accuser, BEFORE any disciplinary action is undertaken or any condition assigned.

While this may slow the processes of justice, the personal security of the individual is totally dependent upon establishing the full truth of any accusation before any action is taken.

Harsh discipline may produce instant compliance but it smothers initiative.

Positive discipline is in itself a stable datum. People are unhappy in an area which is not *well* disciplined because they do not know where they stand.

An area where only those who try to do their jobs are disciplined encourages people to hide and be inactive.

But all discipline must be based on truth and must exclude acting on false reports.

Therefore we get a policy: Any false report leading to the unjust discipline of another is an act of TREASON by the person making the false report and the condition should be assigned and its penalties fully apply.

A condition of DOUBT should be assigned any person who accepts and disciplines another unjustly on the basis of a report which subsequently turns out to have been false.

This then is the primary breakdown of any justice system—that it acts on false reports, disciplines before substantiation and fails to confront an accused with the report and his accuser before any discipline is assigned, or which does not weigh the value of a person in general against the alleged crime even when proven.

3 Third Party Investigations Procedure

*BPL 25 August 1969
Third Party Investigations

An R-factor is necessary before the investigation is begun. It must be understood by the persons involved (a) what a third party is, (b) how the third party will be located, and (c) it may be necessary to indicate that it is not an auditing activity.

How Many?

Many names will come up. They were influenced by the third party. They went into agreement with him. By going into agreement with him, they spread the activity which was originated by the third party. There will be only one third party at the basic of the chain.

THIRD PARTY = FALSE REPORT. ANYONE THAT WENT INTO AGREEMENT WITH HIM CARRIED IT FORWARD, USUALLY BELIEVING IT TO BE TRUE.

Example

Third party investigation with Jill and Alan:

"A." Questions asked to Jill and Alan.

1a. Have you been told you were in bad?
 b. What was said?
 c. Who said it?
2a. Have you been told someone was bad?
 b. What was said?
 c. Who said it?
3a. Have you been told someone was doing wrong?
 b. What was said?
 c. Who said it?
4a. Have you been told a group was bad?
 b. What was said?
 c. Who said it?

"B." Questions asked Jill:

1a. Have you been told you were in bad with Alan (Jill)?
 b. What was said?
 c. Who said it?
2a. Have you been told Alan (Jill) was in bad?
 b. What was said?
 c. Who said it?
3a. Have you been told Alan (Jill) was doing wrong?
 b. What was said?
 c. Who said it?

After asking these questions of Jill, they are asked of Alan.

"C." Any person coming up on both sides, for instance Roger, is noted. You then ask the "B" questions, using Roger's name. Ask them of Jill, then of Alan.

As a new name comes up, use it in "B."

This is continued until you come up with a name, use it in "B," and Jill and Alan cannot find anyone that told you they were in bad with . . . " or "told you . . . was in bad" or "told you . . . was doing bad."

THAT IS YOUR THIRD PARTY. THERE WAS NO ONE SAYING THINGS ABOUT THIS PERSON BECAUSE HE STARTED IT ALL.

As long as they can give you answers to "B," there is someone earlier. This is how you get the BASIC third party.

Indicators

If you have indicated the wrong third party, you will see it in the absence of good indicators. Continue until you hit THE ONE, at which time good indicators will come in on both individuals.

4

HCO PL 15 March 1969

Third Party How to Find One

The way NOT to find a third party is to compile a questionnaire that asks one and all in various ways, "Have you been a VICTIM?" "Do you feel ARC broken about ethics?"

Anyone who uses this approach (1) Does not find any third party and (2) Caves in people.

A third party is ONE WHO BY FALSE REPORTS CREATES TROUBLE BETWEEN TWO PEOPLE, A PERSON AND A GROUP OR A GROUP AND ANOTHER GROUP.

The questionnaire should have a limiter such as "In this group __________." Or "In your marriage___________."

This is also a considerable process! And it may have a lot of answers. So a lot of space should be left for each question.

By then combining names given you have one name appearing far more often than the rest. This is done by counting names. You then investigate this person.

5

*BPL 6 January 1970

Third Party Investigations

The liability of a third party investigation is that a person in the area who has been diligently making reports on outnesses observed or reported to him becomes the most obvious target for declaration as the third party.

An example of this would be the branch manager of a car sales company paying the salesmen only a portion of their commissions and pocketing the balance. The salesmen consider they are underpaid. A conflict arises between them and the branch manager. Sales statistics fall. The chief sales representative realizing the dangerousness of the situation to the survival of the business and his own pay pocket, gathers information which indicates the branch manager is embezzling and sends reports to the accountant at head office for checking. The general manager, having heard of the third party law and noticing the conflict between branch manager and salesmen, commences an investigation, finds the chief sales representative has been sending reports to head offices concerning the branch manager and had previously made reports to the branch manager concerning some of the salesmen misusing company vehicles. The branch manager denies the reports against him and the salesmen state the reports against them to be false. Good indicators on both sides as their denials are accepted and the chief sales representative gets fired. Oddly enough, the pay doesn't go up, sales statistics crash further and the company goes up in smoke.

The matter would have been resolved by full ethics investigation and replacement of the branch manager instead of the one person, trying to protect his job and the company by proper ethics reports, being fired.

It is possible for a third party to use the standard report lines, but this is not usual and, as the reports are in writing and signed, they are easily investigated for validity.

A third party can make all sorts of wild false reports verbally.

When a written report is found to contain false information, don't immediately accuse the person who wrote the report of being a third party—check up on who was maliciously spreading the rumor in the first place.

One staff member aware of a very out-ethics situation in an organization that had been affluent and now was crashing into ruin made very proper reports to a higher authority. The reports were neglected. A later third party investigation said the reporting staff member was the third party even though his reports gave all available information, sources of data, who else knew about it and could give data, etc. All reports were in writing and signed. Whenever a report was based on rumor and not proven, he stated so. When "revealed as the third party," he assigned himself a condition of enemy, cognited that he had exceeded his duties and promised to keep to the standard duties of his post.

In fact, he was the only person taking responsibility for the organization and trying to handle the out-ethics situation which was collapsing statistics. He should have been commended. Instead his reach was cut and it became unsafe for staff members to make reports.

When a third party investigation cannot conclusively find a third party, but an out-ethics situation is revealed, the matter must be handled with proper ethics actions adequate to handle the situation.

There may be a third party, but it could require an ethics clean-up of the area first. The source of the out-ethics situation in such a case will probably also be the third party.

P

Targets

Targets Checksheet

Purpose:

To help the Volunteer Minister create and get compliance to programs for his community.

a	Study Section 1 Target Types.	________
b	Drill: Write out examples of each type of target.	________
c	Study Section 2 OT Orgs.	________
d	Drill: Locate someone with a failed purpose and rekindle his purpose.	________
e	Drill: With your demo kit, demonstrate why a Volunteer Minister wouldn't set an unreal target.	________
f	Study Section 3 Targets, Types of.	________
g	Drill: Find a local situation and create targets which would handle it.	________
h	Study Section 4 Purpose & Targets.	________
i	Drill: With your demo kit demonstrate how failed purposes are dramatized.	________
j	Study Section 5 Ethics Presence.	________
k	Drill: With your demo kit show how a Volunteer Minister would create ethics presence.	________
l	Study Section 6 Compliance.	________
m	Study Section 7 Compliance Reports.	________
n	Drill: Compile a Compliance Report with all necessary components.	________

o	Study Section 8 The Key Ingredients.	________
p	Drill: Draw a huge diagram which shows how to make planning an actuality.	________
q	Study Section 9 Planning and Targets.	________
r	Study Section 10 Program Drill.	________
s	Drill: Dummy Project 1.	________
t	Drill: Dummy Project 2.	________

Target Pack

1

HCO PL 24 January 1969

Target Types

You should learn the names and types of targets for quick use and classification of what you are trying to do.

MAJOR TARGET—The broad general ambition, possibly covering a long, only approximated period of time. Such as "To attain greater security" or "To get the organization up to 50 staff members."

PRIMARY TARGET—The organizational, personnel communication type targets.

These have to be kept *in.* These are the terminals and route and havingness and organizing board type targets. Example: "To put someone in charge of organizing it and have him set the remaining primary targets." Or "To re-establish the original communication system which has dropped out."

CONDITIONAL TARGETS—Those which set up EITHER/OR to find out data or if a project can be done or where or to whom.

OPERATING TARGETS—Those which lay out directions and actions or a schedule of events or timetable.

PRODUCTION TARGETS—Those which set quantities like statistics.

PROGRAM—The complete or outline of a complete target series containing all types.

While there may be other types of targets, these should be studied and every target set should be classed as one or more of the above.

"Complete Planning" and "Programs" are synonymous at this time and PROGRAMS is the preferred word.

2

HCO PL 14 January 1969

OT Orgs

What it takes to make an org go right is the intelligent assessment of what *really* needs to be done, setting these as targets and then getting them actually fully DONE.

We have all the data necessary to make organizations boom.

Therefore we find that when they don't, these faults must be present:

1. Completely unreal analysis of what needs to be done to make things really go.
2. Cross orders—juniors setting other targets *across* vital targets.
3. Non-compliance with vital target accomplishment.
4. False reports on actions or false data concerning targets.
5. Failure to doggedly follow through on one action and get it done fully and completely.
6. Distractions leading to any of the above.

Major Target

The desirable overall purpose being undertaken. This is highly generalized such as "To become an Auditor."

Vital Target

By definition a VITAL Target is something that must be done to operate at all.

Man's worst difficulty is his inability to tell the important from the unimportant. "Every target is the same as every other target" is part of A=A=A.

It takes good sense to be able to survey an area and find out:

1. What MUST be done.
2. What SHOULDN'T be done.
3. What is only desirable to be done.
4. What is trivial.

As Man all too easily specializes in stops he tends to stress what SHOULDN'T be done. While this enters into it, remember that it's a STOP.

STOPS ALL OCCUR BECAUSE OF FAILED PURPOSES.

BEHIND EVERY STOP THERE IS A FAILED PURPOSE.

A stuck picture or a motionless org are similar. Each has behind it a failed purpose.

THERE IS A LAW ABOUT THIS—ALL YOU HAVE TO DO TO RESTORE LIFE AND ACTION IS TO REKINDLE THE FAILED PURPOSE. THE STOPS WILL AT ONCE BLOW.

That law is so powerful it would practically revive the dead!

It applies to orgs.

It applies to cities or nations.

When you diverge from a constructive purpose to "stop attacks," the purpose has been abandoned. You get a *stop.* The real way to stop attacks is to widen one's zone of responsibility. And pour the coal on the purpose. Thus all attacks one makes should be in THE DIRECTION OF ENLARGING ONE'S SCOPE AND AUGMENTING BASIC PURPOSE.

Thus, in the case of Scientology Churches one should attack with the end in view of taking over the whole field of mental healing. If our purpose was this then it had to be this on all dynamics. We only got into trouble by failing to take responsibility for the whole field!

We'll win back by reasserting that responsibility and making it good.

Targets to that degree are purposes.

Purposes must be executed. They are something to DO.

OT

Let us look at the definition of OT—cause over Thought, Life, Form, Matter, Energy, Space and Time.

As one falls away from that one becomes a SPECTATOR, then one becomes an effect. Then one is *gone.*

One causes things by *action.* Not by thinking dim thoughts.

One can be doing an IN basket as simply a spectator.

In the society today *spectatorism* is very common. Magazine writers, reporters write weird pieces that look at how odd things are. The writer doesn't understand them at all. He just watches them.

Spectatorism is not so low as total effect.

The total effect—no cause—person has mainly a case. He doesn't even *look*.

Thus there is a gradient scale of OT. It's not an absolute. One is as OT as he can CAUSE things.

One of the things to cause is target attainment. When somebody can push through a target to completion he's to that degree OT.

People who don't push targets are either just spectators or they are total effect.

Organization State

An organization of any kind is somewhere on the OT scale.

An organization can figure out the vital targets and push them through to completion or it can't.

It's a gradient scale.

An organization succeeds or fails to the degree its individual executives and staff members can measure up to the OT formula: Cause.

Scientology churches must become cause over their environments.

They do this by each executive and each staff member *accomplishing* targets, small and large.

Thus:

(a) If the targets of what MUST be done to operate at all are set and

(b) are carried out with no non-compliance and

(c) if no false reports are entered into it,

Then

That org is way high on the OT scale

AND IT WILL CONQUER ITS ENTIRE ENVIRONMENT COMPLETE.

That's really all there is to it.

One way to fail at it is to do (a) with things that are so general that they invite no doingness.

Some guys are so bad off they set targets like "Move the mountain" and give one and all a big failure. Since there's no way to do it and probably no reason to either, that's an SP target. So what MUST be done means just that. What is vital and necessary. Not what is simply a good idea.

Here's some MUST targets as examples:

A. Get tech delivered 100% in the Church itself.

B. Get the public aware of its being delivered and wanting it.

C. Get the admin machinery in to get the public in and out.

Or another series:

D. Get 10,000 trained auditors into the org field.

E. Get the public aware of the project and wanting training.

F. Set up terrific 100% snap-pop courses to handle the flow.

Or another:

G. Get a $100,000 reserve cushion.

H. Get all accounts staff and executives checked out on finance policy.

I. Shove the throttle down on promotion.

J. Deliver fantastic service.

K. Get enough tech people in training to handle the flows.

L. Find bigger, more posh quarters to handle the flow *when* it rises.

M. Get all staff onto the Organization Executive Course to diminish flow line flubs.

You get the idea.

An executive who is just a spectator to his In Basket flow is doing nothing but cultivating Dev-T.

You *can* assess the situation.

You can drive targets home to full completion.

Every executive and every staff member is somewhere on the OT Scale. And he can rise higher just by setting up the targets and plowing them through to done, done, done.

Yes, it requires ideas. But ideas come from interested looking and sizing it all up before you set the target in the first place.

You can even raise an organization by gradients so as not to overwhelm it. Set and *make* small targets. Then bigger and bigger ones.

Well, you get the idea.

It's any organization's road to OT.

3 Targets, Types of

HCO PL 16 January 1969

There are several VALUES of targets. Not all targets are the same value or importance.

Primary Targets

There is a group of "understood" targets which if overlooked, bring about inaction.

The first of these is:

SOMEBODY THERE

Then

WORTHWHILE PURPOSE

Then

SOMEBODY TAKING RESPONSIBILITY FOR THE AREA OR ACTION

Then

FORM OF ORGANIZATION PLANNED WELL

Then

FORM OF ORGANIZATION HELD OR REESTABLISHED

Then

ORGANIZATION OPERATING.

If we have the above "understood" targets we can go on BUT IF THESE DROP OUT OR ARE NOT SUBSTITUTED FOR then no matter what targets are set thereafter they will go rickety or fail entirely.

In the above there may be a continual necessity to reassert one or more of the "understood" targets WHILE trying to get further *targets* going.

Vital Targets

Under this heading comes WHAT WE MUST DO TO OPERATE AT ALL.

This requires an inspection of both the area one is operating into and the factors or materiel or organization with which we are operating.

One then finds those points (sometimes WHILE operating) which stop or threaten future successes. And sets the overcoming of the vital ones as targets.

Conditional Targets

It is interesting that one can go into an art type "perfection" with targets and groom up Primary Targets *far* beyond the need to accomplish purposes.

You've seen chaps work all their lives to "get rich" or some such thing in order to "tour the world" and never make it. Some other fellow sets Tour the world and goes directly at it and *does* it. So there is a type of Target known as a *Conditional* Target: If I could just ________then we could ________ and so accomplish ________. This is all right of course until it gets unreal.

There is a whole class of conditional targets that have no IF in them. These are legitimate targets. They have lots of WILL in them "We *will* ________ and then ________."

Sometimes sudden "breaks" show up and one must quickly take advantage of them. This is only "good luck." One uses it and replans quickly when it *happens.* One is on shaky ground to count on "good luck" as a solution.

A valid conditional target would be:

"We will go there and see if the area is useful."

All conditional targets are basically actions of gathering data first and if it is okay, then go into action on a vital target and operating target basis.

This could add up like this:

Conditional Target 1. Survey Lower Slobovia to see if it would be a suitable place for an org.

This survey done, if it is positive, one then goes into primary targets and operating targets.

The Primary Targets would be:

Lower Slobovia One:	Appoint Local Organization Officer for Lower Slobovia.
Lower Slobovia Two:	Form up Lower Slobovian Organization. Personnel Officer.
Lower Slobovia Three:	Train up Organization Personnel. Staff Training Officer.
Lower Slobovia Four:	Translate Texts. Translation Section.
Lower Slobovia Five:	Finance Formation. Finance Section.
Lower Slobovia Six:	Transport Lower Slobovian Organization. Transport Section.
Lower Slobovia Seven:	Prepare Lower Slobovian Building in Lower Slobovia. BEFORE ORGANIZATION ARRIVES. Lower Slobovia Organization Officer.

Thus we would establish Lower Slobovia. AND IT WOULD ALL GO OFF WELL TO THE DEGREE THE PRIMARY TARGETS WERE MADE, DONE, COMPLETED.

Primary targets setting on Lower Slobovia would fail if some primary target were omitted in the first place (never set) or if the conditional target findings on Lower Slobovia were a false report.

Thus we are very hot on "false report" and very hot on "non-compliance."

Operating Targets

An operating target would set the *direction* of advance and qualify it. It normally includes a scheduled TIME by which it has to be complete so as to fit into other targets.

Sometimes the time is set as "BEFORE." And there may be no time for the event that it must be done "before." Thus it goes into a rush basis "just in case."

To get all the shoe salesmen in Boston enrolled on a Personal Efficiency Course would be an operating target. This would *then* go into the framework of a *primary* target as to the remaining targets set.

Operating targets often look like "basic purpose." They can come before or after primary targets. But an Operating Target has its *own* series of primary targets. To enroll all the shoe salesmen you need somebody in charge of it, a Personal Efficiency supervisor, literature, a handbook for salesmen etc., etc. which are all set as Primary Targets.

Sometimes an elaborate operating and primary target series falls apart because there was no conditional target set, i.e. to find out if Boston had any salesmen and *which* types were responsive. You might find the operating target had been set with no inspection.

So, again, we can move backward and find that an Operating Target needs a Conditional Target ahead of it—to wit, an inspection.

Production Targets

Setting quotas, usually against time, are *production* targets.

These often fail because they are unreal or issued for other reasons than production (i.e. propaganda).

As *statistics* most easily reflect production, an organization or activity can be so PRODUCTION TARGET conscious that it fails to set Conditional, Operating or Primary Targets. When this happens, then production is liable to collapse for lack of planning stated in other types of targets.

Production as the only target type can become so engulfing that conditional targets even when set are utterly neglected. Then operating and primary targets get very unreal and stats go DOWN.

YOU HAVE TO INSPECT AND SURVEY AND GATHER DATA AND SET OPERATING AND PRIMARY TARGETS BEFORE YOU CAN SET PRODUCTION TARGETS.

A normal reason for down statistics on production is the vanishment of primary targets. These go out and nobody notices that this affects the production badly. Production depends on other prior targets being kept *in*.

Programs

Programs are made up of all types of targets coordinated and executed. ON TIME.

Programs extend in time and go overdue to the extent the various types of targets are not set or not pushed home or drop out.

Programs fail only because the various types of targets are not executed or are not kept in.

Summary

You can get done almost anything you want to do if types of targets are understood, set with reality, held in or completed.

People whose own purposes have failed often cannot either set or complete targets. The remedy is to rehabilitate their own purposes which then blows off the stops.

People who stop targets actively have failed so badly that they can only think in terms of stops.

This whole subject of targets and purposes is probably a large one. These are just rough notes and the naming of the different types which itself is a considerable advance.

It is of help in grasping what is going on and gets one somewhere.

4 Purpose & Targets

HCO PL 24 January 1969
Issue II

The reason we are fought where we are fought is contained in its major part in Purposes.

Purposes often fail and wind up in *stop*.

Stopped purposes can then be dramatized.

In Scientology we use (quite correctly) FREEDOM. While not the most basic purpose TO BE FREE is a common purpose to all thetans.

This tends to key-in (restimulate) in some persons, the stop of being free. They themselves wanted to be free. They were stopped, they dramatize the STOP of being free and try then to stop us. We restimulated (keyed-in) their own purpose to be free or free others and where we are opposed the person or persons dramatizes the stop or disagreement.

Also where we not only restimulate the stop but oppose and deny him *as well,* we get an enemy.

We are then stopping stoppers. While this is necessary to save the day, it is *preventable* if begun early enough.

The psychiatrist is not the only "freedom stopper" we will ever meet. Many people who have been in healing and mental treatment in the times before we came along had only failures. So anything offered to them (including their own) will be looked on as a failure at best or at worst a fraud.

That it really *can* be done in Scientology is not only outside their reality but regenerated the failed purpose they have had to be free and free others and they dramatize STOP.

While this is not the total reason (interrelations also restimulate ethnic values meaning customs) it is a big reason for dedicated opposition to us.

We restimulate their failed freedom efforts and they dramatize what stopped *them.* So they irrationally seek to stop Scientology.

This would also be true for products of a commercial nature. It is good advertising technology.

Freedom is one of the buttons that gets us forward. It is also the button that restimulates the opposition into efforts to stop us.

In dissemination then to such people, theoretically one need only get them remembering when *they* wanted to be free or free others to blow their stops. But as they may have many crimes now built up on top of it some may just spin.

But in all discussions with persons opposing Scientology, one should try the approach of getting them to remember their efforts to be free or to free others and let them talk. As you listen you will realize they were without Scientology to help them and they didn't have a chance.

Led in from that point you *may* get a very receptive person.

5
Ethics Presence

HCO PL 4 October 1968

The reason an executive can get compliance is because he has ethics presence. If you haven't got it, you won't.

When you issue orders you are using power and force.

If you are also *right* in what you get compliance with and your programs are clear, correct and beneficial—boy do you win.

But it is not the rightness of a program that gets compliance. It is ethics presence.

Rightness does not get compliance because there are always counter-intentions in the way. If you go on the assumption that one and all want things to go right you are going to make a dog's breakfast out of it.

There are only a few with a good forward look and who are relatively unaberrated.

Men will keep the accounts straight only because you can muster bayonets to enforce that they do.

Ethics presence is an X quality made up partly of symbology, partly of force, some "now we're supposed to's" and endurance.

Endurance asserts the truth of unkillability. We're still here, can't be unmocked. This drives the SP wild.

As an executive you get compliance because you have ethics presence and persistence and can get mad.

The way you *continue* to have ethics presence is to be maximally right in your actions, decisions and dictates. Because if you're wrong the other fellow gets wrapped around a pole for complying. And the *pain* of *that* starts to outweigh your own Ethics Presence.

So, when you issue orders you are using force and power. You can, however, get in such a frame of mind you cease to use the softer arts as well. Against non-compliance you add ferocity with the aim of continuing your communication line.

Wrath *is* effective but used in moderation and only in moments of urgency.

*BPL 20 February 1973
The Theory of
Compliance—1
What is Compliance?
The Parts of Compliance

6
Compliance

Compliance by definition is: acting in accordance with, or the yielding to a desire, request, condition, direction, etc.; a consenting to act in conformity with, an acceding to; practical assent.

Compliance can only occur in the presence firstly of communication in order for the above definition to have practical meaning.

The obvious purpose of the activity of compliance is to complete the cycles of action requested or ordered by another.

Often compliance is obtained through force of character, by holding to established customs, or by persuasion, either gentle or violent, pleasant or devious, direct or indirect. These forms are not usually called compliance, at least insofar as organizations are concerned with the exception that on occasion persuasiveness is used to overcome a resistance on a personal basis rather than a direct order. But this is usually part of a PR campaign rather than an action involving orders.

Compliance is expected from a staff member to originations from a senior or seniors which are expressed as orders, targets or programs.

7
Compliance Reports

*BPL 26 January 1969RA

Essentially there is a command communication cycle.

HE WHO GIVES THE ORDER GETS AN ANSWER!

They are never routed off the lines before they reach the originator of the order. To do so creates an atmosphere of non-compliance. The originator knowing only that he has never heard thinks the order has not been done, or is forced to listen to rumor, or has to use other lines to get the data.

And thus no real coordination of orders can occur.

And the originator is driven into apathy on getting compliance to even the most simple orders.

Compliance reports are very explicit, never generalized and must not rely upon supposed knowledge of the recipient. Give full name, rank, serial number type data, never Major Jones called today type information. That relies on the recipient remembering who Major Jones is. It's Major Jones of the American Trade Association. Enough data to clearly identify WHO. And in the same way of course enough data to identify WHAT or WHAT ABOUT.

And never use confusing type abbreviations. For example, C/S can mean Case Supervisor or Church of Scientology.

What a Compliance Report Is

A compliance report is exactly that. It is a *REPORT OF COMPLIANCE*, a complete cycle reported to the originator DONE.

It is not a cycle begun, it is not a cycle in progress. It is a cycle completed AND REPORTED BACK TO THE ORIGINATOR AS DONE so that the command comm cycle is completed.

To merely commence a cycle is not to comply. To merely make some progress is not to comply. To drive it through to completion is. And to then report DONE to the originator is to put in a compliance report.

A compliance report has to be answered with the order and get logged *and* the answer goes to whomever issued the order. Standard TRs.

In practice a compliance report takes the following form. It is in standard dispatch form routed through the usual channels. It is headed at the top of the page in the middle COMPLIANCE REPORT. It has a brief concise description of what was done.

1. It is in standard dispatch form routed through the usual channels.
2. It is headed at the top of the page in the middle COMPLIANCE REPORT.

3. It has a brief concise description of *what* was done.
4. It has clipped to it *ALL* the original orders so that the originator and communicators on the line can see at a glance what was ordered, and comparing this with what was done, see that it is in fact compliance, a completed cycle.
5. Any other relevant information is also clipped behind. Such as a carbon of a letter written if that was what was ordered.
6. AND IT IS ADDRESSED AND GOES TO THE PERSON ORIGINATING THE ORDER, via any communicator who logs it as a compliance.
7. It contains an attestation that what was done has been completed; such as "order attached completed."

Compliances On Targets, Programs and Projects

The above applies strictly to compliances on orders in dispatch or telex or verbal form—those that are not divided up into targets in program or project format.

The administration of compliances on program and project targets is different.

Here the primary consideration is that of speed and teamwork, as it is usually necessary to complete the targets quickly in order to handle an emergency or to effect an opportune expansion.

The responsibility for the completion of the whole program is assigned to a specific terminal—a communicator or Program Coordinator or another. This person's part in the team is to simply collect reports attesting "I have done Target Number ______ of Program ______," in a large accessible basket prominently displayed for that purpose, and to then himself inspect and collect or report on the evidence which indicates whether or not the target was done.

If he cannot verify that the target was done, or finds that it is falsely reported done, then he takes appropriate ethics action and intervenes to obtain the full compliance.

But usually he will find it has been done, and makes it his business to collect the evidence and write up his observations on the compliance.

The compliance reports, evidence and observations are placed in the folder for the program which also contains his master copy of the program stapled to the inside front cover of the folder.

The program folder is presented in due course to the originator, together with all debug actions and their results.

Amendment

The preceding steps on how to handle compliance on programs is practical for locally originated programs.

However, where a program has been originated from a source EXTERNAL and not local to that organization, such as a Head Office originating a program to be done by a Branch, for example, the following steps are added:

The person in the Branch verifying a target compliance when writing up his verification, does so in DUPLICATE. One copy goes to the local Program folder and one copy goes to the terminal in charge at the Head Office for seeing to the execution of the Program.

In cases where a second terminal or set of terminals needs to also be advised of the target compliances—as specified in the program or by specific separate groups—the verification should be written up in TRIPLICATE. The extra copy can then be routed to those designated.

This then allows those external to the Branch who are also responsible for observation and execution of the program in the Branch to be kept adequately informed without disrupting the Branch's local program folder for such compliances.

Nothing else is otherwise changed in the preceding steps of this section.

8

HCO PL 14 September 1969
Admin—Know—How 22

The Key Ingredients

When we look at organization in it's most simple form, when we seek certain key actions or circumstances that make organizations work, when we need a very simple, very vital rundown to teach people that will produce results, we find only a few points we need to stress.

The purpose of organization is TO MAKE PLANNING BECOME ACTUALITY.

Organization is not just a fancy, complex system, done for its own sake. That is bureaucracy at its worst. Organizing boards for the sake of organizing boards, statistic graphs for the sake of graphs, rules for the sake of rules only add up to failures.

The only virtue (not always a bad one) of a complex unwieldy, meaningless, bureaucratic structure is that it provides jobs for the friends of those in control. If it does not also bring about burdensome taxation and threatened bankruptcy by reason of the expense of maintaining it and if it does not saddle a people or production employees with militant inspections and needless control, organization for the sake of providing employment is not evil but beyond providing employment is useless, and only when given too much authority is it destructive.

The kings of France and other lands used to invent titles and duties to give activity to the hordes of noble hangers-on to keep them at court, under surveillance, and out of mischief out in the provinces where they might stir up their own people. "Keeper of the Footstools," "Holder of the Royal Nightgown" and other such titles were fought for, bought, sold and held with ferocity.

Status seeking, the effort to become more important and have a personal reason for being and for being respected gets in the road of honest efforts to effectively organize in order to get something done, in order to make something economically sound.

Organization for its own sake in actual practice usually erects a monster that becomes so hard to live with that it becomes overthrown. Production losses, high taxes, irritating or fearsome interference with the people or actual producers invites and accomplishes bankruptcy or revolt, usually both even in commercial companies.

Therefore to be meaningful, useful and lasting, an organization has to fit into the definition above:

TO MAKE PLANNING BECOME ACTUALITY.

In companies and countries there is no real lack of dreaming. All but the most depraved heads of companies or states wish to see specific or general improvement. This is also true of their executives and, as it forms the basis of nearly all revolts, it is certainly true of workers. From top to bottom, then, there is in the large majority, a desire for improvement.

More food, more profit, more pay, more facilities, and in general more and better of whatever they believe is good and beneficial. This also includes less of what they generally consider to be bad.

Programs which obtain general support consist of more of what is beneficial and less of what is detrimental. "More food less disease," "More beautiful buildings, less hovels," "More leisure, less work," "More activity, less unemployment" are typical of valuable and acceptable programs.

But only to have a program is to have only a dream. In companies, in political parties, useful programs are very numerous. They suffer only from a lack of execution.

All sorts of variations of program failure occur. The program is too big. It is not generally considered desirable. It is not needed at all. It would benefit only a few. Such are surface reasons. The basic reason is lack of organization know-how.

Any program, too ambitious, partially acceptable, needed or not needed could be put into effect if properly organized.

The five year plans of some nations which were in vogue in the late 1960's were almost all very valuable and almost all fall short of their objectives. The reason is not that they were unreal, too ambitious or generally unacceptable. The reason for any such failure is lack of organization.

It is not Man's dreams that fail him. It is the lack of know-how required to bring those dreams into actuality.

Good administration has two distinct targets:

1. To perpetuate an existing company, culture, or society
2. To make planning become actuality.

Given a base on which to operate, which is to say land, people, equipment and a culture, one needs a good administrative pattern of some sort just to maintain it.

Thus 1 and 2 above become 2 only. The plan is "to continue the existing entity." No company or country continues unless one continues to put it there. Thus an administrative system of some sort, no matter how crude, is necessary to perpetuate any group or any subdivision of a group. Even a king or headman or manager who has no other supporting system to whom one can bring disputes about land or water or pay is an administrative system. The foreman of a labor gang that only loads trucks has an astonishingly complex administrative system at work.

Companies and countries do not work just because they are there or because they are traditional. They are continuously put there by one or another form of administration.

When a whole system of administration moves out or gets lost or forgotten, collapse occurs unless a new or substitute system is at once moved into place.

Changing the head of a department, much less a general manager and much, much less a ruler can destroy a portion or the whole since the old system, unknown, disregarded or forgotten may cease and no new system which is understood is put in its place. Frequent transfers within a company or country can keep the entire group small, disordered and confused, since such transfers destroy what little administration there might have been.

Thus, if administrative shifts or errors or lack can collapse any type of group, it is vital to know the basic subject of organization.

Even if the group is at effect, which is to say originates nothing but only defends in the face of threatened disaster, it still must plan. And if it plans, somehow it must get the plan executed or done. Even a simple situation of an attacked fortress has to be defended by planning and doing the plan no matter how crude. The order "Repel the invader who is storming the south wall" is the result of observation and planning no matter how brief or unthorough. Getting the south wall defended occurs by some system of administration even if it only consists of sergeants hearing the order and pushing their men to the south wall.

A company with heavy debts has to plan even if it is just to stall off creditors. And some administrative system has to exist even to do only that.

The terrible dismay of a young leader who plans a great and powerful new era only to find himself dealing with old and weak faults is attributable not to his "foolish ambition" or "lack of reality" but to his lack of organizational know-how.

Even elected presidents or prime ministers of democracies are victims of such terrible dismay. They do not, as is routinely asserted, "go back on their campaign promises" or "betray the people." They, as well as their Members of Parliament, simply lack the rudiments of organizational know-how. They cannot put their campaign promises into effect not because they are too high flown but because they are politicians, not administrators.

To some men it seems enough to dream a wonderful dream. Just because they dreamed it they feel it should now take place. They become very provoked when it does not occur.

Whole nations, to say nothing of commercial firms or societies or groups have spent decades in floundering turmoil because the basic dreams and plans were never brought to fruition.

Whether one is planning for the affluence of the Appalachian Mountains or a new loading shed closer to the highway, the gap between the plan and the actuality will be found to be lack of administrative know-how.

Technical ignorance, finance, even lack of authority and unreal planning itself are none of them true barriers between planning and actuality.

Thus, we come to the exact, most basic steps that comprise administration.

First is OBSERVATION. From beginning to end observation must serve both those in charge and any others who plan. When observation is lacking, then planning itself as well as any and all progress can become unreal and orders faulty and destructive. Observation in essence must be TRUE. Nothing must muddy it or color it as this can lead to gross errors in action and training.

Next is PLANNING itself. *Planning* is based on dreams but it must be fitted to what is needed and wanted and what men can do, even with stretched imaginations or misgivings. Planning has to be targeted and scheduled and laid out in steps and gradients or one will be laying railroad tracks that pass through oceans or boring tunnels in mountains that do not exist or building penthouses without putting any building under them to hold them up.

The essence of planning is *COMMUNICATION* and the *communication* must be such that it can be understood and will not be misunderstood. For unless those who oversee and those who do know what their part of the plan is, they cannot execute their share and very well may oversee and do quite some other action, leaving a monstrous gap and even a structure that ate up their time and funds but now has to be torn down.

The next is SUPERVISION and supervision is dually needful. It serves as a relay point to which plans can be communicated and from which observations as reports can be received; and it serves as the terminal which communicates the plans as orders and sees that they are actually done. This gives one the genus of the Organizing Board as a central ordering point which has other relay ordering points taking care of their part of the whole plan or program. These points are often also the points which care for local occurrences which must be handled and their frailty is that they become so involved with local occurrences, oddities and purely local concerns that they do not or can not give any attention to receiving, relaying and overseeing their part of the main plan.

Then there are the PRODUCERS who *produce* the service or the structure or the product required by the plan. Many plans are marvelous in all respects but putting somebody there to actually DO the required actions that make the plan real. The primary fault is to use persons who already have projects and duties to which they are committed and, with their local knowledge, see must be continued at any cost but who are forced to abandon existing programs or duties to start on this new activity solely because the new activity has the stress given it in orders and the old activities are seemingly ordered left alone. Old companies and old countries could be said to be "that collection of incomplete and abandoned projects which is confused and failing."

Finally there is the USER, those who will *use* or benefit from the program when it is realized and completed. When planning fails to take this element into account, only then can the whole program fail utterly, for it, regardless of dreams, labor and expense, is finally seen to be of no value anyway. Thus all great programs begin with an understanding or survey of what is needed and wanted and a nose and value count of those who will use it and a costing action in time, labor, materials and finance, compared to the value of it, even if only aesthetic, of those who will use it in any way, if only to know they have it or to be proud of it or to feel better or stronger because they have done it.

Thus one gets the points which are the true administrative points:

1. OBSERVATION even down to discovering the users and what is needed and wanted.

2. PLANNING which includes imaginative conception and intelligent timing, targeting and drafting of the plans so they can be communicated and assigned.

3. COMMUNICATING which includes receiving and understanding plans and their portion and relaying them to others so that they can be understood.

4. SUPERVISION which sees that that which is communicated is done in actuality.

5. PRODUCTION which does the action or services which are planned, communicated and supervised.

6. USERS by which the product or service or completed plan is used.

Administrative systems or organizations which lack at least the rudiments of the above system will not bring off the dream and will accumulate an enormous lot of uncompleted actions. Not a few failures, bankruptcies, overthrows and revolutions have occurred because one or all of the above points were awry in an existing organization.

The amount of heroic executive overwork which comes from the omission of one or more of these vital essential points accounts for the ulcers which are the occupational disease of those in charge.

When some or all these points are awry or gone, an executive or ruler or his minister is reduced to an anxiety which can only watch for the symptoms of bankruptcy or attack or revolt.

Even if so reduced, an executive who fends off disaster while getting in a system which satisfies the above points has an enormously bettered chance of winning at long last.

The dual nature of an administrative system or an organization now becomes plain.

Let us pry apart 1 and 2 above. The effort to hold an existing organization together is really different than trying to get a plan into actuality. In practice one *has* an organization of some sort. It has functions and it has local concerns and problems. And it has programs and actions from past control centrals or which were locally generated.

To push in upon this plans which, no matter how well conceived or intentioned, are additional to its load will cause a great deal of confusion, incomplete projects left dangling and general upset.

To place new programs into action, two prior actions are necessary:

A. Put in a whole new system paralleling the old existing system.

B. Survey the old system and its existing programs to preserve them, eradicate them or combine them with the new plans.

To leave A and B undone is to court disaster. Whether one is aware of the old programs or the old organization or not THEY REMAIN AND WILL CONTINUE even if only as a pile of undone, unsorted papers nobody knows where to file or as a pile of odd unfinished masonry some future generation can't identify or will identify with scorn of administrations in general.

New leaders are sometimes looked upon as a worse scourge than a foreign enemy and new patterns of rule are often subjected to overthrow simply because they did not, out of ignorance or laziness, do A and B above.

One sometimes finds a company unit or a military officer left in some unheard of place for years, at continuing expense, guarding or nibbling at some project in a bewildered or philosophic fashion.

The activity remained unremembered, unhandled when a new broom and new planners entered the scene.

This can get so bad that a company or a nation's resources can be broken to bits. The old plans, disorganized, not known, discredited are superseded by new plans and new ambitions. The old plans are in the road of the new plans and the new plans prevent old plans from completing. The result is an impasse. And the men in charge, even at the level of junior executives become even more puzzled and bewildered than the workers and begin to believe no new plans can ever be done, blame the ignorance of the populace and the cruelty of fate and give up.

All they had to do was put in a complete new parallel system as in the 1 to 6 outline above for their new plans and to meanwhile preserve and continue the old system while they survey for preservation, eradication or combination of it. It is sometimes even good sense to continue old projects to completion currently with new projects just to maintain stability in the company or country and somehow find new finance and new people for the new plans. It is often far less costly than to simply confuse everything.

Furthermore, all NEW and untried plans should have PILOT PROJECTS which by test and use must be successful before one incorporates them and their new workers into the old system as a parallel dependable activity.

A "chicken in every pot" as a campaign promise could easily succeed if organized as in 1 to 6 above.

There is a lot to organization. It requires trained administrators who can forward the programs. But a "trained" administrator who does not grasp the principles of organization itself is only a clerk.

At this current writing Man has not had administrative training centers where actual organization was taught. It was learned by "experience" or by working in an organization that was already functioning. But as the principles were not the same company to company and nation to nation, the differences of background experiences of any set of administrators differed to such a degree that no new corps could be assembled as a team.

Thus it was said to require a quarter to a half a century to make a company. But the number of ineffective bureaucracies and national failures which existed stated clearly that there were too few skilled administrators and too few training activities.

9 Planning and Targets

HCOPL 18 January 1969
Issue II

Plans are NOT targets.

All manner of plans can be drawn and can be okayed. But this does not authorize their execution. They are just plans. When and how they will be done and by whom has not been established, scheduled or authorized.

This is why planning sometimes gets a bad name.

You could plan to make a million dollars but if when, how and who were not set as targets of different types, it just wouldn't happen. A brilliant plan is drawn as to *how* to convert Boston Harbor into a fuel tanker area. It could be on drawings with everything perfectly placed. One could even have models of it. Ten years go by and it has not been started much less completed. You have seen such plans. World's Fairs are full of them.

One could also have a plan which was targeted—who, when, how—and if the targets were poor or unreal, it would never be completed.

One can also have a plan which had no CONDITIONAL TARGET ahead of it and so no one really wanted it and it served no purpose really. It is unlikely it would ever be finished. Such a thing existed in Corfu. It was a half-completed Greek theatre which had just been left that way. No one had asked the inhabitants if they wanted it or if it was needed. So even though *very* well planned and even partially targeted and half completed, there it is—half finished. And has remained that way.

A plan, by which is meant the drawing or scale modeling of some area, project, or thing, is of course a vital necessity in any construction and construction fails without it. It can even be okayed *as a plan.*

But if it was not the result of findings of a conditional target (a survey of what's needed or feasible) it will be useless or won't fit in. And if no funds are allocated to it and no one is ordered to do it and if no scheduling of doing it exists, then, on each separate count it won't ever be done.

One can define *planning* as the overall target system wherein all targets of all types are set. That would be *complete planning*.

Complete Planning

To get a complete plan okayed one would have to show it as:

(a) A result of a conditional target (survey of what's wanted and needed).

(b) The details of the thing itself, meaning a picture of it or its scope plus the ease or difficulty in doing it and with what persons or materials.

(c) Classification of it as vital or simply useful.

(d) The primary targets of it showing the organization needed to do it.

(e) The operating targets showing its scheduling (even if scheduled not with dates but days or weeks and dovetailing with other actions).

(f) Its cost and whether or not it will pay for itself or can be afforded or how much money it will make.

Complete planning would have to include the targets and the plan of the thing.

Thus, by redefining words and assigning labels to target types we can get a better grip on this.

A *plan* would be the *design* of the thing itself.

Complete planning would be all the targets plus the design.

Thus we see why some things don't come off at all and why they often don't get completed even when planned. The Plan is not put forward in its *target* framework and so is unreal or doesn't get done.

Also it's a great way to lose or waste money.

Sometimes a conditional target fails to ask what obstacles or opposition would be encountered or what skills are available and so can go off the rails in that fashion.

The whole subject of plans, targets, and target types is new in the realm of analyzed thought.

It is a subject to "get the feel of" and "learn to think concerning" rather than a fully "canned" subject.

But if these points are grasped, then one sees the scope of the subject and can become quite brilliant and achieve things hitherto out of reach or never thought of before.

HCOPL 13 June 1972
Establishment Officer
Series 19

10
Program Drill

A majority of people cannot follow a written program. Yet all legal projects are in program form.

The reasons are various. But when programs are not understood they can be cross ordered, abandoned, left half-done and the next thing you know you have a backlog.

There can be (and usually are) other situations that prevent the doing of a program. Out ethics, lack of understanding of a product or exchange, an unmanned or undermanned area are the commonest reasons. But when all these have been handled, there can be two other reasons—the written project itself is bugged so it can't be done (needs special equipment or finance or is outpointy or doesn't apply) or THE PERSONS CONCERNED JUST CAN'T DO A PROJECT. The former of these reasons is seized upon all too often to excuse the latter WHICH USUALLY IS THE CASE. They can't execute a project and prefer cross orders because the orderliness of a project or what it is, is not understood. Therefore, to handle this we have the following project drills.

The person is just to do these, honestly, each one, from targets 1 on.

Dummy Project 1

Purpose: To learn to do a project.
Major Target: To get it done.
Primary Targets:

1. Read this section (Program Drill) down to "Dummy Project 1."

2. Check off each one when done.

Vital Targets:

1. Be honest about doing this.

2. Do all of it.

Operating Targets:

1. Take off your right shoe. Look at the sole. Note what's on it. Put it back on.

2. Go get a drink of water.

3. Take a sheet of paper. Draw three concentric circles on it. Turn over face down. Write your name on the back. Tear it up and put the scraps in a book.

4. Take off your left shoe. Look at the sole. Note what is on it. Put it back on.

5. Go find someone and say hello. Return and write a despatch to your post from yourself as to how they received it.

6. Write a despatch from your post to yourself in proper dispatch form (according to how it is done where you work) correcting how you wrote the despatch in 5 above.

7. Take off both shoes and bang the heels together three times and put them back on.

8. Write a list of projects in your life you have left incomplete or not done.

9. Write why this was.

10. Check this project carefully to make sure you have honestly done it all.

11. List your cognitions if any while doing this project.

12. Decide whether you have honestly done this project.

13. Hand all written papers including the scraps in the book over to the terminal in the Church of Scientology you have been in liaison with; include a proper despatch on top Dummy Project No. 1 Completion.

END OF PROJECT

Dummy Project 2

Purpose: To learn about production.

Major Target: To actually produce something.

Primary Target:

1. Get a pencil and 5 sheets of paper.

2. Situate yourself so you can do this project.

Vital Targets:

1. Read an operating target and be sure to do it all before going on.

2. Actually produce what's called for.

Operating Targets:

1. Look very busy without actually doing anything.

2. Do it again but this time be very convincing.

3. Work out the valuable final product of your post.

4. Straighten up the papers in your IN-basket.

5. Take sheet 1 as per primary targets above. Write whether or not No. 4 was production.

6. Pick over your IN basket and find a paper or despatch that doesn't contribute in any way to your getting out your own product.

7. Answer it.

8. Take a second sheet called for in the primary target. Write on it why the action in 7 is perfectly reasonable.

9. Take the third sheet of paper and draw the correct communication lines of your post.

10. Get out 1 correct product for your post, complete and of high quality.

11. Deliver it.

12. Review operating targets and see which one made you feel the best.

13. Take the 4th sheet of paper and write down whether or not production is the basis of morale.

14. Take the 5th sheet of paper, use it for a coversheet and write a summary of the project.

15. Realize you have completed a project.

16. Deliver the whole project with papers to your Church of Scientology Liaison terminal.

END OF PROJECT

Q

Public Relations

Public Relations Checksheet

Purpose:

To train the Volunteer Minister how to increase his acceptance into the community, and how to enhance community programs.

a	Study Section 1 PR Definition.	________
b	Drill: Think of 5 examples in which the Volunteer Minister would interpret policy for top management.	________
c	Study Section 2 Liabilities of PR.	________
d	Drill: Go through a newspaper and find "out-PR" situations caused by untrained PRs.	________
e	Study Section 3 The PR Personality.	________
f	Drill: Write an essay on why a PR must confront, work and organize.	________
g	Study Section 4 The Missing Ingredient.	________
h	Drill: Listen to the news and spot an obvious lie.	________
i	Drill: Write an essay why it is destructive for a PR to lie.	________
j	Drill: Think of 10 ways a Volunteer Minister can make himself real to the community.	________
k	Drill: Locate three people and make your purpose as a Volunteer Minister real to them.	________
l	Study Section 5 Wrong Publics.	________
m	Drill: List ten different publics in your community.	________
n	Study Section 6 Opinion Leaders.	________

o	Drill: Locate 5 opinion leaders in your community.	______
p	Drill: Put a comm line in to these 5 opinion leaders.	______
q	Study Section 7 Too Little Too Late.	______
r	Drill: Write an essay on how to make an event succeed.	______
s	Drill: Demonstrate the concept of too little too late.	______
t	Drill: Observe a successful event and the steps that went into making it successful.	______
u	Study Section 8 Manners.	______
v	Drill: Observe five people with good manners.	______
w	Drill: Observe five people with bad manners.	______
x	Drill: Write an essay on how your manners can be improved. List your strong points and weaknesses.	______

Public Relations Pack

1 PR Definition

HCOPL 18 November 1970 Issue II
PR Series 5

The definition of public relations is very precise. The definition is not given sufficient importance in PR texts and it is way down in the middle of most books. It is what the subject is all about and without it the subject doesn't make sense. (And doesn't make sense to many PR pros either.)

It took me a whole hour to clear this definition and misunderstoods of it and related words on a PR student. It should be meter cleared. Every word in it should be clay tabled.

THE DUTY AND PURPOSE OF A PUBLIC RELATIONS MAN IS THE INTERPRETATION OF TOP MANAGEMENT POLICY TO THE DIFFERENT PUBLICS OF THE COMPANY—TO ADVISE TOP MANAGEMENT SO THAT POLICY IF LACKING CAN BE SET—TO MAKE THE COMPANY, ITS ACTIONS OR PRODUCTS KNOWN, ACCEPTED AND UNDERSTOOD BY THE DIFFERENT PUBLICS—AND TO ASSIST THE COMPANY TO EXIST IN A FAVORABLE OPERATING CLIMATE SO THAT IT CAN EXPAND, PROSPER AND BE VIABLE.

If a Volunteer Minister understands all that so he can apply it rapidly and perfectly, he will *then* be in a position to know what PR procedures are and do his job.

2 Liabilities of PR

HCOPL 13 August 1970
Issue I
PR Series 1

PR = Public Relations, a technique of communication of ideas.

A casual investigation of the activities and effects of "PR" as practiced in the first 70 years of the 20th century gives one ample data to regard "PR" with caution.

The subject is one which can be said to be dangerous in its incomplete stage of development or in the hands of inexpert or unscrupulous people.

Thus we have 3 major liabilities in PR usage:

1. It is an incomplete technology as developed and used up to 1970.

(a) The human mind was not a known field.

(b) Any early technology of the human mind was perverted by the University of Leipzig studies and animal fixations of a Professor Wundt in 1879 who declared Man a soul-less animal subject only to stimulus-response mechanisms and without determinism.

(c) Further perversions entered upon the scene in the 1894 Libido Theory of Sigmund Freud attributing all reactions and behavior to the sex urge.

PR is essentially a matter of reaching minds. Therefore the above four factors have given PR strange elements and bedfellows which have curtailed its development as a subject.

Naturally you'd have to know something of the mind to handle PR. Yet if a PR man is operating not only without knowledge of the mind but with a corrupt idea of it (as in Wundt or Freud) his use of PR technique can spread a fantastic amount of aberration into the society and can result in an aberrated society. PR men operating in the "mass media" (press, radio, television, magazines and in lobbying parliaments) push strange mental ideas.

2. Inexpert PR men can make a gruesome mess out of the subject and the society.

Working with an incompletely developed subject, yet using the powerful communication systems of the society it is not only not unusual for the work of a PR to recoil on his own employers but is usual to bring them into decay.

3. PR lends itself to the use of unscrupulous persons and cliques.

(a) The extremists such as the Nazis and Stalinists saw in PR techniques the means of subjugating their own people, perpetrating horrors and bringing their opponents into disrepute. Such extremist groups were enormously assisted by PR techniques.

(b) Using PR technique to bring about disrepute of their imagined enemies, unscrupulous persons have brought about an atmosphere of war, crime and insanity on the planet.

These are, of course, harsh words. But it is better to know all sides of a subject.

PR practitioners of course spread PR about PR. But the use of black PR far exceeds its other uses since the year of 1970. Yet teachers of PR in the smokey cloister (smoke from marijuana) give us only the Sunday School version. According to them *PR* is a nicey-nicey way *of bringing good works to public notice* and that is their favorite definition. In actual fact ten times as much PR work is done in getting rid of someone or something imagined to be dangerous to the PR's employer.

Bribing newspapermen and "free lance writers" to write horrible lies about a competitor, bribing or lying to Congressmen or ministers or Members of Parliament to get a law passed to enable a fast buck to be made and countering the ploys of the other firm's PR men are the common duties of a working public relations employee.

This scene doesn't seem to be quite the same as PR as represented in the ivory skulls of its professors.

It's a PR world.

When you read the papers, books and watch the TV of the 20th century, it's not a very nice world. Well, that's PR at work.

The far right PRs against the far left. And in between more moderate groups PR both.

The unsavory history of PR, its use to perpetuate questionable interests and cause needless and murderous quarrels must be confronted as part of the study of PR.

It is not for no reason that PR men are often of pitiful morals and degenerate character.

The countless trillions of volts of radio and TV, the rivers of newsprint and pages tearing through presses, pour fantastic lies into the overwhelmed population of earth.

The prevailing tone of dismay and contempt across the world is stimulated and kept alive by PRs.

So disabuse yourself of any idea of a pleasant scene in the field of PR.

Even if you are engaged in the promotion of the most worthwhile objects pushed by the most altruistic leader, PR work is done cheek by jowl with some pretty questionable characters whose objects are far from worthwhile and whose masters are about as altruistic as a rattlesnake.

Thus PR easily becomes a cynical activity. The PR deeds of the bad hats throw the field into disrepute and throw the whole world into a whirlpool of hate and decay.

So in entering or studying this field do not walk into it like a wide-eyed virgin making an incautious visit to a military brothel.

There is no reason to be disillusioned if one does not start out with illusions.

PR is a partially developed technique of creating states of mind in different types of audiences or publics.

PR can be used or abused.

Thus before proceeding any further with the subject it was necessary to restudy the subject and find out what was wrong with it, add it to the subject and thus make it less dangerous to use.

The liabilities of PR as taught and used before 1970 were:

A. It inevitably recoiled in greater or lesser degree to the harm of its user.

B. It had long repute as a carelessly or badly used subject, full of failures.

C. It is normally used into the teeth of competitive PR.

Unless these objections could be nullified or new discoveries and developments could be accomplished, the basic techniques of PR were about as safe as a cocked Spanish pistol—ready to blow up its user long before it hit anyone else.

This is what has been done with PR in our hands:

1. Its more dangerous points have been located.

2. A *full* study of its texts is required.

3. It is designed now for use that is beneficial as well as offensive and defensive.

Thus the standard texts of PR have to be studied and studied well. And they must be studied WITH THE ADDITIONAL DEVELOPMENTS KNOWN AND GIVEN HIGH IMPORTANCE.

Only then is it safe to use PR techniques. Otherwise PR activities are almost a complete liability and will lead to trouble.

We will bring PR up to date from the liabilities which exist in its purely PR college textbook practice.

HCO PL 9 October 1970
Personnel Series 11
PR Series 4

3 The PR Personality

A public relations personnel has to be spot on in (a) confronting (b) organizing (c) working.

Confront

In confronting, a shy or retiring PR is not about to handle suppressive persons or situations. A PR must be able to stand up to and handle the more wild situations easily and with composure. When he does not, his confront blows and any sense of presentation or organization would go up in smoke. A PTS (Potential Trouble Source) person or one who roller-coasters case-wise or one who tends to retreat has no business in PR. His connections that make him PTS and his case would have to be handled fully before he could make good on PR lines.

Organize

In organizing, a PR has to be able not only to organize something well but to organize it faultlessly in a flash.

Every action a PR takes concerns groups and therefore has to be organized down to the finest detail; otherwise it will just be a mob scene and a very bad presentation.

A PR who can confront, can "think on his feet" and grasp and handle situations rapidly and who can organize in a flash will succeed as a PR.

Work

The last essential ingredient of a PR is the ability to WORK.

The ability to address letters, push around files, haul furniture into place, handle towering stacks of admin in nothing flat are all PR requisites.

To be able to tear out to Poughkeepsie before lunch and set up the Baby Contest and build a scene for a Press Conference on Catfish before two, and get dressed, meet the governor by six is WORK. It takes sweat and push and energy.

A PR should be able to get out a trade paper in hours where an "editor" might take weeks.

The ability to work must be established in a potential PR before wasting any training time as a PR who can't work fails every time.

Delusory Requirements

People *think* a PR must be charming, brilliant, able to inspire, etc., etc.

These are fine if they exist. But they are actually secondary qualities in a PR.

Lack of the (a), (b), (c) qualities is why you see PRs begin to hit the bottle, get sick, fail.

If a PR is *also* charming, brilliant, able to inspire, he is a real winner. Possibly one is born with all these qualities every few generations.

Anyone taking up PR who does so to escape hard work will fail as it IS hard work.

A real top PR wants to be one, has the abilities of (a), (b) and (c) and is trained hard and well on the subject. Then you have a real stat raiser, a real winner, a real empire builder.

HCO PL 13 August 1970
Issue II
PR Series 2

4 The Missing Ingredient

The primary corrective discovery about PR has to do with the ARC triangle of Scientology.

This triangle is Affinity—Reality—Communication. If one corner (say, A) is raised, the other two will rise. If one corner is lowered, the other two are as well.

Thus with high affinity, one also has a high reality and a high communication. With a low affinity, one has also a low reality and a low communication.

With a high or low R one has a high or low A and C.

And so it goes. The whole triangle rises and lowers as one piece. One cannot have a low R and a high A and C.

PR is supposed to be a *communication* technique. It communicates ideas. Suppose one were to try to communicate an out the bottom R. In such a case the communication would possibly at first reach but then it would recoil due to its R.

This is, of course, an advance in the mental technology of Scientology. It was not available to early pioneers of PR. So they talked (and still talk) mainly lies.

Older PR practitioners *preferred* lies. They used circus exaggeration or black propaganda. They sought to startle or intrigue and the easiest way to do it was with exclamation point "facts" which were in fact lies.

"Mental Health" PRs dreamed up out of whole cloth the "statistics" of the insane. "Nine out of every 15 Englishmen will go insane at some period of their lives" is a complete lie. Streams of such false statistics gush from PR lobbyists to get a quick pound from Parliament.

The stock in trade of PRs, whether hired by Stalin, Hitler, the I Will Arise Society, or the International Bank has been black, bald-faced lies.

The "Backfire 8" as the "car of the century" and the parachute exhibition "record delayed drop" are all PR functions—and salted throughout with lies.

You pick up a newspaper or listen in the street and you see PR-PR-PR—all lies.

A battle cruiser makes a "Good Will Visit" to a town it is only equipped to crash and you have more lies.

The tremendous power of newspapers, magazines, radio, TV and modern "mass media" communication is guided by the PRs of special interests and they guide with lies.

Thus PR is corrupted to "a technique of lying convincingly.

It makes a cynical world. It has smashed idealism, patriotism and morality.

Why?

When an enforced communication channel carries only lies then the affinity caves in and you get hate. For the *R* is corrupted.

PR, dedicated to a false reality of lies then becomes low A, low C and recoils on the user.

So the first lesson we can learn that enables us to use PR safely is to KEEP A HIGH R.

The more lies you use in PR, the more likely it is that the PR will recoil.

Thus the law: NEVER USE LIES IN PR.

The trouble with PR then was its lack of *reality.* A lie, of course, is a false reality.

The trouble with PR was R!

In getting out a press release on a new can opener that opens cans easily and you want to say, "A child could use it," find out if it's a fact.

Give one to a child and have him open a can. So it's true. So use the line and say what child. Don't call it the "can opener of the century." It won't communicate.

Just because radios, TVs and press pour out does not mean they communicate. Communication implies that somebody is reached.

Don't tell a lie to city officials when the truth is just as easy to tell. Why go to all the work of dreaming up a lie? If you do, it will weaken you if it is found out that it is a lie. Now you *do* have a PR problem with the "official public."

Any lie will either blunt the C (communication) or end the C off one day with revulsion.

Handling truth is a touchy business also. You don't have to tell everything you know—that would jam the comm line too. Tell an *acceptable truth.*

Agreement with one's message is what PR is seeking to achieve. Thus the message must compare to the personal experience of the audience.

So PR becomes the technique of communicating an acceptable truth—and which will attain the desirable result.

If there's no chance of obtaining a desirable result and the truth would injure then talk about something else.

PR is employed to obtain a result desired by the PR and his group.

Or it is employed to cancel out the undesirable PR of others.

Thus there is offensive and defensive PR.

In defending against hostile PR, once more it is the *R* that counts. Sun Tzu in his book about warfare gives several types of agent. One of these is the "dead agent" because he tells lies to the enemy and when they find out they will kill him.

Hostile (or counter-PR) is usually the usual fabric of lies.

If one finds out the lies being told and documents just one as being false, he has made counter-PR recoil. His hearer will never believe him again. He's dead.

You understand, it's not one PR's word against another's. It's one PR's documents against the other PR's lies! That is correct defensive PR.

So you see that using out-R PR can be very dangerous.

If one is trying to PR an abuse into decay (a dangerous activity in itself) he obtains the desirable result by documenting TRUTH. But using the "dead agent" caper is quite enough almost always.

The use of *R* not only involves truth, it involves acceptable truth and that involves the fixed opinions of another or others and their experience. All this is contained in the subject of REALITY.

What is the R of another or others?

This involves SURVEYS.

Then you know what truth he or they will accept.

Imagination in PR is not limited at all. It takes lots of imagination. But the imagination should be devoted to how the truth is made acceptable to the R of others and how the communication is delivered.

A totally imaginary statement or story is quite useful so long as it is known to be imaginary and not passed off as truth.

In a PR world truth is the almost unknown commodity. This world is full of the "noise" of many lies, many babbles, many old fixations and hates.

But truth has communication value. All the lies will dead end someday.

A (Affinity) supports the R and C.

Therefore PR which seeks to incite hate will not have the C value of a message that carries actual affinity.

But affinity can also be falsified and in the PR world too often is.

A person who is sane has a high ARC value.

So the PR who is sane has a high potential. And those who have corrupted their A, R, and C into a hole, wind up on the bottle or beating their dogs or cynical beyond belief.

Serving mad masters, a PR hasn't much chance.

So there *is* a technique known as public relations. And it has the high liability of abuse through lies and the degrade of its practitioner.

But if one strictly attends to the values of truth and affinity, he will be able to communicate and can stand up to the strain.

Knowing this, PR becomes a far more useful and mature subject.

HCO PL 13 August 1970
Issue III
PR Series 3

5
Wrong Publics

What is a "public"?

One hears "*the* public," a star says "*my* public." You look in the dictionary and you find "public" means an organized or general body of people.

There is a specialized definition of the word "PUBLIC" which is not in the dictionary but which is used in the field of public relations. "PUBLIC" is a professional term to PR people. It doesn't mean the mob or the masses. It means "a TYPE OF AUDIENCE."

The broad population to PR professionals is divided up into separate *publics.* Possibly the early birds in PR should have begun to use "audiences" back in 1911. But they didn't. They used the word "publics" to mean different types of audiences for their communications.

So you won't find this in the dictionaries as a PR professional term. But you sure better wrap your wits and tongue around this term for USE. Otherwise you'll make more PR errors than can easily be computered.

WRONG PUBLIC sums up about 99% of the errors in PR activities and adds up to the majority reason for PR failures.

So what's a "public"?

In PRese (PR slang) use "public" along with another word always. There is no single word form for "public" in PR. A PR never says THE public.

There is the "community public," meaning people in the town not personally grouped into any other special public. There is the "employee public" meaning the people who work for the firm. There's the "shareholder public" meaning the birds who own shares in the PR's company. There's the "teenage public" meaning the under-20 people. There's the "doctor public" meaning the MD audience the PR is trying to reach.

There are hundreds of different types of publics.

An interest in common or a professional or caste characteristic in common—some similarity amongst a special group, determines the type of public or audience.

The PR needs this grouping as he can expect each different type of public to have different interests. Therefore, his promotion to them must be designed especially for each type of public.

In the PR world, there aren't kids, there is a "child public." There aren't teenagers, there's a "teenage public." There aren't elderly people, there's an "elderly public."

The PR man does not think in huge masses. He thinks in group types within the masses.

PR is an activity concerned with *presentation* and *audience.* Even when he writes a news release, he "slants" it for a publication that reaches a type of audience and he writes it *for* that audience (modified by editorial idiosyncrasies).

A PR *surveys* in terms of special publics. Then he presents his material so as to influence *that* particular public.

He doesn't offer stories about wheelchairs to the teenage public or Mickey Mouse prizes to the elderly public. If he is a good PR man.

All releases should be designed to reach a special public.

When you mix it up you fail.

When you get it straight and survey it you succeed.

The "police public" is not going to buy the glories of hash. The "criminal public" isn't going to go into raptures over the "heroes in blue."

All expert PR is aimed at a specific, carefully surveyed, special audience called a "______ public."

When you know that, you can grasp the subject of PR.

When you can use it expertly you are a pro PR!

To give some examples of wrong publics, a lecture by myself was designed as an intimate chat with church staff to let them in on what's going on and what we're planning so that church staffs could be informative to the Scientology public. It was a "staff public" medium of communication.

Somebody broke the rules, played it to the Scientology public. Then somebody else figured it was a substitute for a Congress and dropped Congresses.

The exact end result was to cut totally my comm line to church staffs. The other day I heard how staffs missed hearing from me.

If my line to staffs in churches is going to be played to PE attendees, that's it. Wrong public. No comm line to staffs.

I do a briefing of Sea Organization members on Flag, some dim wit uses it to play to Public Division Public. Wrong public. So that line is cut.

A conclusion someone not knowledgeable in PR technique could reach would be "promotion doesn't work."

Promotion never works on wrong publics.

The System

The PR has to figure out his precise publics. There may be several distinct types.

Then he has to survey and look over the reactions of each different type.

He then plans and designs his communication and offerings for each one.

An orderly Scientology church has each different public categorized and labeled in address.

Then the PR sends the right message to the right public in each case. There may be a dozen different messages if there are a dozen different publics. Each one is right for that public.

The PR is after a result, a call-in, a reply, a response.

The right message in the right form to the right public gets the result.

A wrong message to the wrong public simply costs lots of money and gets no result.

Even if a PR is engaged in "molding public opinion" it still requires a different message to each different public.

6 Opinion Leaders

HCO PL 11 May 1971
Issue II
PR Series 6

An "opinion leader" is that being to whom others look for interpretation of publicity or events. Through wisdom, proximity to data sources, personality or other factors including popularity itself, certain members of the group, company, community or nation are looked to by others for evaluation.

In the teething days of public relations, George Creel, who conducted the massive Liberty Loan drives for the US government considered that it was enough to batter avalanches of publicity down on the heads of the "general public." Given enough money, enough media of communication and no real opposition this proved successful enough.

But as time unreeled, some unsung PR man recognized the fact that the "general" public was made up of smaller groups. Churches, social clubs, factories, and thousands of other large or small groupings of the population were what made up the "general" public.

Each of these groups had its own "opinion leader" and within each group there were smaller groups who each in turn had its own opinion leader.

"To whom do they listen?" "Whose opinion do they accept?" "Whom do they trust?" "On whom do they depend?" are the questions, which answered, identify the opinion leader of the group, large or small.

Further, the opinion leader of a very large group, in turn is interpreted by the opinion leaders of the smaller units which go to make up the larger group.

As an example, government spokesman X puts out Bulletin A on the radio and TV and into the press. He is NOT talking to masses of people. He is in reality talking to opinion leaders. On a crucial question there will not be a reaction to X until the listeners have heard what their opinion leaders have to say about Bulletin A.

If there have been other issuances like Bulletin A, the opinion leaders will have voiced their own opinions. Their groups will then know the attitude. In this case Bulletin A will receive an apparent "general public" reaction. In short, the opinion about Bulletin A will have been preformed by the opinion leaders. This makes it look like there is mass public opinion without opinion leaders.

One of the great dangers of PR practice comes from not really knowing the subject well enough or in twisting it or in losing bits of it.

Having discovered the principle that "opinion leaders" form public opinion not the "general public," many PR people forget it or didn't give it enough importance or even in some cases chose to be willfully destructive of their employers.

It should be very obvious that if general public reaction to an event is dependent upon the reaction and interpretation of opinion leaders, then a PR action's success depends upon favorably influencing the opinion leaders of that part of the population one is trying to reach and calculating what opinion leaders one can neglect or even offend.

This would be almost mathematical in computation. Spokesman X issuing Bulletin A that offended 55% of the opinion leaders would get, roughly, a 55% opposing reaction from the whole public.

Surveys for the identities of opinion leaders would then become a MAJOR activity of PR in any area and for any type of message or event.

Even a rough estimation, which is easily done, would serve better than no thought of it at all.

PR men go for Very Important People. PR wears this out beyond belief. But it is an alter-is. VIPs to PR are only opinion leaders. A government minister is tagged automatically by PR people as a VIP because his car has flags and he *is* a minister. Yet he may be a drunken nephew whose opinion is about as welcome to his colleagues as a hangover. So he may be a VIP but he is not an opinion leader. When he says "blue," his colleagues think "black" and the opinion leaders in the public think "red." The only PR use of this minister would be to get him to embrace and speak up for someone you wanted fired or some cause you wanted opposed!

So it's very lazy PR to assume that a "VIP" is worth knowing or using. Sometimes VIPs are also opinion leaders.

Celebrities are more often opinion leaders as they arrive at their role by popular acclaim. But even here one has to operate with good sense. Paul Robeson, the great American singer, was used by Communists in the 1930s to popularize their cause. It did not achieve this. Paul Robeson, championing his own race, probably would have advanced civil rights legislation greatly. The misuse brought anti-communists to believe that all the Negroes would now become a Communist Fifth Column and brought about strong opposition to Negroes and to Communists.

The rule that should not be violated is to use an opinion leader only to further an opinion he could have visibly. The equation must add up with all factors of a kind, not a strange factor interjected into the sequence. Like music, you don't introduce a wrong note in the scale if you want harmonious rendition. Robeson (black singer)—opinion leader of blacks—Communism. Too odd a sequence. Robeson (black singer)—opinion leader of blacks—black relief. Obvious sequence.

The equation

Bertrand Russell (British philosopher)—Academic opinion leader—Communism: caused a strengthening of the Communist cause because he was a thought symbol and "anybody was free to think" and "they're always forming odd ideas in the halls of learning." His statement "Better red than dead" was a classic PR caper. It was widely quoted. Helped Russell, of whom few ever would have heard, and possibly helped Communism, at least to be talked about, and obviously was picked up by the group in which Russell existed. To the rest of us, this may have sounded like naked atomic war threat and war-mongering. But it was the proper use of a foreign opinion leader by a large group.

Now if the paragraph above jarred on you in any way or seemed to espouse a strange cause, etc., etc., you will have the reason why PR men cannot always see clearly and objectively. They themselves are too involved in causes and pros and cons to remain pan-determined (viewing or handling all sides).

By permitting prejudice to get in the way of handling opinions a PR man loses control of his subject. He becomes so violently partisan that many of his stable data become blurred or abused.

Thus the subject of opinion leaders can become abandoned. Disagreement with the views of some of them remove not only the opinion leaders but the whole subject of opinion leaders out of use.

While conducting themselves like status mad prima donnas, seeking to exist mainly by PR techniques, most people in government power positions are remarkably badly served by their PR men and by their own prejudices or jealousies.

Essentially, a person *in* power is not the same person seeking power.

Maintaining power is a different subject than attaining power.

A politician by definition is someone who handles people. Even the word means "people." Thus the subject of "public relations" does a natural closure with government.

Yet the alteration of the subject of PR and its misuse, neglect or abuse by government PR men could be in itself a considerable study.

A politician commonly is boosted to power by opinion leaders. This could be called the "will of the people." Once he has attained power the garden variety politician of this age finds himself committed to special interests that have little to do with the "will of the people." Few are the politicians who have the integrity to continue to look to the people—the opinion leaders—who put them there. Thus, now apparently serving other masters, they appear to have been false in their earlier pretensions. Not remaining true to their opinion leaders, politicians as a general subject acquire a cynical reputation with the "people."

The general unrest and unpopularity is largely traceable to a violent disregard of the subject of *opinion leaders.*

Attaining power is done usually by the consent of or with the help of the opinion leaders. Arrival in a position of power too often causes the person to shift the basis of his operation. He is now associating with different people in a power strata. It would require quite an effort of will to not be seduced. Having achieved power by opinion leaders the person may forget them and seek to maintain power by other means or by force. This is essentially a violation of the power formula which indicates one should not disconnect. By disconnecting from the previous opinion leaders the person begins his own demise.

This is terribly easy to do in the case of government. It is so easy for a government to use FORCE that a disregard of previous opinion leaders can occur.

Money power is usually available to persons who rise to positions of leadership and can be, like force, a substitute.

Thus a truly suborned leader would desert "opinion leader" as a basis of power and begin to use FORCE and MONEY to hold his position.

But when one assumes a position of power, regard for opinion leaders should *broaden,* not be dropped.

The astute leader on his way up may trod heavily on the opinion leaders of the opposition. This has its benefits in reinforcing the favor of opinion leaders for him. But it also has its liabilities for, now in power, he may have serious enemies who are all the more perturbed now that they too have him as a leader.

Few politicians—indeed few men who move into any kind of power—ever satisfactorily solve this problem. The *very* able ones do solve it and become far more powerful as a result since they do not violate the power formula.

Not only does the brilliant leader refuse to disconnect from the opinion leaders who put him there through "public approval," he also connects with the previously opposing opinion leaders. If truly magnificent he gains the good opinion of former hostile opinion leaders without decreasing the good will of the opinion leaders who put him there. This actually defines the difference between a second rate politician and a real statesman. The genius required to arrive at such solutions cannot be underestimated, but the formula of achieving it is elementary PR.

The leader of the "blues" (supported of course by the opinion leaders of the "blues") rises to power in the teeth of "green" opposition. Now in power, he has sway over both the blues and the greens. The blues opinion is that this should signal a panorama of dead greens. But unless this rule is to be just one long bloodbath it is now necessary to cool off tempers all around, preserve blue support and *win* green support. That is an elementary equation.

Attilas and Huns and Genghis Khans solved this by simply murdering all imagined hostile elements. They may be known in history but politically they built nothing that endured. Even the pyramids of skulls vanished.

Men like Hitler went so far in reverse in handling this problem as to finally slaughter even their adherents.

In the general field of human activities every different or specialized group can be considered a political unit. It elects, with a wide variety of formalities or lack of them, its leaders and when different agencies than themselves elect them (inheritance, appointments from without) the group at least elects its opinion leaders if only by listening.

And people strive to *be* opinion leaders and also back down or otherwise react when someone else is so "elected."

So being an opinion leader involves the responsibility of maintaining the position by remaining well informed or personable or whatever else seems to be required.

One has to decide in some degree what he is an opinion leader for or against or at least about. And one has to set a zone or have one set for him in which he operates.

A usual example is the family. Often someone in it is the opinion leader. It is not necessarily the one with the money or the force. Where one member or clique has the money or force and uses these and the opinion leader is someone else, strife and domestic upset may result.

All the children may look to an aunt for their styles, thoughts and approval. Where this runs counter to the money-force persons, somebody is going to have a broken home or a horrible old age.

Such is human prejudice—or ignorance—that the money-force persons almost never dream of winning the support of the opinion leader aunt by sound but popular policy based on consultation.

The right answer of course is for the money-force power to operate in consultation with the opinion leader.

This is true all the way on up to government sized groups.

Money-force may bribe and break necks but it really never does become the leader in the absence of the approval of a majority of opinion leaders.

Prosperity and easy rule depend utterly upon the cooperation of opinion leaders.

The unrest in the United States and some other countries is

traceable directly to this fantastic omission in their PR technical expertise. They not only do not seek the favor of opinion leaders, they actively harass and seek to destroy them.

In return, the opinion leaders feel endangered and have and state opinions accordingly. The power of the government drops back on money and force only. Governmental survival is thus greatly impaired.

The so-called "mass news media" by which is meant newspapers, TV, radio and magazines, has the fault built into its title. It cannot and never will reach any masses directly. It reaches only through opinion leaders. It has to quote this one and that one which it fancies as an opinion leader. But it never finds out WHO the opinion leaders are.

Newspaper editorials are a direct effort to force opinion. They quote the opinions of other papers just as though these were opinion leaders.

They believe they "mold public opinion" but PR men long since have given up this idea and even greet it with raucous laughter.

Newspapers have ceased to wonder about their rapid demise. They are getting fewer fast. They thought it was radio. Then TV. It wasn't.

Willy Hearst's 1890 yellow journalism and scandal mongering began to dig the grave of the newspaper that many decades ago.

Hear this: While seeking to control public opinion, newspapers began to strike viciously at opinion leaders. Name him, sooner or later any really important opinion leader in the area would be hit with scandal. It happened so often that opinion leaders automatically began to say, "Don't believe the newspapers."

The day of the newspaper is dead. The not mourned London Daily Mail hit one too many opinion leaders one too many times. And nobody believed it anymore and nobody bought it. And it folded.

So government or newspaper or church or hockey club, the same rule applies. The goodwill of the opinion leaders is necessary for survival. *Not* the good opinion of the masses! Since that cannot be reached.

The Russian state talks down about individualism. The "cult of the individual" is a bad thing.

Their internal police is vital to them. They have forgotten that the Czar's Okhrana destroyed the Czar by destroying every opinion leader amongst the people whom they could seize or slay.

So as I said earlier PR is dangerous stuff if one doesn't really know it and if one only applies half of it.

Omitting the opinion leader is bad enough. Seeking to destroy him is far, far worse.

Yes, one says, but how about the violent opposition? How about that fellow?

Well, he's a problem. But he *is* an opinion leader.

One has to decide how much of an opinion leader he is.

If you don't handle a would-be opinion leader who is anti but who is NOT an opinion leader, people get cross.

The decision here stems from (a) is he talking about actual abuse? or (b) is he just lying?

In either case one has certain courses of action. If the abuses are actual, work to remedy them. If he is just lying, lay out the truth. If he really isn't an opinion leader, ignore him.

But one can only interfere with him or remove him if many, many are getting cross because you don't. But that's a risky business.

As a rule, only that dissident person should be removed who is speaking in your name and on your lines and using your power to do you down. And then he can only be removed off your lines as you are under no obligation to finance or empower your own opposition. That's suicide. He is not an opinion leader but a traitor for he owes his power to you.

Usually anti-opinion leaders are *made by neglect*.

PR-wise one has to catch them early and handle.

Abuses by those in charge are never put right by force. They are only worsened.

Perhaps there is no excuse whatever to use force to enforce an opinion. Wars are notorious for failing to solve. You can always find a point years or decades before the war when a point existed that PR and cooperative rule could have solved.

PR imperfectly known or unknown as a subject leads to big trouble.

PR is powerless when it doesn't know.

PR loses when it neglects.

Early enough, PR alone does it.

Later, PR with concessions are needed.

Then, PR is out and only force is thought to serve.

This would be a DETERIORATING SITUATION.

The longer PR takes to catch it up the more imminent loss or force become.

From this, technically adept PR could be seen to have too limited a role in the affairs of nations or groups.

The way to attain a more dominant role with PR is first to know it well, next to be sure others who should understand it and then to use it effectively.

As it is a subject which is meant to reach masses, remember that it must reach them through opinion leaders.

Opinion leaders may or may not by VIPs. But they are, whoever they are, barber or king, VIPs to the PR.

Thus surveys for opinion leaders are necessary. And the opinions of opinion leaders must be known.

And for heaven's sake restrain the boss from shooting opinion leaders no matter how just his wrath.

But also don't tell him Dr. Kutzbrain is an opinion leader just because he talks to two nurses and his wife.

Peace is not necessarily a target of PR. Survival is. And survival requires some control of opinion.

When this becomes control of numbers of people, PR is only accomplished through opinion leaders.

7

HCO PL 28 May 1971
PR Series 8

Too Little Too Late

The hallmark of bad promotion is "too little too late."

Probably the most aggravating and most suppressive error that can be made by those doing promotion or other PR actions, is to plan or announce an event too close to the date for anyone to come.

Typical report "Only 50 came to the Congress. I guess it just wasn't popular."

An exec hearing this can validly suspect "too little too late" as the real WHY. He would be 95% right without even querying further.

"When did you announce the July 1st Congress?"

Usual true answer: "June 25th!"

"How many mailings were sent?"

Usual true answer: "500 because FP . . ."

"What other promotion was done?"

Usual true answer: "None."

Reason for only 50 at the Congress. "Too little promotion announced too late for anyone to come."

Often this factor is hidden. Other more dramatic reasons, not the true WHYs are advanced. "There was a football match the same date." "We were in disrepute." "There is an anti-campaign." "The press . . ." Yap, yap, yap. All lies. It was just too little promotion too late.

"Nobody showed up for the VIP dinner."

The right response to this is "When did you send the invitations?"

"Well, you see, FP wouldn't give us any stamps so . . ."

"WHEN did you send the invitations?"

"The same morning as the dinner was held."

"Were they engraved?"

"No, we sort of ran them off on the mimeograph."

Just *why* event failures are 95% traced "handled at the last moment without proper planning and without proper verified addresses and without enough posh or volume" is itself a mystery.

PR in reality is about 80% preparation of the event and about 20% event.

If the preparation is not planned and prepared fully well in advance of the event, the events fail.

Off the cuff PR is sometimes necessary. But usually made necessary by lack of foresight and hard work.

There is a rule about this:

THE SUCCESS OF ANY EVENT IS DIRECTLY PROPORTIONAL TO THE TIMELY PREPARATION.

In other words, poor preparation made too late gives an unsuccessful event.

PR is hard work. But the hard work mostly occurs before there is any public view of it. The work in the event itself is pie.

You see these beautifully staged affairs, these flawless polished occurrences. They look so effortless. Well, they LOOK effortless because a fantastic amount of preparation went into them ahead of time.

A well attended event is planned and drilled and announced ages ahead of the occurrence.

Even a mere dinner has to be announced at least a week in advance.

PRs who don't work hard to plan and drill and who don't announce in time with enough promotion have flops.

So PR flops come from failures to plan, drill, promote enough and in plenty of time.

Therefore, PR successes are best guaranteed by data gathering, sharp planning, heavy drilling, timely announcement and adequate promotion.

Even a surprise event has to be handled this way for everyone except those for whom the surprise is intended.

So gather the data that will guide planning, plan well, program it, do all the clerical actions necessary, announce it in ample time, drill all those connected with it heavily until they're flawless and then stage it.

And there you are, a "spontaneous," highly successful event.

Whether it's a protest march, a press conference, a new course or dinner for VIPs or even just friends, if it's to be a success, prepare it and announce it widely in plenty of time.

There was this grave where they buried a failed PR man. And on the headstone they put, "George Backlog. Too Little, Too Late." They had to shoot him because he broke the company's leg.

A mediocre event very well prepared and announced well and in time will succeed better than the most splendid event done off the cuff.

The next time you see empty seats remember and use this data. Or better still do it right in the first place.

8 Manners

HCO PL 30 May 1971
PR Series 9

The original procedure developed by man to oil the machinery of human relationships was "good manners."

Various other terms that describe this procedure are politeness, decorum, formality, etiquette, form, courtesy, refinement, polish, culture, civility, courtliness, and respect.

Even the most primitive cultures had highly developed rituals of human relationship. In studying 21 different primitive races, which I did first hand, I was continually impressed with the formalities which attended their interpersonal and intertribal and interracial relationships.

Throughout all races, "bad manners" are condemned.

Those with "bad manners" are REJECTED.

Thus the primary technology of public relations was "manners."

Therefore a public relations man or team that has not drilled and mastered the manners accepted as "good manners" by those being contacted will fail. Such a PR man or team may know all the senior PR tech and yet fail miserably on the sole basis of "exhibiting bad manners."

"Good manners" sum up to (a) granting importance to the other person and (b) using the two-way communication cycle (as in *Dianetics 55!*). Whatever motions or rituals are, these two factors are involved. Thus a PR violating them will find himself and his program rejected.

Arrogance and force may win dominion and control but will never win acceptance and respect.

For all his "mental technology" the psychiatrist or psychologist could never win applause or general goodwill because they are personally (a) arrogant beyond belief (b) hold others in scathing contempt ("man is an animal," "people are all insane," etc.). Born from Bismark's military attitude these subjects have borrowed as well the attitude which made the Nazis an object of worldwide condemnation. No matter how many people were maimed or killed, the Nazi would never have dominated the world anymore than their "mental scientists" will ever win over humanity.

They just don't have "good manners," i.e., they do not (a) consider or give others a feeling of importance and (b) they are total strangers to a comm cycle.

Successful PR

All successful PR, then, is built upon the bedrock of good manners as these are the first technology developed to ease human relations.

Good manners are much more widely known and respected than PR technology. Therefore, NO PR technology will be successful if this element is omitted.

Brushing off "mere guards" as beneath one's notice while one goes after a contact with their boss can be fatal. Who talks to their boss? These "mere guards."

Making an appointment and not keeping it, issuing an invitation too late for it to be accepted, not offering food or a drink, not standing up when a lady or important man enters, treating one's subordinates like lackeys in public, raising one's voice harshly in public, interrupting what someone else is saying to "do something important," not saying thank you or good night—these are all "bad manners." People who do these or a thousand other discourtesies are mentally rejected by those with whom they come into contact.

As PR is basically acceptance then bad manners defeat it utterly.

A successful PR person has to have good manners.

This is not hard. One has to assess his attitude toward others and iron it out. Are they individually important? One has to have his two-way communication cycle perfect, so perfect it is so natural that it is never noticed.

Given those two things, a PR can now learn the bits of ritual that go to make up the procedure that is considered "good manners" in the group with which he is associating.

Then given PR technology correctly used, one has successful PR.

Importance

You have no idea how important people are. There is a reversed ratio—those at the bottom have a self-importance *far* greater than those at the top who *are* important. A char lady's concept of her own importance is far greater than that of a successful general manager!

Ignore people at your peril.

Flattery is not very useful, is often suspect, as it does not come from a sincere belief and the falsity in it is detectable to all but a fool.

A person's importance is made evident to him by showing him respect, or just by assuring him he is visible and acceptable.

To see and acknowledge the existence of someone is a granting of their importance.

To know their name and their connections also establishes importance.

Asserting one's *own* importance is about as acceptable as a dead cat at a wedding.

People have value and are important. Big or small they are important.

If you know that, you are half-way home with good manners.

Thus PR can occur.

Communication

The two-way communication cycle is more important than the content.

The content of the communication, the meaning to be put across to another or others is secondary to the fact of a two-way communication cycle.

Communication exists to be replied to or used.

Communication without the communication cycle being in first must exist before it carries any message.

Messages do not travel on no-line.

Advertising is always violating this. Buy Beanos! Into the empty air. Other things must establish the line. And the line must be such as to obtain an answer, either by use or purchase or reply.

A funny example was a letter writer who without preamble or reason told people to buy a multi-thousand dollar package without even an explanation of its use or value. Response zero. No communication line. He was writing to a name but not really to anyone.

In social intercourse a communication cycle must be established before any acceptance of the speaker can occur. Then one might get across a message.

Good manners require a two-way communication cycle. This is even true of social letters and phone calls.

Out of this one gets "telling the hostess good night as one leaves."

One really has to understand the two-way communication cycle to have really good manners.

Without a two-way communication cycle, PR is pretty poor stuff.

Primitives

If an American Indian's ritual of conference was so exact and complex, if a thousand other primitive races had precise social conduct and forms of address, then it is not too much to ask modern man to have good manners as well.

But "good manners" are less apparent in our times than they once were. This comes about because the intermingling of so many races and customs have tended to destroy the ritual patterns once well established in the smaller units.

So one appears to behold a sloppy age of manners.

This is no excuse to have bad manners.

One can have excellent manners by just observing: (a) importance of people (b) two-way communication cycle (c) local rituals observed as proper conduct.

These are the first musts of a PR man or woman.

On that foundation can be built an acceptable PR presence that makes PR succeed.

R

Surveys

Surveys Checksheet

Purpose

To enable the Volunteer Minister to survey a public to find out what is needed and wanted and valuable to the community, and to optimumly use survey results for dissemination and success.

a	Study Section 1 Breakthrough—PR and Production—Tone Scale Surveys.	________
b	Study Section 2 Creating Survey Questions.	________
c	Study Section 3 How to Do a PR Survey.	________
d	Drill: From what you know so far, make up some sample survey questions for two different surveys.	________
e	Drill: Write three survey questions on the situation found in your community.	________
f	Drill: Survey your community on the situation you found with survey questions above.	________
g	Drill: Examine a newspaper, note various poor advertisements which could have been improved if surveyed beforehand.	________
h	Drill: Demonstrate with your demo kit the mechanics of doing a survey.	________
i	Drill: Write an essay on the beingness the Volunteer Minister should assume when he surveys.	________
j	Study Section 4 Ethnics, Find out What is Needed and Wanted.	________

k Drill: Go out and do a small, 10 people, ethnic survey on your community. ________

l Drill: Go back and tabulate your survey. ________

m Study Section 5 Population Surveys. ________

n Drill: Demonstrate with your demo kit how you handle the idea of "when you are too incredible you become invisible." ________

o Drill: Write an essay on how the Volunteer Minister could use a population survey to the benefit of his community. ________

Surveys Pack

HCO PL 2 June 1971
Issue II
PR Series 10

1

Breakthrough—PR and Production—Tone Scale Surveys

The Laws of PR

THE PRIMARY BARRIER TO PRODUCTION IS HUMAN EMOTION AND REACTION.

PR IS THE SOCIAL TECHNOLOGY OF HANDLING AND CHANGING HUMAN EMOTION AND REACTION.

A LOW PRODUCTION AREA IS OUT-MORALE BECAUSE IT IS LOW PRODUCTION. IF YOU CAN NURSE THE AREA UP TO PRODUCTION YOU HAVE MORALE.

DON'T USE NEGATIVE ARC IN A PR SURVEY. MAKE IT LIGHT SO IT INVOLVES COMMUNICATION.

To get a PR survey done in an area that is barriered against production, you begin by writing down three VERY DIRECT questions that you want answered. One question for each of BE, DO, HAVE.

On a survey of Lower Slobovia central command point, the three direct questions could be:

1. (BE) Do you want this joint to succeed?
2. (DO) Are you personally going to be active in getting this show on the road?
3. (HAVE) Are you going to directly assist Scientology to acquire Lower Slobovia?

Now you translate these into the field of human emotion. Each direct question is concerned with one or more of A, R and C. You put down by your direct question what each question is concerned with.

In the example above,

1. is A
2. is A or C
3. is R.

You now phrase a question to which you will get a reaction, and that reaction you get has to be the reaction of the individual to the *direct* question, but you get that reaction by asking him a different question translated into terms of emotion that will give you his reaction willy-nilly. He can figure his way round the direct question to give you a PR answer. He cannot help but give you his reaction if you involve his emotions. The direct question does not involve his emotions so that he doesn't give a reaction you can observe clearly as *the* reaction to the question.

Having established your BE, DO, HAVE questions and added your connotations of A, R, C, you can translate the direct question into a survey question that involves his emotions and gives you his reactions.

The examples above could translate as follows:

1. Do you think that increased efficiency in management would bring about a more desireable organization?
2. Would it be more pleasant working within such a framework?
3. Have you envisioned improvements that would occur in Lower Slobovia if Scientology were more widely used?

Now you pretest the survey mentally, paying attention to dictation and comprehension, rephrasing to ensure adequate communication without losing any of the sense of your question.

The surveyor contacts the people to be surveyed, asks his questions and makes notes of the answers given; he also makes sure he notes the reaction. He should write down the *tone level* of the reaction to each question. He doesn't handle anything—just the question, recording the answer and the reaction.

Tabulation of the results give you a majority of reactions on one tone level.

You can now design your PR campaign on a tone level half or one notch above that level and be sure to obtain wide agreement, by the rules contained in *Science of Survival.*

Thus the barrier of human emotion and reaction is removed.

The duty and function of PR is to remove the barrier of human emotion and reaction.

You hit at the heart of reaction when you get into human involvement.

You hit at the basic on any production situation when you get into BE, DO, HAVE.

You hit at his emotion when you address his A, R, C.

So you involve him when you get his emotion and thus his reaction.

You can strip off the verbiage in the survey and its tabulation and get a numerical answer (tone level figure) for each question.

Different publics can be PRed. Finance publics for example, as well as production publics—sometimes finance people get into conflicts with production.

PR is always perfectly okay as long as it is real. If not real, it acts as a stop. You find the R by establishing if there is a situation to begin with surveying to get the tone level, figuring out the average response of the group on each question—and design a PR campaign to handle.

There is a 1-2-3 not quite figured out in designing the campaign. But these are the basic concepts of the science of PR. It covers the field of manipulation of human emotion.

2

*BPL 7 January 1972R
PR Series 14R

Creating Survey Questions

The purpose of this section is to fully document *how* survey questions, to evoke human emotion and reaction, are derived. Included are examples of actual surveys done, showing the SITUATION, the SURVEY QUESTIONS, the SURVEY RESULTS and resulting PR

PROGRAM to handle. A good many of the surveys were done within the church to find human emotion and reaction barriers to production amongst staff members. The examples are given in chronological order so that one may see how the survey and PR technology was evolved during the years of 1970 and 1971. (Some of these surveys were done aboard the Sea Organization vessel, *Apollo*.)

SURVEY EXAMPLE 1

SITUATION:

Due to various causes, morale is not what it should be aboard.

The full intention of the Board of Directors is to have things running smoothly and safely for all hands.

Major Target: To interview each individual staff member and obtain his honest state of opinion regarding his post.

Vital Targets:

1. Not to interrupt the work of or worsen the situation.
2. To improve matters by survey.
3. To obtain data so that a new sensible reality can be established by PR programs.

Primary Targets:

1. Provide yourself with paper, clipboard and ballpoints.
2. Work at this at optimum periods.

Operating Targets:

1. To approach persons individually. Draw them out of groups.
2. Just listen and prompt and question. Don't interrupt or interject. Don't comment on what they say to them.
3. Make useful, not necessarily voluminous, notes.
4. Cover each question.
5. Excerpt results.
6. Design programs to handle what is found.

QUESTIONS AND RESULTS:

Survey R-factor: The Board of Directors wants your opinion on certain matters to help handle them.

A. What do you feel command intention really is?

33% 1. Clear the Planet

31% 2. Something planned from the Board or high executives to be carried out by staff members.

16% 3. Everyone doing his job and getting the show on the road.
7% 4. Well trained staff in the technology and policy of Scientology and seamanship.
5% 5. Provide an environment in which L. Ron Hubbard can get on with his research.
5% 6. Successful management of Scientology Churches.
3% 7. Miscellaneous.

B. What do you feel you should know more about to get your job done?

30% 1. Technology, policy and seamanship.
22% 2. Policy.
20% 3. Specifics relating to posts.
14% 4. Nothing in particular.
9% 5. More briefing regarding schedules and senior Church actions with the Churches of Scientology.
5% 6. Scientology technology.
0% 7. Miscellaneous.

C. What do you really need to get your job done?

32% 1. Nothing in particular.
20% 2. More training.
17% 3. Specifics pertaining to posts.
13% 4. More time (without arbitraries and distractions).
8% 5. More personnel.
7% 6. To be left alone to get on with it.
3% 7. More briefing on schedules for planning work cycles.

D. What would you like to see us doing?

31% 1. Expanding Scientology around the planet.
21% 2. Group cooperation and coordination.
16% 3. Staff getting trained and processed.
14% 4. What we are doing.
13% 5. Moving more and to different ports.
3% 6. Getting stats up in Scientology churches.
2% 7. Miscellaneous.

E. What changes should occur?

30% 1. What we are doing is good.
24% 2. More expansion in the field for more flow of recruits to the ship.
20% 3. More trained personnel in technology and policy.

13% 4. More briefing of the staff on operations.

7% 5. Specifics relating to post.

4% 6. No opinion.

2% 7. Miscellaneous.

The following is an item from the Orders of the Day with regard to one tabulated survey.

FRIDAY 24 April 1970

"SURVEY

"The survey of the ship's company purposes and opinions has been completed and all hands are thanked for their contribution to it.

"Results will be issued in due course.

"There is an astonishing similarity in the answers which demonstrates we are all of similar opinion on vital questions.

"It discloses there is far less dissidence in the company than might have been supposed.

"We are a true group.

"The survey will be of great use in future planning."

SURVEY EXAMPLE 2

SITUATION:

"INJURY SURVEY

"Please interview the five people recently injured to discover what's going on?

"We've never had any injured people like this.

"All in this port.

"See if you can two-way comm it and get some common denominator."

RESULTS:

The common denominator found followed this pattern:

1. EXTERIOR at time of injury.
2. Attention OFF the body.
3. Physical contest being engaged in.
4. NO PAIN involved (though two needed stitches!).
5. NO MISEMOTION at having injury, mild interest only.
6. A feeling of POWERFULNESS prior to injury.

Following is an item entered in the next day's Orders of the Day:
4 June 1970

"INJURIES

"Those recently injured were not PTS. Survey showed they were exterior and feeling powerful and didn't watch where they were sending the body."

SURVEY EXAMPLE 3

SITUATION:

A cross-section survey is needed on *what we are thought to be aiming for.*

QUESTIONS AND RESULTS:

1. What is your conception of what we are doing currently?
   - A. Getting staff trained up in specialist seamanship and then administrative functions.
   - B. Getting Scientology technology fully in use and churches running smoothly.
2. What is your idea of the ideal we are working towards?
   - A. Immediately—smooth running ship and Scientology churches.
   - B. Ultimately—a clear and sane planet.
3. What is being done to achieve it?

   Strengthening ourselves internally while keeping our external lines operating.
4. Do you feel we are making it?

   Yes!
5. Does anything need to be changed so we can make it faster?
   - A. More training.
   - B. More processing.
   - C. Any counter-intention removed.
   - D. More promotion.
   - E. Faster and wider acceptance of Scientology.
6. When do you think we will make it?
   - A. Current ship programs, 2-6 months
   - B. Scientology church programs, 1-2 years
   - C. Planetary Scientology influence, 2-5 years

An Orders of the Day item of the next day comments on the survey results.

24 June 1970

"SURVEY

"The cross-section survey just done regarding what we are doing showed 'very good results, and the answers were quite consistent.'

"We sure have group agreement on what we are doing!

"There were very good indicators on this survey. There was an overall feeling of confidence among all those surveyed (a 28 person cross-section of the ship).

"There was confidence that we are progressing on a steady and positive uptrend and that the next few years will show monumental victories in our favor."

Breakthrough

During the month of January 1971, a major advance in the subject of PR and surveying was made. That is—PR surveying in combination with the tone scale technology. I discovered the BASIC LAWS of PR as contained in Section 1, Breakthrough PR and Production Tone Scale Surveys. Thus, ONE SURVEYS TO FIND THE REALITY OF A PERSON *ABOUT* SOMETHING. The person's tone level about this subject is noted. This tone level establishes the affinity or lack of, the person has about the subject. Emotion is A. A is the tone scale. (NOTE: The person's tone level *toward* the SURVEYOR and *about* the SUBJECT may be two entirely different tone bands, so don't get them confused. The person may be in enthusiasm *toward* the surveyor but antagonism *about* the subject being surveyed. It is the latter tone level which is of value. People don't just have a tone. They have a tone *toward* something.

You survey to determine the R (reality) of each person so as to raise the A about the subject through the PR campaign.

You are looking for agreement. To get agreement, you come down to the point where the guy will agree with you. You determine the R (reality) they agreed with. Translate this into A (affinity tone). R is monitored by A attitude. You then raise the R half to one tone band and this establishes the C (comm) level.

The following item in the Orders of the Day of 25 January 1971 summarizes this.

"PR

"Some more PR data has been developed. The same public varies by continent.

"One tests the tone with R questions, reads the A off the tone scale, develops the program at the A half a tone above and uses the R of that tone. R to A, up half, A of that to new R desired. Gives one the program that *communicates,* raises tone.

"A survey of a tone must be a tone *about* something.

"See *Science of Survival's* Chart of Human Emotion. Read the book. The new and future bible of PR followed by *Scientology 0-8* for the graduate PR expert! Finally came into its own!"

On 18 January 1971 I gave a lecture entitled *PR Becomes a Subject* which outlines the basic laws of PR. An excerpt follows:

"PUBLIC RELATIONS IS FOR THE HANDLING AND CONTROL OF HUMAN EMOTION AND REACTION.

"IT'S A THIRD DYNAMIC TECHNOLOGY.

"So how do you make up survey questions? It's simple. You get three questions: One is the equivalent of BE, one is equivalent of DO, one is equivalent of HAVE. BE, DO, HAVE—three questions. Above and below it you could have a couple of null questions. You're trying to find out if somebody on the assembly line likes automobiles. He's building them, does he like them?

"Well, that's an easy one because it's already a human emotion. "Do you like automobiles?"

"Well, let's find out if he's going to work on the assembly line. Let's make it a little bit tougher. Now we're going to find out "Are you going to work on the assembly line?"

"All right, we go around and say, "Are you going to work on the assembly line?" and the guy says, "No," and the next guy says "Yes" and so forth . . . you get no place.

"Therefore, you take the questions you want to know on the subject of BE, DO, HAVE and you encode them into human emotion using the ARC triangle.

"We don't care whether you put A or R or C after each question.

"You're going to translate the basic question that you know into human emotion in order to obtain involvement and you immediately have involvement.

"So you get the true answer, don't you? But the target of your subject is of course the control of human emotion and reaction. So if that is the case, then you would have to have involvement in human emotion and reaction. So how do you put this question together?

"This subject is the control of human emotion and reaction, so therefore the questions of your survey have to be what you want to know transported over into a human emotion and reaction. BE: "Do automobiles exist?" translated once across for an A is "Do you like automobiles?" Now you will get then an emotional response which can be plotted. Now why all this? Because

"THE PRIMARY BARRIER TO PRODUCTION IS HUMAN EMOTION AND REACTION. THAT'S THE PRIMARY BARRIER TO PRODUCTION.

"All at once we know where PR lives.

"There's its use. Not in getting somebody to become a man of "extinction" by drinking Seagram's Whiskey to aid and assist advertising which would be a minor use, but actually to sound out the public to which the campaign is addressed so as to handle the human emotion and reaction.

"Now to trace it back through. The basic law that we're involved with then is: *The primary barrier to production is human emotion and reaction.* Public relations is the technology of handling and changing human emotion, handling and controlling human emotion and reaction.

"So you have to find out what is the human emotion and reaction so you get an encoding of the question, three questions: One BE, one DO, one HAVE. You translate those over into an emotional question by adding the ARC triangle. You plot that now. You get your human emotions in response to these questions. You add them up. You put your program together against the tone scale, one half to one band above. You will have a pretty uniformly successful method of reach.

"So when all seems too grim and you can't seem to get your point across and you can't seem to get your product and it just won't organize that way, then you do have a tool and that tool is called PR. And it has its own technology and we have made a breakthrough in this subject."

EXAMPLE

We're trying to obtain data to popularize and remove barriers from hatting. It may very well be hatting is the least popular function of the Personnel Department.

Developing the Survey Questions

1. You make a statement of a possible situation. (i.e., it may be hatting is the least popular function of the Personnel Department.)
2. You then think up several BLUNT, head-on type questions.
   BE: What is your hat?
   DO: What do you actually do?
   HAVE: What is your product?
3. You then convert those questions so you get a HUMAN ELEMENT. In that way you get an involvement. A PR question must *always* contain a "human" or "being involvement."
   BE: Are you interested in your hat?
   DO: Do your duties align with your own purpose?
   HAVE: Do you consider your product contributes to the group?
   A further question encoded could be:
   DIRECT: Are you being trained in your hat?
   to
   ENCODED: Do you find the training you are getting on your hat interesting?

The purpose of this survey would be to obtain data to popularize and remove the barriers from hatting.

Regarding Production: Validation of accomplishment is garden variety PR.

One rule about a production manager is he has to *want* the product before he gets it.

This is Human emotion and reaction.

Policy-interpreting-wise, does the group want the product?

Thus there is the:

1. ADMINISTRATIVE approach, which the church or production manager uses which is a straight question. (i.e., What is your hat?)
2. HUMAN (or PR) approach, which is used by the PR man to find basic desires and OPINION: (i.e., Are you interested in your hat?)

You hit at the heart of the resistance-to when you get into the human involvement.

The Key PR Datum is of course the greatest barrier to production efficiency is human reaction,

and

A low production area is out-morale because it is low production.

If you can nurse it up to production, you have morale.

SURVEY EXAMPLE 4

SITUATION:

A survey needs to be done in Department X to find out who or what keeps the area upset.

DIRECT QUESTIONS:

BE: Do you want your job?

DO: Are you doing your job?

HAVE: What is wrong in Department X area?

ENCODED QUESTIONS:

BE: Do you enjoy your post?

DO: Are you having any difficulties on your post?

HAVE: What changes are needed, if any, in the Department X set up?

RESULTS: 10 staff out of 17 had good indicators, were willing, having wins and creating their posts.

The other 7 were to varying degrees conservative about their posts, having minor difficulties and upsets.

It was found that unstabilization was coming from external sources to the department, i.e., frequent personnel changes allowed and not ensuring the area was hatted.

HANDLING:

These two factors were gotten in from an executive level and the Department X area stabilized remarkably.

SURVEY EXAMPLE 5

SITUATION:

Three or four days ago an urgent order was given to (*area*). It was not done and the situation went unhandled, causing severe overload to staff in the area.

We are looking for an attitude of defiance and one or more attitudes of helpless child.

RAW QUESTIONS:

1. What hat are you wearing actually if any?
2. Why didn't you handle your post in this emergency?
3. Are you unwilling to have fast lines and stats?

ENCODED QUESTIONS:

Affinity Tone: 1. Did you like the hat you were assigned?
Affinity Tone: 2. What did you feel about the situation?
Affinity Tone: 2A. What was unpleasant about it?
Communication Tone: 3. How do the present (*area*) lines compare with the early ones we had?

RESULTS:

Various terminals in the area were found to be antagonistic and some apathetic. Others were found to have realized their failure to handle the situation that had occurred and had taken steps to prevent reoccurrence.

By isolating these factors it was then possible, by keeping a close eye on the area for the next few days, to observe further instances of non-compliance and resistance to handling the area. In which cases additional actions were taken as necessary to hat and handle confusions and non-compliance.

SURVEY EXAMPLE 6

Personnel Department needs further data for posting personnel optimumly in two departments.

QUESTIONS:

1. When you need to know how to do something, whom do you ask?

2. Who gets the most done?
3. In the department, whom do you feel the most secure about?

RESULTS:

The most upstat of the two departments answered the questions as follows:

Average tone: 4.0 to 20.0

Q1 A. My immediate senior.
B. A reference book.
C. Figure it out myself.

Q2 A. We all do!
B. Our department.
C. The same for all of us.

Q3 A. Our department.
B. All the guys in our department.
C. Myself and the rest in our department.

The less upstat, less productive, low morale department answered accordingly:

Average tone: 2.0

Q1 A. Try to find out for myself then ask the department head.
B. Look in a book.

Q2 Two of the most junior staff in the department named.

Q3 The department head, then the two junior staff members as named in answer 2. (The junior executives not mentioned.)

RESULTS:

This survey confirmed the success of the productive department as having stable leadership from the departmental head, staff who were enthusiastic about their jobs, high morale and continually training on their posts. The department as a unit worked with tremendous team spirit. The downtone, poor production department had an unhappy senior with downtone unstable junior executives. There was no team spirit in this department and little if any post training actions. The most stable terminals in this department were two junior staff members who had enthusiasm for doing their posts and who trained in their study time to increase their abilities.

HANDLING:

Thus we then knew (regarding the unproductive department) who to look to for future executive material, and who would then bring this department to a high operating standard. And the Personnel Department knew what area to concentrate on most heavily with hatting.

Needless to say, nothing was changed in the productive department. As its production increased even higher, it was allotted additional personnel.

SURVEY EXAMPLE 7

SITUATION

Wherewithal. Staff members not adequately aware of their responsibility for viability and income.

Reality and tone level toward this subject needed establishing so further action could be taken to educate staff on the subject of org viability.

ENCODED QUESTIONS

BE: How do you feel about the group making its own way?

DO: What can be done to ensure the group has lots of money to work with?

HAVE: When do you think you'll be receiving full bonus awards?

RESULTS:

The average tone level of those surveyed was 3.5 (strong interest). There was a high degree of reality and agreement that the group make its own way.

Therefore, to support this agreement, the recommendation was to place a 6' x 10' graph in reception showing weekly organization income. This enabled all staff to see viability and to feel more at cause over wherewithal by producing on their own posts.

SURVEY EXAMPLE 8

SITUATION:

More executives were needed. Some on post were not all capable.

The PR survey questions must detect:

BE: Other *status*—status as defense. *Been* something else. IS something else?

DO: Other *involvement*—Involvement in other things or things that don't matter or involvement in contrary actions to a post. Problems would come up.

HAVE: Scene—(omitted or false)—what does he know about it, how real are his data? *Representation.*

Executives fall into two categories.

A. Those who will assume the status or forward the doingness or enhance the scene toward ideal.

B. Those who defend status, have other involvement and have an omitted or falsified scene.

Category A builds things into a smooth prosperous organization.

Category B winds up with an omitted or perverted organization.

SAMPLE SURVEY QUESTIONS:

1. What would be the most ideal post to have if you had total choice? Or what type of life best suits you?

2. What problems or situations would you find easy to handle? Or, what should you be working on? Or, what are you working on?

3. How are things really in your area? Or, what is the organization really doing these days?

QUESTIONS USED:

STATUS	Is there a post you would like to hold sometime in the future for which you feel ideally suited?
INVOLVEMENT	Are you having any problems getting done what you are working on now?
REPRESENTATION	How is your area presently doing on an overall basis?

RESULTS:

The results of this particular survey showed the tone level of the organization executives to be GRIEF. In addition, at least half the executives surveyed volunteered that they really didn't want to be an executive at all, but would prefer to be in a worker position.

The WHY of the area's down statistics was neglect of implementing policy, directives and projects in the organization on the part of the executives.

Short range and immediate handling was to post a staff member in the area who forced in compliance to policy. Long range handling was to move into executive positions junior staff members who were ambitious to hold an executive post competently and to move off the unwilling executives into junior areas where they could produce well until ready to again resume a more senior position.

Spotting Tone

After one has mastered the technique of creating survey questions, the only remaining expertise necessary is accurately spotting tone levels.

The PR man's bible is, of course *Science of Survival* and the *Hubbard Chart of Human Evaluation* and the book *Scientology 0-8*. These materials must be read and thoroughly understood.

To gain proficiency one can do two simple drills.

1. Walk around and spot people on the tone scale. Just say (to yourself) what tone level each person is at until you feel confident that you can tell instantly where any person is on the tone scale. An important datum to grasp is that there is a (1) social tone and (2) an actual thetan tone. And these can be two entirely different tones widely apart in range. This is because a human body is between 0.0 and 4.0 only. A thetan however, can be anywhere from -40.0 and below to +40.0 and infinitely higher.

Thus a thetan can be way way below death on the tone scale and yet his social tone may *appear* to be somewhere around conservatism. But this is where you must be an excellent observer. The person may sit there and conservatively tell you how he just must control bodies in order to get along. He may not say these *exact* words, but amazingly enough, you'll find this really happens. Or the person may go on about how he regrets doing this or that and how it's all someone else's fault. Well, you know he's at shame, blame, regret as a thetan at this point. Yet he or she may at the same time be weeping into a handkerchief. In this case the (1) social tone is GRIEF (.5) and the (2) thetan tone -0.2 to -1.3.

2. Another drill to do is to walk around until you find somebody at a specific tone level. Decide to look for someone at 1.5 for instance. The first person you run into with face flushed from shouting and fists clenched, BINGO you've found your 1.5. Then pick another tone and go from there. If the person you saw at anger was also hitting another, then you would know the person was at 1.5 socially and -1.0 blame (or punishing other bodies) as a thetan.

CONCLUSION

As you can see, the technology of PR surveys and the tone scale in handling and controlling human emotion and reaction is an incredibly powerful tool.

By putting this technology to use on a personal basis, you can literally be in control of your environment on at *least* the first three dynamics! And Scientologists (particularly Scientology staff members) have a monopoly on the entire subject. If there was ever a way to "win friends and influence people," this is it. We as Scientologists are continually jolted by the primitive nature of the general populace around us. So by establishing the local reality and tone we can at least present ourselves and our product in such a way as to be accepted, and then we can bring people up the scale from there. Gone are the days of hit-and-miss promotion and by-guess-or-by-God public events. We now have the know-how to hit the exact target every time. We now have another beautiful tool for UNDERSTANDING.

HCO PL 5 December 1971
Issue II, PR Series 13

3 How to do a PR Survey

SURVEY means "a careful examination of something as a whole and in detail."

The word "survey" as used in Public Relations terminology means to carefully examine public opinion with regard to an idea, a product, an aspect of life, or any other subject. By examining in detail, (person to person surveying) one can arrive at a whole view of public opinion on a subject by tabulating highest percentage of popular response.

The purpose of this section is to describe the two most important aspects of surveying so that 100% successful results can be obtained every time. Though there are many different *types* of surveys, the method used is the same. The two components of surveying are:

1. The mechanics of doing the survey itself.
2. The beingness of the surveyor.

The Mechanics

The actions involved in doing a survey are simple and few. The first thing you do is establish the questions you are going to ask into the public to find out what is wanted and needed, popular or unpopular or whatever. Creating the survey questions is a technology in itself.

After the questions are established they are mimeographed on survey forms or typed on a piece of plain paper for the surveyor to refer to. If one were doing a survey in a city where large numbers of people are interviewed the survey forms might be most practical. However, all that is needed for most surveys is a clipboard with plenty of plain paper and several ball point pens. The survey question page is then placed on top of the pad of paper and flipped back while taking notes of the interview.

The only materials needed for a survey are several ball point pens (so running out of ink in the middle of the survey doesn't cause interruption), plenty of paper and a clipboard.

To begin a survey, you simply walk up to a person and in a friendly manner introduce yourself (if a stranger) and ask to survey them. If additional R-Factor is requested, it is given and then the survey is begun.

Ask the person the first question, flip back the question page and take down the answer. Be sure to number the answers corresponding to the question number being asked. You needn't write down every word as the person speaks to you but get the most important points. You will find, after practice surveying, you can write almost everything down.

After the person has answered the first question, thank him or her with good TRs to acknowledge that comm cycle and go to the next question. All you have to do is BE THERE, be INTERESTED in what the person is saying, and take down his answers.

At the end of the survey thank the person very much. The person will most likely be thanking you by this point as people LOVE to be asked their opinion of things. And having another terminal grant beingness to this and listen attentively is a rare and valuable experience to many.

Then go to the next person and repeat the same procedure. This is all there is to the mechanical action of surveying.

How to Tabulate a Survey

The final tabulation of a survey is very simple. The following data was written and compiled while conducting an Ethnic Survey.

1. Count all the surveys.
2. Establish various categories of answers for each question by listing answers briefly as you go through the surveys.
3. Soon you will be able to merely mark a slant by each category, the slant meaning one more answer of a similar nature.
4. Then you total the answers given for a particular category of answer. Let's say you had 1,500 answers of a similar nature to one question and your total number of surveys is 2,500. This means 60% gave that similar type of answer $\frac{(1500)}{2500}$.
5. You then list each question and under that question list the categories of answers and the percentage from the highest to the lowest.
6. The only mistake you can make is not to realize the similarity of answers and so have a great diversity of categories.

Beingness of the Surveyor

Just as a Volunteer Minister has to have his TRs in, has to abide by Ethical Codes and BE there as a terminal for the pc to communicate to, so must a Surveyor.

Outward appearance of the surveyor must be clean, tidy, and the dress ethnically acceptable for whichever public is being surveyed.

A successful surveyor *must* have a high affinity for other beings—friends or complete strangers. A friendly NATURAL approach to people is required. A sincere smile and good TRs is the door opener. And CONFRONT. You have to reach out to complete strangers and get them interested in themselves enough to let you know where their reality is at so you can help them.

This is completely natural to any trained Scientologist anyway. A Volunteer Minister knows the formula of communication, knows to grant beingness to another, and that ARC = Understanding. With these factors and the basic TRs in, the person being interviewed will feel relaxed about communicating his ideas and realities.

This is all there is to surveying, and you will be amazed with the results attained!

Listed below are some DON'TS just to make sure possible pitfalls are known about and avoided.

1. Don't dress in an unclean or unethnic way. That would automatically make you unwelcome.
2. Don't be short of materials and have to fumble for a pen or survey form. The person might walk off from you in the meantime if you're doing a survey on the street.
3. Don't be backward or shy. Would make you look unconfident of your own product or purpose for being there.
4. Don't overwhelm with forceful overzealous approach or communication.
5. Don't be over-serious or on the other hand giddy. Anything phony is absolutely detrimental.
6. Don't do socially unacceptable practices like chewing gum loudly, biting your fingernails or any one of dozens of other little annoyances.
7. Don't be in too much of a hurry. The person must feel you CARE about what he feels and thinks.
8. Don't be propitiative or, the other extreme, condescending. Be YOURSELF, and confident.
9. Don't cut a person's communication or be gruff in any way.
10. Don't act super-sweet either. Be friendly and BUSINESSLIKE.

As a matter of interest, there is a method of surveying called "depth interview." It is said that this method takes highly trained interviewers and skilled analysts.

Now these fellows think a successful surveyor needs years of training of some kind or another.

But because you have the technology to UNDERSTAND the basics of the mind, yourself and other people, you accomplish what seems miraculous by any other standards.

The miracles of survey results are easily attainable and valuable. But don't be surprised if other people still think you're a genius.

4

HCO PL 21 November 1969

Ethnics
Find out what is needed and wanted

The purpose of this section is to provide a SET FORMAT that can be used over and over again by Volunteer Ministers to find out in their country, area, city, community WHAT IS NEEDED AND WANTED. Once this is known you can angle promotion on it and produce it. For example, an area wants more INTELLIGENT PEOPLE AND ACTIONS and LESS STUPIDITY. The Volunteer Minister of the area finds out and goes into a promotional program of "We can RAISE your IQ!!" or "Tired of being STUPID? We can restore your NATURAL INTELLIGENCE!" Of course, through training and processing an organization can produce this exact result.

If an organization or group or Volunteer Minister does this over and over continually to keep up with the trends and cover new areas its income will ROCKET. A "Needed and Wanted Survey" as laid out below should be done by an organization or group AT LEAST twice a year and again if the trend seems to be changing or a new area is disseminated to. As we expand we repeat the action.

Format

Survey Major Target:

To find out what is needed and wanted by the broad public in a country, area, city or community.

Primary Targets:

1. Those answering the survey, if they ask what it is, should be told it is a survey for social research.
2. Surveys should be conducted in quantity in many parts of the area.

Vital Targets:

1. To conduct the survey as rapidly as possible so results can be tabulated and put into use.
2. To have volunteers asking surveys of any persons they meet.

Operating Targets:

1. The survey questionnaires are printed or mimeographed.
2. The surveys are distributed.
3. All surveys are collected.
4. Survey results are tabulated.

Production Targets:

1. At least 2,700 from any one country for a country tabulation or 1,500 in a big city or 500 to 200 or 100 in a small town.
2. The survey is done at least twice a year or when trends change or when expanding into new areas.

The above is the set format.

What Questions are Used

Questions actually have to be carefully thought out. They have to be something that will tabulate and get the answer. One uses impersonal questions, i.e., "What do people like the best about . . . . ?"

For example, these questions could be used in a Needed and Wanted Survey:

1. What conditions in the . . . (country) society would people like to see changed?
2. What conditions in the . . . (country) society would people like to see unchanged?
3. What improvements in the . . . (country) society do people find needed and wanted?
4. What is the . . . (country) society's greatest problem?

Ethnic Surveys

Are conducted by the above same set format except the MAJOR TARGET is:

To find out the ethnic values of acceptability of a country, area, city or community.

This data is needed so that appearances, conduct, promotion and symbols are in keeping with local ethnic values.

As an example set of questions the ones below could be used:

1. What do people like the most about the . . . (country) society?
2. What do people like the next to the most about the . . . (country) society?
3. What do people like the least about the . . . (country) society?
4. What do people hate or despise about the . . . (country) society?

Exceptions to Broad General Survey

Broad general surveys as above are NOT done in the event an area or country has a strong, successful stable control point which has the area or country under control, i.e., a successful monarchy.

In order for a control point to be successfully in control it must know its people and ethnics pretty well already. The ethnics of this area is what the control point says it is.

The action here is not to do a public survey but to find out all about what the control point says the ethnics values are and what is needed and wanted.

With this data you then use it and follow the trend the control point sets and back up the control point. We back up the upstats, providing what's needed and wanted in keeping with ethnic values and therefore follow the winning line.

If you use and apply this data you can't lose!

5
Population Surveys

*BPL 25 January 1972R
PR Series 15R

Public Divisions of Scientology Churches and Missions specialize in human emotion and reaction—handling it, capturing and controlling it. They get raw public flooding into the church for service. They deal closely with the live wire of public response.

A Public Division by reason of the above has to know what the public will respond to. Without this key datum it can be rough, going around in circles, trying one action after another, hunting and punching with maybe success, maybe disaster but nothing predictable for sure. It becomes a matter of luck stumbling down a blind alley. There is no reason to suffer this way by trial and error and years of hardship not only for the Public Division but the whole church. All you have to do is:

FIND OUT WHAT THE PUBLIC WANTS AND CONSIDERS VALUABLE.

If you promote and deliver what the public wants and considers valuable, you will get public response and by this simple action you are getting out of non-existence with the public. It then becomes a very easy matter for the Public Division to do its job—pushing and promoting what is wanted with guaranteed response and people flooding into churches and missions.

The public will only respond to what is real to them. Here we are centuries ahead of our time and we have even solved death. We can handle anything a person desires from A-Z. We hold a monopoly as the only workable mental technology on the planet and for that matter—the universe. We are incredible. How could we be real? We are unbelievable.

WHEN YOU ARE TOO INCREDIBLE YOU BECOME INVISIBLE.

If you found out what the public wants and then sell and deliver it, you will overcome this reality gap and become real and credible to the public. What they want is real to them. If you deliver what they want, you are real too.

Guessing at public reality levels and what they may consider valuable is complete folly. One can sit guessing for a hundred years and not come up with the right answer. Philosophers in their ivory towers never arrived at any real philosophies. Why should a person sitting behind a desk arrive at any real conclusions on public reality levels and considerations? Guessing can be expensive and when you find yourself guessing: STOP GUESSING AND START SURVEYING.

Sometimes one can be totally amazed and taken by surprise at what comes up in surveys. One can make some real discoveries through surveys. If data was ever dependable, it's the data from a survey. A survey is safe and reliable when all else fails. It is not worth making expensive mistakes when you can do a survey and be right the first time.

Publics are different area by area, city to city. What may be so by survey of one area may not be true of another. Surveys also go out of date as trends change. Always survey the population in YOUR area and survey it REGULARLY.

How to Do It

A population survey is very simple to do. All you are trying to find out is what the public wants and considers valuable. This is a scientific way of finding out.

The Questions

They are exactly verbatim as follows:

1. If you could become anything what would you like to be?
2. What would you like to improve or change about yourself if you really could?
3. If you could have anything you wanted what would you like to have?

R-Factor: If asked, you give the R-factor that this is a survey for social research.

Who and How Many

The public you survey is RAW PUBLIC. You should survey at least

2,000 to 3,000 people. The bigger the number surveyed the more *accurate* your survey results will be.

Method

This is a VERBAL survey. The questions are asked VERBALLY person to person. NEVER by written questionnaire. The questions are asked with Good TR 1 showing interest with intention. TR 1 is natural, not stiff robot style. Fumbling questions or a bad comm cycle can fog up your answers, but only if it's really bad as these questions were built to stand up to such trials. The questions because they are simple are quite powerful.

Procedure

Such a survey is too large to do a "one-man-band." Field Staff Members and volunteers must be called in to help. They must be briefed very thoroughly as follows: tough drilling on the Tone Scale as per Obnosis and the Tone Scale until absolutely certain on spotting tone levels, good drilling with a twin on TR 1 using the questions, how to fill in survey forms, where they turn in filled survey forms, how to dress (neatly and acceptably) and how to use the R-Factor.

The survey forms are mimeographed with spaces to fill in occupation, age, date, the answers to each question and the tone level. The questions are put in full wording on the forms for reference and as a constant reminder. This also helps in tabulating. As many forms as needed are run off. Equip each surveyor with the forms, clipboards and pen. Answers are written in on the forms the instant a person gives them—NEVER after the survey interview—always during it. Establish an agreed upon stable terminal to whom surveyors can turn in their completed forms. It is imperative surveyors keep their admin IN and that they fill in all the required details on the form. Otherwise you'll have a mess to tabulate.

NOTE: If you cannot get any forms mimeographed or it is too expensive you can just have surveyors supplied with blank paper instead. The only liability is that you are leaving the details required to be recorded up to surveyor's memories so extra drilling will have to be done. Using forms is the safest method.

Regarding Tone Scale

Just to make it very clear; you don't need a tone level recording for each question. You just need the one chronic tone level as spotted in the survey interview. Spotting tone levels is a weak point that will have to be drilled well.

Tabulation

This is a key point of the survey. Reliable persons only may be assigned to tabulating the survey. They must be able to see similarities and differences in establishing categories of answers and must not be inclined to arithmetical errors. Once assigned, DON'T musical chair tabulators or it will throw your survey off to that degree.

All you have to have tabulated are (A) each question and (B) the tone level. The procedure is exactly as per How to Tabulate a Survey in Section 3.

Narrow Down

If you really want to get fancy or put the cream on the cake when faced with a somewhat general set of answers from the publics as revealed in your tabulation, you can do a second survey to narrow it down. The first survey is usually informative enough to go about arranging campaign promotion actions. A narrow down would rarely be required as absolutely necessary and more often it would be if one desired an extra fancy, polished, touch on accuracy.

Where it would be absolutely necessary is if you got tabulated answers like: "Everything" or some such real generality. This would show that either your surveyors goofed in demanding specifics or else the public couldn't give any.

As an extra touch on accuracy you could narrow down tabulated answers like: "Happiness" "Freedom." This would be getting very polished and fancy and it's up to you whether you want it that specific. It is true, the more accurate, the bigger the success.

Questions:

1. The first question on the narrowing down survey is the most important. However, it is flexible, depending on what you want to narrow down. Examples:

If it was "Happiness"—
"What would make people unhappy?"

If it was "Freedom"—
"What would deny people freedom?"

If it was "Everything"—
"What would mean everything to a person?"

It's just a matter of using common sense and formulating a coaxing, leading question that *will* get answers.

2. Question two is stable and always:
   "How does that affect people?"
3. Question three is stable and always:
   "If that were resolved, what would happen?"

Procedure

This narrow down survey is conducted using the same procedure as before. As said earlier, your first survey is usually adequate.

Using Results

The survey reveals what the public WANTS. You match up the service to that WANT and promote and sell and deliver it. In other words survey shows people want "thingamabobs." You match up service that will give "thingamabobs," tell the public we do "thingamabobs" and promote and sell and deliver "thingamabobs." You will hit public "R" level and give them a stable datum—"Scientology gives you "thingamabobs" everybody knows that!" Your response will be tremendous.

How to Make up a Campaign

Set the tone level of your campaign half to one tone above that of the survey. This is very important. Everything you do in the campaign will be at that tone level you set. Dig out your Chart of Human Evaluation and study up on the tone level you set for the campaign so you'll have it all aligned.

Look over your survey results. List every button (wants, desires, what's valuable, what they want to get rid of per question 2, etc.) and with technically qualified personnel MATCH UP services that would handle those buttons. You don't have to have a DIFFERENT service for EVERY button—they will be the same service in some cases. You match up whatever service handles.

You then end up with a list of buttons to push with matched up services.

Take this list. On EACH button with matching service, a separate promotion-PR message is formulated.

Rough Example:

Button = other people

Service = processing

Survey tone level = fear

Message = You don't need other people getting in your way. Handle it once and for all. Send them to us for processing. (Antagonism one tone above)

Your list then expands to Button/Service/Message. Each item on this list gets SEPARATE promotion pieces, PR push and advertising. You push each message dogmatically over and over again. A message said just once is never heard.

Look over your lines. Can you deliver the services required?

From the above draw up your campaign covering good preparation, good groove in of volunteers (they're a sales public that can help), volume hitting outflow on promotion, PR actions, press, mass media, rallying up the community etc. It is a population campaign and it's all hands gung-ho!

Get on with it full blast.

IMPORTANT

There are only two crimes in the game of public response. One is not surveying. The other is not using a survey once done.

SUMMARY

So this is the rundown of population surveys. It is basically getting the R of the public by survey, communicating along that R to get ARC, response and agreement with the public on a broad campaign and delivering.

Do it and you can't lose.

S

Being a Field Staff Member

Being a Field Staff Member—Checksheet

Purpose:

To help the Founder of Dianetics and Scientology contact, handle, salvage and bring to understanding the individual and thus the peoples of earth.

a	Study Section 1 Keeping Scientology Working.	______
b	Drill: Write out an example of how you will keep in each of the Ten Points of "Keeping Scientology Working" (a) as a Volunteer Minister and (b) as an FSM.	______
c	Study Section 2 Safeguarding Technology.	______
d	Drill: Find an example in your environment of a Scientologist who is helping to keep Scientology working and safeguarding Scientology and if possible, observe them at their work.	______
e	Study Section 3 Field Auditors Become Staff.	______
f	Drill: Write an essay on the purpose of a field staff member.	______
g	Drill: Write out a dummy Selection Slip according to the instructions in the Field Auditors Become Staff section.	______
h	Study Section 4 Healing Policy in Field.	______
i	Drill: With your demo kit, demonstrate how the data in this section applies to you as a Volunteer Minister and as an FSM.	______

j Study Section 5 Dissemination Drill. ______

k Drill: Practice the Dissemination Drill on friends, associates and those you come into contact with until you can do it comfortably. (Or get trained on it at your local Church of Scientology). ______

l Study Section 6 The FSM Checklist. ______

m Drill: Make out cards now for all the people in your day-to-day life who are prospects, in accordance with the Prospect Finding Checklist instructions. ______

n Study Section 7 FSM Awards. ______

o Study Section 8 FSM of the Year. ______

p Drill: Now look back at the purpose of an FSM as given at the beginning of this checksheet and align it with your own FSM goals. Write down those goals. ______

Being a Field Staff Member—Pack

1

|HCO PL 7 February 1965

Keeping Scientology Working

We have some time since passed the point of achieving uniformly workable technology.

The only thing now is getting the technology applied.

If you can't get the technology applied then you can't deliver what's promised. It's as simple as that. If you can get the technology applied, you *can* deliver what's promised.

The only thing you can be upbraided for by students or pcs is "no results." Trouble spots occur only where there are "no results." Attacks from governments or monopolies occur only where there are "no results" or "bad results."

Therefore the road before Scientology is clear and its ultimate success is assured *if* the technology is applied.

So it is the task of all members of the Church of Scientology, Volunteer Ministers and field staff members to get the correct technology applied.

Getting the correct technology applied consists of:

One: Having the correct technology.

Two: Knowing the technology.

Three: Knowing it is correct.

Four: Teaching correctly the correct technology.

Five: Applying the technology.

Six: Seeing that the technology is correctly applied.

Seven: Hammering out of existence incorrect technology.

Eight: Knocking out incorrect applications.

Nine: Closing the door on any possibility of incorrect technology.

Ten: Closing the door on incorrect application.

One above has been done.

Two has been achieved by many.

Three is achieved by the individual applying the correct technology in a proper manner and observing that it works that way.

Four is being done daily successfully in most parts of the world.

Five is consistently accomplished daily.

Six is achieved by instructors and supervisors consistently.

Seven is done by a few but is a weak point.

Eight is not worked on hard enough.

Nine is impeded by the "reasonable" attitude of the not quite bright.

Ten is seldom done with enough ferocity.

Seven, Eight, Nine and Ten are the only places Scientology can bog down in any area.

The reasons for this are not hard to find. (1) A weak certainty that it works in Three above can lead to weakness in Seven, Eight, Nine and Ten. (b) further, the not-too-bright have a bad point on the button self-importance. (c) The lower the I.Q., the more the individual is shut off from the fruits of observation. (d) The aberrated computations of people make them defend themselves against anything they confront good or bad and seek to make it wrong. (e) The bank seeks to knock out the good and perpetuate the bad.

Thus, we as Scientologists and as an organization must be very alert to Seven, Eight, Nine and Ten.

In all the years I have been engaged in research I have kept my communication lines wide open for research data. I once had the idea that a group could evolve truth. A third of a century has thoroughly disabused me of that idea. Willing as I was to accept suggestions and data, only a handful of suggestions (less than twenty) had long run value and *none* were major or basic; and when I did accept major or basic suggestions and used them, we went astray and I repented and eventually had to "eat crow."

On the other hand there have been thousands and thousands of suggestions and writings which, if accepted and acted upon, would have resulted in the complete destruction of all our work as well as the sanity of pcs. So I know what a group of people will do and how insane they will go in accepting unworkable "technology." By actual record the percentages are about twenty to 100,000 that a group of human beings will dream up bad technology to destroy good technology. As we could have gotten along without suggestions, then, we had better steel ourselves to continue to do so now that we have made it. This point will, of course, be attacked as "unpopular," "egotistical" and "undemocratic." It very well may be. But it is also a survival point. And I don't see that popular measures, self-abnegation and democracy have done anything for Man but push him further into the mud. Currently, popularity endorses degraded novels, self-abnegation has filled the South East Asian jungles with stone idols and corpses, and democracy has given us inflation and income tax.

Our technology has not been discovered by a group. True, if the group had not supported me in many ways I could not have discovered it either. But it remains that if in its formative stages it was not discovered by a group, then group efforts, one can safely assume, will not add to it or successfully alter it in the future. I can only say this now that it is done. There remains, of course, group tabulation or coordination of what has been done, which will be valuable—only so long as it does not seek to alter basic principles and successful applications.

The contributions that were worthwhile in this period of forming the technology were help in the form of friendship, of defense, of organization, of dissemination, of application, of advices on results and of finance. These were great contributions and were, and are, appreciated. Many thousands contributed in this way and made us what we are. Discovery contribution was not however part of the broad picture.

We will not speculate here on why this was so or how I came to rise above the bank. We are dealing only in facts and the above is a fact—the group left to its own devices would not have evolved Scientology but with wild dramatization of the bank called "new ideas" would have wiped it out. Supporting this is the fact that Man has never before evolved workable mental technology and emphasizing it is the vicious technology he *did* evolve—psychiatry, psychology, surgery, shock treatment, whips, duress, punishment, etc., ad infinitum.

So realize that we have climbed out of the mud by whatever good luck and good sense, and *refuse* to sink back into it again. See that Seven, Eight, Nine and Ten above are ruthlessly followed and we will never be stopped. Relax them, get reasonable about it and we will perish.

So far, while keeping myself in complete communication with all suggestions, I have not failed on Seven, Eight, Nine and Ten in areas I could supervise closely. But it's not good enough for just myself and a few others to work at this.

Whenever this control as per Seven, Eight, Nine and Ten has been relaxed the whole organizational area has failed. Witness Elizabeth, N.J., Wichita, the early organizations and groups. They crashed only because I no longer did Seven, Eight, Nine and Ten. Then, when they were all messed up, you saw the obvious "reasons" for failure. But ahead of that they ceased to deliver and *that* involved them in other reasons.

The common denominator of a group is the reactive bank. Thetan's without banks have different responses. They only have their banks in common. They agree then only on bank principles. Person to person the bank is identical. So constructive ideas are *individual* and seldom get broad agreement in a human group. An individual must rise *above* an avid craving for agreement from a humanoid group to get anything decent done. The bank-agreement has been what has made Earth a hell—and if you were looking for hell and found Earth, it would certainly serve. War, famine, agony and disease has been the lot of Man. Right now the great governments of Earth have developed the means of frying every man, woman and child on the planet. That is bank. That is the result of collective thought agreement. The decent, pleasant things on this planet come from *individual* actions and ideas that have somehow gotten by the group idea. For that matter, look how we ourselves are attacked by "public opinion" media. Yet there is no more ethical group on this planet than ourselves.

Thus each one of us can rise above the domination of the bank and then, as a group of freed beings, achieve freedom and reason. It is only the aberrated group, the mob, that is destructive.

When you don't do Seven, Eight, Nine and Ten actively, you are working for the bank dominated mob. For it will surely, surely (a) introduce incorrect technology and swear by it, (b) apply technology as incorrectly as possible, (c) open the door to any destructive idea, and (d) encourage incorrect application.

It's the bank that says the group is all and the individual nothing. It's the bank that says we must fail.

So just don't play that game. Do Seven, Eight, Nine and Ten and you will knock out of your road all the future thorns.

Here's an actual example in which a senior executive had to interfere because of a pc spin: A Case Supervisor told Instructor A to have Auditor B run Process X on Preclear C. Auditor B afterwards told Instructor A that "It didn't work." Instructor A was weak on Three above and didn't really believe in Seven, Eight, Nine and Ten. So Instructor A told the Case Supervisor "Process X didn't work on Preclear C." Now *this* strikes directly at each of One to Six above in Preclear C, Auditor B, Instructor A *and* the Case Supervisor. It opens the door to the introduction of "new technology" and to failure.

What happened here? Instructor A didn't jump down Auditor B's throat, that's all that happened. This is what he *should* have done: Grabbed the Auditor's report and looked it over. When a higher executive on this case did so she found what the Case Supervisor and the rest missed: that Process X was producing good change during the session but that near session end Auditor B Qed and Aed with a cognition and abandoned Process X while it still gave high TA and went off running one of Auditor B's own manufacture, which nearly spun Preclear C. Auditor B's I.Q. on examination turned out to be about 75. Instructor A was found to have huge ideas of how you must never invalidate anyone, even a lunatic. The Case Supervisor was found to be "too busy with admin to have any time for actual cases."

All right, there's an all too typical example. The *Instructor* should have done Seven, Eight, Nine and Ten. This would have begun this way. Auditor B: "That Process X didn't work." Instructor A: "What exactly did *you* do wrong?" Instant attack. "Where's your auditor's report for the session? Good. Look here, you were getting a lot of TA when you stopped Process X. What did you do?" Then the PC wouldn't have come close to a spin and all four of these would have retained certainty.

In a year, I had four instances in *one* small group where the correct process recommended was reported not to have worked. But on review found that each one had (a) increased gains, (b) had been abandoned, and (c) had been falsely reported as unworkable. Also, despite this abuse, in each of these four cases the recommended, correct process cracked the case. Yet they were reported as *not having worked!*

Similar examples exist in instruction and these are all the more deadly as every time instruction in correct technology is flubbed, then the resulting error, uncorrected in the auditor, is perpetuated on every pc that auditor audits thereafter. So Seven, Eight, Nine and Ten are even more important in a course than in supervision of cases.

I recall one student who was squirreling (going off into wierd practices or altering Scientology) on an Academy course and running a lot of off-beat processes on other students after course hours. The Academy students were in a state of electrification on all these new experiences and weren't quickly brought under control and the student himself never was given the works on Seven, Eight, Nine and Ten so they stuck. Subsequently, this student prevented another squirrel from being straighted out and his wife died of cancer resulting from physical abuse. A hard, tough instructor at that moment could have salvaged two squirrels and saved the life of a girl. But no, students had a right to do whatever they pleased.

Squirreling only comes about from non-comprehension. Usually the non-comprehension is not of Scientology but some earlier contact with an off-beat humanoid practice which in its turn was not understood.

When people can't get results from *what they think* is standard practice, they can be counted upon to squirrel to some degree. The most trouble in the past two years came from churches where an executive in each *could not* assimilate straight Scientology. Under instruction in Scientology they were unable to define terms or demonstrate examples of principles. And the churches where they were got into plenty of trouble. And worse, it could not be straightened out easily because neither one of these people could or would duplicate instructions. Hence, a debacle resulted in two places, directly traced to failures of instruction earlier. So proper instruction is vital. The Director of Training and his Instructors and all Scientology Instructors must be merciless in getting Four, Seven, Eight, Nine and Ten into effective action. That one student, dumb and impossible though he may seem and of no use to anyone, may yet some day be the cause of untold upset because nobody was interested enough to make *sure* Scientology got home to him.

With what we know now, there is no student we enroll who cannot be properly trained. As an instructor, one should be very alert to slow progress and should turn the sluggards inside out personally. No *system* will do it, only you or me with our sleeves rolled up can crack the back of bad studenting and we can only do it on an individual student, never on a whole class only. He's slow = something is awfully wrong. Take *fast* action to correct it. Don't wait until next week. By then he's got other messes stuck to him. If you can't graduate them with their good sense appealed to and wisdom shining, graduate them in such a state of shock they'll have nightmares if they contemplate squirreling. Then experience will gradually bring about Three in them and they'll *know* better than to chase butterflies when they should be auditing.

When somebody enrolls, consider he or she has joined up for the duration of the universe—never permit an "open-minded" approach. If they're going to quit let them quit fast. If they enrolled, they're aboard, and if they're aboard, they're here on the same terms as the rest of us—win or die in the attempt. Never let them be half-minded about being Scientologists. The finest organizations in history have been tough, dedicated organizations. Not one namby-pamby bunch of panty-waist dilettantes have ever made anything. It's a tough universe. The social veneer makes it seem mild. But only the tigers survive—and even *they* have a hard time. We'll survive because we are tough and are dedicated. When we *do* instruct somebody properly he becomes more and more tiger. When we instruct half-mindedly and are afraid to offend, scared to enforce, we don't make students into good Scientologists and that lets everybody down. When Mrs. Pattycake comes to us to be taught, turn that wandering doubt in her eye into a fixed, dedicated glare and she'll win and we'll all win. Humor her and we all die a little. The proper instruction attitude is, "You're here so you're a Scientologist. Now we're going to make you into an expert auditor no matter what happens. We'd rather have you dead than incapable."

Fitting that into the economics of the situation and lack of adequate time and you see the cross we have to bear.

But we won't have to bear it forever. The bigger we get the more economics and time we will have to do our job. And the only things which can prevent us from getting that big fast are areas in from One to Ten. Keep those in mind and we'll be able to grow. Fast. And as we grow our shackles will be less and less. Failing to keep One to Ten, will make *us* grow less.

So the ogre which might eat us up is not the government or the High Priests. It's our possible failure to retain and practice our technology.

An instructor or supervisor or executive *must* challenge with ferocity instances of "unworkability." They must uncover what *did* happen, what *was* run and what *was* done or not done.

If you have One and Two, you can only acquire Three for all by making sure of all the rest.

We're not playing some minor game in Scientology. It isn't cute or something to do for lack of something better.

The whole agonized future of this planet, every Man, Woman and Child on it, and your own destiny for the next endless trillions of years depends on what you do here and now with and in Scientology.

This is a deadly serious activity. And if we miss getting out of the trap now, we may never again have another chance.

Remember, this is our first chance to do so in all the endless trillions of years of the past. Don't muff it now because it seems unpleasant or unsocial to do Seven, Eight, Nine and Ten.

Do them and we'll win.

2

| HCO PL 14 February 1965

Safeguarding Technology

For some years we have had a word "squirrelling." It means altering Scientology, off-beat practices. It is a bad thing. I have found a way to explain why.

Scientology is a *workable* system. This does not mean it is the best possible system or a perfect system. Remember and use that definition. Scientology is a *workable system.*

In fifty thousand years of history on this planet alone, Man never evolved a workable system. It is doubtful if, in foreseeable history, he will ever evolve another.

Man is caught in a huge and complex labyrinth. To get out of it requires that he follow the closely taped path of Scientology.

Scientology will take him out of the labyrinth. But only if he follows the exact markings in the tunnels.

It has taken me a third of a century in this lifetime to tape this route out.

It has been proven that efforts by Man to find different routes came to nothing. It is also a clear fact that the route called Scientology *does* lead out of the labyrinth. Therefore it is a workable system, a route that can be travelled.

What would you think of a guide who, because his party said it was dark and the road rough and who said another tunnel looked better, abandoned the route he knew would lead out and led his party to a lost nowhere in the dark. You'd think he was a pretty wishy-washy guide.

What would you think of a supervisor who let a student depart from procedure the supervisor knew worked. You'd think he was a pretty wishy-washy supervisor.

What would happen in a labyrinth if the guide let some girl stop in a pretty canyon and left her there forever to contemplate the rocks? You'd think he was a pretty heartless guide. You'd expect him to say at least, "Miss, those rocks may be pretty, but the road out doesn't go that way."

All right, how about an auditor who abandons the procedure which will make his preclear eventually clear just because the preclear had a cognition?

People have been following the route mixed up with "the right to have their own ideas." Anyone is certainly entitled to have opinions and ideas and cognitions—so long as these do not bar the route out for self and others.

Scientology is a workable system. It white tapes the road out of the labyrinth. If there were no white tapes marking the right tunnels, Man would just go on wandering around and around the way he has for eons, darting off on wrong roads, going in circles, ending up in the sticky dark, alone.

Scientology, exactly and correctly followed, takes the person up and out of the mess.

So when you see somebody having a ball getting everyone to take peyote because it restimulates engrams, know he is pulling people off the route. Realize he is squirreling. He isn't following the route.

Scientology is a new thing—it *is* a road out. There has not been one. Not all the salesmanship in the world can make a bad route a proper route. And an awful lot of bad routes are being sold. Their end product is further slavery, more darkness, more misery.

Scientology is the only workable system Man has. It has already taken people toward higher I.Q., better lives and all that. No other system has. So realize that it has no competitor.

Scientology is a workable system. It has the route taped. The search is done. Now the route only needs to be walked.

So put the feet of students and preclears on that route. Don't let them off of it no matter how fascinating the side roads seem to them. And move them on up and out.

Squirrelling is today destructive of a workable system.

Don't let your party down. By whatever means, keep them on the route. And they'll be free. If you don't, they won't.

3

HCO PL 9 May 1965

Field Auditors become Staff

All field auditors of the level of Hubbard Book Auditor and above are appointed herewith FIELD STAFF MEMBERS of their nearest Scientology church.

Their rank is FIELD STAFF MEMBER (Provisional).

They come directly under the Department of Clearing, Director of Clearing of their nearest Church of Scientology.

The purpose of the Field Staff Member is:

TO HELP ME CONTACT, HANDLE, SALVAGE AND BRING TO UNDERSTANDING THE INDIVIDUAL AND THUS THE PEOPLES OF EARTH.

Their pay shall be in terms of commissions and therefore should be equal to that of general staff members in the churches themselves, depending only on the activity of the Field Staff Member.

The situation is this: the idea of the practitioner setting up a practice to audit preclears must be wrong because it is used with poor success by new doctors and psychiatrists; it also has worked poorly for doctors as groups as they more and more require government subsidy, personally require large borrowed sums to set up new practices and depend for affluence on laws passed to protect them and give them a monopoly; a monopoly held in place by force alone soon vanishes. Further, their system took over 700 years to establish them to a point where they could demand the legislation needed to protect them—proof: examine the status of a medical man in the centuries between the Great Plague and today century by century and see the tiny progress each century in the standing of their profession and their security.

We neither have nor need 700 years.

Civilization is successful only because it is a team. The individual in our present society has a rough time.

We are a team. We have a big job to do. We need every one aboard. Hence the appointment.

This appointment should come as no surprise as we were waiting only for the completion of technology to press the boom buttons. And one of them was to reclaim and enroll as staff members everyone we have ever trained.

Commissions

The official Scientology church to which the Field Staff Member is attached will pay the Field Staff Member a percentage of all training and processing fees received by that organization through its Field Staff Members.

This system has already been piloted some years ago and its administration design is now smoothed out. However it must be followed closely.

The Field Staff Member selects the person to be trained or processed after direct personal contact with the person and issues to that person a paper stating the contacted person has been selected. This paper bears the HOUR, DATE and PLACE of the selection.

The paper is in quadruplicate. The original goes to the person selected (selectee), the second copy is sent promptly to the Field Staff Member's Church of Scientology Advanced Booking Registrar, the third to the Director of Clearing and the fourth copy is held by the Field Staff Member.

If the selectee appears at the church, presents the SELECTION PAPER to the Cashier and enrolls for training and processing, and pays, the church sends at once a commission of 10% for total cash. There is no waiting in sending the commission. The church sends the sum at once. 10% is also paid in memberships bought by the selectee if accompanied by another selection paper marked membership also issued by the Field Staff Member.

Example of Commission: A selectee presents the Selection Paper at the Church Accounts Office and pays for the services bought totally in cash. The Church promptly sends the Field Staff Member 10% of the whole payment.

Example: A selectee presents the Selection Paper of the Field Staff Member at the church accounts office and pays for the service in cash. The church promptly sends the Field Staff Member 10% of the total sum. These both end the transaction. There is no later amount owing the Field Staff Member when the credit extended is paid off. If any

Field Staff Member gave the selectee another later paper the selectee then used, again commission would be paid by the church.

The person selected is directed by the Field Staff Member to Reception at the nearest church, the name and address of which is given to the selectee.

No cash for memberships may be taken by the Field Staff Member as memberships must be paid for only to the church Accounts Cashier.

The preclear or student may be selected as often or as many times as the Field Staff Member can do so.

If the person is not, however, selected again by the Field Staff Member after training or processing, the church may select the person once more and no commission is paid. The church does not have to have a selection paper to train or process a person.

The church will honor and pay commission on the selection papers presented to Accounts by the selectee. It is the responsibility of the Field Staff Member to inform the selectee to present his or her selection paper.

Existing Centers

The Field Staff Member is not attached to unofficial Churches. However, a center or group or group of auditors or mission may send a selectee as a student or pc providing it is a Field Staff Member that signs the selection form. Centers or missions may not have Field Staff Members of their own unless they are owned and operated by Scientology, and Field Staff Members may not send preclears or students to any but official churches. To do so constitutes suppression of Scientology official churches as this is a Scientology Church activity, not designed for centers or mission holders to use until they are officialized and their service can be supervised. Remember, to use this system all a center has to do is become official and meet requirements for a new Church of Scientology.

Forms

Where no forms exist the Field Staff Member can write on plain paper, preferably pink and using carbon or hand copying can make the forms himself.

The form must bear the HOUR, DATE and PLACE, the block printed name and address of the selectee and the block printed name and address and certificate initials and certificate number of the Field Staff Member and what the selectee is selected for (membership, training or processing) and some approximation of arrival date at the Church.

Churches may care to furnish forms, but this is all they contain.

Membership and Rate Cards

The Field Staff Member should be supplied with book lists, membership descriptions and the church rate card. He or she should give copies of these to the selectee if the Field Staff Member has them.

Books

The Field Staff Member may buy books from the Church of Scientology and sell them for his own profit. Any discounts are arranged with the Church.

Commission is also paid on professional rates but not to the auditor himself or a "friend" who will refund the commission. The professional rate applies only to auditing. There is no professional rate for training or courses.

Disputes

Where one Field Staff Member claims he or she sent in a pc or student and another also claims it, the Director of Clearing should be appealed to to settle the dispute.

The church always pays on the selection paper handed in by the selectee, not on the earliest contact.

At least one of the claims *must* be paid. Two commissions may not be paid on the same matter to settle a dispute.

Field Staff Member Regulation

A Field Staff Member comes under the same discipline as any other church staff member and is subject to the same codes of ethics. Auditing church pcs or students is forbidden to all staff members.

Acceptance

The field auditor should write his or her nearest official Church of Scientology addressing his letter to the Director of Clearing, who would be his superior in a church, giving his acceptance of appointment or declining it. In return he will receive his credentials as a Field Staff Member (Provisional) which consist of a letter signed by a church official signifying his or her appointment, to be followed after a year by more formal credentials. In writing the Director of Clearing head the letter "Regarding Field Staff Member Appointment" and give current address and any other particulars. If there are any questions or hitch, write to me at Saint Hill.

Provisional

The first appointment is PROVISIONAL—meaning "not permanent." At the end of one year, the appointment expires unless renewed. On being confirmed at the end of one year, the "Provisional" is removed and more extensive credentials are issued.

When a Field Staff Member (Provisional) has been one for ten months, he or she should write the Director of Clearing requesting the full appointment be made and giving any evidence of good work. At that time the Director of Clearing will cause to be issued a new set of credentials to the Field Staff Member, declaring him or her to be a Field Staff Member. Activity is the criteria of issuing full credentials.

The names or short lists sent to the Field Staff Member for selection or collection are considered to be church prospects. The Field Staff Member may only select them to the church or collect from them for the church, and if the Field Staff Member processes or trains for his own fee prospect names sent by the church he is subject to discipline.

New Courses and Processing

Field Staff Members who are Hubbard Certified Auditor and above may have the professional rate now for Hubbard Guidance Center intensives if International Members in good standing.

Courses for Field Staff Members are given at the same fees as for any other International Member or Staff Member. There is no professional rate for courses, only for intensives. They are however given short briefings on pertinent subjects at such times as the Director of Clearing makes it available. However, the better trained a Field Staff Member is, the better he will succeed and therefore this appointment should not interrupt training plans.

Debts

Field Staff Members may be requested by the Church of Scientology Department of Accounts to collect overdue accounts on which 10% commission of any sums collected will be paid by the Church. But they may not be ordered to do this.

Accounts may release to Field Staff Members in an area lists of overdue accounts in that area. By using ARC break technology and assists the Field Staff Member may collect the sums in check form only payable to the church and forward it with any details to Accounts in the Church. All such assists are given at the Field Staff Member's own discretion without org reimbursement.

Certificate Required

Any auditor who has any certificate including Hubbard Book Auditor may become a Field Staff Member.

No classification is required.

No other stipulations may be locally made.

Pitfall

This is all taken from my own experience when I was the only field auditor there was.

I was hammered at by many to process them and became quite overworked. I was only saved by church formation to which I could turn over my traffic.

The moment a field auditor starts individual processing he becomes too pinned down to promote and in a year or so fails therefore or has to turn to other activities.

I got my pc by casual personal contact and by letting a book circulate (*Dianetics: The Original Thesis*) and by local personal promotion. I ran a Personal Efficiency type course and at one time had even psychiatrists demanding I process their wives after they had heard one lecture.

The demand for my own processing cut back my time and nearly stopped everything until I turned everyone over to the Church and got on with my local public promotion.

I refused to process people myself and therein lies the secret of expansion. Only a church with its organization and facilities and teamwork can handle pcs and students. Even a very small church doesn't dare process pcs or train students. It does best when it only promotes. And it should send its pcs to a higher church. It should limit itself as I did after churches took my pcs over, to short assists and PE courses.

Payment of Commission

Accounts receives the selectee's selection paper from the selectee when that person arrives at the Accounts window. Accounts must write on the invoice the auditor's name who did the selection.

Accounts will at once (or within a week of registration) make out a check for 10% of the cash payment made to the Field Staff Member and mail it to him or her.

When the commission is paid, Accounts sends an invoice copy of the payment and of the pc or student's training, processing or membership payment to the Department of Clearing. The department staples these to the Field Staff Member's copy and files it under the Field Staff Member's name.

The commission is only given on the actual amount the selectee paid. In intensives this should be for at least one intensive. However, if at that appearance the selectee bought several grades worth of intensives or several courses, the commission is also given for those.

Time

There is no time stipulation as to how often selectees may be selected and the Church has no period of grace wherein a person may only be selected by the Church itself. If a Church procures a pc or student however, directly, the Church, not one of its general staff members, gets the commission.

Senior Church Preference

A Field Staff Member trained and certified at a senior Church may be a Field Staff Member of that church even while employed on staff by a junior church but the commission is paid to the junior church. The junior church is paid the commission on any pc or student he sends to the senior church (not his own). Memberships alone are denied commission in such a case as the junior church can also sell them.

Such a Field Staff Member for a senior church employed in a junior church must not distract students or pcs already selected by a Field Staff Member of the junior Church before they can present selection papers.

Being on Two Staffs

Any field auditor can be a Field Staff Member to more than one church but is actually on the staff of the nearest church to his address and may not use another appointment to another church or Saint Hill to set aside the nearer church's requirements of him or her. In changing location the Field Staff Member must inform the Director of Clearing of the Church he has been nearest to and inform the Director of Clearing of the Church he will now be nearest to. In case he is a Field Staff Member Saint Hill also, he should inform the Director of Clearing St. Hill.

4

HCO PL 7 April 1965
Issue II

Healing Policy in Field

Many field auditors do not realize that they damage their own dissemination and usefulness by becoming involved with the very ill and the insane.

The only thing a field auditor or Volunteer Minister can do, really, without going down is to promote, run meetings and do short assists as field staff members of their nearest Church. But whether they are or not, all Field Auditors must abide carefully by this policy and inform those persons who seek to persuade them to help the insane or very *ill* that "it is an offense to break church policy" on this matter and thus get themselves free. I have seen too many field auditors fail by their becoming entangled with psychos and chronically sick cases to fail to protect them from such a mistake.

Healing

Any process labelled 'healing', old or new refers to healing by mental and spiritual means and should therefore be looked upon as the relief of difficulties arising from mental and spiritual causes.

The proper procedure in being requested to heal some complained of physical disability is as follows:

1. Require a physical examination from whatever practioners of the physical healing arts may be competent and available;
2. Clearly establish that the disability does not stem from immediately physical causes;
3. If the disability is pronounced to be curable within the skill of the physical practitioner and is in actual fact a disease or illness which surrenders to contemporary physical treatment, to require the person to be so treated before Scientology processing may be undertaken;
4. If, however, the physical practitioner's recommendation includes surgery or treatment of an unproven nature or the illness or disease cannot be accurately diagnosed as a specific physical illness or disease with a known cure, the person may be accepted for processing on the reasonable assumption that no purely physical illness is proven to exist, and that it is probably mental or spiritual in origin.

5

Dissemination Drill

|HCO PL 23 October 1965

The Dissemination Drill has four exact steps that must be done with a person you are disseminating to.

There is no set patter, nor *any* set words you say to the person.

There are four steps that must be accomplished with the individual and they are listed in the order that they should be done:

1. *Contact* the individual: this is plain and simple. It just means making a personal contact with someone, whether you approach them or they approach you.

2. *Handle:* if the person is wide open to Scientology, and reaching, this step can be omitted as there is nothing to handle. *Handle* is to handle any attacks, antagonism, challenge or hostility that the individual might express towards you and/or Scientology. Definition of "handle"—to control, direct. "Handle" implies directing an acquired skill to the accomplishment of immediate ends. Once the individual has been handled you then—

3. *Salvage:* Definition of salvage: "to save from ruin." Before you can save someone from ruin, you must find out what their own personal ruin is. This is basically—What is ruining them? What is messing them up? It must be a condition that is real to the individual as an unwanted condition, or one that can be made real to him.

4. *Bring to understanding:* Once the person is aware of the ruin, you bring about an understanding that Scientology can handle the condition found in 3. This is done by simply stating Scientology can or, by using data to show how it can. It's at the right moment on this step that one hands the person a selection slip, or one's professional card, and directs him to the service that will best handle what he needs handled.

These are the steps of the Dissemination Drill. They are designed so that an understanding of them is necessary and that understanding is best achieved by being coached on the drill.

Coaching the Drill

POSITION: Coach and student may sit facing each other a comfortable distance apart, or they may stand ambulatory.

PURPOSE: To enable a Scientologist to disseminate Scientology effectively to individuals. To enable one to contact, handle, salvage and bring to understanding, another being. To prepare a Scientologist so that he won't be caught "flat-footed" when being attacked or questioned by another.

PATTER: There is no set patter. The coach plays the part of a non-Scientologist and displays an attitude about Scientology upon being approached by the student. The student must then handle, salvage and bring the coach to understanding. When the student can comfortably do these steps with a given coach's attitude, the coach then assumes another attitude, etc., and the drill is continued until the student is confident and comfortable about doing these steps with any type of person. This drill is coached as follows:

The coach says, "Start." The student must then (1) contact the coach, either by approaching the coach or not, depending upon the mocked-up situation. The student then (2) handles any invalidation of himself and/or Scientology, any challenge, attack or hostility displayed by the coach. The student then (3) salvages the coach. In this step the student must locate the ruin (problem or difficulty the coach has with life), and point out that it is ruinous and get the person to see that it is.

When (3) has been done, you then (4) bring about an understanding that Scientology can do something about it. Example: The coach has admitted a problem with women. The student simply listens to him talk about his problem and then asserts—"Well, that's what Scientology handles. We have processing, etc. etc." When the coach indicates a realization that he did have a problem and that something might be done about it, the student presents him with a selection slip, or a professional card, routing him to the service that would best remedy the condition.

The coach must flunk for comm lags, nervousness, laughter or non-confront. The coach would similarly flunk the student for failure to (1) contact, (2) handle, (3) salvage, and (4) bring to understanding.

TRAINING STRESS: Stress giving the student wins. This is done by using a gradient scale in the coach's portrayal of various attitudes, and staying with any selected until the student can handle it comfortably. As the student becomes better, the coach can portray a more difficult attitude.

Stress bringing about for the student the accomplishment of the purpose of this drill.

A list of things to handle and another of ruins to discover can be made up and used.

Do not specialize in either antagonistic attitudes or an eagerness to know about Scientology. Use both and other attitudes. One meets them all.

6
The FSM Checklist

*The Selectee to Flag Checklist

Use this checklist as a guide to help you effectively and swiftly get your selectee underway.

1. Find a prospect.

2. Through talking with your selectee, determine what service(s) he is going to take.

3. Get him signed up for these services using Registration Forms from your local Church of Scientology. Have him make his first advance donation or a donation in full for the services he will be taking.

4. Take or send these forms and the donation to your local Church of Scientology.

5. Fill out a Selection Slip for your selectee which you may get from your Church of Scientology.

6. Give him a copy to take with him to the Church of Scientology and tell him to give it to the Cashier there. Send another copy to the Church's Director of Clearing, the third copy to the Advance Scheduling Registrar, and keep the fourth copy for yourself.

7. If necessary, work out with your selectee how he is going to pay for his services.

8. Get him fully paid for the service as soon as possible so he can get started on his auditing and/or training program. Checks are made out to the Church of Scientology of California.

9. Keep in communication and see him through all the necessary steps he must take for (8) to be realized.

10. When he goes to the local Church of Scientology for the first time, make sure he takes with him his copy of the selection slip.

11. Await your commission.

7 FSM Awards

HCOPL 10 November 1969

Hereafter, awards based on the numbers of FSM Commissions paid as in FSM Contests MAY BE PAID ONLY TO SINGLE INDIVIDUALS OR SINGLE CHURCHES OR MISSIONS WHICH DID THE ACTUAL SELECTION.

No one may claim an award or bonus or contest prize by reason of multiple franchises or multiple churches or several individuals.

Example: Joe Blow turns in a claim for prizes based on 39 selections which represent 10 missions. The claim is not valid. It must show which mission selected what and that one mission that turned in the most is the potential winner unless some one else turned in more.

Example: Tom Sikes turns in 4 selections as an entry in the contest. Joe Blow turns in 56. But Blow's "56" is made up of selections from 52 FSMs. The most any single FSM selected in that group was 3. Tom Sikes wins the bonus contest.

Staff Members

Church of Scientology staff members are NOT eligible for bonus awards by reason of FSM selections.

Eligibility

Individual missions, Gung-Ho Groups, Official Scientology groups, staffs of these and individual field FSMs are the only ones eligible for FSM contest bonuses. None of these named may combine their selections as an entry in an award contest.

8

*BPL 23 April 1968R
Issue I

FSM of the Year

At the end of every year, each Scientology Church sends in the statistics of their best FSM to CS-6 Flag.

CS-6 then compares all the statistics of the most people sent in and picks the best FSM.

This FSM is then "The FSM of the Year" and a special silver cup is sent and presented at the FSM's Church.

Then a full article is prepared on their wins and successes, methods used and photograph.

The above is then condensed into an interesting leaflet and sent to all FSMs.

T

Scientology Training

Scientology Training Checksheet

Purpose:

To enlighten the Volunteer Minister on the importance of training in Dianetics and Scientology to make him competent in listening and helping people and applying the technology to life.

a Study Section 1 Training for Gain. ________

b Drill: Using the data you learned in the targets pack work out and write up a program for yourself which will get you from your current level of training in Scientology up to (and completed on) the next level. (Consult with the registrar of your Church of Scientology if necessary to ascertain which would be your next course in Scientology.) ________

c Study Section 2 "What do I think of Auditors?" ________

d Drill: Write an essay on why you should be a fully trained auditor. (Be honest with yourself and state only real reasons in your essay.) ________

e Study Section 3 The E-Meter. ________

f Study Section 4 Religion and the E-Meter. ________

g Drill: Go to your local Church of Scientology and request a demonstration of how the E-Meter is operated. ________

Scientology Training Pack

1

The Auditor No. 54

Training for Gain

A trained Scientology auditor, applying standard tech, is one of the most valuable beings on this planet. Auditors have, since the first session in Scientology, been the only individuals on this planet, in this universe, capable of freeing Man. An auditor is a highly trained specialist no matter what level auditor.

The auditor is on a broader career than merely being a capable individual. A slightly trained auditor is superior to *homo sapiens.* He is doing something in the widest field there is which is the inter-relationships of life. An auditor is handling things. It isn't that these other fields are degraded. It's that the field of inter-personal relationships amongst living beings is actually so elevated. It's so elevated that, up until recent times, it was regarded with such awe that nobody ever approached it. It was a total mystery. It was a terrible secret. Well, it doesn't have to be those things to succeed or to be such an elevated field. All it has to be is effective.

A good auditor, skilled, doing his work well, accomplishing his mission, finds himself in the particular position of being at cause point over an awful lot of people. Things don't baffle him anymore. He is totally aware of the fact that he can somehow or other poise himself through almost anything. He has a wider, broader view of life and people than any person regardless of state of case who is not an auditor.

A fully trained Scientologist is in a far better position to understand than a partly trained one. For a Scientologist who really knows is able not only to retain confidence in himself and what he can do, but also can understand why others do what they do and, so knowing, does not become baffled or dismayed by small defeats.

As you begin your training, you will find your life becoming more orderly and your environment easier to handle. Lots of good reasons exist for people to be trained and get their processing from fellow students. A student gets tons of auditing. Only training gives low cost auditing from fellow students. Study is high gain. Students audit students for gain, not for practice, and there are dozens of processes.

How you accomplish an auditing session is based to some degree upon the state of the person accomplishing the session which is the auditor. And when the state of mind is that of an effective person who wishes to help, there's nothing that could stop that session. Training as an auditor, the desire for it, eventually winds up in an ability to give a terrific session and to be very effective.

Naturally, anybody who wants to help his fellow man a bit more could become an auditor. One has to start somewhere. The thing to do is start. No machines can be set up to audit anybody. There's only one person that can audit and that's the auditor himself.

There's a tremendous amount of understanding involved in auditing. There are millions of words written on the subject. There's theory and practice. There are the drills and other things one has to know.

But the moment a person starts training he's already walking a track which is higher than the track to Clear.

An auditor is to be respected. He is very important in clearing this planet and this universe and the only one who can give Man the truth that Man knows. It's a big job and only the auditor will do it. All auditors everywhere are appreciated.

2 What do I Think of Auditors?

Professional Auditor's Bulletin 79

Every now and again somebody tries to get me to say what I think of auditors.

I think of auditors in a rather intense way. As I know more auditors than anybody else and have a better basis for judgment, on this subject I can be for once an authority.

My opinion of auditors in general is fairly well known to several people.

I think of an auditor as a person with enough guts to DO SOMETHING ABOUT IT. This quality is rare and this quality is courageous in the extreme.

It is my opinion and knowledge that auditors are amongst the upper tenth of the upper twentieth of intelligent human beings. Their will to do, their motives, their ability to grasp and to use is superior to that of any other profession.

I think of an auditor as having INITIATIVE. He is able to grasp or make a mock-up and put it into action.

Auditors survive better than other people.

If this world has any faintest chance of surviving it will be not because I write but because auditors can and will think and do.

I think our auditors seeing where earth was going decided to band together to send it elsewhere.

I consider all auditors my friends. I consider them that even when they squirrel. I believe they have a right to express themselves and their own opinions. I would not for a moment hamper their right to think. I think of auditors and Scientologists as free people.

Just as they consider one another their people so I consider them my people.

I think their errors of the past, when they existed, came about because we were new and we were finding out, and I don't think any of their errors were intentional any more than mine were.

I can understand their own reactions because I can understand the counter-effort given them by society and thus I don't hold auditors guilty even when they fold up but simply assume we'd better make a better effort into the society to overcome or bypass the counter-effort.

I don't expect auditors or Scientologists to instantly agree with or seize upon whatever I say. I would be offended if they did and would feel they weren't free people. Since they are intelligent I expect them to think over what's said, try it and if it's good for them, use it. That old auditors sooner or later come back to and use what I have discovered isn't any testimony to our relationship at all, it's only a testimony to my being right because I meant to be right in the first place.

I sorrow when I see somebody accomplishing less than he should because he thinks I wouldn't approve of it. In our churches and out, I count upon initiative and good judgment.

The most decent people I have ever known have been auditors. The best hearted people I know are auditors. They are so decent and good hearted I have to work and argue with them to make enough to keep mock-ups rolling well, a thing they are now beginning to do.

3 The E-meter

Electropsychometric Auditing

The E-meter, apart from the processes of Dianetics and Scientology, is one of the auditor's major tools, and it is fitting that this instrument be remarked upon at this stage.

The measurement of thought with a meter is not new, the understanding and accuracy of measurement is new.

Einstein is reported to have said that all an observer should be permitted to do is to read a meter and report the message of the meter. This is true enough. But the observer of a human mind can read it with a meter only if the meter is an accurate and constant meter, and only if he knows what questions to ask. The constancy of the meter and the questions to ask are subjects thoroughly researched by myself and exist in manuals as part of the materials of Dianetics and Scientology. E-metering is a science and an art.

*BPL 24 September 1973
Issue VII
Religion Requirement: E-Meter Promotion
HCO PL 29 October 1962 Religion

4
Religion and the E-meter

The Hubbard E-meter is a religious artifact developed for the exclusive use of ordained ministers and theological students who are trained in its use in church ministrations. It is not intended for and is forbidden by the Church to be used in any medical or physical treatment or the diagnosis, treatment or prevention of any disease. By itself it does nothing and is strictly not to be employed for medical or scientific purposes. Its purpose is to assist the minister to locate in his parishioner areas of travail so that he can assist in the relief of spiritual suffering. The existence and use of the E-Meter is sanctioned by law, and the copying of it or attempts by unqualified persons, doctors, scientists, psychologists or psychiatrists to obtain or use one are actionable under law in the United States. To obtain an E-meter one must be a sincerely enrolled student of the Church of Scientology or a fully qualified minister of that church and must undertake as well to become wholly skilled in its purpose and use. No other persons are permitted to have E-meters. The church permits the E-meter to be sold, possessed, or owned only under these conditions.

All religions seek truth.

Freedom of the spirit is only to be found on the road to truth.

Sin is composed, according to Scientology, of lies and hidden actions and is therefore untruth.

The electrometer is used to disclose truth to the individual who is being processed and thus free him spiritually.

Only in this way can Man's spiritual self be regained.

A religious confessional fails only when not guided by a modern instrument such as the E-meter.

The electrometer is a religious instrument, used in confessionals, and is in no way diagnostic and does not treat.

Regardless of any earlier uses of psychogalvanometers in Dianetics or psychology or in early Scientology publications when research was in progress, the electrometer in Scientology today has *no* other use than as directed above.

Dianetics used an older instrument to detect engrams. The book, *Electropsychometric Auditing* is entirely a Dianetic manual.

U

Ministerial Qualifications and Ceremonies

Ministerial Qualifications and Ceremonies Checksheet

Purpose:

To give the Volunteer Minister sufficient knowledge of the great religions of the world and of the Creeds, Codes and Ceremonies of the Church of Scientology, so that he meets the Ministerial Qualifications of the Church of Scientology.

a	Study Section 1 The Background to the Religion of Scientology and Ceremonies of the Church of Scientology of California.	______
b	Study Section 2 Ministerial Qualifications.	______
c	Study Section 3 Religion All Auditors—Ministers Ministerial Board of Review.	______
d	Study the book, "The Religions of Man" by Huston Smith or "The Living Religions of the World" by F. Spiegelberg.	______
e	Study The Bible—The Gospel according to St. John.	______
f	Study the book, "Background and Ceremonies of The Church of Scientology"—Part 1.	______
g	Study the book, "Background and Ceremonies of The Church of Scientology"—Part 2.	______
h	Drill: Practice the following ceremonies until you are confident you can perform them. A Prayer for 'Total Freedom'	______

	A Recognition and Naming Ceremony	________
	A Wedding Ceremony	________
	A Funeral Service	________
i	Drill: Draw up two different sermon outlines and practice giving them until you are confident that you could give one at a Sunday Service.	________
j	Drill: Draw up an outline for a full Sunday Service and practice giving it until you are confident that you can conduct a full Sunday Service for the church.	________
k	Drill: Read the Church Creed aloud until you can recite it verbatim.	________
l	Study Section 4 "Code of A Scientologist"	________
m	Drill: Write an essay on how the "Code of a Scientologist" applies to you.	________
n	Study Section 5 "Code of Honor."	________
o	Drill: Write an essay on how the "Code of Honor" applies to you and how you will use it.	________
p	Study Section 6 Religion, The Spirit, The Mind.	________

Ministerial Qualifications And Ceremonies Pack

*BPL 27 October 1970R
Issue I
A Book: The Background to the Religion of Scientology and Ceremonies of the Church of Scientology of California World Wide

1
The Background to the Religion of Scientology and Ceremonies of the Church of Scientology of California

There has been a gradual standardization of Sunday Church services and other ceremonies over the last few years.

There is an increasing interest in the religious philosophy of Scientology amongst Scientologists and indeed non-Scientologists.

Currently there is an increasing number of individuals entering missions, Churches and organizations who before Scientology had no religious practice or persuasion.

It is therefore an entirely predictable evolutionary step to produce a standard ministerial and lay reference book for study and corporate prayer. The above mentioned book is this text.

It is to be used by all Ministers and Volunteer Ministers in all Sunday services and ceremonies in all Churches of Scientology.

Founding Church Policy Letter of 15 August 1958 (Second Revision of 12 June 1958)

2
Ministerial Qualifications

A Minister of the Church of Scientology must meet the following requirements:

(1) Must have a Validated certificate in Scientology. (The Volunteer Minister receives a certificate upon completion of study and examination on this Handbook).
(2) Must know the Church Creed verbatim.
(3) Must be capable of giving the various ceremonies.
(4) Must be able to pass an examination on the great religions.
(5) Must have a knowledge of St. John.
(6) Must be of good moral character.
(7) Must be able to conduct a Sunday service for the Church.
(8) Must have moral and ethical codes by which he can live and abide.

*BPL 24 September 1973R Issue III

3
Religion
All Auditors — Ministers
Ministerial Board of Review

All auditors must hold a valid Certificate of Ordination in order to practice auditing, whether for a church, a mission or as an independent missionary in the field.

The certificate granted upon completion of any training course, does not entitle anyone to practice pastoral counselling (auditing) unless the individual satisfactorily completes the requirements for ordination and has in fact been ordained.

As a student minister of Scientology, you may elect to become a minister of the church in which case you must complete the checksheet of this pack and pass the examination on it at a Church of Scientology. You can then be ordained as a minister. Upon proof of ordination, you are granted permission to practice by the local church.

Missions are not authorized to ordain ministers. Their student ministers who wish to practice auditing may apply to the nearest local church for any necessary training and ordination.

A Ministerial Board of Review is established in the Church of Scientology. It shall be composed of no less than three persons who shall themselves be ministers of the church. The Board of Review will be headed by the Assistant Guardian or other Guardian Office personnel assigned by the Assistant Guardian. The purpose of this Board of Review is to help safeguard Scientology, Scientology Churches and Scientologists by ensuring that ministers of the church are and remain of good moral character, continue to uphold the Codes of Scientology and apply standard technology in their counselling of parishioners.

Ministerial certificates may be withdrawn by the Ministerial Board of Review when this board finds cause within the framework of the above purpose.

HCO PL 5 February 1969R
Press Policy
Code of a Scientologist

4
Code of A Scientologist

The Code of a Scientologist as per *The Creation of Human Ability* was recently updated and it is reissued as follows:

As a Scientologist, I pledge myself to the Code of Scientology for the good of all:

1. To keep Scientologists, the public and the press accurately informed concerning Scientology, the world of mental health and society.
2. To use the best I know of Scientology to the best of my ability to help my family, friends, groups and the world.
3. To refuse to accept for processing and to refuse to accept money from any preclear or group I feel I cannot honestly help.
4. To decry and do all I can to abolish any and all abuses against life and Mankind.
5. To expose and help abolish any and all physically damaging practices in the field of mental health.
6. To help clean up and keep clean the field of mental health.
7. To bring about an atmosphere of safety and security in the field of mental health by eradicating its abuses and brutality.
8. To support true humanitarian endeavors in the fields of human rights.
9. To embrace the policy of equal justice for all.
10. To work for freedom of speech in the world.
11. To actively decry the suppression of knowledge, wisdom, philosophy or data which would help Mankind.
12. To support the freedom of religion.
13. To help Scientology orgs and groups ally themselves with public groups.
14. To teach Scientology at a level it can be understood and used by the recipients.
15. To stress the freedom to use Scientology as a philosophy in all its applications and variations in the humanities.
16. To insist upon standard and unvaried Scientology as an applied activity in ethics, processing and administration in Scientology organizations.
17. To take my share of responsibility for the impact of Scientology upon the world.
18. To increase the numbers and strength of Scientology over the world.
19. To set an example of the effectiveness and wisdom of Scientology.
20. To make this world a saner, better place.

5
The Code of Honor from *The Creation of Human Ability*

Creation of Human Ability

No one expects the Code of Honor to be closely and tightly followed.

An ethical code cannot be enforced. Any effort to enforce the Code of Honor would bring it into the level of a moral code. It cannot be enforced simply because it is a way of life which can exist as a way of life only as long as it is not enforced. Any other use but self-determined use of the Code of Honor would, as any Scientologist could quickly see, produce a considerable deterioration in a person. Therefore its use is a luxury use, and which is done solely on self-determined action, providing one sees eye to eye with the Code of Honor.

1
Never desert a comrade in need, in danger or in trouble.

2
Never withdraw allegiance once granted.

3
Never desert a group to which you owe your support.

4
Never disparage yourself or minimize your strength or power.

5
Never need praise, approval or sympathy.

6
Never compromise with your own reality.

7
Never permit your affinity to be alloyed.

8
Do not give or receive communication unless you yourself desire it.

9
Your self-determinism and your honor are more important than your immediate life.

10
Your integrity to yourself is more important than your body.

11
Never regret yesterday. Life is in you today, and you make your tomorrow.

12
Never fear to hurt another in a just cause.

13
Don't desire to be liked or admired.

14
Be your own adviser, keep your own counsel and select your own decisions.

15
Be true to your own goals.

6

| Book List

Religion, The Spirit, The Mind

Further recommended reading for you in order to enhance your knowledge and understanding of religion, the spirit of man, human behavior and the mind are the following books:

In the entirety of Scientology literature, *Scientology: A World Religion Emerges in the Space Age* stands unique. Among the millions of words devoted to the philosophy, technology and application of Scientology, here is offered the full illumination of its antecedents and background and ascending evolvement of the Church of Scientology's doctrines, scriptures, ceremonies, practices, ethics and justice system and its many social reform programs from institutional psychiatric reform to drug abuse rehabilitation to mental retardation.

The book is dedicated to the Founder of Scientology, L. Ron Hubbard, whose lifelong work in the fields of the humanities, religious research and the broad spectrum of Man's enduring search for higher realizations and awarenesses qualify him as one "whose unique genius has united the realms of Spirit and Natural Science to enhance immeasurably the life and consciousness of our Time, as well as Ages and Civilizations yet unborn."

A certainty of spiritual values whose breadth and scope of thought impels beyond all physical boundaries, pervades this book and radiates an aura that is galaxies wide. In its radiance is recreated and reaffirmed the spirit of Man in ageless equation with Life itself.

The Religions of Man by Huston Smith or *The Living Religions of The World* by F. Spiegelberg will provide you with knowledge of some of the beliefs and practices of many religions. Man has a 10,000 year history of religion, these works can give you an insight into the scope of religion as a subject.

Dianetics: The Evolution of a Science is an exposition of the Dianetic breakthrough on the subject of the anatomy of the human mind, how it works, what happens to it under stress, shock, pain or unconsciousness and the basic single answer to the resolution of aberration. This will enlighten you on the subject of aberration, the characteristics and "mysterious" behavior of the people you are dealing with which might have once balked you instead will be understandable.

Dianetics: The Modern Science of Mental Health, the basic text book of Dianetics gives the discoveries about the human mind which resulted from a quarter of a century of research. The human mind *is* understandable. The knowledge of it you will gain from this book will wipe out any fear of consequence of effect on the individual from the mind in your endeavors to help.

Science of Survival gives a thorough analysis of the characteristics common to people of different levels of awareness and emotional tone. Included are chapters on social, ethical, physical and emotional characteristics, courage, responsibility and many, many more covering the full range of human behavior. You will be able to understand any behavior of any individual and be able to predict behavior once you have gained a full knowledge of the subject.

Epilogue
Your Role in Society

All communication lines should have a purpose. The purpose of this communication line is the advising and orienting of Volunteer Ministers and Scientologists everywhere on the subject of Scientology, the formation and the direction of its churches and the creation of space in which Man can walk upright with respect for himself and others.

We are the only people and the only religion on earth which have the technology and the ambition to attempt a clarification of situations which in other hands are considered entirely out of control, to wit, the atomic bomb and the decay and confusion of societies.

There are those who would tell us that our ambitions are too high, that no single group much less a single man could bring about a change in the dangerous career of earth. But such people do not know their history. Single men and determined groups have been the only makers of space in which Man could live in peace. Left to the multitude, each inverted with his own selfishness and greed, the affairs of man do not prosper. Left to an anarchy of nations with no international responsibility, earth and mankind cannot prosper.

The Anglo-American civilization was the first new civilization since the Roman Empire. All civilizations between the last collapse of Rome in the fourth century A.D. and the present moment were some fragment of the Roman Empire or its conquerors. Rome possessed certain technologies which conquered the world. In company with these technologies there was a philosophy and a willingness to do. When the philosophy had faded or had been changed for one far less workable, when the technologies of Rome had been scattered before the hordes of barbarians who now from Moscow once more seek to spread confusion, man was left to drift, to interpret the word "freedom" as he would and in the main for his own purposes. The disciplines that were Rome faded away. Today the European countries are beginning to function once more.

Various portions of civilization are alert. For over a century a new technology has been making space. That technology is Anglo-American in its development. Leaders of the new industrial age in the United States and Great Britain have pressed upon the world know-how and machinery and ways of living which have revolutionized almost every society on earth. In Berlin, in Paris, in Madrid and Tangiers and Cairo and indeed in Moscow itself we see the evidences of this onslaught. Anglo-American mechanization has even driven the Chinese from its background and in the European pants and hats. In India and Burma and Buenos Aires we see the cinema, the automobile, the clock, the booklets and the rifle created by or modeled upon Anglo-American industrial might. Technologically, the United States and Great Britain have conquered the world. Philosophically, they have failed.

The original impetus of the Anglo-American industrial push was carried along with Protestant Christianity. Somewhere on the way there is one spiritual message which, packaged in with the clock and the cinema and the guns, was lost. Unlike earlier Jesuit successes with native peoples, Protestants' successes have been few for some reason, possibly because the Jesuit incorporated the religion he found with the religion he brought, and Protestantism remained entirely itself. The spiritual philosophy which should have prepared the way for the proper use of the technology did not succeed.

We are left then with a world of confusion, for the tools and the weapons have gone out and no message has gone with them even to the United States and Great Britain themselves to use them properly. We are confronted then with the picture of Man's failure to keep pace with his humanities alongside the onslaught of his technology. We have humanities in the Dark Ages and technologies in the next century. We are, therefore, confronted within our own nations with strikes, crimes, upsets, insanity, juvenile delinquency and problems beyond count. We are confronted at the same time with many rebellious peoples across the planet. We are confronted then with a United States and Great Britain which having delivered the weapons of slaughter into the hands of others seemingly have no will to continue their regulation.

The white man within his own countries and within all the countries of earth has solved the problem technologically. Guns, furniture, linoleum, weaving machines, harvesters, air conditioning, medical advances have each and every one conquered their environments. Though the machine has penetrated such distance and though the machine has made each and every United States citizen and British citizen more independent and capable, it has not been accompanied by a philosophy of use adequate to its potential for harm. Thus we have a chaotic world condition.

We have uncounted communication devices and have not had until Scientology any formula for communication itself. We have a thousand tongues, the phonograph, the motion picture, the radio, the television to talk about affinity and we do not even know what it is. We have numberless realities being created daily in huge antiseptic factories without any understanding of what reality might be and thus we have created beyond the ability of man to understand, and unless the understanding of man can be brought to the level of his own creations man is doomed as the conquering animal of earth.

So desperate has man become that he will buy almost any ideology whether it is communism or druidism. He will buy the garbage of Marx and even write it unsuspectingly into the United States Constitution under the heading of "income tax." He will seek solutions to his overpowering problems from indigestible sources such as Russian psychiatry or Wundtian German psychology, neither one of which were intended to free man from insanity or to give him understanding and which were intended only to enslave, debase, and give one a "freedom from death." Counterfeited ideologies and humanities are not good enough in this age of atomic fission and jet planes. These two alone unless handled sentiently can bring about the wipe out of modern man.

If you have questioned where you were going with Scientology, if you did not know exactly what you intended to do with Scientology, if you had no real understanding of what Scientology was for, read the above again. You will readily recognize that the typist sitting in some office overwhelmed by routine is equipped immediately with the means of writing letters faster than any amanuensis of past ages but has no understandings of why she should be there or what she should be doing beyond the fact that she "has to have a job." What hope is there for this girl?

Like the operator of a drill press in a factory, like the pilot of a jet plane or like the man himself who designs atomic missiles, she does not know what she is doing or why she is doing it. Therefore, she cannot hope to understand the motives of those around her nor can she understand any need for any team work in the execution of a better civilization. She is being overpowered and engulfed by the business machinery with which she is surrounded. Work and happiness, or comfort or pride exist in such surroundings. From the highest head of state to the lowest menial saving only Scientologists in the United States, Great Britain, Europe, Australia, Africa, Asia, South America, Southern Africa, Canada, Mexico, New Zealand, or the rest of the world, there is no exact understanding of life itself, thus livingness itself has become as automatic as machinery.

Machines do not bleed, they do not suffer. It is only because Man conceives Man to be an incomprehensible machine that makes Man willing to destroy with such weapons as atomic fission. Only men without purpose, without understanding, men who cannot play the game would so attack their fellows.

What craven cowardice is it that requires a weapon as great as an H-bomb to command compliance with one's bad temper. One can only gaze with contempt upon a person who in a relatively peaceful society will overarm himself and overthreaten his fellows.

If man cared more, if man had a better understanding of his own purpose, man would make a better effort to survive, but lost in the confusions of ideologies which were intended to do nothing but confuse him what chance does he have?

The chance he has is Scientology. We're giving him that chance and if you do not pass along to him what you know, you yourselves are failing that man, failing yourselves, and failing us. This is man's one chance. You must give it to him, otherwise he faces other planets, other times, other elsewheres, but no more here. Scientology is not so much man's first real applied religious philosophy as his last call to reason.

If you cannot see this as a necessity, the religious technology to fit in with man's mission of the machine then you cannot view man's further survival, for it will not exist.

Were we to straighten out on its lower and middle strata the thinkingness of man, he would have a chance to live. You would give that chance to a person dying in an automobile accident. You would give that chance to a dog; you would give the chance to breathe again and look at the sun to your deadliest enemy. Then why not give it to a man at large? Is it because you cannot see him as an entirety, because you cannot see him as units made up in a similar image to those of your immediate family and friends? You must give man that chance. Given that chance he can live out his destiny. If that chance is withheld from him he will be no more.

Where earth pursues her gentle way in her orbit about the sun today there will be a black orb seared, scorched and defaced with ruin. Its air polluted by radiation, its surface gouged by pocks, the skeletons of its cities standing black and ruined against a sun which was allowed to set upon the Anglo-American civilization.

Perhaps there are other planets, perhaps there will be other times but here we are right now, our urgings and our strivings ought to carry forward the civilization which we have about us. Perhaps it would be better to start all over and make another one. I do not happen to think so. I think that we can and will continue to create this civilization and continue to bring Man through despite his folly in creating industrially and technologically far beyond his ability to understand and then borrowing from those who hated him the technologies he hoped would permit him to survive.

We know how with Dianetics and Scientology and we can do. It is up to us. It is up to you, Volunteer Ministers and Scientologists all, and only then we can say with honesty that it is up to Man.

Appendix 1

Reference Summary

A
Study Pack

1	**Vital Data on Study**	*The Organization Executive Course Basic Staff Volume 0* page 9
2	**Definition of a Student**	*Board Technical Bulletin 26 October 1970, Issue II Reissued 8 July 1974 as BTB Cancels HCO Bulletin 26 October 1970, Issue II same title
3	**The Intention of the Student**	*Board Technical Bulletin 27 October 1970 Reissued 7 July 1974 as BTB Cancels HCO Bulletin 27 October 1970, same title (Extracted from Study Tapes)
4	**Learning Processes Education by Evaluation of Importance**	*Board Technical Bulletin 14 September 1969 Issue I
5	**Barriers to Study**	Hubbard Communications Office Bulletin 25 June 1971 Word Clearing Series 3
6	**Study Phenomena**	Hubbard Communications Office Policy Letter 24 September 1964 *Instruction & Examination: Raising the Standard of*

		Hubbard Communications Office Policy Letter 4 October 1964, Reissued 21 May 1967 Modifies HCO Policy Letter 24 September 1964 *Theory Check-out Data*
7	**Simple Words**	Hubbard Communications Office Bulletin 4 September 1971, Issue III, Word Clearing Series 20
8	**Words, Misunderstood Goofs**	Hubbard Communications Office Bulletin 10 March 1965 Scientology 0, Scientology VI
9	**How to use a Dictionary**	*Board Technical Bulletin 4 September 1971R Revised 15 December 1973 Reissued 20 July 1974 as BTB Cancels HCO Bulletin 4 September 1971R Word Clearing Series 22R, same title
10	**Dinky Dictionaries**	Hubbard Communications Office Bulletin 19 June 1972 Word Clearing Series 37
11	**Demo Kits**	*Board Technical Bulletin 29 October 1970R Revised & Reissued 26 June 1974 as BTB. Cancels HCO Bulletin 29 October 1970 same title
12	**What is a Checksheet**	Board Policy Letter 27 July 1969R Revised 16 October 1974 Cancels HCO Policy Letter 27 July 1969, same title

B
Orientation Pack

1	**Conditions**	*Ability Magazine* 174
2	**Volunteer Minister**	Excerpts from Briefing Tapes 7312TC10 and 7402MC19

3	**Abilities of a Volunteer Minister**	Excerpts from Briefing Tapes 7312TC10 and 7402MC19
4	**Technology**	Excerpts from Briefing Tapes 7312TC10 and 7402MC19

C
The Eight Dynamics Pack

1	**The Dynamics**	*The Fundamentals of Thought* by L. Ron Hubbard, Chapter 4 page 36

D
ARC Pack

1	**Understanding**	*Sea Organization Worldwide Executive Directive 54 INT 6 October 1971 *Campaign Org Friendliness!*
2	**Affinity**	*Sea Organization Worldwide Executive Directive 54 INT 6 October 1971 *Campaign Org Friendliness!*
3	**What is Communication?**	Hubbard Communications Office Bulletin 21 June 1971 Issue II, (Extracted from HCOB 23 March 1965 Materials and Axiom 28)
4	**This is how to communicate!**	Hubbard Communications Office Bulletin 21 June 1971 Issue II, (Extracted from HCOB 23 March 1965, Level 0 Materials and Axiom 28) *What is Communication?*
5	**Reality**	*Sea Organization Worldwide Executive Directive 54 INT 6 October 1971 *Campaign Org Friendliness!*

E
Tone Scale Pack

1	**The Tone Scale**	*The Auditor* No. 60 *Science of Survival,* page 91
2	**Emotional Tone Scale**	Hubbard Communications Office Bulletin 18 September 1967 correcting HCOB 3 February 1967, Corrected 4 April 1975, *Scales*
3	**Tone Scale Expanded**	Hubbard Communications Office Bulletin 25 September 1971 RA, Revised 4 April 1974 *Tone Scale in Full*
4	**Obnosis and the Tone Scale**	*Board Technical Bulletin 26 October 1970, Issue III Reissued 4 July 1974 as BTB Cancels HCO Bulletin 26 October 1970, Issue III same title

F
Assists Pack

1	**Assists in Scientology**	Hubbard Communications Office Bulletin 21 October 1971, Reissued 21 September 1974
2	**Assist Summary**	Hubbard Communications Office Bulletin 11 July 1973
3	**Touch Assists—Correct Ones**	*Board Technical Bulletin 7 April 1972R, Revised & Reissued 23 June 1974 as BTB Cancels HCO Bulletin 7 April 1972, same title
4	**Assists for Injuries**	*Board Technical Bulletin 9 October 1967R Revised 18 February 1974 Cancels & Revises HCO Bulletin 9 October 1967
5	**Unconscious Person Assist**	Hubbard Communications Office Bulletin 5 July 1971R Revised & Reissued 8 June 1974 C/S Series 49R, *Assists*

6	**Sickness**	Hubbard Communications Office Bulletin 14 May 1969
7	**Emergency Assists**	Tape Lecture 5406C17 6ACC-50, *Assists*
8	**How to Make a Person Sober**	*Board Technical Bulletin 7 June 1969, Reissued 27 July 1974 as BTB. Cancels HCO Bulletin 7 June 1969 same title
9	**Touch Assist: An Improvement on Spinal Adjustment for Medical Doctors and Practitioners**	*Board Technical Bulletin 22 July 1970 (Issued 28 March 1974). Cancels HCO Bulletin 22 July 1970
10	**Exercises One, Two, and Three**	*Ability Magazine* 114A, 1963

G
Training Routines Pack

1	**Confronting**	*Ability Magazine* Issue 54 *More Confronting*
2	**Training Drills Modernized**	Hubbard Communications Office Bulletin 16 August 1971, Issue II
3	**Coaching**	Hubbard Communications Office Bulletin 24 May 1968
4	**Premature Acknowledgments**	Hubbard Communications Office Bulletin 7 April 1965
5	**Tone of Voice—Acknowledgment**	Hubbard Communications Office Bulletin 12 January 1959
6	**Upper Indoc TR's**	Hubbard Communications Office Bulletin 7 May 1968
		*Board Technical Bulletin 22 May 1971R, Revised & Reissued 10 November 1974 as BTB. Cancels HCO Bulletin 22 May 1971, same title *TR-8 Clarification*

Hubbard Communications Office Bulletin 16 November 1965, Issue II, *Commands for Upper Indoctrination TR 6, TR 7, TR 9*

H
Drug Rehabilitation Pack

1	**Pain Association**	Hubbard Communications Office Bulletin 16 July 1970 *The Psychiatrist at Work*
2	**Drug Data**	Hubbard Communications Office Bulletin 29 August 1968 (Corrected & Reissued 10 June 1975)
3	**TRs and Drugs**	*Board Technical Bulletin 25 October 1971R, Issue II Revised 26 August 1972 Revised 30 June 1974 Reissued 29 August 1974 as BTB. Cancels HCO Bulletin 25 October 1971, same title *The Special Drug Rundown*
4	**Drugs**	Hubbard Communications Office Bulletin 28 August 1968 Issue II
5	**Withdrawal Symptoms**	Hubbard Communications Office Bulletin 5 November 1974, *Drugs, More about*
6	**Drugs, Aspirin and Tranquilizers**	Hubbard Communications Office Bulletin 17 October 1969
7	**Antibiotics**	Hubbard Communications Office Bulletin 27 July 1969

I
Handling The Dangerous Environment Pack

1	**The Dangerous Environment**	Tape Lecture 6309C25 SH Spec 310 *Summary II, Scientology Zero* Tape Lecture 6312C10 SH Spec 328, *Scientology Zero*

J
Investigations Pack

1	**Logic**	Hubbard Communications Office Policy Letter 11 May 1970, Data Series 2
2	**Investigatory Procedure**	Hubbard Communications Office Policy Letter 19 September 1970 Issue I, Data Series 16
3	**Narrowing the Target**	Hubbard Communications Office Policy Letter 19 September 1970, Issue II Data Series 17
4	**Summary of Out-points**	Hubbard Communications Office Policy Letter 19 September 1970 Issue III, Data Series 18, *Summary of Out-points, Omitted Data*
5	**More Outpoints**	Hubbard Communications Office Policy Letter 26 November 1970, Data Series 20
6	**Outpoints, More**	Hubbard Communications Office Policy Letter 30 September 1973, Issue I Data Series 29
7	**The Real Why**	Hubbard Communications Office Policy Letter 13 October 1970, Issue II, Data Series 19
8	**The Why is God**	Hubbard Communications Office Policy Letter 31 January 1972, Data Series 22
9	**The Product as an Overt Act**	Hubbard Communications Office Policy Letter 14 November 1970 Org Series 14
10	**Organization Misunderstoods**	Hubbard Communications Office Policy Letter 20 November 1970 (Corrected 29 August 1970), Personnel Series 12, Org Series 15

11	**Third Dynamic De-aberration**	Hubbard Communications Office Policy Letter 6 December 1970, Personnel Series 13, Org Series 18
12	**Group Sanity**	Hubbard Communications Office Policy Letter 14 December 1970, Personnel Series 14, Org Series 19
13	**Organization and Morale**	Hubbard Communications Office Policy Letter 1 November 1970 Org Series 11

K
PTS/SP Pack

1	**Psychosis**	Hubbard Communications Office Bulletin 28 November 1970, C/S Series 22
2	**The Anti-Social Personality The Anti-Scientologist**	Hubbard Communications Office Bulletin 27 September 1966
3	**Handling the Suppressive Person, The Basis of Insanity**	Hubbard Communications Office Policy Letter 5 April 1965, HCO Justice Data Re: Academy and Hubbard Guidance Center
4	**Suppressed Pcs and PTS Technology**	Hubbard Communications Office Bulletin 20 April 1972 Expanded Dianetics Series 4
5	**Search and Discovery**	Hubbard Communications Office Bulletin 24 November 1965, Level IV
6	**Suppressives and Hidden Standards**	Hubbard Communications Office Bulletin 8 November 1965
7	**Mistakes, Anatomy of**	Hubbard Communications Office Bulletin 12 March 1968
8	**PTS Handling**	Hubbard Communications Office Bulletin 10 August 1973
9	**PTS Type A Handling**	Hubbard Communications Office Policy Letter 5 April 1972, Issue I

10	**Policies on "Sources of Trouble"**	Hubbard Communications Office Policy Letter 7 May 1969 (Revises HCO Policy Letter 27 October 1964)
11	**Robotism**	Hubbard Communications Office Bulletin 10 May 1972
12	**Alter-is and Degraded Beings**	Hubbard Communications Office Bulletin 22 March 1967 *Important: Admin Know-How Alter-Is and Degraded Beings*

L
Ethics and Justice Pack

1	**Ethics**	Hubbard Communications Office Policy Letter 18 June 1968 (Corrected & Reissued 26 January 1974)
2	**Ethics, the Design of**	Hubbard Communications Office Policy Letter 7 December 1969
3	**Administering Justice**	Hubbard Communications Office Policy Letter 17 March 1965, Issue III *HCO (Division I), Justice Hat*
4	**Exchange**	Hubbard Communications Office Policy Letter 3 December 1971 Executive Series 4
5	**Rewards and Penalties**	Hubbard Communications Office Policy Letter 6 March 1966 *Rewards and Penalties How to Handle Personnel and Ethics Matters*
6	**Criminality**	Hubbard Communications Office Policy Letter 4 April 1972, Establishment Officer Series 14, *Ethics*
7	**The Volunteer Minister His Character**	Hubbard Communications Office Policy Letter 7 December 1969, Issue II, *The Ethics Officer His Character*

8 Conditions	Hubbard Communications Office Policy Letter 14 March 1968, *Corrected Table of Conditions*
	Hubbard Communications Office Policy Letter 9 February 1974, *Ethics Condition Below Treason*
	Hubbard Communications Office Policy Letter 16 October 1968, *Formula for the Condition of Treason*
	Hubbard Communications Office Policy Letter 23 October 1967, *Enemy Formula*
	Hubbard Communications Office Policy Letter 6 October 1967, *Condition of Liability*
	Hubbard Communications Office Policy Letter 9 April 1972. (Cancels HCO Policy Letter 7 February 1970 Danger Condition 2nd Formula) *Ethics Correct Danger Condition Handling*
	Tape Lecture 6505C25 SH Spec 62, *The Five Conditions*
	*Board Policy Letter 27 April 1974, *Power Formulas, First and Third Dynamics*
9 Non-Existence Formula Expanded	Hubbard Communications Office Policy Letter 8 November 1975

M
Integrity Pack

1 Integrity	*Board Technical Bulletin 4 December 1972 Reissued 3 July 1974 as BTB Cancels HCO Bulletin 4 December 1972 Integrity Processing Series 1, *Historical*

2	**Fundamentals**	*Board Technical Bulletin 10 December 1972 Reissued 12 July 1974 as BTB Cancels HCO Bulletin 10 December 1972 Integrity Processing Series 7, same title
3	**Overt—Motivator Definitions**	Hubbard Communications Office Bulletin 1 November 1968, Issue II
4	**The Continuing Overt Act**	Hubbard Communications Office Bulletin 29 September 1965, Issue II, All Levels
5	**Effectiveness of Overts in Processing**	Hubbard Communications Office Bulletin 9 December 1974. Cancels HCO Bulletin 10 July 1964, Reissued 5 December 1974 as Integrity Processing Series 6R HCO Bulletin 10 July 1964 "Overts—Order of Effectiveness in Processing" remains as originally issued. Cancels BTB 9 December 1972 "Why Overts Work" Integrity Processing Series 6RA, *Effectiveness of Overts in Processing—ARC Breaks*
6	**Irresponsibility**	Hubbard Communications Office Bulletin 14 December 1972R, Revised 12 February 1973, Integrity Processing Series 11R, *Generalities Won't Do*
		Hubbard Communications Office Bulletin 10 July 1964 *Overts—Order of Effectiveness in Processing*
7	**Justification**	Hubbard Communications Office Bulletin 21 January 1960
8	**Some Famous Justifications**	Hubbard Communications Office Bulletin 8 July 1964 *Scientology III & IV More Justifications*

9	**What is a Missed Withhold?**	Hubbard Communications Office Bulletin 8 February 1962 *Urgent, Missed Withholds*
10	**ARC Breaks, Missed Withholds**	Hubbard Communications Office Bulletin 3 May 1962
11	**Withholds, Missed and Partial**	Hubbard Communications Office Bulletin 22 February 1962
12	**Withholds, Other People's**	Hubbard Communications Office Bulletin 31 January 1970
13	**Blow-offs**	Hubbard Communications Office Bulletin 31 December 1959

N
Marriage and Children Pack

1	**Pregnancy and Auditing**	*Board Technical Bulletin 24 July 1973 Reissued 8 July 1974 as BTB Cancels HCO Bulletin 24 July 1973, same title (Cancels HCO Bulletin 27 February 1972 Revised 30 May 1973)
2	**Healthy Babies**	*The Auditor* No. 6
3	**Marriage**	Tape Lecture 6001C02 SMC-5
4	**Be-Do-Have**	Hubbard Communications Office Policy Letter 13 November 1970 Org Series 13, *Planning by Product*
5	**Child Scientology**	*Scientology Journal* Issue 14-G

O
Third Party Pack

1	**The Third Party Law**	Hubbard Communications Office Bulletin 26 December 1968

2	**Justice**	Hubbard Communications Office Policy Letter 24 February 1969 *An Ethics Policy Letter—Justice*
3	**Third Party Investigations Procedure**	*Board Policy Letter 25 August 1969, Reissued 8 July 1975 as BPL. Cancels HCO Policy Letter 25 August 1969, same title, *Third Party Investigations*
4	**Third Party, How to find one**	Hubbard Communications Office Policy Letter 15 March 1969
5	**Third Party Investigations**	*Board Policy Letter 6 January 1970, Reissued 8 July 1975 as BPL. Cancels HCO Policy Letter 6 January 1970 same title

P
Targets Pack

1	**Target Types**	Hubbard Communications Office Policy Letter 24 January 1969
2	**OT Orgs**	Hubbard Communications Office Policy Letter 14 January 1969 (Corrected per Policy Letter 23 January 1969, OT Orgs Correction)
3	**Targets, Types of**	Hubbard Communications Office Policy Letter 16 January 1969
4	**Purpose & Targets**	Hubbard Communications Office Policy Letter 24 January 1969, Issue II
5	**Ethics Presence**	Hubbard Communications Office Policy Letter 4 October 1968

6	**Compliance**	*Board Policy Letter 20 February 1973 Reissued 16 August 1975 as BPL. Cancels HCO Policy Letter 20 February 1973, same title, The Theory of Compliance 1, *What is Compliance? The Parts of Compliance*
7	**Compliance Reports**	Board Policy Letter 26 January 1969RA Revised 10 May 1975 Cancels HCO Policy Letter 26 January 1969, same title
8	**The Key Ingredients**	Hubbard Communications Office Policy Letter 14 September 1969 Admin Know How 22
9	**Planning and Targets**	Hubbard Communications Office Policy Letter 18 January 1969, Issue II
10	**Program Drill**	Hubbard Communications Office Policy Letter 13 June 1972, Establishment Officer Series 19

Q
Public Relations Pack

1	**PR Definition**	Hubbard Communictions Office Policy Letter 18 November 1970, Issue II PR Series 5
2	**Liabilities of PR**	Hubbard Communications Office Policy Letter 13 August 1970, Issue I, PR Series 1
3	**The PR Personality**	Hubbard Communications Office Policy Letter 9 October 1970, Personnel Series 11 PR Series 4
4	**The Missing Ingredient**	Hubbard Communications Office Policy Letter 13 August 1970, Issue II, PR Series 2
5	**Wrong Publics**	Hubbard Communications Office Policy Letter 13 August 1970, Issue III, PR Series 3

6	**Opinion Leaders**	Hubbard Communications Office Policy Letter 11 May 1971, Issue II, PR Series 6
7	**Too Little Too Late**	Hubbard Communications Office Policy Letter 28 May 1971, PR Series 8
8	**Manners**	Hubbard Communications Office Policy Letter 30 May 1971, PR Series 9

R
Surveys Pack

1	**Breakthrough PR and Production Tone Scale Surveys**	Hubbard Communications Office Policy Letter 2 June 1971, Issue II, PR Series 10
2	**Creating Survey Questions**	*Board Policy Letter 7 January 1972R, Revised & Reissued 9 September 1975 as BPL. Cancels HCO Policy Letter 7 January 1972, Issue II same title, PR Series 14R
3	**How to do a PR Survey**	Hubbard Communications Office Policy Letter 5 December 1971, Issue II PR Series 13
4	**Ethnics, Find out what is Needed and Wanted**	Hubbard Communications Office Policy Letter 21 November 1969
5	**Population Surveys**	*Board Policy Letter 25 January 1972R, Revised & Reissued 3 July 1974 as BPL. Cancels HCO Policy Letter 25 January 1972, same title, PR Series 15R

S
Being a Field Staff Member Pack

1	**Keeping Scientology Working**	Hubbard Communications Office Policy Letter 7 February 1965, Reissued 15 June 1970

2	**Safeguarding Technology**	Hubbard Communications Office Policy Letter 14 February 1965, Reissued 7 June 1967
3	**Field Auditors become Staff**	Hubbard Communications Office Policy Letter 9 May 1965 Revised & Reissued 14 January 1968 (Cancels HCO Policy Letters 26 March 1965 & 30 March 1965)
4	**Healing Policy in Field**	Hubbard Communications Office Policy Letter 7 April 1965, Issue II
5	**Dissemination Drill**	Hubbard Communications Office Policy Letter 23 October 1965
6	**The FSM Checklist**	**The Selectee to Flag Checklist*
7	**FSM Awards**	Hubbard Communications Office Policy Letter 10 November 1969
8	**FSM of the Year**	*Board Policy Letter 23 April 1968R, Issue I Revised & Reissued 19 July 1975 as BPL. Cancels HCO Policy Letter 23 April 1968, Issue I

T
Scientology Training Pack

1	**Training for Gain**	*The Auditor* No. 54
2	**What do I think of Auditors?**	*Professional Auditor's Bulletin* 79
3	**The E-meter**	*Electropsychometric Auditing*
4	**Religion and the E-meter**	*Board Policy Letter 24 September 1973, Issue VII Reissued 24 August 1975 as BPL. Cancels HCO Policy Letter 24 September 1973

Issue VII, same title, *Religion Requirement: E-meter promotion,* Hubbard Communications Office Policy Letter 29 October 1962, *Religion*

U
Ministerial Qualifications and Ceremonies Pack

1	**The Background to the Religion of Scientology and Ceremonies of the Church of Scientology of California**	*Board Policy Letter 27 October 1970R, Issue I Revised & Reissued 19 July 1975 as BPL. Cancels HCO Policy Letter 27 October 1970 Issue V, same title *A Book: The Background to the Religion of Scientology and Ceremonies of the Church of Scientology of California World Wide*
2	**Ministerial Qualifications**	Founding Church Policy Letter 15 August 1958 (Second revision of 12 June 1958)
3	**Religion All Auditors—Ministers Ministerial Board of Review**	*Board Policy Letter 24 September 1973R, Issue III Revised 15 May 1975 (Cancels HCO Policy Letter 24 September 1973, same title)
4	**Code of a Scientologist**	Hubbard Communications Office Policy Letter 5 February 1969R (Revised 15 May 1973) *Press Policy* *Code of a Scientologist*
5	**Code of Honor**	*Creation of Human Ability*
6	**Religion, The Spirit, The Mind**	Book List

Appendix 2

Religious Status of the Church of Scientology

The religious status of the Church of Scientology has consistently been upheld by the Courts of the United States and has never been successfully challenged in any court where the issue has been raised, in the United States or elsewhere.

Judicial, Governmental, Ministerial and Administrative decisions in different parts of the world have accepted that Scientology is a religion.

Founding Church of Scientology -v- United States

1. In *Founding Church of Scientology of Washington, D.C. v. United States of America* (409 F2D 1146) a decision of the United States Court of Appeals for the District of Columbia Circuit, decided on 5th February, 1969, it fell to be determined whether or not Scientology is a religion and as such entitled to the protection afforded to religions by the First Amendment to the United States Constitution. In finding for the Appellants, Church of Scientology, and against the Appellee, the United States of America, the Court said, *inter alia:*

> "Appellants (Scientology) have argued from the first that the entire case must fall as an unconstitutional religious persecution. In their view, auditing or processing is a central practice of their religion, akin to confessions in the Catholic Church, and hence entirely exempt from regulation or prohibition. They have made no attempt to contradict the expert testimony introduced by the Government. They have conceded that the E-meter is of no use in the diagnosis or treatment of disease as such, and have argued that it

was never put forward as having such use. Auditing or processing, in their view, treats the spirit of man, not his body, though through the healing of the spirit the body can be affected. They have culled from their literature numerous statements disclaiming any intent to treat disease and recommending that Scientology practitioners send those under their care to doctors when organic defects may be found. They have introduced through testimony a document which they assert all those who undergo auditing or processing must sign which states that Scientology is 'a spiritual and religious guide intended to make persons more aware of themselves as spiritual beings, and not treating or diagnosing human ailments of body or mind, and not engaged in the teaching of medical arts or sciences. . . .'

"Finally, with respect to their claim to be a religion and hence within the protection of the First Amendment, they have shown that the Founding Church of Scientology is incorporated as a Church in the District of Columbia, and that its ministers are qualified to perform marriages and burials. They have introduced their Creed into evidence. The Government has made no claim that the Founding Church is not a *bona fide* religion, that auditing is not part of the exercise of that religion, or that the theory of auditing is not a doctrine of that religion.

* * * * * *

"Finally, we come to the vexing question: Is Scientology a religion? On the record as a whole, *we find that appellants have made out a prima-facie case showing that the Founding Church of Scientology is a religion.* It is incorporated as such in the District of Columbia. It has ministers, who are licensed as such, with legal authority to marry and to bury. Its fundamental writings contain a general account of Man and his nature comparable in scope, if not in content, to those of some recognized religions. The fact that it postulates no deity in the conventional sense does not preclude its status as a religion.

"Appellants have contended that their theories concerning auditing are part of their religious doctrine. We have delineated in detail the evidence on which this claim is based. Again the Government has not contested this claim. . . . We cannot assume as a matter of law that all theories describing curative techniques or powers are medical and therefore not religious. Established religions claim for their practice the power to treat or prevent disease, or include within their hagiologies accounts of miraculous cures. In the circumstances of this case *we must conclude that the literature setting forth the theory of auditing, including the claims for curative efficacy contained therein, is religious doctrine of Scientology. . . .*"

2. Marriages may lawfully be solemnized by duly appointed Ministers of the Founding Church of Scientology of Washington, D.C. within the District of Columbia, U.S.A. by virtue of authority granted by the Superior Court of the District of Columbia or the District of Columbia Court of General Sessions.

3. Marriages may lawfully be solemnized by duly appointed Ministers of the Church of Scientology of California, within the State of California U.S.A. under authority of license issued by the County Clerk of Los Angeles, California.

4. Marriages may lawfully be solemnized by duly appointed Ministers of the Church of Scientology of Hawaii, U.S.A. under the authority of the State of Hawaii.

5. Marriages may lawfully be solemnized by duly appointed Ministers of the Church of Scientology of New York, within the State of New York, U.S.A. under the authority of the State of New York.

6. Marriages may lawfully be solemnized by duly appointed Ministers of the Church of Scientology of Washington, within the State of Washington, U.S.A. under the authority of the State of Washington.

7. Marriages may lawfully be solemnized by duly appointed Ministers of the Church of Scientology of Michigan, within the State of Michigan, U.S.A. under the authority of the State of Michigan.

8. Marriages may lawfully be solemnized by duly appointed Ministers of the Church of Scientology of Minnesota, within the State of Minnesota, U.S.A. under the authority of the State of Minnesota.

9. Marriages may be lawfully solemnized by duly appointed Ministers of the Church of Scientology of Florida, within the State of Florida, U.S.A. under the authority of the State of Florida.

10. Marriages may lawfully be solemnized by duly appointed Ministers of the Church of Scientology of Oregon, within the State of Oregon, U.S.A. under the authority of the State of Oregon.

11. Marriages may lawfully be solemnized by duly appointed Ministers of the Church of Scientology of Texas, U.S.A. under the authority of the State of Texas.

12. Marriages may lawfully be solemnized by duly appointed Ministers of the Church of Scientology of Missouri, within the State of Missouri, U.S.A. under the authority of the State of Missouri.

13. Since June 1973, marriages may lawfully be solemnized by duly appointed Ministers of the Church of Scientology of Boston, within the State of Massachusetts, U.S.A. under the authority of the State of Massachusetts.

14. The United States Department of the Treasury Internal Revenue Service exempts ministers of religion from liability to pay self-employment tax.

For the purpose of exemption from self-employment tax, the Internal Revenue Service recognizes Ministers of the Church of Scientology as Ministers of Religion.

15. The New York State Board of Social Welfare in a letter dated 26th October, 1972, to the Church of Scientology of California acknowledged that the Church is a "religious agency" and as such exempt from registration under the Social Services law.

16. The State of Missouri, Department of Revenue, in granting the Church of Scientology of Missouri, exemption from Missouri Sales-Use Tax by letter dated 9th March, 1973, wrote:

> "(The Law) exempts educational, religious and charitable institutions and political subdivisions from the payment of sales-use tax on purchases for use in the conduct of their regular functions and activities. In our opinion your institution would qualify for exemption."

17. Ministers of the Church of Scientology of Hawaii have, at the invitation of the Senate of the State of Hawaii, taken morning prayers (read the prayer of invocation) in the Senate, which is the first order of business in the Senate before proceeding to the day's work.

United States
Barr -v- Weise

18. In *Barr v. Weise* 293 F.Sup.7 (1968) a decision of the United States District Court for the Southern District of New York, decided on 26th August, 1968 by Tenney, District Judge, the Petitioner Aaron Barr sought a writ of habeas corpus to restrain his alleged unlawful detention by the United States Army and to obtain judicial review of the denial by the Army of his application for discharge based on his status as a full-time student of the Ministry in the Church of Scientology. In granting the application for a writ of habeas corpus and ordering the discharge of the

petitioner from the United States Army Reserve forthwith, the Court said, *inter alia:*

"By denying petitioner's application solely on the basis of the exclusion of the Academy of Scientology from the 'approved list' an exclusion that may have resulted from the school's failure to submit the required information rather than from academic deficiency, *the Army capriciously neglected to consider either the standards set by the Academy of Scientology or the established character of the Church of Scientology of New York.*

"As noted herein, the Church of Scientology of New York is a duly recognized religious corporation under the laws of the State of New York. It has been in existence since November 15th, 1955. . . . The duties and functions of its ministers are similar to those of the clergy of other religious denominations. Their ministers hold services every Sunday, officiate at funerals, christenings and weddings, counsel their parishioners, and conduct confessionals. The Church has three ministers duly licensed by the State of New York as well as other ministers licensed by other states. There are some 50 full-time students in the Academy of Scientology who devote approximately 35 to 40 hours per week to their training. Their course of study includes instruction in the basic tenets of their Church and its system of ethics, and on the methods of counseling parishioners as to their personal, spiritual and ethical affairs. In order to qualify as a minister, students must pass oral and written examinations.

"Inasmuch as petitioner complied in all respects with the applicable Army regulations, and since the Army's determination was arbitrarily reached, this Court directs that petitioner's application for a writ of habeas corpus be granted and petitioner be discharged from the United States Army Reserve forthwith."

This decision was upheld on appeal by the U.S. Court of Appeals for the Second Circuit (412 f.2d 338 (1969)).

United States -v- Engle

19. In *United States of America v. Richard Joseph Engle,* an action in the United States District Court, Southern District of Indiana, Indianapolis Division, the Defendant Engle was indicted for failing to report for military service; he defended the indictment on the grounds that he was a duly ordained Minister in the Church of Scientology. By a motion to dismiss dated 21st September,

1972, the United States Attorney, the prosecuting authority, moved to dismiss the indictment in the following terms:

"Motion to Dismiss

"Comes now the United States of America, by Counsel, and moves the Court to dismiss the indictment in the above captioned cause.

"In support of this motion, the United States of America, by Counsel, shows the Court that:

1. The Defendant, Richard Joseph Engle, alleges that he is a duly ordained Minister in the Church of Scientology.

2. The Defendant Richard Joseph Engle, alleges that he executes his ministerial duties from seventy to eighty hours per week.

3. *Some of the Circuits* which have had occasion to examine the religious status of the Church of Scientology have determined that the organization should be recognized as a religious organization, and*

4. It appears that the Selective Service System** should recognize the Church of Scientology as a religious organization, even though the Selective Service System does not now do so.

"Wherefore, the United States of America, by Counsel moves the Court to dismiss the indictment filed in the above captioned cause."

The Court duly granted the motion and dismissed the indictment.

20. The United States Army by its Chaplain School situated at Fort Hamilton, New York, has accepted the religious status of the Church of Scientology. The policy of the U.S. Army is that "Commanders at all levels have a responsibility to provide religious activities which serve the needs of persons of all faiths within their commands."*** In accordance with this policy, the Army Chaplain School publication *The Newer Religions* contains information concerning Scientology for the use of Army Chaplains.

21. In the United States, the Military Selective Service Act of 1967 permits persons, who conscientiously object to military service, to be assigned by the Selective Service System to "civilian work contributing to the maintenance of the national health, safety or interest" for a period of two years.

*United States Federal Circuit Courts.

**The responsible body for drafting persons into the U.S. Armed Services.

***Student Handout H 22026/12-1 U.S. Army Chaplain School: *The Newer Religions*, July, 1972.

The Selective Service System recognizes employment with the Church of Scientology as work "contributing to the maintenance of the national health, safety or interest."

Lake -v- United States

22. In *June Margaret Lake v. United States of America, in Rescission Proceedings under Section 246 of the Immigration and Nationality Act,* a decision of the United States Department of Justice, Immigration and Nationality Service, decided on 19 October, 1972, by oral decision of the Special Inquiry Officer, (File A 18-232-265; Kansas City) Lake, an Australian citizen, applied for permanent residence status in the United States on the grounds that she was a Minister in the Church of Scientology of Missouri. Her application was at first granted, but subsequently revoked on the grounds that the Church of Scientology was not a *bona fide* religious organization in the United States. Lake appealed, the sole issue being whether the Church of Scientology is a *bona fide* religious organization. Allowing the appeal, the Special Inquiry Officer of the Immigration and Nationality Service gave judgment in the following terms:

"These proceedings were brought about by a Notice of Intention to Rescind*, dated December 15th, 1970. On January 4th, 1971, Mrs. Lake requested the present hearing. The Notice of Intention contains 13 numbered factual allegations in support of the conclusion that Mrs. Lake was not in fact a minister of religion of a *bona fide* religious organization. There is no question raised in the enumerated paragraphs as to Mrs. Lake's qualifications as a minister. *The only question is whether the Church of Scientology is a bona fide religious organization in the United States?* I will limit my decision to that issue.

"*I am at a loss to understand on the basis of 13 numbered factual allegations how one could draw the conclusion that the Church of Scientology is not a bona fide religious organization.*

"The burden of proof upon the Service in a rescission proceeding is a heavy one (*Waziri v. U.S.* INS. 392 F.2d 55. (9 Cir 1968)).

"In *Matter of M.,* 5 I & N Dec 172, the Salvation Army was held to be a *bona fide* religious organization in the United States within the meaning of the predecessor statute to 101(a) (27) (D) (1). The criteria in making that determination was set out as follows:

*i.e. the Notice of Intention to Rescind Mrs. Lake's previously granted immigrant status, on a number of stated grounds.

> . . . has been incorporated under the laws of many of the states in this country; is a world-wide religious organization having a distinct legal existence; a recognized creed and form of worship; a definite and distinct ecclesiastical government; a formal code of doctrine and discipline; a distinct religious history; a membership, not associated with any other church or denomination; officers ministering to their congregation, ordained by a system of selection after completing prescribed courses of training; a literature of its own; established places of religious worship; religious congregations and religious services; a Sunday school for the religious instruction of the young; schools for the preparation of its ministers, who in addition to conducting religious services, perform marriage ceremonies, bury the dead, christen children, and advise and instruct the members of their congregation.
>
> "I believe that this criteria has been substantially met by the respondent's (Mrs. Lake's) presentation. The Service failed to establish by clear, convincing, and unequivocal evidence that the Church of Scientology is not a *bona fide* religious organization in the United States. I am satisfied therefore that the respondent was lawfully accorded permanent residence status."

United Kingdom

1. In the United Kingdom, Ministers of the Church of Scientology have been held to be persons exempted, as Ministers of Religion, from liability to Jury service, by virtue of the provisions of Section 9 of the Juries Act 1870.

2. In a report on the Church of Scientology in Great Britain by Sir John Foster he states, "The mere fact that someone is a Scientologist is . . . no reason for excluding him from the United Kingdom when there is nothing in our law to prevent those of his fellows who are citizens of this country from practising Scientology here." On the subject of earlier restricted practice of Scientology Sir John wrote: "Such legislation appears to me to be discriminatory and contrary to the best tradition of the Ango-Saxon legal system."

Commonwealth of Australia

1. By a Proclamation of the Governor-General of Australia published in the Commonwealth Gazette No. 20 on 15th February, 1973, the Government of Australia gave offical recognition to the Church of the New Faith* as a religious body. Further the Church of the New Faith* was

*The name of the Church of Scientology in Australia.

declared to be a recognized denomination for the purpose of the solemnization of marriages by virtue of the Marriage Act 1961-1966.

2. In pursuance of the Proclamation, Ministers of the Church in Australia have been licensed to perform marriages in accordance with the provisions of the Marriage Acts in various states. Ministers of Religion licensed in this fashion are empowered to celebrate marriages anywhere in Australia.

3. Tax Exemption. In a letter dated 12th December, 1973, the Deputy Commissioner of Taxation of the Australian Taxation Office confirmed that the Church of the New Faith is tax exempt as a religious body.

4. In a letter dated the 27th July, 1973, to the Secretary of the Church of the New Faith the Payroll Tax Office of New South Wales recognized that the Church was exempt from payroll tax because of the religious nature of its activities.

5. In *An Application by J. Gellie for Exemption from Liability to Render Service under the National Service Act,* a decision of the Court of Petty Sessions held at Perth, Western Australia, decided on 2nd December, 1970, by Zempilas, Senior Magistrate, the applicant Jonathan Gellie claimed that he was entitled to exemption from military service on the grounds that he was a Minister of the Church of the New Faith, which is the name of the Church of Scientology in Australia. In allowing his claim to exemption the Court said, *inter alia:*

> "Section 29 of the National Service Act 1951-1968 provides that certain persons are exempt from liability to render service under the Act so long as the condition, or status on which the exemption is based, continues. One class of persons so exempted are "Ministers of Religion."
>
> "The applicant in this matter, Jonathan Gellie, a person registered under the Act, applied to the Department of Labour and National Service for exemption from liability to render service on the ground that he was a Minister of Religion.
>
> "In support of his application the applicant gave evidence and stated that he had completed a course of training with the Hubbard Association of Scientology in Perth and obtained a certificate dated the 30th May, 1970, from an organization called "The Church of Scientology of California" indicating that he had

been selected and ordained as a 'Minister of the Church.'

"He later received a certificate from the Church of the New Faith Incorporated, Adelaide South Australia dated the 18th August, 1969, which indicated that Jonathan Gellie had been selected and ordained as a Minister of the Church with power to practice Divine Counselling to give Special Advice to hear confessions and to officiate at Marriages, Funerals, Baptisms and other sacraments and to perform all other duties that may devolve thereon as a Minister of the Church.

"The applicant said that there was no significant difference between the Church of the New Faith and the Church of Scientology. Evidence to this effect was also given by a Mr. Marc Harrison a Barrister and Solicitor of South Australia.

"The applicant stated that since March 1970 he had been employed on a full-time basis as a Minister of the Church of the New Faith and apart from casual labouring work once a month his sole source of income was from the Church. Most of his time is spent in counselling the members and also visiting those who were sick. He and three other Ministers conduct services once a week on a Sunday in premises in Hay Street for a group of people of an average number of 60. Since March 1970 he has conducted about one service in four. These services are commenced by a chaplain who preaches to the congregation and reads the Creed of the Church of Scientology. There is a reference in this creed to God and the soul of man. After this a minister reads texts from the writings of Lafayette Ron Hubbard, the Founder of Scientology and explains it to the group. A prayer for "Total Freedom" is then read. This prayer says "May the author of the Universe enable all men to reach an understanding of their spiritual nature. May awareness and understanding of life expand, so that all may come to know the author of the Universe. And may others also reach this understanding which brings Total Freedom." Notices are then read and the minister moves among the group discussing various matters and the formal part of the service is then concluded.

"Having carefully considered the evidence, called on behalf of the applicant which evidence was not contradicted and which I accept, the submissions made by counsel and the various authorities quoted, *I came to the conclusion that in the context of the National Services Act the Church of the New Faith is a religion. It has a creed which makes reference to God, its objects speak of God and a human spirit and it believes in the immortality of the spirit. Its creed and objects indicate a belief in and a reverence for a divine power.*

"Marriage Christening and burial services are conducted by its ministers who dress in a similar fashion to the ministers of other religions and when the adherents meet, their services are conducted in an orderly and dignified manner.

"From the evidence that has been produced I consider that, on the balance of probabilities the Church of the New Faith is a religion."

6. In *Church of Scientology of California and Church of the New Faith Incorporated v. City of Caulfield* a decision of the Town Planning Appeals Tribunal, Victoria, Australia, decided on 14 April, 1973, the Appellant Churches appealed against the refusal of the Council of the City of Caulfield to grant them a permit to use certain premises for the purpose of 'Church Mission (including Chapel, Mission Staff Offices, Reading Room, etc.).' In allowing the appeal, the Appeals Tribunal said, *inter alia:*

"The only non-residential purposes which should be permitted within a residential zone are such as are reasonably necessary for the proper enjoyment in the broad sense of the residential use of land in the zone . . . In our opinion, a Place of Worship is a use consistent with surrounding residential use. The advancement of religion is a purpose which is generally recognized as being advantageous to the community as a whole and a purpose for which there is a need sufficient to override the primary zoning of the land.

* * * * * *

"The moral philosophy of the Western world demands freedom of religion and it is not proper for a judicial body to judge the tenets of any particular religion.

* * * * * *

"It appeared from evidence given on behalf of the appellants, the four rooms labeled as relating to the Church Administration and Offices of the Church would be used mainly for discussing matters relating to the faith of the Church with its adherents. The reading room would be used for the reading of church literature, while the rooms on the first floor would mainly be used for discussion of matters relating to the Church with its adherents.

"A Place of Worship is defined in the Ordinance as including 'buildings used primarily for the religious and social activities of a Church but not such buildings as are used for primary, secondary or higher education or as residential.

"It appears to us that the rooms referred to . . . as offices would, in fact, be *primarily used for the religious and social activities of the Church and consequently would form part of a 'Place of Worship.'* Even if they were used to some extent for the administration of Church business, this would not, in our opinion, detract from the general purpose of the whole complex which, in our opinion, *can be classed as a Place of Worship. . . .*"

Canada

1. The Church of Scientology, British Columbia, is a religious body within the meaning of the Marriage Act of British Columbia, and marriages may be lawfully solemnized by duly appointed Ministers of the Church of Scientology, British Columbia, under the authority of the Province of British Columbia.

2. The Alberta Department of Health and Social Development stated on 10th July, 1973, that the Church of Scientology of Calgary, Alberta had fulfilled "the requirements for recognition as a religious denomination as provided for under the Marriage Act."

3. On October 1st, 1973, the Registrar General of the Government of the Northwest Territories advised the Church of Scientology of Toronto that it had been granted permission to have its Ministers registered to perform marriages and burials in the Northwest Territories.

4. The Deputy Registrar-General of Nova Scotia formally placed the name of a Minister of the Church of Scientology on the Civil Register authorizing him to solemnize marriages in the Province of Nova Scotia, on the 1st October, 1973.

5. The Province of British Columbia has recognized clergymen of the Church of Scientology of British Columbia, being a religious body within the meaning of the Marriage Act, for the purposes of celebrating marriage ceremonies.

6. The Department of Health and Social Development of the Province of Manitoba have accepted the Registration of Clergymen of the Church of Scientology for the purposes of the celebration of marriages under the Provisions of the Manitoba Marriage Act.

7. The Church of Scientology has been granted permission to register ministers for the purpose of celebrating marriages under the Marriage Ordinance of the Yukon Territory in the Yukon.

8. The Department of Revenue of the Province of Ontario has recognized the Church of Scientology of Toronto's religious bona fides for the purposes of the Retail Sales Act. (Exemption from the payment of tax on the purchase price of admission to entertainments whose proceeds will be devoted to religious purposes.)

9. The Ontario Ministry of Revenue recognized the Church of Scientology of Toronto as a religious organization for the purpose of exemption from certain aspects of retail sales tax, in a statement of the 27th June, 1973.

10. The Sheriff of the Judicial center of Regina, Province of Saskatchewan has confirmed that Ministers of the Church of Scientology listed in City Directories are exempt from Jury Duty under the provisions of Section 4 of the Saskatchewan Juries Act.

11. The Sheriff of the Supreme Court of the Province of Newfoundland has confirmed that Ministers of the Church of Scientology are exempt from Jury Service under the provisions of Section 70(1) (f) of the Newfoundland Judicature Act 1970.

12. The Sheriff of the Yukon Territory has confirmed that Ministers of the Church of Scientology are entitled to exemption from Jury Service under the provisions of Section 7F, Ordinances of the Yukon Territory.

13. The Judicial Offices of the Government of the Province of Alberta have confirmed in a statement of the 16th of October, 1973, that Ministers of the Church in Canada are exempted from serving as common jurors, in accordance with Section 5 of the Jury Act (c.165 of the Revised Statutes of Alberta).

14. The Church of Scientology in Vancouver, British Columbia has been officially exempted from license fees for its operation because of its religious nature by the Department of Permits and Licenses.

Denmark

1. On 19th September, 1973, in giving judgment for the Church of Scientology of Denmark in its action for libel against a reporter of the Danish newspaper *Ekstra Bladet,*

the Frederiksburg District Court Copenhagen said *inter alia:*

"When considering the content of the articles in question, of which the defendant is the named author, the fact that the Plaintiff is a religious or philosophical movement working publicly and wishing to gain followers in this country must be taken into consideration. . . ."

2. The Educational Department of the Danish Armed Forces has recognized the Church of Scientology as having a bona fide religious educational function in agreeing to contribute funds to the Church in exchange for courses delivered to personnel in its charge.

(Statement of the Military College of Civilian Education of 21st November, 1972.)

Germany

1. The Bavarian Ministry of Education and Culture decided after consideration in October, 1973, that the Church of Scientology of Germany, situate (sic) in Bavaria, was indeed a bona fide Church organization. It has stated in a letter dated 23rd October, 1973:

"The Church of Scientology has . . . submitted further materials concerning its basic beliefs. From these materials it can now be seen that the corporation cannot in any event be denied the status of a religious community any longer. The Church of Scientology has, according to its own extant literature, a belief in God, (and) Teachings concerning the Last Things and of the Fate of Man after Death."

2. The municipal authorities of Stuttgart partially exempt from liability to pay taxes, organizations organized for religious purposes.

Stuttgart recognizes the Church of Scientology Mission, in Stuttgart as a religious organization for this purpose.

3. The municipal authorities of Heilbronn partially exempt from liability to pay taxes, organizations organized for religious purposes.

Heilbronn recognizes the Church of Scientology Mission in Heilbronn as a religious organization for this purpose.

Theologians and scholars in the field of Comparative Religion in different parts of the world have concluded that Scientology is a Religion.

For example:

1. Professor E. G. Parrinder, the Professor of the Comparative Study of Religions at the University of

London, made the following statement on 25th November, 1971.

"1. I am the Professor of the Comparative study of Religions at the University of London.

"2. I am the author of more than twenty books on the subject of comparative religion and other subjects including:

Worship in the World's Religions
Comparative Religion
The World's Living Religions
Avatar and Incarnation (based on the Wilde Lectures delivered at Oxford University)
Witchcraft etc. etc.

and I have edited an Encyclopedia and a Dictionary on the world's religions, just being published.

"3. I have read a number of books on Scientology including *Scientology, The Fundamentals of Thought, Science of Survival, The Phoenix Lectures, Scientology 8-8008, Notes on the Lectures of L. Ron Hubbard, Axioms and Logics, A New Slant on Life.*

"4. I have also attended a service in the Chapel of the Church of Scientology at Saint Hill Manor, East Grinstead, Sussex.

"5. I am particularly interested in the age-old discussion on the definition of a religion.

"E. O. James, author of the work *Comparative Religion,* Emeritus Professor at the University of London and an outstanding living authority has defined religion as 'Primarily the recognition of an order of reality which transcends the ordinary and commonplace and is responsive to human needs.'

"Another famous definition is that of Dr. E. B. Tylor—'Belief in spiritual beings.'

"In my opinion Scientology may be properly regarded as a religion. It has striking parallels with a number of Eastern religions.

"6. I am also interested in the question of what constitutes worship and the definition of worship. There is an almost infinitely wide variety of forms of worship. In my opinion the services held by the Church of Scientology may be regarded as forms of religious worship.

"7. The work *Ceremonies of the Founding Church* has influenced me particularly in coming to this conclusion—in particular, the Christening and the Funeral Services described therein.

"I am particularly impressed by the teaching of the self or spirit, the so-called Thetan. Further, that this is immortal. This is a basic element of nearly all religions, and even Buddhism which refuses to define a soul yet holds to reincarnation and the ultimate goal of Nirvana for whatever there is of purified being.

"8. This emphasis upon the spiritual clearly distinguishes religion from a secular or humanist or political society. The Jain religion, for example, one of the oldest though small religions of India, does not believe in a Supreme Being but believes in countless immortal souls, and it is an undoubted religion, with innumerable temples and priests.

"9. Belief in a Supreme Being seems to be taught by Scientology, though since the Supreme Being is only the "Eighth Dynamic" which is primarily defined as "the urge toward existence as infinity," this does not seem to be a strong belief in a personal God. But I note that there are other mentions of God in the literature. Also Jains and Buddhists might be cited as religions without a personal God, though I believe in practice this should be qualified by recognizing their use of images of their founders, Jinas and Buddhas."

2. Dr. Marcus Bach, eminent theologian and scholar in the field of comparative religion, made the following statement on 8th June, 1970.

"I, Dr. Marcus Bach, am an acknowledged authority in the field of comparative religions and intercultural relations. I hold a Ph.D. from the State University of Iowa, and four Honorary Degrees from other Universities and Colleges. I am the Founder and Director of the Foundation for Spiritual Understanding in Palos Verdes, California.

"I am the author of twenty books, including *Major Religions of the World, Report to Protestants, Of Faith and Learning* and *Spiritual Breakthrough for our Time.*

"My biographical sketch appears in *Who's Who in America,* and the reference work *Who Knows—And What* lists my scholarly work in the field of contemporary religious movements.

"I have encountered and studied the Creeds and Doctrines of the Church of Scientology, and have concluded, to my satisfaction, that the Church of Scientology is a valid and vital pan-denominational religion which does not conflict with other religious beliefs, but is stimulating and enhancing to all religious pursuits. The Church of

Scientology is eclectic in that it has taken many great spiritual truths common to all religions and redefined them in a life style which makes them accessible and usable in daily life, particularly in our contemporary time.

"It is my opinion that governmental representations against the Church of Scientology parallel reactions experienced by many major religions in their historical genesis and that such repressions have usually contributed materially to the rapid growth and spread of religious movements so suppressed."

3. K. B. Leaver, Principal of Parkin Congregational Theological College in Adelaide, South Australia, made the following statement on 1st December, 1970:

"I hold the qualifications of Bachelor of Arts, Bachelor of Divinity, Master of Sacred Theology.

"I have held the position of Principal of Parkin Congregational Theological College, Adelaide 1958 to 1968 and I currently hold the position, from 1968 to the present date, of Co-Principal of Parkin Wesley Congregational-Methodist Theological College, Adelaide in the State of South Australia.

The Church of the New Faith incorporated in South Australia on the 31st day of January, 1969 is a bona fide Church showing the institutional characteristics of a Church.

"I hold that the Church of the New Faith, formally teaching Scientology, is a religion for the following reasons:

> It requires a belief in God. Although the New Faith does not define the characteristics of this belief very closely, it nevertheless is quite as specific as, for example, the Hindu or the Buddhist faiths—the latter religion has no belief in a personal deity at all.
>
> The Church of the New Faith gathers its believers into a fellowship which seems not to differ significantly from normal church worship and fellowship meetings, which are almost characteristic of religious bodies. Individuals are committed to each other, to the support of the church and answerable to the fellowship.
>
> Worship is conducted in a way which is indistinguishable from, say, Unitarian worship the world over. God is invoked and reverenced and a way of thought and life proclaimed.
>
> A professional ministry has been appointed. Although in the early stages of the development of the New Faith ministers were not fully supported by their

churches, like most other denominations, the development of their institutions has enabled them to set aside full-time leaders for this ministry.

"I would submit, therefore, that the Church of the New Faith is a religion in every main consideration which would be applied to any other church or faith. In fact it has more of the characteristics of a religion than some other faiths which are universally accepted as such. The Quakers do not have a ministry, the Unitarians and even the Salvation Army do not have an enunciated theology, the Buddhists do not even have a God. This church has the essential characteristics of a religion and in my opinion should have the rights adhering to such a designation."

4. Professor Kingsley J. Joblin, the Professor of Religious Studies at the University of Toronto, Canada, having undertaken a study of Scientology, made the following statement on 28th July, 1972:

"I have perused six or seven books and pamphlets issued by "The Church of Scientology" and written for the most part by its founder, L. Ron Hubbard. I offer the following considerations:

I. The Title. It may be thought that the term "Church" is misleading, since it was originally a distinctively Christian term and seekers might assume the sect to be under Christian auspices. This would be incorrect; I found no mention of Jesus Christ in the literature.

But this term is now used loosely for any religious organization, e.g., "The Buddhist Church of Toronto" as well as by authors such as Arnold Toynbee for any religious society.

Since among those societies at least one other legally recognized one is "The Church of Christian Science" we can hardly quarrel with the word "Scientology."

II. The Question Whether this Organization Should be Called A Religion. The literature shows that the central concern is the development of the individual soul or psyche called the "thetan." My first reaction to a consideration of the methods, the use of a machine called the "E-Meter," and the disciplines undertaken was that the closest parallel was not a religious denomination so much as one of a chain of clubs for the development of the body. But other aspects, notably contained in *The Background and Ceremonies of the Church of Scientology* (1970) show that it shares many marks of normative religion.

1. The corporate fellowship meeting every Sunday open to all, plus frequent meetings of members.
2. A ministry trained in the use of material written by the founder, with particular emphasis on counseling.
3. A commitment to a way of life as evidenced by signed testimonials in the pamphlet *The Character of Scientology*.
4. Orders of Service: A weekly Church Service, including Prayer; Marriage; Child-Naming; Funerals.
5. The assumption that man is primarily Soul.
6. The assumption that the ultimate reality is Deity described as Infinity.

III. MATURITY AND SPREAD. This organization is comparatively recent, having been incorporated in 1954, and its founder is still alive. But with the printing of the *Ceremonies* in 1970 it seems to have reached a point of maturity, and its spread to 38 centers points to future growth.

IV. TWO QUESTIONS. Normally, religious denominations have social concerns that involve extensive charitable works. The material perused gave no evidence of this or the use to which fees and book profits are put, though this information might be obtainable.

2. Status as a "Church" might be clouded by the approach evidence in these words by Mary Sue Hubbard from the Supplement to *Communication*, Sept. 1964:

> It is non-denominational. By that is meant that Scientology is open to people of all religious beliefs and in no way tries to persuade a person from his religion, but assists him to better understand that he is a spiritual being.'

"CONCLUSION: The balance of the evidence, indicates in my judgment, that "The Church of Scientology," qualifies as a religious denomination as those words are understood in our present culture."

5. Professor H. J. McSorley, of St. Michael's College, University of Toronto, Canada, made the following written statement on 23 February, 1973:

"I, Harry J. McSorley, B.C., M.A., Dr. Theol. (Munich), am associate professor in the Combined Department of Religious Studies at the University of Toronto. I am a member of the Roman Catholic Church.

"After examination of some of the books and literature published by the Church of Scientology, most notably *The Background and Ceremonies of the Church of Scientology of California, World Wide,* (London 1970), I think it can reasonably be concluded, and I so conclude, that "the Church of Scientology" is a religion or a religious denomination as these terms are used in contemporary culture."

* * *

About the Author

L. Ron Hubbard was born on the 13th of March, 1911, in Tilden, Nebraska, USA, to Commander Harry Ross Hubbard of the US Navy and Dora May Hubbard (Nee Waterbury de Wolfe).

He grew up in Montana with old frontiersmen and cowboys, and had an Indian medicine man as one of his best friends. Here in Montana, L. Ron Hubbard had his first encounter with another culture, the Blackfoot (Pikuni) Indians. He became a blood brother of the Pikuni and was later to write about them in his first published novel, Buckskin Brigades.

By the time he was twelve years old, he had read a good number of the world's greatest classics and began to take interest in the fields of religion and philosophy. During this time, while living in Washington, D.C., he became a close friend of President Calvin Coolidge's son, Calvin Jr., whose early death accelerated L. Ron Hubbard's interest in the mind and spirit of Man.

From 1925 to 1929, his father's career took the family to the Far East where L. Ron Hubbard journeyed throughout Asia, exploring out-of-the-way places, and saw many new peoples and customs.

In 1929 with the death of his grandfather, the Hubbard family returned to the United States and there L. Ron Hubbard continued his formal education. He attended Swavely Prep School in Manassas, Virginia, and went to high school at Woodward School for Boys in Washington, D.C.

In 1930, he graduated from Woodward with honors, and enrolled at George Washington University Engineering School in the fall. He became the associate editor of the university newspaper and was a member of many of the university's clubs and societies, including the Twentieth Marine Corps Reserve and the George Washington College Company.

While at George Washington University, he learned to fly and discovered a particular aptitude as a glider pilot. Here, also, he was enrolled in one of the first nuclear physics courses ever taught in an American university.

As a student, barely twenty years old, he supported himself by writing, and within a very few years he had established himself as an essayist in the literary world.

Even though he was very busy during these college years, L. Ron Hubbard still found time for his exploring. In 1931, at the age of twenty, he led the Caribbean Motion Picture Expedition as a director, and underwater films made on that journey provided Hydrographic

Office and the University of Michigan with invaluable data for the furtherance of their research. And again in 1932, at twenty-one years of age, L. Ron Hubbard led another expedition conducting the West Indies Mineralogical Survey and made the first complete mineralogical survey of Puerto Rico.

Although very active now in several areas, L. Ron Hubbard continued his writing. Under about twenty different pen names millions of words poured from his pen and into print, including both fact and fiction, travel articles, stories of exploration and adventure, essays and anecdotes, science fiction, and western stories appearing in over ninety magazines and journals.

In 1935, L. Ron Hubbard went to Hollywood and worked under motion picture contracts as a scriptwriter. He is still very active in Hollywood's movie production.

While in Hollywood he continued his study of "What makes men tick," and in his own statement, L. Ron Hubbard dates the discovery of the primary law of life, summarily expressed by the command "Survive!" at 1938.

In 1940, as a duly elected member of the Explorers Club of New York, L. Ron Hubbard conducted the Alaskan Radio Experimental Expedition. He was awarded the Explorers Club flag for conducting this expedition. Also, in 1940, he earned his "License to Master of Steam and Motor Vessels," and within four and a half months obtained a second certificate attesting to his marine skill: "License to Master of Sail Vessels" ("Any Ocean").

Between the years of 1923 and 1928, he received an extensive education in the field of the human mind from Commander Thompson of the Medical Corps of the US Navy, a friend of his father and a personal student of Sigmund Freud. Some of his early research was spent determining whether the mind regulated the body or the body regulated the mind. If the mind was capable of putting restraint upon the physical body, then obviously the fact that was commonly held to be true, that the body regulated the mind, was false. He went about proving this.

And so, L. Ron Hubbard continued studying, researching, and synthesizing this knowledge with what he had learned of Eastern philosophy, his understanding of nuclear physics, and his experiences among men, to form some of the basic tenets of Dianetics and Scientology.

The study, work, writing and research continued at a rapid pace. And then in 1948, he wrote Dianetics: The Original Thesis, his first formal report of the mysteries of the mind and life, which was a thirty-thousand word revelation.

The interest in Dianetics spread like wildfire. Letters asking for clarifications and advice and more data poured in, and just answering them was becoming a full-time occupation.

So the work continued, work, on an extensive popular text on the subject of Dianetics that would answer all questions. In May of 1950, Dianetics: The Modern Science of Mental Health exploded onto the booklists, leapt to the top of the New York Times Best-Seller List and stayed there. It is still a best seller today.

L. Ron Hubbard then founded in 1950 the Hubbard Dianetic Foundation in Elizabeth, New Jersey to facilitate auditing and training the public in Dianetics.

During the next twenty-six years many, many churches and missions were established all over the planet to professionally deliver L. Ron Hubbard's technology standardly to the peoples of the world.

The founder of Dianetics and Scientology, L. Ron Hubbard, lives with his wife, Mary Sue, and their children: Quentin, twenty-two; Suzette, twenty-one; and Arthur, seventeen. Their eldest daughter, Diana, twenty-three, is happily married.

Today, L. Ron Hubbard continues his life's work unabated, writing, researching and exploring new avenues and hitherto unexplored realms of life and the human spirit.

Abbreviations List

A	Affinity
ACC	Advanced Clinical Course
Ack	Acknowledgment
Admin	Administration
A/Guardian	Assistant Guardian
AO	Advanced Organization
ARC	Affinity, Reality and Communication
Assn Sec	Association Secretary
BPC	Bypassed charge
BPL	Board Policy Letter
BTB	Board Technical Bulletin
C	Communication
Cal-Mag	Calcium-Magnesium
CCHs	Communication, Control and Havingness
CF	Central Files
CO	Commanding Officer
Cog	Cognition
Comm	Communication
Comm Ev	Committee of Evidence
C/S	Case Supervisor
CS-6	Commodore's Staff for Division 6
DC	Refers to the Scientology church in Washington, D.C.
Dept.	Department
Div	Division
D of P	Director of Processing
D of T	Director of Training
EC	Executive Council
ED	Executive Director, Executive Directive
8-C	Control
E/O	Ethics Officer
EP	End phenomena
Est O	Establishment Officer
Eval	Evaluation
Exec	Executive
Exp	Expanded

F/N	Floating Needle
FP	Financial Planning
FSM	Field Staff Member
GIs	Good Indicators
HAS	Hubbard Apprentice Scientologist Course
H.A.S.	Hubbard Association of Scientologists
HBA	Hubbard Book Auditor
HCA	Hubbard Certified Auditor
HCO	Hubbard Communications Office
HCO Area Sec	Hubbard Communications Office Area Secretary
HCO B	Hubbard Communications Office Bulletin
HCO P/L	Hubbard Communications Office Policy Letter
HCO Sec	Hubbard Communications Office Secretary
HDC	Hubbard Dianetic Counselor
H E and R	Human emotion and reaction
HPA	Hubbard Professional Auditor
HQS	Hubbard Qualified Scientologist Course
Indoc	Indoctrination
INT	International
Issue I	First issue of that date
LRH	L. Ron Hubbard
MEST	Matter, energy, space and time
OCA	Oxford Capacity Analysis
OES	Organization Executive Secretary
0-IV	Scientology Grades 0-IV
OODay	Orders of the Day
Op Pro by Dup	Opening Procedure by Duplication
Org	Organization, organizing
Org Bd	Organizing Board
Org Sec	Organization Secretary
OT	Operating Thetan
OTL	Operation and Transport Liaison Office
O/W	Overt/withhold
Pc	Preclear
PES	Public Executive Secretary
P/L	Policy Letter (Hubbard Communications Office Policy Letter)
Pol Ltr	Hubbard Communications Office Policy Letter
PR	Public Relations
Promo	Promotion

PT	Present time
PTS	Potential Trouble Source
Q and A	Question and Answer
Qual	Qualifications Division
R	Reality
R	A letter used to designate that a mimeographed issue has been revised, as in C/S Series 48*R*.
RD	Rundown
Rehab	Rehabilitation, rehabilitate
R-factor	Reality factor
Remimeo	Churches which receive this must mimeograph it again and distribute it to staff
R3R	Routine 3 Revised
S and D (S&D)	Search and Discovery
Scn	Scientology
S-C-S	Start-Change-Stop
Sec checking	Security checking
Sect	Section
SH	Saint Hill
SH Spec	Saint Hill Special (refers to a Saint Hill Special Briefing Course Tape Lecture)
SMC	State of Man Congress
SO	Sea Organization
SP	Suppressive Person
Stat	Statistic
TA (or T/A)	Tone Arm
Tech	Technical, technology
TR	Training Regimen or Routine (often referred to as a training drill)
VGIs	Very Good Indicators
Vol	Volume
WFMH	World Federation of Mental Health
W/H	Withhold
WW	World Wide (or Worldwide)

Glossary

A = A = A, Anything equals anything equals anything. This is the way the reactive mind thinks, irrationally identifying thoughts, people, objects, experiences, statements, etc., with one another where little or no similarity actually exists.

Aberration, 1. a departure from rational thought or behavior. From the latin *aberrare,* to wander from; Latin, *ab,* away, *errare,* to wander. It means basically to err, to make mistakes, or more specifically to have fixed ideas which are not true. The word is also used in its scientific sense. It means departure from a straight line. If a line should go from A to B, then if it is "aberrated," it would go from A to some other point, to some other point, to some other point, to some other point, to some other point and finally arrive at B. Taken in its scientific sense, it would also mean the lack of straightness or to see crookedly as, in example, a man sees a horse but thinks he sees an elephant. Aberrated conduct would be wrong conduct, or conduct not supported by reason. When a person has engrams, these tend to deflect what would be his normal ability to perceive truth and bring about an aberrated view of situations which then would cause an aberrated reaction to them. Aberration is opposed to sanity, which would be its opposite. 2. An aberrated person wanders from his self-determined course. He no longer goes where he wants to go now, but goes where he has wanted to go in the past. His course is, therefore, not rational, and he seems to go wherever the environment pushes him. He has as many aberrations as he has hidden contra-survival decisions in his past. 3. mental derangement, any irrational condition. 4. the aberree's reaction to and difficulties with his current environment. 5. the manifestation of an engram and is serious only when it influences the competence of the individual in his environment. 6. the degree of residual plus or minus randomity accumulated by compelling, inhibiting or unwarranted assisting of efforts on the part of other organisms or the physical (material) universe.

Ability, to observe, to make decisions, to act.

Academy, in Scientology the Academy is that department of the Technical Division in which courses and training are delivered; Department 11, Division 4.

Accounts, See DEPARTMENT OF ACCOUNTS.

Acknowledgement, something said or done to inform another that his statement or action has been noted, understood and received. "Very good," "okay," and other such phrases are intended to inform another who has spoken or acted that his statement or action has been accepted. An acknowledgement also tends to confirm that the statement has been made or the action has been done and so brings about a condition not only of communication but of reality between two or more people. Applause at a theater is an acknowledgement of the actor or act plus approval. Acknowledgement itself does not necessarily imply an approval or disapproval or any other thing beyond the knowledge that an action or statement has been observed and is received. In signaling with the Morse Code, the receiver of a message transmits an R to the sender as a signal that the message has been received, which is to say acknowledged. There is such a thing as over-acknowledgement and there is such a thing as under-acknowledgement. A correct and exact acknowledgement communicates to someone who has spoken that what he has said has been heard. An acknowledgement tends to terminate or end the cycle of a communication, and when expertly used can sometimes stop a continued statement or continued action. An acknowledgement is also part of the communication formula and is one of its steps. The Scientologist, sometimes, in using Scientologese abbreviates this to "ack": He "acked" the person.

Administration (Admin), a contraction or shortening of the word administration, admin is used as a noun to denote the actions involved in administering an organization. The clerical and executive decisions, actions and duties necessary to the running of an organization, such as originating and answering mail, typing, filing, dispatching, applying policy and all those actions, large and small which make up an organization. Admin is also used to denote the action or fact of keeping auditor's reports, summary reports, worksheets and other records related to an auditing session. "He kept good admin" meaning that his summary report, auditor's report and worksheets were neat, exactly on pattern, in proper sequence and easily understood as well as complete. "His admin was bad," from the scribble and disorderly keeping of records of the session while it was in progress one could not make out what had happened in the session. You will also see the word admin in connection with the three musts of a well-run organization. It is said that its ethics, tech and admin must be "in," which means they must be properly done, orderly and effective. The word derives from minister, which means to serve. Administer means to manage, govern, to apply or direct the application of laws or discipline, to conduct or execute religious offices, dispense rights. It comes from the Latin, *administrare,* to manage, to carry out, accomplish, to attend, wait, serve. In modern English, when they use administration they mean management or running a government or the group that is in charge of the organization or the state.

Admin Scale, I have developed a scale for use which gives a sequence (and relative seniority) of subjects relating to organization. Goals, Purposes, Policy, Plans, Programs, Projects, Orders, Ideal Scenes, Stats, Valuable Final Products. This scale is worked up and worked down until it is (each item) in full agreement with the remaining items. In short, for success all these items in the scale must agree with all other items in the scale on the same subject.

Advance Booking Registrar, that person in a Scientology Church who, by mail, services and secures people in advance for Scientology training or processing.

Advanced Clinical Course, basically a theory and research course which gives a much further insight into the phenomena of the mind and the rationale of research and investigation.

Advanced Organization, that organization which runs the advanced courses. Its products are Clears and OTs.

Advance Scheduling Registrar, the prime purpose of the Advance Scheduling Register is: To schedule and secure individuals by mail in advance for technical services and ensure the future prosperity of the Church.

Affinity, 1. the feeling of love or liking for something or someone. Affinity is a phenomena of space in that it expresses the willingness to occupy the same place as the thing which is loved or liked. The reverse of it would be antipathy, "dislike" or rejection which would be the unwillingness to occupy the same space as or the unwillingness to approach something or someone. It came from French, *affinite,* affinity, kindred, alliance, nearness and also from the Latin, *affinis* meaning near, bordering upon. 2. The ability to occupy the space of, or be like or similar to, or to express a willingness to be something. 3. The relative distance and similarity of the two ends of a communication line. 4. emotional response; the feeling of affection or the lack of it, of emotion or misemotion connected with life. 5. the attraction which exists between two human beings or between a human being and another life organism or between a human being and mest or theta or the supreme being. It has a rough parallel in the physical universe in magnetic or gravitic attraction. The affinity or lack of affinity between an organism and within the theta (including entheta) of the organism brings about what we have referred to as emotions. 6. in its truest definition which is coincident of location and beingness, that is the ultimate in affinity.

Alter-is, 1. a composite word meaning the action of altering or changing the reality of something. Is-ness means the way it is. When someone sees it differently, he is doing an alter-is; in other words, is altering the way it is. 2. to introduce a change and therefore time and persistence in an as-is-ness to obtain persistency. An introduction of an alter-is is therefore the addition of a lie to the real which causes it to persist and not to blow or as-is.

Analytical, capable of resolving, such as problems, situations. The word analytical is from the Greek, *analysis* meaning resolve, undo, loosen, which is to say take something to pieces to see what it is made of. This is one of those examples of the shortcomings of the English language since no dictionary gives the word analytical any connection with thinking, reasoning, perceiving, which in essence is what it would have to mean, even in English.

Analytical mind, 1. the conscious aware mind which thinks, observes data, remembers it and resolves problems. It would be essentially the conscious mind as opposed to the unconscious mind. In Dianetics and Scientology, the analytical mind is the one which is alert and aware and the reactive mind simply reacts without analysis. 2. that mind which combines perceptions of the immediate environment, of the past (via pictures) and estimations of the future into conclusions which are based upon the realities of situations. The analytical mind combines the potential knowingness of the thetan with the conditions of his surroundings and brings him to independent conclusions. This mind could be said to consist of visual pictures either of the past or the physical universe, monitored by, and presided over, by the knowingness of a thetan. The keynote of the analytical mind is awareness, one knows what one is concluding and knows what he is doing. 3. the awareness of awareness unit plus some evaluative circuit or circuits or machinery to make the handling of the body possible. 4. we say the analytical mind is kind of a misnomer because most people think it's some kind of computing machine, and it's not, it's just the pc, the thetan.

Anaten, an abbreviation of analytical attenuation meaning diminuation or weakening of the analytical awareness of an individual for a brief or extensive period of time. If sufficiently great, it can result in unconsciousness.

Anchor points, assigned or agreed-upon points of boundary which are conceived to be motionless by the individual.

Appetite over tin cup, *slang,* a pioneer Western US term used by riverboat men on the Missouri; it means thrown away violently, like "head over heels," "bowled over."

ARC, 1. a word from the initial letters of affinity, reality, communication which together equate to understanding. It is pronounced by stating its letters, A-R-C. To Scientologists it has come to mean good feeling, love or friendliness, such as "He was in ARC with his friend." One does not, however, fall out of ARC, he has an ARC break. 2. ARC = understanding and time. A = space and the willingness to occupy the same space of. R = mass or agreement. C = energy or recognition.

3. affinity is a type of energy and can be produced at will. Reality is agreement; too much agreement under duress brings about the banishment of one's entire consciousness. Communication, however, is far more important than affinity or reality, for it is the operation, the action by which one experiences emotion and by which one agrees. 4. the triagonal manifestation of theta each aspect affecting the other two.

ARC break, a sudden drop or cutting of one's affinity, reality or communication with someone or something. Upsets with people or things come about because of a lessening or sundering of affinity, reality or communication or understanding. It's called an ARC break instead of an upset because, if one discovers which of the three points of understanding have been cut, one can bring about a rapid recovery in the person's state of mind. It is pronounced by its letters A-R-C break. When an ARC break is permitted to continue over too long a period of time and remains in restimulation, a person goes into a "sad effect" which is to say they become sad and mournful, usually without knowing what is causing it. This condition is handled by finding the earliest ARC break on the chain, finding whether it was a break in affinity, reality, communication or understanding and indicating it to the person, always, of course, in session.

ARC breaky pc, an anti-social act done and then withheld sets the pc up to become "an ARC breaky pc." It isn't an accurate remark really since one has a pc with withholds who on being audited ARC breaks easily. So the accurate statement is "the pc is a withholdy type pc that ARC breaks a lot." If you have a pc, then, who seems to have a lot of ARC breaks, the pc is a "withholdy pc" *not* an "ARC breaky pc."

ARC triangle, it is called a triangle because it has three related points: affinity, reality and the most important, communication. Without affinity there is no reality or communication. Without reality or some agreement, affinity and communication are absent. Without communication, there can be no affinity or reality. It is only necessary to improve one corner of this very valuable triangle in Scientology in order to improve the remaining two corners. The easiest corner to improve is communication; improving one's ability to communicate raises at the same time his affinity for others and life, as well as expands the scope of his agreements.

As-is, to view anything exactly as it is without any distortions or lies, at which moment it will vanish and cease to exist.

Assess (in Dianetics), choose, from a list or statement which item or thing has the longest read or the pc's interest.

Assist, 1. an action undertaken by a minister to assist the spirit to confront physical difficulties which can then be cared for with medical methodology by a medical doctor as needful. 2. anything which is done to alleviate a present time discomfort. 3. simply, easily done processes that can be applied to anyone to help them recover more rapidly from accidents, mild illness or upsets. 4. the processing given to a recently injured person in order to relieve the stress of live energy which is holding the injury in suspension. See also CONTACT ASSIST, TOUCH ASSIST, AUDITING ASSIST.

Assistant Guardian, See GUARDIAN.

Association Secretary, procures people, puts them bodily on post, puts the person's hands on the equipment or mest of the job, handles pay, supervises the actual conduct of the work (get the work done), sees that the proper hours are kept, etc., and changes, transfers or dismisses the personnel.

Attention, 1. when interest becomes fixed, we have attention. 2. a motion which must remain at an optimum effort. Attention is aberrated by becoming unfixed and sweeping at random or becoming too fixed without sweeping.

Auditing, 1. the application of Scientology processes and procedures to someone by a trained auditor. 2. the action of asking a preclear a question (which he can understand and answer), getting an answer to that question and acknowledging him for that answer. Auditing gets rid of unwanted barriers that inhibit, stop or blunt a person's natural abilities as well as gradiently increasing the abilities a person has so that he becomes more able and his survival, happiness and intelligence increase enormously. 3. Scientology processing is called auditing by which the auditor (practitioner) listens, computes and commands. 4. to get a result on a pc. 5. an activity of an auditor taking over the control of and shepherding the attention of a pc so as to bring about a higher level of confront ability. 6. directing the pc's attention on his own case and directing his ability to talk to the auditor. 7. the reversing of other-determined flows by gradient scales, putting the pc at cause again. 8. a communication process or a communication process with the end goal of raising the ability of another person so that he can handle his bank, body, others and environment in general. 9. the process of bringing a balance between freedom and barriers. Auditing is a game of exteriorization versus havingness.

Auditing command, a certain, exact command which the preclear can follow and perform.

Auditing command cycle, auditor asks, pc replies and knows he has answered, auditor acknowledges. Pc knows auditor has acknowledged. That is a full auditing command cycle.

Auditing communication cycle, this is the auditing comm cycle that is always in use: (1) is the pc ready to receive the command? (appearance, presence), (2) auditor gives command/question to pc (cause, distance, effect), (3) pc looks to bank for answer (4) pc receives answer from bank, (5) pc gives answer to auditor (cause, distance, effect), (6) auditor acknowledges pc, (7) auditor sees that pc received ack (attention), (8) new cycle beginning with (1).

Auditing session, a period in which an auditor and preclear are in a quiet place where they will not be disturbed. The auditor gives the preclear certain and exact commands which the preclear can follow.

Auditor, The, The Journal of Scientology. Journal means a daily newspaper; a periodical dealing especially with matters of current interest.

Auditor, one who has been trained in the technology of Scientology. An auditor applies standard technology to preclears.

Auditor Report Form, an auditor's report form is made out at the end of each session. It gives an outline of what actions were taken during the session.

Auditor's Code, a collection of rules (do's and don'ts) that an auditor follows while auditing someone, which ensures that the preclear will get the greatest possible gain out of the processing that he is having.

Automaticity, non-self-determined action which ought to be determined by the individual. The individual ought to be determining an action and he is not determining it. That's a pretty broad consideration. It's something not under the control of the individual. But if we said, something not under the control of the individual, as a total, unqualified definition of automaticity, we would have this, then: that car that just went down the street would be an automaticity to you. You didn't have control of it. So this is not a precision definition. The precision definition has "which ought to be under the control of the individual."

Bank, 1. the mental image picture collection of the pc. It comes from computer technology where all data is in a "bank." 2. a colloquial name for the reactive mind. This is what the procedures of Scientology are devoted to disposing of, for it is only a burden to an individual and he is much better off without it.

Basic auditing, the fundamental and most important elements of auditing—the skill of handling and keeping the preclear in session, proper use of the auditing communication cycle, the repetitive use of the auditing communication cycle to flatten a process, the correct application of the technology of Scientology, and the ability to use and read an E-meter correctly.

Basic personality, 1. a person's own identity. 2. the individual himself.

Be-Do-Have, there are three conditions of existence. These three conditions comprise life. They are be, do and have. The condition of being is defined as the assumption (choosing) of a category of identity. An example of beingness could be one's own name. Another example would be one's profession. The second condition of existence is doing. By doing, we mean action, function, accomplishment, the attainment of goals, the fulfilling of purpose, or any change of position in space. The third condition is havingness. By havingness we mean owning,

apable of commanding, positioning, taking charge
or spaces. These three conditions are given in an
importance) where life is concerned.

sumption or choosing of a category of identity.
ed by oneself or given to oneself, or is attained.
ess would be one's own name, one's profession, one's
stics, one's role in a game—each and all of these
led one's beingness.

R is used for the destruction of ideals or institutions
, it is called traditionally black PR. This is usually
ion of truth or a whole cloth fabrication.

uthorized departure from an area, usually caused
ata or overts. 2. the sudden dissipation of mass in
ccompanying feeling of relief.

e, sudden and relatively unexplained from sessions,
s and areas.

rs, these are similar in content to HCO PLs but are
other than L. Ron Hubbard and issued on Flag by
Directors of the Churches of Scientology. BPLs are
or revised. Distribution is as indicated on the BPL.
buff paper with green ink.

ulletins, these are similar in content to HCOBs but
ne other than L. Ron Hubbard and issued on Flag
of Directors of the Churches of Scientology. BTBs
lled or revised. Distribution is as indicated on the
ted on buff paper with red ink.

groggy and seem to go to sleep.

ugged is slang for snarled up or halted.

ching certain drills, the coach attempts to find
s, phrases, mannerisms or subjects that cause the
ll to become distracted from the drill by reacting
ullfighter attempts to attract the bull's attention
so does the coach attempt to attract and control

The sun is in the sky
The stars are in the heavens
Life lives.
And I am here to wish you a happy holiday season.
With inexorable promptitude 1983 is upon us!
What will it bring?
For some, I trust, a revitalized purpose and shining life.
For others not so fortunate, another step deeper in the black pit of oblivion.
Some conceive they are in the toils of fate.
But others, having achieved insight know that is not so.

the student's attention, however, the coach flunks the student whenever he succeeds in distracting the student from the drill and then repeats the action until it no longer has any effect on the student. Taken from a Spanish and English sport of "baiting" which means "to set dogs upon a chained bull," but mainly "to attack or torment especially with persistent insult, criticism or ridicule." Also "to tease."

Button, 1. items, words, phrases, subjects or areas that cause response or reaction in an individual by the words or actions of other people, and which cause him discomfort, embarrassment or upset or make him laugh uncontrollably. 2. the primary thing you get from your survey is a "button." This is the answer that was given the most number of times to your survey question.

Bypass, ignore the junior or juniors normally in charge of the activity and handle it personally.

Bypassed charge, mental energy or mass that has been restimulated in some way in an individual, and that is either partially or wholly unknown to that individual and so is capable of affecting him adversely.

Can't have, it means just that—a depriving of substance or action or things.

Capers, public relations events or actions.

Case, the whole sum of bypassed charge.

Case gain, the improvements and resurgences a person experiences from auditing.

Case supervisor, that person in a Scientology Church who gives instructions regarding and supervises the auditing of preclears.

Cause, could be defined as emanation. It could be defined also, for purposes of communication, as source-point.

"Cave in" (*noun*), **"Caved in"** (*adjective*), mental and/or physical collapse to the extent that the individual cannot function causatively. The individual is quite effect. A US Western term which symbolized mental or physical collapse as like being at the bottom of a mine shaft or in a tunnel when the supports collapsed and left the person under tons of debris.

Chain, incidents of similar nature strung out in time.

Chaos merchant, the slave master, the fellow who's trying to hold everybody down, the fellow who's trying to keep everybody shook up one way or the other and so he can't ever get up again, the fellow who makes his money and his daily bread out of how terrible everything is.

Charge, harmful energy or force accumulated and stored within the reactive mind, resulting from the conflicts and unpleasant experiences that a person has had. Auditing discharges this charge so that it is no longer there to affect the individual.

Chart of Human Evaluation, see HUBBARD CHART OF HUMAN EVALUATION.

Checklist, a list of actions or inspections to ready an activity or machinery or object for use or estimate the needful repairs or corrections. This is erroneously sometimes called a "checksheet" but that word is reserved for study steps.

Checkout, the action of verifying a student's knowledge of an item given on a checksheet.

Checksheet, a list of materials, often divided into sections, that give the theory and practical steps which, when completed, give one a study completion. The items are selected to add up to the required knowledge of the subject. They are arranged in the sequence necessary to a gradient of increasing knowledge on the subject. After each item there is a place for the initial of the student or the person checking the student out. When the checksheet is fully initialed, it is complete, meaning the student may now take an exam and be granted the award for completion. Some checksheets are required to be gone through twice before completion is granted.

Circuit, a part of an individual's bank that behaves as though it were someone or something separate from him and that either talks to him or goes into action of its own accord, and may even, if severe enough, take control of him while it operates. A tune that keeps going around in someone's head is an example of a circuit.

Classification, Gradation and Awareness Chart, the route to Clear, the Bridge. On the right side of the chart there are various steps called the States of Release. The left-hand side of the chart describes the very important steps of training on which one gains the knowledge and abilities necessary to deliver the grades of release to another. It is a guide for the individual from the point where he first becomes dimly aware of a Scientologist or Scientology and shows him how and where he should move up in order to make it. Scientology contains the entire map for getting the individual through all the various points on this gradation scale and for getting him across the Bridge to a higher state of existence.

Clay demo, abbreviation for clay demonstration. A Scientology study technique whereby the student demonstrates definitions, principles, etc., in clay to obtain greater understanding by translating significance into actual mass.

Cleaning a Clean, attempting to clean up or deal with something that has already been cleaned up or dealt with or that wasn't troublesome to the person in the first place.

Clear, a thetan who can be at cause knowingly and at will over mental matter, energy, space and time as regards the first dynamic (survival for self). The state of Clear is above the release grades (all of which are requisite to clearing) and is attained by completion of the Clearing Course at an Advanced Scientology Organization.

Clearing, a gradient process of finding places where attention is fixed and restoring the ability of the pc to place and remove attention under his own determinism.

Clearing Course, the state of Clear is above the Release Grades (all of which are requisite to Clearing) and is attained by completion of the Clearing Course at an Advanced Organization.

Co-auditing, an abbreviation for cooperative auditing. It means a team of any two people who are helping each other reach a better life with Scientology processing.

Cognition, as-ising aberration with a realization about life.

Command communication cycle, he who gives the order gets an answer.

Commands, See AUDITING COMMAND.

Comment, a statement or remark aimed only at the student or the room.

Commodore, head of the flotilla and related organizations as well as the immediate Flag Organization above the level of Captains, which carry out and help him to carry out his duties.

Communication, the consideration and action of impelling an impulse or particle from source point across a distance to receipt point with the intention of bringing into being at the receipt point a duplication and understanding of that which emanated from the source point.

Communication Bridge, it simply closes off the process you were running, maintains ARC, and opens up the new process on which you are about to embark.

Communication Course, because the HAS course is a course about communication, it is often called the Comm Course (comm being short for communication).

Communication Cycle, a cycle of communication and two-way communication are actually two different things. A cycle of communication is not a two-way communication in its entirety. In a cycle of communication we have Joe as the originator of a communication addressed to Bill. We find Bill receiving it and then Bill originating an answer or acknowledgement back to Joe and thus ends the cycle.

Communication Formula, the formula of communication is: Cause, Distance, Effect with Intention, Attention and Duplication with Understanding.

Communication Lag, the length of time intervening between the asking of the question by the auditor and the reply to that specific question by the preclear. The question must be precise; the reply must be precisely to that question. It does not matter what intervenes in the time between the asking of the question and the receipt of the answer.

Communication Line, the route along which a communication travels from one person to another.

Communicator, one who keeps the lines (body, dispatch, letter, intercomm, phone) moving or controlled for the executive he assists.

Compliance Report, a compliance report is exactly that. It is a report of compliance. A completed cycle reported to the originator of the order as done.

Conditional target, those which set up either/or find out data or if a project can be done or where or to whom.

Condition, ethics, in Scientology the term also means the ethics conditions (Confusion, Treason, Enemy, Doubt, Liability, Non-existence, Danger, Emergency, Normal, Affluence, Power Change, Power). The state or condition of any person, group or activity can be plotted on this scale of conditions which shows the degree of success or survival of that person, group or activity at any time.

Confessional, sec checking done in session not for security purposes is called a confessional.

Confront, the ability to be there comfortably and perceive.

Contact assist, the patient is taken to the area where the injury occurred and the injured member is made to gently contact it several times. A sudden pain will fly off and the injury, if minor, lessens or vanishes.

Control, when we say control we simply mean willingness to start, stop and change.

Cope, to handle whatever comes up. In the dictionary it means "to deal successfully with a difficult situation." We use it to mean "to handle any old way whatever comes up, to handle it successfully and somehow."

Counter-intention, a determination to follow a goal which is in direct conflict with those known to be the goals of the group.

Counter-policy, a local policy that demands a procedure or sequence of actions be followed that prohibits or inhibits the carrying out of the origination that is expected to be followed by a source which is senior to the originators of the counter-policy.

Course Supervisor, the instructor in charge of a course and its students.

Cracked case, case unmistakably improved and the person is fully aware of it.

Cramming, 1. a section in the Church of Scientology where a student is given high pressure instruction after being found slow in study or when failing his exams. 2. the cramming section teaches students what they have missed. This includes trained auditors who wish to be brought up to date on current technical developments.

Cross order, an order received from a local person who is junior to the originator of the order or policy that is to be duplicated and complied with, which is contrary to the senior order but is not cancelled (as it should be) in favor of the senior order.

CS-6, Commodore's staff for Division Six. CS-6 is an Aide to L. Ron Hubbard, Commodore of the Sea Organization, and assists him to run the Public Divisions (Division Six) of Scientology Churches all over the world. The title Distribution Aide was at one time also used to designate CS-6 but Distribution Aide now designates a separate and lower position which is also responsible for Public Divisions.

Cutative, an invented word to mean the impulse to shorten or leave out or the thing left out.

Cycle of action, the sequence that an action goes through wherein the action is started, is continued for as long as is required and then is completed as planned.

Data, 1. the information one has received that alerts one to the situation. 2. facts, graphs, statements, decisions, actions, descriptions which are supposedly true.

Data analysis, see SITUATION ANALYSIS.

Data Series, a series of policy by L. Ron Hubbard on management and concerning the subject of logic.

Dear Alice, see TR 1.

Debug, to get the snarls or stops out of something.

Declare, an action done in Qual after a pc has completed a cycle of action or attained a state. The pc or pre-OT who knows he made it must be sent to exams and certs and awards to attest. A declare completes his cycle of action and is a vital part of the action.

Degraded being, the degraded being is not a suppressive as he can have case gain. But he is so PTS that he works for suppressives only. He is a sort of super-continual PTS beyond the reach really of a simple S&D. The degraded being is not necessarily a natively bad thetan. He is simply so PTS and has been for so long that it requires our highest level of tech to finally undo it after he has scaled up all our grades.

Demo kit, demonstration kit. Consists of various small objects such as corks, caps, paper clips, pen tops, batteries—whatever will do. These are kept in a box or container. Each student should have one. The pieces are used while studying to represent the things in the material one is demonstrating. It helps hold concepts and ideas in place. A demo kit adds mass, reality and doingness to the significance and so helps the student to study.

Department of Accounts, headed by the Director of Accounts, the Department of Accounts receives, safeguards and expends funds in the organization. No other person can expend money, though others can receive it if it is promptly handed to accounts.

Department of Clearing, Department 18, Distribution Division. Its product is active field Scientologists.

Deputy, a deputy is assigned where the appointment is already filled by another. A deputy is a second in command who acts in the absence of the actual appointed person.

Deputy system, training on post is a second stage of any training—and processing—action. This is essentially a familiarization action. To have a person leave a post and another take it over with no "apprenticeship" or groove-in can be quite fatal. The deputy system is easily the best system. Every post is deputized for a greater or lesser period before the post is turned over and the appointment is made. When the deputy is totally familiar he becomes the person on the post.

Dev-t, "developed traffic," means unusual and unnecessary traffic.

Dianetic assist, running out the physical painful experience the person has just undergone, accidents, illness, operation or emotional shock. This erases the "physical trauma" and speeds recovery to a remarkable degree.

Dianetic auditing, includes as its basic principle, the exhaustion of all the painfully unconscious moments of a subject's life. By eradicating pain from the life of an individual, the auditor returns the individual to complete rationality and sanity.

Dianetics, *Dia* (Greek), through, *Nous* (Greek), soul, deals with a system of mental image pictures in relation to psychic (spiritual) trauma. The mental image pictures are believed on the basis of personal revelation to be comprising mental activity created and formed by the spirit, and not by the body or brain.

Differentiation, the ability to locate things in time and space.

Director of Clearing, Director of Department 18, Department of Clearing. The Director of Clearing hats Scientologists by drilling and mini-courses and will use whatever training tool is to hand needed to get a person to produce the four products of a Scientologist (purchased books, disseminated knowledge, environmental control and a cleared planet).

Director of Processing, the HGC is headed by the Director of Processing, under whom come all individual cases, (public and staff).

Director of Training, that person who is the head of the Department of Training in a Scientology church and who ensures that all people enrolled on courses are well and properly trained.

Distribution Aide, same as CS-6.

Double acknowledgement, this occurs when the pc answers up, the auditor then acknowledges and the pc then finishes his answer, leaving the auditor with another acknowlegement to do.

Double hatted, the individual is wearing more than one hat (has more than one post).

Down stats (statistic), a low or non-producing individual whose personal ethics is also normally out.

Dramatization, to repeat in action what has happened to one in experience. That's a basic definition of it, but much more important, it's a replay now of something that happened then. It's being replayed out of its time and period.

Dwindling spiral, one commits overt acts unwittingly. He seeks to justify them by finding fault or displacing blame. This leads him into further overts against the same terminals which leads to a degradation of himself and sometimes those terminals.

Dynamics, there could be said to be eight urges (drives, impulses) in life. These we call dynamics.

Effect Scale, a scale which tells you how much cause the individual dare be by measuring how much effect he's willing to suffer. At the top of the scale the individual can give or receive any effect and at the bottom of the scale he can receive no effects but he still feels he must give a total effect.

8-C, name of a process. Also used to mean good control.

Electrometer, Hubbard, is called an E-meter for short. Technically it is a specially developed wheatstone bridge well known to electrically minded people as a device to measure the amount of resistance to a flow of electricity.

E-meter, the E-meter is a religious artifact used as a spiritual guide in the church confessional. It is an aid to the auditor (minister, student, pastoral counselor) in two-way communication locating areas of spiritual travail and indicating spiritual well-being in an area.

Emotional Tone Scale, See TONE SCALE.

End Phenomena, those indicators in the pc and meter which show that a chain or process is ended.

Engram, a mental image picture which is a recording of a time of physical pain or unconsciousness. It must by definition have impact or injury as part of its content.

Engramic, adjective of engram. See ENGRAM.

Entheta, enturbulated theta (thought or life); especially refers to communications, which, based on lies and confusions are slanderous, choppy or destructive in an attempt to overwhelm or suppress a person or group.

Enturbulate, cause to be turbulent or agitated and disturbed.

Erasure, the act of erasing, rubbing out, locks, secondaries or engrams.

Ethics, 1. ethics actually consists, as we can define them now in Dianetics and Scientology, of rationality toward the highest level of survival for the individual, the future race, the group and mankind and the other dynamics taken collectively. Ethics are reason. The highest ethic level would be long-term survival concepts with minimal destruction, along any of the dynamics. 2. the term used to denote ethics as a subject, or the use of ethics, or that section of a Scientology church which handles ethics matters.

Ethics bait, someone who is "out-ethics" is said to be ethics bait. See OUT-ETHICS.

Ethics case, SPs and PTSes.

Ethics Officer, when ethics isn't in, it's put in. Ethics Officers put ethics in. An Ethics Officer removes counter-intention from the environment.

Ethics presence, an X quality made up partly of symbology, partly of force, some "now we're supposed to's" and endurance. The way to continue to have ethics presence is to be maximally right in your actions, decisions and dictates.

Ethics record, the known facts about a person's behavior, integrity and out-ethics situations he has been involved in, etc. An ethics record also includes data concerning the value of the individual—his awards and commendations received, attainments of affluence and power statistics.

Ethnic surveys, surveys finding out what is needed and wanted in different subjects or areas of interest, i.e., education, health, etc.

Ethnic values, publicly admired values and publicly detested values.

Evaluate, (evaluating, evaluation, evaluative), 1. evaluation for a person could be defined as the action of shaking his stable data without giving him further stable data with which he can agree or in which he can believe. 2. telling the pc what to think about his case.

Evaluation, the purpose of an evaluation is to isolate and handle the cause of a non-optimum situation so as to reverse and improve it toward an ideal scene. An evaluation is also done to isolate the cause of a scene which is going well and to reinforce it.

Evil purpose, destructive intentions.

Examiner, that person in a Scientology Church assigned to the duties of noting pc's statements, TA position and indicators after a session or when pc wishes to volunteer information.

Executive Directives, are issued by any executive council and named for the area it applies to. Thus ED WW, meaning issued to Worldwide. They are valid for only one year. They contain various immediate orders, programs etc. They are blue ink on blue paper.

Expanded Dianetics, is not the same as Standard Dianetics as it requires special training and advanced skills. The main difference between these two branches is that Standard Dianetics is very general in application. Expanded Dianetics is very specifically adjusted to the pc. Some preclears, particularly heavy drug cases, or who have been given injurious psychiatric treatment or who are physically disabled or who are chronically ill or who have had trouble running engrams (to name a few) require a specially adapted technology.

Exterior, the fellow would just move out, away from the body and be aware of himself as independent of a body but still able to control and handle the body.

Exteriorization, the act of moving out of the body with or without full perception.

Facsimile, 1. a simple word meaning a picture of a thing, a copy of a thing, not the thing itself. 2. the physical universe impression on thought and it means that section of thought which has a physical universe impression on it and it has a time tag on it.

Fact, a fact is something that can be proven to exist by visible evidence.

Falsehood, when you hear two facts that are contrary, one is a falsehood or both are. A false anything qualifies for this outpoint. A false being, terminal, act, intention, anything that seeks to be what it isn't is a falsehood and an outpoint. So the falsehood means "other than it appears" or "other than represented."

False motivator, when a person commits an overt or overt of omission with no motivator, he tends to believe or pretends that he has received a motivator which does not in fact exist. This is a false motivator.

False overts, the person has been hit hard for no reason. So they dream up reasons they were hit.

False perception, one sees things that don't exist and reports them as fact.

Field auditor, that means "a man who is running PE Courses and who is actively active in the field." It doesn't mean "just any auditor." But somebody we know is busy, somebody who is doing things. We give him the label of field auditor and that means he's running a little office of his own.

Field Staff Member, gets people into Scientology by disseminating to bring about an understanding of what Scientology can do thus creating a desire for service, and selecting the person for that service.

Financial planning, in essense is the *sensible* allocation of funds on necessities.

Fixed idea, 1. the "idée fixe" is the bug in sanity. Whenever an observer has fixed ideas he tends to look at them not at the information. Prejudiced people are suffering mainly from an "idée fixe." A fixed idea is something accepted without personal inspection or agreement. It is the perfect "authority knows best." It is the "reliable source." A fixed idea is uninspected. It blocks the existence of any contrary observation. Most reactionaries (people resisting all progress or action) are suffering from fixed ideas which they received from "authorities" which no actual experience alters. 2. some people have a method of handling a downstat which is a fixed idea or cliché they use to handle all downstat situations in their lives. These people are so at effect they have some idea sitting there "that handles" a down statistic. "Life is like that." "I always try my best." "People are mean." "It will get better." "It was worse last year." They know it isn't any use trying to do anything about anything and that it is best just to try to get by and not be noticed—a sure route to suicide. Instead of seeking to prevent or raise a declining stat in life such people use some fixed idea to explain it. This is a confession of being in apathy. We can always make stats go up. Hard work, foresight, initiative, one can always make stats go up. That's the truth of it and it needs no explanations.

Flag, the Church of Scientology of California operates a marine mission aboard a chartered vessel. This marine mission is commonly referred to as Flag. It is operated under the aegis (protection, support) of the Church of Scientology of California.

Flatten, flattening something means to do it until it no longer produces a reaction.

Floating needle, the idle uninfluenced movement of the needle on the dial without any patterns or reactions in it. The E-meter ceases to register on the pc's bank.

Flow, an impulse or direction of energy particles or thought or masses between terminals.

Flow lines, refers to the administrative lines of an organization which facilitate delivery of an organization's products.

Flunk, (verb) to make a mistake. Fail to apply the materials learned. Opposite of pass.

Folder, a folded sheet of cardboard which encloses all the session reports and other items. The folder is foolscap size, light card, usually blue or green in color.

Formula of communication, see COMMUNICATION FORMULA.

Game, a game consists of freedoms, barriers, and purposes.

General staff member, any staff member who is not an executive.

Goal, a long, long-term matter.

Good indicators, those indicators of a person (or group) indicating that the person is doing well, e.g., fast progress, high production statistics, person happy, winning, cogniting are said to be good indicators.

Good roads and good weather, (letter writing) whatever else you do, however keep it a warm good roads and good weather. That's the golden rule. Calm, warm, friendly. No "thank you for yours of the 19th instant." Sounds like we sell shoes. To a letter about a compliment on a church and a win, it's "Dear Bill, yes, things are going along okay. Tell me about your next big win. Tell Agnes hello."

Grade, the word used to describe the attainment of a level achieved by a preclear. Grade is the personal points of progress on the Bridge. A preclear is Grade 0, 1, 2, 3, 4, 5, 5A, 6, depending on the technology successfully applied.

Grade Chart, see CLASSIFICATION, GRADATION AND AWARENESS CHART.

Gradient, something that starts out simple and gets more and more complex. The essence of a gradient is just being able to do a little bit more and a little bit more and a little bit more until you finally make the grade.

Gradient scale, the term can apply to anything, and means a scale of condition graduated from zero to infinity. Absolutes are considered to be unobtainable.

Grant beingness, the ability to assume or grant (give, allow) beingness is probably the highest of human virtues. It is even more important to be able to permit (allow) other people to have beingness than to be able oneself to assume it.

Groove-in, the action of showing a person how to operate something. It especially applies to showing a person how to do a new post.

Group auditor, one who administers techniques, usually already codified, to groups of children or adults.

Group justice, the action of the group against the individual when he has failed to get his own ethics in.

Guardian, the purpose of the Guardian is to enforce and issue policy, to safeguard Scientology churches, Scientologists and Scientology.

Guardian Office, they have the guardianship and the defense of Scientology in general. The purpose of that organization is basically protection.

HAS Course, a course in elementary communication and control. Consists of training drills on communication and to put the student at cause over the environment. There are no prerequisites. The graduate is awarded the certificate of Hubbard Apprentice Scientologist.

Hat, *noun* a term used to describe the write-ups, policies and instructions that outline the purposes, know-how and duties of a post. It exists in folders and packs and is trained in on the person on the post. "Hats" developed in 1950 for use in the Church of Scientology as a special technology. The term and idea of "a hat" comes from conductors or locomotive engineers, etc., each of whom wear a distinctive and different type of headgear. A "hat" therefore designates particular status and duties in an organization. A "hat" is a speciality. It handles or controls certain particles in various actions and receives, changes and routes them. *Verb,* putting a person on post (the job), showing him his post position in relationship to his department and rest of the organization; giving him his post title, his duties, his statistic and seeing to the performance of those duties, through his study and application of the policies and written instructions of his post.

Hatted, each church staff member is a specialist in one or more similar functions. These are his specialties. If he is fully trained to do these he is said to be hatted.

Havingness, 1. havingness is the concept of being able to reach or not being prevented from reaching. 2. the feeling that one owns or possesses.

Havingness process, a process designed to increase one's havingness. An example of such a process is "point out something." This process is usually run in the auditing room with the preclear pointing out things in the room.

"Hey you" organization, what is sometimes called a "hey you" organization is one that takes orders from anyone.

Hidden standard, a problem a person thinks must be resolved before auditing can be seen to have worked. It's a standard by which to judge Scientology or auditing or the auditor. This hidden standard is always an old problem of long duration. It is a postulate—counter-postulate situation. The source of the counter-postulate was suppressive to the pc.

High school indoctrination, an extremely precise activity which consists of teaching an auditor not to let a preclear stop him.

Hit, punished, hurt, etc.

HSDC, Hubbard Standard Dianetics Course.

Hubbard Apprentice Scientologist, the graduate of the HAS course is awarded the certificate of Hubbard Apprentice Scientologist.

Hubbard Book Auditor, this level teaches about application of Dianetic and/or Scientology data in life. Processes taught are application of data in Dianetics and Scientology books. End result is ability to help self and others through the application of data contained in books of Dianetics and Scientology.

Hubbard Certified Auditor, a Class II auditor. This level teaches about overt acts and withholds. The end result is an ability to audit others to Grade 2 Relief Release.

Hubbard Chart of Human Evaluation, application of the human evaluation chart permits the student to estimate with some exactness the behavior and reactions he can expect from the human beings around him and what can happen to him as a result of association with various persons. Additionally, the use of human evaluation permits the individual to handle and better live with other human beings.

Hubbard Communications Office, it's in charge of the org boards, in charge of the personnel, it's in charge of hatting, it's in charge of the communication, which gives it communication lines, because an organization consists of the lines. It's in charge of inspection and it's in charge of ethics. HCO builds, holds, maintains, mans and controls the organization and it's the orders issue section.

Hubbard Communications Office Bulletins, are written by L. Ron Hubbard only. These are the technical issue line. They are valid from first issue unless specifically cancelled. All data for auditing and courses is contained in HCOBs. A Church of Scientology needs a master file of them from which to prepare course packs. These outline the product of the church. They are distributed as indicated, usually to technical staff. They are printed red ink on white paper, consecutive by date.

Hubbard Communications Office Policy Letters, are written by L. Ron Hubbard only. This is a permanently valid issue of all third dynamic, organization and administrative technology. These regardless of date or age, form the know-how in running an organization, group, church or company. The bulk of hat material is made up from HCO PLs. They are printed in green ink on white paper. They are filed by consecutive date. More than one issued on the same date are marked Issue I, II, III etc.

Hubbard Dianetic Auditor, an HDA is a graduate of the Dianetic Auditor's Course, forerunner to the HSDC. A graduate of the HSDC is known as an HDC which is the current certificate awarded to a Dianetic Auditor.

Hubbard Dianetic Counselor, a graduate of the Hubbard Standard Dianetics Course.

Hubbard Standard Dianetics Course, teaches about the human mind, mental image pictures, the time track, locks, secondaries and engrams. The processes taught are Standard Dianetic auditing and Dianetic assists.

Hubbard Guidance Center, that department of the Technical Division of a Scientology church which delivers auditing. Department 12, Division 4.

Human emotion and reaction, blow-ups, tempers.

Ideal scene, the state of affairs envisioned by policy or the improvement of even that.

Identification, the inability to evaluate differences in time, location, form, composition, or importance.

Illogic, illogic occurs when one or more data is misplaced into the wrong body of data for it. An example would be "Los Angeles smog was growing worse so we fined New York." That is pretty obviously a misplace.

Implant, an unwilling and unknowing receipt of a thought. An intentional installation of fixed ideas, contra-survival to the thetan.

Implanter, one who engages in the techniques of implanting.

In, things which should be there and are or should be done and are, are said to be "in," i.e., "We got scheduling in."

In basket, each administration personnel is to have a stack of three baskets. The top basket, labelled "IN" should contain those items which are still to be looked at. The middle basket, labelled "PENDING" is to contain those items which have been looked at but cannot be dealt with immediately. The bottom basket, labelled "OUT" is to contain those items which have been dealt with and are now ready for distribution into the communication lines again, or to files, etc.

Incident, an experience, simple or complex, related by the same subject, location, perception or people that takes place in a short or finite time period such as minutes, hours or days; also, mental image pictures of such experiences.

Inflow, the three primary flows are outflow (self to another), inflow (another to self) and crossflow (another to another or others to others).

Injustice, a penalty for an unknown crime or a non-existent crime.

Insane (Insanity), the overt or covert but always complex and continuous determination to harm or destroy.

Integrity Processing, that processing which enables a person, within the reality of his own moral codes and those of the group, to reveal his overts so he no longer requires to withhold and so enhances his own integrity and that of the group.

Intelligence, the ability to recognize differences, similarities and identities.

Intention, the command factor as much as anything else. If you intend something to happen it happens if you intend it to happen. Verbalization is not the intention. The intention is the carrier wave which takes the verbalization along with it.

International Membership, the cost is $15.00 per year for International Membership. This gives a 10% discount on all bookstore items over $1.25 and 20% discount on E-meters. An International Membership is membership in the main International Organization.

Introversion, looking in too closely.

Introvert, *noun,* someone who has looked in on himself too closely. *Verb,* the action of looking in too closely.

Invalidate (Invalidating) (Invalidation), a refuting or degrading or discrediting or denying something someone else considers to be fact.

Irreducible minimum, the principle of the irreducible minimum of a post. A post tends to reduce to only its visible points. In other words, all of the hidden or not too visible actions or the preparatory actions that make a good product tend to drop away from a post and tend to drop away from an organization. You wind up with the irreducible minimum and that is merely the visible.

Is-ness, something that is persisting on a continuum. That is our basic definition of is-ness.

Issue authority, prior approval from the Office of LRH to issue or publish (whether or not previously issued). I.e.: "new" books, booklets, magazines, all proposed promo pieces, handouts, mailings, HCO Bs, HCO PLs, Ethics Orders, etc.

Itsa, the action of the pc saying "It's a this or it's a that." A pc who is itsa-ing is simply looking at and identifying something.

Justice, could be called the adjudication of the relative rightness or wrongness of a decision or an action.

Justification, explaining away the most flagrant wrongnesses. Most explanations of conduct, no matter how far fetched, seem perfectly right to the person making them since he or she is only asserting self-rightness and other-wrongness.

Key-in, a moment when the environment around the awake but fatigued or distressed individual is itself similar to the dormant engram. At that moment the engram becomes active. It is keyed-in and can thereafter be dramatized.

Key-out, release or separation from one's reactive mind or some portion of it.

Knowingness, 1. being certainness. 2. a capability for truth; it is not data. 3. knowingness would be self-determined knowledge.

Letter registrar, the prime purpose of the letter registrar is "to guide individuals by letter into correct channels to obtain Scientology and to increase the size of Churches."

Life, a fundamental axiom of Dianetics is that life is formed by theta compounding with mest to make a living organism. Life is theta plus mest.

Lines, see FLOW LINES.

Locational, "locate the ________." The auditor has the preclear locate the floor, the ceiling, the walls, the furniture in the room and other objects and bodies.

Locational Processing, the object of locational processing is to establish the adequacy of communication terminals in the environment of the preclear. It can be run in busy thoroughfares, parks, confused traffic or anywhere that there is or is not motion of objects and people Example command: "Notice that (*person*)."

Lock, a mental image picture of a non-painful but disturbing experience the person has experienced; they depend for their force on secondaries and engrams.

Logged, the record of the issuance of orders, etc. and the recording of receipt of compliance reports to such orders.

Logic, the subject of reasoning.

Major target, the broad general ambition, possibly covering a long only approximated period of time, such as "to attain greater security" or "to get the organization up to fifty staff members."

Mass, it's electronic standing waves actually, and they usually appear black to the pc and these become visible.

Memory, a recording of the physical universe. Any memory contains a time index (when it happened) and a pattern of motion. As a lake reflects the trees and moving clouds, so does a memory reflect the physical universe. Sight, sound, pain, emotion, effort, conclusions and many other things are recorded in this static for any given instant of observation. Such a memory we call a facsimile.

Mental image pictures, copies of the physical universe as it goes by.

Merchant of chaos, see CHAOS MERCHANT.

Merchant of Fear, 1. probably the truly aberrative personalities in our society do not number more than five or ten per cent. They have very special traits. Where you find in the preclear's bank a person with one or more of these characteristics, you will have the person who most thoroughly tried the preclear's sanity. Such people would be better understood if I called them the "Merchants of Fear." 2. we can now technically call the suppressive person.

Mere explanation, a "why" given as the why that does not open the door to any recovery.

MEST, a coined word meaning matter, energy, space and time, the physical universe. All physical phenomena may be considered as energy operating in space and time. The movement of matter or energy in time is the measure of space. All things are MEST except theta.

Meter, see E-METER.

Meter check, the procedure whereby an Ethics Officer or trained auditor establishes the state of a person in regard to ethical or technical matters by using the technology of the E-meter.

Mind, a network of communications and pictures, energies and masses, which are brought into being by the activities of the thetan versus the physical universe or other thetans. The mind is a communication and control system between the thetan and his environment.

Ministerial Board of Review, established in the HCO Division. It shall be composed of no less than three persons who shall themselves be ministers of the church. The Board of Review will be headed by the Assistant Guardian or other Guardian Office personnel assigned by the Assistant Guardian. The purpose of this Board of Review is to safeguard Scientology, Scientology Churches, and Scientologists by ensuring that ministers of the Church are and remain of good moral character, continue to uphold the codes of Scientology and apply standard technology in their counseling of parishioners.

Misemotion, anything that is unpleasant emotion such as antagonism, anger, fear, grief, apathy or a death feeling.

Missed withhold, an undisclosed contra-survival act which has been restimulated by another but not disclosed.

Mission, a group granted the privilege of delivering elementary Scientology and Dianetic services. Does not have church status or rights.

Mock-up, any knowingly created mental picture that is not part of a time track.

Model session, the same exact pattern and script (patter) with which an auditing session is begun and ended; the overall form of all Scientology auditing sessions which is the same anywhere in the world.

Motivator, an aggressive or destructive act received by the person or one of the dynamics. It is called a motivator because it tends to prompt that one pays it back—it "motivates" a new overt.

Natter, sometimes pcs who have big overts become highly critical of the auditor and get in a lot of snide comments about the auditor. Such natter always indicates a real overt.

Neurotic, 1. a person who has some obsession or compulsion which overmasters his self-determinism to such a degree that it is a social liability. 2. a person who is mainly harmful to himself by reason of his aberrations, but not to the point of suicide.

No case gain, no case-change despite good tries with routine processes.

No-gain-case, this case performs continual, calculating, covert, hostile acts damaging to others. This case puts the enturbulence and upset into the environment, breaks the chairs, messes up the rugs and spoils the traffic flow with "goofs" done intentionally.

Noise, the amount of disturbance and offline actions and chatter and general dev-t in an area.

No-situation, a situation is something that applies to survival and if you evaluate the word "situation" against survival, you've got it. A good situation is a high level of survival; a bad situation is a threatened survival and a no-situation is something that won't affect survival.

Not-is-ness, the effort to handle is-ness by reducing its condition through the use of force. It is an apparency and cannot entirely vanquish an is-ness.

Objective processes, processes dealing with body motions and observing and touching objects in the auditing room.

Obnosis, this is a coined (invented) word meaning observing the obvious. There is no English or any other language precise equivalent for it.

Office of L. Ron Hubbard, this office handles the affairs of L. Ron Hubbard and has the signature and seals of the Church.

Offline, a dispatch is offline when it is sent to the wrong person.

Off-policy, an org run by those ignorant of policy has collapsed to the degree it went "off-policy." "Off-policy" (not knowing, not applying our procedures) has been the common denominator of every church or continental area collapse.

Operating target, those which lay out directions and actions or a schedule of events or timetable.

Operating thetan, a being who can be at cause knowingly and at will over thought, life, form, matter, energy, space and time, subjective and objective.

Opinion leader, that being to whom others look for interpretation of publicity or events. Through wisdom, proximity to data sources, personality or other factors including popularity itself, certain members of the group, company, community or nation are looked to by others for evaluation.

Orders, the verbal or written direction from a lower or designated authority to carry out a program step or apply the general policy.

Orders of the day, a type of ship's "newspaper" containing an item from the Commodore, the daily schedule for that day, news and notices, as well as orders necessary to administration of the ship's business. A copy of the "OODs" is delivered every morning to each in-basket on the ship.

Organism, a life organism is composed of matter and energy in space and time, animated by *theta.*

Organization Executive Course, this course contains the basic laws of organization. Primarily intended for Scientology organization executives, its policy letters are slanted toward a Scientology organization. However, it covers any organization and contains fundamentals vital to any successful or profitable activity.

Organizing board, shows the pattern of organizing to obtain a product. It is a flow chart of consecutive *products* brought about by terminals in a series.

Org rudiments, for some time, I have been advocating that you get one piece of organizational data in before you do another. This has been a very rewarding action. Orgs have become better off at once by doing this. Therefore, let's call it rudiments of an organization. And . . . let's get them in one at a time.

Origin, origination.

Originate, by originate is meant a statement or remark referring to the state of the coach or fancied case.

Origination, in TR-4, all originations concern the coach, his ideas, reactions or difficulties, none concern the auditor. By originate is meant a statement or remark referring to the state of the coach or fancied case.

Other-determinism, simply something else giving you orders or directions.

Other-intentionedness, a state of mind of wanting to follow a different goal than those known to be the goals of the group (either a big or little goal).

Other-intentionness, see OTHER-INTENTIONEDNESS.

OT TR 0, a drill to train students to be there comfortably and confront another person. The idea is to get the student able to be there comfortably in a position three feet in front of another person, to be there and not do anything else but be there. Student and coach sit facing each other with eyes closed.

Out, things which should be there and aren't or should be done and aren't are said to be "out"; i.e., "Enrollment books are out."

Out-ethics, an action or situation in which an individual is involved contrary to the ideals and best interests of his group. An act or situation or relationship contrary to the ethics standards, codes or ideals of the group or other members of the group. An act of omission or commission by an individual that could or has reduced the general effectiveness of a group or its other members. An individual act of omission or commission which impedes the general well-being of a group or impedes it in achieving its goals.

Outflow, a person talking to someone else, communicating to that person.

Outpoint, any one datum that is offered as true that is in fact found to be illogical when compared to the five primary points of illogic.

Out of valence, a person whose ethics have been out over a long period goes out of valence. They are "not themselves."

Out reality, see OUT and REALITY.

Overt, overt act. An overt act is not just injuring someone or something; an overt act is an act of omission or commission which does the least good for the least number of dynamics or the most harm to the greatest number of dynamics.

Overt-motivator sequence, the sequence wherein someone who has committed an overt has to claim the existence of motivators. The motivators are then likely to be used to justify committing further overt acts.

Overt product, called so because they are not in actual fact useful products but something no one wants and are overt acts in themselves, such as inedible biscuits or a "repair" that is just further breakage.

Overwhelm, to push in too tight.

Ownership, that area being covered and protected by the preclear.

Oxford Capacity Analysis, a specially prepared graph which plots ten traits of a pc's personality from a personality test taken by the pc.

Pack, a pack is a collection of written materials which match a checksheet. It is variously constituted—such as loose-leaf or cardboard folder or bulletins in a cover stapled together. A pack does not necessarily include a booklet or hard cover book that may be called for as part of a checksheet.

Pan-determinism, determining the activities of two or more sides in a game simultaneously.

Past lives, times lived before this life. Past lives are not "reincarnation." That is a complex theory compared to simply living time after time, getting a new body, eventually losing it and getting a new one.

Pastoral counseling, Dianetics practiced in the Church of Scientology as pastoral counseling, addresses the spirit in relation to his own body and intended to increase well-being and happiness.

Perception, the process of recording data from the physical universe and storing it as a theta facsimile.

Personal Efficiency Course, curriculum should consist of a mixture of drills and lectures. The first evening lecture should talk about definitions in life as found in Scientology. The dynamic principle of existence, the eight dynamics, a preview of the next evening's lecture should be given and this lecture should consist of a very rapid survey of communication course TRs 0 and 1 and should sail in the second hour into the ARC triangle, and all data for the rest of the week used in lectures should consist of ARC triangle data taking up the whole subject and one corner at a time. The remainder of the week previews TRs 2 and 3 and says how the TRs are used in life and how people can't do them. The last lecture's last part sells the HAS Communication Course.

Pilot projects, in new programs the bugs have not been worked out. It's like a newly designed piece of machinery. The clutch slips or the horsepower is sour. New programs are undertaken on a small scale as pilot projects. If they work out, good. Spot the bugs, streamline them and prove them. Only then is it all right to give them out as broad orders.

Plans, the general bright idea one has to remedy the "why" found and get things up to the ideal scene or improve even that.

Pluspoint, a datum of truth when found to be true compared to the five points of illogic.

Policy, the rules of the game, the facts of life, the discovered truths and the invariable procedures.

Post, (a position of employment) a post or terminal is an assigned area of responsibility and action which is supervised in part by an executive.

Postulate, *noun,* a self-created truth would be simply the consideration generated by self. Well, we just borrow the word which is in seldom use in the English language, we call that postulate. And we mean by postulate, self-created truth. He posts something. He puts something up and that's what a postulate is. *Verb,* in Scientology the word postulate means to cause a thinkingness or consideration. It is a specially applied word and is defined as causative thinkingness.

Potential Trouble Source, a person connected to a suppressive person. All sick persons are PTS. All pcs who roller-coaster (regularly lose gains) are PTS. Suppressive persons are themselves PTS to themselves.

Power, the ability to maintain a position in space. If you can't maintain a position in space you will never have power. An individual's ability to withhold, his ability to hold, and his ability to keep something from going away, is part and parcel of his ability to maintain his own position, situation or location.

PR (Public Relations), 1. *slang,* to cover up, putting up a lot of false reports to serve as a smoke screen for idleness or bad actions. 2. the duty and purpose of a public relations man is the interpretation of top management policy to the different publics of the company; to advise top management so that policy if lacking can be set; to make the company, its actions or products known, accepted and understood by the different publics; and to assist the company to exist in a favorable operating climate so that it can expand, prosper and be viable.

PR Area Control, keeping the area handled so the church is well thought of.

Precipitation, the factors which cause the sickness to manifest itself.

Preclear, a spiritual being who is now on the road to becoming clear, hence preclear.

Predisposed, a previous inclination or tendency, susceptibility or liability; before the fact a person is disposed to get sick.

Predisposition, the factors which prepared the body for sickness.

Premature acknowledgement, occurs when you "coax" a person to talk after he has begun with a nod or a low "yes"; you ack, make him forget, then make him believe you haven't got it and then make him tell you at great length. He feels bad and doesn't cognite and may ARC break. Any habit of agreeable noises and nods can be mistaken for acknowledgement, ends cycle on the speaker, causes him to forget, feel dull, believe the listener is stupid, get cross, get exhausted explaining and ARC break. The missed withhold is inadvertent. One didn't get a chance to say what one was going to say because one was stopped by premature acknowledgement. Result, missed withhold in the speaker, with all its consequences.

Present time, the time which is now and which becomes the past almost as rapidly as it is observed. It is a term loosely applied to the environment existing in now, as in "The preclear came up to present time," meaning the preclear became aware of the existing matter, energy, space and time of now. The point on anyone's time track where his physical body (if alive) may be found. "Now."

Present time problem, technically a special problem that exists in the physical universe now, on which the pc has his attention fixed.

Primary target, the organization, personnel, communication-type targets.

PRO, 1. Public Relations Office(r). 2. Professional.

Problem, postulate, counter-postulate resulting in indecision. That is the first manifestation of problems, and the first consequence of a problem is indecision.

Process, a set of questions asked by an auditor to help a person find out things about himself or life. More fully, a process is a patterned action, done by the auditor and preclear under the auditor's direction, which is invariable and unchanging, composed of certain steps or actions calculated to release or free a thetan. There are many processes and these are aligned with the levels taught to students and with grades as applied to preclears, all of which lead the student or the preclear gradiently to higher understanding and awareness. Any single process is run only so long as it produces change and no longer.

Processing (auditing), the principle of making an individual look at his own existence, and improve his ability to confront what he is and where he is.

Product, a finished high quality service or article in the hands of the consumer as an exchange for a valuable.

Production target, those which set quantities like statistics.

Program, the complete or outline of a complete target series containing all types.

Projects, the sequence of steps necessary to carry out one step in a program.

Prolongation, a lengthening in time or space; extension; when a person is sick and then he doesn't get well, that's called prolongation, in other words, it's just continuously gone on with.

Proportionate pay, the staff of the organization except for "part-time" staff is paid in units under the following system: Staff is paid 50% of the gross income less congress fees, books and tapes, of the organization. A staff member is assigned units of pay. The value of the unit varies from week to week.

Psychosis, is simply an evil purpose. It means a definite obsessive desire to destroy.

Psychosomatic, psycho of course refers to mind and somatic refers to body; the term psychosomatic means the mind making the body ill or illnesses which have been created physically within the body by derangement of the mind.

Psychosomatic illness, those which have a mental origin but which are nevertheless organic.

Psychotic, a person who is physically or mentally harmful to those about him out of proportion to the amount of use he is to them.

PTS Type A, a person intimately connected with persons (such as marital or familial ties) of known antagonism to mental or spiritual treatment or Scientology.

Public Division, that division of a Scientology church which handles communication to and contact with the broad public to bring the religion of Scientology to them.

Purpose, 1. a survival route chosen by an individual, a species or a unit of matter or energy in the accomplishment of its goal. 2. a lesser goal applying to specific activities or subjects.

Q and A, means "Question and Answer," When the term Q and A is used it means one did not get an answer to his question. It also means not getting compliance with an order but accepting something else. Example: Auditor: "Do birds fly?" Pc: "I don't like birds." Auditor: "What don't you like about birds?" Flunk. It's a Q and A. The right reply would be an answer to the question asked and the right action would be to get the original question answered.

Qualifications, the Qualifications Division is the division in the Church of Scientology which has the purpose to ensure the results of Scientology, correct them when needful and attest to them when attained.

Quickie, in the dictionary you will find quickie also quicky: something done or made in a hurry. Also: a hurriedly planned and executed program (as of studies). Anything that does not fully satisfy all requirements is quickie. So "quickie" really means "omitting actions for whatever reason that would satisfy all demands or requirements and doing something less than could be achieved." In short, a quickie is not doing all the steps and actions that could be done to make a perfect whole.

Rational conflict, while man is concerned with any of the eight dynamics, any one of them may become antipathetic to his own survival. This is rational conflict and is normally and commonly incidental to survival. It is non-aberrative in that it is rational within the education limitation.

Reach and Withdraw, to grasp and let go.

Reactive mind, a portion of a person's mind which works on a totally stimulus-response basis, which is not under his volitional control, and which exerts force and the power of command over his awareness, purposes, thoughts, body and actions. Stored in the reactive mind are engrams, and here we find the single source of aberrations and psychosomatic ills.

Read, the action of the needle on the E-meter dial falling (moving to the right).

Reality, the degree of agreement reached by two ends of a communication line. In essence, it is the degree of duplication achieved between cause and effect. That which is real is real simply because it is agreed upon, and for no other reason.

Reality-factor, 1. explanation in information, data, etc., given to a person in order to bring about sufficient understanding for him to be able to perform a specific action. 2. telling the pc what you are going to do at each new step.

Real why, a real why opens the door to handling. If it does not, then it is a wrong why. When you have a right why, handling becomes simple. The more one has to beat his brains for a bright idea to handle, the more likely it is that he has a wrong why. The why will be how come the situation is such a departure from the ideal scene and will open the door to handling.

Reasonable, reasonableness, 1. a staff member or an executive can be "reasonable" and accept reasons why something cannot be done, accept incomplete cycles as complete, and fail to follow through and get completions. 2. faulty explanations. 3. an objective can always be achieved. Most usually, when it is not being achieved, the person is finding counter-intention in the environment which coincides with his own (this is reasonableness), and his own attention becomes directed to his own counter-intention, i.e., he has interiorized into the situation.

Recall, present time remembering something that happened in the past. It is not re-experiencing it, re-living it or re-running it. Recall does not mean going back to when it happened. It simply means that you are in present time, thinking of, remembering, putting your attention on something that happened in the past—all done from present time.

Registrar, in a Scientology Church, the registrar is the person who signs people up for Scientology services.

Rehabilitation, when the person was originally released he had become aware of something that caused the reactive mind to de-stimulate at that point or become weak. And so he released. You have to find that point of sudden awareness again.

Release, *noun,* one who knows he or she has had worthwhile gains from Scientology processing and who knows he or she will not now get worse. *Verb,* the act of taking the perceptions or effort or effectiveness out of a heavy facsimile or taking away the preclear's hold on the facsimile.

Religious philosophy, implies study of spiritual manifestations; research on the nature of the spirit and study on the relationship of the spirit to the body; exercises devoted to the rehabilitation of abilities in a spirit.

Religious practice, implies ritual, faith-in, doctrine based on a catechism and a creed.

Responsibility, 1. the discovery of the direct anatomy of responsibility is as follows: "able to admit causation," "able to withhold from." 2. the concept of being able to care for, to reach or to be.

Responsibility (a process), "What part of that incident could you be responsible for?"

Restimulate, to cause restimulation.

Restimulation, the reactivation of an existing incident.

Restimulator, those approximations in the environment of an individual of the content of an engram.

Ridge, a ridge is caused by two energy flows coinciding and causing an enturbulence of energy, which, on examination, is found to take on a characteristic which in energy flows is very like matter, having its particles in chaotic mixture.

Robot, the individual with an evil purpose has to withhold himself because he may do destructive things. When he fails to withhold himself he commits overt acts on his fellows or other dynamics and occasionally loses control and does so. This, of course, makes him quite inactive. To overcome this he refuses any responsibility for his own actions. Any motion he makes must be on the responsibility of others. He operates then only when given orders. Thus he *must* have orders to operate. Therefore, one could term such a person a robot and the malady could be called robotism.

Robotism, the malady a person termed a robot is suffering from.

Roller-coaster, a case that betters and worsens. A roller-coaster is always connected to a suppressive person and will not get steady gains until the suppressive is found on the case or the basic suppressive person earlier. Because the case doesn't get well he or she is a potential trouble source to us, to others and to himself.

Run, undergo processing.

Rundown, a series of steps which are auditing actions and processes designed to handle a specific aspect of a case and which have a known end phenomena.

Run out, erase.

Saint Hill, the name of L. Ron Hubbard's home in East Grinstead, Sussex, England, and location of the worldwide headquarters of Scientology, and the UK Advanced Organization and SH (AOSH UK). Ron taught the original Saint Hill Special Briefing Course at Saint Hill from 1961 to 1965. The term SH now applies to any organization authorized to deliver those upper level Scientology services hence we also have the "American Saint Hill Organization" (ASHO), and the "Advanced Organization and Saint Hill in Denmark" (AOSH DK).

Sanity, the ability to recognize differences, similarities and identities.

Sanity Scale, hiring, training, apprenticeships, utilization, production, promotion, sales, delivery, finance, justice, morale. These eleven items must agree with and be in line with the Admin Scale. Where these subjects are not well handled and where one or more of these are very out of line, the organization will suffer a third dynamic aberration. This then is a Sanity Scale for the third dynamic of a group.

Scan, scanning, the action of rapidly glancing through an incident from beginning (earliest moment of the incident) to the end of the incident.

Scene, the way things ought to be or are.

Scientology, 1. formed from the Latin word, *Scio,* which means know or distinguish, being related to the word *Scindo,* which means *cleave.* (Thus the idea of differentiation is strongly implied.) It is formed from the Greek word, *Logos,* which means THE WORD OR OUTWARD FORM BY WHICH THE INWARD THOUGHT IS EXPRESSED AND MADE KNOWN: also THE INWARD THOUGHT OR REASON ITSELF. Thus, SCIENTOLOGY MEANS KNOWING ABOUT KNOWING, or science of knowledge. 2. a religious philosophy in its highest meaning as it brings man to total freedom and truth.

Scientology Zero, the problems and confusions and wrongnesses, zones of chaos of existence and the identification of those zones of chaos. At Scientology Zero you merely want the people to become aware of the fact of what the problem is.

Sea Organization, a fraternal organization existing within the formalized structure of the Churches of Scientology. It consists of highly dedicated members of the church. These members take vows of eternal service. The Sea Organization life style of community living is traditional to religious orders.

Search and Discovery, a Scientology process which locates the SP the preclear was connected to in the past.

Secondary, a mental image picture of a moment of severe and shocking loss or threat of loss which contains misemotion such as anger, fear, grief, apathy or "deathfulness." It is a mental image recording of a time of severe mental stress. It may contain unconsciousness. Called a secondary because it itself depends upon an earlier engram with similar data but real pain, etc.

Selection paper, the field staff member selects the person to be trained or processed after direct personal contact with the person and issues to that person a paper stating the contacted person has been selected. The form must bear the hour, date and place, the block printed name and address of the selectee and the block printed name and address and certificate initials and certificate number of the field staff member and what the selectee is selected for (membership, training or processing) and some approximation of arrival date at the church.

Selection slip, see SELECTION PAPER.

Self-coaching, the student tending to introvert and look too much at how he is doing and what he is doing rather than just doing it.

Self-analysis, a group technique aimed at the rehabilitation of one's own universe so as to bring it up to a level of comparability with one's own observation of the mest universe, and can be delivered to groups of children or adults by a person trained only through the text of *Self-Analysis in Scientology.*

Self-determinism, the ability to locate in space and time, energy and matter; also the ability to create space and time in which to create and locate energy and matter. 2. the ability to direct himself.

Session, a precise period of time during which an auditor audits or processes a preclear.

Short-sessioned, running a session for only a short period of time, but more than one session done in the same day.

Single-hand, to run it all by himself performing all vital functions. The term comes from a sailor who runs a boat or vessel by himself alone with no other crew.

Situation, the broad general scene on which a body of current data exists. A major departure from the ideal scene.

Situation analysis, in confronting a broad situation to be handled we have of course the problem of finding out what's wrong before we can correct it. This is done by data analysis followed by situation analysis. We do this by grading all data for outpoints. We now have a long list of outpoints. This is data analysis. We sort the outpoints we now have into the principle areas of the scene. The majority will appear in one area. This is situation analysis. We now know what area to handle.

Slow gain case, not everyone is a continuous overt committer by about a thousand to one. But this phenomenon is not confined to the no-gain case. The slow gain case is also committing overts the auditor doesn't see. Therefore a little discipline in the environment speeds the *slow* gain case.

Social machinery, action without awareness. He's doing it all the time but he never noticed it. What the individual is aware of and what the individual is doing are not the same thing, ever.

Somatic, 1. this is essentially body sensation, illness or pain or discomfort. *Soma* means body; hence psychosomatic or pains stemming from the mind; a pain or ache, sensation and also misemotion or even unconsciousness. 2. this is a general word for uncomfortable perceptions coming from the reactive mind. Its genus is early Dianetics and it is a general, common-packaged word, used by Scientologists to denote "pain" or "sensation" with no difference made between them. To the Scientologist anything is a SOMATIC if it emanates from the various parts of the reactive mind and produces an awareness of reactivity.

Spin bin, slang term for "insane asylum" or mental institution.

Spins, (spinning), slang term meaning going insane.

Spirit, the thetan, after the Greek symbol of thought (θ) and spirit—theta.

Squirrel (squirreling), those who engage in actions altering Scientology, and offbeat practices. It is a bad thing.

Stable datum, any body of knowledge, more particularly and exactly, is built from one datum. That is its stable datum. Invalidate it and the entire body of knowledge falls apart. A stable datum does not have to be the correct one. It is simply the one that keeps things from being in a confusion and on which others are aligned.

Stable terminal, pushes the actions that belong to his area on the org board and handles or suppresses the confusions of that area or aligns them with the correct flows.

Standard Dianetics, modern Dianetic auditing is called Standard Dianetics, and new Dianetics. It is a precision activity.

Standard tech, is not a process or a series of processes. It is following the rules of processing.

Static, something without mass, without wavelength, without time, and actually without position.

Statistic, the relative rise or fall of a quantity compared to an earlier moment in time. If a section moved ten tons last week and twelve tons this week, the statistic is rising. If a section moved ten tons last week and only eight tons this week, the statistic is falling.

Stuck picture, when a pc can't audit the chain he should be on because the picture keeps coming in.

Sub-products, those necessary to make up the valuable final products of the organization.

Suppressive person, 1. The person is in a mad, howling situation of some yesteryear and is "handling it" by committing overt acts today. I say condition of yesteryear but this case thinks it's today. 2. is one that actively seeks to suppress or damage Scientology or a Scientologist by suppressive acts.

Survey, "a careful examination of something as a whole and in detail." The word "survey" as used in public relations terminology means to carefully examine public opinion with regard to an idea, a product, an aspect of life, or any other subject. By examining in detail (person to person surveying) one can arrive at a whole view of public opinion on a subject by tabulating highest percentage of popular response.

Sweetness and light, a person who cannot conceive of ever having done anything bad to anybody or anything.

Tapes, these are an issue line of both policy and technology as designated and are recopied at the Publications Organization of the Church of Scientology and issued for courses, congresses and other purposes.

Technical Division, that part of a Scientology Church which routinely delivers auditing and training services. It handles the technology of Dianetics and Scientology, thus it is the Technical Division.

Technology, the methods of application of an art or science as opposed to mere knowledge of the science itself.

Terminal, anything used in a communication system; something that has mass in it. Something with mass, meaning and mobility. Anything that can receive, relay or send a communication.

Theetie-weetie, *slang,* it's from England, means "sweetness and light" (but they can't face mest or any outness). Cannot go deeper into the bank than a thought.

Theta, energy peculiar to life or a thetan which acts upon the material in the physical universe and animates it, mobilizes it and changes it; natural creative energy of a thetan which he has free to direct toward survival goals, especially when it manifests itself as high-tone, constructive communications.

Thetan, from the Greek letter, *theta* (θ), traditional symbol for thought or spirit, the thetan is the individual himself, not his body, mind or anything else.

Third party, one who by false reports creates trouble between two people, a person and a group or a group and another group.

Time track, the consecutive record of mental image pictures which accumulates through the preclear's life or lives. It is very exactly dated.

Tone, the emotional condition of an engram or the general condition of an individual.

Tone 40, defined as "giving a command and just knowing that it will be executed despite any contrary appearances."

Tone Scale, under affinity we have the various emotional tones ranging from the highest to the lowest and these are, in part, serenity (the highest level), enthusiasm (as we proceed downward towards the baser affinities), conservatism, boredom, antagonism, anger, covert hostility, fear, grief, apathy. This in Scientology is called the Tone Scale.

Touch assist, an assist which brings the patient's attention to injured or affected body areas.

Tough case, (is also the difficult student), is the sole reason one has an urge to alter a process. The poor TA type case or the "no change" response to routine processes.

Track, the time track, the endless record, complete with fifty-two perceptions of the pc's entire past.

Training drill, a precise training action putting a student through laid out practical steps gradient by gradient, to teach a student to apply with certainty what he has learned.

TR-0, a drill to train students to confront a preclear with auditing only or with nothing. The whole idea is to get the student able to be there comfortably in a position three feet in front of a preclear, to be there and not do anything else but be there.

TRs 1-9, see the TRs PACK.

Two-way communication, a two-way cycle of communication would work as follows: Joe, having originated a communication, and having completed it, may then wait for Bill to originate a communication to Joe, thus completing the remainder of the two-way cycle of communication. Thus we get the normal cycle of communication between two terminals.

Unconscious, any person who is unaware, to a great degree is unconscious.

Understanding, composed of affinity, reality, communication.

Unmock, 1. take down or destroy. 2. make nothing of.

Unreality, the consequence and apparency of the practice of not-isness.

Upper indoctrination, training processes 6 to 9.

Upstat, high producing, responsible and ethical person.

Valence, the assumption at the reactive level by one individual of the characteristics of another individual. An individual may have a number of valences which he puts on and off as he might hats. Often these changes are so marked that an observant person can notice him dropping one valence and putting on another. The shift from valence to valence is usually completely outside the awareness and control of the individual doing so. In other cases an individual has one valence, not his own, in which he is thoroughly stuck.

Valuable Final Product, something that can be exchanged with other activities in return for support. The support usually adds up to food, clothing, shelter, money, tolerance and cooperation (good will).

Very Good Indicators, 1. it means good indicators to a very marked degree. Extremely good indicators. 2. Preclear happy.

Via, via means a relay point in a communication line. To talk via a body, to get energy via eating alike are communication byroutes. Enough vias make a stop. A stop is made out of vias.

Victim, the individual has done to other dynamics those things which other dynamics now seem to have the power to do to him. Therefore, one can become in fact a zero of influence and a vacuum for trouble.

Viewpoint, a point of awareness from which one can perceive.

Vital target, something that must be done to operate at all.

Whole track, the moment to moment record of a person's existence in this universe in picture and impression form.

Why, the basic outness found which will lead to a recovery of statistics.

Win, intending to do something and doing it or intending not to do something and not doing it.

Withhold, 1. an undisclosed harmful (contra-survival) act. 2. an unspoken, unannounced transgression against a moral code by which the person was bound.

Word Clearer, one who is qualified in and uses the technology of word clearing.

Word Clearing, a technique for locating and handling (clearing) misunderstood words. There are nine methods of word clearing.

Worldwide, the corporation that owns and controls Scientology Churches, currently under the advices of the Sea Organization.

Wrong Why, the incorrectly identified outness which when applied does not lead to recovery.

Subject Index

Bibliography

Buy these Books by L. Ron Hubbard

Dianetics: The Original Thesis
Written two years before public release of the discoveries of Dianetics. *$5.00*

Dianetics: The Evolution of a Science
L. Ron Hubbard's exciting story of the first quarter century of Dianetic research. *$4.00*

Dianetics: The Modern Science of Mental Health
A spectacular international best seller from the moment of its publication in May, 1950, this is *the* book of Man's most advanced knowledge and technology in the field of the human mind. *$7.00*

Notes on the Lectures
From a major lecture series by the Founder of Dianetics given in the autumn of 1950. *$5.00*

Child Dianetics
Compiled by the technical staff of the Hubbard Dianetic Research Foundation (1951) from the research files and lecture materials of L. Ron Hubbard, and with an introduction by him. *$5.00*

Science of Survival
The book which is startling the scientific world with its accurate methods of predicting human behavior, and its insight into the activities of Man. Included with the book of over 500 pages is the famous Hubbard Chart of Human Evaluation. *$8.00*

Self Analysis
A simple self-help volume of tests and processes based on the discoveries contained in Dianetics. *$5.00*

Advanced Procedure and Axioms
Advanced Dianetic discoveries and techniques comprising a research breakthrough by L. Ron Hubbard beyond the field of the mind into codification of the basic principles of existence. *$4.00*

Handbook for Preclears

Designed for use as a self-help volume, and for use by the trained auditor and intelligent layman to apply to others. *$5.00*

A History of Man

A list and description of the principal incidents to be found on the time track of a human being. "This is a cold-blooded and factual account of your last sixty trillion years." *$4.00*

Scientology 8-80

The discovery and increase of life energy in the genus Homo sapiens. *$4.00*

Scientology 8-8008

The complete treatise of the anatomy of universes and the role played in them by a spiritual being—the beingness of Man in relation to the universe of matter, energy, space and time, subjective and objective. *$5.00*

How to Live Though an Executive

A must for any executive or anyone who works near one. Hundreds of applications in every phase of life. L. Ron Hubbard's earliest work on the subject of organization. *$4.00*

The Creation of Human Ability

A huge number of processes for use by Scientology auditors, with full elucidation of the major philosophical and technical breakthroughs by L. Ron Hubbard from which the techniques were derived. *$6.00*

Dianetics 55!

This best seller gives clearly the defined scope of Dianetics related to what, by 1955, the impetus of Dianetics discoveries and successes had produced—which is Scientology. Much newly codified theory and auditor technology. The Six Levels of Processing, Communication Formula. Indispensable auditor know-how. *$5.00*

Scientology: The Fundamentals of Thought

Basic book of the theory and practice of Scientology for beginners. *$4.00*

The Problems of Work

Scientology applied to the workaday world. *$4.00*

All About Radiation

By a nuclear physicist and a British medical doctor. Bluntly informative. A vital application of Scientology observations and discoveries. *$5.00*

Fortress in the Sky

The first article written in English on the military aspects of the moon in an atomic age. *$.50*

Control and the Mechanics of S.C.S.

Edited from the tape lectures of L. Ron Hubbard. *$2.00*

Scientology: Clear Procedure

1957 Clearing procedures. *$2.00*

Have You Lived Before This Life?

When Dianetics touched off the Bridey Murphy craze, conservative investigators were justifiably upset. Now quite conservative, trained Scientologists have tested a series of seventy cases. Their fascinating findings are given in this book. *$5.00*

Axioms and Logics

The Axioms of Scientology, the Prelogics, the Logics, The Axioms of Dianetics. *$2.00*

E-Meter Essentials

L. Ron Hubbard's standard text for all students and trained auditors on the precision use of the E-meter. *$3.00*

The Book of Case Remedies

The trained auditor's and student's manual covering preclear difficulties and their remedies. Loaded with brilliant LRH case resolutions and technical notes, the book is as fascinating as it is important. *$3.00*

The Book of E-Meter Drills

Practical training in the exact skills that make students (all levels) fully skilled in successful E-meter use. *$3.00*

Scientology: A New Slant on Life

A collection of all-time favorite essays by the Founder of Scientology. *$4.00*

The Book Introducing the E-Meter

Beginner's first familiarization with the use of the Hubbard Electrometer. Fully photo-illustrated throughout. *$3.00*

The Phoenix Lectures

The celebrated 1954 Phoenix Professional Course Series now in book form. L. Ron Hubbard's first and comprehensive discussion of the Axioms of Scientology and other fundamentals on the subject. *$7.00*

Introduction To Scientology Ethics
How to make a safe environment in which the individual and organizations can continue to succeed in his or their lives and jobs. *$3.00*

Scientology 0-8
The fundamentals of Scientology: the codes, scales and axioms. *$5.00*

Background and Ceremonies of the Church of Scientology
The background and religious antecedents of the Church of Scientology, the Creed of the Church, instructions for service, general sermon outlines, many ceremonies as originally given in person by the Founder of Scientology. *$15.00*

The Basic Scientology Picture Book Volume I
A visual aid to a better understanding of Man and the material universe. *$3.00*

The Basic Dianetics Picture Book
A visual aid for a quicker understanding and dissemination of Standard Dianetics and Dianetic Pastoral Counseling. *$2.00*

Mission Into Time
In 1968, L. Ron Hubbard led an unusual expedition into the past, with a crew to check on his recall of incidents occurring several thousand years ago. *$6.00*

Dianetics Today
The book which gives the technical breakthroughs in Dianetics since 1950, a follow-up to **Dianetics: The Modern Science of Mental Health.** *$18.00*

Hymn of Asia
Ron's famous poetic address to the world. Destined to be among the greatest of religious classics of Mankind. Contains colorful and splendid art work and photography. *$14.00*

Dianetics and Scientology Technical Dictionary
Released in 1975 this book is the key to greater awareness and a fuller understanding of the technology of Dianetics and Scientology. *$15.00*

APPLY FOR YOUR FREE SIX-MONTH SCIENTOLOGY MEMBERSHIP TODAY!

As an International Member of Scientology you receive a 10 percent discount on all books priced over $1.25, tape recorded L. Ron Hubbard lectures and other items. You also receive free magazines with vital data, world Scientology news and modern technical information. New members are eligible for all International Membership privileges (including 10 percent discount) as of date of application.

Apply to:
MEMBERSHIP OFFICER, your nearest Church of Scientology.

Church and Mission List

Contact Your Nearest Church of Mission

UNITED STATES

ADVANCED ORGANIZATION

Church of Scientology of California
Advanced Organization of Los Angeles
5930 Franklin Avenue
Los Angeles, California 90028

SAINT HILL ORGANIZATION

Church of Scientology of California
American Saint Hill Organization
2723 West Temple Street
Los Angeles, California 90026

PUBLICATIONS ORGANIZATION

Church of Scientology of California
Publications Organization
2723 West Temple Street
Los Angeles, California 90026

LOCAL CHURCHES

AUSTIN

Church of Scientology
2804 Rio Grande
Austin, Texas 78705

BOSTON

Church of Scientology
448 Beacon Street
Boston, Massachusetts 02215

BUFFALO

Church of Scientology
1116 Elmwood Avenue
Buffalo, New York 14222

CHICAGO

Church of Scientology
1555 Maple Street
Evanston, Illinois 60201

DENVER

Church of Scientology
1640 Welton
Denver, Colorado 80202

DETROIT

Church of Scientology
19 Clifford Street
Detroit, Michigan 48226

HAWAII

Church of Scientology
143 Nenue Street
Honolulu, Hawaii 96821

LAS VEGAS

Church of Scientology
2108 Industrial Road
Las Vegas, Nevada 89102

LOS ANGELES

Church of Scientology of California
2005 West 9th Street
Los Angeles, California 90006

Church of Scientology
Celebrity Centre Los Angeles
1551 North La Brea Avenue
Hollywood, California 90028

MIAMI

Church of Scientology
1235 Brickell Avenue
Miami, Florida 33131

NEW YORK

Church of Scientology
28-30 West 74th Street
New York, New York 10023

PHILADELPHIA

Church of Scientology
8 West Lancaster Avenue
Ardmore, Pennsylvania 19003

PORTLAND

Church of Scientology
333 South West Park Avenue
Portland, Oregon 97205

SACRAMENTO

Church of Scientology
819 19th Street
Sacramento, California 95814

SAN DIEGO

Church of Scientology
926 "C" Street
San Diego, California 92101

SAN FRANCISCO

Church of Scientology
414 Mason Street, Rm. 400
San Francisco, California 94102

SEATTLE

Church of Scientology
1531 4th Avenue
Seattle, Washington 98101

ST. LOUIS

Church of Scientology
3730 Lindell Boulevard
St. Louis, Missouri 63108

TWIN CITIES

Church of Scientology
730 Hennepin Avenue
Minneapolis, Minnesota 55403

WASHINGTON, D.C.

Founding Church of Scientology
2125 "S" Street N.W.
Washington, D.C. 20008

CANADA

LOCAL CHURCHES

MONTREAL

Church of Scientology
15 Notre Dame Quest
Montreal, Quebec H2Y 1B5

OTTAWA

Church of Scientology
292 Somerset Street West
Ottawa, Ontario K2P 9Z9

TORONTO

Church of Scientology
124 Avenue Road
Toronto, Ontario M5R 2H5

VANCOUVER

Church of Scientology
4857 Main Street
Vancouver 10, British Columbia

UNITED KINGDOM

ADVANCED ORGANIZATION/ SAINT HILL

Hubbard College of Scientology
Advanced Organization Saint Hill
Saint Hill Manor
East Grinstead, Sussex RH19 4JY
England

LOCAL CHURCHES

EAST GRINSTEAD

Saint Hill Foundation
Saint Hill Manor East Grinstead
Sussex RH19 4JY
England

LONDON

Hubbard Scientology Organization
68 Tottenham Court Road
London W.1.
England

MANCHESTER

Hubbard Scientology Organization
48 Faulkner Street
Manchester M1 4FH
England

PLYMOUTH

Hubbard Scientology Organization
39 Portland Square
Sherwell
Plymouth
Devon
England PL4 6DJ

EDINBURGH

Hubbard Academy of Personal Independence
Fleet House
20 South Bridge
Edinburgh
Scotland EH1 1LL

EUROPE

ADVANCED ORGANIZATION

Church of Scientology
Advanced Organization Denmark
Jernbanegade 6
1608 Copenhagen V
Denmark

SAINT HILL ORGANIZATION

Church of Scientology
Saint Hill Denmark
Jernbanegade 6
1608 Copenhagen V
Denmark

PUBLICATIONS ORGANIZATION

Scientology Publications Organization Demark
Jernbanegade 6
1608 Copenhagen V
Denmark

LOCAL CHURCHES

AMSTERDAM

Church of Scientology
Singel 289-293
Amsterdam C,
Netherlands

COPENHAGEN

Church of Scientology
Hovedvagtsgade 6
1103 Copenhagen K
Denmark

Church of Scientology of Copenhagen
Frederiksborgvej 5
2400 Copenhagen V
Denmark

GOTEBORG

Church of Scientology
Magasinsgatan 12
S-411 18 Goteborg
Sweden

MALMO

Church of Scientology
Skomakaregatan 12
S-211 34 Malmo
Sweden

MUNICH

Church of Scientology
8000 Munchen 2
Lindwurmstrasse 29
Munich
West Germany

PARIS

Church of Scientology
12 Rue de la Montagne
Ste Genevieve 75005
Paris
France

STOCKHOLM

Church of Scientology
Kammakaregatan 46
S-111 60 Stockholm
Sweden

AFRICA

LOCAL CHURCHES

BULAWAYO

Church of Scientology
508 Kirrie Bldgs.
Cnr Abercorn & 9th Avenue
Bulawayo
Rhodesia

CAPETOWN

Church of Scientology
3rd Floor Garmour House
127 Plein Street
Capetown
South Africa 8001

DURBAN

Church of Scientology
57 College Lane
Durban
South Africa 4001

JOHANNESBURG

Church of Scientology
99 Polly Street
Johannesburg
South Africa 2001

PORT ELIZABETH

Church of Scientology
2 St. Christopher's
27 West Bourne Road
Port Elizabeth
South Africa 6001

PRETORIA

Church of Scientology
224 Central House
Cnr Central & Pretorius Streets
Pretoria
South Africa 0002

AUSTRALIA/NEW ZEALAND

LOCAL CHURCHES

ADELAIDE

Church of the New Faith
57 Pulteney Street
Fullarton
Adelaide 5000
South Australia

MELBOURNE

Church of the New Faith
724 Inkerman Road
North Caulfield 3161
Melbourne
Victoria
Australia

PERTH

Church of the New Faith
Pastoral House
156 St. George's Terrace
Perth 6000
Western Australia

SYDNEY

Church of the New Faith
1 Lee Street
Sydney 2000
New South Wales
Australia

AUCKLAND

Church of Scientology
New Imperial Buildings
44 Queen Street
Auckland 1,
New Zealand

CELEBRITY CENTERS

UNITED STATES

Church of Scientology
Celebrity Centre Los Angeles
1551 North La Brea Avenue
Hollywood, California 90028

Celebrity Center Baton Rouge
7939 Jefferson Hwy
Baton Rouge, Louisiana 70809

Celebrity Center Boulder
Marine Street No. 1
Boulder, Colorado 80302

Celebrity Center
1912 E. Yandell
El Paso, Texas 79903

Celebrity Center Las Vegas
2004 Western Avenue
Las Vegas, Nevada 89102

Celebrity Center Lewisburg (Greensbriar)
Laird House, Underwood Estates
Lewisburg, West Virginia 24901

Celebrity Centre Maine
Boot Cove
Lubec, Maine 04652

Celebrity Center Mountainview
2483 Old Middlefield Way
Mountain View, California 94040

Celebrity Center New York
65 East 82nd Street
New York, New York 10021

Celebrity Center San Antonio
2120 San Pedro Avenue
San Antonio, Texas 78212

Celebrity Centre San Francisco
2456 Clay St.
San Francisco, California 94115

Celebrity Center Santa Fe
330 Montezuma
Santa Fe, New Mexico 87501

Celebrity Center Steamboat Springs
P.O. Box 1987
Steamboat Springs, Colorado 80477

Celebrity Center Washington, D.C.
3411 Massachusetts Avenue N.W.
Washington, D.C. 20007

CANADA

Celebrity Center Toronto
67 Pembroke Street
Toronto, Ontario

AUSTRALIA

Celebrity Center Melbourne
46 Clingin
E. Rosewain
Melbourne, Victoria
Australia 3073

MEXICO

Celebrity Centre Mexico
Centro Cultural Latino Americano
Plaza Rio de Janeiro 52
Col. Roma, Mexico 7DF
Mexico

SWEDEN

Celebrity Centre Sweden
Malmvagen 4C, 9TR
191 61 Sollentuna, Sweden

MISSION LIST

UNITED STATES

ALASKA

Scientology Mission of Anchorage
155 E. Potter Street
Anchorage, Alaska 99502

ARIZONA

Scientology Mission of Flagstaff
4469 Mountain Meadow Drive
Flagstaff, Arizona 86001

Scientology Mission of Phoenix
331 North 1st Avenue
Phoenix, Arizona 85003

Scientology Mission of Phoenix
1722 East Indian School Road
Phoenix, Arizona 85016

Scientology Mission of Tucson
2100 East Speedway
Tucson, Arizona 85719

CALIFORNIA

Scientology Mission of Adams Avenue
6911 El Cajon
San Diego, California 92115

Scientology Mission of Berkeley
1918 Bonita
Berkeley, California 94704

Scientology Mission of Burbank
124 N. Golden Mall
Burbank, California 91502

Scientology Mission of Castro Valley
20730 Lake Chabot Road
Castro Valley, California 94546

Scientology Mission of Chula Vista
192 Landis Street
Chula Vista, California 92010

Scientology Mission of Davis
1046 Olive Drive
Davis, California 95616

Scientology Mission of East Bay
411 15th Street
Oakland, California 94612

Scientology Mission of Fresno
1350 "O" Street, Room 200
Fresno, California 93721

Scientology Mission of Goldengate
1807 Union Street, No. 2
San Francisco, California 94128

Scientology Mission of Lake Tahoe
P.O.Box 1540
South Lake Tahoe, California 95705

Scientology Mission of Long Beach
1261 Long Beach Boulevard
Long Beach, California 90813

Scientology Mission of Los Angeles
(Los Feliz)
1570 N. Edgemont, No. 107
Los Angeles, California 90027

Scientology Mission of Los Gatos
10 Jackson Street, No. 111
Los Gatos, California 95030

Scientology Mission of Orange County
1451 Irvine Boulevard, No. 30
Tustin, California 92680

Scientology Mission of Palo Alto
600 Middlefield Road
Palo Alto, California 94301

Scientology Mission of Pasadena
634 East Colorado Boulevard
Pasadena, California 91101

Scientology Mission of Riverside
3485 University Street
Riverside, California 92501

Scientology Mission of Sacramento
1725 23rd Street
Sacramento, California 95816

Scientology Mission of Sacramento
5136 Arden Way
Carmichael, California 95608

Scientology Mission of Santa Barbara
20 W. Della Guerra Street
Santa Barbara, California 93101

Scientology Mission of Santa Clara
4340 Stevens Creek, No. 180
San Jose, California 95129

Scientology Mission of Santa Monica
(Coast Line)
309 Santa Monica
Santa Monica, California 90401

Scientology Mission of Santa Rosa
806 Sonaoma Avenue
Santa Rosa, California 95402

Scientology Mission SCS
3802 Riverside Drive
Burbank, California 91505

Scientology Mission of South Bay
607 South Pacific Coast Highway
Redondo Beach, California 90277

Scientology Mission of Stockton
47 West Acadia
Stockton, California 95202

Scientology Mission of Sunset Strip
8863 Sunset Boulevard
Hollywood, California 90069

Scientology Mission of Valley
13561 Ventura Boulevard
Sherman Oaks, California 91403

Scientology Mission of Vista
1027 East Vista Way
Vista, California 92083

Scientology Mission of Walnut Creek
2363 Boulevard Circle, No. 5
Walnut Creek, California 94595

Scientology Mission of Westwood/Wilshire
10930 Santa Monica Boulevard
Los Angeles, California 90025

COLORADO

Scientology Mission of Boulder
2049 Broadway, P.O. Box 995
Boulder, Colorado 80302

Scientology Mission of Colorado Springs
712 N. Weber Street
Colorado Springs, Colorado 80905

CONNECTICUT

Scientology Mission of Berlin
1240A Farmington Avenue
Berlin, Connecticut 06037

Scientology Mission of New Haven
109 Church Street, No. 505
New Haven, Connecticut 06520

Scientology Mission of New London
183 Williams Street
New London, Connecticut 06320

Scientology Mission of Waterbury
42 Bank Street
Waterbury, Connecticut 06702

FLORIDA

Scientology Mission of Coral Gables
4615 Ponce de Leon Boulevard
Coral Gables, Florida 33134

Scientology Mission of Fort Lauderdale
423 North Andrews Avenue
Fort Lauderdale, Florida 33301

Scientology Mission of Orlando
P.O. Box 14045
Orlando, Florida 32807

Scientology Mission of Tampa
12205 Dale Malory, Suite B
Tampa, Florida 33609

GEORGIA

Scientology Mission of Atlanta
2979 Grandview Avenue
Atlanta, Georgia 30305

HAWAII

Scientology Mission of Hawaii
1282 Kapiolani Boulevard
Honolulu, Hawaii 96814

ILLINOIS

Scientology Mission of Carbondale
417 South Illinois Avenue
Carbondale, Illinois 62901

Scientology Mission of Chicago
108 East Oak Street
Villa Park, Illinois 60181

Scientology Mission of Lakeview
1928 West Montrose
Chicago, Illinois 60613

Scientology Mission of Peoria
920 West Main Street
Peoria, Illinois 61606

Scientology Mission of Urbana
1004 South Fourth Street
Champaign, Illinois 61820

INDIANA

Scientology Mission of Anderson
1111 Meredian Plaza, P.O. Box 664
Anderson, Indiana 46016

Scientology Mission of Indianapolis
6728 Everglades Court
Indianapolis, Indiana 46217

MARYLAND

Scientology Mission of Bethesda
4823 Fairmont at Woodmont
Bethesda, Maryland 20014

MASSACHUSETTS

Scientology Mission of Cambridge
8 Essex Street
Cambridge, Massachusetts 02139

Scientology Mission of Marshfield
34 Flames Road
Marshfield, Massachusetts 02050

Scientology Mission of Worchester
16 Front Street
Worchester, Massachusetts 01608

MICHIGAN

Scientology Mission of Huron Valley
203 East Ann Street
Ann Arbor, Michigan 48108

MINNESOTA

Scientology Mission of Excelsior
21 Water Street
Excelsior, Minnesota 55331

MISSOURI

Scientology Mission of Kansas City
4528 Main Street
Kansas City, Missouri 64111

Scientology Mission of St. Charles
138A North Main Street
St. Charles, Missouri 63301

NEBRASKA

Scientology Mission of Omaha
5061 California Street
Omaha, Nebraska 68132

NEVADA

Scientology Mission of the Meadows
1326 Las Vegas Boulevard
Las Vegas, Nevada 89101

Scientology Mission of Washoe Valley
319 East 6th Street
Reno, Nevada 89501

NEW JERSEY

Scientology Mission of Delaware Valley
1 Cherryhill Mall, Suite 924
Cherryhill, New Jersey 08034

Scientology Mission of Flemington
27 Church Street
Flemington, New Jersey 08822

NEW MEXICO

Scientology Mission of Albuquerque
613 San Mateo Boulevard, N.E.
Albuquerque, New Mexico 87108

NEW YORK

Scientology Mission of Albany
141 Brunswick Road
Troy, New York 12180

Scientology Mission of Bayshore (Long Island)
7 Smith Avenue
Bayshore, New York 11706

Scientology Mission of East Manhattan
17 East 79th Street
New York, New York 10021

Scientology Mission of Elmira
111 North Main Street
Elmira, New York 14902

Scientology Mission of Fifth Avenue
434 6th Avenue, 2nd Floor
New York, New York 10011

Scientology Mission of New York
500 West End Avenue
New York, New York 10024

Scientology Mission of North Manhattan
Apt. 2A, 251 West 98th Street
New York, New York 10025

Scientology Mission of Putnam Valley
Dunderberg Road
Putnam Valley, New York 10579

NORTH CAROLINA

Scientology Mission of Charlotte
1000 Dilworth Road
Charlotte, North Carolina 28209

OHIO

Scientology Mission of Central Ohio
3894 North High Street
Columbus, Ohio 43214

Scientology Mission of Cincinnati
3352 Jefferson Avenue
Cincinnati, Ohio 45220

Scientology Mission of Cleveland
2055 Lee Road
Cleveland Heights, Ohio 44118

Scientology Mission of Columbus
1074 East Broad Street
Columbus, Ohio 43205

Scientology Mission of Toledo
3257 West Bancroft
Toledo, Ohio 43606

OREGON

Scientology Mission of Portland
709 South West Salmon Street
Portland, Oregon 97205

Scientology Mission of Sheridan
Route 2, Box 195
Sheridan, Oregon 97378

PENNSYLVANIA

Scientology Mission of Chaddsford
Box 171, Brintion Bridge Road
Chaddsford, Pennsylvania 19317

Scientology Mission of Erie
528 West 18th Street
Erie, Pennsylvania 16502

PUERTO RICO

Scientology Mission of Puerto Rico
P.O. Box 211
Old San Juan Post Office
San Juan, Puerto Rico 00902

RHODE ISLAND

Scientology Mission of Rhode Island
264 Wey Bosset
Providence, Rhode Island 02903

TENNESSEE

Scientology Mission of Norris
P.O. Box 66
Norris, Tennessee 37828

TEXAS

Scientology Mission of Amarillo
2046 South Hayden
Amarillo, Texas 79109

Scientology Mission of Houston
4034 Westheimer
Houston, Texas 77027

Scientology Mission of Richardson
114 North McKinley
Richardson, Texas 75080

Scientology Mission of San Antonio
Colony North Mall
3723 Colony Drive
San Antonio, Texas 78230

Scientology Mission of South West
P.O. Box 8386
Dallas, Texas, 75205

UTAH

Scientology Mission of Salt Lake City
253 East 2nd Street
Salt Lake City, Utah, 84111

VERMONT

Scientology Mission of Putney
Wabena Stables
Putney, Vermont 05346

VIRGINIA

Scientology Mission of Arlington
818 North Taylor Street
Arlington, Virginia 22203

CANADA

Scientology Mission of Calgary
335 11th Avenue SW.
Calgary, Alberta T2R 0C7

Scientology Mission of Edmonton
9610 82nd Avenue
Edmonton, Alberta

Scientology Mission of Halifax
Suite 208, 1585 Barrington Street
Halifax, Nova Scotia B3J 1Z8

Scientology Mission of Hamilton
28½ John Street North
Hamilton, Ontario L8R 1G9

Scientology Mission of Kitchener
Apt. 14 241 King Street
Kitchener, Ontario N2G 1B3

Scientology Mission of North Vancouver
146 West 15th Avenue 15N
Vancouver, British Columbia

Scientology Mission of Quebec
224½ St. Joseph Est.
Quebec, P.Q. G1K 349

Scientology Mission of Regina
2023 St. John Street
Regina, Saskatchewan

Scientology Mission of St. Catharines
455 St. Pauls Street
St. Catharines, Ontario

Scientology Mission of St. John
15 Charlotte Street
St. John, New Brunswick

Scientology Mission of Vancouver
1562 West 6th Avenue
Vancouver, British Columbia V6J 1R2

Scientology Mission of Windsor
437 Ouelette Avenue
Windsor, Ontario N9A 4J2

Scientology Mission of Winnipeg
410 Spence Street
Winnipeg, Manitoba R3B 2R6

UNITED KINGDOM

Scientology Mission of Birmingham
3 Saint Mary's Road
Moseley
Birmingham, 13
England

Mission of Botley (Southampton)
16 Rectorey Court
Holmesland, Garden Est.
Botley, England

Scientology Mission of Bournemouth
43 Markham Rd.
Winton Bornemouth,
Dorset, England

Scientology Mission of Charnwood Forest
109 Meeting Street
Quorn, Loughborough
Leicestershire
England

Scientology Mission of Helensborough
121 West King Street
Helensborough
Dunbartonshire G84 8DQ
Scotland

Scientology Mission of Hove
Flat 1, 56 Wilbury Road
Hove, Sussex
England

Scientology Mission of Kirkwood
"Kirkwood House"
Biggar
Lanarkshire
Scotland

Scientology Mission of Leeds
27 Manor Drive
Leeds
Yorkshire LS6 IDE
England

Scientology Mission of Reading
"St. Michael's" Shinfield Road
Reading
Berkshire RG2 9B4
England

Scientology Mission of Swansea
1 High Pool Close
Newton
Mumbles
Swansea
Wales

EUROPE

AUSTRIA

Scientology Mission of Vienna
Museumstrasse 5/18
1070 Vienna
Austria

BELGIUM

Centre de Scientology du Brabant
Rue Du Pacifique 4
B-1180 Bruxelles
Belgium

Eglise de Scientology
45A Rue de l'Ecuyer
B-1000 Bruxelles
Belgium

DENMARK

Scientology Mission of Virum
Kaplevej 301
DK 2830
Virum, Denmark

FRANCE

Scientology Mission of Angers
43 Rue Proust
49000 Angers
France

Scientology Mission of Paris
147 Rue St. Charles
Paris
F-75015, Paris
France

Scientology Mission of Versailles
29 Bis Rue Des Noailles
F-78000 Versailles
France

SWEDEN

Scientology Mission of Helsingborg
Sodergaten 4
S-252/25 Helsingborg
Sweden

SWITZERLAND

College fur Angewandte Philosophie
Haldenstrasse 37
6006 Luzern
Switzerland

Scientology Mission of Basel
Gerberleinstrasse 25
CH-4051 Basel
Switzerland

Scientology Bern
2 Sudbanhofstrasse
CH-3007 Bern
Switzerland

Scientology Zentrum Bern
Hotelgasse 3
CH-3011 Bern
Switzerland

Scientology Mission of Geneva
8 Rue Masbov
1205 Geneva
Switzerland

Scientology Mission of Luzern
Grossweidstrasse 1
CH-6010 Kriens
Switzerland

Scientology Mission of Zurich
Mulibachstrasse 423/6
CH-8185 Winkelruti
Zurich
Switzerland

Scientology Mission of Zurich
Lowenstrasse 69
CH-8001
Zurich
Switzerland

WEST GERMANY

College fur Angewandte Philosophie
Kennedy Allee 33
D-6000 Frankfurt Am Main
West Germany

College fur Angewandte Philosophie
Fleinerstrasse 37
D-71 Heilbronn
West Germany

College fur Angewandte Philosophie
Widenmayer 28
8 Munchen 28
West Germany

College fur Angewandte Philosophie
Kidlerstr. 10
8 Munchen 70
West Germany

Dianetic College
Stegstrasse 37
D-6000 Frankfurt 70
West Germany

Dianetic Stuttgart
Hauptsatterstr. 126A
D-7000 Stuttgart 1
West Germany

Scientology Center Hamburg
Gerhofstrasse 18
D-2 Hamburg 36
West Germany

Scientology Kirche Stuttgart
Neue Brucke 3
D-7000 Stuttgart 1
West Germany

Scientology Mission of Berlin
Giesebrechtstr. 10
D-1000 Berlin 12
West Germany

AFRICA

Scientology & Dianetics Center
11 First Avenue
Highlands North
Johannesburg 2001
South Africa

AUSTRALIA/NEW ZEALAND

The New Faith Mission of Melville
15 Birdwood Road
Melville
West Australia 6156

Scientology Mission of Christchurch
35 Rapaki Road
Christchurch 2
New Zealand

Scientology Mission of Ellerslie
1 Ranier Street
Ellerslie
Auckland
New Zealand

OTHER ORGANIZATIONS OF DIANETICS & SCIENTOLOGY

MEXICO

Academia de Dianetica
Ave. Revolucion 591-B1
Mexico 18DF, Mexico

Associación de Dianetica
Matamoros No. 5
A.P. 21875
Mexico 21DF, Mexico

Centro de Dianetica A.C.
Campos Eliseos 205
Mexico 5DF
Mexico

Instituto de Dianetica en Guadalajara A.C.
Mexicaltzingo No. 1985
Sector Juarez
Guadalajara, Jalisco
Mexico

Organización de Dianetica A.C.
Provencia No. 1000
Col. de Valle
Mexico 12DF
Mexico

Scientology Centre Empalme
AP 181 Guaymas
Empalme
Sonora
Mexico

Scientology Organization Mexico A.C.
Avenida Nuevo Leon 159 1°
Piso, Mexico 11DF
Mexico

ISRAEL

Scientology Centre of Negev
P.O. Box 2098
Beer Sheva
Israel

Scientology Center of Tel Aviv
7 Fichman Street
Tel Aviv, Israel

PHILIPPINES

Scientology Centre of Philippines
P.O. Box 1182
Makati
Rizal
Philippines

BRAZIL

Scientology Centre of Rio De Janeiro
Praia de Botafogo 472, Apt. 913
Rio de Janeiro, GB
Brazil